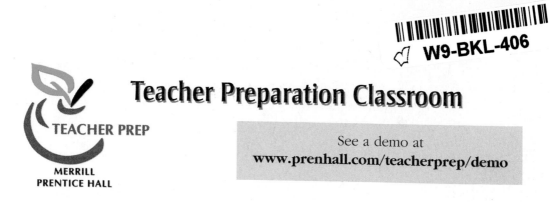
Teacher Preparation Classroom

TEACHER PREP

MERRILL
PRENTICE HALL

See a demo at
www.prenhall.com/teacherprep/demo

Your Class. Their Careers. Our Future. Will your students be prepared?

We invite you to explore our new, innovative and engaging website and all that it has to offer you, your course, and tomorrow's educators! Preview this site today at www.prenhall.com/teacherprep/demo.

Organized around the major courses pre-service teachers take, the Teacher Preparation site provides media, student/teacher artifacts, strategies, research articles, and other resources to equip your students with the quality tools needed to excel in their courses and prepare them for their first classroom.

This ultimate online education resource will provide you and your students access to:

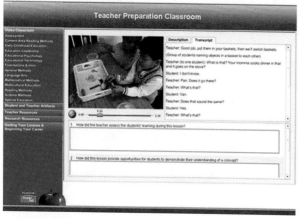

Online Video Library. More than 250 video clips—each tied to a course topic and framed by learning goals and Praxis-type questions—capture real teachers and students working in real classrooms.

Student and Teacher Artifacts. More than 200 student and teacher classroom artifacts—each tied to a course topic and framed by learning goals and application questions—provide a wealth of materials and experiences to help make your students observe children's developmental learning.

Lesson Plan Builder. Offers step-by-step guidelines and lesson plan examples to support students as they learn to build high quality lesson plans.

Articles and Readings. Over 500 articles from ASCD's renowned journal *Educational Leadership* are available. The site also includes Research Navigator, a searchable database of additional educational journals.

Strategies and Lessons. Over 500 research supported instructional strategies appropriate for a wide range of grade levels and content areas.

Licensure and Career Tools. Resources devoted to helping your students pass their licensure exam, learn standards, law, and public policies, plan a teaching portfolio, and succeed in their first year of teaching.

Access Code previously been used?
Students: To purchase or renew an access code, go to www.prenhall.com/teacherprep and click on the "Register for Teacher Prep" button.
Instructors: Email Merrill.marketing@pearsoned.com and provide the following information:
- Name and Affiliation
- Author/Title/Edition of Merrill text

Upon ordering *Teacher Prep* for their students, instructors will be given a lifetime *Teacher Prep* Access Code.

Teaching Children to Read

The Teacher Makes the Difference

Fifth Edition

D. RAY REUTZEL

Utah State University

ROBERT B. COOTER, JR.

University of Memphis

With Contributions by

BRETT ELIZABETH BLAKE

St. John's University

PEARSON

Merrill
Prentice Hall

Upper Saddle River, New Jersey
Columbus, Ohio

Library of Congress Cataloging in Publication Data

Reutzel, D. Ray (Douglas Ray)
   Teaching children to read: the teacher makes the difference / D. Ray Reutzel, Robert B.
Cooter, Jr.—5th ed.
          p. cm.
   Includes bibliographical references and index.
   ISBN-13: 978-0-13-613806-8
   ISBN-10: 0-13-613806-3
1. Reading (Elementary) 2. Reading (Elementary)—Language experience approach.
3. Language arts (Elementary) I. Cooter, Robert B. II. Title.

   LB1573.R48 2008
   372.41—dc22

                                                                        2007015707

Vice President and Executive Publisher: Jeffery W. Johnston
Senior Editor: Linda Ashe Bishop
Senior Development Editor: Hope Madden
Senior Production Editor: Mary M. Irvin
Senior Editorial Assistant: Laura Weaver
Design Coordinator: Diane C. Lorenzo
Project Coordination: Carlisle Publishing Services
Cover Image and Design: Kellyn E. Donnelly
Production Manager: Pamela D. Bennett
Director of Marketing: David Gesell
Marketing Manager: Darcy Betts Prybella
Marketing Coordinator: Brian Mounts

This book was set in ITC Garamond by Carlisle Publishing Services Ltd. It was printed and bound by
Courier/Kendallville. The cover was printed by Phoenix Color Corp.

Chapter Opener Photo Credits: Anthony Magnacca/Merrill, Chapter 1; Maria B. Vonada/Merrill, Chapter 2; David
Mager/Pearson Learning Photo Studio, Chapter 3, 4, and 5; Patrick White/Merrill, Chapter 6, 8, and 12; Krista Greco/
Merrill, Chapter 7; Scott Cunningham/Merrill, Chapter 9 and 11; Lori Whitley/Merrill, Chapter 10.

Pearson Education Ltd.   Pearson Education Australia Pty. Limited
Pearson Education Singapore Pte. Ltd.   Pearson Education North Asia Ltd.
Pearson Education Canada, Ltd.   Pearson Educación de Mexico, S.A. de C.V.
Pearson Education—Japan   Pearson Education Malaysia Pte. Ltd.

10 9 8 7 6 5 4
ISBN-13: 978-0-13-613806-8
ISBN-10:   0-13-613806-3

For my wife, Pam, my children, and my grandchildren who are my life's inspiration.

—*DRR*

For Kathy

—*RBC*

PREFACE

Why is preparation so critical for literacy teachers? Because research tells us it's the teacher who makes the difference in effective reading instruction. As a capable literacy teacher, you will need to think about your teaching decisions, and understand and meet the literacy needs of every student in your class. That is a tall order, but this text will provide you the guidance you need to succeed.

Teaching Children to Read: The Teacher Makes the Difference, Fifth Edition, emphasizes the teacher's role in literacy instruction. We thoroughly examine five pillars of effective instruction, which provide a structure for closely examining the critical elements that well-prepared literacy teachers know, understand, and are able to implement in classrooms. By organizing every chapter around these pillars of effective instruction, the concept of *teacher as lynchpin in literacy learning* is reinforced and cemented. Using these pillars to ground your teaching, you will be able to recognize your role in developing your students' literacy education.

Five Pillars of Effective Instruction

Teacher Knowledge

Chapters thoroughly examine how teacher knowledge leads to wise teaching decisions. Purple headings, figures, tables, and features mark the chapter sections that cover the important elements of teacher knowledge. This material shares the foundational knowledge and research that you need to know and understand to build your background knowledge and assure you are well-prepared as an informed literacy decision maker.

Assessment

The role of assessment as an ongoing tool that informs instruction is carefully considered in every chapter. Because teachers must be able to gauge their students' grasp of literacy skills to make informed instructional decisions, orange sections in each chapter are designed to help you create an instructional roadmap of where children are in their literacy development. These assessment sections also guide you in the use of evaluation and assessment tools that will steer you to instruction or intervention, helping you meet specific instructional goals for each child.

Effective Practice

The steps of effective practice are uncovered and illustrated chapter after chapter, topic after topic. As research guides, the material provided in the red Effective Practice sections lays out practical methods for *teaching essential literacy skills and strategies*. Great teachers have a large assortment of tools in their educational toolbox, allowing every child to reach their literacy potential. The applications in these sections provide procedural strategies you can take directly into your classroom.

Differentiated Instruction

Each chapter provides guidance toward differentiating instruction to meet all students' needs. Children come to school with diverse learning needs. Your goal must be to help all the students in your classroom succeed, including students who struggle because English is not their first language or because they have a learning disability or other special need. Green sections in every chapter provide the guidance and specific recommendations you need to focus on the individual needs of striving students. You'll find valuable ideas for adapting instruction to help *all* your students succeed in literacy.

Family/Home Connections

The value of connections made between the classroom and home is clarified in blue sections in each chapter, leading to recommendations for creating and nurturing these important links. These sections help teachers make powerful learning links between the classroom and the home environment. The goal is to help you communicate with parents and other caregivers, involving them in their children's ongoing literacy success.

Text Organization

In preparing the fifth edition of *Teaching Children to Read*, we looked closely at the information teachers need to develop into master literacy teachers. We believe that a foundation in the scientific research that informs teacher decision making is pivotal. Building on that knowledge with an understanding of how children develop their earliest skills in literacy led to the inclusion of a new chapter on oral language, which leads logically to the needs of the emergent reader. This understanding of the needs of early learners leads naturally to the principal literacy topics of phonics, fluency, vocabulary, and comprehension, and then on to reading and writing connections.

With that in place, we build on the chapter-by-chapter focus on assessment with a full, dedicated chapter on the topic, including a focus on meeting contemporary guidelines of No Child Left Behind, a federal mandate for improving student and school literacy progress.

We then turn our attention to the reality of today's reading classrooms and the programs and standards teachers are asked to examine and follow. Lastly, because classroom organization and management is an important consideration in setting up

literacy programs, we offer you insight into the observations and recommendations we have made to K–8 teachers to help them prepare and organize their literacy materials to meet students' developmental needs.

1. Effective Reading Instruction: The Teacher Makes the Difference
2. Developing Children's Oral Language
3. Early Reading Instruction: Teaching the Essentials
4. Phonics and Word Identification
5. Developing Children's Reading Fluency
6. Increasing Reading Vocabulary
7. Teaching Reading Comprehension
8. Writing
9. Assessment
10. Programs and Standards for Reading Instruction
11. Effective Reading Instruction and Organization in Grades K–3
12. Effective Reading Instruction and Organization in Grades 4–8

Special Text Features

Getting to Know English Learners
The literacy learning of ELs is protected under Title VI of the Civil Rights Act of 1964—an important guarantee as one in five children in the United States today speaks a language other than English at home.

Getting to Know English Learners In addition to our differentiated instruction focus, chapters are peppered with margin features that offer explicit connections to the needs of English learners. These provide contemporary information and research-based applications to help you meet the needs of students whose first language is not English.

Model Lessons for Literacy Instruction: Virtual Classroom Experiences CD-ROM This CD-ROM is packaged with the text and offers real classroom examples to ground your teacher knowledge. The CD contains video clips of four different classrooms, each following a master teacher through the stages of a reading lesson.

- Kindergarten teacher Heather Clark conducts a lesson on phonemic awareness.
- Second grade teacher Rhonda Blake works through guided reading.
- Cover comprehension strategies with second grade teacher DiAnn Sundin.
- Fourth grade teacher Jean Turner conducts a writing workshop lesson.

Unlike any field experience, you can watch each lesson as many times as you'd like, reflecting on the decisions made and the strengths and weaknesses in each procedure.

TEACHER PREP　Learn how to use dialogic reading to assist English Learners. Visit our Teacher Prep Website (*www.prenhall.com/ teacherprep*) for a link to *Language Arts Methods*. Read the article titled "Generating Stories."

Teacher Prep Margin Notes These margin notes make use of the robust website available free with this text. The Teacher Prep Website contains video, student artifacts, research articles, teaching strategies, lesson planning software, national and state standards links, and guidance for your licensing and first year of teaching. The Teacher Prep notes throughout chapters link you to the specific artifacts, strategies, standards, and research that will enrich and demonstrate the chapters' content and strategies.

Video Classroom This feature leads you to the clips on the accompanying CD-ROM and on the *Teacher Prep Website* that illustrate the text's effective practices in action. You'll be asked to think critically about the video model and consider points that will impact your teaching.

Video Classroom

Visit a primary grades classroom to view vocabulary instruction

Refer to our Teacher Prep Website (*www.prenhall.com/teacherprep*) for a link to Video Classroom. Select Reading Methods to view "Introducing Words to Young Readers—Vocabulary.

As you view the clip, note how the teacher introduces the vocabulary words in this lesson.

- Why might the teacher select the words "she" and "inside" to introduce for the story of "Hermit Crab"?
- What word learning techniques are utilized? Why are they powerful?
- What other alternate forms might be used for vocabulary introduction?

Instructor Resource Center The Instructor Resource Center at *www.prenhall.com* has a variety of print and media resources available in downloadable, digital format—all in one location. As a registered faculty member, you can access and download passcode protected resource files, course management content, and other premium online content directly to your computer. Digital resources available for *Teaching Children to Read: The Teacher Makes the Difference,* Fifth Edition, include:

- A test bank with multiple choice and essay tests
- PowerPoints specifically designed for each chapter
- Chapter-by-chapter materials, including chapter objectives, suggested readings, discussion questions, and in-class activities
- CD integration ideas to help you utilize the CD that accompanies the text
- Teacher Prep correlation guide to help you make the best use of the Teacher Prep Website in your classes

To access these items online, go to *www.prenhall.com* and click on the Instructor Support button and then go to the Download Supplements section. Here you will be able to log in or complete a one-time registration for a user name and password. If you have any questions regarding this process or the materials available online, please contact your local Prentice Hall sales representative.

Acknowledgments

We owe a great deal of credit to the many teachers, parents, and children of the classrooms where we have visited over several editions and continually experiment to try out new ideas and strategies. The insights we gain from teachers and learners, both in Utah and in Tennessee, profoundly influence our understanding of how children solve the language learning puzzle. We are especially thankful for the support of our colleagues at Utah State University and the University of Memphis. You who have been reactors to our evolving ideas have offered many hints for improvement. We appreciate your wisdom and advice.

We also wish to express our gratitude to our reviewers for this edition: Julie Coppola, Boston University; Shirley Ermis, Texas A&M University, Kingsville; Claudia McVicker, Ball State University; Laura Pardo, Michigan State University; Margaret Pope, Mississippi State University.

We are deeply grateful to Brett Elizabeth Blake, St. John's University, for her help in keeping us focused on the needs of English learners. We also extend our gratitude to Bonnie Turner of Ball State University for her contributions in thoughtfully integrating technology throughout the chapters and in providing excellent instructors' resources to fill out the *Teaching Children to Read* package.

BRIEF CONTENTS

Note: Every effort has been made to provide accurate and current Internet information in this book. However, the Internet and information posted on it are constantly changing, so it is inevitable that some of the Internet addresses listed in this textbook will change.

CONTENTS

CHAPTER 11   Effective Reading Instruction and Organization
in Grades K–3 **406**

Teaching Children to Read

1 Effective Reading Instruction

The Teacher Makes the Difference

Chapter Questions

1. Why is learning to read considered so important for young children?
2. What is reading?
3. What are the seven characteristics of highly effective reading teachers?
4. What do effective teachers know and do to promote success in reading for all students?

The First Day

Selena is a college student preparing to become an elementary school teacher. For her, this is not just another class, but the real beginning of her teaching career. Without doubt, teaching reading will be the centerpiece of her classroom. Selena recalls fondly her own first grade teacher, Mrs. Roberts, who introduced her to the world of books and reading. Selena hopes she will be a "Mrs. Roberts" to the children she will teach over the course of her career.

Though there are several professors who teach the introductory reading course, Selena has chosen Dr. Favio's class. Professor Favio is known for her many years of successful teaching in public schools and her rigorous, hands-on instructional methods that get her students ready for their first year of teaching. The professor begins by asking students to read a scenario printed on the cover of the course syllabus.

On one occasion, Frank Smith (1985), a well-known literacy expert who had never taught a child to read in a classroom, was confronted with a taunting question by a group of exasperated teachers: "So, what would you do, Dr. Smith, if you had to teach a room full of 30 five-year-olds to read?" Dr. Smith's response was quick and decisive. He first indicated that children learn to read from people—and the most important of these people are teachers. As teachers, therefore, you need to comprehend the general processes of how children develop and learn. And teachers need to understand the specific processes whereby children learn to read.

After everyone has finished reading the quote, Dr. Favio continues the class with a question clearly intended to provoke discussion: "How did *you* learn to read? What do you remember about learning to read? Who helped you? Turn to your neighbor, introduce yourself, and share your thoughts in response to this question." Immediately the room fills with the buzz of students sharing their ideas about how they learned to read. Selena shares her memories with her "elbow partner," Terrence. She tells him how she was first introduced to books by her mom and grandma. "Did they ever read *Clifford, the Big, Red Dog* to you?" asks Terrence. "He was my favorite!"

After a few minutes of discussion, Dr. Favio asks the class to share some of their ideas and records them on a white board at the front of the classroom.

- *Little kids learn to read from someone who reads to them.*
- *I learned to read from my older sister.*
- *I remember writing letters and asking my mother what they spelled.*
- *I had a favorite book I memorized because my grandmother read it to me over and over again.*
- *I remember my teacher reading a great big book to us in kindergarten called* Mrs. Wishy Washy. *I loved that book!*
- *I watched* Sesame Street, Barney, *and* Reading Rainbow. *I learned the letters and some words from watching TV.*

Next, Dr. Favio asks her students to define what it really means to *read*. They are to take one minute of think time, and then share their ideas with their elbow partner. This question makes Selena remember how she struggled in learning phonics. Terrence remarks, "Well, I agree that reading has to include phonics, but I don't see how you can call it "reading" if you don't understand what you are reading. I mean, I can call out all of the words in my geology book, but *understanding* what they mean is another thing. For me, that takes some work!"

Dr. Favio invites comments from the class and records these statements about the nature of reading.

- *I think reading is when you sound out letters to make words.*
- *Reading involves understanding what's on the page.* (This was Terrence's contribution.)
- *I learned to read from little books that used the same pattern over and over again.*
- *Learning phonics is the first part of reading and comprehension is the last.*
- *Reading is about learning information that makes you smarter.*
- *Reading is the ability to put together what you know with what the author wants you to know.*

Dr. Favio stops the discussion at this point. She comments in sincere tones, "While these are critical issues for all teachers to reflect upon, when we look at scientific research there can be no doubt that the teacher's skill and the teacher's knowledge make the greatest difference in whether or not a young child learns to read. And because reading is, in a very real way, the gateway to social justice, your role as a reading teacher has the potential of changing lives and, therefore, our society."

That, thinks Selena, *is why I have chosen to become a teacher.*

Why Is Learning to Read So Important?

The ability to read is a key factor in living a healthy, happy, and productive life. In fact, the ability to read has recently been declared the "new civil right" on the Web site of the National Right to Read Foundation (2001). Without the ability to read, a child cannot fully access his or her democratic rights. Nonreaders and poor readers cannot fully consider political positions and issues; they cannot take complete advantage of available societal or governmental institutions for themselves or their children or thoroughly access their rights and responsibilities as citizens. Stated differently, we believe that the ability to read is—for all America's citizens—the essential hinge upon which the centrally important gate of social justice swings.

Conversely, the *inability to read* has been listed recently as a national health risk. The National Institutes of Health (NIH), an agency of the federal government, has recently registered *reading disability* or *the inability to read* on the nation's list of "life-threatening diseases" because of the devastating and far-reaching effects that reading failure has upon the quality of our citizens' lives. To clearly understand the full impact that reading failure has upon the life of an individual, we offer the following quote from *The 90% Reading Goal,* by Fielding, Kerr, and Rosier (1998):

> The most expensive burden we place on society is those students we have failed to teach to read well. The silent army of low readers who move through our schools, siphoning off the lion's share of administrative resources, emerge into society as adults lacking the single prerequisite for managing their lives and acquiring additional training. They are chronically unemployed, underemployed, or unemployable. They form the single largest identifiable group of those whom we incarcerate, and to whom we provide assistance, housing, medical care, and other social services. They perpetuate and enlarge the problem by creating another generation of poor readers". (pp. 6–7)

Ernest Boyer (1995), former president of the Carnegie Foundation for the Advancement of Teaching, once asserted that the success of every elementary school is judged by its students' achievement in reading and writing. He continued by emphasizing that ". . . learning to read is without question the top priority in elementary education" (p. 69).

What Is Reading?

A substantial task in becoming a teacher is learning what particular terms mean and how to use these terms with other professionals in the field. The term *reading* has been used for many years in a narrow sense to refer to a set of print-based decoding and thinking skills necessary to understand text (Harris & Hodges, 1981). Snow, Burns, and Griffin contend that "Reading is a complex developmental challenge that we know to be intertwined with many other developmental accomplishments: attention, memory, language, and motivation, for example. Reading is not only a cognitive psycholinguistic activity but also a social activity" (1998, p. 15).

Nowadays our understanding of the act of reading has been broadened to include the visual and thinking skills necessary to acquire information from digital video, handheld data assistants, computers, or other technological learning environments (Hobbs, 2005; Messaris, 2005). Add to this broadened definition of reading the idea that the visual and thinking skills needed for acquiring information today are situated in and shaped by increasingly diverse social or cultural settings found in schools, homes, communities, or ethnic groups (Tracey & Morrow, 2006). As a result, the term **reading** is currently interpreted far more broadly and encompasses the learning of a complex set of skills and knowledge that allows individuals to understand visual and print-based information. The goal of reading instruction, then, is to empower *readers* to learn, grow, and participate in a vibrant and quickly changing information-based world.

As children begin the process of learning to read, they need to acquire a set of skills and strategies that will help them reach the ultimate goal associated with learning

Getting to Know English Learners
The literacy learning of ELs is protected under Title VI of the Civil Rights Act of 1964—an important guarantee as one in five children in the United States today speaks a language other than English at home.

to read: comprehending what they read whether in traditional print forms or more technology-based formats. On the way to the goal of reading comprehension—that is, understanding the author's message—children must acquire a set of early reading skills or tools that include the following:

- Hearing individual sounds in spoken words (known as *phonemic awareness*)
- Recognizing and identifying letters
- Understanding concepts about how printed language looks and works
- Increasing oral language (speaking) vocabularies
- Understanding that sounds in spoken language "map" onto letters in written language
- Decoding words with accuracy, speed, and expression

Shanahan (2006) and others (e.g., Durkin, 1966), indicate that the desire and ability to learn to read often grow out of a child's initial curiosity about how to write letters and words. Consequently, writing very often represents not only the beginning point in many a young child's journey to learn to read but the finish line as well. At first, young children become aware of letters and words in the world around them. Eventually they may ask how to write their name or spell some other personally significant word or concept (e.g., their pet's name or the name of a relative). When children are able to write letters and words, a "cognitive footprint" or *memory trace* left in the brain is deep and long-lasting—much longer-lasting than that engendered by mere letter or word recognition alone. Similarly, when children can string words together to construct meaning such as that found in a story, they have "comprehended" text at a deeper and longer-lasting level. In a very real sense, children's understanding of what they read is deepened and cemented when they can write about it.

As children learn to write, they must learn a similar set of enabling skills to send them on their way to the ultimate goal of writing: *composition*. To acquire proficiency in writing, younger children need to acquire such skills as:

- handwriting (upper and lower case letters).
- understanding writing conventions such as punctuation, headings, paragraph indents, and the like.
- being able to "encode" thoughts into print (i.e., spelling words).

As you can readily see, the components of reading instruction are complementary and reflect a strong and supportive relationship between reading and writing processes (Tierney & Shanahan, 1991). Stated differently, it would be most difficult and terribly ineffective to separate reading from writing in an effective reading instruction program.

Teachers Make the Difference

Question: What is the primary ingredient in the recipe for every child's reading success? Answer: A classroom teacher with the expertise to support the teaching of reading to children having a variety of abilities and needs (Braunger & Lewis, 2006; National Education Association (NEA) Task Force on Reading, 2000; National Research Council, 2001; Snow, Griffin, & Burns, 2005; Strickland, Snow, Griffin, Burns, & McNamara, 2002).

In 1985, the National Academy and Institute of Education issued *Becoming a Nation of Readers: The Report of the Commission on Reading*. In this famous report, commission members concluded that teacher knowledge, skill, and competence is absolutely essential in helping all learners become strong readers. They added:

> An *indisputable* [italics added] conclusion of research is that the quality of teaching makes a considerable difference in children's learning. Studies indicate that about 15 percent of the variation among children in reading achievement at the end of the school year is attributable to factors that related to the skill and effectiveness of the teacher. In contrast, the largest study ever done comparing approaches to beginning reading found that about 3 percent of the variation in reading achievement at the end of the first grade was attributable to the overall approach of the program. Thus, the prudent assumption for educational policy is that, while there may be some 'materials-proof' teachers, there are no 'teacher-proof' materials. (Anderson, Hiebert, Scott, & Wilkinson, 1985, p. 85)

Competent teachers make the difference in effective reading instruction, a fact that has been verified time and again through research. For instance, The National Commission on Teaching and America's Future, or NCTAF, in 1996 declared that by the end of the year 2006, the nation must "provide all students in the country with what should be their educational birthright: access to competent, caring, and qualified teachers" (p. 5), a goal that, sadly, has not yet been achieved (NCTAF, 2006). Likewise, the National Education Association's Task Force on Reading 2000 noted, "The teacher, not the method, makes the real difference in reading success" (p. 7).

From experience, we know parental attitudes confirm that "It all comes down to the teacher,"—since they [parents] are notorious for competing to get their children into classes taught by the current faculty stars of the school! And why shouldn't they? Nothing in this world can replace the power of a great classroom teacher . . ." (Strickland, Snow, Griffin, Burns, & McNamara, 2002, p. 4). In a national survey by Haselkorn and Harris (2001), 89 percent of Americans responded that it is very important to have a well-qualified teacher in every classroom. These same researchers found that 80 percent of parents agreed strongly that fully qualified teachers should be provided to all children, even if that meant spending more money. Seventy-seven percent said it is a high national priority to develop the professional skills and knowledge of teachers throughout their careers. The National Commission on Teaching and America's Future (1996) reported that, "Without telling parents they are doing so, many districts hire unqualified people as 'teachers' and assign them full responsibility for children. More than 12 percent of all newly hired 'teachers' enter without any training at all, and another 14 percent enter without having fully met state standards" (p. 14). Though these data may have improved somewhat since 1996, it is clear that the problem has not been adequately addressed, especially in large, urban districts having high numbers of disadvantaged children. The poorest children and the most powerless families often receive the least our educational system has to offer (NCTAF, 2006)—what Jonathan Kozol (1991) labels "savage inequalities."

Teacher Development Is a Worthwhile Investment. In a national study of 1,000 school districts, Ferguson (1991) found that every additional dollar spent on more highly qualified teachers netted greater improvement in student achievement than did any other use of school resources. We also know that teachers' general instructional ability and knowledge are strongly related to student achievement (Greenwald, Hedges, & Laine, 1996). And an increasing number of studies now show a strong link between what teachers know about the teaching of reading and their students' achievement in reading (Darling-Hammond, Wise, & Klein, 1999; Snow, Griffin, & Burns, 2005). In fact, research also suggests that teachers influence student academic growth more than any other single factor, including families, neighborhoods, and the schools students attend (Sanders & Rivers, 1996). Successful schools that produce high student reading and writing achievement test scores, regardless of socioeconomic status or the nature of reading and writing instruction, have teachers who are knowledgeable and articulate about their work (Mosenthal, Lipson, Torncello, Russ, & Mekkelsen, 2004; McCardle & Chhabra, 2004).

The Seven Characteristics of Highly Effective Reading Teachers

Emerging from a synthesis of research on effective reading instruction and the practices of exemplary reading teachers in elementary schools, we have determined that there are seven important characteristics that guide us in the central message of this book: The teacher's knowledge about effective reading instruction makes the single greatest difference in whether or not every child will have an equal and effective opportunity to learn to read successfully in elementary school!

Each characteristic of exemplary reading instruction is stated in terms of what highly effective reading teachers must know and be able to do to provide an effective reading instructional program in early childhood and elementary school classrooms. Highly effective reading teachers:

- understand how children learn oral language and how children learn to read.
- are excellent classroom managers.
- begin reading instruction by first assessing what students already know and can do.
- know how to adapt instruction to meet the needs of diverse learners.
- teach the essential components of reading using evidence-based instructional practices.
- model and encourage reading and writing applications throughout the day.
- partner with other teachers, parents, and community members to ensure children's learning.

We outline each characteristic here, but they will be discussed in much greater detail in the remaining chapters of this book.

Characteristic 1: Highly Effective Reading Teachers Understand How Children Learn Oral Language and How Children Learn to Read

The development of oral language is directly linked to success in reading and writing abilities. Children who come to school with thousands of "words in their head"—

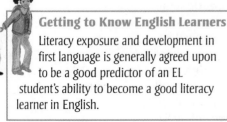

Getting to Know English Learners
Literacy exposure and development in first language is generally agreed upon to be a good predictor of an EL student's ability to become a good literacy learner in English.

words they can hear, understand, and use in their daily lives—are already on the path to learning success (Allington & Cunningham, 1996). Similarly, children from what could be termed "language-deprived backgrounds" must receive immediate attention if they are to have any real chance at reading success (National Research Council, 1998; Johnson, 2001; Reutzel & Cooter, 2005). Thus, we have concluded that highly effective reading teachers know and understand the value of early language development.

Language is mainly a verbal (speech sounds) and visual symbol (printed letters/words) system used in human society that is capable of representing the full range of our knowledge, experiences, and emotions. All humans use language as a tool for having needs met, for thinking and solving problems, and for sharing ideas and feelings (Halliday, 1975). Language is both expressive and receptive. *Expressive language* requires the sender of a message to *encode* or to put his or her thoughts into symbolic systems (verbal and visual) of the language. *Receptive language* requires the receiver of a message to *decode* or unlock the code of the language symbol systems used by the sender in order to construct meaning. Both expressive and receptive forms of language typically take the forms of spoken sounds or written symbols, but may also be represented visually through gestures, art, pictures, video, or dramatization.

The English language is an *alphabetic language*. An alphabetic language is one in which the sounds of spoken or oral language and the symbols or print found in written language relate to one another in more or less predictable ways. For example, the sound /buh/ *maps* onto or is represented by the letter *b*. In some languages the symbols used do not represent sounds in the language at all, but instead represent unified concepts or events such as words or phrases. For example, English uses an alphabetic or orthographic system where symbols represent sounds; Chinese, on the other hand, uses a logographic system that represents entire concepts (words) or events (phrases) with pictures.

The Structure of Language

The structure of language is typically divided into seven interrelated components: (1) phonology, (2) orthography, (3) morphology, (4) syntax, (5) semantics, (6) etymology, and (7) pragmatics.

1. **Phonology** refers to the study of the sound structures of oral language and includes both understanding speech and producing speech.
2. **Orthography** refers to patterns linking letters or **graphemes** to sounds or phonemes in spoken language to produce conventional word spellings (Snow, Griffin, & Burns, 2005).
3. **Morphology** refers to the study of word structure (Carlisle, 2004; Piper, 1998).
4. **Syntax** refers to the rule system of how words are combined into larger language structures, especially sentences. Many persons use the term **grammar** as nearly synonymous with *syntax.*
5. The **semantic** component of language involves connecting one's background experiences, knowledge, interests, attitudes, and perspectives with spoken or written language to comprehend the meaning of that language (Anderson & Pearson, 1984; Kintsch & Kintsch, 2005; Rumelhart, 1980).
6. **Etymology** (Snow, Griffin, & Burns, 2005) is the study of how word meanings and language meanings change over time in popular culture. For example, the meaning of the word *bad* has been changed from "undesirable" or "awful" to "desirable" or "high-quality."
7. **Pragmatics** is the study of how language is used by people in societies to satisfy their need to communicate. Research over the past decade has shown that a teacher's knowledge

Getting to Know English Learners
Children who are learning to become literate in English face a dual task. Besides the characteristics of written language, they have to learn an unfamiliar language that in part refers to an unfamiliar cultural background. In fact, the written system from which these students' home language, culture, and identity is embedded may not even be one that uses alphabetic script as represented by the Greek alphabet. Chinese students, for example, may read symbols that represent whole phrases; Arabic students may read from bottom to top and from right to left.

of language structure and language components relates to and moderately predicts students' early reading achievement (Cunningham, Perry, Stanovich, & Stanovich, 2004; Moats, 1994).

Teachers need to understand how children acquire their ability to speak. There are essentially four major views of how children come by their oral language ability: (1) behaviorist, (2) innatist, (3) constructivist, and (4) social interactionist. **Behaviorists** believe that oral language is learned through *conditioning* and *shaping*— processes that involve a stimulus and a reward or a punishment. **Innatists** believe that language learning is natural or "in-born" for human beings. **Constructivists** believe that language development is built over time and linked to overall thinking ability or cognitive development. **Social interactionists** assume that oral language development is greatly influenced by physical, social, and, of course, linguistic factors found in the child's immediate environment. Whether teachers work with slow learners, gifted students, English Learners (EL), or typically developing children living in the suburbs, they find that oral language among young children develops along a fairly predictable continuum. However, we also know that language development can be slowed through such external influences as poverty.

Getting to Know English Learners
By socially interacting with oral language, ELs not only adjust their language to be better understood by others, but seek ways to nudge native speakers to modify their speech as well.

Research tells us that reading teachers who are aware of the oral language developmental stages and average rates of oral language development are more likely to be effective in raising children's oral language development to new and higher levels (Braunger & Lewis, 2006; Burns, Griffin, & Snow, 1999; Snow, Burns, & Griffin, 1998; Snow, Griffin, & Burns, 2005; Strickland, Snow, Griffin, Burns, & McNamara, 2002). Also, highly effective reading teachers understand that rates of oral language development vary radically among children (Smith, 2001) and are able to adjust their instructional pacing and expectations accordingly (Braunger & Lewis, 2006; Burns, Griffin, & Snow, 1999; Snow, Burns, & Griffin, 1998; Snow, Griffin, & Burns, 2005; Strickland, Snow, Griffin, Burns, & McNamara, 2002). Finally, highly effective reading teachers understand the varying explanations of the reading process and are better able to adapt their reading instruction to meet the diverse learning needs of all children (Tracey & Morrow, 2006).

Characteristic 2: Highly Effective Reading Teachers Are Excellent Classroom Managers

The term *classroom management* refers to the ability of a teacher to organize, direct, and supervise the classroom environment so that effective student learning is made possible (Snow, Griffin, & Burns, 2005). Excellent classroom management (Morrow, Reutzel, & Casey, 2006; Reutzel & Morrow, in press) requires teachers to know and use a complex set of skills and strategies to accomplish tasks such as the following:

- Allocate classroom space for multiple uses
- Supply and arrange classroom materials
- Clearly communicate expectations and rules within a positive classroom climate
- Employ effective instructional practices
- Effectively train students in classroom routines and procedures
- Establish a predictable and familiar daily classroom schedule

A supportive and well-thought-out classroom environment is integral to achieving the goals of an effective reading program. When planning for an effective classroom environment, teachers must consider the literacy materials available in the classroom. They may need to think about the quantity of genres (e.g., nonfiction, mysteries, poetry), reading levels, and content of materials provided to children. They see classroom walls as blank palettes for instructional displays and student work. The maintenance of a classroom library, the grouping and accessibility of reading and writing tools, written invitations and encouragements, and directions on how to participate in upcoming literacy events are just a few of the many considerations teachers must deal with to be excellent classroom managers (Hoffman, Sailors, Duffy, & Beretvas, 2004; Wolfersberger, Reutzel, Sudweeks, & Fawson, 2004).

Characteristic 3: Highly Effective Reading Teachers Begin Reading Instruction by First Assessing to Find Out What Students Already Know and Can Do

Reading assessment refers to the observations, record keeping, and ongoing performance tests that a teacher uses to gather information about each student's reading progress (Flippo, 2003). Classroom assessment should be broadly interpreted to allow examination of students' literacy *processes* as well as the *products* they create. The goal of literacy assessment should be to provide sufficient information for teachers to make decisions about "next steps" for students in their literacy learning, and for the selection of effective, evidence-based teaching strategies.

> **Getting to Know English Learners**
> The use of alternative assessment techniques like literacy portfolios maximize the EL's chance for success, as literacy growth can be documented in powerful and positive ways.

Excellent reading assessment and careful analyses of data (McKenna & Stahl, 2003; Reutzel & Cooter, 2007) are necessary for effective reading instruction and require that teachers know how to use a variety of assessment skills and strategies such as the following:

- Determining what children *can do,* not just what they *cannot do*
- Understanding the multiple purposes for which assessment strategies may be used (i.e., screening, diagnosis, progress monitoring, and outcome assessments)
- Using assessment data to inform the selection of reading instructional strategies
- Gaining insight into the processes students use when reading and writing, not just the final products of their reading and writing
- Documenting children's reading growth and development over time in relation to established benchmarks or standards
- Examining the entire context (the school, the home, and the classroom) of a child's opportunities to learn to read
- Developing a year-long assessment plan for multiple assessment strategies
- Integrating reading assessment data gathering into ongoing reading instruction and practice
- Using computers and electronic technology to collect, store, organize, and analyze assessment data

Teachers must have a well-thought-out assessment plan to achieve the goals of an effective reading program. When planning for reading assessment, teachers may need to consider the purposes for the test(s), testing conditions, and time needed to collect and, most especially, to analyze the data to shape, adapt, and inform later teaching. Great reading teachers think about how to infuse their data gathering into instruction so as to minimize the amount of time taken from teaching. Masterful teachers plan how to use informal data-gathering strategies during whole-group, small-group, and individual instruction. Sometimes, if the school district provides them, teachers are able to use computer software and electronic technological tools like personal data assistants (PDAs) to collect data (Wepner, Valmont, & Thurlow, 2000).

Characteristic 4: Highly Effective Reading Teachers Know How to Adapt Instruction to Meet the Needs of Learners with Special Needs

Meeting every student's needs in learning to read in today's increasingly diverse classroom environments can be complex and challenging. Children's ability to flourish from reading instruction can be influenced by any number of factors, including physical, emotional, behavioral, and intellectual disabilities; differences between the language of instruction and students' primary language, as with English Learners (EL); access to print materials in the home; parenting styles; previous schooling experiences; cultural differences; economic strata; and more. Unfortunately, there is an increasing tendency in some schools to engage in a "one-size-fits-all" reading curriculum that will not address the learning needs of all children (Raphael et al., 2003; Tyner, 2004). However, the only way to provide solid instruction that meets the needs of learners having special needs in today's classrooms is to pursue what is called "differentiating instruction" (Gregory & Chapman, 2002; Tomlinson, 1999). Excellent teachers provide instruction that is responsive to the *specific* needs of every child based on ongoing assessment findings. How one goes about differentiating reading instruction to meet each child's needs is of critical importance for all teachers (Gregory & Chapman, 2002; Tomlinson, 1999).

Today's teachers will need to know how to:

- use a variety of assessment tools for multiple purposes, and then translate their student data into effective teaching plans.
- implement teaching interventions using multiple instructional strategies because one size does NOT fit all.
- make use of multiple organizational and classroom management techniques.

A workable model for many teachers is to begin with a simple, limited, and manageable small-group differentiated instructional system. Small-group differentiated instruction requires that teachers group children by similar abilities and needs for instruction in groups numbering four to eight. Over time and with experience, these same teachers can gradually expand their practice using a range of instructional strategies to include:

- daily, intensive, small-group, teacher-guided reading instruction in appropriately challenging text levels.
- the use of student-selected books and other readings at appropriate reading levels.
- sensibly selected classroom spaces accompanied by clear rules, directions, schedules, and familiar routines.

Of course, there are many other ways effective reading teachers adapt instruction for children with special needs. In this book we show you (1) how to use research-based strategies to help students work collaboratively and develop language skills; (2) how to weave in successful experiences in reading history, science, mathematics, health, and other nonfiction texts; and (3) how to encourage children to become more independent literacy learners (Gregory & Chapman, 2002; Raphael et al., 2003; Tomlinson, 2001; Tyner, 2004).

Video Classroom

Visit a Second Grade Classroom on the Companion CD
"Model Lessons for Literacy Instruction"—
Grouping Students

Begin by viewing the Orientation portion of the CD to under-stand all the options available to you on this CD.

View *Grouping Students,* Clip 3 under "Second Grade Guided Reading." Follow-ing viewing, read about the grouping of students through Experts, Literature, Teachers, and Students. Their comments are located in the tabbed box below the video viewing window.

Review the video and ask yourself the following:

- How are the Five Pillars of Effective Reading Instruction reflected in current approaches of flexible grouping with students? Cite examples as evidence for each connection.
- What are the three assumptions that teachers keep in mind as they prepare to group students? How do these relate to flexible grouping and the moni-toring of progress?
- What examples of grouping did you experience in elementary school? Do these reflect the current characteristics of effective reading instruction? Why or why not?

Learn more about meeting individual needs within the classroom. Visit our Teacher Prep Website (*www.prenhall.com/teacherprep*) for a link to "Getting Your License" and "Beginning Your Career." Select *Field Experiences* and *Accommodating Student Differences and Equality in the Classroom.* You will find practical resources to assist you in becoming an active professional who meets the needs of diverse learners.

Characteristic 5: Highly Effective Reading Teachers Teach the Essential Components of Reading Using Evidence-Based Instructional Practices

In the past decade or so, a series of reports has been commissioned dealing with the **essential components of reading** that young children need to learn and be taught to become successful readers. One of the early reports was sponsored by the National Academy of Sciences and the National Research Council. Prominent read-ing and education experts were convened to review existing research studies to determine which skills must be taught to young children when they are learning to read to prevent them from falling into early reading difficulties or eventual reading failure. This panel issued a report titled *Preventing Reading Difficulties in Young Children* (Snow, Burns, & Griffin, 1998). A companion document, published in 1999 and intended to make the findings of the earlier report more accessible to parents and teachers, was titled *Starting Out Right: A Guide to Promoting Children's Reading Success* (Burns, Griffin, & Snow, 1999). In these two reports, the National Research Council spelled out several essential reading instruction components that simply must be taught to prevent early reading failure.

Two years later, in direct response to a U.S. Congressional mandate to examine the status of "scientific" research on teaching young children to read, the report of the National Reading Panel on Teaching Children to Read (2000) was jointly pub-lished by the National Institute of Child Health and Human Development, the National Institutes of Health, and the U.S. Department of Education. Like the previously published reading research report, a companion document, titled *Put Reading First: The Research Building Blocks for Teaching Children to Read* (Armbruster & Osborn,

2001), was distributed with the intent to widely disseminate the findings of the National Reading Panel (2000) report to parents and educators. (Note: You can receive a free copy of these reports on the Web from *www.nationalreadingpanel.org.*)

What we now know is that highly effective reading programs focus on (1) curriculum essentials, (2) providing students access to print materials, and (3) effective instruction. Curriculum essentials of evidence-based reading instruction include teaching the following (Burns, Snow, & Griffin, 1999; National Reading Panel, 2000):

- oral language development
- concepts of printed language
- letter name knowledge and production
- sight word recognition
- phonemic awareness
- phonics
- fluency
- vocabulary
- comprehension
- writing/spelling

An equally important component of evidence-based reading instruction is providing children access to various kinds of print materials (e.g., books, poetry, graphic novels, etc.) and print-making supplies (Neuman, 1999; Neuman & Celano, 2000, 2006). Print and print-making supplies or materials include but are not limited to:

- a variety of interesting and appropriately challenging reading and writing materials to include both good literature and information books.
- supportive and assistive technologies for learning to read and write.
- sociodramatic, literacy-enriched play in kindergarten.
- adequate time for reading and writing instruction.
- adequate time for reading and writing practice.
- extra time and expert help for those who struggle.
- outreach to and involvement of parents in interacting with their children around reading and writing.

The third essential component of an evidence-based reading instructional program is, not surprisingly, quality instruction. As noted earlier in this chapter, the quality of instruction provided by the teacher is the single most significant determiner of a child's reading achievement once he or she enters school (Sanders & Rivers, 1996). Evidence-based, high-quality reading instruction includes:

- reading and writing *to, with*, and *by* children.
- making use of captioned television to aid in reading practice at home.
- encouraging the viewing of educational television programming and use of the Internet to increase world knowledge.
- modeling comprehension strategies and encouraging children and teachers to talk about texts to improve comprehension.
- connecting literature study to content learning in other curriculum areas, (i.e., science, math, and history).
- creating print-rich, well-organized, and highly interactive classroom environments.
- providing systematic, explicit, and sustained skill and strategy instruction in each of the essential curriculum components of reading instruction.

Characteristic 6: Highly Effective Reading Teachers Model Reading and Writing Applications Throughout the Day

In 1975, New Zealand's renowned reading educator Marie Clay wrote a book titled *What Did I Write?* Children often ask this question while holding up their scribbles and drawings, catching adults off-guard as they begin to explore the world of print. The powerful connection between writing and reading has long been recognized by teachers and researchers alike (Farnan & Dahl, 2003). In 1966, Dolores Durkin wrote the following in her now classic *Children Who Read Early* about how young children become readers:

> In fact, for some early readers, the ability to read seemed almost like a by-product of the ability to print and to spell. For these "pencil and paper kids," the learning sequence moved from (a) scribbling and drawing, to (b) copying objects and letters of the alphabet, to (c) questions about spelling [writing], to (d) ability to read. (p. 137)

Similarly, Clay discovered that

> "In the early child's contact with written language, writing behaviours seem to play the role of organizers of reading behaviors . . . which appear to help the child come to grips with learning to attend to the significant details of written language". (1975, p. 3)

Here's what we now know about reading/writing connections: As children read, they learn about how authors structure their writing. They learn about indenting, word spellings, headings, subheadings, and more. They also learn about how authors select words to convey an idea or feeling as well as gain greater insight into how authors organize and present their thoughts in print. No evidence-based reading instructional program is complete without daily, planned opportunities for children to engage in "reading like a writer" and "writing like a reader."

Characteristic 7: Highly Effective Reading Teachers Partner with Other Teachers, Parents, and Community Members to Ensure Children's Learning

Reading teachers in the twenty-first century no longer have the luxury of viewing home involvement as merely a good or even an important idea. There is now substantial agreement among literacy researchers and master teachers that parents can make powerful contributions to their children's success in early literacy learning (Dickinson & Tabors, 2001; Paratore, 2003). Therefore, the teacher's reaching out to parents and homes is vital to young children's progress in learning to read successfully.

For example, in a large-scale, federally funded study of 14 schools in Virginia, Minnesota, Colorado, and California; teachers, administrators, and parents were interviewed, surveyed, and observed to determine the characteristics of effective schools and classroom teachers who were *Beating the Odds in Teaching All Children to Read* (Taylor, Pearson, Clark, & Walpole, 1999). One of the six key school-level factors in this study that was clearly associated with the most effective schools in teaching at-risk children to read successfully was outreach to homes and parents. According to the researchers, "The four effective schools made a more concerted effort to reach out to parents than the other schools. Efforts included conducting focus groups, written or phone surveys, and having an active site council on which parents served" (p. 2).

The findings of the Virginia study were echoed in other research in a major urban school district having high poverty conditions. In *Perspectives on Rescuing*

Urban Literacy Education, R. Cooter (2004) described results of a privately funded "failure analysis" to learn what teachers must know and be able to do to reverse a 76 percent reading failure rate for this school district's third graders. Five "pillars" or instructional supports, the report concluded, were necessary to ensuring reading success—one of which was family and community involvement. "Most parents help their children at home [with reading] if they know what to do; thus, teachers must be supported in their efforts to educate families in ways they can help their children succeed in the home" (p. 22).

There are many examples of excellent family literacy programs that may serve as models for teachers as they make plans to reach out to families. Perhaps one of the best-known family literacy programs nationally is the **Even Start** program which has involved over 80,000 children and adults (St. Pierre, Gamse, Alamprese, Rimdziux, & Tao, 1998). **Project FLAME** (Family Literacy Aprendiendo, Mejorando, Educando), a program designed for English Learner (EL) parents and children, is yet another example of a nationally recognized family literacy program (Rodriquez-Brown, Fen Li, & Albom, 1999; Rodriquez-Brown & Meehan, 1998; Shannahan, Mulhern, & Rodriquez-Brown, 1995). Parents involved with the **Intergenerational Literacy Project** (ILP) (Paratore, 2003) as well as those trained in **Project EASE** (Jordan, Snow, & Porche, 2000) significantly influenced their children's early literacy development prior to school and substantially impacted their children's early reading progress once in school.

Getting to Know English Learners
Projects include taking parents and their children to the local library to meet the librarian, tour the children's book section, and get library cards so that parents could aid in their ELs children's literacy growth in English.

Effective teachers of reading focus on building strong, sturdy, and easily traversed bridges between the classroom and the homes of the children they serve in order to help every child have a successful experience in learning to read and write.

The Five Pillars of Effective Reading Instruction

In each chapter of this book, we include five sections we think of as the **pillars of effective reading instruction,** derived from the seven characteristics of highly effective reading teachers we have just discussed. We call these "pillars" because these five elements (see Figure 1.1) are like the pillars found in many great buildings that support the integrity of the entire structure.

In the context of our discussion of effective reading instruction, the five pillars provide an integral supporting structure. The five pillars will help you organize your understanding of effective reading instruction like other master teachers of reading. What follows is a brief description of each of the five pillars of effective reading instruction that guide the organization of succeeding chapters in this book.

- *Teacher Knowledge.* Educational research over recent decades has verified the basic skills and strategies of reading and the approximate order in which they should be taught. Effective teachers know this sequence of skills and approach their teaching with this important knowledge.
- *Classroom Assessment.* Teachers must know which reading skills each child has already developed and which he or she has not. Master teachers are able to quickly assess each student's knowledge, create instructional roadmaps of what children know, and then teach students according to their specific needs. Assessment happens in these classrooms *before, during,* and *after*

Figure 1.1   The Five Pillars of Effective Reading Instruction

(Pillars labeled: TEACHER KNOWLEDGE · CLASSROOM ASSESSMENT · EFFECTIVE PRACTICE · DIFFERENTIATING INSTRUCTION · FAMILY / COMMUNITY CONNECTIONS)

instruction has taken place. Assessment is essential for making sure every student receives appropriate instruction, and then verifying that learning has taken place.

- *Effective Practice.* There is a veritable mountain of research evidence on the preferred ways of teaching each of the important reading skills and strategies. Great teachers have a plethora of tools in their educational toolbox to ensure that every child is helped to reach his or her full potential.
- *Differentiating Instruction for Diverse Student Needs.* Children come to school with diverse learning needs. For example, in many school districts English is not the first language for a large percentage of students; these students speak

Getting to Know English Learners

The home-school connection—where adults interact with children in a print-rich environment—is crucial for ELs' literacy learning as well. Too often, though, the culture of the EL's home is unlike the culture of the school and ELs' literacy learning can suffer.

Spanish, Chinese, Korean, Arabic, Hmong, and so on. Teachers need to know a variety of ways to help these students learn to read and write in English. In addition, it has been estimated that up to 20 percent of students come to school with various learning differences, such as attention deficit disorder (ADD), dyslexia, cognitive challenges (i.e., "slow learners"), language deficiencies, and behavioral disorders (BD). Our goal must be to help *all* students succeed. Effective reading teachers must have the necessary tools for adjusting instruction to children with diverse learning needs if all are to reach their potential.

- *Family/Community Connections.* It has been said that 80 percent of what students learn occurs outside of school. We know from research, for instance, that children who have been read to a great deal before entering kindergarten have a much stronger language base and are far more likely to succeed in reading (Snow, Burns, & Griffin, 1998). Parents and many involved others in the child's extended family and community are often interested in helping children develop as readers—*if they know what to do.* Thus, teachers can add great power to a child's literacy learning program by educating the adults in their lives in proven reading development strategies that make sense in our busy world.

Summary: Reading Teachers Make the Difference!

So then, we return full circle to our earlier question: *What is the primary ingredient in the recipe for every child's reading success?* We hope that by now you understand the significant role you play in the reading success of each and every child you teach or will teach. You are the hero in every child's literacy learning drama! Research absolutely confirms that your knowledge and skill in the teaching of reading is incredibly important, and we conclude our opening chapter with a little more proof (Braunger & Lewis, 2006; Clark & Peterson, 1986; National Education Association (NEA) Task Force on Reading, 2000; National Research Council, 2001; Snow, Griffin, & Burns, 2005; Strickland, Snow, Griffin, Burns, & McNamara, 2002).

In an interesting reversal of research perspective, students in grades K–12 were asked about the characteristics of their most influential reading teachers. The studies were conducted to discover student perceptions of what teachers do in exemplary reading instruction that helps them succeed (Ruddell, 1995; Ruddell & Harris, 1989; Ruddell & Kern, 1986). The results of the studies indicated that exemplary reading teachers (a) use highly motivating and effective teaching strategies; (b) build strong affective relationships with their students (this relates to interest, attitude, and motivation); (c) create a feeling of excitement about what they are teaching; (d) adjust instruction to meet the individual needs of their students; (e) create rich classroom environments to support their teaching; and (f) have strong organization and management skills.

Taylor and colleagues (1999) studied the literacy practices of exemplary teachers in high-poverty schools that "beat the odds" in teaching children to read. Students in this study were considered at-risk because they came from low-income families, but had average or above-average scores on reading achievement tests. Two teachers each from grades K–3 in 14 schools from across the United States participated in the study. Each teacher was observed five times from December to April for an hour of reading instruction. Teachers also completed a written survey, kept a weekly log of reading and writing activities in their classrooms, and were interviewed at the end of the school year. These masterful teachers focused their reading instruction on small-group instruction, provided time for students to read independently, monitored students' on-task behaviors, and provided strong links to homes with consistent communication. These tremendous teachers also included in their reading instruction a focus on explicit phonics instruction and the application of phonics while reading and writing connected text. They asked high-level comprehension questions, and were more likely to ask students to record their responses to reading in writing.

Metsala and Wharton-McDonald (1997) carefully collected survey and interview data about the most important reading instructional practices among 89 K–3 regular education and 10 special education teachers identified by their school principals as "outstanding." These first-rate reading teachers were described by their peers and supervisors as "masterful" classroom managers who handled time, materials, and student behavior with finesse. These superior reading teachers held high expectations for their students and had a real sense of purpose, direction, and objective. At the top of the list of common practices was a print-rich classroom environment. They also provided daily doses of skill and strategy instruction, access to varied types of text, and adapted their classroom reading instruction to the ability levels or needs of their students. These extraordinary teachers worked to motivate their students to engage in reading and writing regularly and consistently monitored student progress.

In yet another study of primary level exemplary reading teachers, Morrow, Tracey, Woo, and Pressley (1999) found that these teachers, as we saw in earlier studies, created print-rich classroom environments. See a pattern forming? In these print-rich classrooms, teachers orchestrated a variety of learning activities involving the whole class, small groups, and independent seatwork. Instruction was often individualized and occurred on a one-to-one basis. Learning was sometimes teacher-directed; sometimes self-directed through the use of learning centers. Classrooms were rich with student conversation and interaction. Teachers planned and implemented regular times for writing, word analysis instruction, and comprehension strategy instruction. They also made consistent efforts to connect reading and writing instruction to the content taught at other times of the day in core subjects like science, math, and social studies. Many of these same effective practices were reported and confirmed by Cantrell (1999a, 1999b) two years later in her study of the effects of reading instruction on primary students' reading and writing achievement.

In summary, a synthesis of several case studies of exemplary reading teachers in the early childhood and elementary grades found that effective reading teachers share several important characteristics (Allington & Johnston, 2002; Block, 2001; Cantrell, 1999a, 1999b; Morrow, et al., 1999; Morrow & Casey, 2003; Pressley et al., 1996; Pressley, Allington, Taylor et al., 1999; Taylor et al., 2002; Wharton et al., 1997; Wharton-McDonald, Collins-Block, & Morrow, 2001). Masterful reading teachers:

- provide clear explanations and model how to perform specific reading and writing skills, strategies, and behaviors.
- engage students in constructive conversations with teachers and with other students.
- create a supportive, encouraging, and nurturing classroom climate.
- weave reading and writing throughout the curriculum and throughout the day.

- integrate content area topics into literacy instruction.
- create print-rich classroom environments with a variety of literacy materials that support instruction readily accessible.
- meet individual needs in whole-class, small-group, and independent settings.
- implement excellent organization and management decisions.
- develop strong connections with their students' families, homes, and communities.

A common myth about teachers goes something like this: "Those who can, do. Those who can't, teach." Another equally distasteful myth alleges that "Teachers are born, not made." Neither could be farther from the truth. Teachers today must understand a great deal about how children develop and learn generally, about how they develop and learn to read specifically, and about how to assess and teach children in a classroom filled with diversity that did not seem to exist in the past. Today's teachers are expected to know more and do more than teachers at any other time in our history. Teachers must know how to teach by mastering and implementing a body of knowledge related to language development, children's literature, curriculum standards, classroom management, and learning. They must be able to assess students' strengths and needs, plan effective instruction that focuses on the essential components of reading, and ensure that every child makes adequate yearly progress so that no child is left behind. In the end, the expert teaching of reading requires some of the best minds and talent to be found in our nation. Like Louisa Moats (1999), we too, believe that teaching reading is rocket science!

Classroom Applications

1. Read *Using Research and Reason in Education: How Teachers Can Use Scientifically Based Research to Make Curricular and Instructional Decisions.* Working with other members of a small group, list ten reasons why teachers should rely on the results of scientific research to inform their instructional and curricular choices. Share your group's list with the rest of the class. Collapse all of the small-group charts into a single class chart.
2. Read "Beginning Reading Instruction: The Rest of the Story from Research" at *http://www.nea.org/reading/images/beginningreading.pdf.* Compile a list of practices in reading instruction that research supports in addition to those found in the Report of the National Reading Panel: Teaching Children to Read (2000).
3. Organize into small research groups. Select a grade level from kindergarten to third grade. Read *Starting Out Right: A Guide to Promoting Children's Reading Success.* Prepare a class presentation on student accomplishments in reading and writing at the grade level you selected.
4. Read "Beating the Odds in Teaching All Children to Read" (Ciera Report No. 2–006), available on the Web at *www.ciera.org.* In small groups, prepare a brochure or pamphlet that explains to parents, teachers, and school administrators the characteristics of schools and teachers who succeed in teaching all children to read. Share your pamphlet with your class or with parents at your first open house.

Recommended Readings

Armbruster, B. B., Lehr, F., & Osborn, J. (2001). *Put reading first: The research building blocks for teaching children to read.* Washington, DC: U.S. Department of Education. Available at *http://www.nifl.gov/partnershipforreading/publications/reading_first1.html*

Burns, M. S., Griffin, P., & Snow, C. E. (1999). *Starting out right: A guide to promoting children's reading success.* Washington, DC: National Academy Press.

National Institute of Child Health and Human Development. (2000). *Report of the National Reading Panel: Teaching children to read.* Washington, DC: Available at *www.nationalreadingpanel.org/Publications/researchread.htm*

Pressley, M. (2002). Beginning reading instruction: The rest of the story from research. Washington, DC: National Education Association. Available at *http://www.nea.org/reading/images/beginningreading.pdf*

Pressley, M. (2003). A few things reading educators should know about instructional experiments. *The Reading Teacher, 57*(1), 64–71.

Shannahan, T. (2003). Research-based reading instruction: Myths about the National Reading Panel Report. *The Reading Teacher, 56*(7), 646–654.

Slavin, R. E. (2003, February). A reader's guide to scientifically-based research. *Educational Leadership,* pp. 12–16.

Snow, C. E., Burns, M. S., & Griffin, P. (1998). *Preventing reading failure in young children.* Washington, DC: National Academy Press.

Snow, C. E., Griffin, P., & Burns, M. S. (2005). *Knowledge to support the teaching of reading: Preparing teachers for a changing world.* San Francisco, CA: Jossey-Bass.

Stanovich, P. J., & Stanovich, K. E. (2003). *Using research and reason in education: How teachers can use scientifically based research to make curricular and instructional decisions.* Washington, DC: National Institute for Literacy. Available at *www.nifl.gov/partnershipforreading/publications/pdf/Stanovich_Color.pdf*

U.S. Department of Education. (2001). *No Child Left Behind.* Washington, DC: U.S. Department of Education. Available at *http://www.ed.gov/index.jhtml*

U.S. Department of Education. (2003). Identifying and implementing educational practices supported by rigorous evidence: A user-friendly guide. Washington, DC: Coalition for Evidence-Based Policy. Available at *http://www.ed.gov/rschstat/research/pubs/rigorousevid/guide.html*

chapter 2

Developing Children's Oral Language

Chapter Questions

1. What do teachers need to know about oral language?
2. What does research say about the relationship between oral language and reading?
3. What are some ways to assess oral language development and use?
4. What are some ways to develop children's oral language?
5. How can oral language experiences meet the diverse needs of children and families?

A Trip to the Zoo . . . and a Hairy Question

It was a beautiful spring morning in Mr. Cantwell's kindergarten class at Adams Elementary School. Earlier in the week, Mr. Cantwell, a second-year teacher, had taken the children on a field trip to a local petting zoo to learn about baby animals. The children had been learning about life cycles of young animals including birds, insects, fish, and mammals. This morning, Mr. Cantwell was reading books aloud and talking with the children about mammals. After reading and discussing several baby mammal books, the class made a language experience chart based on what they learned at the zoo. As the children dictated their ideas aloud, Mr. Cantwell recorded each child's comments onto the chart using a different colored marker to identify each child's contribution.

When ready to contribute, the children made the gesture Mr. Cantwell established on the first day of school that signaled they had something to say—a hand placed over their mouth meaning, in his words, "O Great One, I have something to say." (None of this waving hands in the air stuff!) Mr. Cantwell called on a bright-eyed little boy named Jamal, who blurted out, "Mammals are born alive."

"That's very good," said Mr. Cantwell, and he wrote the words *born* and *alive* on the chart.

"Austin, what do you know about mammals?"

Austin thoughtfully replied, "Mammals don't hatch from eggs like birds and bugs."

"Way to go. Excellent thinking!" Mr. Cantwell added *egg* to the chart.

Amalia was nearly ready to explode when called upon. "Mammal moms feed their babies milk."

"Wow! You children are *so* smart! Amalia, you are absolutely right. Good job!" Mr. Cantwell added *milk* to the language experience chart.

Rosa chimed in next: "Mammals have hair!" Mr. Cantwell wrote *hair* on the chart.

Ray Reutzel

Braxton, when recognized, removed his hand from his mouth and asked, "Mr. Cantwell, are boys mammals, too?"

Pointing to key words on the chart as he spoke, Mr. Cantwell responded, "Why, yes, they are, Braxton. Think about it. Boys are *born alive;* they don't hatch from *eggs* like birds and bugs, their mothers feed them *milk* when they are little, and they have *hair.* Why do you ask if boys are mammals, Braxton?"

"Well," replied Braxton, "I was just wondering because my grandpa doesn't have any hair. He's bald!"

Mr. Cantwell smiled and patiently explained that Braxton's grandpa was a mammal because when he was younger he used to have hair, and that when boys become men they sometimes lose the hair on their heads. Mr. Cantwell noticed a few of the children leaning forward to check their teacher for early signs of this mysterious hair loss some men experience.

As illustrated by this classroom story, teachers frequently encounter children's attempts to construct meaning around their own experiences and words. Young children often misinterpret words or ideas they do not fully understand, like the child who recites the Pledge of Allegiance saying *invisible* rather than *indivisible* and *liverty* rather than *liberty*. Understanding children's language development is important because **oral language,** the spoken form of communication, has been shown to be strongly related to children's early reading success and in predicting their ability to comprehend what they read. "Oral language is the foundation not only of learning and schooling but of our living together as people of the world. . . . Oral language development is inextricably related to literacy development" (Pinnell & Jaggar, 2003, p. 881).

What Do Teachers Need to Know About Oral Language?

Research confirms that a rich and extensive oral language foundation is critical to the later development of reading and writing (Dickinson & Tabors, 2001; Hart & Risley, 1995, 2002; Scarborough, 2001; NLP, 2006). Children must be relatively fluent in oral language use to communicate effectively with the teacher and with other students in their "learning networks" found in the classroom and in life (Pinnell, 1998; Pinnell & Jaggar, 2003). Also, oral language paves the way for learning such reading skills as phonemic awareness, alphabetic principle, phonics and decoding, and reading comprehension. (Do not be concerned if you are unfamiliar with these terms; they will be explained later.) In fact, oral language ability is the bedrock foundation upon which all future literacy learning is built (Scarborough, 2001; Shanahan, 2006; Smith, 2001; Vygotsky, 1978). As Allington and Cunningham (1996) put it, children who come to school with thousands of "words in their head"—words they can hear, understand, and use in their daily lives—are already on the path to learning success.

Children who come to school with thousands of "words in their head"—words they can hear, understand, and use in their daily lives—are already on the path to learning success.

Similarly, children who have small listening and speaking vocabularies—who come from what might be termed "language-deprived backgrounds"—must receive immediate attention if they are to have any real chance at reading success (National Research Council, 1998; Johnson, 2001).

What Is Language?

Language is essentially an agreed-upon "symbol system." People who share a common vocabulary are able to understand each other when they speak. Oral language is used in human society to represent our full range of knowledge, experiences, and emotions. All humans use language as a tool for getting their needs met, for learning, for thinking, for problem solving, and for sharing ideas and feelings.

Language is both expressive and receptive. **Expressive language** requires the *sender* of a message to "encode" or to put his or her thoughts into a symbolic form. Expressive language most often takes the form of spoken words or written words, but may also be represented visually through gestures, art, pictures, video, or dramatization. **Receptive language** requires the *receiver* of a message to "decode" or unlock the code of the spoken or written communication used by the sender in order to understand the message.

The structure of language is typically divided into six interrelated components:

1. Phonology
2. Orthography
3. Morphology
4. Syntax
5. Semantics
6. Pragmatics

We will now discuss each of these six components of language to help you become a better-informed and more effective reading teacher. You might be asking, "Do I really need to know all of this information about language to effectively teach children to read?" In short, yes! Research over the past decade has shed new light on how teachers' knowledge of language structure relates to their students' success (Moats, 1994; Cunningham, Perry, Stanovich, & Stanovich, 2004).

Phonology: Sounds in Spoken Words

Phonology is a component of language that refers to sounds in speech. There are two major categories in phonology: (1) *prosodic features* or what we sometimes call "speaking with expression," and (2) *articulatory units* or elements such as individual speech sounds, syllables, and words (Snow, Burns, & Griffin, 1998).

Prosodic or expressive features of spoken language include intonation, stress, and juncture. **Intonation** refers to how one's voice rises or falls when one is speaking. For example, vocal pitch usually drops at the end of a statement. (We use a period in writing so that the reader "hears" that drop.) On the other hand, vocal pitch generally rises at the end of a question. (In writing, of course, we use the question mark so the reader "hears" that rise in pitch.) **Stress** refers to speech intensity—the loudness or softness of spoken words. For example, when a speaker wants to emphasize a particular point, he or she will articulate a word or phrase more loudly. (In writing, an exclamation point may be used.) **Juncture** refers to the time between words; note, for example, the difference between "I scream" and "ice cream."

Articulatory features of spoken language include words, syllables, and phonemes. We assume that most of our readers are familiar with the spoken concept of *word*. However, syllables may not be as clearly understood. All words in spoken English are made up of at least one syllable. A single syllable can also be a word. For example, the single-syllable, spoken words *sat, run, dot,* and *cat* are both words and syllables. Of course, many spoken words contain more than one syllable. For example, the word *window* contains two syllables, /win/ and /dow/.

Every syllable in English must contain a rime. A **rime** is defined as the vowel sound and every other sound that follows the vowel sound in a spoken syllable. The spoken words *an, it, a, of,* and *I* all contain a rime that includes the vowel sound (/a/, /e/, /i/, /o/, or /u/) and the other sounds that follow the vowel sound. Some spoken syllables may also contain an onset. An **onset** is defined as all sounds in a spoken syllable that come before the vowel sound. For example, /st/ in *street* or /f/ in *fit* are onsets.

A **phoneme** is the smallest unit of sound in a spoken word (Piper, 1998). The spoken word *wake* contains three phonemes: /w/, /ā/, and /k/. The word *wake* differs by only one phoneme from the words *wade* (/w/, /ā/, /d/) and *make* (/m/, /ā/, /k/), thus showing how changing a single phoneme can alter meaning. Linguists estimate that spoken English is composed of 44 speech sounds. Additional information about the phonological structure of language is provided in Chapters 3 and 4, which deal with phonological awareness (early literacy) and phonics.

An abundance of research over the past two decades has shown that young children who are aware of the phonemes in spoken words, as well as alphabet letters and their associated sounds, are more likely to succeed in early reading and writing (Burns, Snow, & Griffin, 1998; National Reading Panel, 2000, pp. 2–11). By the way, the term we use in our profession for students' awareness of phonemes is called, not surprisingly, **phonemic awareness.** It seems that young children benefit more from early phonics instruction and are able to create "invented spellings" (e.g., TRK for *truck*) in early writing if they have phonemic awareness (Armbruster, Lehr, & Osborn, 2001; Burns, Griffin, & Snow, 1999).

Orthography: Connecting Letters and Sounds

Orthography refers to the patterns used in English linking letters (graphemes) to sounds (phonemes) in spoken language to produce conventional word spellings (Snow, Griffin, & Burns, 2005). A **grapheme** is a printed or visual symbol, usually a letter such as *a, r, m, s,* or *o,* that represents a phoneme. Because English is an alphabetic language, its spelling or orthographic structure is represented by 26 letters or graphemes that relate in somewhat predictable ways to the 44 spoken sounds, or phonemes.

Getting to Know English Learners
English Learners who come from a language background, like Spanish, tend to want to try to pronounce all the sounds in English like in the word, "knight," which retains its spelling from Old English.

To understand orthography, teachers and students must know how the 44 speech sounds are matched with or "mapped" onto the 26 alphabet letters. English, unlike many other languages, has a less predictable relationship between sounds and letters. In languages like Spanish, French, and German, letters and corresponding sounds form one-to-one matches of sound to symbol with few or no exceptions. On the other hand, the 44 sounds of spoken English can be spelled using more than 500 letters or letter combinations! Not surprisingly, this can make learning to read and write in English a bit of a challenge for many children.

Alphabetic Principle. Knowing that speech sounds and letters link to one another, sometimes called the **alphabetic principle,** is a critical insight that young children must achieve in learning to read and write (National Reading Panel, 2000). When students have grasped the alphabetic principle, research has shown they will be able to grasp the relationships between letters and sounds, or **phonics,** which can lead to significant increases in reading and writing achievement, especially for children of poverty (National Reading Panel, 2000). With these facts in mind, highly effective teachers offer very explicit instruction on the alphabetic principle and phonics. A more thorough discussion of how the orthographic system works in reading and writing is provided in Chapter 4: Phonemic Awareness and Phonics.

Morphology: The Building Blocks of Meaning in Words

Morphology refers to the study of word structures that create meaning (Piper, 1998; Carlisle, 2004). Some people mistakenly believe that a word is the smallest unit of meaning in language; however, it is not the word but rather the **morpheme** that comprises the smallest unit of meaning. There are two major types of morphemes: free and bound. A free morpheme is a word that stands alone and has meaning. Words like *ball, peninsula,* and *chain* consist of a single morpheme. A bound morpheme, on the other hand, is an equally meaningful unit of language, but must be connected to another morpheme. Examples include *-ocracy, -ante,* and *bio-* as well as other prefixes and suffixes like *re-, -ed,* and *-es.* In some cases, a bound morpheme can be attached to another bound morpheme to form a meaningful word. Two bound morphemes making a word, for example, are *bio-* and *-ology,* which together form the word *biology.* A bound morpheme, *anti-,* connected with the free morpheme, *thesis,* forms the word *antithesis.*

Linguists also classify morphemes as inflected, derivational, and compound. Inflected morphemes are words with an added suffix or meaningful word ending, such as *-s, -ed, -ing,* and *-est.* Derivational morphemes involve adding a letter to or changing letters within a word, thereby changing the part of speech. For example, changing the words *rust* to *rusty* by adding a *y* to the noun *rust* changes the part of speech to an adjective. Compound words are single words created by joining two words together in various ways (e.g., *bathroom, wallpaper, deerskin, bluebird*).

When children first enter preschool, they are still developing morphological understanding. Word study is critical in the early years (pre-K through second grade) and is strongly related to early word reading ability (Baumann, Edwards, Boland, Olejnik, & Kame'enui, 2003; Carlisle, 2004, 2005) Word study lays the groundwork for all elementary reading, and becomes even more important through students' secondary schooling.

Syntax and Grammar: The "Rule Book" in Language

Syntax involves an understanding of how words are combined into larger language structures, especially sentences. Many people use the term *grammar* as nearly synonomous with *syntax,* and we will do so here for the sake of simplicity. The term **grammar** is defined as a rule system for describing the structure or organization of a language. Thus, English grammar is a system of rules for describing the structure

> **Getting to Know English Learners**
> Many languages around the world do not use the same word order as English. Spanish is just one example, where in most cases the adjective follows the noun, rather than preceding it as it normally is in English.

or organization of the English language. Each language has its own syntax, grammatical system, structure, or organization.

Although the term *grammar* may conjure up visions of learning the names of the parts of speech, it is actually syntax that is more concerned with the conventional ways words are strung together to communicate meaning than with identifying the part of speech of a word. Proper use of syntactic rules results in the production of grammatically acceptable phrases and sentences in speech and writing. In short, knowledge of syntax involves an understanding of the system of rules for organizing words to communicate. Using accepted word order in language is important because it relates to how meaning (comprehension) is constructed. Suppose you were to read or hear the following:

> A is saying individual the is our aloud ability our in rarely purposes respond reader the silently only skill upon our is word of called conducted reading reading it Most by is private fluent that for element of to to use course one each to. (Chapman & Hoffman, 1977, p. 67)

Although each word can be understood in isolation, the meaning of the passage is unclear because the word order is jumbled. When correct word order is restored, meaning is easier to construct:

> The ability to respond to each individual word by saying it aloud is, of course, only one element in reading. It is a skill that the fluent reader is rarely called upon to use. Most of our reading is conducted silently for our own private purposes. (Chapman & Hoffman, 1977, p. 67)

Syntactic, or grammatical, knowledge also enables readers to predict what comes next in a sentence or phrase. For example, read the following sentence.

Hopalong Hank is the name of my green pet _____.

Even young children will fill in the blank with a noun. Although children may not be able to state a grammatical rule that accounts for the fact that a noun follows an adjective in a phrase, they are competent enough to know that only certain kinds of words are allowed in the blank. Moffett (1983) learned through his research that by the time children enter school they have mastered basic grammar and syntax. Moffet further discovered that young children can use their basic grammar and syntax knowledge to help them identify words in reading and to select grammatically correct phrases and sentences in writing.

On the other hand, English learners (ELs) may find the syntax of English quite different from that of their primary language. As teachers, we need to be aware of this fact and clearly model for children English syntax using full sentences in our spoken language.

Semantics: Connecting Past Experiences to Reading

Semantics involves connecting one's background experiences, knowledge, interests, attitudes, and perspectives with spoken or written language to construct meaning (Anderson & Pearson, 1984; Kintsch & Kintsch, 2005; Rumelhart, 1980). Essentially, our total collection of prior experiences and knowledge are connected in the mind in a vast network of related concepts and events. The belief that new knowledge is connected to related ideas one already knows is known as **schema theory** (the plural of *schema* is *schemas* or *schemata*). This enormous quantity of our stored memories is perhaps best seen in the vocabulary words we know. As we encounter new experiences in life, we store this new information in our minds by connecting new words to our known words.

The labeling of new knowledge and experiences with words provides a shared system for language users when communicating or in comprehending a message from someone else (Kintsch & Kintsch, 2005). Prior knowledge and experiences, or the lack thereof, can affect our understanding of language in many ways. For example, you may have prior knowledge about the content of the text shown below but be unable to retrieve (remember) your stored knowledge (Kintsch & Kintsch, 2005). Read the following passage taken from an experiment conducted by Bransford and Johnson (1972):

> If the balloons popped the sound wouldn't be able to carry since everything would be too far away from the correct floor. A closed window would also prevent the sound from carrying, since most buildings tend to be well insulated. Since the whole operation depends upon a steady flow of electricity, a break in the middle of the wire would also cause problems. Of course, the fellow could shout, but the human voice is not loud enough to carry that far. An additional problem is that a string could break on the instrument. Then there could be no accompaniment to the message. It is clear that the best situation would involve less distance. Then there would be fewer potential problems. With face to face contact, the least number of things could go wrong. (p. 719)

Did you experience difficulty in understanding the content or topic of this excerpt? If you did, you are not alone. Bransford and Johnson's (1972) experimental subjects had great difficulty connecting the content of this passage to anything they already knew. Pause for a moment and try to make a mental note of your best guess about the meaning of this passage. Then turn to page 30 and look at the picture in Figure 2.1. Finally, go back and reread the passage.

After your first reading, were you able to recognize that the passage was a modernized version of the Romeo and Juliet serenade? Or did you think the passage was about physics or electricity? Were you thinking about someone making a phone call? Although you could understand all the language in the passage, there was not enough information provided to allow you to retrieve knowledge you had stored in your mind to comprehend its meaning. However, once you were able to retrieve the correct schema, you were able to figure out the passage's meaning.

Here's another interesting fact: When you encounter new language, your brain will often modify your existing knowledge network (schema). For example, as you read the following sentences, pause after each one and think about what you see in your mind. Then move on to the next sentence and do the same. At each point, make note of which schema or "package" of knowledge and experiences you are retrieving to construct meaning.

> John was on his way to school.
> He was terribly worried about the math lesson.
> He thought he might not be able to control the class again today.
> It was not a normal part of a janitor's duties.
>
> (Sanford & Garrod, 1981, p. 114)

Did you notice a change in your understanding of the passage as you stopped each time? Did your schema selection (i.e., the direction your comprehension took) change from that of:

1. a young boy on his way to school
2. who was worried about his math class and lesson
3. to that of a concerned teacher
4. and finally a worried janitor?

Figure 2.1   The Romeo Scene

The more you know about a topic or event, the clearer a written message becomes (Pearson, Hansen, & Gordon, 1979). Researchers have also found that the prior knowledge one has that is *contrary* to the information found in what one hears or reads can actually result in decreased understanding (Alvermann, Smith, & Readence, 1985; Collins-Block, Gambrell, & Pressley, 2002; Collins-Block & Pressley, 2002; Hollingsworth & Reutzel, 1990; Lipson, 1984; Reutzel & Hollingsworth, 1991a). Suppose someone told you that the world was flat rather than round, as with a recent book by Tom Friedman (2005) titled *The World Is Flat!* You might tend to dismiss Friedman as some kind of nut for thinking the Earth is flat when you know good and well from past learning this is not true. But if you later discovered that Mr. Friedman crafted his title to grab readers' attention and to point out that twenty-first century governments and societies must realize that we are all economically connected as never before and must adapt to this "flattening" of world economies, then your schema for a "flat" world would be changed—broadened, really.

Finally, one's point of view or perspective can influence what is understood from language. Goetz, Reynolds, Schallert, and Radin (1983), for example, found that people who read a test passage from the perspective of a burglar recalled very different details than those who were told to read it from the perspective of a burglary victim. It is clear, then, that our prior knowledge, experiences, and perspectives help us anticipate and interpret meaning in language. The more we experience both directly and vicariously, the more our schemas grow. The more we use our schemas, the easier it is for us to retrieve our past knowledge and understand spoken or written language.

> **Getting to Know English Learners**
> ELs may have different knowledge, experiences, and perspectives than their English speaking peers and therefore may have initial trouble with matching their schema to that of the school's.

Pragmatics: Using Language to Get What We Need

The study of how language is used in society to satisfy the needs of human communication is called *pragmatics*. Hymes (1964) defined *pragmatics* as knowing how language works and is used in one's culture. In other words, children's and adults' language-related knowledge, habits, and behaviors are directly influenced by the culture or society in which they live and interact.

M. A. K. Halliday (1975) described three pragmatic language functions in our day-to-day lives: (a) ideational, (b) interpersonal, and (c) textual. F. Smith (1977) expanded Halliday's three aspects of pragmatic language functions into 10 purposes for which language may be used in Figure 2.2.

As children interact with their environment and other people, they discover that language is power! They learn that they can control others and what they do through language. They learn that language can be used to get what they want and need. In short, they learn that language serves a wide variety of purposes. Once children understand the many uses for language in their lives, they begin to see the purposes of written language. In fact, success in reading depends very much on the degree to which the language children encounter in their early speaking and reading experiences mirror one another (Pinnell & Jaggar, 2003; Watson, 2001).

Great teachers realize that children must have experiences with quality literature, extended discussions about important topics in their reading, and opportunities to write and respond to literature for reading success (Morrow & Gambrell, 2001). It is in this setting that children begin to make the critical connections between oral and written language uses. When texts support and relate to children's oral language experiences, children discover that written and oral language are mirror forms of language that serve similar purposes.

Figure 2.2 Pragmatic Language Functions

1. *Instrumental:* "I want." (Getting things and satisfying material needs.)
2. *Regulatory:* "Do as I tell you." (Controlling the attitudes, behaviors, and feelings of others.)
3. *Interactional:* "Me and you." (Getting along with others, establishing relative status.) Also, "Me against you." (Establishing separateness.)
4. *Personal:* "Here I come." (Expressing individuality, awareness of self, pride.)
5. *Heuristic:* "Tell me why." (Seeking and testing world knowledge.)
6. *Imaginative:* "Let's pretend." (Creating new worlds, making up stories, poems.)
7. *Representational:* "I've got something to tell you." (Communicating information, descriptions, expressing propositions.)
8. *Divertive:* "Enjoy this." (Puns, jokes, riddles.)
9. *Authoritative/contractual:* "How it must be." (Statutes, laws, regulations, and rules.)
10. *Perpetuating:* "How it was." (Records, histories, diaries, notes, scores.)

From "The Uses of Language" by F. Smith, 1977, *Language Arts, 54(6)*, p. 640. Copyright 1977 by the National Council of Teachers of English. Reprinted with permission.

Getting to Know English Learners

Even ELs have dialects! In fact, in China it is thought that there are many more dialects than the two most of us are familiar with: Mandarin Chinese and Cantonese Chinese. And in Mexico, there are indigenous dialects spoken by country dwellers that some city dwellers say they cannot understand!

Dialect, or speech variations associated with various regions of the United States or ethnic groups, also impact children's ability to understand and use the sounds of spoken English. Regional speech differences also are reflected in word choices, as in "We are getting ready to go" versus "We are fixin' to go." Even grammatical changes can be found in dialects—regional or cultural—across the nation. For example, grammatical changes such as "He be goin'" for "He is going" might be heard in some African-American communities. Thus, language change and variation is evidence of how language is used in various cultures and regions of the nation.

Children reared in the Midwest are not always accustomed to the way speech sounds and words are produced in the South or Northeast, and vice versa. So a child living in the Midwest who is taught by a teacher who has recently moved from the South might experience some difficulty in perceiving that teacher's speech sounds and understanding his or her word choice. Similarly, children who are raised in other English-speaking cultures—African-American or Native American, for example—might also experience difficulty in hearing the sounds of spoken English or in understanding specific word choices. Consequently, teachers (1) must be aware that everyone speaks in a particular dialect and (2) must develop sensitivity to the differences between their particular articulation of spoken sounds and words and those of their students. We summarize the components of language in Table 2.1.

How Do Children Develop Oral Language?

As indicated in Chapter 1, there are essentially four major views on how children gain oral language ability: (1) behaviorist, (2) innatist, (3) constructivist, and (4) social interactionist. We have found that all of these views help to explain one or more aspects of how children acquire and use oral language.

Table 2.1   Six Components of Language Structure

Component	Concepts	Examples
Phonology	*Prosodic Features*	Expression
	• Pitch	• Highness or lowness of speech
	• Juncture	• Pauses within or between words
	• Stress	• Emphasis or intensity of speech
	Articulated Speech Units	Spoken words and parts of words
	• Words	*duck, college, elephant*
	• Syllables	*win-dow, Mc-Don-alds*
	• Onset	*r, t, sl, pl, ch, str*
	• Rime	*an, un, ick, ake, on*
	• Phonemes	/s/, /r/, /t/, /m/, /a/, /uh/
Orthography	*Grapheme*	Written symbols/letters
	Phoneme	Spoken sounds
	Grapheme-Phoneme Correspondence	The means by which spoken sounds are represented by specific letters
Morphology	*Morpheme*	Smallest unit of meaning
	• Free	*ball, peninsula, chain*
	• Bound	*anti, pre, ology, bio*
	• Derivational	*rust → rusty*
	• Inflected	*big, bigger, biggest, walk → walked*
	• Compound	*wallpaper, cowboy, towboat*
Syntax	*Grammar*	System of rules for language
	• Parts of speech	verbs, nouns, adjectives, adverbs
	• Sentence structure	The dog ran after the bone.
	• Sentence combining	The dog ran. The cat ran. The dog and cat ran.
	• Cohesion	*because, therefore, but, or, and*
	• Word order	The dog ran *vs.* Dog the ran
Semantics	*Meaning*	To signify or represent an idea, concept, or action
	• Words	How many meanings are there for the word *run?*
	• Connected language	jokes, songs, books, stories
Pragmatics	*Purpose*	Using language to satisfy human needs or to represent human situations
	• Instrumental	To get one's needs met
	• Regulatory	To control the behavior of others
	• Interactional	To establish relationships with others
	• Personal	To share oneself with others
	• Heuristic	To seek answers to questions
	• Imaginative	To make believe
	• Representational	To communicate information
	• Divertive	For humor and recreation
	• Authoritative	For contracts, statutes, laws, rules
	• Perpetuating	For journals, diaries, notes, personal histories
	Variation	Changes in language forms and function resulting from geographical and cultural influences
	• Dialect	*apartment* vs. *flat* *morning* vs. *mawnin'* *Yo!* vs. *Hey!* vs. *Hello!*

The Behaviorist View of Oral Language Development

Behaviorists believe that oral language is learned through conditioning and shaping, processes that involve a stimulus and a reward or a punishment. Recall from your study of psychology the concept of stimulus–response training, one of the principles of behaviorism. Behaviorists contend that human role models in an infant's environment provide the stimuli and responses (i.e., rewards or punishments) that shape the learning of oral language. Parents' and other caregivers' speech tends to act as the stimulus in the social/cultural speech environment. When baby imitates the sounds or speech of adult models, she receives praise and affection as rewards. Thus, the **behaviorist theory** of language development states that infants learn oral language from other human role models through a process involving stimulation/modeling, imitation, rewards, punishment, and practice.

However, behaviorist theories of language development fail to answer a number of important questions associated with children's language acquisition. For example, if a parent is hurried, inattentive, or not present when the child attempts speech, then rewards for the desired speech responses are not always provided. Thus, if baby's language learning were only motivated by rewards, speech attempts would cease where regular rewards (the parent's smile or other responses) are absent.

Another problem with the behaviorist theory of oral language acquisition centers on the fact that young children do not simply imitate other human speech. Imitation implies certain behaviors. For example, when mother says, "Baby, say 'Mama,'" baby does not imitate or echo Mama by saying, "Baby, say 'Mama.'" Even in the earliest stages of language acquisition, children are not mere echo chambers. They are processing language meaning and sorting out the relevant from the irrelevant. Behaviorist theories of language learning fail to account for this kind of selective or strategic cognitive processing.

Behaviorist language acquisition theories also do not account for words and sounds invented by infants. For example, one girl we know used to call a sandwich a "weechie" even though no one in her home called a sandwich by any such name. Another failure of behaviorist theories to fully explain oral language development is the "jargon" that often emerges between identical twins and no one else. Although behaviorist theories may explain to some extent the role of the social environment and the importance of role models in shaping children's language learning, they seem incomplete. Arguments that counter behaviorist language acquisition theories include the following (Piper, 1998):

- Evidence of regression in pronouncing sounds and words previously pronounced correctly
- Evidence of novel forms of language not modeled by others
- Inconsistency of reinforcement or rewards provided
- Learning the use and meaning of abstract words
- Uniformity of language acquisition in humans
- Uniqueness of human language learning

The Innatist View of Oral Language Development

A second theory about oral language development is referred to as **innatist theory.** Innatist theorists believe that language learning is natural for human beings. In short, babies enter the world with a biological propensity (inclination)—an inborn device as it were—to learn language. Lenneberg (1964) refers to this human built-in device for learning language as the *language acquisition device* (LAD). Thus, the innatist theory explains to some degree how children can generate or invent language they have never heard before.

Chomsky (1974, 1979) maintained that children use the language acquisition device to create an elaborate rule system for inventing complex and interesting speech. Put another way, just as wings allow birds to fly, LAD allows infant humans to speak. Although the innatist theory provides what appears to be a believable explanation for some aspects of oral language acquisition, researchers have failed to discover supporting evidence. Menyuk (1988) wrote, "Despite the apparent logic of this position, there is still a great deal of mystery that surrounds it" (p. 34). Several arguments against innatist language acquisition theories are listed here (Piper, 1998).

- The timing of language learning varies greatly within cultures.
- Feedback from other language users affects language acquisition.
- Environment shapes the language learned and how much language is learned.

The Constructivist View of Oral Language Development

Constructivist theories of oral language development emerged from the work of Jean Piaget (1959). Piaget believed that language development is linked to cognitive development (i.e., thought processes and abilities). Even though he contended that cognition and language operate independently of each other, Piaget believed that language development was deeply rooted in the development of cognition or thinking, and that concept or cognitive development preceded the development of language ability (Cox, 2002).

Cox (2002) offers a summary of the stages of language development using (as was the case with Piaget) her own children as examples. These stages are presented here, with Piaget's cognitive stages noted in parentheses.

1. *Preverbal* (Piaget's *Sensorimotor Stage*). 0–2 years. Preverbal language, from birth to 6 months, is characterized by crying and babbling. Approximation of others' speech also occurs. From 12 to 18 months, children repeat one-syllable sounds typically beginning with consonant phonemes, such as "na-na-na-na." First "words" such as *Da-da, Ma-ma*, and *bye-bye* begin to appear.

2. *Vocabulary and True Language* (Piaget's *Preoperational Stage*). 2–7 years. From 18 months to 2 years of age, children become skillful at naming things in their environment, using one-word utterances called *holophrases* to communicate a complex set of needs or ideas. They then move to two-word sentences, called *telegraphic speech,* as they grow in their ability to use very simple sentences. Children 3 to 4 years of age continue using simple sentences, and begin using compound sentences; they understand present and past tenses, but overgeneralize sometimes (e.g., *goed* for *went*); they understand concepts like *few* and *many, first* and *second;* and they may have a speaking vocabulary of up to 1,500 words. Children at this stage are still quite egocentric and do not always use words correctly—like Rob, who after fake-coughing a few moments said, "I have a carburetor stuck in my throat!" From ages 4 to 7 years, children use sentences that grow in terms of both length and complexity. They commonly use grammatically correct sentences, learn the rudiments of reading and writing, and expand their speaking vocabularies to between 3,000 and 8,000 words.

3. *Logical and Socialized Speech* (Piaget's *Concrete Operational Stage*). 7–11 years. During this stage, children's speech becomes more adult-like. Language is essentially mastered, although linguistic skills continue to grow in complexity. At ages 7 and 8, children use more symbolic language, such as that of expressing concepts (e.g., *courage, freedom, time, seasons*). From 8 to 10 years, their language becomes more flexible, and they are able to engage in abstract discussions, facilitate and nurture less-developed language users, and expand ideas into lengthy discourse. Children respond to questions more logically and often use language to establish and cement relationships.

4. *Abstract Reasoning and Symbolism* (Piaget's *Formal Operations Stage*). 11–15 years and beyond. At this stage, children's speech becomes, at least in function and form, indistinguishable from adult speech. As with abstract thought, some learners seem to never quite reach this level of sophistication, which is why we have inserted the phrase "and beyond" as a caveat.

Two key points in Piaget's constructivist theory are (1) children move through cognitive stages at fairly predictable times, and (2) external influences, such as schooling, have very little effect on their evolution. In other words, children progress through these stages according to a biologically determined timetable, and external influences (e.g., parents and teachers) have very little effect on the pace of growth. These notions are very much at odds with the social interactionist perspective.

The Social Interactionist View of Oral Language Development

One's environment and the people in it play a critical role in the development of language according to **social interactionist** explanations of oral language development. Social interactionist theory assumes that language development is greatly influenced by physical, social, and, of course, linguistic factors (Cox, 2002).

Vygotsky (1986, 1990) demonstrated that adult interactions with children could not only assist in language development, but could also change the pace of language learning (a point Piaget eventually embraced in his later years). Vygotsky assessed cognitive development in terms of how well a child could perform a specific task *in collaboration with others*. The difference between what a child can do alone and in collaboration with others is what Vygotsky called the **zone of proximal development** (ZPD). Smith (1988) described the zone of proximal development (ZPD) this way: "Everyone can do things with assistance that they cannot do alone, and what they can do with collaboration on one occasion they will be able to do independently on another" (pp. 196–197). For a ZPD to be useful, there must be a joint task that creates a learning situation for learner/expert interaction. The "expert" (one who has more experience and skill doing the assigned task) can then use different strategies to help the learner succeed in the learning situation (Tharpe & Gallimore, 1988). Instead of withholding certain tasks from a child until a particular stage of cognitive development is reached, as suggested by Piaget (1955), Vygotsky (1978) argued that once the zone of proximal development is identified, teachers, parents, or more advanced peers should help a learner perform a task he or she is not capable of doing alone. With much practice and support, the learner will ultimately master the new task.

Vygotsky (1978) also explained that learners internalize language activities, like reading and writing, by going through a three-stage process. **Internalization,** as Vygotsky called it, begins with the learner observing others as they perform a language task. For example, a child who continually asks for the same book to be read aloud again and again by an experienced reader is studying what the reader is doing and learning some of reading's most basic structures. The experienced reader is **modeling** a skill. Modeling can be performed by the teacher or another student who has mastered the desired skill. The next stage of internalization begins when the learner mimics the language task, like a child pretending to read a book aloud when she is really only looking at the pictures and repeating what was read aloud to her on previous occasions. In teaching, we call these first attempts by a novice at performing a task with support from an expert **guided practice.** The third stage of internalization comes when a learner, after benefiting from a great deal of skillful instruction and guided practice, is able to perform a specific reading task without further help. Examples of this stage of internalization are shown in the developmental reading and writing descriptions found later in this chapter. In teaching we refer to this final stage of learning as **independent practice.**

Internalization and the zone of proximal development are depicted in Figure 2.3.

The idea that social interaction plays a significant role in developing a child's cognitive growth and language ability is extremely relevant to current trends in reading instruction. If children are immersed in reading and writing early in their schooling experience and receive support from peers and adults while they are learning, they will begin to internalize more mature reading and writing behaviors. Put into practice, Vygotsky's theory, which advocates a child-centered and activity-oriented reading curriculum, enables children to learn the meaning of language while also using language as a tool for exploration. This concept is at the heart of the social interactionist view and is the means by which teachers are able to create a kind of **scaffolding** (Bruner, 1978), or temporary support, that helps students construct new oral language.

Video Classroom

Visit an Early Childhood Classroom to View Children Developing Oral Language

Refer to our Teacher Prep Website (*www.prenhall. com/teacherprep*) for a link to Video Classroom.

Select *Early Childhood* and *Intelligence and Infancy*. As you view the clip, note how the child is responding to the experiences using blocks and pictures.

- Create a chart with the headings for the four major views of language acquisition as presented in this chapter (behaviorist, innatist, constructivist, social interactionist).
- How does the child's beginning language acquisition align with the four major views presented in this chapter? Record your observations on your chart. (Note: All of these views help to explain one or more aspects of how children acquire and use oral language.)

The Developmental Stages of Oral Language Development

Teachers need to be aware that children develop oral language in stages. Recognizing the average rates of children's oral language development allows teachers to help scaffold or structure oral language development and assist children in reaching higher

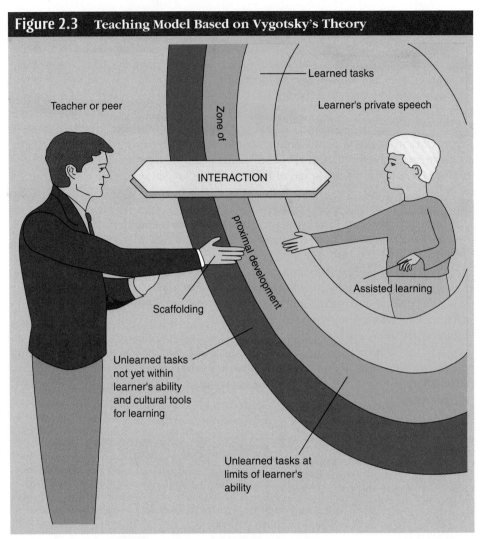

Figure 2.3   Teaching Model Based on Vygotsky's Theory

From *Educational Psychology* (4th ed., p. 50) by R. E. Slavin, 1994. Needham Heights, MA: AB Bacon. Reprinted by permission.

levels of knowledge. Bear in mind that oral language developmental rates can vary dramatically among children.

Getting to Know English Learners

It has been documented by linguists all over the world, that adults use "caretaker speech" to modify their oral language when talking to their infants and toddlers. It is thought that this "caretaker speech," is a universal phenomenon that adults use to help children learn language.

Parents' Baby Talk: One Way of Getting Attention. Many parents use a special type of speech commonly called "baby talk" with their infants up to about 24 months of age (Stern & Wasserman, 1979). Characteristics of baby talk include higher pitch and special intonation patterns. Studies have shown that infants respond best to high-pitch levels and to varied rhythms in speech (Gopnik, Meltzoff, & Kuhl, 1999; Kearsley, 1973; Kessen, Levine, & Wendrich, 1979). Other research has shown that the ways in which infants react to adult speech affect the subsequent speech and behavior of their adult caretakers. In fact, adults usually use shorter speech patterns with significant periods of pausing to encourage the infant to respond (Gleason, 1989). Thus, it appears that parents and adult caregivers intuitively are intense kid watchers (Goodman, 1986). They seem to structure their speech demonstrations carefully in response to their child's responses and suspected needs (Harste, Woodward, & Burke, 1984). In short, parents and adult caregivers change their normal speech structures during interactions with their infants to encourage verbal interaction.

The First 12 Months: A Time for Hope. During the first 2 months of life, babies cry to indicate their need to be fed, changed, or otherwise attended to in some manner. Because their tiny mouths are almost entirely filled with the tongue, and because the vocal cords are still quite high in the throat, children at this age are unable to produce much variation in vocalization. As time passes, the growth of the head and neck allows infants to vary their vocalizations to produce sounds already responded to and experienced in the environment. During this early stage of speech development, young infants also make what linguists call "vegetative sounds," such as burps, coughs, and sneezes.

From about 2 to 5 months of age, babies begin to coo, uttering sounds much like those made by pigeons. During this period, they may also begin to vary the consonant sounds attached to the pure /oo/ vowel sound typical of cooing. These cooing sounds, along with sustained laughter, typically seem to occur during social and speech interactions with caregivers in the environment. Cooing and laughter, however, may also occur when baby is alone or even asleep. D'Odorico (1984) has discovered that during this period, babies develop three distinct types of crying associated with three distinct needs: (1) a need for comfort, (2) a need for attention, and (3) a need for rescue from distress. All of these speech developments seem to provide great pleasure and even a sense of relief and encouragement for parents and caregivers.

From 6 months to 1 year of age, babies enter a period of oral language development called *vocal play* or *babbling*. This stage of development is marked by the ability to utter single syllables containing a consonant sound followed by a prolonged vowel sound, such as "Maa maa." Although many other syllables (e.g., "Laa laa") may be uttered during this period of development, only a few of these syllables will be retained into the next stage (e.g., "Ma-ma" and "Da-da"). These syllables are retained primarily because their use seems to bring a quick, delighted reaction from parents or adult caregivers. It is also during this period of speech development that children begin to use single words *(holophrases)*, sounds, or invented words to represent complete ideas (Au, Depretto, & Song, 1994; Gleason, 1989). For example, an eleventh-month-old may point to a picture of a cow and squeal in delight "Mooooo!" This same child may point at the sink and say, "Wa wa," indicating that he or she wants a drink of water.

From 1 to 2: By Leaps and Bounds. Language expands rapidly during the second year of development. Children continue to approximate the speech of their parents to the point of duplicating their gestures and intonation patterns. Children in this stage continue to make hypotheses about the rules that govern language use, and they try out and refine these rules as they use language. During this year, toddlers achieve a significant linguistic milestone when they begin to put two words together. These words typically are selected from the large, open classes of words known as nouns, verbs, and adjectives. Because these two-word utterances sound much like the reading of a telegram, linguists have called this stage of speech development *telegraphic speech*. Typical utterances of the telegraphic type include "Mommy down!" or "Go potty?" One recognizes readily the ability of these two-word, cryptic speech patterns to communicate an entire complex idea or need.

From 2 to 3: What Does It Mean When I Say No?! Oral language development continues to progress rapidly during the third year. The broken and incomplete nature of telegraphic speech begins to give way to more complex and natural forms of speech. The use of descriptives such as adjectives and adverbs dramatically increases (Fields & Spangler, 2000; Glazer, 1989; Morrow, 2005).

One linguistic discovery made by the two-year-old is the effect of negation. For many months the child has heard the word *no*. Although over time she has learned what "No-no" implies for her behavior, she has not yet come to understand what *no* means when applied to the behavior of others. When asked, "Does baby want an ice cream cone?" she quickly responds, "No!" But when she discovers that the ice cream cone (to which she had said "No") is denied, she begins to cry. Over time, the two-year-old learns what *no* means and how it affects the behavior of others. In a sense, children at this age begin to establish their own identity—separate from others in their environment—and the "No!" response is evidence of this. Use of the words *no* and *not* signals an important change in young children's language development.

From 3 to 4: The Why Years. By age 3, children begin using complex sentences that include the use of prepositions, pronouns, negatives, plurals, possessives, and interrogatives. Children at this age have a speaking vocabulary of between 1,000 and 1,500 words (Morrow, 2005). Also at this age, children begin to use analogical substitutions in their speech. An **analogical substitution** is the overgeneralization by analogy of a language rule, which often results in using an incorrect substitute word in speech. For example, a child may say, "Mom, will you put my boots on my foots?" In this case, the child has overgeneralized the rule for pluralizing nouns by adding an *-s* to the irregular noun *foot*. Another example of an analogical substitution is the overgeneralization of the language rule for changing verbs to their past-tense form. For example, Lee rushes into the house and yells, "Daddy, come quick. I digged up that mean bush with flowers and thorns on it!" Language "errors" such as these reveal the language rules children have been internalizing and how they go about refining their language hypotheses.

During this fourth year of oral language development, children begin to transform basic sentence structures into interrogative sentences (questions). Before this time, these same children indicated that a question was being asked by making a statement followed by a rising intonation pattern. Thus, questions were framed without the use of interrogatives or by transforming basic sentence structures. However, by the time the child is 3, parents have become well acquainted with the interrogative "Why?"

For statements that appear to be perfectly obvious to adults, the 3-year-old will begin the typical line of questioning with "Why, why, why?" After several answers to this question, parents realize they are trapped in a linguistic situation from which it is nearly impossible to escape with dignity. Bill Cosby once offered a simple solution that we tried with our own 3-year-old children with reasonable success: You ask "why?" first! Regardless of the questioning nature of the 3-year-old, language development during the third to fourth year is an exciting experience for parents and caregivers.

From 4 to 6: Years of Growth and Refinement. At 4 years of age, children seem to have acquired most of the elements of adult language (Morrow, 2001). Vocabulary and syntactical structures continue to increase in variety and depth. Children at this age possess a vocabulary of about 2,500 words, which by age 6 will have grown to 6,000 words

(Clark, 1993; Johnson, 2001; Norton & Norton, 2003). Some children at age 4 or 5 continue to have trouble articulating the /r/ and /l/ sounds and the /sh/ at the end of words, although the vast majority of children are 90 to 100 percent intelligible by age 4.

Cody, son of one of the authors, has provided many examples of imaginative and generative language. With his hard-earned money, Cody purchased several plastic clips for his belt. He could hang his flashlight and plastic tools on these clips and make believe he was a workin' man. When Cody's father saw these clips on his belt, he inquired, "Cody, what are those things on your belt?" The child responded, "Those are my *hookers,* Dad!"

On entering the world of school, kindergarten children often discover a genre of speech known as "toilet talk" or "curse words." One day, a young boy overheard his kindergarten teacher reprimanding some other boys for using inappropriate language. Sometime later during the day, his teacher overheard him remark regarding the subject of taboo words: "She means those words your daddy uses when he gets real mad!" According to Seefeldt and Barbour (1986), adults find the way in which children of this age group use language imaginative and amusing. We certainly concur with these observations!

Understanding the development of oral language among children can be a source of increased enjoyment for parents and teachers. Knowing how children develop language helps adults recognize and appreciate the monumental achievement of learning to speak—especially when it occurs so naturally and in a space of just six short but very important years.

What Does Research Say About the Relationship Between Oral Language and Reading?

Deficits in oral language can ultimately limit a child's learning of reading and writing. This is true whether the child is a first or second language learner (Biemiller, 2006; Lyon, 1999; NLP, 2006; Pinnell & Jaggar, 2003; Scarborough, 2001; Shannahan, 2006; Snow, Scarborough, & Burns, 1999). Language deficits also are the most common root causes for referrals to special education (Warren, 2001). Research shows that children with weak oral language abilities tend to (1) have small vocabularies characterized by lots of short words that are used frequently, (2) make frequent use of nonspecific words, and (3) use fewer complex sentences and less elaboration (Beimiller, 2006; Greenhalgh & Strong, 2001; Paul, 2001; Wiig, Becker-Redding, & Semel, 1983).

Viewed from another perspective, research confirms that good readers "bring strong vocabularies and good syntactic and grammatical skills to the reading comprehension process" (Biemiller, 2006; Lyon, 1999, p. 10). We also know that early and intensive intervention with children having underdeveloped language can enhance literacy learning (Dickinson & Tabors, 2001; Warren & Yoder, 1997).

Poverty, a condition in which an individual or group does without resources (Payne, 1998), is highly correlated with underdeveloped oral language. Children of poverty are often denied exposure to many language-growing experiences that are common to children from more affluent families, from a trip to Taco Bell or McDonalds, to participating in youth clubs, to going on summer vacations. Because the working poor often have to maintain several jobs just to make ends meet, parents frequently have little or no time to interact with their children. A common result of poverty for these children is poorly developed oral language. According to the 2002 report of the National Assessment of Educational Progress (NAEP) for reading, children from poverty score significantly lower in reading proficiency than their more affluent counterparts. These children are often at greatest risk of failing in school and eventually dropping out.

Hart and Risley (1995, 2002) recorded every word spoken at home between parents and children in 42 families from various socioeconomic status (SES) backgrounds for 2 1/2 years. These families were categorized according to SES as professional, working class, or welfare level. In comparing language interactions between professional level (SES) parents and their children versus welfare level parents' interactions, data revealed the following:

- Professional parents spent more than 40 minutes daily interacting with their young children while welfare parents spent 15 minutes each day.
- Professional-class parents verbally responded to their children 250 times per hour, as compared to welfare-level parents, who verbally responded 50 times per hour.
- Professional-level parents approved and encouraged their children's actions an average of 40 times per hour. Welfare-level parents approved and encouraged their children's actions an average of four times per hour.
- In their interactions, professional families usually spoke more than 3,000 words per hour as compared to 500 words per hour in welfare homes.
- Access to oral language in both quantity and quality was so consistent within families that the differences in children's language experience were enormous by age 3.

Results showed that children in professional families would have had experiences with 42 million words, children in working-class families would have had experience with 26 million words, and welfare family children would have had experience with 13 million words. In professional families, the extraordinary volume of verbal exchanges and exposure to many different words—greater richness of nouns, modifiers and past-tense verbs—suggest a language culture focusing on symbols and analytic problem solving. In welfare families, fewer verbal exchanges focused on the teaching of socially acceptable behavior: obedience, politeness, and conformity. The volume of early oral language interactions between parents and children and particularly the language interactions of parents and children with regard to the books parents read to or with their children are major predictors of later reading success (Dickinson & Tabors, 2001; Watson, 2001).

Assessing Children's Oral Language Development and Use

Oral language assessment is a very difficult undertaking because, as Walter Loban (1976) once said, "no published tests measure power over the living language, the spoken word. . . . [teachers should] devise ways of assessing oral language using cassettes, tape recorders, and video tapes" (p. 1).

What part of oral language should one assess? Should teachers assess the breadth and depth of children's oral language vocabularies? Should teachers assess children's ability to retell stories? Should teachers assess children's use of language in classrooms and on the playground? Should teachers assess children's acquisition of each of the language structures previously described in this chapter? Should teachers assess children in English only or also in their primary language? The answer to this set of questions is a resounding "Yes!" Realistically, however, teachers do not have the time or resources necessary to engage in all of these types of oral language assessment. Many currently published oral language tests are expensive and time-consuming. On the other hand, teachers can and should assess children's oral language as part of the everyday classroom environment (Smith, 2001).

To help you with the assessment process, we recommend two free and widely available oral language assessment tools we find useful. A teacher using these two instruments can quickly gauge children's expressive language development.

- *Teacher Rating of Oral Language and Literacy (TROLL)*. This tool allows teachers to simultaneously assess children's expressive (spoken) oral language along with their early reading and writing development.
- *Get It, Got It, Go!—Picture Naming Test*. This is a reliable and valid assessment of children's expressive (spoken) oral language.

We also favor a third instrument, the *Oral Language Acquisition Inventory* (OLAI), which can be used to assess children's acquisition of oral language structures and components (Gentile, 2003). Following are descriptions of these useful tests.

Teacher Rating of Oral Language and Literacy (TROLL)

As we have seen, children must develop strong oral language skills to learn to read and write effectively (Shanahan, 2006). According to Dickinson, McCabe, and Sprague (2003), the TROLL rating system measures skills critical to speaking and listening in today's classrooms. The TROLL can be used to track children's progress in language and literacy development, to inform curriculum, and to encourage communication between parents and teachers. Oral language skills relevant to later literacy development include the ability to tell stories, to use talk while pretending during play, and to vary vocabulary usage (Dickinson & Tabors, 2001).

The TROLL assessment compares favorably to formal and more costly oral language assessments such as the well-established Peabody Picture Vocabulary Test (PPVT-III), a measure of receptive (listening) vocabulary. In about five minutes and with no special training, teachers themselves can index what trained researchers would spend roughly 25 to 30 minutes per child assessing (Dickinson, McCabe, & Sprague, 2003).

To administer the TROLL you will need a copy of the rating form (see Figure 2.4) for each student you plan to observe.

While no formal training is required to use the TROLL instrument, it is most effective if teachers know about how language and literacy develops. The TROLL requires only 5 to 10 minutes of observation per child. Use of the TROLL need not disrupt classroom activities.

You can use information yielded by the TROLL to inform your teaching. The instrument identifies children who show evidence of serious oral language developmental delays, those who may need formal assessment by speech professionals, and/or children who are showing high levels of literacy development and could benefit from additional challenges. By completing the TROLL several times over the course of a year, you can track the progress of all your students' oral language development.

Figure 2.4   Teacher Rating of Oral Language and Literacy (TROLL)

Language Use

1. **How would you describe this child's willingness to start a conversation with adults and peers and to continue trying to communicate when he or she is not understood on the first attempt? Select the statement that best describes how hard the child works to be understood by others.**

1	2	3	4
Child almost never begins a conversation with peers or the teacher and never keeps trying if unsuccessful at first.	Child sometimes begins conversation with either peers or the teacher. If initial efforts fail, he or she often gives up quickly.	Child begins conversations with both peers and teachers on occasion. If initial efforts fail, he or she will sometimes keep trying.	Child begins conversations with both peers and teachers. If initial efforts fail, he or she will work hard to be understood.

2. **How well does the child communicate personal experiences in a clear and logical way? Assign the score that best describes this child when he or she is attempting to tell an adult about events that happened at home or some other place where you were not present.**

1	2	3	4
Child is very tentative and offers only a few words, requires you to ask questions, has difficulty responding to questions you ask.	Child offers some information, but information needed to really understand the event is missing (e.g., where or when it happened, who was present, the sequence of what happened).	Child offers information and sometimes includes the necessary information to understand the event fully.	Child freely offers information and tells experiences in a way that is nearly always complete, well sequenced, and comprehensible.

3. **How would you describe this child's pattern of asking questions about topics that interest him or her (e.g., why things happen, why people act the way they do)? Assign the score that best describes the child's approach to displaying curiosity by asking adults questions.**

1	2	3	4
To your knowledge, the child has never asked an adult a question reflecting curiosity about why things happen or why people do things.	On a few occasions the child has asked adults some questions. The discussion that resulted was brief and limited in depth.	On several occasions the child has asked interesting questions. On occasion these have led to an interesting conversation.	Child often asks adults questions reflecting curiosity. These often lead to interesting, extended conversations.

4. **How would you describe this child's use of talk while pretending in the house area or when playing with blocks? Consider the child's use of talk with peers to start pretending and to carry it out. Assign the score that best applies.**

1	2	3	4
Child rarely or never engages in pretend play or else never talks while pretending.	On occasion the child engages in pretending that includes some talk. Talk is brief, may only be used when starting the play, and is of limited importance to the ongoing play activity.	Child engages in pretending often and conversations are sometimes important to the play. On occasion child engages in some back-and-forth pretend dialogue with another child.	Child often talks in elaborate ways while pretending. Conversations that are carried out "in role" are common and are an important part of the play. Child sometimes steps out of pretend play to give directions to another.

Figure 2.4   (Continued)

5. How would you describe the child's ability to recognize and produce rhymes?			
1 Child cannot say if two words rhyme and cannot produce a rhyme when given examples (e.g., *rat, cat*).	2 Child occasionally produces or identifies rhymes when given help.	3 Child spontaneously produces rhymes and can sometimes tell when word pairs rhyme.	4 Child spontaneously rhymes words of more than one syllable and always identifies whether words rhyme.

6. How often does child use a varied vocabulary or try out new words (e.g., heard in stories or from teacher)?			
1 Never	2 Rarely	3 Sometimes	4 Often

7. When child speaks to adults other than you or the teaching assistant, is he or she understandable?			
1 Never	2 Rarely	3 Sometimes	4 Often

8. How often does child express curiosity about how and why things happen?			
1 Never	2 Rarely	3 Sometimes	4 Often

Language Use Subtotal ( )

Reading

9. How often does child like to hear books read in the full group?			
1 Never	2 Rarely	3 Sometimes	4 Often

10. How often does child attend to stories read in the full group or small groups and react in a way that indicates comprehension?			
1 Never	2 Rarely	3 Sometimes	4 Often

11. Is child able to read storybooks on his or her own?			
1 Does not pretend to read books	2 Pretends to read	3 Pretends to read and reads some words	4 Reads the written words

12. How often does child remember the story line or characters in books that he or she heard before either at home or in class?			
1 Never	2 Rarely	3 Sometimes	4 Often

(continued)

Figure 2.4   (Continued)

13. How often does child look at or read books alone or with friends?

1 Never	2 Rarely	3 Sometimes	4 Often

14. Can child recognize letters? (Choose one answer.)

1 None of the letters of the alphabet	2 Some of them (up to 10)	3 Most of them (up to 20)	4 All of them

15. Does child recognize his or her own first name in print?

1 No	2 Yes

16. Does child recognize other names?

1 No	2 One or two	3 A few (up to four or five)	4 Several (six or more)

17. Can child read any other words?

1 No	2 One or two	3 A few (up to four or five)	4 Several (six or more)

18. Does child have a beginning understanding of the relationship between sounds and letters (e.g., the letter _b_ makes a _/buh/_ sound)?

1 No	2 One or two	3 A few (up to four or five)	4 Several (six or more)

19. Can child sound out words that he or she has not read before?

1 No	2 Once or twice	3 One-syllable words often	4 Many words

Reading Subtotal ( )

Writing

20. What does child's writing look like?

1 Only draws or scribbles	2 Some letter-like marks	3 Many conventional letters	4 Conventional letters and words

Figure 2.4   (Continued)

21. How often does child like to write or pretend to write?			
1 Never	2 Rarely	3 Sometimes	4 Often

22. Can child write his or her first name, even if some of the letters are backward?			
1 Never	2 Rarely	3 Sometimes	4 Often

23. Does child write other names or real words?			
1 No	2 One or two	3 A few (up to four or five)	4 Several (six or more)

24. How often does child write signs or labels?			
1 Never	2 Rarely	3 Sometimes	4 Often

25. Does child write stories, songs, poems, or lists?			
1 Never	2 Rarely	3 Sometimes	4 Often

Writing Subtotal ( )

Writing Subtotal	( ) (out of 24 possible)
Oral Language Subtotal	( ) (out of 32 possible)
Reading Subtotal	( ) (out of 42 possible)
Total TROLL Score	( ) (out of 98 possible)

Note: Copyright © 1997 Education Development Center, Inc., *www.edc.org.*

Finally, you can combine results for all your students to determine which students need additional oral language experiences and which are in need of more systematic instruction. For example, if all of your students score relatively low on asking questions, you will want to begin providing numerous opportunities to listen and ask questions during the daily routine in your classroom.

Get It, Got It, Go!—Picture-Naming Test

The *Get It, Got It, Go!* Individual Growth and Development Indicators are a set of several standardized, individually-administered measures of early language and literacy development. The Picture-Naming Test (PN) was specifically designed to assess

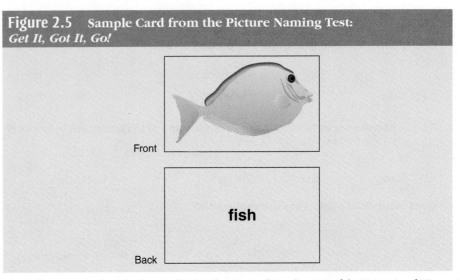

Figure 2.5   Sample Card from the Picture Naming Test: *Get It, Got It, Go!*

Front

fish

Back

Used with permission from the Center of Early Education and Development of the University of Minnesota.

children's expressive (speaking) language development at ages 3 to 5 by asking them to look at picture cards drawn from their home, classroom, and community environments. An example can be found in Figure 2.5. Throughout this test, children are directed to look at pictures and name each. The PN test, administration guidelines, and the pictures to be named are available at no cost on the Internet at *http://ggg.umn.edu/*.

A *Get It, Got It, Go!* free data reporting service is also available on the Internet, but users must enter their own data. Using this Internet-based system, teachers can enter assessment data directly into the *Get It, Got It, Go!* database and generate class reports as often as desired. The Picture Naming Test has not yet become available in Spanish. Missal & McConnell (2004) report reliability and validity data for the IGDI Picture Naming test that show a strong correlation with the Peabody Expressive Vocabulary Test, a standard oral language assessment tool widely accepted and used by school psychologists. Free *Picture Naming Test* directions, picture cards, and scoring forms are all available on the Internet at *http://ggg.umn.edu/*. Directions for administration of the Picture Naming Test are shown in Table 2.2.

The *Oral Language Acquisition Inventory (OLAI)*

The *Oral Language Acquisition Inventory* (OLAI), the third oral language assessment instrument we discuss, is a commercially available test developed to provide teachers key information to help English learners (ELs) and children of poverty achieve oral language proficiency and literacy. The pre K–3 version of the OLAI was constructed after analyzing nearly 2,000 oral dictations by 60 first grade children during their Reading Recovery lessons. The common sentence structures drawn from sampling these oral dictations included (1) simple sentences, (2) sentences containing prepositional phrases, (3) sentences containing two phrases or clauses linked by a conjunction, (4) sentences containing two phrases or clauses linked by a relative pronoun, and (5) sentences containing two phrases or clauses linked by an adverb.

The *Oral Language Acquisition Inventory* is an informal, repeated measure assessment that "provides teachers, in a short period of time, information related to the most common language structures children control in their expressive speech. It

Table 2.2 Directions for Administration of the Picture Naming Test

---

Remember

- This is a timed, 1-minute task. Be sure to use your stopwatch!
- Shuffle cards prior to each administration.
- Separate correctly named pictures into one pile and incorrectly named or skipped pictures into another pile.
- Follow directions below *exactly* as written.
- Read aloud all words in bold.

Standardized Procedure

1. Say, "**Now we're going to look at some other pictures. This time, name them as fast as you can!**"
2. Start the stopwatch and immediately show the first card to the child.
3. If the child does not respond within 3 seconds, point to the picture and say: "**Do you know what that is?**" or "**What's that?**"
4. If the child still does not respond within an additional 2 seconds, show the next card.
5. As soon as the child names a picture, show the next card.
6. After *1 minute,* STOP showing cards to the child. Record the total number of correctly named pictures on the appropriate form.

Used with permission from the Center of Early Education and Development of the University of Minnesota.

helps identify stages of linguistic development for instruction" (p. vi). The inventory is published by Dominie Press, Inc., and can be found at the following Web address: *http://plgcatalog.pearson.com.* Test materials include an accompanying curriculum guide for teachers—the *Pre-K–3 Oracy Instructional Guide*—that features oral language experiences and instruction related to strengths and weaknesses revealed by administration of the inventory.

Review an assessment artifact on our Teacher Prep Website (*www.prenhall.com/teacherprep*). Select *Teacher and Student Artifacts* for a link to *Early Childhood.* Select *Assessment* and *Group Participation.* View an informal classroom assessment and respond to questions relating to the connection of this assessment to effective instruction. (These are two of the Five Pillars presented in Chapter 1.) Your responses can be printed and/or sent to your instructor directly from this site.

Principles of Effective Oral Language Instruction

Oral language ability is directly related to reading development and is the primary tool for human thinking and communicating. Nevertheless it continues to take a back seat to reading and writing in the elementary school curriculum (Pinnell & Jaggar, 2003). Like others before us, we have read compelling arguments about the importance of developing children's oral language skills and their link to reading development. We have also studied long lists of loosely connected oral language instructional activities. Teachers must provide oral language instruction at all levels, and a research-based framework for oral language instruction is urgently needed. However, we have found very little research available for guiding the development of a curricular framework for effective oral language instruction. So what are we to do?

In the absence of a strong research base to support oral language curriculum development and instructional decision making, Stanovich and Stanovich (2003) suggest teachers use the best research-based reasoning currently available. We have taken as our guide the language instructional framework proposed by Dutro and Moran (2003), which is comprised of three interrelated components:

1. language functions
2. forms of language
3. language fluency

Language functions may be best defined as real world and classroom-based oral language practice. Table 2.3 summarizes how pragmatics form the basis of the oral language instruction conceptual framework.

Children also need oral language instruction that focuses attention on the **forms of language.** Dutro and Moran (2003) identify the forms of language as vocabulary, verb tense, parts of speech, and sentence structure. As stated earlier in this chapter, the teacher's knowledge of the components of language strongly influences children's oral language development. Just as an artist must understand how various paints and painting surfaces function to create an appealing image, so must a teacher understand the way English works in its various forms (Fillmore & Snow, 2000; Moats, 2000; Snow, Griffin, & Burns, 2005). Teachers must also understand the general sequence of how children acquire oral language. Knowledge of words that are both rich and varied is critical to developing a child's language proficiency and to later reading and writing success (Dutro & Moran, 2003).

Table 2.3　A Pragmatics-Based Conceptual Framework for Oral Language Instruction

Pragmatic Category	Function Served	Oral Language Instruction Strategies and Activities
Instrumental	I want; I need.	Dramatic play: "House," "Store," "Hospital" Interviews
Regulatory	Do as I tell you!	Simon Says Copy Cat
Interactional	Let's talk together.	Telephone conversations Face-to-face conversations
Personal	It's all about me.	Introductions Me Box Me Book Show and Tell
Heuristic	Tell me why?	Persuasion Discussions Debates
Imaginative	Let's pretend . . .	Dramatization Puppetry Storytelling Wordless picture books
Representational	Let me tell you how to . . .	Treasure hunt Following directions
Divertive	That's funny!	Jokes Riddles Singing songs
Authoritative	This is how it has to be!	Following the rules Role play justice system
Perpetuating	Let me tell you about how it used to be.	Pick a photograph Memorable moments

Language fluency is defined by Dutro and Moran as varying the ways oral language can be used. For example, one reads aloud a folktale in a different way than he or she does a math story problem. Being able to use oral language in different ways certainly takes training and practice. Therefore, children need to experience a wide range of settings, purposes, and tasks for developing fluent oral language. They need to develop conversational and academic language, for example. For this reason, supportive elementary classrooms provide a wide range of oral language practice and performance activities to teach, use, and refine children's oral language functions and forms.

We believe Dutro and Moran's (2003) framework for oral language instruction is theoretically consistent and defensible for two reasons. First, the functions or pragmatics of language reflect the real purposes for which human beings learn and use language in their daily lives. Second, the demand for children to understand increasingly complex forms of language increases as they progress through the grades and largely determines their later academic success. Next, we discuss how to promote oral language learning in the school and classroom.

Promoting Oral Language Learning in the School and Classroom

Elementary schools and classrooms should offer ample opportunities for real conversations. Unlike classrooms of old that saw children sitting silently in rows doing seatwork, twenty-first century classrooms are roiling with activity and productive oral language is encouraged. As K.S. Cooter (2006) asserts, "*Learning* is noisy, *death* is silent!" So, you ask, how do you tell the difference between productive conversations and activity versus chaos?

Establishing Instructional Conversations. Roland Tharp and his colleagues at the Center for Research on Education, Diversity, and Excellence (CREDE) describe five standards for effective pedagogy (i.e., teaching and learning) (2006). You can learn more about these standards online at *http://crede.berkeley.edu/standards/standards.html.* They were developed by researchers interested in helping "students at risk of educational failure due to cultural, language, racial, geographic, or economic factors . . . [but] are effective with both majority and minority students in K–16 classrooms across subject matters, curricula, cultures, and language groups." (CREDE, 2006, p. 1).

The fifth CREDE standard, "Emphasizing Dialogue Over Lectures," offers insights into the thinking behind productive instructional conversations and ways teachers can achieve them. **Instructional conversations** (CREDE, 2006) involve teacher-student dialogue instead of lecture; are especially academically focused on key areas like math, science, and social studies; are explicitly goal-directed; and are typically conducted in small-group discussions. Several indicators of instructional conversation offered by CREDE to help teachers better understand what they may do to promote these exchanges are shown in Figure 2.6.

Oral Language Instructional Strategies

Perhaps the most important question elementary teachers ask us is, "How do we *teach* listening and speaking vocabulary?" In the next section, we present a few common strategies and activities for enhancing children's oral language development

Figure 2.6 CREDE Indicators of Instructional Conversation (2006)

Indicators of Instructional Conversation

The teacher:

- arranges the classroom to accommodate conversation between the teacher and a small group of students on a regular and frequent basis.
- has a clear academic goal that guides conversation with students.
- ensures that student talk occurs at higher rates than teacher talk.
- guides conversation to include students' views, judgments, and rationales using text evidence and other substantive support.
- ensures that all students are included in the conversation according to their preferences.
- listens carefully to assess levels of students' understanding.
- assists students' learning throughout the conversation by questioning, restating, praising, encouraging, etc.
- guides the students to prepare a product that indicates the instructional conversation's goal was achieved.

---

using a pragmatics-based conceptual framework. We begin with instructional strategies focused on instrumental uses of oral language.

Instrumental Oral Language Instruction: Interviews

Recall that the instrumental function of language relates to meeting personal needs. Having personal needs met usually involves requesting information or services from others. Interviewing is an engaging oral language activity that helps children meet personal needs by refining their ability to ask questions and make requests of others (Tompkins, 2005). Interviewing can be formal or informal. During informal interviews, children ask questions and make requests of others in day-to-day classroom settings. Informal interviews might be conducted during the first week of school with students working as partners in interviewing each other. The interview can be modeled initially by the teacher in the large group. Interview questions might include the following:

What is your name?
What is your favorite food?
What is your favorite game or sport?
What do you like to do for fun?
What do you want to be when you grow up?
If you could go anywhere in the world, where would you go?

An effective way to introduce children to formal interviewing in the intermediate years is to share with them videos of recorded interviews or to have them watch real-time interviews on television. Discuss with children the purpose of the interview and the kinds of questions that were asked. Point out that good interview questions require more than a "yes" or "no" response, and that effective questions prompt people to give information, state their opinions, and express their feelings.

Children should be taught how to plan and conduct effective formal interviews through teacher modeling of the process. First, the interview time and location should be arranged. These should be convenient for the interviewee and free from distractions. The types and sequence of questions to be asked should be carefully planned. This is accomplished through brainstorming, and the teacher should model this prewriting process.

Questions selected for the interview can be written on 3″ × 5″ note cards, which can be ordered and reordered until an effective sequence is achieved.

Second, the teacher should model how to conduct the actual interview. The school principal or a community member might be invited to class to act as the interviewee. Students should learn how to greet the person they interview, how to properly introduce themselves, and how to request permission to take notes or record the interview on videotape or audiotape. They should be taught to be polite and respectful of their interviewee's responses. The teacher should model how to end the interview by thanking the interviewee.

A natural follow-up to the formal interview activity is to have students share the results of their interviews with an audience. They might be invited to deliver an oral report about the interview to the class or to record their report on videotape for playback to the class at a later time.

Teaching children interviewing skills helps them develop their ability to ask good questions and listen for answers. These basic skills are essential to obtaining information or services they might need.

Regulatory Oral Language Instruction: Giving and Following Commands

You will recall from earlier in this chapter that the regulatory language function focuses on using language to manage the behavior of others. Two classic and engaging activities that provide experience with the regulatory functions of oral language are "Simon Says" and "Copycat."

In playing "Simon Says," children learn both the receptive and expressive facets of regulatory oral language. As Simon, children learn to give commands to others. As participants in the game, they learn to listen and follow commands. For this activity, someone is chosen to be Simon, while the remaining players are the recipients of Simon's commands. The game has two simple rules: (1) If Simon gives a command prefaced by "Simon says," players are to follow the command; and (2) If Simon gives a command without prefacing it with "Simon says," players should *not* follow the command. For example, if Simon says, "Jump up and down," players would do nothing. On the other hand, if Simon says, "Simon says 'touch your nose,'" players would touch their noses. Participants are eliminated from the game when they do not listen carefully to what Simon says. The last person remaining in a round becomes Simon in the next round.

In the game "Copycat," players are to say exactly—or copy—what the "top cat" says. Children can be asked to copycat a word, a phrase, a sentence, or several connected sentences. This activity is usually begun with the teacher in the role of "top cat." After a few minutes of play, the teacher chooses a student to be the "top cat." As the game progresses, the role of "top cat" is assumed by each player.

Both of these oral language activities help children develop skills in awareness, structure, and use of regulatory words, phrases, and connected language.

Interactional Oral Language Instruction: "Phone" and Small-Group Conversations

The interactional language function focuses on using oral language to talk or interact with others. The activity we call "Phone" requires two battery-operated telephones (these can be purchased at toy stores and often resemble cellular phones). It is helpful if the teacher develops a series of direction cards that give examples of phone calls for different purposes. For example, one card might require the student to make a phone call to his or her parent to tell the parent about a school event. One student plays the role of the student; a second student plays the role of the parent. Another card might direct the student to call a classmate to invite him or her to a birthday party. A partial list of ideas for starting phone conversations in the elementary classroom follows.

> Ordering pizza
>
> Calling the fire station to report a fire
>
> Arranging a party at a local bowling alley
>
> Reporting to the police an escaped boa constrictor in your backyard
>
> Calling a friend to invite him or her to come over to watch a DVD or video
>
> Calling a grandparent who lives far away

Like other oral language instructional activities, phone conversations are most successful when initially modeled by the teacher and several students. After modeling a few phone conversations focusing on telephone etiquette, the teacher can invite students to practice conversations with their classmates. Initial guided practice should be supervised by the teacher; later, students can work independently. Throughout their practice on the telephone, students can be encouraged to learn how to begin and end conversations, how to respond politely, and how to listen actively.

Children also learn to use oral language effectively when they have guidance and support while engaging in small-group conversations. Such conversations are usually begun by someone asking a question or making a comment. Responses to the initial question or comment follow, with members of the conversational group taking turns asking other questions or expanding on the comments of others. Again, children should be taught the skills of polite, active listening and respectful responding. They should also learn that good conversations do not focus on only one of the speakers or put others down.

Conflict in conversations is inevitable, and students need to learn how to resolve such conflict peacefully. The teacher might model how people can agree to disagree with one another, or how humor can "defuse" a tense conversational situation. Students also need to be taught acceptable ways to end a small-group conversation, perhaps by asking questions such as "Is that about it?" or "What do you think: Have we about said all we can on this?" A partial list of prompts for small-group conversations follows.

> Talking about characters in a book
>
> Discussing what students like to do for fun after school
>
> Discussing what students have learned today in school
>
> Sharing current events in the news or on TV
>
> Planning what students will do during recess time that day
>
> Discussing the lunch menu and students' favorite foods

Personal Oral Language Instruction: "About Me!"

The personal language function focuses on using oral language to tell others about oneself and one's interests. A daily time set aside in many classrooms to use oral language for personal reasons is found in the time-honored activity called "Show and Tell."

Children bring favorite objects to school and tell their classmates what the object is, how they obtained it, why they like it, and what they do with it. Although some teachers may think of this daily ritual as "Bring and Brag," "Show and Tell" daily time is ideal for bridging the home and school cultures. Here, again, teacher modeling is paramount in teaching students to use language to share what they bring to class and to listen and respond appropriately. "Show and Tell" guidelines for speakers might include the following:

Tell us about what you brought today.

Tell us how or where you got it.

Tell us why it is important to you.

Tell us what you do with it.

Tell us about one of the experiences you've had with it.

Guidelines for listeners are listed here:

Listen.

Pay attention.

Ask questions.

Thank the speaker for sharing.

Say something nice about the speaker or his or her presentation.

As an alternative to "Show and Tell," students might create and share a "Me Box." Each day a child is given a decorated "Me Box" to take home and bring back the next day. On one side of outside of the "Me Box" is a clear acrylic picture frame titled "When I Was Little." On another side of the outside of the "Me Box" is a clear acrylic frame for "My Name." On the third side of the outside of the "Me Box" is a clear acrylic picture frame titled "My Family." On the fourth side of the outside of the "Me Box" is a clear acrylic frame labeled "My favorite thing to do is __." Inside the "Me Box," students should place no more than six meaningful pictures or objects they want to share with the class. When a student shares his or her "Me Box" with the class, he or she begins by sharing the outside of the box and then proceeds to the objects/pictures inside the box. The rules for sharing are very similar to those for speaker and listener during "Show and Tell." Children enjoy telling others about who they are and what they like, and they appreciate having their classmates express interest. With both "Show and Tell" and the "Me Box," children have daily opportunities to share information about who they are in a personal way with the teacher and their peers in the classroom.

Heuristic Oral Language Instruction: Explaining and Convincing

The heuristic language function focuses on using oral language to debate, explain, and convince. The ability to use oral language to persuade others is a critical language function. Two oral language activities well suited to supporting its development are debates and TV commercials.

Debates are most engaging when children are enthused about a current issue. When children participate in debates, they learn how to use oral language to articulate their points of view and persuade others. In debates, students in grades 3–6 determine an issue or problem for discussion. This issue or problem might emerge from books the teacher has read aloud, from current events, or from real classroom experience. For example, one issue that might provoke a debate is the preference among some students for more than one vegetable in school hot lunch offerings. Children on one side of the issue move to one area of the room; children on the other side of the issue move to a different area of the room. Children who choose not to take sides remain in their seats and become the judges for the debate, determining which side's argument is most persuasive.

The teacher acts as moderator of the debate. To begin, the teacher asks one child from the supporting side of the issue under debate to come up to the front of the class, indicate his or her position on the issue, and then comment on or explain that position. Next, the teacher asks a child with an opposing point of view to come up to the front of the class, indicate his or her position, and then comment on or explain that position. Depending on the amount of time allotted to the debate, several children can present their views. After the time allotted has run out, the teacher asks the judges to vote either by a show of hands or a written ballot on which "team" won the debate.

To prepare children to be successful in debates, teachers might show several examples of televised debates. Children should also be taught how to debate effectively: this is helpful not only for debaters, but also for those children who serve as debate judges. Tompkins (1998) recommends that children be taught to use a rubric for evaluating debates. A debate rubric is found in Figure 2.7.

Another effective oral language activity for developing students' skill in explaining and persuading is producing television commercials. To begin this activity, students learn about several propaganda techniques (see Table 2.4).

Figure 2.7 Debate Rubric*

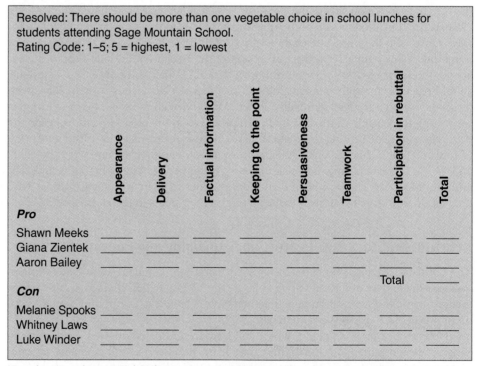

*Based on Tompkins, G. E. (1998), *Language arts: Content and teaching strategies* (5th ed.), © 2002, p. 58. Adapted by permission of Upper Saddle River, NJ: Merrill Prentice-Hall.

Table 2.4 Propaganda Techniques

Name	Characteristics	Example
1. Snob appeal	Makes us want a product because superior or wealthy people have it. Association with a small, exclusive group.	L'Oreal Haircolor: Because I'm worth it. BMW: the ultimate driving machine.
2. Name calling	Creates a feeling of dislike for a person or product by associating it with something disliked or undesirable. May appeal to hate and fear. Asks people to judge without first examining the evidence.	My opponent is a tax-spending liberal! My opponent is a flip-flop man who cannot make up his mind. He changes his mind with the breeze! How could anyone follow such a weak-willed flip-flopper? In a campaign speech to a logging company, the Congressman referred to his environmentally conscious opponent as a "tree hugger."
3. Glittering generalities	Uses broad general statements, whose exact meanings are not clear. Appeals to emotions of love, generosity, brotherhood. Words suggest ideals such as truth, freedom, and the American way.	Be all that you can be . . . in the Army. Our world-class employees and their commitment to innovative ideas continue to drive our success in today's fast-paced business environment.
4. Plain folks	Identifies the person or product with the average person. Politicians may try to win confidence by appearing to be like the good folks in your town.	Motel 6: We'll leave the light on for you. Wendy's "Where's the beef?" campaign.
5. Transfer	Creates a good or bad impression by associating with a product or person with something respected or not respected. The feeling for the symbol is supposed to transfer to the new product or person.	Texaco ad: You can trust your car to the man who wears the star. Hanes Underwear: Wait 'til we get our Hanes on you.
6. Testimonial	A respected person, such as a movie star or athlete, recommends a product and suggests that you buy it because he or she used it.	Brooke Shields: Know what comes between me and my Calvins? Nothing. Indy 500 Michael Schumacher's Choice: Omega Speedmaster Automatic. Life cereal: Hey, Mikey! He likes it.
7. Bandwagon	Follow the crowd and buy what everyone else is buying, or vote for the winner.	The Pepsi Generation. The president says, "We must unite in the fight against terrorism."

From Norton, Donna E., *Effective Teaching of Language Arts, The,* 6th edition, © 2004, p. 149. Adapted by permission of Pearson Education, Inc., Upper Saddle River, NJ.

We have found that the teaching of propaganda or persuasion techniques is much more effective when these are illustrated using multiple examples, such as magazine advertisements, radio spots, and TV commercials. Students can reinforce their knowledge about propaganda techniques by creating a series of posters identifying and explaining specific techniques and giving examples from magazine advertisements and/or TV commercials.

Once several propaganda techniques have been taught, we suggest dividing students into TV commercial-production groups, with no more than four students per group. Groups select a propaganda technique to implement in making their commercial, develop a script, and collect props and other materials for production. After groups have rehearsed their commercial several times, they perform it in front of the video camera. When all of the commercials have been recorded, students view them and identify the propaganda technique used.

Imaginative Oral Language Instruction: "Let's Pretend"

The imaginative language function finds expression in using oral language for pretend or fantasy play. Dramatizing a story from a book is an excellent expressive oral language development activity and is a favorite among children. We have found several alternatives for dramatizing a story, whether it is one children have heard before or one they themselves have composed during play. Although many children are too shy to speak up in front of their peers, they open up when they use puppets to talk in their place. There are many types of puppets, from simple finger, paper bag, sock, paper cup or plate, and stick puppets, to more elaborate, commercially produced puppets. Teachers can demonstrate how to make a puppet character come alive by using a distinct voice and interesting actions. Flannel board cut-out characters can also be used to tell stories, while wordless picture books can stimulate children to fabricate stories based on illustrations.

The key elements to model for children when telling stories are found in narrative structures: setting, characters, problem, goal, events, and resolution. (We will discuss story structure in greater detail in Chapter 6 of this book.) Younger children need to know that a good story has a beginning, middle, and end. To help children internalize the structure and language associated with storytelling, teachers need to read aloud traditional tales such as *The Little Red Hen, The Three Little Pigs, Goldilocks and the Three Bears, The Three Billy Goats Gruff,* and *Jack and the Beanstalk.*

Children develop greater ability to use oral language when they have many opportunities to retell and dramatize stories using props such as dress-up clothes, puppets, and flannel board cut-out characters (Tompkins, 2006). In Figure 2.8, we show a variety of puppets children can make for dramatizing stories from books they have read or that they have composed on their own.

Representational Oral Language: Instructions and Directions

The representation language function focuses on using oral language to give others instructions for performing a task successfully or directions to find a location. Treasure hunts are ever-popular activities for developing these abilities. Hide two "treasure chests" (boxes containing granola bars) in two locations. Pair students with partners; show the first child in each pair where one of the treasure chests is hidden. Mark the starting place for the treasure hunt with an "X." Have the first child in each pair give oral directions for finding the treasure to the other child. Once the second child in the pair finds the treasure, have the children exchange roles. Show the second child the location of the other "treasure chest," and direct partners to return to the starting spot. The second child then gives oral directions to the first.

Another excellent activity for developing skill in giving oral directions can be conducted in small groups. Decide on a task, such as making instant chocolate pudding.

Figure 2.8 Types of Puppets Students Can Make

Stick Puppet   Paper Bag Puppet   Cylinder Puppet

Sock Puppet   Styrofoam Puppet   Paper Plate Puppet

Finger Puppet (with tabs)   Finger puppet (from glove finger)   Cloth Puppet

Arrange four to six children into two groups of two to three students each. Blindfold one group of two to three students, and have them give oral directions for carrying out the task to the two to three students who are not blindfolded. The members of the group carrying out the task follow the oral directions exactly as given by the students who are blindfolded. For the task to be carried out successfully, the students in the blindfolded group must first discuss the directions they wish to give so that they are complete and sequential. On another day, the two groups can exchange roles in carrying out another activity (e.g., making a peanut butter and jelly sandwich).

Divertive Oral Language Instruction: "That's Funny!"

The divertive language function points to the use of oral language for enjoyment, amusement, and recreation—i.e., using language as a diversion. Children love to tell jokes and riddles. In fact, they love telling jokes and riddles so much they will go to great lengths to find as many willing listeners as they can! To help children develop both a repertoire of jokes and riddles as well as the ability to tell them well, teachers need to read aloud a variety of joke and riddle books. After reading a joke or riddle book aloud to the large group, the can teacher invite students to "turn to a neighbor" and tell her or him a favorite joke or riddle. In Table 2.5 we list several joke and riddle books that are favorites.

For older children, "Pundles" and "Sniglets" are wonderfully rich divertive oral language activities. "Pundles" are configurations of letters, lines, and symbols used to spell out familiar words and phrases. (See, for example, *Pundles* or *Pundles II* by Bruce and Greg Nash [1983]). A "pundle" for the familiar breakfast cereal Cheerios™ might be represented as follows:

A "sniglet" is a word that does not appear in the dictionary, but should. A listing of some "sniglets" (see Table 2.6) from the Web site *http://bertc.com/sniglets.htm* are drawn from the very popular books *Sniglets,* by Rich Hall (1984).

Singing humorous songs is another means by which elementary-aged students can share in divertive oral language. One of our favorite humorous songbooks is *A Prairie Home Companion Folk Song Book* by Garrison Keillor, Jon Pankake, and Marsha Pankake (1988). As children build up a store of jokes, riddles, and other humorous language, provide opportunities for them to share these with the class. "Joke, Song, or Riddle of the Day" is a favorite activity in many classrooms. Jokesters, singers, and riddlers are given an opportunity to tell their joke or riddle or sing their song with a microphone and karaoke box. Regardless of the activity, children should have opportunities to share in humorous oral language activities regularly in the elementary classroom.

Authoritative Oral Language Instruction: Now Hear This!

The authoritative language function focuses on using oral language to provide others with important information or to enforce rules, statutes, laws, and ordinances. Because children are often reminded about rules for behavior in class, on the playground, and in the lunchroom, authoritative language is a daily experience at school. Invite children to

Table 2.5 Childrens' Jokes and Riddles Sources

Children's Joke and Riddle Web Sites

www.kidsjokes.co.uk
www.brownielocks.com/jokes.html
www.fun4children.com

Children's Joke and Riddle Books

Bonham, T. (1997). *The Treasury of Clean Children's Jokes.* Broadman & Holman Publishing, ISBN 080546364X.

Cerf, B. (1999). *Riddles and More Riddles* (Beginner Books). Random House, ISBN 0679889701.

Dahl, M. (2003). *A Book of Rhyming Riddles.* Picture Window Books, ISBN 1404802274.

Dahl, M. (2002). *The Everything Kids' Joke Book: Side-Splitting, Rib-Tickling Fun.* Adams Media Corporation, ISBN 1580626866.

Davis, J. (1997). *Garfield's Book of Jokes and Riddles.* Troll Communications, ISBN 0816742901.

Hills, T. (2000). *Knock-Knock—Who's There?: My First Book of Knock Knock Jokes.* Little Simon, ISBN 0689834136.

Horsfall, J. (2003). *Kids' Silliest Jokes.* Sterling Publishing Company, ISBN 1402705980.

Keillor, G. (2000). *Pretty Good Jokes.* Highbridge Publishing, ISBN 1565113683.

Keller, C. (2004). *Kids' Bathroom Book: Riddles.* Sterling Publishing Company, ISBN 1402717105.

Keller, C. (1997). *The Little Giant Book of Knock-Knocks.* Sterling Publishing Company, ISBN 0806981083.

Krull, K. (2003). *You Must Be Joking! Lots of Cool Jokes, Plus 17 1/2 Tips for Remembering, Telling, and Making Up Your Own Jokes.* Cricket Books, ISBN 0812626613.

Lederer, R. (1996). *Pun and Games: Jokes, Riddles, Rhymes, Daffynitions, Tairy Fales, and More Wordplay for Kids.* Chicago Review Press, ISBN 1556522649.

Leno, J. (2005). *How to Be the Funniest Kid in the Whole Wide World (or Just in Your Class).* Simon & Schuster Children's Publishing, ISBN 1416906312.

Mauterer, E. (2005). *Laugh Out Loud: Jokes and Riddles from* Highlights for Children. Boyds Mills Press, ISBN 1590783484.

McCory, Martin, J. (2004). *Vocabulary-Boosting Jokes and Riddles.* Scholastic Professional Books, ISBN 0439542561.

O'Donnell, R. (1997). *Kids Are Punny: Jokes Sent by Kids to* The Rosie O'Donnell Show. Warner Books, ISBN 0446523232.

Peterson, S., Walton, R., Walton, A., & Schultz, S. (Eds.). (2004). *Ivan to Make You Laugh: Jokes and Novel, Nifty, and Notorious Names.* Carolrhoda Books, ISBN 1575056593.

Phillips, B. (2001). *Extremely Good Clean Jokes for Kids.* Harvest House Publishers, ISBN 0736903097.

Phunny, U. R. (2004). *Animal Jokes.* Buddy Books, ISBN 1591976200.

Rosenbloom, J. (2004). *696 Silly School Jokes and Riddles.* Sterling Publishing Company, ISBN 140271095X.

Rosenbloom, J. (1999). *Great Book of Riddles and Jokes.* Sterling Publishing Company, ISBN 0806999342.

Thomas, Lyn. (2004). *Ha! Ha! Ha!: 1,000 + Jokes, Riddles, Facts, and More.* Maple Tree Press, ISBN 1897066120.

Weintraub, A. (2005). *Everything Kids' Gross Jokes Book: Side-Splitting Jokes That Make Your Skin Crawl.* Adams Media Corporation, ISBN 1593374488.

Weitzman, I. (2000). *Jokelopedia.* Workman Publishing Company, ISBN 0761112146.

Table 2.6 Examples of "Sniglets"

- *Accordionated* (ah kor' de on ay tid)—*adj.* Being able to drive and refold a road map at the same time.
- *Orosuctuous* (or oh suk' chew us)—*adj.* Being able to hold a glass to one's face by sheer lung power.
- *Pigslice* (pig' slys)—*n.* The last unclaimed piece of pizza that everyone is secretly dying for.
- *Tilecomet* (tyl Kom' it)—*n.* the piece of toilet paper that clings to your foot after you've left a public restroom.

Figure 2.9   "Memorable Moments" Story Starter Cards

The happiest moment of my life was _____.	It all started when _____.
I was terrified when _____.	I was so embarrassed when _____.
You won't believe this, but _____.	How was I to know that _____?
The worst day of my life began _____.	The funniest thing that ever happened to me was _____.
Late last night, _____.	I expected it to happen, and it did _____.
The best day of my life began _____.	The saddest thing I ever saw was _____.

listen for oral language during the day that is used to remind them of class or school rules. At the end of the day, share the reminders of school and class rules they heard. Brainstorm with students places outside of school where authoritative oral language is used, such as in homes, stores, courtrooms, police stations, and so on. We have also found it effective to have students dramatize authoritative roles: a police officer informing a child that she should cross the street at a marked crosswalk; a lunchroom worker or teacher telling a child what to do before he can leave the lunchroom to go out to recess; a parent telling a child she can watch TV only after her homework is finished.

A less frequent authoritative oral language opportunity is to have students give oral reports about experiences they have had, books that someone read to them, or TV programs or movies they have watched. Modeling for children how to give well-presented oral reports and then having them engage in oral reporting is an excellent way to help them learn to use authoritative oral language.

Perpetuating Oral Language Instruction: Remember This!

The perpetuating language function uses oral language to tell others about historical events that are worthy of preserving and being passed on to others. Gordon (2001) offers two excellent activities that support the perpetuating function of oral language: "Memorable Moments" and "Pick a Picture."

The teacher makes a set of "Memorable Moments" cards featuring story starters similar to those in Figure 2.9. Next, he or she models choosing a card and telling a story from his or her past that uses the story starter on the card. Student storytellers follow suit.

The "Pick a Picture" oral language activity is similar to the "Memorable Moments" activity. The teacher collects a boxful of old personal and magazine photographs, old postcards, greeting cards, and newspaper photographs. Next, she or he models choosing an old photograph or other item from the box and telling a story from her or his past experiences that connects in some way to the photo, postcard, or greeting card. Children are invited to follow suit, telling stories from their own lives.

Create a lesson through the Teacher Prep Website. You will be guided through the alignment of standards, lesson objectives, your introduction, planning for and sequencing lesson activities and procedures, planning for ongoing assessment throughout the lesson, and planning end-of-lesson assessment. You will also choose and list lesson materials/resources and create adapted instruction to meet the needs of all students. This lesson can be sent to your instructor through this link. Using the pragmatics-based conceptual framework for oral language instruction, create a lesson to enhance oral language development.

Differentiating Oral Language Instruction

Effectively teaching English learners (ELs) to read and write well in English is an important responsibility in today's elementary schools. A growing number of students come from homes where English is not the primary language or where children are exposed to limited amounts of oral language usage (Hart & Risley, 1995). According to the National Literacy Panel Report on Language-Minority Children and Youth (2006), in 1979 there were 6 million language-minority students; by 1999, the number of EL students had swelled to 14 million. The panel concluded

> Language-minority students who cannot read and write proficiently in English cannot participate fully in American schools, workplaces or society. They face limited job opportunities and earning power. Nor are the consequences of low literacy attainment in English limited to individual impoverishment. U.S. economic competitiveness depends on workforce quality. Inadequate reading and writing proficiency in English relegates rapidly increasing language-minority populations to the sidelines, limiting the nation's potential for economic competitiveness, innovation, productivity growth, and quality of life (National Literacy Panel Executive Summary, 2006, p. 1).

Dutro and Moran (2003) offer six excellent principles for providing effective oral English language instruction for English learners (ELs). These general principles extend far beyond benefiting only the EL population of oral language learners and provide excellent suggestions for planning and adapting oral language instruction for children of poverty and other diverse language learners who struggle. To develop high levels of oral language ability among young learners, teachers should:

1. Build on students' prior knowledge of both language and content
2. Create meaningful contexts for functional use of language
3. Provide comprehensible input and model forms of language in a variety of ways connected to meaning
4. Provide a range of opportunities for practice and application so as to develop fluency
5. Establish a positive and supportive environment for practice, with clear goals and immediate corrective feedback
6. Reflect on the forms of language and the process of learning

Activating and building on children's prior knowledge is essential. Gersten & Baker (2000) say that strategic use of some native language terms and phrases can help address specific problems in connecting new knowledge to students' existing knowledge and language abilities. When creating meaningful contexts for diverse learners to develop oral language, moving from the concrete to the abstract is another principle of importance. Whether children are learning a first or second language, the use of visuals, objects, diagrams, labels, simulations, gestures, and dramatization of situations and roles are extremely helpful for early language learners (Gersten & Baker, 2000; Marzano, 1998).

Another principle for teaching English learners involves teacher and peer modeling within a "communicative context" (Long, 1991). Such instruction involves clear modeling, slower pacing, information presented in smaller chunks, and frequent checking for understanding and feedback. Also, modeling is best if it occurs in relation to specific or defined tasks such as applying for a job, talking to the doctor, renting an apartment, or buying food at the store.

Working cooperatively in the classroom offers increased opportunities for children to use language purposefully and appropriately. Moran (1996) suggests that small-group work that is cooperative in nature increases the incentives for children to use oral language in

> **Getting to Know English Learners**
> Differentiated learning environments are crucial for the English language learner because it is here that the teacher makes sure that the ELs language learning is always supported and growth is documented in authentic ways so that the EL can use language as a tool to enter into other areas of learning, like the content areas.

greater amounts and more appropriately. Also, small-group work encourages children to help one another by providing corrective feedback in positive and helpful ways that are low risk (Lightbrown & Spada, 1999).

Finally, for oral language development to flourish, children need to feel that the classroom is a safe place for risk taking when trying to use new language patterns (Krashen, 1985). Dutro and Moran (2003) also emphasize that, even though classrooms should be safe for trying out new language, teachers should provide clear communication about learning goals and offer positive corrective feedback so that students can improve.

Making Family and Community Connections

Parents are their children's first teachers, and homes are children's first schools where the foundations of oral language development are begun (Biemiller, 2006). Parents who talk while playing with their children, who often use rare (infrequent and mature) vocabulary words while interacting with their children, and who take time to engage in rich mealtime conversations provide many of the essential elements for developing oral language (Dickinson & Tabors, 2001; Snow, Scarborough, & Burns, 1999; Watson, 2001). More than three decades of research, unfortunately, indicates that most parents spend very little time having real conversations with their children. Our goal as teachers, then, is to buttress language development at school with ways of teaching parents how they can help children at home through conversations.

Perhaps the most effective practice for developing children's oral language at home is for parents to read books aloud to their children regularly, and provide access to books and other print materials in the home (Dickinson & Tabors, 2001; Straub, 2003). It is, however, a mistake for teachers to assume that because parents can read for their own purposes, they know how to effectively interact with their child around the reading of a book. Straub and DeBruin-Parecki (2002) note that many parents were not read to as children themselves. Following are two guidelines for effective parent-child read-alouds teachers can use in training parents.

1. *Books should be read aloud interactively.*   This means readers should stop to discuss parts of the text, the storyline, information, or a picture during the reading. In fact, recent evidence (Dickinson & Tabors, 2001) suggests that interaction is the most important part of making reading aloud effective! An interactive parent-child read-aloud starts with a brief introduction and discussion of the book that helps children recall their background knowledge and personal experiences with the topic or theme of the book. Background knowledge can be built through field trips, movie viewing, or searching for pictures and information on the Internet or in books. When reading aloud, parents should stop at various points in the book to ask the child open-ended questions. They should invite children to inquire about concepts they do not understand and help them make connections between the text read and their own life experiences. Parents should be sure that an adequate amount of time is allowed for discussion during and after the reading. Too often, parents talk too much, rush through the reading, and do not allow sufficient time for their listeners to express themselves or their ideas.

Reading books aloud to children should be an important part of each day's family and home routine. Reading aloud before going to bed at night is a wonderful way for parents and children to bond; it is also helpful in settling children down for a good night's sleep.

2. *Look for books that provide children information about their world.* Young children love fiction (stories), but they also love nonfiction—books about real facts, objects, and events such as butterflies, magnets, weather, and transportation (Mohr, 2003). Information books help children grow new concept knowledge and vocabulary (listening and speaking).

Taking parent training one step further, we have created a list of the "do's" and "don'ts" of reading aloud based on Trelease's (1995) *The New Read-Aloud Handbook* (see Figure 2.10).

Involving Parents Having Limited English or Reading Ability

Teachers, particularly those serving in rural or urban areas, will sometimes discover that some of their students' parents have limited English or reading abilities. Nevertheless, there are some research-proven strategies these parents can be taught to help their children develop oral language.

Increasing Mean Length of Utterance (MLU): Dialogic Reading. A mother's **mean length of utterance (MLU),** the average number of words spoken together, is predictive of her child's later language development (Cooter, 2006; Murray, 1990; Reutzel & Cooter, 2007). As parents speak in longer word chains—sentences that are longer and more complex—children tend to imitate and create longer sentences, too. Vocabulary becomes more complex and expressive as well.

Research on increasing a child's mean length of utterance (MLU) provides some valuable insights for teachers who are coaching language-limited parents.

- Parents who speak or question using complete sentences are more likely to have children who respond in longer word chains or longer utterances (Peterson, Carta, & Greenwood, 2005).
- Parents who read books or talk through books that are both narrative and manipulative—those where children can touch, pull, or handle the book—can increase their children's questions and length and number of utterances (Kaderavek & Justice, 2005).
- Simply giving children models and opportunities of lengthening and elaborating their sentences significantly increases their oral language ability (Farrar, 1985; Remaly, 1990).

In an article titled "When Mama Can't Read: Counteracting Intergenerational Illiteracy," K. S. Cooter (2006) offers a proven strategy parents can use with their children to help increase their MLU: dialogic reading. **Dialogic reading** is often thought of as simple picture book reading, but it has a much different face. It transfers the book's oral language responsibility to the child, who leads a dialogue with his parent around the pictures he chooses. Some of the original dialogic reading research was conducted by Whitehurst, Falco, and Lonigan (1988) and replicated many times in the ensuing years, each time with results that are educationally and statistically significant (Huebner, 2001; Huebner & Meltzoff, 2005; Scarborough & Dobrich, 1994; Whitehurst, Arnold & Epstein, 1994).

Find out more about how parents can create storytelling activities. You will enhance family and community connections by sharing this idea for use outside of the classroom. Children can tell or write stories based on pictures. Refer to the Teacher Prep web site (*www.prenhall.com/teacherprep*) for a link to *Reading Methods.* Select the article titled "Storytelling."

Learn how to use dialogic reading to assist English Learners. Visit our Teacher Prep Website (*www.prenhall.com/teacherprep*) for a link to *Language Arts Methods.* Read the article titled "Generating Stories."

George Dodson/PH College

Figure 2.10   Do's and Don'ts of Reading Aloud

DO

- Begin reading to children as early in their lives as they can be supported to sit and listen.
- Use rhymes, raps, songs, chants, poetry, and pictures to stimulate oral language development, listening, and interaction with others.
- Read aloud to children at least 10–15 minutes daily, more often if possible.
- Set aside a time for daily reading aloud in the family's schedule.
- Read picture books to all ages, but gradually move to reading longer books without pictures as well.
- Vary the topics and genre of read-aloud selections.
- Read books that stretch children's intellectual and oral language development.
- Allow plenty of time for interaction before, during, and after the reading.
- Read aloud with expression and enthusiasm.
- Add another dimension to reading by occasionally using hand movements or puppets or by dressing up in costume.
- Carry a book with you at all times to model your love of books and reading.

DON'T

- Don't read aloud too fast.
- Don't read aloud books children can read independently—give a "book talk" instead!
- Don't read aloud books and stories you don't enjoy yourself.
- Don't read aloud books and stories that exceed children's emotional development.
- Don't continue reading a book you don't like. Admit it, and choose another.
- Don't impose your interpretations and preferences on children.
- Don't confuse quantity with quality.
- Don't use reading aloud as a reward or punishment.

Based on Trelease (1995).

Build family and community connections by sharing ways to stimulate reading at home and at school. Visit our Teacher Prep Website (*www.prenhall.com/teacherprep*) for a link to *Reading Methods*. Read the article titled "Ways to Stimulate Reading in Young Children."

Any picture book that has illustrations that effectively tell the story may be used in dialogic reading. Examples we often use to demonstrate this strategy are *Flossie and the Fox* (McKissack, 1986) and *Chicken Sunday* (Polacco, 1992). Either fiction or nonfiction books may be used, but we favor a heavy diet of nonfiction books for improving language and vocabulary. It is recommended that the text be read aloud first to the child, but sending home a cassette tape recording (and player) of the teacher reading the book aloud will do just fine. The child leads the conversation with the parent, focusing on and responding to the pictures in the book. The parent is open to the child's remarks, uses "what" questions, and rephrases and extends the child's utterances, but remains at all times the follower in the dialogue. As one child put it, "I talk the book." The parent can be helped to learn how to engage the child in this child-led dialogue as well. The American Library Association, for instance, hosts parent trainings and can help teachers locate trainers throughout the nation in their Every Child Ready to Read @ Your Library program (for more information, see their *http:// www.ala.org* Web site).

Picture book dialogic reading seems to yield the best results in improving the length of children's sentences (Cooter, 2006; Whitehurst, Falco & Lonigan, 1988). Vocabulary becomes more complex and expressive as well. Sometimes just adding gestures is valuable. Mothers who pointed as they talked established joint attention and help children learn object names.

Huebner (2000) found that parents must be *taught* to use a book in this language-rich manner. Parents without training typically resort to the more traditional page-turning and labeling of pictures with their children. This can lead to parents who are increasing their efforts to read to their children at home, but the quality or nature of the reading has not changed.

Parents with limited English literacy skills can easily partner with their child in dialogic reading in that the book itself is a tool in the parent-child dialog.

One of the Five Pillars refers to differentiating instruction. Reference our Teacher Prep Website (*www.prenhall.com/teacherprep*) for a link to *Reading Methods.* You can learn to deliver effective instruction in "Differentiating Instruction for Second Language Learners."

Summary: Oral Language Instruction— A World Difference

Oral language is the foundation for all learning in school and out. Teaching oral language effectively may mean the difference between success in school and life for many children, especially those at risk due to poverty. To teach oral language effectively, teachers must understand six inter-related components of language structure: (1) phonology, (2) orthography, (3) morphology, (4) syntax, (5) semantics, and (6) pragmatics. Teachers also need to understand theories and the developmental trajectory of language acquisition in the early years of children's lives. Each theory of language acquisition, Behaviorist, Innatist, Constructivist, and Social Interactionist, explains some facet of how children learn to speak their native language and other languages as well. Children's language acquisition follows a fairly predictable path in its development throughout the early years of life if children receive support for doing so. These stages were each discussed in broad descriptive terms in this chapter. However, when children do not receive this support in the early years, they begin school with a tremendous deficit in oral language which often translates into later school frustration and failure.

Adequately assessing children's oral language development is desirable but impractical due to expense in terms of time and money. Several simple, reliable, and inexpensive oral language assessments were described in this chapter to help teachers get a reasonable handle on children's oral language growth. An instructional framework was presented based upon the pragmatics of language use for teaching elementary school children oral language. Within this framework several effective and motivating instructional strategies were described to develop oral language within each of ten different pragmatic language categories. Finally, we offered some thoughts on how to differentiate oral language instruction to meet diverse student learning needs as well as how to connect the teaching of oral language in the classroom to families and the larger community. Woven together, these elements will help you, the teacher, to become much more effective in planning and providing rich and focused oral language instruction in your elementary school classroom.

Classroom Applications

1. Divide into groups of four to six students. Refer to Table 2.1, Six Components of Language Structure. With your group, make a poster featuring examples of the six components of language.

2. Read Chapter 9, pages 191–216, of Hart and Risley's (1995) *Meaningful Differences in the Everyday Experience of Young American Children.* Pair with another student in the class. Share five important ideas you learned from reading this chapter with your partner. As a class, discuss the significant concerns, issues, and problems raised in this chapter and what classroom teachers can do. Develop a list of oral language instruction do's and don'ts based on your discussion.

3. Work with a partner in identifying the propaganda techniques used in several magazine or television advertisements. Join with another pair of students to jigsaw your findings in groups of four. Collaborate with another group of four students to achieve consensus on the propaganda techniques employed in the advertisements examined by each group.

Recommended Readings

Dickinson, D. K., & Tabors, P. O. (2001). *Beginning literacy with language.* Baltimore, MD: Paul H. Brookes.

Dutro, S., & Moran, C. (2003). Rethinking English language instruction: An architectural approach. In G. G. Garcia (Ed.), *English learning: Reaching the highest level of English literacy* (pp. 227–258). Newark, DE: International Reading Association.

Halliday, M. A. K. (1975). *Learning how to mean: Explorations in the development of language.* London: Edward Arnold.

Hart, B., & Risley, T. R. (1995). *Meaningful differences in the everyday experience of young American children.* Baltimore, MD: Paul H. Brookes.

Hart, B., & Risley, T. R. (2002). *The social world of children: Learning to talk.* Baltimore, MD: Paul H. Brookes.

Moats, L. C. (2000). *Speech to print: Language essentials for teachers.* Baltimore, MD: Paul H. Brookes.

Payne, R. K. (1998). *A framework for understanding poverty.* Highlands, TX: RFT Publishing Co.

Pinnell, G. S., & Jaggar, A. M. (2003). Oral language: Speaking and listening in elementary classrooms. In J. Flood, D. Lapp, J. R. Squire, & J. M. Jensen (Eds.), *Handbook of research on teaching the English language arts* (2nd ed.), (pp. 881–913). New York: MacMillan.

Piper, T. (1998). *Language and learning: The home and school years* (2nd ed.). Upper Saddle River, NJ: Merrill/Prentice-Hall.

Scarborough, H. S. (2001). Connecting early language and literacy to later reading (dis) abilities: Evidence, theory, and practice. In S. B. Neuman & D. K. Dickinson (Eds.), *Handbook of early literacy research* (Vol. 1, pp. 97–110). New York: Guilford.

Shannahan, T. (2006). Relations among oral language, reading, and writing development. In C. A. MacArthur, S. Graham, & J. Fitzgerald (Eds.), *Handbook of writing research.* NY: Guilford.

Smith, F. (1977). The uses of language. *Language Arts, 54*(6), 638–644.

Smith, P. G. (2001). *Talking classrooms: Shaping children's learning through oral language instruction.* Newark, DE: International Reading Association.

Watson, R. (2001). Literacy and oral language: Implications for early literacy acquisition. In S. B. Neuman & D. K. Dickinson (Eds.) *Handbook of Early Literacy Research.* NY: Guilford.

chapter **3** Early Reading Instruction

Teaching the Essentials

Chapter Questions

1. What are three early reading essentials discussed in this chapter?

2. What are print concepts?

3. What are phonological and phonemic awareness?

4. What is letter name recognition?

5. What are three assessment tools for assessing the early reading essentials?

6. What are three instructional strategies for helping children learn letter names?

Inviting Them In

(Authors' Note: The following is based on an event that happened when one of the authors was a child.)

Ms. Allen looked over her new class of kindergarten children at Emerson School. It was Thursday of the first week of school, and she was seeing the first signs of children becoming comfortable with their new and strange environment. To be sure, some of the children were practically pros—the ones who had attended the neighborhood preschool. But most of the twenty-two youngsters had not had that opportunity: they were from working-class families or from poverty, and preschool had not been a possibility for many of them in their small, rural town.

The one child she was most determined to reach today was Charles. On the first day, right after being walked to the school's front door by his mom, Ms. Jefferson, Charles had fled school and actually beat his mom home. This may have been an indication that school was not a place to be, in Charles's mind. On the second day of school, the principal had called Ms. Jefferson and asked her to please come back to school and see her son. When she arrived at Principal Henderson's office, he asked her to look out the back window, which faced the playground. There Ms. Jefferson saw Charles . . . happily walking along the four-foot-high stone wall at the perimeter of the schoolyard about a hundred yards away. He had evidently gone straight to the wall at the opening bell. "You think he's a little reluctant about coming to school?" the principal asked with a grin. After much coaxing by his mother, Charles stoically took his place in Ms. Allen's class that day and was there again this morning.

Ms. Allen's goal was to make Charles feel at home at all costs. Perhaps a good way to achieve that goal, she told herself, was to help him feel some success in early reading. Later that day, when she was able to have all of the children working at stations, she called Charles aside for a little one-on-one assessment. "Charles," Ms. Allen began, "I'm so happy I have you in my class this year. I can tell you are very smart and you'll probably be one of my kindergarten leaders!" She gave Charles a genuine smile as she spoke and the lad beamed.

Ms. Allen continued by laying an index card between them. On it she had written his name in block letters. "Do you know what this says?"

"That's my name, Ms. Allen!" Charles responded with pride.

"That's right! I knew you were a reader the first day I saw you." Charles smiled, but she saw some puzzlement in his face. *A reader?*

"Yes," she said, anticipating his puzzlement. "One of the very first steps in becoming a reader is to know your own name when you see it. Good job!"

Charles relaxed slightly and Ms. Allen could see the tension starting to ebb. She had him! Next Ms. Allen asked, "Charles, can you tell me what any of the letters are in your name?"

Charles responded by pointing and saying, "This is *c*." He glanced up for affirmation.

"Correct!" said Ms. Allen. "What other letters do you know?"

Skipping over *h* and *a*, Charles confidently proclaimed, "This letter is *r*. It says *rrrrrrr*. My mom taught me that!"

"Your mom is a *great* teacher, Charles," said Ms. Allen. He nodded his agreement.

After continuing with this exercise, and then later with a short phonemic awareness and letter-naming test, Ms. Allen concluded her ten-minute session saying, "Charles, I am so pleased with how much you know about sounds and letters. You know so many! This year we will learn together *all* of the sounds and letters, and before you know it, you'll be able to read just about any book you want! How's that sound?"

"I like that, Ms. Allen." Charles returned her smile. He went back to his center activity, this time with a little more spring in his step. *I think Charles will be just fine,* thought Ms. Allen.

Primary grade teachers, like Ms. Allen, know well the fundamentals of early reading instruction. Nested in a classroom environment resplendent with great books, and where children engage in abundant amounts of reading and writing, there are critical skills and strategies young children must learn to become readers. Not only do children need to have books read aloud, print displayed around the room, and opportunities to write, but they also need to have a teacher like Ms. Allen, who knows what is important to teach young children in order to get them off to a good start—from the very beginning.

Over many decades, research has been converging on what primary grade teachers need to know—and children need to learn—in order to make progress in early reading instruction. In this chapter, we focus our attention on three of these essential early reading concepts, skills, and strategies: phonological and phonemic awareness, letter name knowledge, and print concepts.

What Is Early Reading and How Do Young Children Become Readers?

The question "What is early reading?" or perhaps more appropriately, "What should early reading instruction include?" has been at the heart of a long debate in the early childhood and elementary school teaching profession. In the late 1920s and early

1930s, early reading was thought to be the result of reading readiness (N. B. Smith, 2002). The concept of **reading readiness** distinguished readiness for reading from a general readiness for learning. During the reading readiness era of early reading instruction, researchers attempted to determine a threshold or point in time at which children could be taught to read with the largest success rates. In practice, however, reading readiness often led to withholding reading and writing instruction from young children until they were thought to be "ready."

In the early 1970s, the definition of early reading as "reading readiness" was challenged by a new concept: emergent literacy. **Emergent literacy** is a term that implies children are becoming literate beginning from birth and continue to develop as literate beings throughout life. Emergent literacy, like its predecessor reading readiness, has been challenged in recent years. Many of those who embraced the concept of emergent literacy believed that because literacy learning begins at birth and extends throughout life, children learn to read and write as naturally as they learn to speak. As a result, some educators and teachers during the **whole language** movement spurned direct reading skill instruction in the 1980s and early 1990s. Many thought it was only necessary to immerse children in print or provide them experiences with books, literature, and opportunities to read and write (Goodman, 1984; Smith, 1985; Tunnell & Jacobs, 1989). This extreme, too, became largely discredited when, in the mid-1990s, it was found in the 1994 National Assessment of Educational Progress (NAEP) that large numbers of school children were failing to learn to read "proficiently" at grade level (Reutzel & Mitchell, 2005).

An overwhelming sense of frustration in the nation and within the profession of education itself led the U.S. Congress and then-President Clinton to appoint a National Reading Panel to determine what scientific evidence suggested would be effective for teaching young children to read. The National Reading Panel (2000) found sufficient evidence to support five essentials of early reading instruction:

1. Phonemic awareness
2. Alphabetics (to include letter knowledge and phonics instruction)
3. Fluency
4. Vocabulary
5. Comprehension

Many educators and scholars have criticized the National Reading Panel's (2000) findings as being too narrow in scope (Allington, 2002, 2006; Coles, 2000; Garan, 2002; McQuillan, 1998; Pressley, 2002). However, we, like T. Shanahan (2004), find it difficult indeed to imagine early reading instruction without these five essentials!

Evidence today clearly indicates that although children do emerge into reading and writing, this emergence rarely occurs naturally. Instead, success in early reading requires knowledgeable teachers who know *what* and *how* to teach young children in terms of reading and writing. Strickland et al. noted this in 2002 when they pointed out that not all children were succeeding as early readers, which, they believed, reaffirmed the need for improved early reading instruction and intervention. In a document titled, *Teaching Reading IS Rocket Science,* the American Federation of Teachers cited NAEP test evidence that "the rate of reading failure for some groups [e.g., African-American, Hispanic, Native American] is 60 to 70 percent" (p. 9). Research also indicates that a pattern of school failure starts early and persists throughout a child's school career. Juel (1988) found that there is approximately a 90 percent chance that a child who is a poor reader in first grade will be a poor reader in fourth grade.

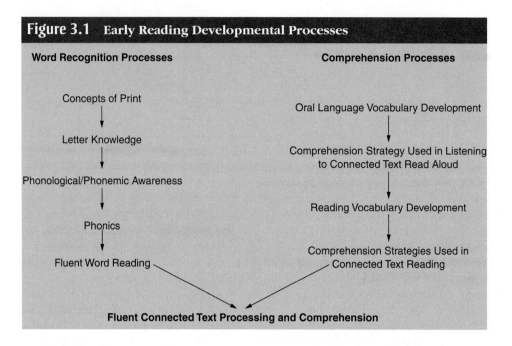

Figure 3.1 **Early Reading Developmental Processes**

Word Recognition Processes

Concepts of Print
↓
Letter Knowledge
↓
Phonological/Phonemic Awareness
↓
Phonics
↓
Fluent Word Reading

Comprehension Processes

Oral Language Vocabulary Development
↓
Comprehension Strategy Used in Listening to Connected Text Read Aloud
↓
Reading Vocabulary Development
↓
Comprehension Strategies Used in Connected Text Reading

Fluent Connected Text Processing and Comprehension

The evidence at hand today indicates that early reading is a developmental process that requires explicit instruction by a knowledgeable teacher. When we reviewed the research on early reading development (e.g., Lomax & McGee, 1987; Morris et al., 2003; Rasinski, 2003; Stahl, 2004), the evidence seemed to converge mainly in the areas of word recognition and comprehension. This early reading developmental process is represented in Figure 3.1.

What Does Research Say About the Essentials of Early Reading Instruction?

Getting to Know English Learners

Remember this is especially crucial for ELs as their language may not use the Greek alphabet (i.e., a, b, c . . .) nor may it use letters at all—as in the Chinese language where symbols are used.

Some children enter school already knowing a great deal about how books work, while others do not (e.g., Burns, Griffin, & Snow, 1999; Early Childhood-Head Start Taskforce, 2002; Reutzel, Fawson, Young, Morrison, & Wilcox, 2003; Yaden & Templeton, 1986). Some children know the difference between a word and a letter; others know where a story begins in a book; and others have had little access to books and guided experiences with print (Neuman, 1999; Neuman & Celano, 2001). Concepts associated with printed language, such as directionality (reading left to right, top to bottom), concepts of word or letter, book handling, voice-print matching, and punctuation, are known as **print concepts** (also *concepts about print*). These are an essential part of early reading development for beginning readers.

Research also clearly shows that young children must develop **phonological** and **phonemic awareness** to succeed in learning to read (e.g., Adams, 2001; Armbruster, Lehr, & Osborn, 2001; National Reading Panel, 2000). Phonological and phonemic awareness involve the conceptual understanding that spoken language can be broken down into smaller units such as sentences, phrases, words, syllables, onsets, rimes, and phonemes (sounds). We know from the work of Marilyn Adams (2001) that children's phonological awareness begins with an awareness of individual words in spoken language, followed by an awareness of the syllables within words. Next, children become aware that syllables are made up of **onsets** (all the sounds in the syllable *before* the vowel) and **rimes** (the vowel sound in a syllable and everything following it). Third, young children become aware of individual sounds, or **phonemes,** in spoken language. Finally, children develop the ability to manipulate (delete and substitute) individual sounds in spoken words. From these research findings, the teacher of reading realizes that children's awareness of spoken language progresses from the whole (ideas shared through speech) to the parts (individual words, syllables, onsets and rimes, and then phonemes).

In addition to phonological and phonemic awareness, the National Reading Panel (2000) pointed out the equally important contribution that **letter name knowledge** makes to early reading success: ". . . correlational studies identified PA [phonemic awareness] and letter knowledge as the two best school-entry predictors of how well children will learn to read during the first 2 years of instruction" (p. 7). The Early Childhood–Head Start Task Force (2000), in a report titled *Teaching Our Youngest,* added, "Children who enter kindergarten knowing many letter names tend to have an easier time learning to read than do children who have not learned these skills" (p. 21). Burns, Griffin, and Snow (1999), in a document for the National Research Council titled *Starting Out Right,* listed "recognizes and can name all uppercase and lowercase letters" (p. 85) as one of several kindergarten outcomes with regard to reading instruction. Finally, Stage, Sheppard, Davidson, and Browning (2001) found that letter naming fluency, or accurate and effortless letter naming ability, is a unique predictor of children's reading fluency at the end of first grade. Thus, letter name recognition is an essential skill to be taught and learned in early reading instruction. Taken together, research evidence clearly points out that print concepts, phonological/phonemic awareness, and letter name knowledge are critical stepping stones toward early reading success.

How Is Young Children's Early Reading Assessed?

There are many purposes for conducting early reading assessment (Miesels & Piker, 2001). For most elementary classroom teachers, reading assessment is used either to (1) monitor students' progress, and/or (2) inform the teacher's instructional decisions. Given these twin purposes for early reading assessment, the natural question to ask next is "*Which* early reading skills should teachers assess?" Answer:

- ✓ Oral language development
- ✓ Concepts about print
- ✓ Phonological and phonemic awareness
- ✓ Letter name knowledge
- ✓ Sight word recognition
- ✓ Phonics knowledge
- ✓ Vocabulary
- ✓ Comprehension

Because we describe assessment tools for measuring oral language, phonics, sight word recognition, fluency, vocabulary, and reading comprehension in Chapters 2, 4, 5, 6, and 7 we will confine our discussion of early reading assessment tools in this chapter to those that can be used to assess print concepts, phonological and phonemic awareness, and letter name knowledge. Many tools are available for assessing these three essentials of early reading, and we recommend that our readers obtain a copy of our companion book, *Strategies for Reading Assessment and Instruction: Helping Every Child Succeed,* 3rd edition (Reutzel & Cooter, 2007) if more assessment tools are needed than we are able to provide here.

Print Concepts

In recent years, researchers and research reports have emphasized the importance of print concepts to early reading (Burns, Griffin, & Snow, 1999; Clay, 2000b; Early Childhood–Head Start Taskforce, 2002; Hiebert, Pearson, Taylor, Richardson, & Paris, 1998; Lomax & McGee, 1987; McGee & Richgels, 2003; Morris, Bloodgood, Lomax, & Perney, 2003; Reutzel, Fawson, Young, Morrison, & Wilcox, 2003; Yaden & Templeton, 1986). Not all young children have had equal access to printed language in their everyday experiences, homes, and communities (Neuman, 1999; Neuman & Celano, 2000). We appraise one informal classroom assessment, the Metalinguistic Interview, and one commercially published assessment, the *Concepts About Print Test* (Clay, 2000a, b), for examining young students print concepts for teaching early reading.

The Metalinguistic Interview.   The metalinguistic interview is an informal measure of young children's print concepts. It consists of a set of questions designed to assess children's understanding of academic or instructional language—the language teachers use in instruction as they talk about printed language in books and print displayed elsewhere. Young children often do not have a clear understanding of many of the common academic or instructional terms used in beginning reading instruction, such as *alphabet, letter, word,* and *sentence* (Clay, 1966; Denny & Weintraub, 1966; Downing, 1970, 1971, 1972; Reid, 1966). Obviously, knowledge of these terms is most likely linked to how well children understand and respond to early reading instruction. Academic or instructional language terms/concepts assessed in the metalinguistic interview include:

Getting to Know English Learners
Don't forget that an EL whose language uses a different directionality (e.g., Arabic) may have difficulty, at first, with this assessment.

- Concept of a single letter, word, or sentence
- Directionality L → R (left to right), T → D (top/down), and so on
- Punctuation
- How to differentiate uppercase and lowercase letters
- Terms such as the *front* and *back* of a book, and an understanding of *page(s)*

Any children's trade book or literature book containing both pictures and print may be used to administer a metalinguistic interview. For kindergarten assessment, locate a book that has print on one page and a full-page picture on the facing page. A scoring sheet can easily be constructed by duplicating Figure 3.2.

Begin your assessment by seating the child comfortably next to you. Hand the child a picture book such as *The Gingerbread Man* (Schmidt, 1985) or *The Little*

Figure 3.2   The Metalinguistic Interview

1. "What are books for? What do books have in them?" _____
2. "Show me the front cover of the book. Show me the back cover of the book." _____
3. "Show me the title of the book." _____
4. "Show me the author's name." _____
5. "Open the book to where I should begin reading." _____
6. "Show me which way my eyes should go on the page when I begin reading." _____
7. "Show me the last line on the page." _____
8. Begin reading the book. At the end of the first page ask, "Where do I go next?" _____
9. "Show me where to begin reading on this page. Will you point to the words with your finger as I say them?" _____
10. "Show me a sentence on this page." _____
11. "Show me the second word in a sentence on this page." _____
12. "Show me a word." _____
13. "Show me the first letter in that word." _____
14. "Show me the last letter in that word." _____
15. "Show me a period on this page." _____
16. "Show me a question mark on this page." _____
17. Show the child a quotation mark and ask, "What is this? What is it used for?" _____
18. Ask the child to put his fingers around a word. _____
19. Ask the child to put his fingers around a letter. _____
20. Ask the child to point to an uppercase letter and then a lowercase letter. _____

Correct responses are given a 1 score. Incorrect responses are scored 0.

Total Score _____

Red Hen (McQueen, 1985) upside down, with the spine of the book facing the child. Once the child has taken the book, tell him that the two of you are going to read the book together. Ask him to respond to the 20 tasks listed in Figure 3.2. Mark responses on your copy of Figure 3.2.

When scoring a *metalinguistic interview*, write 0 or 1 following each of the 20 questions. Scores on the interview range from a low of 0 to a high of 20. Carefully examine which items were missed in order to determine potential areas for print concepts instruction.

The Concepts About Print Test.   The *Concepts About Print Test* (CAP), developed by Marie Clay (1972, 2000a), is a commercially published instrument that can be used to assess children's knowledge of concepts about printed or written language such as letter, word, sentence, directionality, text versus picture, and punctuation. The CAP test makes use of four small test-like booklets, two published in 1972 and two published in 2000. The two test-like booklets published in 1972 are titled *Sand* and *Stones*; the two published in 2000 are titled *New Shoes* and *Follow Me, Moon*. All four are read aloud by the teacher as he or she works with individual students. We suggest that *Sand* and *Stones* be used for pre- and post-testing in kindergarten, while *New Shoes* and *Follow Me, Moon* be used for pre- and post-testing during first grade.

> **Getting to Know English Learners** 
> Marie Clay's, "Sand and Stones" is a wonderful assessment to determine an EL's baseline not only in print awareness but in beginning English language ability as well.

Directions for administering, scoring, and interpreting the *Concepts About Print Test* are found in Clay's (2000b) book, *Concepts About Print: What Have Children*

Learned About the Way We Print Language? More information about the test and the manual for administration, scoring, and interpretation can be found on the Internet at *www.heinmann.com.*

Print concepts assessed in the CAP test include front of book; proper book orientation to begin reading; beginning of book; print rather than pictures carry the message; directional rules of left to right; top to bottom on a page; return sweep to the beginning of a line of print; matching spoken words with written words; concepts of first and last letters in a word; mapping spoken word and letter order onto print; beginning and ending of a story; punctuation marks; sight words; and identifying printed letters, words, and upper- versus lowercase letters.

In order to adequately test children's print concepts, the *Sand, Stones, New Shoes* and *Follow Me, Moon* booklets make use of some rather unusual features. For example, at certain points the print or pictures in the test-like booklets are upside down, letter and word order are changed or reversed (*saw* for *was*), line order is reversed, and paragraph indentions are removed or inverted. Because of the somewhat tedious nature of this test and its tasks, children need to be tested in a calm environment by an examiner with whom they have a trusting relationship. The CAP test has established a long and excellent record as valid and reliable when used in conjunction with other tools in assessing reading skills, concepts, and strategies in the early years (Denton, Ciancio, & Fletcher, 2006).

Phonemic Awareness

In recent years, researchers and research reports have emphasized the importance of phonemic awareness among early readers (Adams, 1990, 2001; Adams, Foorman, Lundberg, & Beeler, 1998; Bear, Templeton, Invernizzi, & Johnston, 2004; Blevins, 1997, 1998; Cunningham, 2005; Ericson & Juliebo, 1998; Fox, 2004; Goswami, 2000, 2001; Goswami & Bryant, 1990; Lyon, 1998; Mustafa, 1997; National Reading Panel, 2000; Snow, Burns, & Griffin, 1998; Strickland, 1998; Wilde, 1997). It is estimated that roughly 20 percent of young children lack phonemic awareness (Blevins, 1997). Though phonemic awareness is not a "magic bullet" for preventing or fixing all reading problems (Shanahan, 2003a), it is certainly an essential component of early reading instruction (Shaywitz & Shaywitz, 2004). Two critical skills for young children to acquire in relation to early reading ability are blending and segmenting (Yeh, 2003). *Blending* refers to matching a spoken sound to each letter in print and putting these sounds together to figure out an approximate pronunciation for an unknown word. *Segmenting* refers to stretching out the sounds heard in a spoken word and representing each sound heard with a letter in writing or spelling. We present one tool for assessing students' blending and segmenting abilities.

Auditory Blending Test. Much like the *Roswell-Chall Auditory Blending Test* (1963), an auditory blending test (ABT), an informal assessment tool, requires students to say a word after hearing its individual sounds slowly articulated by the teacher. In other words, teachers stretch out the written word into segmented sound units, i.e., *m-an* or *sh-i-p*, and the child responds by blending the sounds mentally and then saying the word—*man* or *ship*. According to Griffith and Olson (1992), the ability to guess what the word is from its blended form demonstrates a high level of phonemic awareness. Yeh (2003) found that blending was one of two

Figure 3.3 Auditory Blending Test Sample Word List

at	l-ap	l-o-ck
two	t-ip	s-t-e-m
in	m-an	b-ea-k
if	st-ate	h-i-de
be	b-ox	c-a-sh
as	sc-ab	m-i-c-e
sea	r-ug	sh-ee-t
now	m-ind	f-r-o-g
go	th-ink	j-u-m-p
sew	p-ig	t-ur-key

phonemic awareness tasks that caused kindergarten children to reach high levels of early reading achievement.

To administer an auditory blending test (ABT), prepare a list of 30 words divided into three sets of 10 as follows (see Figure 3.3):

- The first 10 words should be two-phoneme words.
- The second set of 10 words should be three- to four-phoneme words that are divided before the vowel, demonstrating the onset and rime, e.g., *c* (onset) -*ap* (rime).
- The third set of 10 words should be three- to four-phoneme words that are segmented completely, e.g., *ch-i-p*.

Begin administering the ABT by telling the child that you will be stretching words out by saying the sounds in them slowly. Model several of these stretched words for the child and blend the words you have stretched. For example, stretch the word *s-i-t*. Then say the word: *sit*. Do this several times. Next, stretch a word and ask the child to tell you the word. Once this has been accomplished, tell the child you are going to play a game where you say a word stretched out and they are to answer the question you will then ask: "What am I saying?" According to Yopp's (1988) research, kindergarten children achieve a mean score of 66 percent, or correctly identify 20 out of the 30 target words blending tasks.

Phoneme Segmenting Test. Yeh (2003) found that segmenting was the second phonemic awareness ability that enabled kindergarten children to reach high levels of early reading achievement. In a phoneme segmenting test (PST), students are asked to listen to and isolate sounds in spoken words. A child's ability to isolate the sounds in spoken words is an excellent indication of whether he or she will profit from initial phonics instruction. The test should be comprised of 15 words consisting of three phonemes each. Target sounds in the beginning, middle, and ends of the words should be like the ones shown in Figure 3.4.

The teacher begins by modeling how phonemes can be pronounced, showing how *sit* starts with /*s*/, *hike* has the /*i*/ sound in the middle, and *look* ends with the /*k*/ sound. Next, the teacher tells the child they are going to play a quick game together: "I will say a word, and then you tell me the sound you hear in a certain place in the word, such as the beginning, the middle, or the end." As an example, the teacher might say, "*Slam*. Say the sound at the end of the word *slam*." The child would respond correctly by articulating the sound /*m*/.

Learn how to connect student names and nursery rhymes to help students develop phonemic awareness. A helpful sequence chart is included in this article as you reference the *Reading Methods* link in the Teacher Prep Website. (*www.prenhall.com/ teacherprep*). Select the article titled "Activities that Foster Phonemic Awareness."

Figure 3.4   Auditory Blending Phoneme Segmenting Test Sample Word List

	f-ool
	l-*oo*-p
	r-ode
	h-ome
	yar*d*
d-ime	k-*i*-ss
hu*sh*	g-*e*-t
fi-ve	raf*t*
clo*ck*	*b*-ike
c*u*-t	mu-*g*

The teacher should record each of the student's responses. According to Yopp's (1988) research, young children achieve a mean score of 9 percent, or one to two correct responses out of 15 target words, at the beginning of kindergarten.

Letter Name Knowledge

Recall earlier that we discussed the significance of recognizing and being able to name the letters of the alphabet in early reading acquisition. The National Reading Panel (2000) identified letter name knowledge as one of the two best predictors of early reading achievement. The letter naming task shown here is based on the work of Marie Clay (1993) and can be used to determine if young children can identify the letters of the alphabet.

Teachers begin this assessment by first reproducing a randomized alphabet letter display like the one shown in Figure 3.5 on a sheet of paper or chart paper. Next, the teacher invites the student to sit beside him and explains that he would like to find out which letters of the alphabet the student can name. The teacher then points to the letters on the randomized letter display chart, beginning at the top of the display working line by line and left to right to the bottom of the display. The teacher uses a photocopy of the randomized letter display shown in Figure 3.5 to mark the letters the child correctly names. The teacher then reverses the process, asking the child to point to the letter he names in the randomized letter display. The teacher also records this information.

Most young children should be able to identify 100 percent of the letters requested at the end of kindergarten. However, students who have little familiarity with letters at the beginning of kindergarten may perform poorly on this task.

What Are the Characteristics of Effective Early Reading Instruction?

Children who get off to a good start in early reading rarely fall behind. Those who do fall behind tend to stay behind for the rest of their academic lives (Burns, Griffin, & Snow, 1999). It is imperative, then, that early reading instruction be based on

Figure 3.5 Randomized Alphabet Letter Display

```
               E
             P  v
           r D f o
         A m I X T
          i Y w K
            u C
             J
```

research so that all children have an equal chance in school to get off to that good start and not fall behind!

Effective early reading instruction has been the focus of several research studies throughout the past two decades. These studies have focused on the variables that lead to student achievement in early reading (Block, Oaker, & Hurt, 2002; Morrow, Tracey, Woo, & Pressley, 1999; Pressley, Allington, Wharton-McDonald, Block, & Morrow, 2001; Rogg, 2001; Taylor, Pearson, Clark, & Walpole, 1999; Taylor, Pearson, Peterson, & Rodriguez, 2005). We provide an extensive discussion of these research-based characteristics in Chapter 11, but we will offer a few additional insights from research in this chapter as well. So in addition to our insistence in this chapter that teachers focus early reading instruction on the "right stuff" for early readers to succeed—such as print concepts, phonological/phonemic awareness, and letter name recognition—we also believe other conditions should be in place for young children to flourish in early reading instruction.

Morrow et al. (1999) identified the characteristics of effective early reading instruction by studying the practices of six exemplary first-grade reading teachers in New Jersey. These teachers produced exceptional reading achievement in their classrooms. These classrooms were happy places—communities of learning founded upon the principles of respect, cooperation, and high expectations for hard work and achievement. The classrooms were rich with access to printed materials for reading and print production supplies for writing. The exemplary teachers understood that in order to meet the diverse needs of their students, they would be called on to employ different instructional strategies involving the whole group, small groups, partners, and one-to-one instruction. The early reading essentials we have discussed in this chapter were explicitly and systematically taught. Teachers immersed children in abundant guided reading practice using appropriately selected texts: authentic literature, leveled books, decodable books, and big books. They read books aloud to students. Their instruction was carefully planned, but these teachers also responded spontaneously to "teachable moments" as they occurred. Exemplary early reading teachers were consistent in their expectations, training, and daily execution of classroom management procedures, routines, and schedules. Learning activities were engaging, varied, and involved children actively, often playfully. Instruction took a variety of forms: writing activities, shared reading and writing, reading aloud, modeled or shared writing, interactive writing, word study, word analysis, reading performances, guided reading, and independent reading and writing. Students often acquired content knowledge in themed cycles or units of study focused on exciting topics in social studies, science, and mathematics. Finally, exemplary teachers were students themselves, always seeking opportunities to learn how to teach early reading more effectively in grade level team meetings, in professional development trainings, and at professional conferences.

Much of what these researchers found is the substance of this chapter and the remaining chapters of this book. We remind you, however, that Chapter 11 is intended to help you organize all that you will learn as you study this book into an effective, evidence-based reading instructional program that will meet the diverse needs of all learners.

Video Classroom

Refer to our Teacher Prep Website (*www.prenhall. com/teacherprep*) for a link to Video Classroom.
Select Reading Methods and Module 3. View "The Second Rereading in a K-3 Multilingual Classroom."
As you view this clip, note how shared reading is conducted and the role of the teacher in this lesson.

- How does shared reading contribute to fluency development?
- How are the children supporting each other?
- Are there any problems that might inhibit this approach from being successful?

*Responses may be completed online to be printed or sent to your instructor.

What Are Effective Strategies for Teaching Early Reading?

Effective early reading instruction focuses on teaching young children the essential skills, concepts, and strategies necessary for developing fluent, expressive, and strategic reading. As discussed previously, these essentials include (1) oral language development, (2) concepts about print, (3) phonological and phonemic awareness, (4) letter name knowledge, (5) sight word recognition, (6) phonics knowledge, (7) vocabulary, and (8) comprehension. Because we deal with oral language, phonics, fluency, vocabulary, and reading comprehension in Chapters 2, 4, 5, 6, and 7, we will confine our discussion of early reading instructional strategies in this chapter to print concepts phonological and phonemic awareness, and letter name knowledge, and reorder list to match presentation. For each of these three, we will offer effective strategies for introducing and reinforcing skills. We begin with instruction in print concepts.

Print Concepts Instruction

An understanding of print concepts can be divided into three distinct and different print aspects (Clay, 2000b; Taylor, 1986): (1) the functional aspects of print, (2) the mapping aspects of print, and (3) the technical aspects of print.

Functions of Print. Children learn early that written language, like oral language, is useful for a variety of purposes. Halliday's (1975) landmark research describes how oral and written language functions in our daily lives. The purposes children and adults have for using language can be divided into three categories: (1) ideational, or expressive of one's thought; (2) interpersonal, or intimate/social; and (3) textual, or informational. Smith (1977) expanded on Halliday's theories about purposes for which language can be used. Each of Smith's ten purposes or functions of language, whether oral or written (Smith, 1977, p. 640), is detailed in Chapter 2: instrumental, regulatory, interactional, personal, heuristic, imaginative, representational, divertive, authoritative/contractual, and perpetuating. Children make varied use of oral language in their lives, at least in a subconscious way. As you help students become aware of these oral language functions, they will readily apply this knowledge in their written language as well.

Mapping Speech onto Print. The ability to match or "map" speech sounds onto printed symbols or letters develops rather slowly. Some researchers believe that the ability to map speech sounds onto printed language and knowledge of the sound-symbol code, or phonics knowledge, may develop simultaneously (Lomax & McGee, 1987). Important concepts for students to learn include the following.

1. Speech can be written down and read. What is written down can also be spoken.
2. Print is in our environment in the form of signs and logos.
3. The message of a text is constructed from the print rather than from the pictures.
4. Written language uses different structures (see Halliday, 1975, and Smith, 1977, mentioned above) than spoken language.
5. The length of a spoken word is usually related to the length of the written word.
6. One written word equals one spoken word.
7. Correspondences exist between spoken sounds and written symbols.
8. Using context and other language-related clues can help readers construct meaning and identify words.

Mapping speech onto print helps students become successful readers and benefit from further experiences with written language (Reutzel, Oda, & Johnston, 1992; Moore, 1989). For some readers, failing to acquire an understanding of mapping principles can slow their progress in reading and writing development (Clay, 1991; Ehri & Sweet, 1991; Johns, 1980).

Technical Aspects of Print. The term *technical aspects of print* refers to the rules or conventions that govern written language. These aspects include directionality (left to right/top to bottom progression across the page in reading), spatial orientation, and instructional terms used in classrooms to refer to written language elements. Because many of these technical concepts are commonsense matters for adults, it is little wonder that sometimes teachers and parents mistakenly assume that children already understand them. There is, however, ample evidence that knowledge of the technical

Think about all Five Pillars of Effective Reading Instruction as you read more about Guided Reading procedures. Information regarding learning patterns that produce increased student engagement and the parent/home connection are included in this article.

Refer to the Teacher Prep Website (*www.prenhall.com/ teacherprep*) and select the *Reading Methods* link to locate the article titled "Guided Reading."

aspects of written language is an important part of learning to read and write (Clay, 1979; Day & Day, 1979; Denton, Ciancio, & Fletcher, 2006; Downing & Oliver, 1973; Johns, 1980; Meltzer & Himse, 1969; Morris, Bloodgood, Lomax, & Perney, 2003; Reutzel, Fawson, Young, Morrison, & Wilcox, 2003). The technical aspects of print are summarized in Table 3.1.

Using Environmental Print to Teach Print Concepts. Researchers have examined the value of using environmental print to teach children print concepts and have consistently shown it to be useful in initiating children's awareness of print in their world (Proudfoot, 1992; Neuman & Roskos, 1993; Orellana & Hernandez, 1999; Kuby & Aldridge, 1994; Reutzel et al., 2003; Vukelich, 1994; West & Egley, 1998). Environmental print is not only useful for giving children experiences with print that they see in the world outside of the classroom, but it can also be used to build children's confidence in their ultimate ability to learn to read (Reutzel et al., 2003).

The term *environmental print* refers to print that is frequent and commonly accessible in children's community, school, and home environments. Examples include signs in the school building and on school grounds, such as STOP, EXIT, and NO SMOKING. Other examples of environmental print include signs on, in, and around businesses and stores, and on products children and families commonly consume, such as *McDonalds, Cheerios, Diet Coke,* and so forth. To use environmental resources to teach print concepts to early readers, you will need to gather product labels and logos. One strategy for using environmental print to teach print concepts involves creating "I Can Read" books. Titles for environmental print "I Can Read" books might include "My Favorite Foods," "I Spy: Signs I See," "A Trip to the Supermarket," and "My Favorite Things."

To prepare students for creating their own "I Can Read" books, present to them a read-aloud book that will serve as a template. If the selected topic is "Going Shopping," you might use as a template book Lobel's *On Market Street* (1981). After selecting a template book, gather environmental print and product labels that can be used in the children's "I Can Read" books.

To present a lesson focused on the theme of "Going Shopping," read the template book *On Market Street* aloud to students, pausing to discuss each of the things the main character purchases while shopping on Market Street. After reading, tell

Getting to Know English Learners

In a global world as today's, many of the products we are so familiar with are also familiar cross-culturally, thus aiding ELs in their abilities to interact with environmental print as part of their emergent awareness of print.

Table 3.1   Technical Aspects of Print Concepts

Ordinal	Visual Clues Embedded in Books and Print	Location Concepts
• First, second, third, etc. • Beginning • Last • Book • Paragraph • Sentence • Word • Letter	• Cover, spine, pages • Margins, indentations • Spacing • Print size • Punctuation	• Top • Bottom • Left • Right • Beginning (front, start, initial) • Middle (center, medial, in between)

students they are going to make their own "Going Shopping" book using *On Market Street* as a pattern. Model for students how to select different products for inclusion in their books: They must pay attention to the alphabet letter on the bottom of the page and select an item that begins with that letter as indicated on the product label. For example, the page featuring an *A* might be matched with an *All* detergent label or an *Alphabits* cereal label. You may want to pick just a few, perhaps no more than five to ten, familiar letters you have been learning to include in the children's *On Market Street* (Lobel, 1981) books. Once you have explained and modeled how to create your own *On Market Street* (Lobel, 1981) book, children can be invited to create their own "I Can Read" *On Market Street* (Lobel, 1981) book by selecting product labels from a classroom collection or from several copied pages of product labels they can cut out. This is just one example of how children can use print they often recognize in their world to learn more about print concepts such as words and letters, matching letters, and so on.

You might also create a bulletin board featuring the 26 letters of the alphabet with an area for each letter where product logos can be displayed. Involve students in collecting, sharing, and displaying on the board the print they read in their environment. One quick caution, however: Be sure to tell children that before they can remove a label from something at home, they need to get a parent's or caregiver's permission. It is most annoying to open a can without a label expecting to find corn and discovering refried beans!

Using Shared Reading Experiences to Teach Print Concepts. **Shared reading,** or what is sometimes called the **shared book experience,** is used with very young readers to model how readers look at, figure out, and understand print. During shared reading, the teacher typically uses a large-print text with a group of children, rather than a traditional-sized book with an individual child (Slaughter, 1993). In a shared book experience, children and teachers must be able to share the print simultaneously. As noted, this requires that the print be enlarged so that every child can see it and process it together under teacher guidance (Barrett, 1982; daCruz Payne, 2005). When selecting **big books,** be sure the print is large enough for children to see from 20 feet away. Shared reading books should have literary merit, engaging content (both fiction and nonfiction), and high interest. Illustrations in shared reading books should augment and expand upon the text. Books chosen for shared reading should also put reasonable demands on younger readers' capabilities. The number of unknown words in a book selected for shared reading should not overwhelm students.

Begin a shared book experience by inviting children to look at the book cover while you read the title aloud. Display and discuss the front and back covers of the book; point out certain features of the cover and title page, such as the author and illustrator names, publisher, and copyright date. Read the book with "full dramatic punch, perhaps overdoing a little some of the best parts" (Barrett, 1982, p. 16). While reading the story, invite children to join in reading any repeated or predictable words or phrases. They positively love doing this! At key points during shared reading, pause to encourage children to predict what is coming next in the story and to explain their predictions ("That's an interesting prediction. What made you think that?"). After reading, invite children to share their responses to the story. Ask them to talk about their favorite parts and connect the story to their experiences. Discuss how well they were able to predict and participate.

Visualize shared reading as you read "A First Grade Shared Reading Lesson Plan." The use of *wikki stiks*, highlight tape, word cards, pocket charts, and self-stick notes are incorporated within these five lessons. Learn more about shared reading teaching strategies in the Teacher Prep Website (*www.prenhall.com/teacherprep*), *Language Arts Methods* link.

Once a shared reading book has been presented, you might select something from the print in the book to examine in a **print concept reading.** For example, using the book *The Carrot Seed* (Krauss, 1945) (available in big book format), you might decide that students should understand the print concept of *word*—the visual detail that printed words are separated by spaces on either side. To direct students' attention to the spaces between the words in the text, you might use 2-inch lengths of wax-covered strings called *wikki stiks*. These adhere to the pages of a book without leaving a residue. During the lesson, engage students in the second reading of a text, pointing to and talking about the spaces between words. Insert *wikki stiks* between the words on the first page of the text, and then count the words. Turn to the next page of the text, and invite a child to come forward and place *wikki stiks* between the words. This time, direct the whole class to count the words with you. This process of sharing the identification and counting of words on pages is repeated for the rest of the book. Eventually, ask volunteers to place the *wikki stiks* between words independently and to count words without your assistance.

We have found that teachers need the following tools to teach print concepts during a shared reading experience in their classroom.

Large-print text

Post-it notes

Highlighting tape

Pointer

Fixed and sliding print frames

Lap-sized white board

Word and sentence strips

Chart or big book easel

Pocket charts

Print concepts that might be the focus of shared reading experiences include the following:

- The print carries the message, not the picture.
- Books have fronts and backs.
- The reader must be properly oriented to the print.
- The reader must know where to begin reading.
- Text is read left to right, top to bottom.
- Voice can be matched to print.
- Concept of word: A word is a unit of meaning.
- Concept of letter: A letter is a symbol for a sound.
- Concept of *first* and *last:* These words indicate sequence.
- Letters are written in both uppercase and lowercase.
- Reversible words such as was and saw or not & on!
- Print has certain required characteristics.
- Punctuation carries meaning.

The teacher can use a variety of techniques during shared readings to direct children's eyes to the print concepts to be observed. *Smooth pointing* underneath print on a page demonstrates for children that (a) print, not picture, is how the message of reading is carried; (b) one begins reading at a particular point on a page; and (c) one reads

TEACHER PREP   Create a lesson through the Teacher Prep Website.

- You will be guided through the alignment of standards, lesson objectives, your introduction, planning for and sequencing lesson activities and procedures, planning for ongoing assessment throughout the lesson, and planning end of lesson assessment. You will also choose and list lesson materials/resources and create adapted instruction to meet all needs of students.
- This lesson can be sent to your instructor through this link.
- Plan a shared reading experience using a big book. Review information provided in this chapter along with articles located in the Teacher Prep Website (*www.prenhall.com/ teacherprep*) in Teacher Resources and Research Resources.

left to right, sweeps the eye across the page to the next line, and proceeds from top to bottom. *Word-by-word pointing* underneath print demonstrates for children (a) concept of word, and (b) voice-print matching, sometimes called *finger point reading*. When selecting a pointer to be used for print concept instruction, it is important to remember that it is the print children are to look at—not the pointer. Elaborate and distracting pointers—those with footballs, trees, moons, and snowmen on the ends—often deflect children's attention from print. The best pointers are simple. A plain wooden dowel approximately 2–2.5 feet in length with a black or white rubber tip or pencil eraser tip will hold students' attention without distracting them from the task at hand.

Another technique for directing children's eyes during shared reading to the print on the page is to use fixed or sliding print frames as shown here.

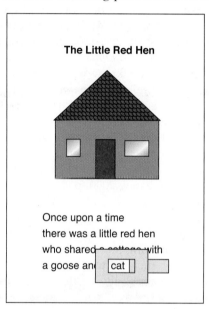

Sticky notes might also be used as shown here.

Some teachers have found that colored, transparent highlighter tape and arrows are useful in directing the eyes of young students to the features of print under study. Others create sentence strips or word and letter cards featuring text from the page(s) of a shared reading; these materials are then displayed to the group and become the focal point for instruction in print concepts.

In short, the shared reading experience is a logical context for teachers to explicitly teach print concepts (daCruz-Payne, 2005; Reutzel, Oda, & Moore, 1989).

Phonological and Phonemic Awareness Instruction

Adams (1990) reminds us that a child's level of phonemic awareness upon entering school "may be the single most powerful determinant of the success he or she will experience in learning to read" (p. 304). We begin our discussion of phonological and phonemic awareness by answering a most important question: What do the terms *phonological awareness* and *phonemic awareness* mean? If you are going to teach these essentials, then you must know what they are and what they are not. *Phonological awareness* is an umbrella term that includes hearing and manipulating larger parts of spoken language such as words, syllables, rhyming elements in syllables, and alliteration (Armbruster, Lehr, & Osborn, 2001; National Reading Panel, 2000; Snow, Burns, & Griffin, 1998). For example, the word *willow* has two syllables and rhymes with *pillow*. *Phonemic awareness,* in contrast, refers to the ability to focus on and manipulate phonemes (roughly equivalent to individual sounds) in spoken words (National Reading Panel, 2000, p. 2–10). For example, the word *rope* has three individual phonemes: /r/, /o/, and /p/. One common misunderstanding among practicing educators is that phonological awareness and phonemic awareness are synonymous. Clearly, this is not so. *Phonological awareness* is a much broader term that pertains to hearing and manipulating units of spoken language larger than a single phoneme, such as words, syllables, and rhyming elements. *Phonemic awareness* pertains specifically to the ability to hear and manipulate individual or single phonemes in spoken words and syllables.

Another common misunderstanding about phonemic awareness is that it is the same as phonics. As we have just discussed, phonemic awareness is the understanding that spoken words are made up of individual speech sounds, or what are called *phonemes.* Phonics, on the other hand, is the understanding that letters and letter combinations can be used in print to *represent* phonemes in spoken language that can be blended together to create spoken words from printed language. In other words, phonemic awareness does not involve the use of written symbols. Rather, it involves hearing spoken sounds. Phonics, on the other hand, involves written symbols, spoken sounds, and the connections between the two.

One thing is certain: Building children's phonemic awareness will help them acquire phonics skills later on. The reason is simple, really. When students are phonemically aware and can hear individual sounds (phonemes) in spoken words, learning that letters or letter combinations *represent* sounds in speech makes perfect sense—because there is a relationship between many spoken sounds and individual letters.

According to Adams (1990), the path to phonemic awareness is "top down." It begins with awareness of spoken words, then moves to an awareness of syllables within words, and then to an awareness of small units within syllables called onsets and rimes. We discussed onsets and rimes in Chapter 2, but a brief summary may be useful at this point: An onset involves the sounds in syllables that come before the vowel, as the /w/ sound in the syllable *win*. The rime includes the vowel sound and every other sound that follows it, as /in/ in the syllable *win*.

TEACHER PREP Observe choral response as children fill in rhyming words following a class wipe off board activity on the CD ROM that accompanies this text. Click on *Phonemic Awareness Kindergarten* and then select *Choral Reading*. Think about how this is helpful for ESL learners and why this approach is a source of on-going assessment for the teacher.

Adams (1990) describes how the movement from phonological to phonemic awareness occurs developmentally, in ascending order of difficulty. Step one involves becoming aware of spoken words. Surprising as it may seem, research suggests that children do not naturally think of spoken language as a string of individual words or understand words as individual units of meaning. When children listen, they attend to the full meaning of an utterance—and this meaning is only available after the meanings of the individual words have been combined, automatically and without their attention. Step two in developing phonemic awareness involves becoming aware of spoken syllables. An awareness of syllables in words constitutes an essential link between the seemingly natural ability of many young children to hear similarities between initial word sounds and ending rhyming elements in words and that more sophisticated ability to hear and recognize individual phonemes. Step three involves becoming aware of phonemes. Remember that syllables divide into two primary parts: the *onset* and the *rime*. Once a spoken word is broken down into syllables and then into onset and rime, children need to be able to identify each sound in the syllables and words. These individual sounds are called phonemes. Phonemic awareness occurs when teachers and children focus their attention on individual sounds in spoken words.

Numerous studies have confirmed the effectiveness of several kinds of learning activities that help children develop phonological and phonemic awareness. These activities will help students who come to school without these essential skills fill in that gap and become better readers (Adams, 1990; Blevins, 1997).

According to Armbruster, Lehr, and Osborn (2001), children can demonstrate their phonological awareness in a number of ways.

- Identifying and making rhymes orally
  *"Hickory, dickory **dock,***
  *The mouse ran up the **clock."***
- Identifying and working with syllables in spoken words
  "I can tap out the sounds in *kindergarten:* **kin-der-gar-ten!**"
- Identifying and working with onsets and rimes in spoken syllables or one-syllable words
  The first sound in *tall* is */t/,*
  and the last part is *-all*
- Identifying and working with individual phonemes in spoken words
  The first sound in *dog* is */d/.*

Next we present evidence-based categories to use in selecting learning activities related to children's developing phonemic awareness.

- ***Phoneme isolation***—Recognizing individual sounds in words.
  Teacher: What is the first sound in *boy?*
  Student: The first sound in *boy* is /b/.
- ***Phoneme identity***—Hearing the same sound in different words.
  Teacher: What sound is the same in *boy, bake,* and *butter?*
  Student: The first sound /b/ is the same.
- ***Phoneme categorization***—Recognizing the word having a different sound in a group of three or four words.
  Teacher: Which word doesn't belong? *run, rake, toy*
  Student: *Toy* doesn't belong because it begins with /t/.
- ***Phoneme blending***—Children listen to phonemes spoken separately, then blend them together to form a word.
  Teacher: What is this word? /m/ /a/ /k/
  Student: /m/ /a/ /k/ is *make.*

- **Phoneme segmentation**—Breaking a spoken word into its separate phonemes while tapping or counting on the fingers each sound.
  Teacher: Say the sounds you hear in the word *cup* slowly.
  Student: *Cccccccc uhhhhhhhh pppppppp.*
  Teacher: How many sounds did you count in *cup?*
  Student: Cup has three sounds.
- **Phoneme deletion**—Recognizing that a phoneme can be removed from a spoken word and that part of the word remains.
  Teacher: If I take away the sound /*b*/ in the word *brook,* what word is left?
  Student: *Brook* without /*b*/ is *rook.*
- **Phoneme addition**—The ability to create a new word by adding a phoneme.
  Teacher: If I add the sound /*s*/ to the word *tree,* what new word would I have?
  Student: *Tree* with /*s*/ added to the end would be *trees.*
- **Phoneme substitution**—Exchanging a phoneme for one in a spoken word to create a new word.
  Teacher: The word is run. Change /*n*/ to /*t*/. What's the new word?
  Student: The new word is *rut.*

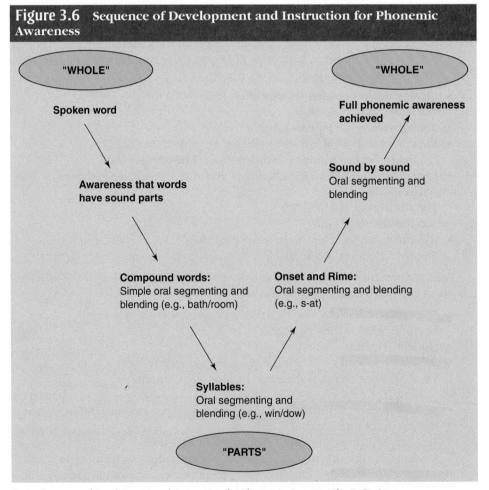

Figure 3.6   Sequence of Development and Instruction for Phonemic Awareness

"WHOLE"

Spoken word

Awareness that words have sound parts

Compound words:
Simple oral segmenting and blending (e.g., bath/room)

Onset and Rime:
Oral segmenting and blending (e.g., s-at)

Syllables:
Oral segmenting and blending (e.g., win/dow)

"PARTS"

Sound by sound
Oral segmenting and blending

Full phonemic awareness achieved

"WHOLE"

From *Sequence of Development and Instruction for Phonemic Awareness* by R. B. Cooter, Jr., D. R. Reutzel, and K. S. Cooter. 1998, unpublished paper.

Matching the Instructional Sequence to the Developmental Difficulty of Phonological and Phonemic Awareness Tasks. In phonological and phonemic awareness instruction, teaching should move from the simplest, most well-understood or familiar concepts toward the more complex, least well-understood or unfamiliar concepts. Figure 3.6 shows that the starting point is helping students understand that spoken words are made up of individual speech sounds. Word-stretching activities such as "rubber banding" can help students begin to hear word parts, such as two words in compound words. For example, the compound word *frogman* consists of two sound units familiar to children—*frog* and *man.* Young children are able to catch on quickly that compound words like *airport, bloodhound, clothespin,* and *rainbow* are just two smaller words "glued" together. They can hear and segment the two spoken words easily! If compound words are chosen so that each word part is a one-syllable word that carries a meaning students easily understand, both the sound and meaning connections can be understood at once by most students. Learning simple segmenting and blending with compound words is the first major jump from phonological awareness toward phonemic awareness.

Syllables are the next speech unit for students to orally segment and blend in this instructional sequence. This next step moves students from simply segmenting smaller words in compound words to dividing words by sound units that seem more abstract. Clapping or counting syllables heard in words like *window* and *kindergarten* helps them to segment sound elements (i.e., *win-dow, kin-der-gar-ten*). Blending activities are also effective: "I will say the first part of a word, and then the rest of the word—*sha . . . dow.* Then I will say the whole word blended together—*shadow.* Next, I will say the first part of a word, and then the rest of the word—*win . . . dow.* Now you say the word as a whole."

While blending syllables is one way to help children along the path from phonological to phonemic awareness, segmenting is also important. Consider the following segmenting sequence: "I will say the whole word—*shadow.* Next, I will stretch the word to count the speech parts—*ssshhhaaa dooo.* I count two. Now you try it. I will say the whole word—*mustache.* Now, let's stretch the word together and clap the speech parts—*mus tache.* How many times did we clap?" Yeh (2003) found that instructional time in kindergarten is best spent on blending and segmenting tasks rather than on rhyming tasks to develop phonemic awareness that will impact reading acquisition.

The next phonological awareness level calls for segmenting and blending onsets and rimes. As noted earlier, an onset is the part of a syllable that comes before the vowel; the rime is the rest (Adams, 1990, p. 55). For example, in the word *sat, s* is the onset and *-at* is the rime. Similarly, in the first syllable of the word *turtle, t* is the onset and *-ur* is the rime. This activity is easily done in the context of poetry (teaching *rimes* with *rhymes*).

Segmenting and blending spoken words sound-by-sound is the most abstract task and is the first and only level of phonemic awareness. Segmenting individual sounds in spoken words is a necessary precursor to children's developing the ability to spell words in writing. Blending, on the other hand, is a necessary precursor to children's developing the ability to blend or "sound out" words in reading. The difference is that we blend individual sounds to say whole words while we segment whole words into individual sounds.

The final phonemic awareness skills to be taught help children use phonemic blending and segmenting in more sophisticated and fun ways. At this point students are ready for phoneme manipulation activities such as phonemic categorization, deletion, addition, and substitution tasks described earlier.

Notice how a teacher models stretching sounds in words on the CD ROM that accompanies this text. Click on *Phonemic Awareness Kindergarten* and then select *Identifying Sounds.* She and the students use *slinkys* as they slowly say a prompted word. The teacher writes the word on a white board for beginning letter association with the sounds.

Some Other Tips for Planning Phonological and Phonemic Awareness Instruction. Blevins (1997, pp. 7–8) has summarized some important points that teachers of kindergarten through second grade should keep in mind as they plan for phonological and phonemic awareness instruction.

1. *Phonemic awareness is not related to print.* Oral and aural (listening) activities are what phonemic awareness teaching and learning are all about. Once children can name and identify the letters of the alphabet, they are ready to move into learning the alphabetic principle.

2. *Many, if not most, poor readers in the early grades have weak phonemic awareness skills.* Thus, phonemic awareness may be an important issue (on a limited basis) for teachers well beyond the K–2 years. Indeed, phonemic awareness training may well be indicated throughout K–12 education for students considered "remedial" readers.

3. *Model, model, model!* Children need to see you, their teacher, and other students actually performing phonemic awareness activities.

> **Getting to Know English Learners**
> Just like mainstream students, ELs will vary not only in their phonemic awareness, but also in their general language awareness and abilities. According to Cummins (1981), there are two types of language proficiency: BICS, or Basic Interpersonal Communication Skills, which takes ELs generally two years to achieve and CAPL, or Cognitive Academic Language Proficiency, which takes ELs five to seven years to achieve.

Several other recommendations for phonemic awareness activities are presented here (National Association for the Education of Young Children (NAEYC), 1986; Yopp & Troyer, 1992).

1. *Learning activities should help foster positive feelings toward learning through an atmosphere of playfulness and fun.* Drill activities in phonemic awareness should be avoided, as should rote memorization.

2. *Interaction among children should be encouraged through group activities.* Language play seems to be most effective in group settings.

3. *Curiosity about language and experimentation should be encouraged.* Teachers should react positively when students engage in language manipulation and might do so themselves occasionally. We like to read familiar stories aloud using spoonerisms to alert children to phonemic elements in spoken language. A spoonerism exchanges initial sounds in two words, for example, "Once upon a time, deep in the woods, there lived a family of **bee threars** (three bears)." Almost always children will hear these changes and want to correct the teacher's reading!

4. *Teachers should be prepared for wide differences among students in their acquisition of phonemic awareness.* Some children will catch on quickly, whereas others will need a great deal of guided practice. Teachers should avoid making quick judgments about children based on how they perform in phonemic awareness activities. In Figure 3.7 we summarize the levels of language through which phonological and phonemic awareness develops, the developmental sequence of tasks, and examples of those tasks.

Finally, research yields several important cautions for phonological and phonemic awareness instruction. First, the National Reading Panel (2000) advises teachers not to assume that *all* children need phonological and phonemic awareness (PPA) instruction. Rather, teachers should begin by assessing what young children may already know about PPA to be able to target instruction to meet students' needs. Second, research has determined that PPA instruction should require approximately 18 total hours of instruction for most children during their primary grade years. This means that PPA

Figure 3.7 Overview of Phonemic Awareness

Developmental Level Tasks	Phonological Awareness →			Phonemic Awareness →			Phonemic Awareness with Phonics →
Linguistic Levels	Word → Awarness	Syllables →	Onset and Rime →	Single Sound →	Blending →	Segmenting →	Manipulation
Introduced (Approx.)	Pre → K		K review first five weeks of 1st grade	K–1st Grade			1st Grade
Instruction Sounds Like	Model how many words heard in this sentence: The cat runs quietly (4)	Model how many syllables heard in this word: *skateboard* (2) or *windy* (2)	Model what the sound(s) is/are before the vowel in this syllable: *sit* -/s/ Model what the sound unit is, including the vowel and the sounds after the vowel in a syllable: *sit* -/it/	Model how many sounds heard in this word: *sit* (3)	Model what word we say when we blend the sounds /m/+/a/+/n/ - *man*	Model individual sounds heard in the word *sit*— /s/ /i/ /t/	Model Manipulating sounds in words by taking the /k/ sound off *cat–at*. Model manipulating sounds in words by substituting the /t/ sound for the /s/ sound in the word *son–ton*
Child's Response Looks Like	• Count • Clap • Manipulate markers	• Count • Clap • Manipulate markers	• Recognize • Manipulate	Count sounds they heard (not letters)	Elongate the sounds, getting faster each time	• Count • Clap	• Delete sound to make new word • Substitute sound(s) to make new word
Helpful Hints	The dog ran 1 2 3	Best to start with compound words— *cow/boy* 1 2	Use words families, rhyming words, alliteration *s + at* *w + in / d + ow*	*W i n d o w* 5 sounds (6 letters)	Clap when it's fast enough to be a word: *man*	Use a rubber band to "stretch" the word *c - a - t* /k/ /a/ /t/	*cat - /k/ = at* */t/on - /t/ + s = son*

Total: 18 hours of instruction unless indicated otherwise via assessment.

instruction should occur in rather quick lessons of no more than 5 to 7 minutes over several months in kindergarten and first grade. It may be necessary in some cases of diagnosed need to review PPA instruction in second grade. Third, the National Reading Panel (2000) found that phonemic awareness instruction, especially that focused on blending and segmenting, works best when combined with letter naming and phonics instruction in small groups as shown in Figure 3.7.

Letter Name Instruction

Recall that the National Reading Panel (2000) found that the two best predictors of early reading achievement were (1) letter name knowledge, and (2) phonemic awareness. Other researchers have found that letter name knowledge is a unique predictor of first-grade reading achievement (Stage, Sheppard, Davidson, & Browning, 2001). Consequently, in kindergarten and early first grade, teachers need to be concerned with developing fluent letter recognition—letter recognition that is both rapid and accurate.

Many teachers ask whether there is an evidence-based, optimal order for teaching the alphabet letters. The answer to this question is "no." Some educators prefer to teach the letters in the order of the alphabet. This approach allows children to hook their learning of alphabetical order on having sung the alphabet song, having seen the alphabet frieze above the board in the classroom, and on having heard alphabet books read aloud. On the other hand, some educators prefer to teach letter recognition as a way to get children quickly into blending and writing words using phonics. These teachers usually select one to three vowels along with some high-frequency consonants to teach initially, moving through the remaining letters in order of their frequency. To review comparative letter frequencies in words, we recommend that teachers consult the list compiled by Fry (2004), as shown in Table 3.2.

Still other teachers prefer to teach children to recognize alphabet letters by beginning with their names, as recent research has shown this to be a powerful source of letter name learning among four-year-olds (Justice, Pence, Bowles, & Wiggins, 2006). An excellent resource for teaching children letter recognition using children's names is Krech's *Teaching with Kids' Names* (2000).

In our work with kindergarten and early first-grade children, especially those from poverty, we have found that flash cards featuring letters and the alphabet frieze above the chalkboard are not sufficient in developing letter-naming fluency. We have found that for kindergarten and early first-grade children to identify letter names accurately and quickly, they need to *search* to find specific letters in a variety of print displays such as those found in small, easy-to-read books. They also need to *write* letters as their teachers dictate them. To help you teach letter recognition more effectively, we provide examples of each of these processes—letter recognition, letter searching, and letter writing—as well as offering some evidence-based advice about the pacing of letter recognition instruction and review cycles.

Teachers relate names and classroom objects as they help children learn the alphabet. "Understanding Alphabet Letters" will provide you with additional ideas for instruction. You can locate this article in the Teacher Prep Website (*www.prenhall.com/teacherprep*) *Reading Methods* Link.

Recognizing Letters. To help children recognize alphabet letters (both uppercase and lowercase) quickly and accurately, we recommend teachers avoid relying on the alphabet frieze displayed in the classroom. An alphabet frieze is the block print or script display of uppercase and lowercase letters found in nearly every classroom in the nation. We do not recommend using the alphabet frieze for practicing letter recognition for one important reason: Children recall their knowledge of alphabetical order to help them recognize the letters when those letters are practiced using

Table 3.2   Vowels and Consonants Ranked by Frequency

Vowels	Consonants
Short i—*pill*	r
Short a—*cat*	t
Short e—*get*	n
Schwa r—*girl*	s
Long o—*rope*	l
Long e—*me*	c
Short u—*cup*	d
Short o—*pot*	p
Long a—*ate*	m
Long u—*tune*	b
Long i—*like*	f
Broad a—*are*	v
Broad o—*for*	g
ou—*out*	h
oo—*look*	k
oi—*oil*	w
ar—*fair*	th
	sh
	ng
	ch
	x
	z
	j
	qu
	wh
	y

the alphabet frieze. For example, if you were to point to the letter *A* in the alphabet frieze, children would identify it accurately and quickly because this letter is at the beginning of alphabetical order. However, point to the letter *V* in the alphabet frieze, and note that children are slower in responding and less accurate in their identification. Careful observation will also reveal that children subvocalize the letters in alphabetical sequence and match each subvocalized letter with the next one in the alphabet frieze. Hence, practicing letters in this fashion is excellent for learning alphabetical order, but not for recognizing letters out of the sequence of the alphabet. When teaching letter recognition, teachers should present children letters for practice tasks in random order so that learners rely on the physical characteristics of the letter rather than its place in the alphabet to identify it.

Young children enjoy matching activities. Create decks of letter cards using letters you have focused on; be sure each letter is used more than once. Deal out several cards to students, and have them match letters. This activity can be played in a way similar to the old favorite, Go Fish! Each of several players is dealt five letter cards. The remaining letter cards become the draw pile. The first player says, "Do you have the letter *p?* If another player has that letter card in his or her hand, he or she must give it to the player requesting it. If the player gets a pair, he or she lays the pair on the table. If the other players do not have the letter requested, they say, "Go fish!" The first player takes a card from the draw pile and the next player gets to

Ray Reutzel

take a turn. The game is finished when a player is able to match all of the letter cards in his or her hand.

Searching for Letters. One engaging way for students to search for letters is to play an adaptation of the game I Spy. Required materials are several copies of the same book, an overhead transparency, and a washable ink overhead pen for each student. Place the transparency over the book pages. Direct students to look carefully at the print on the first page of their book. Start the game by saying, "I spy with my little eye————." Fill in the blank with a letter that occurs several times on the page, e.g., "five lowercase *m's*." To increase the challenge of the game, tell children you will set a timer for 1 minute. Challenge them to accurately and quickly identify using the overboard pen and transparency all of the *m's* on the page in the time alloted. Once children have learned a few letters, they can assume the role of "spy." The process can be repeated using different letters on the same page.

Writing Letters. The most important practice for ensuring that children can identify uppercase and lowercase alphabet letters quickly and accurately is through the use of writing. We use a game called Beat the Clock. This game requires that children have paper and pencil or, better yet, a gel board or white board and dry erase markers for writing. Set a timer for three minutes. Start the game by saying, "GO!" Tell students: "Write an uppercase *b*." Count off ten seconds and then say: "Write a lowercase *m*." Continue the process with a variety of letters until the timer alarm sounds. Then have students show you their letters. Make brief notes about each student's performance on the dictation task. Then tell students: "Let's see if we can beat the clock." This time, count to nine between each letter dictated. This slightly faster pace challenges children to write their letters as dictated more quickly, yet legibly and accurately. A simple graph can be created for each child showing his or her times across rounds of the game.

Pacing of Letter Recognition Instruction. We recommend teaching a new letter each day in kindergarten. Review cycles for the letters already taught should occur using the "law of 10–20" recently researched by Pashler (2006). This "law" proposes that if one wants to remember something for six months or more, then a spaced review should take place between 10 and 20 percent of the time period for which the thing is to be remembered, i.e., colors, dates, letters, words, math facts, and so on. Six months is equivalent to 183 days. The law of 10–20 suggests that a complete review of the 26 letters taught in the first five weeks of school should occur between 10 and 20 percent of 183 days, or every 18 to 36 days. Reviewing all of the 26 letters every five weeks falls well within the law of 10 to 20 percent used with other memory tasks. There is no question that letters are best learned through distributed practice and review rather than from massed practice. This goes against the grain in many kindergarten classrooms, where a letter a week is the traditional practice. Five letters a week can be taught quickly over time, with spaced reviews every 5 weeks for a total of seven review cycles in the kindergarten year. Such teaching is far more effective in helping children learn to quickly and accurately identify their alphabet letters.

How Can Early Reading Instruction Be Adapted to Meet the Needs of Diverse Learners?

As teacher educators, we have worked for over three decades with teachers who teach young children to read in many diverse elementary school settings: urban, rural, suburban; affluent, middle-class, and lower socioeconomic status. Regardless of the stratum or the school's diversity, young children who struggle in learning to read require several special considerations.

First, children who struggle with learning to read need more instructional time (Shanahan, 2003b). Struggling readers need double or triple the teacher-guided reading instruction that normally developing readers receive. But increasing allocated reading instruction time is not the key factor in success. Rather, spending more time on-task during allocated instructional time is the key factor. Struggling readers remain on-task better when they are in small-group or one-to-one teaching situations. Thus, small-group differentiated reading instruction is critical for helping struggling readers (Mathes et al., 2005). Increasing on-task reading behaviors can also be accomplished by increasing the pacing of instruction; by reviewing skills, strategies, and concepts at regular intervals; by reducing transition time between daily learning activities; and by redeploying key personnel such as special educators, Title I teachers, and ESL/ELL teachers to help increase small-group reading instructional opportunities within the classroom. Some schools also provide before-school, after-school, and summer reading programs to increase instructional time for struggling readers.

> **Getting to Know English Learners**
> Instructional time in ESL instruction, especially in reading, in many states has been doubled. For example, in New York State, beginning ELs in K–8, must not only have two periods of ESL but one period of ELA.

Struggling readers also need structure and routine. This means that their daily schedule should be predictable, with few unannounced or unexpected changes. Assigned reading practice tasks should be clearly and explicitly taught previous to application in independent practice. Struggling readers need support through instructional scaffolds such as graphic organizers (see Chapter 7) and guided practice. They often benefit from peer tutoring.

Struggling readers are often, as we discussed in Chapter 2, well behind in their oral language vocabularies. As a consequence, they need exposure to more opportunities to listen to and use language—not fewer. Reading both fiction and nonfiction aloud to children is critical in building their knowledge and background experiences (Duke & Bennett-Armistead, 2003). Unfortunately, many younger readers are not given enough access to information books even though they prefer to read them rather than story books (Mohr, 2003; 2006). One of the most powerful commercial series we have seen to date is from the National Geographic Society. Their school publishing division (*www.ngschoolpub.org*) has a wide selection of themed books on different reading levels that, when used as read-aloud books, can help early/emergent readers learn new vocabulary and concepts.

Early intervention to catch reading problems before they become insurmountable has been shown in many studies to have the greatest impact on student outcomes (Ramey & Ramey, 2006). Instruction offered struggling readers needs to be targeted to their needs; it needs to be clear and explicit, provide "scaffolding" (i.e., structured learning experiences) over time, and occur every day in the relentless pursuit of success (Duffy, 2004).

Struggling readers require more clearly articulated reading feedback from teachers and peers. They need to know exactly what they are doing well and precisely where they need to focus their attention to do better. Generic feedback such as, "Gee, that was really good!" will not be of much help to struggling readers (National Reading Panel, 2000: Reutzel, 2006). Explicit feedback like, "Your phrasing was very good because you paused at the commas and stopped at the periods in each sentence" ultimately is more meaningful to these students. Constructive criticism should also be specific: "When a sentence ends in a period, you need to lower your pitch and stop at the period like this."

Finally, struggling readers are helped the most in schools where school-wide assessment occurs and where the approach to reading instruction is consistent across and within grades (Taylor, Pearson, Clark, & Walpole, 1999; Taylor, Pearson, Petersen, & Rodriquez, 2005). Successful schools that help at-risk, struggling readers succeed have school-wide, well-articulated assessment and instructional approaches that all teachers use and honor. Remember: For struggling readers, remediation is not the main goal. Rather, *acceleration of learning* is the paramount goal. Struggling readers need to make larger gains each year to catch up to their peers in reading. Failure to do so can cause them to remain behind in school and in attaining life's opportunities (Fielding, Kerr, & Rosier, 1998; Juel, 1988). But most of all, good reading instruction has the potential to help all children (August & Shanahan, 2006).

What Families and Communities Can Do to Develop Children's Early Reading

Parents look for ideas to extend learning experiences at home. Find tips for parents as you read "Ways to Stimulate Reading in Young Children." Visit the Teacher Prep Website (*www.prenhall.com/teacherprep*) to locate this article in the *Language Arts Methods.*

Parent involvement with young children as they learn to read is a critical component of any good school or classroom reading instructional program (DeBruin-Parecki & Krol-Sinclair, 2003; Enz, 2003). One successful approach for teaching parents how to implement effective early literacy activities in the home is called **Project EASE** (**E**arly **A**ccess to **S**uccess in **E**ducation). Research has shown that children whose parents were trained in Project EASE to implement structured activities to improve their children's early literacy knowledge at home demonstrated statistically significant gains over those of control group students on measures of both language and literacy growth (Jordan, Snow, & Porche, 2000). The data also indicate that the more parents participated in using the literacy activities in Project EASE, the better their children performed. One finding of significance is that the children who began the project with the lowest scores on language and literacy made the greatest gains.

Project EASE states four goals on their Web site (*www.gseweb.harvard.edu/~pild/description.htm*):

1. All students should have a strong beginning to their educational career.
2. Each student should have a plan to meet his or her individual needs.
3. Parents are integral to the success of their children in reading.
4. Early efforts will yield long-range success in school.

Effective schools and classrooms do not operate in isolation. Young children's early reading success requires the combined efforts of both home and school (DeBruin-Parecki & Krol-Sinclair, 2003). Literacy development plays a critical role in assuring academic success (Fielding, Kerr, & Rosier, 1998; Snow, Burns, & Griffin, 1998).

The parent component of Project EASE includes scripted and structured activities that address the critical early reading components of vocabulary development, decoding, narrative and information text reading, and others. These structured lessons require parents to be highly engaged in helping their child develop reading ability. The creators of Project EASE indicate that the parent activities are designed to foster "de-contextualized" language skills such as decoding that not only support early reading behaviors but also reading fluency in later years.

Parents are asked to commit to five monthly parent education sessions with follow-up weekly parent-child activities or lessons that are available on the Project EASE Web site. Parents can attend these educational sessions at different times depending on how their child's school sets them up. For example, morning, afternoon, or evening sessions may be set up to correspond with kindergarten schedules and allow at least one session for working parents. Typically, the parent education sessions for Project EASE begin in October and continue until April of the kindergarten year. Title I aides and other school staff have been used to facilitate the parent education component and assist in the classroom on the designated Project EASE parent education days. Each session includes (1) parent education, (2) modeled activities for parent and child, and (3) structured weekly activities completed at home. Parents are invited to participate in kindergarten classroom activities after attending the parent educational sessions.

Parent-child activities focus on five monthly topics that have been shown to significantly impact early reading development. Topics include (1) storybook reading, (2) working with words, (3) letter recognition and sound awareness, (4) retelling family narratives, and (5) talking about the world (using information books). Each of the five parent activity units contains background information for parents, parent education session information, at-school activities, at-home activities, book titles, and flash cards. These five parent involvement activities, available at the Project EASE Web site, have been shown to successfully build beginning print skills by establishing strong letter recognition and sound awareness. Other activities such as storybook and information book readings, retellings, and so on have been shown to positively influence children's reading comprehension.

Project EASE is just one of many possible parent involvement programs for early reading success. There are several others, including Project FLAME (Shanahan, Mulhern, & Rodriguez-Brown, 1995), the Intergenerational Literacy Project (ILP) (Paratore, 2003); The Parent Project (Vopat, 1994), and Keeping Up with Children (Brookes et al., 2002). No early reading instructional program can be considered comprehensive and complete without serious attention given to the use of a parent and community involvement program.

Summary: Teaching Early Reading Essentials—Getting Children Off to a Great Start!

In this chapter we learned how young children take their first steps in becoming readers. Part of our journey in this chapter was to learn about the developmental stages young readers typically go through as beginning readers. Phonological and phonemic awareness, print concepts, and letter recognition are but a few of the early skills learned as children move through literacy development stages. We also saw how the twin skills of *segmenting* and *blending* spoken words become the bedrock supporting future phonics, decoding, and spelling instruction.

Next, we presented several important assessment tools that help teachers monitor student progress in early reading development. For example, we learned how to use the Metalinguisitic Interview and the *Concepts About Print test* for assessing and supervising children's emerging understanding about how print works. Finally, we discussed how to monitor children's acquisition of letter recognition and letter-naming ability."

We followed the discussion of assessing early reading essential skills with a detailed description of how to teach children phonological and phonemic awareness, concepts about print, and letter recognition. We stressed the importance of young children receiving explicit, systematic instruction for each of these early reading essential skills through teachers' informed and systematic application of a variety of effective, evidence-based instructional strategies.

We described specific adaptations of instructional interventions and necessary accommodations for young children's diverse reading and writing learning needs including: increased time allocations, small group differentiated reading instruction, classroom structure and routine, feedback, early intervention, knowledge and concept development, and school wide assessment. Finally we presented information dealing with one evidence-based program, Project EASE, among several for supporting young readers' early development in the home and broader community.

To conclude this chapter, we reiterate the fact that the overwhelming evidence today indicates that although some children can emerge into reading and writing without systematic early reading skill instruction, this emergence rarely occurs naturally. Instead, success in early reading requires knowledgeable teachers who know *what* to teach and *how* to teach the early reading skills of phonological and phonemic awareness, concepts about print, and letter recognition in order for young children to successfully and efficiently learn to read and write.

Classroom Applications

1. Work with a partner. Teach one another a 3–5-minute phonemic awareness lesson focused on phoneme blending, segmenting, or manipulation.
2. Administer the *Concepts About Print Test* (Clay, 2000b) to another student in the class. Discuss insights you have gained from using this test. How would you apply these insights in selecting appropriate strategies for teaching print concepts?
3. Working in groups of four to six students, make a visual or graphic organizer showing the way in which early word reading ability develops according to the research of Lomax and McGee (1987). Present your group's work to the class. What does research tell you about early reading instruction?
4. In your class, arrange three brainstorming groups and one synthesis group. Brainstorming group 1 should develop an instructional strategy for using names to develop children's letter-recognition skills. Brainstorming group 2 should devise a strategy for teaching letter recognition by focusing on searching for letters in names. Brainstorming group 3 should generate a strategy for

teaching letter recognition through writing of names. The synthesis group should develop a handout for the class that summarizes the other groups' ideas.

Recommended Readings

Adams, M. J. (1990). *Beginning to read: Thinking and learning about print—a summary*. Urbana, IL: Center for the Study of Reading.

Armbruster, B. B., Lehr, F., & Osborn, J. (2001). *Put reading first: The research building blocks for teaching children to read*. Washington, DC: National Institute for Literacy. Available free online at *www.nifl.gov*.

Barone, D. M. (2006). *Narrowing the literacy gap: What works in high-poverty schools*. New York: Guilford Press.

Burns, M. S., Griffin, P., & Snow, C. E. (Eds.). (1999). *Starting out right: A guide to promoting children's reading success*. Committee on the Prevention of Reading Difficulties in Young Children, Commission on Behavioral and Social Sciences and Education, National Research Council. Washington, DC: National Academy Press.

Cole, A. D. (2004). *When reading begins: The teacher's role in decoding, comprehension, and fluency*. Portsmouth, NH: Heinemann Educational Books.

DeBruin-Parecki, A., & Krol-Sinclair, B. (2003). *Family literacy: From theory to practice*. Newark, DE: International Reading Association.

Dickinson, D. K., & Tabors, P. O. (2001). *Beginning literacy with language*. Baltimore, MD: Paul H. Brookes.

Dragan, P. B. (2001). *Literacy from day one*. Portsmouth, NH: Heinemann Educational Books.

Learning to read and write: Developmentally appropriate practices for young children. Newark, DE: International Reading Association/Washington, DC: National Association for the Education of Young Children.

Prior, J., & Gerard, M. R. (2004). *Environmental print in the classroom: Meaningful connections for learning to read*. Newark, DE: International Reading Association.

Vaughn, S., & Linan-Thompson, S. (2004). *Research-based methods of reading instruction, grades K–3*. Alexandria, VA: Association for Supervision and Curriculum Development.

Venn, E. C., & Jahn, M. D. (2004). *Teaching and learning in preschool: Using individually appropriate practices in early childhood literacy instruction*. Newark, DE: International Reading Association.

chapter **4**

Phonics and Word Identification

Chapter Questions

1. How do children learn to decode words?

2. How do effective teachers assess students' letter and word identification abilities?

3. What does research show are the best ways of teaching phonics?

4. Who has difficulty learning phonics and what can be done to assist them?

5. What strategies can parents use to help their child learn phonics skills?

Mr. Bill and Emily

Mr. Bill, as his students like to call him, is a second grade teacher beginning his third year of teaching at Doolittle Elementary in downtown Chicago. As is his practice, Mr. Bill conducts a number of short assessments in the first two weeks of school to get a better handle on where his students are in their reading development and to help in planning small-group instruction. While his students are engaged in independent work, Mr. Bill invites Emily, apparently one of his more precocious readers, to join him in the reading center. He had asked her to pick a favorite book or two and show him her "very best reading."

"Emily," asks Mr. Bill, "what book did you choose to share with me today?"

Emily proudly holds up a copy of *The Summer of the Swans* by Betsy Byars and says, "I'm ready to show you my very best reading, Mr. Bill."

"Go for it!" responds Mr. Bill. "Let's do it! Pick out a page and show me your very best reading." He then turns on the tape recorder.

Emily opens her book to page 46, where she had placed her bookmark, and begins reading. At one point, Emily reads tentatively: "'Already he had started shhh—aaakkk—ing, *shaking* his head again, all the while waaa—chh—ing the swans gliding across the dark water.'" Emily looks up for a reaction from her teacher.

Mr. Bill says, "I like how you stretched out those words you didn't know like a rubber band so you could *hear* the sounds and blend them. Well done! Let's continue."

Emily reads, "'Sss—kwint—ing, *squinting!*'" then quickly looks up with a mix of anticipation and dread in her eyes.

"Right again! You're quite a reader, Miss Emily!" says Mr. Bill. Emily beams at Mr. Bill's words of praise.

When Emily's recitation is finished, she looks up, obviously hoping for some sign of approval from the room's best reader. Mr. Bill says, "Emily, I've already noticed this year how much you enjoy poetry." When Emily nods, Mr. Bill says, "Me, too! I love poetry that rhymes and also tells a story. One of my favorite poems is by a man named Pek Gunn. He was from Tennessee and liked to tell stories from his childhood."

Mr. Bill continues. "Pek Gunn wrote a poem called 'June Bug on a String'* that talks about how children a hundred years ago used to catch June bugs. They're bugs kind of like bumblebees, except they don't sting. Kids would tie a thread around a June bug and then let it fly around while they held the string and watched."

"That sounds mean," responds Emily.

"I see your point. But they didn't hurt the bug—they just watched it fly slowly around."

"I guess that's okay," says Emily. "As long as they let the June bug go after they played awhile."

"They did. The point of the poem is that whoever holds the string in life is in control. So, the child in the poem holding the string was in control!"

"Mr. Bill, I see what you mean. But what are you trying to tell me?" Emily queries.

"Only this. When I see how well you are coming along with your reading, I see a girl who is getting control over reading like a grown-up! This year we are

David Mager/Pearson Learning Photo Studio

* The poem "Junebug on a String" was written by the late poet laureate of Tennessee, Richard "Pek" Gunn. His two self-published books of poetry, *Keep On Laughin'; It's Good for What Ails You: Nostalgic in Verse and Short Story,* and *Tumblin' Creek Tales and Other Poems* are out of print, but can be found for purchase from online bookstores.

going to learn new ways to make sure that, whenever you come to a new word in a book, you'll be able to pronounce that new word as fast as lightning. That way, *you* will be the one holding the string. You'll be in control of reading all the time!"

How Do Children Learn to "Decode" Words?

What do you think of when you hear the word *phonics?* Does it call to mind the old phrase "sounding out words"? If so, you're not alone. But the truth is, there is much more to learning to unlock the code of written language than you may think. An understanding of the development of phonics and other decoding skills is essential for effective assessment and teaching. In this chapter we take a close, evidence-based look at what children must know and be able to do to effectively "decode" words using phonics and related word identification skills, and the teacher's role in fostering the learning process.

What Is *Phonics?*

Phonics refers to how alphabet spellings relate to speech sounds in systematic and predictable ways (letter-sound relationships or **graphophonemic knowledge**), and how this knowledge can be used to identify words in print (National Research Council, 1999; Rasinski & Padak, 1996). Before we go further in this conversation about phonics, let's clarify the difference between two important skills: word identification and word recognition.

   Word identification has to do with the skills students learn that help them to figure out the pronunciation of a word in print. This is what the old phrase, *sound out* means. When a reader sees a new word in print (for example, *preamble*), he or she must be able to blend the speech sounds together that are represented by the letters *pre/am/ble* to pronounce the word correctly. The act of correctly pronouncing the word in print is what we mean by *word identification.* Word identification skills are sometimes referred to as *word attack skills* because the purpose is to break the code of written words and translate the letters, affixes, syllables, and so forth back to a spoken word.

   Word recognition, on the other hand, has to do with connecting a printed word's pronunciation with its meaning. It is possible for a student to use word identification skills to pronounce a word in print, yet not be able to connect the pronunciation of the word to its meaning, thereby failing at word recognition. For instance, a child may well be able to use word identification skills to pronounce the word *mordant,* yet have no idea what the word means. By the way, do *you* know the meaning of the word *mordant?* If not, then you now know the difference between word identification (the ability to pronounce a word in print—*mordant* is pronounced /more•dent/), and word recognition (the ability to understand the word's meaning). Thus, when we think of phonics, structural analysis, application of onset and rime, and so forth, we are talking about word identification.

Learning the Alphabetic Principle

Getting to Know English Learners
While the spelling of most words in American English remains the same, some ELs have learned English in countries that use British English spelling (like Canada and India), so words like "color" are spelled "colour," "recognize" is "recognise," and "judgment" is "judgement."

In Chapters 2 and 3, we saw how children begin learning oral language (which never stops, of course) then learn, either on their own or with help, that spoken words have individual speech sounds called *phonemes*. By developing an awareness of phonemes in words, they have learned to hear the parts of spoken words. We call this ability to pull apart spoken words and attend to the individual phonemes as **segmentation.** Next in children's literacy learning journey comes an awareness of the alphabetic principle.

The **alphabetic principle** is the concept that letters or letter combinations represent speech sounds in whole, spoken words. Understanding of the alphabetic principle is the first step toward learning to decode words using phonics. It is a critical conceptual connection between spoken language and written language that young children must acquire to profit from phonics instruction. Primary grade teachers create instructional strategies that help children learn the following:

- Speech is made up of individual speech sounds (phonemes) that are represented by specific letters (graphemes) and letter combinations (e.g., the speech sound /r/ is always written using the letter *r*).
- The 26 letters of the English alphabet represent certain sounds.
- The spelling of most words remains the same across the various books and texts students will encounter (i.e., the words *open* and *weather* are always spelled the same in print).

In summary, when phonemic awareness is combined with letter–name knowledge, students attain a new conceptual understanding—the alphabetic principle (Byrne & Fielding-Barnsley, 1989). This understanding is necessary for students to progress in their reading development, particularly in learning phonics. As students become aware of the alphabetic principle, teachers can expect to effectively provide them phonics instruction.

Phonics and Related Word Attack Skills

Surveys conducted by the International Reading Association (IRA) found that "phonics" is one of the most talked-about subjects in the field of reading education. Before we plunge into an "executive briefing" for teachers of phonics and related decoding and word recognition skills, we invite you to take a short pretest to find out what you already know—or what you need to know—about phonics. Complete the *Phonics Quick Test* (Figure 4.1) before reading further. The results may surprise you!

Important Phonics Patterns

Most states and local school districts have either developed or purchased a reading program with a *scope and sequence* of reading skills to help teachers know which reading skills should be taught at each grade level. The primary value of a scope and sequence of skills is that it helps teachers approach decoding instruction systematically. A secondary value is that it helps coordinate instruction across the state, which

Figure 4.1   The Phonics Quick Test

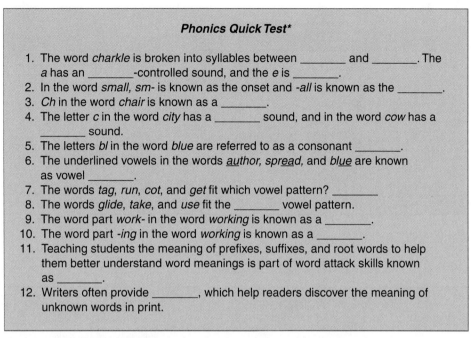

Phonics Quick Test*

1. The word *charkle* is broken into syllables between _____ and _____. The *a* has an _____-controlled sound, and the *e* is _____.
2. In the word *small, sm-* is known as the onset and *-all* is known as the _____.
3. *Ch* in the word *chair* is known as a _____.
4. The letter *c* in the word *city* has a _____ sound, and in the word *cow* has a _____ sound.
5. The letters *bl* in the word *blue* are referred to as a consonant _____.
6. The underlined vowels in the words *author, spread,* and *blue* are known as vowel _____.
7. The words *tag, run, cot,* and *get* fit which vowel pattern? _____
8. The words *glide, take,* and *use* fit the _____ vowel pattern.
9. The word part *work-* in the word *working* is known as a _____.
10. The word part *-ing* in the word *working* is known as a _____.
11. Teaching students the meaning of prefixes, suffixes, and root words to help them better understand word meanings is part of word attack skills known as _____.
12. Writers often provide _____, which help readers discover the meaning of unknown words in print.

*Answers to the *Phonics Quick Test* are found at the end of this chapter, on p. 140.

is especially useful in maintaining continuity in learning for highly mobile students. Texas, California, Mississippi, Kansas, and Oklahoma are just a few states that have developed their own scope and sequence of reading skills. Following are a few phonics skills that seem to be included in virtually all commercial or locally developed scope and sequence charts of reading skills.

Beginning Consonant Sounds in Words.   Arguably the single most efficient phonics generalization to teach has to do with identifying beginning consonant sounds in words. This is the best starting point for phonics instruction because consonants more regularly represent consistent phonemes than do vowels. It is easy to see this consistency of grapheme-phoneme relationship of consonants with the sounds they represent in the Fry letter frequency study we discuss in Chapter 3. In other words, consonant sounds tend to be more constant or reliable compared to vowel sounds. However, not all consonants are created equal—some are much more stable than others! The most consistent or stable consonants and their sounds are listed in Table 4.1

Just to prove the point that not all consonants are created equal (i.e., some consonants are not as consistent as others), we share in Table 4.2 some of the not-very-consistent consonants that should not be taught until after students make some significant gains in phonics knowledge.

The C Rule.   The letter *c* is an irregular consonant because it represents more than one phoneme. Rather, it can be used to represent two other phonemes that are already represented by the letters *k* and *s*. In general, when the letter *c* is followed by the letters *a, o,* or *u,* it will represent the sound we associate with the letter *k,* also known as the *hard c* sound. Some examples are the words *cake, cosmic,* and *cute.*

Table 4.1   Most Consistent Consonants

Sound	Spelling and Percentage of Use in English	Example(s)
/b/	b (97%)	ball
/d/	d (98%)	doll
/h/	h (98%)	hall
/l/	l (91%)	lost
/m/	m (94%)	Molly
/n/	n (97%)	not
/p/	p (96%)	put
/r/	r (97%)	road
/t/	t (97%)	tell
/v/	v (99.5%)	vault

Table 4.2   Some Not-Very-Consistent Consonants

Sound	Spellings and Percentage of Use in English	Example(s)
/f/	f (78%), ff, ph, lf	fun, staff, phone, wolf
/g/	g (88%), gg, gh	good, egg, ghost
/j/	g (66%), j (22%), dg	giraffe, jelly, judge
/k/	c (73%), cc, k (13%), ck, lk, q	can, stucco, rock, Chuck, chalk, bisque
/s/	s (73%), c (17%), ss	some, cent, stress
/y/	i (55%), y (44%)	onion, yell
/z/	z (23%), zz, s (64%)	zip, jazz, easy

On the other hand, the letter *c* can sometimes represent the sound associated with the letter *s*. This is referred to as the *soft c* sound. The *soft c* sound is usually produced when *c* is followed by *e, i,* or *y.* Examples of the *soft c* sound are found in the words *celebrate, circus,* and *cycle.*

The G Rule.   *G* is the key symbol for the phoneme we hear in the word *get* (Hull, 1989, p. 35). The consonant *g* is also irregular, having both a soft and a hard sound. The rules are the same as for the letter *c:* When *g* is followed by the letters *e, i,* or *y,* it represents a soft *g* or /j/ sound, as with the words *gently, giraffe,* and *gym.* If *g* is followed by the letters *a, o,* or *u,* then it usually represents the hard or regular sound, as with the words *garden, go,* and *sugar.*

The CVC Pattern.   When a vowel comes between two consonants, it usually represents what is referred to as a *short* vowel sound. Examples of words following the CVC pattern include *sat, ran, let, pen, win, fit, hot, mop, sun,* and *cut.*

Vowel Digraphs (CVVC). When two vowels come together in a word, the first vowel usually carries what is referred to as a *long* sound and the second vowel is silent. This occurs especially often with the *oa, ee,* and *ay* combinations. Some examples are *toad, fleet,* and *day*. A common slogan used by teachers to help children remember this generalization is "When two vowels go walking, the first one does the talking."

The VCE (Final Silent E) Pattern. When two vowels appear in a word and one is an *e* at the end of the word, the first vowel is generally long and the final *e* is silent. Examples include *cape, rope,* and *kite*.

The CV Pattern. When a consonant is followed by a vowel, the vowel usually produces a long sound. This is especially easy to see in two-letter words such as *be, go,* and *so*.

R–Controlled Vowels. Vowels that appear before the letter *r* are usually neither long nor short but tend to be overpowered or "swallowed up" by the /r/ sound. Examples include *person, player, neighborhood,* and *herself.*

Other Important Phonics Terms and Skills to Be Taught

Even though the phonics generalizations above are some of the most useful, most commercially published reading programs focus attention on many others. Following are several more terms, definitions, and examples of other phonics skills related to consonants and vowels not already discussed in this chapter.

Consonant Digraphs. Two consonants that produce only one speech sound *(th, sh, ng)* are called **consonant digraphs.** Examples of words containing consonant digraphs follow.

> *ch—children, change, merchant, search, which, branch*
>
> *th—thank, author, both, that, mother, smooth*
>
> *ng—sling, gang, long, fang, hung, wrong*

Review a consonant digraphs lesson by visiting our Teacher Prep Website (*www.prenhall.com/teacherprep*). Select "Discovering Consonant Diagraphs" in *Strategies and Lessons-Reading Methods/Module 2* to increase your teaching knowledge.

Consonant Blends or Clusters. Two or more consonants coming together in which the speech sounds of all the consonants may be heard *(bl, fr, sk, spl)* are referred to as **consonant blends** *or clusters.* Examples of words containing consonant blends follow:

> *bl—black, block, blast, blur, oblige, nimbly*
>
> *fr—frost, fruit, afraid, befriend, leapfrog, refresh*
>
> *sk—sky, skunk, outskirts, desk, task*
>
> *spl—splash, splat, split, splotch*

Vowel Digraphs. Two vowels together in a word that produce only one speech sound *(ee, oo, ie, ai)* are called **vowel digraphs.** The usual rule is "When two vowels go walking, the first one does the talking," but this is not always so. Examples of words containing vowel digraphs follow:

> *ee—eel, sleep, week, three, spree*
>
> *ea—head, each, threat, heaven*
>
> *oa—houseboat, oak, coat, loaf, toad*

Schwa. Some vowel letters produce the /*uh*/ sound (*a* in *America*). The schwa is represented by the backward upside-down *e* symbol: ə. Examples of words containing the schwa sound follow:

a—about, ago, several, canvass, china, comma

e—effect, erroneous, happen, children, label, agent

o—other, mother, atom, riot, second, objection

Diphthongs. Two vowels together in a word that produce a single, glided sound (*oi* in *oil*, *oy* in *boy*) are known as **diphthongs.** Here are some examples:

ow—down, flower, crowd, towel, how, bow, avow

oi—oil, voice, exploit, soil, void, typhoid

ou—out, hour, doubt, our, around, count

Onset and Rime

Children hear, read and create new words through rhyming activities. Learn more about how to relate language development through rhyme as you locate "Rhyming Time" in *Strategies and Lessons-Reading Methods/Module 8, 10, or 11.* This article may be found on the Teacher Prep Website (*www.prenhall.com/ teacherprep*).

Because many phonics generalizations are not as consistent in English as we would like, teachers buttress their instruction with other word attack strategies. Adams (1990b) states that linguistic researchers have found an instructionally useful alternative form of word identification involving onsets and rimes. An **onset** is that part of the syllable that comes before the vowel; the **rime** is the rest (Adams, 1990b, p. 55). Although all syllables must have a rime, not all have an onset. The following are a few examples of onsets and rimes in words.

Word	Onset	Rime
a	—	*a*
in	—	*in*
aft	—	*aft*
sat	*s-*	*-at*
trim	*tr-*	*-im*
spring	*spr-*	*-ing*

One may wonder about usefulness of onset and rime in the classroom, at least as far as word identification instruction is concerned. First, some evidence indicates that children are better able to identify the spelling of whole rimes than of individual vowel sounds (Adams, 1990b; Barton, Miller, & Macken, 1980; Blevins, 1997; Mustafa, 1997; Treiman, 1985). Second, children as young as 5 and 6 years of age can transfer what they know about the pronunciation of one word to another that has the same rime, such as *call* and *ball* (Adams, 1990b). Third, although many traditional phonics generalizations with vowels are very unstable, even irregular phonics patterns seem to remain stable within rimes! For example, the *ea* vowel digraph is quite consistent within rimes, with the exceptions of *-ear* in *hear* compared to *bear,* and *-ead* in *bead* compared to *head* (Adams, 1990b). Finally, there appears to be some utility in the learning of rimes for children. Nearly 500 primary-level words can be derived through the following set of only 37 rimes (Adams, 1990b; Blachman, 1984):

-ack	-at	-ide	-ock	-ain	-ate
-ight	-oke	-ake	-aw	-ill	-op
-ale	-ay	-in	-or	-all	-eat
-ine	-ore	-ame	-ell	-ing	-uck
-an	-est	-ink	-ug	-ank	-ice
-ip	-ump	-ap	-ick	-ir	-unk
-ash					

The application of onset and rime to reading and word identification instruction seems almost obvious. Many students will find it easier to identify new words in print by locating familiar rimes. Spelling efficiency may also increase as rimes are matched with onsets to construct "invented" spellings. (We prefer to call them "temporary" spellings so that children and parents understand that we intend to develop correct spellings.)

One teacher remarked that the easiest way to teach rimes is through *rhymes!* She was exactly right. Children learn many otherwise laborious tasks through rhymes, songs, chants, and raps. Any of these that use rhyming words can be very useful to teachers. For example, a teacher may wish to use an excerpt like the one shown below from the book *Taxi Dog* by Debra and Sal Barracca to emphasize the *-ide* and *-ill* rimes. The rimes are noted in bold type for easy identification by the reader.

> It's just like a dream,
> Me and Jim—we're a team!
> I'm always there at his s**ide.**
> We never stand st**ill,**
> Every day's a new thr**ill**—
> Come join us next time for a r**ide!** (1990, p. 30)

From *The Adventures of Taxi Dog* by Debra and Sal Barracca, pictures by Mark Buehner, copyright © 1990 by Debra and Sal Barracca, Text. Used by permission of Dial Books for young Readers, A Division of Penguin Young Readers Group, A Member of Penguin Group (USA) Inc., 345 Hudson Street, New York, NY 10014. All rights reserved.

Structural Analysis: An Important Decoding Tool

Another strategy readers use to decode unfamiliar words in print is called **structural analysis.** Rather than attacking words on the letter-phoneme level or on the onset and rime level, this kind of word identification uses a reader's knowledge of meaning "chunks" in words. Here's how it works. A reader encounters a word, usually a multi-syllabic word, that is unknown to him in print (that is, the word is known to him when he hears it; just not familiar in print)—let's say the word is *unbelievable*. Let's say our reader in this example has heard the word part or root word *believe* dozens of times in conversations and has seen it in print (e.g., in sentences like "Yes, I believe you" or "I believe that all children should have a nice birthday party") and immediately recognizes it. The prefix *un-* is likewise very familiar to the reader from other words he has learned to read, such as *untie, unreal,* and *unhook.* He is able to infer from his prior knowledge of words that *un-* means something like "not" or "to reverse." Finally, the reader's mind focuses briefly on the suffix (and word) *-able* and its meaning, also deduced from his prior knowledge of words like *workable.* In our example, then, the reader has found a new way of decoding words at something larger than the sound–symbol level. He progressed from the root word *(believe),* to the prefix *(un-),* to the suffix *(-able).* Furthermore, it was the meaning of these word parts that led to successful decoding. Structural analysis of words takes decoding to a new and higher

"Jeopardy Game" is a model for practicing the use of word patterns, spelling, and decoding skills as you customize your own categories and questions. Reference our Teacher Prep Website (*www.prehall.com/ teacherprep*) to locate this example in *Strategies and Lessons-Reading Methods/Module 2.*

level. This is a particularly important strategy for children in second and third grade, during which multisyllabic words become more common and must be decoded in chunks!

How Structural Analysis Works.   Words are made up of basic meaning units known as **morphemes**. Morphemes may be divided into two classes—bound and free. Bound morphemes must be attached to a root word (sometimes called a base word) to have meaning. Prefixes and suffixes are bound morphemes (e.g., *pre-, un-, dis-, en-, inter-, extra-, -ed, -ies, -er, -ing*). Free morphemes (base words or root words) are meaning units that can stand alone and have meaning. The word *replay* has both a bound and free morpheme: *re-*, the bound morpheme (prefix) meaning "again," and *play,* the free morpheme that has meaning on its own. Sometimes two free morphemes combine to form a new compound word, such as *doghouse, outdoors, playground,* and *tonight.*

> **Getting to Know English Learners**
>
> ELs may apply their knowledge of cognates when they come across unfamiliar vocabulary words. Romance languages like Spanish, Italian, French, and Germanic-based English have a large number of cognates. (Latin heavily influenced English and the romance languages' linguistic roots are distinctly Latin). Examples of Spanish/English cognates are: curioso/curious, decidir/to decide, naturalmente/naturally, and novelas/novels.

Teachers can help children begin to practice structural analysis of words in the same ways as they do onset and rime. The idea to get across to students is that whenever a good reader comes to a word she cannot identify through context and phonics alone, she sometimes looks within the word for a recognizable base (root) word and its accompanying prefix, suffix, or endings (Durkin, 1989; Lass & Davis, 1985). In other words, we tell our students to "look for something you know within the word."

Figure 4.2 shows selected examples of affixes adapted from *The Reading Teacher's Book of Lists* (Fry, Kress, & Fountoukidis, 2000).

Figure 4.2   Examples of Affixes

Prefixes

Prefix	Meaning	Example	Prefix	Meaning	Example
intro-	inside	*introduce*	*ad-*	to, toward	*adhere*
pro-	forward	*project*	*para-*	beside, by	*paraphrase*
post-	after	*postdate*	*pre-*	before	*predate*
sub-	under	*submarine*	*per-*	throughout	*pervade*
ultra-	beyond	*ultramodern*	*ab-*	from	*abnormal*
dis-	opposite	*disagree*	*trans-*	across	*transatlantic*

Suffixes

Suffix	Meaning	Example	Suffix	Meaning	Example
-ant	one who	*servant*	*-ee*	object of action	*payee*
-ist	one who practices	*pianist*	*-ary*	place for	*library*
-ence	state/ quality of	*violence*	*-ity*	state/ quality of	*necessity*
-ism	state/ quality of	*baptism*	*-ette*	small	*dinette*
-s, -es	plural	*cars*	*-ard*	one who	*coward*
-kin	small	*napkin*	*-ing*	material	*roofing*

Putting It All Together: A Sequence for Phonics and Word Identification Skill Instruction

Evidence-based reading research allows us to suggest a general sequence of early literacy skills that directly relate to word identification. This sequence is shown in Figure 4.3. Children who become proficient in these word identification skills by the end of grade 3 and who practice them regularly in reading for pleasure will attain a high degree of fluency. Note that these benchmark skills are appropriate for children learning to read in English or Spanish. We also include benchmark skills for the closely related areas of spelling and writing.

Visit *Reading On-Line* through the Internet link on the text accompanying CD and read an article titled "Effects of Traditional Verses Extended Word-Study Spelling Instruction on Students' Orthographic Knowledge" by Mary Abbott. You will also benefit from linking to the related postings from archives at this site to increase your knowledge about how words work.

Figure 4.3   End-of-year benchmark skills: K–3

Kindergarten End-of-Year Benchmarks for English and Spanish

DECODING AND WORD RECOGNITION

✓ Recognizes and names all uppercase and lowercase letters

✓ Knows that the sequence of written letters and the sequence of spoken sounds in a word are the same

✓ (Spanish only) Applies letter sound knowledge of consonant-vowel patterns to produce syllables

SPELLING AND WRITING

✓ Writes independently most uppercase and lowercase letters

✓ Uses phonemic awareness and letter knowledge to spell independently (invented/temporary spelling)

ORAL READING

✓ Recognizes some words by sight, including a few common words

First Grade End-of-Year Benchmarks for English and Spanish

DECODING AND WORD RECOGNITION

✓ Decodes phonetically regular one-syllable words and nonsense words accurately

✓ (Spanish only) Decodes two-syllable words, using knowledge of sounds, letters, and syllables including consonants, vowels, blends, and stress

SPELLING AND WRITING

✓ Spells three- and four-letter short vowel words correctly (English only)

✓ Uses phonics to spell independently

✓ Uses basic punctuation and capitalization

✓ Uses graphic organizers to plan writing with guidance

✓ Produces a variety of types of compositions like stories, descriptions, journal entries, and so on.

(continued)

Figure 4.3 (Continued)

✓ (Spanish only) Recognizes words that use specific spelling patterns such as *r/rr, y/ll, s/c/z, q/c/k, g/j, j/x, b/v, ch, h, i/y, gue,* and *gui*

✓ (Spanish only) Spells words with two syllables using dieresis marks, accents, *r/rr, y/ll, s/c/z, q/c/k, g/j, j/x, b/v, ch, h,* and *i/y* accurately

✓ (Spanish only) Uses verb tenses appropriately and consistently

ORAL READING

✓ Reads aloud with fluency any text that is appropriate for the first half of grade one

✓ Comprehends any text that is appropriate for the first half of grade one

✓ Uses phonic knowledge to sound out unknown words when reading text

✓ Recognizes common, irregularly spelled words by sight

Second Grade End-of-Year Benchmarks for English and Spanish

DECODING AND WORD RECOGNITION

✓ Decodes phonetically regular two-syllable words and nonsense words

✓ (Spanish only) Decodes words with three or more syllables using knowledge of sounds, letters, and syllables including consonants, vowels, blends, and stress

✓ (Spanish only) Uses structural cues to recognize words such as compounds, base words, and inflections such as *-mente, -ito,* and *-ando*

SPELLING AND WRITING

✓ Spells previously studied words and spelling patterns correctly in own writing

✓ Represents the complete sound of a word when spelling independently

✓ Begins to use formal language patterns in place of oral language patterns in own writing

✓ Uses revision and editing processes to clarify and refine own writing with assistance

✓ Writes informative, well-structured reports with organizational help

✓ Attends to spelling, mechanics, and presentation for final products

✓ Produces a variety of types of compositions like stories, reports, correspondence, and so on.

✓ Uses information from nonfiction text in independent writing

✓ (Spanish only) Spells words with three or more syllables using silent letters, dieresis marks, accents, verbs, *r/rr, y/ll, s/c/z, q/c/k, g/j, j/x, b/v, ch, h,* and *i/y* accurately

ORAL READING

✓ Reads aloud with fluency any text that is appropriate for the first half of grade two

✓ Comprehends any text that is appropriate for the first half of grade two

Figure 4.3   (Continued)

✓ Uses phonic knowledge to sound out words, including multisyllable words, when reading text

✓ Reads irregularly spelled words, diphthongs, special vowel spellings, and common word endings accurately

Third Grade End-of-Year Benchmarks for English and Spanish

DECODING AND WORD RECOGNITION

✓ Uses phonic knowledge and structural analysis to decode words

SPELLING AND WRITING

✓ Spells previously studied words and spelling patterns correctly in own writing

✓ Uses the dictionary to check and correct spelling

✓ Uses a variety of formal sentence structures in own writing

✓ Incorporates literary words and language patterns in own writing (elaborate descriptions, figurative language)

✓ Uses all aspects of the writing process in compositions and reports with assistance

✓ Combines information from multiple sources in written reports

✓ Suggests and implements editing and revision to clarify and refine own writing with assistance

✓ Reviews written work for spelling, mechanics, and presentation independently

✓ Produces a variety of written work (response to literature, reports, semantic maps)

✓ Uses graphic organizational tools with a variety of texts

✓ (Spanish only) Writes proficiently using orthographic patterns and rules such as *qu*, use of *n* before *v, m* before *b, m* before *p*, and changing *z* to *c* when adding *-es*

✓ (Spanish only) Spells words with three or more syllables using silent letters, dieresis marks, accents, verbs, *r/rr, y/ll, s/c/z, q/c/k, g/j, j/x, b/v, ch, h*, and *i/y* accurately

ORAL READING

✓ Reads aloud with fluency any text that is appropriate for the first half of grade three

✓ Comprehends any text that is appropriate for the first half of grade three

How Do Effective Teachers Assess Letter and Word Identification?

We have seen in this chapter that word identification skills proceed from grasp of the alphabetic principle to early phonics skills, then to structural analysis and onset and rime. In this section we present essential assessment strategies used by effective teachers in determining student needs.

Letter Naming Test (LNT)

A critical first step for children moving from phonemic awareness to alphabetic principle and phonics is letter naming. *Rapid* letter-naming ability is the goal. Based on the work of Marie Clay (1993), this task determines whether readers can identify letters of the alphabet in uppercase and lowercase forms. Walsh, Price, and Gillingham (1988) found that letter naming was strongly related to early reading achievement in kindergarten children. Cooter, Flynt, and Cooter (2007) include in their new *Comprehensive Reading Inventory* several letter-naming subtests for this purpose. We present one of these subtests here for your use in the classroom.

Administration of the Letter-Naming Test. Ask the student to be seated next to you and explain that you would like to find out which letters of the alphabet she can name as you point to them on the chart found in the alphabet letter display in Figure 4.4. Begin by pointing to the top of the form and ask the student to identify each letter work line by line and left to right to the bottom of the display, keeping letters below your line of focus covered. Using a photocopy of the alphabet letter display, mark the letters the student correctly identifies. Also make note of those letters the students cannot identify and whether the case of the letter appears to be an issue. Ask the child to point to the letter you named in the display. Record this information. Most children, even readers with special learning needs, will be able to identify at least 50% of the letters requested (Reutzel & Cooter, 2007).

Determining the Student's Developmental Level. Cooter, Flynt, and Cooter (2007) explain that the developmental levels derived from their assessment tool are indications of students' skill in performing a particular task. **Proficient** means that the student has attained relative mastery of the skill being assessed and does not require further instruction. **Developing** means that the student has demonstrated a degree of skill in the task being assessed, but has not yet achieved mastery. **Emergent** essentially means that the student has little or no skill in the task assessed and requires instruction.

In relation to the Letter-Naming Test (LNT), we are interested in (1) whether the student can name all 26 letters of the alphabet, and (2) how quickly he or she can identify each letter (rapid letter naming). Perfect letter identification is the goal. While research-based criteria for speed of letter identification is unavailable at this time, we believe teachers should consider how long students take to identify each letter. A pause of more than, say, 5 seconds is viewed as problematic and indicates that more practice is in order for the student.

Developmental Level	Items Correct
Proficient	26
Developing	20–25
Emergent	0–19

Word Attack Survey

Sometimes teachers choose to conduct a quick, informal assessment of students' phonics and word attack skills. Reutzel and Cooter (2007) have developed an instrument to assess these skills titled the *Reutzel/Cooter Word Attack Survey* (WAS). This tool has been tested extensively in classroom trials since 1999. Like many

Figure 4.4 Alphabet Letter Display (Mixed Case Letters)

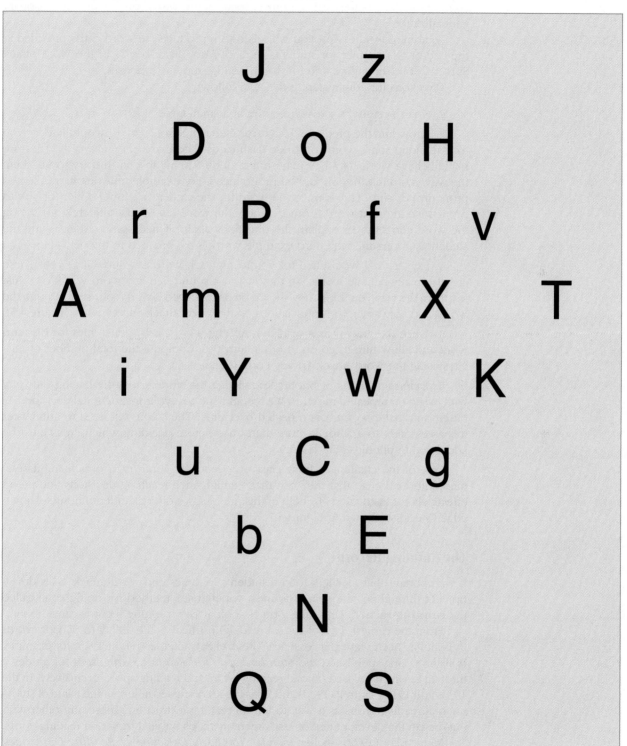

commercially available word attack tests, the WAS uses "nonsense" words that fit common spelling patterns. The primary focus of the WAS is on vowel and consonant generalizations.

To administer the WAS you will need to reproduce the word cards provided at the end of this chapter for students to read. Also, make copies of the Word Attack Survey Form (see Figure 4.5) for use in noting student responses.

Directions for administering the WAS follow:

1. Seat the student across from you at a small table.

2. Show him the premade flash cards (see Figure 4.6). Say: "I would like for you to read aloud some words on these flash cards. These are not real words. They are make-believe words, so they may sound kind of funny to you. Just try to say them the way you think they should be pronounced. For example, this first word *(sim)* is pronounced "sim." (Pronounce the word for the student.) "Now I'd like for you to pronounce the next word for me." (Show the word *cip.*) Praise the child for saying the word correctly (or explain the directions again, if necessary). After asking the student to pronounce the third example word *(sar),* proceed to the next step.

3. Say: "Now I would like for you to say each word as I show it to you. These are also make-believe words, so they will not sound like any word you know. Just say them the way you think they should be pronounced." Work your way through the words and note any mispronunciations on the Word Attack Survey Form (Figure 4.5).

4. Once the student has read through the word cards, praise him for his hard work and allow him to go on to other activities. Compute the total number of miscues using the Word Attack Survey Form (Figure 4.5).

5. Determine areas of phonic knowledge the student may be having difficulty with based on repeated miscues. We recommend that your instructional decisions be based on a pattern of errors repeated over time. Thus, you will need to administer this assessment to a student more than once before deciding which areas must be addressed in phonics mini-lessons.

One of the challenges busy classroom teachers confront is organizing assessment information so that they can make enlightened teaching decisions and group effectively for instruction. To help in this process, we offer a Student Phonics Knowledge Checklist, shown in Figure 4.7.

The Running Record

It is important that teachers follow students' phonics and word attack skills development throughout the year. The most widely used method for doing so is called the **running record.** Let's take a quick look at how running records came about.

From the earliest days of formal reading instruction, the ability to decode words in print has been viewed as essential (Reutzel & Cooter, 2005). In 1915, for example, William S. Gray published the *Standardized Oral Reading Paragraphs* for grades 1 through 8, which focused on oral reading errors and reading speed exclusively. In the 1930s and 1940s, Durrell (1940) and Betts (1946) discussed at length the value of studying oral reading errors as a way to inform reading instruction. These and other writings began the development of assessment methods for analyzing oral reading errors.

Marie Clay (1972), in her manual *The Early Detection of Reading Difficulties,* sought to formalize methodology for teachers conducting decoding assessments. Clay's running records for analyzing oral reading errors proved to be functional for

Figure 4.5   The Reutzel/Cooter Word Attack Survey Form

Student Name _____ Date _____

Part 1: Vowel Generalizations

Sample Item	sim	cip	sar

A. CVC/Beginning Consonant Sounds

1. tat _____
2. nan _____
3. rin _____
4. mup _____
5. det _____
6. sim _____
7. loj _____
8. cal _____
9. pif _____
10. fek _____

B. Vowel Digraphs

11. geem _____
12. hoad
13. kait _____
14. weam _____

C. VCE Pattern

15. jape _____
16. zote _____

17. gipe _____
18. tope _____

D. CV Pattern

19. bo _____
20. ka _____
21. fi _____
22. tu _____

E. R-Controlled Vowels

23. sar _____
24. wir _____
25. der _____
26. nur _____

F. Schwa Sound

27. ahurla _____
28. thup _____
29. cremon _____
30. laken _____

Part 2: Consonant Generalizations

G. Hard and Soft *C*

31. cale _____
32. cose _____
33. cimmy _____
34. cyler _____

H. Hard and Soft *G*

35. gare _____
36. gob _____
37. gime _____
38. genry _____

I. Consonant Digraphs

39. ohur _____
40. thim _____
41. shar _____
42. whilly _____
43. thar _____

J. Double Consonants

44. nally _____
45. jpple _____
46. attawap _____
47. urrit _____

K. Ph (f sound)

48. phur _____
49. phattle _____
50. phenoblab _____

L. Single Consonants*
M. Syllabication Rule**

51. lappo _____
52. pabute _____
53. larpin _____
54. witnit _____

*See section A
**Besides Items 51–54, there are many other syllabication examples throughout the *R/CWAS*.

Comments:

Reutzel, D. Ray; Cooter, Robert B. *Strategies for Reading Assessment and Instruction: Helping Every Child Succeed*, 3rd Edition, © 2007. Reprinted by permission of Pearson Education, Inc.

Figure 4.6   Word Cards for the Reutzel/Cooter Word Attack Survey

tat
nan
rin
mup

det
sim
loj
cal
pif

fek
geem
hoad
kait

weam
jape
zote
gipe
tope

bo
ka
fi
tu

sar
wir
der
nur
ahurla

Figure 4.6 (Continued)

Figure 4.7 Student Phonics Knowledge Checklist

Student Phonics Knowledge Checklist

Student Name _____

Skill(s)	Date Observed
Level 1: Phonemic Awareness	
1. Rhyming	_____
2. Alliteration	_____
3. Oddity tasks	_____
4. Oral blending syllables, onset/rime, phoneme by phoneme	_____
5. Oral segmentation syllables, onset/rime, phoneme by phoneme	_____
6. Phonemic manipulation substitution *(i, f, v)*; deletion *(s, i, f)*	_____
Level 2: Alphabetic Principle	
7. Making the connection between sounds and symbols	_____
Level 3: Explicit Phonics Instruction	
8. Specific letter sounds/Specific letter names	_____
a. Onset/consonants and rimes	_____
b. Continuous consonants	_____
c. Short vowel sounds	_____
d. Continue teaching both vowels and consonants	_____
e. Consonant digraphs *wh, ch, th, sh,* etc.	_____
f. Vowel dipthongs *ol, oy, ou*	_____
g. Vowel digraphs *ee, ea, ai, ay,* etc.	_____
9. Word play with onset and rime blending	_____
10. L → R blending of letter-sounds in words	_____
11. Segmentation of sounds in words and writing segmented sounds	_____

Source: From Phonemic Awareness for Early Reading Success, by W. Blevins, 1997. Reprinted by permission of Scholastic, Inc.

many classroom teachers. A New Zealand educator and former president of the International Reading Association, Clay described the running record as an informal assessment procedure with high reliability (.90 on error reliabilities) that informs teachers regarding students' decoding development.

The procedure for maintaining a running record is not difficult, but does require practice.

In essence, the teacher notes everything the student says while reading a selected passage, including all words read correctly as well as all miscues (Wiener & Cohen, 1997). Clay recommends that three running records be obtained for each child on various levels of difficulty for initial reading assessment. Her criteria for oral reading evaluation are based on words correctly read aloud:

> ***Independent Level*** (easy to read)   95–100% correct
> ***Instructional Level*** (ideal for teaching)   90–94% correct
> ***Frustration Level*** (too difficult)   80–89% correct

Running records using Clay's method are taken using books on different reading levels; student errors (miscues) can be recorded on a sheet of paper. In recent research

(Fawson, Ludlow, Reutzel, Sudweeks, & Smith, in press), it was found that reliable scores are obtained when teachers take three running records within the same reading level of text and average the three scores.

Guidelines for generating running records follow:

1. Gather passages from a number of reading materials representing a variety of reading levels. Each reading level should be represented by three passages; passages should be 100 to 200 words in length (for early readers, texts may fall below 100 words).

2. Have the student read the passage one or two times orally before you begin the running record.

3. Sit alongside the student while she reads so that both of you can see the page of text. Record a check mark on a sheet of blank paper for each word the student says correctly. Miscues (errors) should be recorded using the notations indicated in Figure 4.8. Figure 4.9 shows an example of a running record based on a passage from the *Flynt-Cooter Reading Inventory for the Classroom* (Flynt & Cooter, 2004).

Understanding Miscues: MSV Analysis.   Clay (1985) developed a way of interpreting miscues for use in her widely acclaimed Reading Recovery program, commonly referred to as **MSV analysis.** This interpretive strategy enables you to determine whether the student uses three primary **cueing strategies** when she encounters a new word and a miscue occurs: meaning cues (M), syntax cues (S), and visual cues (V). Here is a summary of Clay's work compiled by Flynt and Cooter (2004).

> **Getting to Know English Learners**
> Word order and syntax may vary by language and may, therefore, cause confusion among ELs. A modern example of a language with a different word order is German; Latin is an antiquated example.

M = Semantic (Meaning—Does it make sense?).   In reviewing each miscue, consider whether the student is using meaning cues in her attempt to identify the word. Context clues, picture cues, and information from the text are examples of meaning cues used by the reader.

S = Structure (or Syntax—Does it sound right?).   A rule system, or *grammar*, governs all languages. The English language is essentially based on a "subject-verb" grammar system. *Syntax* is the application of this subject-verb grammar system in creating sentences. The goal of studying syntax cues as part of your miscue analysis is to determine the extent to which the student unconsciously uses rules of grammar in attempting to identify unknown words in print. For example, if a word in a passage causing a miscue for the reader is a verb, ask yourself whether the student's miscue was also a verb. Consistent use of the appropriate part of speech in miscues (i.e., a noun for a noun, a verb for a verb, articles for articles, etc.) is an indication that the student has internalized the rule system of English grammar and is applying that knowledge in attacking unknown words.

V = Visual (Graphophonic—Does it look right?).   Sometimes a miscue looks a good bit like the correct word appearing in the text. The miscue may begin with the same letter or letters, for example, *top* for *toy*, or *sit* for *seat*. Another possibility is that the letters of the miscue may look very similar to the word appearing in text (e.g., *introduction* for *introspection*). Use of visual cues is essentially the student's ability (or inability) to apply phonics skills. The extent to which students use visual cues is an important factor to consider when trying to better understand the decoding skills employed by developing readers.

Figure 4.8　Notating Miscues in a Running Record

Reading Behavior	Notation	Explanation
Accurate Reading	✓ ✓ ✓ ✓ ✓	*Notation:* A check is noted for each word pronounced correctly.
Self-Correction	✓ ✓ ✓ ✓ attempt │ SC —————————— word in text │	The child corrects an error himself. This is not counted as a miscue. *Notation:* "SC" is the notation used for self-corrections.
Omission	———— —————————— Word in text	A word or words are left out during the reading. *Notation:* A dash mark is written over a line above the word(s) from the text that has been omitted.
Insertion	Word inserted —————————— ————	The child adds a word that is not in the text. *Notation:* The word inserted by the reader is placed above a line and a dash placed below it.
Student Appeal and Assistance	———— │ A —————————— Word from text │	The child is "stuck" on a word he cannot call and asks (verbal or nonverbal) the teacher for help. *Notation:* "A" is written above a line for "assisted" and the problem word from the text is written below the line.
Repetition	✓ ✓ ✓ R ✓ ✓ ✓	Sometimes children will repeat words or phrases. These repetitions are not scored as an error, but *are* recorded. *Notation:* Write an "R" after the word repeated and draw a line back to the point where the reader returned.
Substitution	Substituted word —————————— Word from text	The child says a word that is different from the word in the text. *Notation:* The student's substitution word is written above a line under which the correct word from text is written.
Teacher Assistance	———— │ —————————— Word from text │ T	The student pauses on a word for five seconds or more, so the teacher tells him/her the word. *Notation:* The letter "T" is written to the right of a line that follows the word from text. A blank is placed above a cross-line to indicate that the student didn't know the word.

Figure 4.9   Running Record Example

Student	Paco (Grade 2)

Title: The Pig and the Snake

One day Mr. Pig was walking to	✓ ✓ ✓ ✓ ✓ ✓ ✓
town. He saw a big hole in the	✓ ✓ $\frac{sam\mid sc}{saw\mid}$ ✓ ✓ ✓ ✓ ✓
road. A big snake was in the	✓ ✓ $\frac{=}{big}$ ✓ ✓ ✓ ✓ ✓
hole. "Help me," said the snake,	✓ ✓ ✓ $\frac{ouT}{-}$ ✓ ✓ ✓
"and I will be your friend." "No, no,"	✓ ✓ ✓ ✓✓ $\frac{-\mid A}{friend\mid}$ ✓ ✓
said Mr. Pig. "If I help you get	✓ ✓ ✓ ✓ ✓ ✓ ✓ ✓
out you will bite me. You're	✓ ✓ ✓ R ✓ ✓
a snake!" The snake cried and	✓ ✓ ✓ ✓ ✓ ✓
cried. So Mr. Pig pulled the	✓ ✓ ✓ ✓ $\frac{popped}{pulled}$
snake out of the hole.	✓ ✓ ✓ ✓ ✓
Then the snake said, "Now I am	✓ ✓ ✓ ✓ ✓ ✓ ✓
going to bite you, Mr. Pig."	✓ ✓ ✓ ✓ ✓ ✓
"How can you bite me after	✓ ✓ ✓ ✓ ✓ $\frac{-\mid}{after\mid T}$
I helped you out of the hole?"	✓ ✓ ✓ ✓ ✓ ✓ ✓
said Mr. Pig. The snake said, //	✓ ✓ ✓ ✓ ✓ ✓
"You knew I was a snake	✓ ✓ ✓ ✓ ✓ ✓
when you pulled me out!"	✓ ✓ ✓ ✓ ✓

Source: Flynt, E. S., & Cooter, R. B. (2004). *The Flynt/Cooter Reading Inventory for the Classroom* (5th ed.), Upper Saddle River, NJ: Merrill/Prentice Hall. Used with permission of the authors.

Applying MSV thinking is fairly simple once you get the hang of it. In Figure 4.10 we return to the miscues noted in Figure 4.9 and conduct an MSV analysis on each. Do you see why each interpretation was made?

An Alternative Running Records System.   Flynt and Cooter (2004) developed a method of generating running records that makes the process both efficient and useful to classroom teachers. This system involves what they call a "miscue grid" and can be extremely effective when used with reading passages that are matched to student interests.

Figure 4.11 shows how miscues can be noted on the left side of the grid over the text, then tallied in the appropriate columns to the right according to miscue type. This process expedites administration and enables teachers to identify error patterns for each oral reading. The "grid method" can easily be adapted by teachers for use with excerpts from any piece of literature.

Teachers should select passages representing a range of reading levels (or have students select the passage(s) to be read) one day prior to assessment so that the first 100 words can be transcribed onto the left-hand side of a blank grid patterned after the one shown in Figure 4.11. Tape record the student's oral reading so that it can be reviewed later for accuracy of transcription. Miscues should be noted in the left-hand column over the text facsimile using the symbols described earlier. After all miscues are noted, examine each and make a final determination about its type (mispronunciation, substitution, insertion, etc.). Then make a mark in the appropriate grid box on the right side of the form. Only one mark is made for each miscue. Once this process is completed, each column is tallied.

In Figure 4.11 you will note that the reader had two mispronunciations, four substitutions, and so on. When the student has read several passages for the teacher over a period of weeks and months, it becomes easy to identify "error patterns"— types of miscues that happen regularly—and to plan appropriate instruction for small groups or individuals.

If you decide to use the grid system, be sure to conduct an MSV analysis on each miscue to better understand which cueing systems the reader is using.

A Running Record Self-Assessment.   It is critical that all assessments be carried out with precision. When we are learning how to do a running record, which takes six or so practice sessions, it is helpful to have a way of judging for ourselves how we are doing and make corrections as needed. If a literacy coach is available to help us with modeling and feedback, so much the better; but that is not always an available resource. R. Cooter and colleagues (Cooter, Mathews, Thompson, & Cooter, 2004) developed a self-assessment tool to help teachers with "fidelity of implementation" in administering running records. Their running record self-assessment is offered in Table 4.3 for your use in the classroom.

Commercial Diagnostic Reading Tests.   Teachers sometimes believe it necessary to assess an individual student's reading ability using norm-referenced measures. This often happens when new students move into a school district without their permanent records, or when struggling readers are being considered for extra assistance programs such as Title 1 or special education services provided in inclusive classrooms. Here we describe for you one such measure, a diagnostic tool called the *Woodcock Reading Mastery Tests–Revised* (Woodcock et al., 1987, 1997).

Figure 4.10 Running Record with MSV Analysis

Student	Paco	(Grade 2)		

Title: **The Pig and the Snake**		E MSV	SC MSV
One day Mr. Pig was walking to	✓ ✓ ✓ ✓ ✓ ✓ ✓		
town. He saw a big hole in the	✓ ✓ $\frac{sam \mid sc}{saw \mid}$ ✓ ✓ ✓ ✓ ✓		Ⓜ Ⓢ Ⓥ
road. A big snake was in the	✓ ✓ $\frac{—}{big}$ ✓ ✓ ✓ ✓ ✓	M S V	
hole. "Help me," said the snake,	✓ ✓ ✓ $\frac{ouT}{—}$ ✓ ✓ ✓	Ⓜ Ⓢ V	
"and I will be your friend." "No, no,"	✓ ✓ ✓ ✓✓ $\frac{— \mid A}{friend \mid}$ ✓ ✓	M S V	
said Mr. Pig. "If I help you get	✓ ✓ ✓ ✓ ✓ ✓ ✓ ✓		
out you will bite me. You're	✓ ✓ ✓ R ✓ ✓		Ⓜ Ⓢ Ⓥ
a snake!" The snake cried and	✓ ✓ ✓ ✓ ✓ ✓		
cried. So Mr. Pig pulled the	✓ ✓ ✓ ✓ $\frac{popped}{pulled}$	Ⓜ Ⓢ Ⓥ	
snake out of the hole.	✓ ✓ ✓ ✓ ✓		
Then the snake said, "Now I am	✓ ✓ ✓ ✓ ✓ ✓ ✓		
going to bite you, Mr. Pig."	✓ ✓ ✓ ✓ ✓ ✓		
"How can you bite me after	✓ ✓ ✓ ✓ ✓ $\frac{—}{after \mid T}$	M S V	
I helped you out of the hole?"	✓ ✓ ✓ ✓ ✓ ✓ ✓		
said Mr. Pig. The snake said, //	✓ ✓ ✓ ✓ ✓ ✓		
"You knew I was a snake	✓ ✓ ✓ ✓ ✓ ✓		
when you pulled me out!"	✓ ✓ ✓ ✓ ✓		

Source: Flynt, E. S., & Cooter, R. B. (2004). *The Flynt/Cooter Reading Inventory for the Classroom* (5th ed.). Upper Saddle River, NJ: Merrill/Prentice Hall. Used with permission of the authors.

Figure 4.11 Sample of a Miscue Grid

	ERROR TYPES					Error Totals	Self-Correct.	ERROR ANALYSIS		
	Mis-pronun.	Sub-stitute	Inser-tions	Tchr. Assist	Omis-sions			Meaning (M)	Syntax (S)	Visual (V)
Hot Shoes										
The guys at the I. B. Belcher										
Elementary School loved all the new sport *lived*		1								
shoes. Some wore the "Sky High" *wear*		1				1		1	1	
model by Leader. Others who *mobil*		1				1				
couldn't afford Sky Highs would settle					2	2		1 / 1	1 / 1	
for a lesser shoe. Some liked the "Street *sc*							1			
Smarts" by Master, or the										
"Uptown-Downtown" by Beebop.										
The Belcher boys got to the point										
with their shoes that they could										
identify their friends just by *in-duh-fee*	1					1				
looking at their feet. But the boy who										
was the envy of the entire fifth *enemy*		1				1		1	1	
grade was Jamie Lee. He had a										
pair of "High Five Pump'em Ups"							1			
by Superior. The only thing Belcher // *sooner* *sc*	1				1	2		1	1	
boys loved as much as their										
shoes was basketball.										
TOTALS	2	4			3	9	2	5	5	

Summary of Reading Behaviors (Strengths and Needs)

Source: Cooter, R. B., Flynt, E. S. & Cooter, K. S. (2007). *Comprehensive reading inventory.* Upper Saddle River, NJ: Pearson/Merrill/Prentice Hall. Used with permission of the authors.

Table 4.3   Self-Assessment/Goal Continuum: Running Records

Directions: Using a red marker, draw a vertical line after the description on each row that best describes your current implementation of each aspect of running record. Using a yellow marker, indicate your end-of-the-year goal for each aspect.

Conventions: marking system	I have never received training on a universal marking system.	I created my own marking system.	I use markings that can be interpreted by my grade level.	I use markings that can be interpreted by my school. Some markings can be universally read.	I use markings that can be interpreted by district teachers. Most markings can be universally read.	I use markings that can be interpreted universally by teachers.
Scoring • Accuracy rate • Error rate • Self-correction	I do not score running records.	I score for accuracy rate.	I use the conversion chart to score for accuracy rate to group my students.	I use the conversion chart to score for accuracy rate and error rate to group my students.	I use the conversion chart to calculate accuracy rate, error rate, and self-correction rate for grouping.	I use the conversion chart to calculate accuracy, error rate, and self-correction rates daily to inform my instruction.
Analysis: cueing systems (MSV) • Meaning • Structure • Visual	I do not analyze my running records.	I sometimes analyze errors on running records.	I analyze all errors on each running record.	I analyze all errors and self-corrections on each running record.	I analyze all errors and self-corrections for meaning, structure, and visual on each running record to guide and inform instruction.	I analyze all errors and self-corrections for meaning, structure, and visual on each running record. In addition, I look for patterns over time to further guide instruction.
Frequency	I do not use running records.	I use running records two times a year, at the beginning and end of school.	I do running records occasionally throughout the year.	I do one running record on my struggling students once per six weeks.	I do one running record on all my students once per six weeks.	I perform running records daily so that each student is assessed every six weeks. My struggling students are done twice every six weeks.

From "Searching for Lessons of Mass Instruction," by Cooter, R., Matthews, B., Thompson, S., and Cooter, K. *Reading Teacher, 58*(4), December, 2004. Copyright 2004 by International Reading Association. Reproduced with permission of International Reading Association in the format Textbook via Copyright Clearance Center.

The WRMT–R/NU is a battery of six individually administered subtests intended to measure reading abilities from kindergarten through adult levels. Subtests cover visual-auditory learning, letter identification, word identification, word attack, word comprehension, and passage comprehension. The test's design aligns with a skills perspective of reading. The assessment is divided into two sections according to age and ability levels: readiness and reading achievement. The WRMT–R/NU reports norm-referenced data for both of its forms and offers insights into remediation. Results may be calculated either manually or by using the convenient scoring program developed for personal computers (PCs). The WRMT–R/NU is frequently used by teachers in special education and Title I reading programs.

Commercial Reading Assessment Tools

There are a number of commercial products on the market to help teachers gather information about students' reading skills. While such products may be helpful, they can also be expensive. In this section we present products that have been useful in our classroom practices and that meet with our general approval. We begin with the most valid instruments of all: informal reading inventories or IRIs.

Informal Reading Inventories. An **informal reading inventory** (IRI) is normally individually administered (though some can be given to groups of children), and is usually comprised of graded word lists and story passages. Emmett A. Betts is generally considered to be the developer of the first IRI; however, several other individuals contributed to its development in concept as far back as the early 1900s (Johns & Lunn, 1983).

The Teacher's Guide to Reading Tests (Cooter, 1990) lists several advantages and unique features of IRIs that help explain why teachers continue to find them useful. One benefit is that IRIs provide for authentic assessment of the reading act: that is, an IRI closely resembles real reading. Students are better able to "put it all together" by reading whole stories or passages. Another advantage of IRIs is that they usually provide a systematic procedure for studying student miscues or reading errors.

IRIs are rather unusual when compared to other commercial forms of reading assessment. First, because they are informal, no norms, reliability data, or validity information are usually available. This is often seen as a disadvantage by some public school educators, especially when assessing students enrolled in federally funded remedial programs where reliability data are often required. Second, IRIs are unusual (in a positive way) because they provide a great deal of information that is helpful to teachers in making curricular decisions, especially teachers who place students into needs-based or guided reading groups (Fountas & Pinnell, 1996). IRIs provide an approximation of each child's ability in graded or "leveled" reading materials, such as basal readers and books used for guided reading.

IRIs tend to be somewhat different from each other. Beyond the usual graded word lists and reading passages, IRIs vary a great deal in the subtests offered (e.g., silent reading passages, phonics, interest inventories, concepts about print, phonemic awareness, auditory discrimination) and in the scoring criteria used to interpret reading miscues. Some argue (we include ourselves among them) that the best IRIs are those constructed by classroom teachers themselves using their own reading materials. Several examples of IRIs now used in many school systems follow.

The Comprehensive Reading Inventory (CRI) (Cooter, Flynt, & Cooter, 2007). The CRI is a research-based version of the traditional IRI. The authors incorporate phonemic awareness, letter naming, word identification, comprehension processes, reading fluency, and miscue analysis into an authentic reading assessment. Unlike most other commercial IRIs, the new CRI offers validity and reliability data based on scientific research. The CRI includes appropriate length passages, both expository and narrative, and an efficient miscue grid system for quick analyses of running records. The CRI also includes a spanish version for bilingual teachers use with EL students.

Developmental Reading Assessment (DRA) (Beaver, 2001). This is an informal reading inventory offering graded reading passages, rubrics for evaluating students' oral reading, and a storage box for student portfolios.

The English * Español Reading Inventory (Flynt & Cooter, 1999). This easy-to-use tool offers complete informal reading inventories for prekindergarten through grade 12 students in both Spanish and English. The Spanish passages were carefully developed and field-tested with the aid of native Spanish-speaking teacher-researchers from the United States, Mexico, and Central and South America to avoid problems with dialect differences and to maximize their usefulness in U.S. classrooms.

Qualitative Reading Inventory–3 (Leslie & Caldwell, 2000). This IRI includes both narrative and expository passages, has pictures for each level passage, and methods for assessing prior knowledge. This IRI also includes a text link to the Internet.

Dynamic Indicators of Basic Early Literacy Skills (DIBELS). The *Dynamic Indicators of Basic Early Literacy Skills,* or DIBELS, is a set of standardized, individually administered measures of early literacy development. DIBELS was specifically designed to assess three of the "five big ideas" of early literacy development: phonological awareness, alphabetic principle, and oral reading fluency (measured as a corrected reading rate) with connected text. Because of its prominence in schools today, we discuss DIBELS in detail in Chapter 9.

What Does Research Show Are the Best Ways of Teaching Phonics?

Phonics: What Do We Know from Research and Practice?

Research confirms that systematic and explicit phonics instruction is more effective than nonsystematic instruction or programs that ignore phonics (National Reading Panel, 2000). When delivered as part of a comprehensive reading program—one that includes expansive vocabulary instruction, reading practice in great books, and writing development—by a skillful teacher, phonics instruction can help children become enthusiastic lifelong readers.

Approaches to Phonics Instruction

Several approaches to phonics instruction have found support in the research (National Reading Panel, 2000). These approaches are sometimes modified or combined in reading programs.

Synthetic Phonics Instruction. Traditional phonics instruction in which students learn how to change letters or letter combinations into speech sounds, then blend them together to form known words ("sounding out").

Embedded Phonics Instruction. The embedding of phonics instruction in text reading, which results in a more implicit approach that relies to some extent on incidental learning (National Reading Panel, 2000, p. 8).

Analogy-Based Phonics Instruction. A variation of onset and rime instruction that encourages students to use their knowledge of word families to identify new words that have that same word part. For example, students learn to pronounce *light* by using their prior knowledge of the *-ight* rime from three words they already know: *right, might*, and *night*.

Analytic Phonics Instruction. A variation of the previous two approaches; students study previously learned whole words to discover letter–sound relationships. For example, *Stan, steam*, and *story* all include the *st* word element (*st* is a consonant blend).

Phonics-Through-Spelling Instruction. Students segment spoken words into phonemes and write letters that represent those sounds to create the word in print. For example, *rat* can be sounded out and written phonetically. This approach is often used as part of a process writing program.

Favorite Strategies for Teaching Phonics

Letter–Sound Cards. Letter–sound cards are intended as prompts to help students remember individual and combination (i.e., digraphs and blends) letter sounds that have been introduced during mini-lessons or other teachable moments. You will need to have a word bank for each child (children's shoe boxes, recipe boxes, or other small containers in which index cards can be filed), alphabetic divider cards to separate words in the word bank, index cards, and colored markers.

The idea is to provide students with their own word cards on which you (or they) have written a key letter sound or sounds on one side and a word that uses that sound on the other. Whenever possible, it is best to use nouns or other words that can be depicted with a picture, so that, for emergent readers, a drawing can be added to the side having the word (as needed). Two examples are shown in Figure 4.12.

Phonics Fish (or Foniks Phish?) Card Game. Remember the children's card game Fish (sometimes called Go Fish)? This review activity helps students use their growing awareness of phonics sounds and letter patterns to construct word families (i.e., groups of words having the same phonetic pattern). It can be played in small groups, at a learning center with two to four children, or during reading groups with the teacher.

You will need a deck of word cards. The words can be selected from the students' word banks or chosen by the teacher or parent/teaching assistant from among those familiar to all students. The word cards should contain ample examples of at least three or four phonetic patterns that you wish to review (e.g., beginning consonant sounds, *r*-controlled vowels, clusters, digraphs, rime families, etc.).

Before beginning the game, explain which word families or sound patterns are to be used. Next, explain the rules of the game.

1. Each child will be dealt five cards.
2. The remaining cards (deck of about fifty) are placed facedown in the middle of the group.
3. Taking turns in a round-robin fashion, each child can ask any other if he or she is holding a word having a particular sound or pattern. For example, if one of the patterns included is the */sh/* sound, then the first student may say something

Figure 4.12 **Letter–Sound Card Examples**

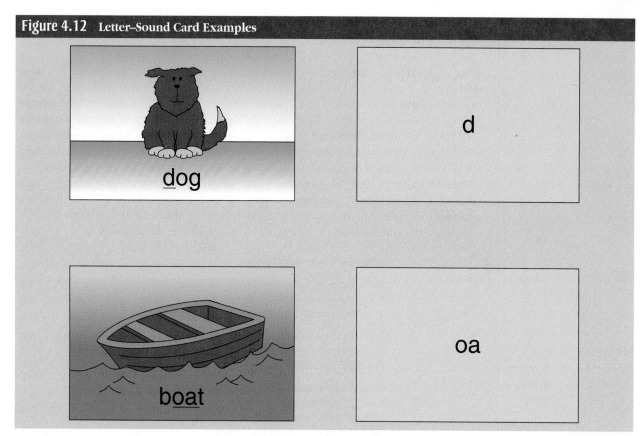

Reutzel, D. Ray; Cooter, Robert B., *Strategies for Reading Assessment and Instruction: Helping Every Child Succeed,* 3rd Edition, © 2007, Reprinted by permission of Pearson Education, Inc.

like, "Juanita, do you have any words with the /*sh*/ sound?" If the student being asked does not have any word cards with that pattern, he or she says, "Go Fish!" The student asking the question then draws a card from the deck.

4. Cards having matching patterns (two or more) are placed faceup in front of the student asking the question.
5. The first student to get rid of all his or her cards wins the game.

Stomping, Clapping, Tapping, and Snapping Sound. Helping children hear syllables in words enables them to segment sounds. This knowledge can be used in myriad ways to improve writing/spelling, increase awareness of letter combinations used to produce speech sounds, and apply knowledge of onsets and rimes. All these skills and more enable students to sound out words in print more effectively. Many teachers have found success in helping children hear syllables by clapping them out when reading nursery rhymes: "Mar-y had a lit-tle lamb, lit-tle lamb, lit-tle lamb. . . ."

We prefer to use rhyming poetry, songs, chants, or raps for these syllabication activities. Use an enlarged version produced for an overhead projector, a big book version, or simply rewrite the text on large chart paper using a watercolor marker. First, model-read the enlarged text aloud in a normal cadence for students. Reread the selection, again at a normal cadence, inviting students to join in as they wish. Next, explain that you will reread the selection, but this time you will clap (or snap, stomp, etc.) the syllables in the words. (Note: If you have not already explained the concept of syllables, you will need to do so at this point.) Finally, invite students to clap (or make whatever gesture or sound you have chosen) as you reread the passage.

Tongue Twisters. Many students enjoy word play. Tongue twisters can be a wonderful way of reviewing consonants (Cunningham, 1995) in a way that is fun for students. We have found that tongue-twister activities can combine reading and creative writing processes to help children deepen their understanding of phonic elements.

There are many traditional tongue twisters in published children's literature that may be used. However, we find that children enjoy creating their own tongue twisters. All you need to do is decide which sounds/letter pattern families are to be used.

Cunningham (1995) suggests that you begin by simply reciting some tongue twisters aloud and inviting students to join in. We recommend that you produce two or three examples on chart paper and post them on the wall as you introduce the concept of tongue twisters. For example, you might use the following.

> Silly Sally sat in strawberries.
>
> Peter Piper picked a peck of pickled peppers.
> If Peter Piper picked a peck of pickled peppers,
> Then how many peppers did Peter Piper pick?
>
> Peter Piper panhandles pepperoni pizza,
> With his pint-sized pick-up he packs a peck of pepperoni pizzas,
> For Patti, his portly patron.
>
> Simple Simon met a pieman going to the fair,
> Said Simple Simon to the pieman,
> "Let me taste your wares!"
> Said the pieman to Simple Simon,
> "Show me first your penny!"
> Said Simple Simon to the pieman,
> "I'm afraid I haven't any."

Children especially love it when teachers create tongue twisters using names of children in the class, such as the following example:

> Pretty Pam picked pink peonies for Patty's party.

Challenge students to create their own tongue twisters to "stump the class." It may be fun to award students coupons that can be used to purchase take-home books for coming up with clever tongue twisters.

Creating Nonsense Words

Many popular poets, such as Shel Silverstein and Jack Prelutsky, have tapped into children's fascination with word play in their very creative poetry. For instance, when Silverstein speaks of "gloppy glumps of cold oatmeal," we all understand what he means, even though *gloppy* and *glumps* are nonsense words. Having students create nonsense words and then apply them to popular poetry is a motivating way to help them practice phonic patterns.

First decide which phonic sound/letter pattern families you wish to emphasize. For instance, it may be appropriate to review the letter/sound families represented by *-ack, -ide, -ing,* and *-ore.* You will also need books of poetry or songs with rhyming phrases, chart paper or overhead transparencies, and markers.

As with all activities, begin by modeling what you expect students to do. On a large sheet of chart paper or at the overhead projector, write the word family parts that you wish to emphasize (for this example, we used *-ack, -ide, -ing,* and *-ore*). Illustrate how you can convert the word parts into nonsense words by adding a consonant, consonant blend, or consonant digraph before each one, such as shown here.

-ack	-ide	-ing	-ore
gack	spide	gacking	zore
clack	mide	zwing	glore
chack	plide	kaching	jore

In the next phase of the demonstration, select a poem or song that rhymes and review it with students (use enlarged text for all of your modeling). Next, show students a revised copy of the song or poem in which you have substituted nonsense words. Here is one example we have used with the song "I Know an Old Lady Who Swallowed a Fly." We show only the first verse here, but you could use the entire song, substituting a nonsense word in each stanza.

> I know an old lady who swallowed a fly,
> I don't know why,
> she swallowed the fly,
> I guess she'll die.

A nonsense-word version follows:

> I know an old lady who swallowed a **zwing,**
> I don't know why,
> she swallowed the **zwing,**
> I guess she'll die.

Online Phonics and Word Attack Activities

Many wonderful phonics activities are available on the Internet. The following Web sites offer useful, creative, and pedagogically sound activities.

First School Years—*www.firstschoolyears.com*

Reading Rockets—*www.readingrockets.org/*

BBCEducation—*www.bbc.co.uk/schools/wordsandpictures/*

EdHelper.com—*www.edhelper.com/phonics/Phonics.htm*

Phonics Link—*www.sdcoe.k12.ca.us/SCORE/Phonics_Link/phonics.html*

Who Has Difficulty in Learning Phonics and What Can Be Done to Assist Them?

There are many reasons why children may have difficulty learning phonics and other word identification skills. As we have seen in the past two chapters, if students have not developed phonemic awareness knowledge of letter names and an understanding

TEACHER PREP Tips for effective instruction with EL students can be found on the Teacher Prep Website (*www.prenhall.com/ teacherprep*). Spelling patterns, teaching phonics within context, the use of pictures to enhance understanding and exploring cognates (words similar in spelling in English and the native language) are included in "Diversity Issue: Helping EL Students with Phonics." This article can be located in *Strategies and Lessons-Reading Methods/Modules 2, 8, or 11.*

of concepts of print, learning phonics will be difficult if not impossible. Research also suggests that most students who have reading difficulties may have deficits in oral language, language comprehension, and background knowledge (Snow, Burns, & Griffin, 1998; Stanovich & West, 1989). We have seen that this is often the case with many children living at the poverty level. Other factors affecting the learning of phonics include challenges faced by English learners (ELs), issues of focusing attention on learning activities (as with children having attention deficit disorder [ADD]), dyslexia, language impairments affecting sound perception, and children who are less cognitively able ("slow learners"). In this section we offer strategies for meeting the needs of many of these learners.

Interactive Strategies

Vellutino and Scanlon (2002) developed and field-tested a sequence of instructions for struggling readers called **interactive strategies.** These strategies for providing differentiated instruction appear to be adapted in part from the Reading Recovery model originally developed by Marie Clay (2003). Aimed at improving decoding skills, interactive strategies are comprised of five "lessons" in the intervention format. Walpole and McKenna (2004) recommend this sequence as one that provides "strategic integration" of new decoding skills. Here are the five steps in the integrative strategies model.

1. *Five minutes of rereading familiar texts.* Repeated readings of familiar texts is an effective way to improve word identification skills and automaticity in decoding (National Reading Panel, 2000). Daily rereading of familiar or decodable texts can be a powerful reinforcement in phonics acquisition.
2. *Five minutes of phonics skills instruction.* This focused and intensive instruction is based on individual student needs in learning phonics and related skills. In the research by Vellutino and Scanlon (2002), students received short, focused "bursts" of instruction and practice in such areas as phonemic awareness, alphabet recognition, phonics, studying word families (onset and rime), and producing spelling patterns.

Laura Bolesta/Merrill

3. *Ten minutes of reading and applying decoding skills to new text.* Children read a new text each day on their **instructional reading level** (90–95 percent correct word identification). Before reading, the teacher introduces the book in an enticing way (sometimes referred to as a "book talk"). As the child reads the text aloud, the teacher may intervene to offer prompts when the child encounters an unknown word.
4. *Five minutes of word work using high-frequency words in isolation.* We have long been proponents of students having **word banks** or

vocabulary notebooks in which they keep the most frequently occurring words in print (e.g., *was, the, run, are, and, there, this,* etc.), or **high-frequency words,** as well as other content-related words the teacher has selected from science, social studies, and mathematics curricula. We discuss high-frequency words in Chapter 5, in the context of fluency. In the interactive strategies model, teachers have students spend five minutes each day identifying high-frequency words and others selected by the teacher. These practice sessions can be conducted easily with students working in pairs.

5. *Five minutes of writing.* In the final step of the interactive strategies model, teachers begin (as they always should for any practice activity) with building background or activating students' prior experiences that are related to the task students are being asked to do. The writing activity may involve dictation by the teacher or student, spelling practice with the target words, or sentence writing according to criteria established by the teacher.

Students with Dyslexia

Dyslexia is defined by the International Dyslexia Association (2006) as a

specific learning disability that is neurological in origin. It is characterized by difficulties with accurate and/or fluent word recognition and by poor spelling and decoding abilities. These difficulties typically result from a deficit in the phonological component of language that is often unexpected in relation to other cognitive abilities and the provision of effective classroom instruction. Secondary consequences may include problems in reading comprehension and reduced reading experience that can impede growth of vocabulary and background knowledge . . . Many people who are dyslexic are of average to above average intelligence.

Recommended instruction for students with dyslexia typically involves individualized, intensive, **multisensory** (i.e., visual, tactile, auditory, kinesthetic) methods and writing and spelling components. Remedial teaching of phonics for dyslexic students may include direct instruction in phonics and structural analysis.

It is recommended that instruction for students with dyslexia be individualized to meet their specific learning needs. Materials used should be matched to each student's individual ability level. Following are key recommendations of the International Dyslexia Association (IDA):

- *Linguistic.* Instruction should be aimed at insuring fluency with the patterns of language in words and sentences.
- *Meaning-based.* All instruction should lead to an emphasis on comprehension and composition.
- *Multisensory.* The simultaneous use of two or more sensory pathways (auditory, visual, kinesthetic, tactile) during presentation and practice are often effective.
- *Phonemic awareness.* It can be beneficial to offer instruction that reteaches students to detect, segment, blend, and manipulate sounds in spoken language.
- *Explicit direct instruction.* Phonics instruction should be systematic (structured), sequential, and cumulative, and presented in a logical sequential plan that fits the nature of language (alphabetic principle), with no assumption of prior skills or language knowledge.

TEACHER PREP Learn more about supporting ELs in alphabet knowledge, phonological awareness, book/print concepts, vocabulary knowledge, and discourse skills through reading "Supporting English Learners' Language and Literacy Skills" on the Teacher Prep Website (*www.prenhall.com/ teacherprep*). Click on the *Strategies and Lessons-Reading Methods/Module 8* links.

English Learners

Recently, the *Report of the National Literacy Panel on Language-Minority Children and Youth* (August & Shanahan, 2006) was released, shedding new light on the reading instruction needs of English learners (EL). First, it was found that evidence-based reading research confirms that focusing instruction on key reading components—phonemic awareness, decoding, oral reading fluency, reading comprehension, vocabulary, and writing—has clear benefits. The researchers went on to say that differences due to children's second-language proficiency make it important to adjust instruction to meet the needs of second-language learners.

A second finding was that language-minority students who become literate in their first language are likely to have an advantage in the acquisition of English literacy. This finding was supported by studies demonstrating that language-minority students taught in both their native language and English performed, on average, better on English reading measures than language-minority students instructed only in English. Unfortunately, it is often difficult for large school districts to find enough well-qualified bilingual teachers to serve these children.

This important study makes it clear that phonics instruction is critical to English learners and must be delivered by a knowledgeable teacher.

TEACHER PREP "Beginning, Middle, and End—Finding Phonemes," offers a lesson example to increase awareness of the placement of sounds in words. Access the Teacher Prep Website (*www.prenhall.com/ teacherprep*). Select *Strategies and Lessons-Reading Methods/Module 2*.

English Learners (Spanish). Native Spanish speakers are the most rapidly growing population of English learners (EL) in many states. Some basic similarities and differences between English and Spanish languages may cause some problems in the learning of phonics. Table 4.4 shows a few points for you to consider in planning phonics instruction with EL students, adapted from Honig, Diamond, and Gutlohn (2000).

More similarities and exceptions are noted earlier in this chapter. Happily, most phonics generalizations in English and Spanish are the same. If anything, Spanish is far more consistent than English!

Table 4.4 Planning Phonics Instruction

Sound	Explanation	Examples
/s/	This sound is spelled with *s* in English and Spanish.	English: *seed, secret* Spanish: *semilla, secreto*
/m/	This sound is spelled with *m* in English and Spanish.	English: *map, many* Spanish: *mapa, mucho*
Spanish *e*	The letter *e* in Spanish has the long -*a* sound, as in *eight*.	
/ch/	In Spanish, the digraph *ch* also make the /ch/ sound. However, *ch* only appears in the beginning or medial positions in Spanish.	English: *church, each* Spanish: *chico, ocho*
/sh/	The *sh* digraph does not exist in Spanish. Sorting new words with *sh* and *ch* will be helpful. Be sure to also focus on the meaning of each word.	

What Strategies Can Parents Use to Help Their Child Learn Phonics Skills?

Activities for Parents to Increase Children's Print and Phonological Awareness

The Public Library Association (*www.pla.org*) and the Association for Library Service to Children conduct a joint project known as Every Child Ready to Read @ Your Library. In this section we paraphrase some of this project's excellent ideas. We have worded them in language you might use with parents. The activities listed below are arranged, like our benchmark skills, from easiest to most difficult. It is wisely recommended that parents be sure that their children can perform tasks at the simpler level before moving on to a higher level.

Words from Pictures. Have your child glue pictures cut from magazines donated for this purpose onto paper. Have him or her tell a "story" about the picture *as you write* what he or she says. You can teach new words at this time, but be sure to draw the child's attention to the printed word. After the story is written, go back and take turns "reading" the story to each other. Collect these pictures and stories and make them into a book that can be looked at again and again.

Nursery Rhymes. A somewhat lost tradition in the United States is reading nursery rhymes to children, though hearing rhymes helps children later learn rimes (and onsets). Read nursery rhymes to your child. After he or she can say the rhyme and is very familiar with it, practice counting the words in one sentence at a time. Focus on hearing like sounds in words and how the sounds look in print.

Rhyming Picture Cards. Create picture cards with words beneath and practice categorizing the rhyming words. If your child has trouble matching rhyming words, provide help by drawing attention to the fact that words that rhyme have the same sound at the end. For example, *cat* and *rat* rhyme because they both have the *at* sound at the end; *clock* and *block* rhyme because they both have the *ock* sound at the end (emphasize the ending that makes the words rhyme when saying them). Adding some examples that do not rhyme may help your child understand (e.g., *clock* and *ball* do not rhyme because they have different ending sounds).

Silly Words. Make up "silly" words by changing the first letter in a known word. Play a game of seeing how many silly words you and your child can create and then have your child tell you whether or not the silly word is a real word. To play this game at the easiest level, you should make up several words by changing the first sound (e.g., *cook—sook, book, wook, took*) and then asking your child whether or not each is a real word. At a more advanced level, you can model and ask your child to change the first sound in a word from one word to another. For example, say: "My word is *be* and the new sound is /*m*/." (Say the sound, not the word.) "What is the new word?" *(Me.)* There are many familiar words in which the first sound can be changed to make a new word (*light–night, boat–goat, pail–sail, cat–rat, ball–wall*).

Many states have established their own collaborative Web sites featuring valuable information about family involvement in early reading development. You can find many more activities like these online at *www.ala.org/ala/pla/plaissues/earlylit/ workshopsparent/workshopsparents.htm.*

Create a Word identification lesson plan through the Teacher Prep Website.

- You will be guided through the alignment of standards, lesson objectives, your introduction, planning for and sequencing lesson activities and procedures, planning for ongoing assessment throughout the lesson, and planning end of lesson assessment. You will also choose and list lesson materials/resources and create adapted instruction to meet all needs of learners.

- This lesson can be sent to your instructor through this link.

- Review the Teacher Prep Website links, the text CD links and recommended Online Phonics and Word Attack Activities Links from this chapter to create a Word Identification Lesson Plan.

- As you create your plan, consider effective instruction by reviewing what we know from research and practice as discussed early in this chapter.

- Please note if materials for this activity could be transported home for parental reinforcement.

Summary

Reading research has confirmed the importance of teaching children alphabetic principle, phonics, and other word attack skills explicitly. In this chapter, we have offered an evidence-based sequence for teaching phonemic awareness skills, moving from a simple understanding that, as competence in phonemic awareness is reached, students are helped to gain an understanding that the sounds in spoken words can be symbolically represented by letters (alphabetic principle). This level of understanding brings students to the point of development where they are ready to acquire basic phonics skills.

After basic phonics skills have been learned, readers are ready to learn an even higher level of word identification called *structural analysis*. Here the reader uses prior knowledge of word parts and their meaning to both pronounce and understand unfamiliar words in print. This chapter presents a practical sequence of instruction leading to fluent word identification. In later chapters we present evidence-based strategies teachers can use to teach each of these important reading skills.

Classroom Applications

1. Conduct a library and Internet search for books that could be used to help you introduce the alphabetic principle to emergent readers. Prepare an annotated bibliography of your sources to share with your colleagues in class.

Phonics Quick Test*

1. The word *charkle* is broken into syllables between ___r___ and ___k___. The *a* has an ___r___-controlled sound, and the *e* is __silent__.
2. In the word *small,* sm- is known as the onset and -*all* is known as the __rime__.
3. *Ch* in the word *chair* is known as a __consonant digraph__.
4. The letter *c* in the word *city* has a __soft__ sound, and in the word *cow* has a __hard__ sound.
5. The letters *bl* in the word *blue* are referred to as a consonant __blend__.
6. The underlined vowels in the words *author, spread,* and *blue* are known as vowel __digraphs__.
7. The words *tag, run, cot,* and *get* fit which vowel pattern? __CVC__
8. The words *glide, take,* and *use* fit the __VCE__ vowel pattern.
9. The word part *work-* in the word *working* is known as a __root or base word, or free morpheme__.
10. The word part -*ing* in the word *working* is known as a __suffix or bound morpheme__.
11. Teaching students the meaning of prefixes, suffixes, and root words to help them better understand word meanings is part of word attack skills known as __structural analysis__.
12. Writers often provide __context clues__, which help readers discover the meaning of unknown words in print.

2. Locate the Web page for your state's education department. Print out the scope and sequence of recommended skills in the areas of alphabetic principle and phonics. Compare this list to the curriculum guide or map from the school district in which you plan to carry out your internship (student teaching). Prepare a "Comprehensive Decoding Checklist" to use in profiling each child's decoding abilities. This will be useful to you later, when we discuss reading assessment in this text. More importantly, you will have created a valuable tool for informing your teaching.

3. Develop your own *Words to Go!* activity for parent involvement. Use new examples. Find a resource for making all materials for the activity available in both English and Spanish.

4. Through your college or university teacher-preparation program, find a teacher who will allow you to perform running records on two of his or her students. Analyze your findings using MSV analysis. Be sure to do three running records on each level of difficulty with each child as recommended by research cited in this chapter.

5. With a classmate, assemble a PowerPoint presentation summarizing important concepts from this chapter that could be shared with parents. Share your presentation with two or three adults; solicit their feedback.

Recommended Readings

American Federation of Teachers. (1999). *Teaching reading is rocket science: What expert teachers of reading should know and be able to do.* Washington, DC: American Federation of Teachers.

Burns, M. S., Griffin, P., & Snow, C. E. (1999). *Starting out right: A guide to promoting children's reading success.* Washington, DC: National Academy Press.

Cooter, R. B., Matthews, B., Thompson, S., & Cooter, K. S. (2004). Searching for lessons of mass instruction? Try reading strategy continuums. *The Reading Teacher, 58*(4), 388–393.

Cunningham, P. M. (2004). *Phonics they use: Words for reading and writing* (4th ed.). Boston: Pearson/Allyn & Bacon.

Fry, E. B., Kress, J. E., & Fountoukidis, D. L. (2000). *The reading teacher's book of lists* (4th ed.). New York: Jossey-Bass.

Leu, D. J., Kinzer, C. K., Wilson, R. M., & Hall, M. A. (2006). *Phonics, phonemic awareness, and word analysis for teachers: An interactive tutorial* (8th ed.). Upper Saddle River, NJ: Pearson/Merrill/Prentice Hall.

National Institute for Literacy. (2003). *Put reading first: The research building blocks for teaching children to read.* Washington, DC: National Institute for Literacy at Ed Pubs. Free download available at *www.nifl.gov/partnershipforreading.*

Reutzel, D. R., & Cooter, R. B. (2007). *Strategies for reading assessment and instruction: Helping every child succeed* (3rd ed.). Upper Saddle River, NJ: Pearson/Merrill/Prentice Hall.

chapter 5

Developing Children's Reading Fluency

Chapter Questions

1. According to evidence-based research, what is fluent reading?

2. What is the nature of the relationship between fluency and reading comprehension?

3. How do young children develop fluency in reading?

4. How is reading fluency assessed?

5. What are evidence-based instructional practices or strategies for developing reading fluency?

"One Minute of Reading"

Michelle, a second grade student, settles in next to Mrs. Chang, who is waiting to take a one-minute reading sample. Mrs. Chang hands her the second grade passage and sets a one-minute timer. "Michelle, I am glad to spend some time today listening to you read. Are you ready?" queries Mrs. Chang.

"Yes, I think so," answers Michelle.

"I want you to read the passage aloud as quickly as you can without making mistakes. Do you understand?"

"Yes, Mrs. Chang, I understand," replies Michelle.

"Okay, then. When I say 'Start,' you may begin reading."

Michelle nods and clears her throat.

"Start!" says Mrs. Chang.

Michelle begins reading. "My Friend. I have a new friend at school. She can't walk so she uses a wheelchair to get around. She comes to school in a special van. . . ."

When Michelle finishes the reading, Mrs. Chang praises her: "Michelle, you are reading very fluently. You made only two errors, read quickly enough for a second grader, had expression in your voice, and read more than word at a time!"

Michelle beams with pride. "Thanks," she says quietly.

"Can you tell me what you remember from the pages you read?"

"I think so," responds Michelle.

When Michelle finishes retelling what she can remember, Mrs. Chang praises her again. "Would you like to add anything to what you remember from your reading?" she questions.

"Uh-huh."

Mrs. Chang listens while Michelle adds one more detail she has remembered to her oral retelling.

"Michelle, I'm going to ask you a few questions about what you have just read. I would like for you to answer the questions as best you can."

"Okay," responds Michelle.

Mrs. Chang probes Michelle's comprehension of the passage with a few well-chosen questions to see if she remembers more than she has retold.

That afternoon, Mrs. Chang looks at the record she made of Michelle's earlier oral reading. She read the text with 95 percent accuracy, so Mrs. Chang knows that decoding this text wasn't a problem for Michelle. She had timed Michelle's reading and calculated her reading rate in words read correctly per minute. She now compares Michelle's words read correctly per minute (wcpm) to a chart showing expected oral reading rate ranges by grade level. Michelle scores near the 75th percentile for her grade level. Next, Mrs. Chang reviews the oral reading expression rating scale she had filled out right after listening to Michelle read. Michelle averaged three out of four points on expression, pacing, smoothness, and phrasing using this rating scale as a measure. Finally, Mrs. Chang carefully reviews what she wrote down while listening to Michelle's oral retelling of the pages she had read aloud. Michelle remembered the major ideas and more than half of the details in the passage, evidencing her comprehension of the text.

All things considered, Michelle has performed well! There is no doubt in Mrs. Chang's mind that Michelle is progressing well toward the goal of becoming a fluent reader!

For many years, fluency has been acknowledged as an important goal in becoming a proficient and strategic reader (Allington, 1983, 1984, 2001; Klenk & Kibby, 2000; Opitz & Rasinski, 1998; Rasinski, 2000; Rasinkski & Padak, 1996; The Report of the National Reading Panel, 2000). As a result of the publication of the *Report of the National Reading Panel* in 2000, there has been a marked increase in attention given to teaching, practicing, and assessing reading fluency in the elementary school grades. To help children become fluent readers, teachers need to know the answer to four important questions. First, what is fluency? Second, how do children develop fluency in reading? Third, how is reading fluency assessed to determine which elements of fluent reading require instruction and practice? And finally, what are evidence-based strategies for fluency instruction and practice that will assist all children to develop fluent reading behaviors? This chapter develops teacher knowledge in the area of reading fluency, describes valid and reliable fluency assessment instruments and procedures, and explains evidence-based reading fluency instructional strategies.

What Is Reading Fluency?

Fluency is defined as (1) accuracy and ease of decoding (automaticity); (2) age- or grade-level-appropriate reading speed or rate; (3) appropriate use of volume, pitch, juncture, and stress (prosodic features) in one's voice; and (4) appropriate text phrasing or "chunking." There seems to be a high degree of agreement among researchers as to the skills one must develop to become a fluent reader (Allington, 2001; Juel, 1991; National Reading Panel, 2000; Richards, 2000; Samuels & Farstrup, 2006). These skills include the following:

- **Automaticity**—Translating letters to sounds to words effortlessly and accurately
- **Expression**—Using proper intonation (i.e., prosodic features such as pitch, juncture, and stress) in one's voice

Figure 5.1   A Model of Fluent Reading

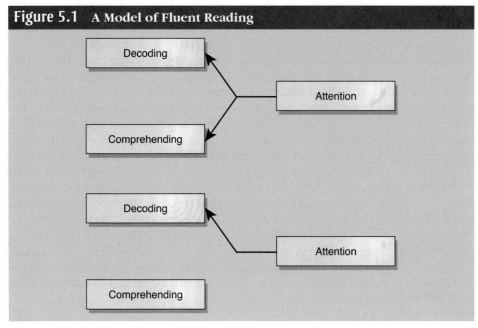

Adapted from Chall, 1967.

- **Rate**—Attaining appropriate reading speed according to the reader's purpose or the type of passage
- **Phrasing**—Reading orally large chunks of text such as phrases or sentences smoothly without hesitating, stopping to decode, or rereading

In summary, fluent readers can decode the words in text accurately and effortlessly, and read with correct volume, phrasing, appropriate intonation, and at a reasonably rapid rate so that their reading has become "automatic." When fluent readers read aloud effortlessly with speed, accuracy, and proper expression, their mind is free to focus on comprehension of text. The top half of Figure 5.1 presents a model reflecting the automaticity of fluent readers.

On the other hand, less fluent readers struggle through text in a labored, word-by-word manner. They focus most of their attention on decoding or figuring out how to pronounce the words, so reading comprehension suffers. The bottom half of Figure 5.1 shows how comprehension can be virtually ignored when readers devote most of their mental energies to decoding. Thus, reading fluency is important because it provides a much-needed bridge between word recognition and reading comprehension (National Reading Panel, 2000; Rasinski, 1989; Reutzel & Hollingsworth, 1993; Samuels & Farstrup, 2006).

How Do Children Develop Reading Fluency?

The answer to this question has been the focus of many years of research and theory development (Jenkins, Fuchs, Van den Broek, Espin, & Deno, 2003; Kame'enui & Simons, 2001; National Reading Panel, 2000; Stahl, 2004; Wolf & Katzir-Cohen, 2001).

Perhaps the most prominent theory devised to explain how readers become fluent is the the LaBerge and Samuels (1974) theory of automatic information processing, or *automaticity theory*. This popular and well-researched explanation of how reading fluency develops hypothesizes that the human mind functions much like a computer, and that visual input (letters and words) is sequentially entered into the mind of the reader. Almost without exception, humans have the ability to perform more than one task at a time (computer specialists sometimes call this "multitasking"). Because each computer—and, by extension, the human mind—has a limited capacity for multitasking, attention must be shifted from one job to another. If one job requires a large portion of the available computer's attention capacity, then capacity for another job is limited. The term *automaticity* implies that human minds of readers, like computers, have a limited amount of ability to shift attention between the processes of decoding (sounding out words) and comprehending (thinking about the meaning of the author's message in the text). If readers are too bogged down in decoding the text, they will not be able to focus on the job of comprehending the author's message. Particularly in the earliest stages of reading development, the relationship between fluency and comprehension is relatively high (Paris, Carpenter, Paris, & Hamilton, 2005).

> **Getting to Know English Learners**
>
> a. Human beings have an innate ability to acquire language, almost without exception, when appropriate socio cultural factors, such as socialization, are in place.
>
> b. Automaticity also occurs when a speaker of a language acquires his or her language fluently, and can, therefore, "automatically" draw upon this knowledge in most situations.

An example of automaticity in action can be seen in the skill of riding a bike. Novice bike riders focus so intently on balancing, turning the handlebars, and pedaling that they sometimes fail to attend to other important tasks like direction and potential dangers. Similarly, a reader who is a poor decoder focuses so much of his attention on phonics and other sounding out strategies that he has little brainpower left for comprehending. When this happens the reading act, like an overloaded computer or a novice bike rider, "crashes." In contrast, children who are accomplished bike riders can ride without hands, carry on a conversation with a friend, dodge a pothole in the road, and chew gum at the same time. Like the accomplished bike rider, fluent readers can rapidly shift attention and focus on the author's message because decoding no longer demands the lion's share of their attention capacity. LaBerge and Samuels's theory of automaticity predicts that if reading can occur automatically without too much focus or effort devoted to the decoding process, then reading comprehension, while not guaranteed, is at least made possible (Samuels, 2006).

Chall's Stages of Reading Fluency

Jeanne Chall (1983) proposed six stages of becoming a fluent, accomplished reader as shown in Figure 5.2. In the first stage, or Stage 0, children have not yet begun to pay much attention to the letters and words on the page. Rather, they ask for books to be read aloud repeatedly so that they can internalize both the language and structure of the stories. They also rely rather heavily on pictures for making their way through a text. During this prereading or nonreading stage, children often need someone to read to or with them in order to successfully navigate their way through text.

> **Getting to Know English Learners**
>
> Remember, print direction may differ for certain ELs.

Stage 0. In Stage 0, children engage in a kind of pseudo-reading— the "reading" common among preschoolers who retell a familiar story with the aid of pictures, recognizing an occasional word to help them remember the events and language of the story.

Figure 5.2 Stage Model of Reading Development

Children pass through stages of reading development one at a time in order. Each stage must be completed before the child moves on to the next stage of reading development.

- *Stage 0: Children love to hear books read aloud to them again and again, enjoying the language and repetition. They can pretend read by retelling the story with the aid of the pictures in the book.*
- *Stage 1: Children start to notice letters and sounds and how these connect. When this happens they may recognize that they cannot read the print and refuse to read aloud. They first try to guess words based on meanings. Next they pay so much attention to how words look that they may not care about meaning. Eventually they become concerned with how the words look and what they mean.*
- *Stage 2: Children love to read familiar books again and again to gain fluency and confidence.*
- *Stage 3: Children want to read books to learn new information about the world.*
- *Stage 4: Children learn to read books that present more than a single point of view.*
- *Stage 5: Children learn to selectively sample print to get what they want for their own purposes. They also know what they don't want to read. They become critical readers who use print to think and reason.*

Stage 1. Once children understand that reading requires more than listening to a story read aloud repeatedly and following along with the pictures, they begin to focus their attention on the print on the page. As they do so, they come to understand that reading involves looking at and understanding how to process that print. At this point, children move into Stage 1 of reading development, which involves learning the ways in which letters and sounds connect to form words that may be spoken. Chall (1983) says that Stage 1 reading has been referred to pejoratively as a "guessing and memory game," or as "grunting and groaning," "mumbling and bumbling," or "barking at print," depending on whether the prevailing and currently popular methodology for teaching beginning reading is a sight word or a phonics approach.

As children focus intently on reading the print on the page, they will often say that they can't read and refuse for a time to try to do so. They may even retreat to old habits of guessing the words using pictures. When children begin to attend to the print on the page, they often make errors while reading that are semantically or syntactically acceptable, such as substituting the word *home* for *house.* Later on, as they focus more intently on decoding the actual print on the page, their errors shift to saying words that "look" about the same but do not mean the same, such as *horse* rather than *house.* This shift in errors signals that children are now paying greater attention to how words appear rather than focusing on what they mean. As children's reading development progresses and they can more quickly assign sounds to letters and blend these sounds together to form spoken words, they begin to return to a concern for not only how a word *looks* but also what it *means.* Chall indicates that children need to temporarily unglue from meaning in language to focus their attention on the print in order to later process print well enough (accurately, quickly, effortlessly, and expressively) or fluently to unglue from the print and return again to meaning. Chall also indicates that all children seem to move through the learning-to-read process in the same way. Better readers progress through these stages faster, and poor readers continue to make the first type of reading error—substituting or guessing the word on the basis of meaning and syntax. Chall insists that it is only when the children appear to let go of "meaning" substitutions and work instead on what words look and sound like that they make substantial progress.

Stage 2. In Stage 2, children consolidate what they have learned about reading in Stage 1—the connections between letters and sounds—by reading easy books that are familiar or well-known to gain a sense of fluency. For children of low socio-economic status (SES), Chall notes that discrepancies between good and poor readers reported in Stages 0 and 1 seem to widen at Stage 2. Chall assumes the reasons for this widening of the fluency gap to be that the parents of children in poverty cannot afford to buy books, and that their patterns of recreation and work do not include borrowing books and magazines from a public library. As a result, children of poverty lose access to needed time for reading practice in appropriately challenging texts. They also are deprived of opportunities to develop their oral language and to enjoy emotionally confirming responses that reading books with caregivers can bring.

Getting to Know English Learners
ELs may also lose time with reading books because their parents may not yet be able to read in English.

Stages 3–5. Once children can read fluently or with automaticity, Chall contends, reading development progresses on to Stage 3, during which children read for knowledge or for information, and then to Stage 4, during which children and adolescents read books that require dealing with more than one point of view. This means Stage 4 readers gradually become able to look beyond the literal meaning of text and consider content from more than a single point of view. In other words, they become critical readers, both learning from and questioning the text. In the final stage of development, Stage 5, readers are self-directed and have learned to read many genres of text. They know what not to read as well as what to read: they selectively use printed material in pursuit of areas of knowledge central to their own learning and responsibilities. They know how to skim and scan text to find information they want or need. They understand that various types of printed materials are organized differently, and they know how to make efficient use of search strategies in relation to this knowledge of text organization.

Thus, children develop reading fluency in a whole-to-parts-to-whole manner. They begin by using pictures to memorize texts that are repeatedly read aloud. This process encourages them to pay attention to the meaning of spoken language. Eventually, children understand that the story is not coming from the pictures on the page and begin to pay attention to the print. As they pay greater attention to the print, they continue to try to figure out the meaning of text using picture clues, a few known sight words, and their emerging understandings of letter, sound, and blending processes. They make meaning-related and grammatically acceptable errors as they read. As they progress, they understand that they need to learn letter names to connect these with sounds in spoken language.

The Stages of Reading in Action

In kindergarten and early first grade, children benefit from learning to decode easy words, for example, CVC or consonant-vowel-consonant words such as *fat, sit,* or *run*. Fluency in decoding and writing these simple CVC words in kindergarten leads to increased reading achievement and oral reading fluency at the end of first grade, helping children move successfully through Chall's (1983) Stage 1 reading development (Good, Simmons, & Kame'enui, 2001). In Stage 2, children need to read large amounts of text that are appropriately selected for challenge. This means that texts should support students' abilities to continuously add new words to their reading vocabularies. Most scholars currently agree that children should practice their fluency in texts that are written at the instructional level—90–94% known words—with guidance or feedback from peers, teachers, or other caregivers (Stahl, 2004). Hiebert & Fisher (2006) caution teachers to consider how many unfamiliar words are found in texts children read and the balance between sight words and decodable words as they work their way into uncontrolled texts for fluency practice. We have found that Dr. Seuss books typically present young readers with an appropriate balance of sight words to decodable words for beginning reading fluency practice (Hiebert, 2006).

Fluency involves a developmental process that looks different over time. It begins with fluent letter and sight word recognition, then moves to fluent decoding or automaticity, and then to fluent access to vocabulary and comprehension strategies (Pikulski, 2006). Fluency develops differently across text difficulty levels and genres, and teachers must not take for granted that fluent reading at one level of text difficulty or within one type of text genre indicates that fluency is fully developed for other levels of text difficulty or genres (Pikulski, 2006; Reutzel, 2006).

Finally, teachers need to know what to expect from children as they develop reading fluency. The Committee on the Prevention of Reading Difficulties in Young Children included in their report, titled *Preventing Reading Difficulties in Young Children* (Snow, Burns, & Griffin, 1998), desired "benchmarks" for kindergarten through third grade in reading and writing. Figure 5.3 presents fluency benchmark standards from their report.

Figure 5.3 Fluency Benchmark Standards*

Kindergarten: "Reads" familiar texts emergently, i.e., not necessarily verbatim from the print alone.

Grade 1: Reads aloud with accuracy any text that is appropriately designed for the first half of grade 1.

Grade 2: Accurately decodes orthographically regular multisyllable words and nonsense words. Accurately reads many irregularly spelled words and such spelling patterns as diphthongs, special vowel spellings, and common word endings.

Grade 3: Reads aloud with fluency any text that is appropriately designed for grade level.

*Criteria derived for the research by the *Committee on the Prevention of Reading Difficulties in Young Children*. Snow, C. E., Burns, M. S., & Griffin, P. (Eds.). (1998). *Preventing reading difficulties in young children*. Washington, D.C.: National Academy Press.

What Does Research Say About Fluency and Reading?

The history of fluency instruction in reading is characterized by the swinging of the pendulum of fashion (Rasinski, 2006). Prior to and during the early part of the twentieth century, oral reading ability and performance were highly valued as a cultural asset (Rasinski, 2006; Smith, 2002). But modern research disclosed that reading silently seems to hold an advantage for readers in terms of reading rate and comprehension (Huey, 1908). Moreover, the utility and superiority of silent reading seemed apparent, since most adult readers engage almost exclusively in silent reading as opposed to oral reading (Rasinski, 2003). Allington (1983) indicated that fluency instruction was often neglected in reading programs. Results of this neglect were highlighted in a large-scale study of fluency achievement in U.S. education, in which the National Assessment of Educational Progress found that "44% of fourth grade students tested were disfluent *even with grade-level stories that the student read under supportive testing conditions*" (National Reading Panel, 2000, pp. 3–1; emphasis added). Due to the analyses and findings of the National Reading Panel (2000) about effective fluency practice, the importance of oral reading practice—at least in the earliest stages of fluency development—has been called to our collective attention once again.

The National Reading Panel's (2000) meta-analysis of fluency studies showed that fluency practice is most effective when (1) the reading practice is oral; (2) when it involves repeated readings of a text (more than twice); and (3) when students receive guidance or feedback from teachers, parents, volunteers, and peers (pp. 3–11). The National Reading Panel was unable to locate sufficient evidence showing a significantly positive impact for silent reading practice on students' reading fluency acquisition. Of the 14 studies that met the National Reading Panel's selection criteria dealing with silent reading practice, only three showed any evidence of gains in reading achievement from more time spent in silent reading practice, and the size of the gains were so small as to be "of questionable educational value" (pp. 3–26). The Panel further noted that none of the 14 silent reading studies even attempted to measure the impact of increased amounts of silent reading on children's development of reading fluency. From these findings, we have concluded that younger students will likely benefit far more from oral, repeated reading practice with feedback during the early stages of reading fluency acquisition, instruction, and practice than from silent reading.

More recently, Stahl (2004) reported an investigation of the effects of FORI (fluency-oriented reading instruction) using two variations of practice: monitored, wide silent reading practice compared with oral repeated readings with feedback. He also used a control group to determine whether one form of reading practice was superior to the other in terms of fluency acquisition of second grade readers. Stahl found that repeated oral readings with feedback *and* wide silent readings with monitoring were *both* superior to the control group performance. On the other hand, the two variations—oral readings with feedback and wide silent readings with monitoring—were roughly equivalent to one another, suggesting that "the increased amount of reading and the support given during the reading are what underlie the success of the two approaches" (p. 205). This finding has been replicated in a more recent study of struggling readers by M. Kuhn (2005b).

Hasbrouck and Tindal (2006) provide a study of oral fluency reading rates that span grades 1–8. These reading rate norms adjust reading rate for accuracy using a metric called *words correct per minute (wcpm)*. Their research suggests that children ought to be able to read about 53 wcpm by the end of first grade (Hasbrouck & Tindal, 2006). Rates for other grades and ages will be discussed later in this chapter as they relate to assessing oral reading fluency.

There is precious little research available about how expression and intonation affect fluency or comprehension (Dowhower, 1991; Reutzel, 2006). Most measures of expression in the reading literature make use of informal scales (Rasinski, 2003; Zutell and Rasinski, 1991) that ask teachers to make judgments about the prosodic features of oral reading rather than more exacting prosodic measures similar to those used by speech-language pathologists.

At present, research is unclear about which levels of text to use for fluency practice and instruction. In answer to this continuing concern, Kuhn and Stahl (2000) recommend the use of instructional-level text for fluency instruction and practice in their review of fluency developmental and remedial practices. Fluency, much like reading comprehension, also needs to be developed across text types. An ability to read narrative or poetry texts fluently does not necessarily imply an ability to read information or expository texts with similar facility. These findings suggest that fluency when reading different text genres and difficulty levels is not a perfectible process—at least not in the primary grades.

Even though most research indicates that fluency practice and instruction are an essential component of high-quality reading instruction in the elementary years (Stahl, 2004), too much of a good thing can be a bad thing! In one short-term study, Anderson, Wilkinson, and Mason (1991) reported that too much attention and time spent on developing fluency, especially when the emphasis is largely focused on accuracy and rate, may detract from students' ability to comprehend text. The National Reading Panel (2000) found in its review of fluency instruction that fluency lessons ranging in length from 15 to 30 minutes showed positive effects on students' fluency development.

Finally, research on fluency has generally shown there is a strong relationship between fluency development in the early grades and children's later reading comprehension (Carpenter, Paris, & Hamilton, 2005). Recent studies show, however, that this relationship between fluency and comprehension is transitory, diminishing over time. Some educators believe that fluency is the key that unlocks the door to comprehension. But this is only partially true. Fluency may *unlock* the door, but it does not *open* the door to reading comprehension. Rather, it is best to think of fluency as necessary but insufficient for children to comprehend what they read. To comprehend, children must be more than fluent. They must learn how to select and use a variety of cognitive strategies to help them understand text (Pressley, 2000; 2006).

How Is Reading Fluency Assessed?

Assessing fluency is the first step in understanding and planning effective fluency instruction. With a wide variety of fluent reading levels within classrooms and across grade levels, it is highly unlikely that a single approach to fluency instruction will address the diverse needs of all children. To begin fluency assessment, we focus on children's ability to read high-frequency sight words.

Assessing Sight Word Fluency

We suggest beginning sight word fluency assessment with the Thorndike-Lorge Magazine Count list of 25 high-frequency words shown in Table 5.1. This tool is typically used with kindergarten children. Neatly print each of the 25 words onto individual cards using white card stock and black block printing or computer-produced print. Shuffle the deck of 25 sight word cards to randomize the order. Next, invite a student to be seated next to you. Explain that you would like to find out which words the child knows by sight. Begin by showing the child the first card in the deck and continue until all 25 randomly presented words from the list are shown to the child.

Progress monitoring of early readers' accurate and fast recognition of these 25 highly frequent words should occur at least monthly in the second half of kindergarten and early half of first grade. By the end of kindergarten or early first grade, children should be able to accurately and quickly recognize all 25 sight words.

Table 5.1   The Thorndike-Lorge Magazine Count

	Word	Frequency of Use	Cumulative % of Use
1	the	263,472	.0515
2	and	138,672	.0817
3	a	117,222	.1072
4	to	115,358	.1323
5	of	112,601	.1568
6	I	89,489	.1763
7	in	75,253	.1926
8	was	58,732	.2055
9	that	55,667	.2176
10	it	52,107	.2290
11	he	49,268	.2397
12	you	42,581	.2490
13	for	39,363	.2576
14	had	34,341	.2651
15	is	33,404	.2723
16	with	32,903	.2795
17	her	31,824	.2884
18	she	31,087	.2932
19	his	30,748	.2999
20	as	30,693	.3066
21	on	30,244	.3132
22	at	26,250	.3189
23	have	24,456	.3242
24	but	23,704	.2392
25	me	23,364	.3345
	Sum = 1,535,783		
	Total Number of Words = 4,591,125		

Reprinted by permission of Teachers College Press from *Teacher's word book of 30,000 words.*

To expand the assessment of early readers' sight words into the first and second grade levels, we suggest using the 107 High-Frequency Word List by Zeno, Ivens, Millard, and Duvvuri (1995), shown in Table 5.2.

Neatly print each of the 107 words onto individual cards using white card stock and black block printing or computer-produced print. Shuffle the deck of 107 sight word cards to randomize the order. Next, invite a student to be seated next to you. Explain that you would like to find out which words the child knows by sight. Begin by showing the child the first card in the deck and continue until 25 randomly presented words from the list of 107 are shown to the child.

Progress monitoring of early readers' accurate and fast recognition of these 107 highly frequent words should occur at least monthly in the second half of first grade and into second grade. By the end of second grade, children should be able to accurately and quickly recognize all 107 sight words.

If children have difficulty recognizing the sight words in the instruments we have presented here, they can be assisted in commiting the words to memory through the use of instructional strategies presented later in this chapter.

Assessing Oral Reading Fluency

Assessing oral reading fluency has for many years focused somewhat exclusively on how quickly students could read a given text. This is known as **reading rate** or **reading speed.** More recently, reading teachers have used **words correct per minute** (wcpm) to indicate reading rate. Although wcpm is one indicator of fluent oral reading, it is *only*

Table 5.2 The 107 Most Frequently Used Words in Written English (Zeno et al., 1995)

the	at	we	many	first	know
of	or	what	these	new	little
and	from	about	no	very	such
to	had	up	time	my	even
a	I	said	been	also	much
in	not	out	who	down	our
is	have	if	like	make	must
that	this	some	could	now	
it	but	would	has	way	
was	by	so	him	each	
for	were	people	how	called	
you	one	them	than	did	
he	all	other	two	just	
on	she	more	may	after	
as	when	will	only	water	
are	an	into	most	through	
they	their	your	its	get	
with	there	which	made	because	
be	her	do	over	back	
his	can	then	see	where	

Excerpt from "The 107 most frequently used words in wrtitten English" from Zeno, S. M., Ivens, S. H., Millard, R. T., & Duvvuri, R. (1995). *The educator's word frequency guide.* New York: Touchstone Applied Science Associates, Inc. Used with permission.

one. To adequately assess fluency, teachers should consider at least four different components: (1) accurate decoding of text; (2) reading rate or speed; (3) use of volume, stress, pitch, and juncture (prosodic markers); and (4) mature phrasing or "chunking" of text.

Teachers have in recent years begun to discuss how they might more efficiently and authentically assess the ability to read fluently (Kuhn & Stahl, 2000). Most teachers believe that paper and pencil assessment tools such as standardized reading tests are inadequate or at least incomplete measures of reading fluency. Another significant issue for many teachers today is accessing valid and reliable estimates of reading rates appropriate for children of differing ages and grades.

One of the simplest and most useful means of collecting fluency data is the **one-minute reading sample** (Rasinski, 2003). A one-minute reading sample is typical of that used in the Oral Reading Fluency (ORF) test drawn from the *Dynamic Indicators of Basic Early Literacy Skills* (DIBELS) battery (Good & Kaminski, 2002).

To take a one-minute reading sample, teachers need a grade-level text of between 200 and 300 words, a one-minute cooking timer with an alarm sounding at zero or a stop watch, and a pencil for marking the text. Children are asked to read aloud a grade-level passage for one minute. Words omitted, substituted, or hesitations of more than three seconds are scored as errors. Words self-corrected within three seconds are scored as accurate. After one minute, the student stops reading. The teacher subtracts the total number of errors from the number of words read by the student to obtain a score of words correct per minute (wcpm). This number constitutes the student's reading rate. Using more than one passage to assess fluency rates helps to control for any text-based or genre-type differences or variations. However, if standardized passages are used, such as those from published sources of CBM materials (e.g., *DIBELS, Reading Fluency Monitor, AimsWEB*), a score from a single passage is considered valid (Hintze & Christ, 2004). The final wcpm score can then be compared to the ORF norms (see Table 5.3) for making screening, diagnostic, or progress-monitoring decisions. By using words correct per minute (wcpm), reading rate is corrected for the accuracy of the reading. The new ORF norms align closely with those published in 1992, and also closely match the widely used DIBELS norms for fall, winter, and spring.

If you want to use the DIBELS oral reading fluency test to augment one-minute fluency samples you take during the year, the full directions for using the ORF measurement can be obtained by going to the DIBELS Web site at *http://dibels.uoregon.edu/,* registering as a user, and downloading grade-level passages and administration and scoring procedures.

Assessing Expressive Reading

As we mentioned earlier in this chapter, reading fluency is not just described or defined as accurate reading at an age-appropriate rate. It also includes reading that is appropriately expressive. To augment one-minute reading sample measurement of accuracy and rate, Rasinski (2003) provides a practical measurement of students' oral reading fluency, the *Multidimensional Fluency Scale* (see Figure 5.4). This rating tool provides more extensive and reliable information about four components of fluent reading: (a) volume and expression, (b) phrasing, (c) smoothness, and (d) pace. Rasinski's (2003) recent revision of the original Zutell and Rasinski's (1991)

Table 5.3 Grades 1–8 Oral Reading Fluency Norms*

Grade	Percentile	Fall WCPM	Winter WCPM	Spring WCPM
1	90	XX	81	111
	75	XX	47	82
	50	XX	23	56
	25	XX	12	28
	10	XX	6	15
2	90	106	125	142
	75	79	100	117
	50	51	72	89
	25	25	42	61
	10	11	18	31
3	90	128	146	162
	75	99	120	137
	50	71	92	107
	25	44	62	78
	10	21	36	48
4	90	145	166	180
	75	119	139	152
	50	94	112	123
	25	68	87	98
	10	45	61	72
5	90	166	182	194
	75	139	156	168
	50	110	127	139
	25	85	99	109
	10	61	74	83
6	90	177	195	204
	75	153	167	177
	50	127	140	150
	25	98	111	122
	10	68	82	93
7	90	180	192	202
	75	156	165	177
	50	128	136	150
	25	102	109	123
	10	79	88	98
8	90	185	199	199
	75	161	173	177
	50	133	146	151
	25	106	115	124
	10	77	84	97

*Compiled by Jan Hasbrouck, Ph.D. & Gerald Tindal, Ph.D. (2006). Oral reading fluency norms: A valuable assessment tool for reading teachers. *The Reading Teacher, 59(7)*, 636–645.
Count 5546 3496 5335
WCPM: Words correct per minute
TABLE SUMMARIZED FROM: Behavioral Research & Teaching (2005, January). Oral Reading Fluency: 90 Years of Assessment (BRT Technical Report No. 33), Eugene, OR: Author.
Data available at: *http://brt.uoregon.edu/*TECHNICAL REPORTS
Table available at: *www.jhasbrouck.com/*Q&A: Fluency

Figure 5.4 Multidimensional Fluency Scale

Use the following scale to rate reader fluency on the five dimensions of accuracy, expression and volume, phrasing, smoothness, and pace.

A. Accuracy

1. Word recognition accuracy is poor, generally below 85%. Reader clearly struggles in decoding words. Makes multiple decoding attempts for many words, usually without success.
2. Word recognition accuracy is marginal: 86–90%. Reader struggles with many words. Many unsuccessful attempts at self-correction.
3. Word recognition accuracy is good: 91–95%. Reader self-corrects successfully.
4. Word recognition accuracy is excellent: 96%–100%. Self-corrections are few but successful, as nearly all words are read correctly on initial attempt.

B. Expression and Volume

1. Student reads with little expression or enthusiasm. Reads words as if simply to get them out. Little sense of trying to make text sound like natural language. Tends to read in a quiet voice.
2. Student reads with some expression. Begins to use voice to make text sound like natural language in some areas of the text, but not others. Focus remains largely on saying the words. Still reads in a voice that is quiet.
3. Student's reading sounds like natural language throughout the better part of the passage. Occasionally slips into expressionless reading. Voice volume is generally appropriate throughout the text.
4. Student reads with good expression and enthusiasm throughout the text. Sounds like natural language. Reader is able to vary expression and volume to match his/her interpretation of the passage.

C. Phrasing

1. Monotonic with little sense of phrase boundaries; frequent word-by-word reading.
2. Student uses frequent two- and three-word phrases, giving the impression of choppy reading; improper stress and intonation that fails to mark ends of sentences and clauses.
3. Student reads in mixture of run-ons, with mid-sentence pauses for breath and possibly some choppiness; reasonable stress/intonation.
4. Reading is generally well-phrased, mostly in clause and sentence units, with adequate attention to expression.

D. Smoothness

1. Student reads with frequent extended pauses, hesitations, false starts, sound-outs, repetitions, and/or multiple attempts.
2. Student experiences several "rough spots" in text, where extended pauses, hesitations, etc., are more frequent and disruptive.
3. Reader experiences occasional breaks in smoothness caused by difficulties with specific words and/or structures.
4. Generally smooth reading with some breaks, but word and structure difficulties are resolved quickly, usually through self-correction.

E. Pace (during sections of minimal disruption)

1. Slow and laborious.
2. Moderately slow.
3. Uneven mixture of fast and slow reading.
4. Consistently conversational.

Multidimensional Fluency Scale (MFS) adds assessment of reading volume and expression. Zutell and Rasinski (1991) report a .99 test-retest reliability coefficient for the original MFS.

To use the *Multidimensional Fluency Scale,* teachers take a one-minute reading sample as previously described and fill in the required ratings using a paper copy of the MFS. The MFS can also be used to rate group performances such as plays, readers' theater, and radio readings (Reutzel & Cooter, 2004).

What Are the Characteristics of Effective Fluency Instruction?

In this section we provide seven characteristics of effective fluency instruction and practice drawn from evidence-based research.

1. *Explicit Instruction.* Hoffman (2003) asserts that teachers should "Work to develop the meta-language of fluency with . . . students, which includes concepts of expression, word stress, and phrasing" (p. 6). Young readers need to know that fluency is an important goal of their reading instruction. They need to know what fluency is. They need to know the academic language or terms used by teachers and researchers to describe fluency, so that they, too, can think and talk specifically about fluency as a concept and skill with their peers and their teachers. They also need the language of fluency to be able to examine and regulate their own reading fluency as an independent reader. Students must develop an awareness of the various elements of fluency in order to monitor them, fix them, and improve their fluency. Students must know how to use fluency fix-up strategies and understand the varying purposes of fluency in order to self-regulate and improve it. As classroom teachers, we must not only facilitate reading fluency practice but also cultivate a deeper appreciation among students of the importance of fluency as a personal goal of reading improvement. Equally important, we need to develop students' understanding of what we mean when we say that reading is fluent so that they can go about fixing fluency up when it isn't going along as it should (Rasinski, Blachowizc, & Lems, 2006; Reutzel, 2006; Worthy & Broadus, 2002).

Getting to Know English Learners
Modeling oral reading to ELs may be especially helpful if their parents do not yet read English. Assigning a capable reading buddy in the classroom may help alleviate this problem.

2. *Modeling.* Exposure to rich and varied models of fluent oral reading helps *some* children. For other students, modeling of nonfluent oral reading seems to alert attention to the specific characteristics of fluent reading that are sometimes transparent or taken for granted when teachers only model fluent oral reading. In other words, some students need to know what fluency *is* and *is not* to achieve clarity on the concept of fluency and its attendant characteristics (Reutzel, 2006). In this case, parents, teachers, or siblings spend significant amounts of time reading aloud to children while modeling fluent oral reading. Through this process of modeling fluent (and sometimes nonfluent) oral reading, children learn the behaviors of fluent readers as well as the elements of fluent oral reading. Many researchers have documented the significant impact of modeling on the acquisition of fluency in reading (Rasinski, 2003; Rasinski, et al., 2006; Reutzel, 2006; Stahl, 2004).

3. *Reading Practice.* Good readers are given more opportunities to read connected text for longer periods of time than are students having reading problems. This dilemma led Allington (1977) to ask, "If they don't read much, how are they ever gonna get good?" The National Reading Panel (2000) has emphasized the need for children to experience regular, daily reading practice.

4. *Access to Appropriately Challenging Reading Materials.* Proficient readers spend more time reading appropriately challenging texts than students having reading problems (Gambrell et al., 1981). Reading appropriately challenging books with instruction and feedback may help proficient readers make the transition from word-by-word reading to fluent reading, whereas poorer readers often spend more time in reading materials that are relatively difficult. Doing so denies those students who are having reading problems access to reading materials that could help them develop fluent reading skills. For the most part, children need to be reading in instructional level texts with instruction, modeling, support, monitoring, and feedback (Bryan, Fawson, & Reutzel, 2003; Kuhn, 2005a; Kuhn & Schwanenflugel, 2006; Kuhn & Stahl, 2000; Rasinski & Hoffman, 2006; Stahl, 2004). Menon and Hiebert (2005) and Hiebert and Fisher (2006) found that texts for supporting early readers' fluency development need to be controlled to contain fewer unfamiliar words than is typical in many beginning reading texts as well as a balance between high-frequency words and decodable words. When children read in such texts, they made weekly gains of over 3.4 words correct per minute! Carefully selected texts, in a very real way, are the scaffolding teachers use to support students' reading fluency practice (Brown, 1999). Teachers need to increase the volume of students' reading in appropriately designed, controlled reading texts in the early stages of fluency development (Hiebert & Fisher, 2006).

5. *Use of Oral and Silent Reading.* The *Report of the National Reading Panel* (2000) indicated there was ample scientific evidence to support reading practice for fluency that included the following elements: (a) oral reading, (b) repeated reading of the same text, and (c) feedback and guidance during and after reading of a text. On the other hand, silent reading of self-chosen books without monitoring or feedback did not have substantial scientific evidence to support its exclusive use for reading practice across elementary grades. Recent experimental research suggests that silent, wide reading (across genre or text types) with monitoring seems to produce equivalent or better fluency gains in second and third grade students as compared to oral repeated readings (Kuhn & Schwanenflugel, 2006; Pikulski & Chard, 2005; Reutzel, Fawson, & Smith, 2006 in preparation; Stahl, 2004). There is mounting evidence that the old practice of SSR where the teacher read as a model for children is giving way to a new model of silent reading practice that incorporates book selection instruction, student monitoring and accountability, and reading widely (Bryan, Fawson, & Reutzel, 2003; Kuhn, 2005b; Marzano, 2004; McKenna & Stahl, 2006; Reutzel, Smith, & Fawson, in preparation; Stahl, 2004).

6. *Monitoring and Accountability.* For many years, teachers believed that their sitting and reading a book silently provided modeling sufficient to promote students' desires and abilities to read. This has never been proven to be the case. In recent years, Bryan, Fawson, and Reutzel (2003) have reported that monitoring disengaged readers with quick, stop-in visits to listen to oral reading and discuss a piece of literature during silent reading has a beneficial effect on their engagement during silent reading. Furthermore, having children account for their fluency practice time by reading onto a tape or for a teacher has a positive impact upon fluency engagement and growth (Reutzel, 2006; Reutzel, Smith, & Fawson, in preparation; Stahl, 2004).

7. *Wide and Repeated Reading.* There is considerable evidence that repeated readings of the same text leads to automaticity—fast, accurate, and effortless word recognition (Dowhower, 1991; NRP, 2000). However, once automaticity is achieved, reading widely seems to provide the necessary ingredient to move students' fluency from automaticity to comprehension. Thus, it is important that when a student achieves grade-level automaticity, he or she be encouraged to read widely as well as repeatedly to develop connected text comprehension (Kuhn, 2005a; Kuhn & Schwanenflugel, 2006; Pikulski & Chard, 2005; Reutzel, 2006; Stahl, 2004). From the currently available evidence, this occurs in second or third grade for some children while others may need to continue to read texts repeatedly until they achieve automaticity at grade level into the intermediate years.

An awareness of the seven characteristics of effective fluency instruction and practice can help you, the teacher, create optimal conditions for students to become fluent readers.

Fluency Begins Early

Even though an emphasis on reading fluency is recommended to begin midyear in the first grade, recognizing a few common words by sight is also an important part of early reading development (Burns, Griffin, & Snow, 1999). Young children should be taught to recognize several common, high-frequency words (known as **sight words**) instantaneously and without phonic analysis. Many years ago, Thorndike and Lorge (1944), researchers at Columbia University, reported a study in which they counted the frequency of words found in a 4.5 million-word sample drawn from popularly published U.S. magazines. At the conclusion of this study, these researchers found that a corpus of only 25 words accounted for 1.5 million of the total 4.5 million words in these magazines (see Table 5.1). In fact, three words in this list accounted for nearly 11 percent of frequency of words in the sample; these words were *a, and,* and *the,* with the word *the* accounting for nearly 5 percent of all words in the sample. Years later, Zeno, Ivens, Millard, and Duvvuri (1995) found that a corpus of 107 words accounted for 50 percent of all words typically found in printed materials read by U.S. adults (see Table 5.2).

These studies show that with a relative few words known by sight—somewhere between 25 and 107—young children can fluently recognize approximately 33 to 50 percent of the words they will be likely to encounter in commonplace adult reading materials. Thus it seems reasonable for teachers to focus significant and early attention on helping young children acquire the ability to automatically identify a small corpus of common, high-frequency words by sight in the future service of reading fluency.

What Are Effective Fluency Teaching Strategies?

Careful planning is always crucial for successful teaching. In fluency instruction, as with most other reading skill areas, the teacher must choose a "balanced diet" of reading materials for practice exercises (i.e., stories, nonfiction materials, poetry), and provide explicit, teacher-led instruction, modeling, guided student practice, practice with peers, and independent practice. An effective model for organizing fluency instruction that includes these elements was developed for Title I reading teachers in Kansas

Figure 5.5   The Fluency Formula

The Fluency Formula

A Blueprint for Improving Accuracy, Rate, Expression, and Phrasing

---

Planning for Instruction

A. Identify instructional standards (objectives).
B. List necessary supplies and check-off selection of passage.
C. Introduce passages for modeling and practice (fluency pyramid).
D. Develop explicit fluency instructional plans.

Step I: Explicit Fluency Instruction and Modeling

A. Explain the specific fluency instructional objective—targeted fluency skill.
   • Explain *what* is to be learned about fluency—accuracy, rate, expression, or phrasing.
   • Explain *why* learning this information is important.
   • Explain *when* and *where* this information will be useful.
B. Introduce the passage and concepts.
   • Teach high-frequency sight words.
   • Introduce vocabulary.
   • Introduce the fluency skill to be learned.
C. Model the targeted fluency skill.

Step II: Guided Oral Reading Practice

A. Guided oral reading strategies: teacher with students
   • Choral reading
B. Peer-supported practice: *students helping students*
   • Partner or "buddy" reading
   • Neurological impress method (NIM)

Step III: Independent Practice Reading

   • Assisted repeated oral readings
   • Scaffolded Silent Reading (ScSR)

Step IV: Performance Reading for Fluency Practice

   • Readers' theatre
   • Radio reading
   • Recitation

Step V: Goal Setting and Monitoring Student Progress

   • Fluency assessment rubric
   • Tracking fluency progress
   • Goal setting

(R. Cooter & K. Cooter, 2002) called **the Fluency Formula** (summarized in Figure 5.5). A sample lesson plan for teaching children about phrasing in fluency is shown in Figure 5.6. In the description that follows, you will see that evidence-based elements of effective fluency instruction have been included.

Implementing the Fluency Instructional Plan

An effective teacher always maps out her lesson plan well before implementing it. Lesson planning always begins with the decision about an appropriate objective. Objectives for fluency instruction, as with anything else in any curriculum, should be drawn from three sources:

1. a careful review of grade-level expectations and state standards,
2. an assessment of each child's needs and abilities relative to the standards, and
3. a collation of all students' needs into a classroom profile to better understand more universal group needs.

Identifying Standards for Fluency Instruction. Standards for fluency have been developed by most states for each grade level, as well as by the U.S. Department of Education. In Chapter 9, "Assessment," we discuss ways of developing both individual and group objectives from assessment data. Fluency standards almost invariably pertain to one of three principal areas: accuracy, rate, or expression. These three areas are described later in the description of Stage 1 of the Fluency Formula.

Selecting Reading Materials: Varying Literary Genre. Once you have selected a fluency objective, reading materials should be selected for (1) reading aloud (modeling), and (2) for instruction (guided oral reading). Your primary goal in the first part of fluency instruction should be to *model* fluent reading behavior. As the teacher, you are—theoretically—the *best* reader in the room and your young charges want to see and hear what fluent reading behavior is like. Because you will have a wide range of reading ability represented in your class, you will want to think about modeling for students in two venues: whole class and small groups based on reading level (i.e., guided reading groups).

For whole group modeling, remember the "balanced diet" idea mentioned earlier: *model fluent reading using a variety of genres in children's literature.* Here's what we mean: Think of the balanced reading diet at each grade level as you would the famous food pyramid. At the bottom of the **fluency pyramid** we place the ever-popular narrative selections or stories. Some of your oral reading to the class for fluency modeling and practice should come from high quality children's stories and books. At the center of the fluency pyramid are interesting nonfiction books that not only provide a medium for modeling and practicing fluency, but also help children develop an understanding of new concepts and vocabulary. Notice that nonfiction text examples are almost equal in proportion to narrative texts. At the top of the pyramid, less frequent in comparison to the first two types, is some extra spice for children's fluency diet: songs, poetry, chants, and raps. Figure 5.7 shows a fluency pyramid scheme for passage selection in the elementary grades.

Selecting Appropriately Challenging Reading Materials. Passages *only* read aloud by the teacher during modeling can be at reading levels well above the abilities of the listeners. In these cases, the teacher is

Getting to Know English Learners
It is important to read aloud to ELs, regardless of reading level, so that they can hear the rhythm of the English language as their brains actively process the new language.

Figure 5.6 Sample Lesson Plan: The Fluency Formula

Instructional Standard or Objective: *Children will pay attention to punctuation to help them read expressively.*

Materials

- Book—*In a Tree*, pp. 18–19
- Overhead transparency
- Overhead projector
- Fluency phones
- Three colored overhead markers
- Text types: Narrative ( ) Information Books (x) Poetry ( )

Explain

- **What**

Today, boys and girls, we are going to be learning about how to read expressively. Important parts of reading expressively are pausing, stopping, and raising or lowering our pitch as we read. Pitch is how high or low the sounds are that we make with our voices. *(Demonstrate high and low pitch.)* "Stopping" means we quit reading for a moment, like this. *(Demonstrate.)* "Pausing" means we take a breath and keep reading. Marks on the page called *punctuation marks (point)* help us to know when we need to pause, stop, or raise or lower our pitch.

- **Why**

We need to read expressively with pauses or stops so that we can show that we understand what we are reading. Punctuation tells us what we need to know about how to express the words, phrases, and sentences with the right pauses, stops, and pitch.

- **When/Where**

Whenever we read, we should pay attention to the punctuation so that we know where to pause, stop, and raise or lower our pitch.

Teacher Modeling

- **Example**

I am going to begin by reading this page with good expression, paying attention to what the punctuation tells me to do, such as pause, stop, or raise or lower my pitch. Please look at the page on the overhead. Notice that I have colored each punctuation mark with a different color to help you see it more clearly. Follow what I read with your eyes. Listen very carefully to see if I stop, pause, or change my pitch where I should.

- **Non-example**

Now I am going to read this page with poor expression, paying little or no attention to what the punctuation tells me to do. I won't pause, stop, or raise or lower my pitch. Please look at the page on the overhead. Notice that I have colored each punctuation mark with a different color to help you see it more clearly. Follow what I read with your eyes. Listen very carefully to see where I should have changed my reading to stop, pause, or raise or lower my pitch.

Guided Oral Reading Practice: Teacher and Students; Students with Students

Teacher and Students

Now that I have shown you how and how not to read this page, let's practice it together! We will begin reading this page all together. *(Point.)* Watch my pen so that we can all stay together.

Figure 5.6 (Continued)

Next, we will read this again using echo reading. How many of you have ever heard an echo? If I say, "Hello," the echo will say, "Hello." Now I will read and you will echo me. Let's begin.

Students with Students

Turn to your neighbor. One person will read and the other will echo.

Independent Practice

Take your fluency phone (PVC pipe shaped into a phone as shown in photo) and read this again to yourself, listening carefully to see where you are stopping, pausing, or raising or lowering your pitch.

Take your fluency phone and read this again to yourself, listening carefully to see where you are stopping, pausing, or raising or lowering your pitch.

Ray Reutzel

Performance

Today we will perform our fluency readings by standing and reading the passage aloud in unison in pairs. We will number off into pairs. Get with your partners and prepare to read this aloud for the class. I will roll two or three dice to see which pair is picked to read aloud. After reading, we will ask each pair to use the fluency assessment rubric and evaluate their performance.

Assess

• Rubric for assessment
• Set personal goals
• Graph progress

Reflect

• What went well?
• How would you change the lesson?

simply demonstrating how a passage can be read with proper intonation and rate. When selected for children to read themselves, either with the teacher or with another student, passages should conform to the following guidelines.

• *Use selections within the decoding range of the learner—95 percent or better accuracy.* A good rule of thumb to remember is that the range of readers in a classroom

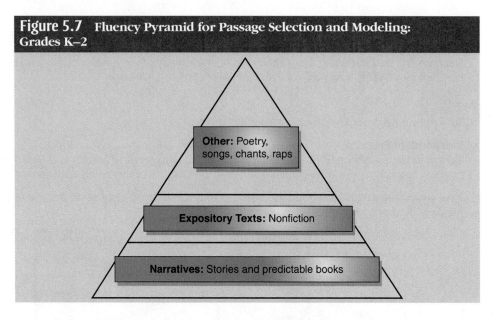

Figure 5.7 Fluency Pyramid for Passage Selection and Modeling: Grades K–2

Other: Poetry, songs, chants, raps

Expository Texts: Nonfiction

Narratives: Stories and predictable books

is usually equal to plus or minus the grade level designation. For example, in second grade classrooms there can be a range of readers from a pre-primer level to fourth grade. In a fourth grade classroom there can be struggling readers at emergent or first grade levels, as well as students reading at an eighth grade level.

• *Text type and your objective should be a good match.* The objective of your lesson, depending on the needs of your students, should fall within the domain of accuracy, rate, or expression. If your purpose is to practice accuracy of decoding, then you may want to choose what is called **decodable text.** Decodable texts are usually short books that use common spelling patterns, or **orthography.** If, on the other hand, your objective is to help readers adjust their reading speeds according to their purpose or type of text, then you may want to choose a variety of text samples for demonstration and practice sessions, such as stories, mathematics word problems, history readings, and poetry.

• *Limit the number of unfamiliar words.* Words that are new to students should appear in the passage rarely—about 1 in 150 words—for children to have a high probability of learning to read these words (Hiebert, 2006).

• *Target oral reading rates.* Identify these rates using grade level, time of year, and 50th percentile performance as desirable goals (see Table 5.3).

• *Practice with a variety of text genres.* A variety of literary genres should be used in balanced proportions (see the Fluency Pyramid in Figure 5.).

Developing an Explicit Lesson Plan. Once you have completed the above tasks, begin lesson planning. Using the sample lesson plan in Figure 5.6 as a template, you will be able to map out in some detail the flow of explicit fluency instruction to offer. It is important that new teachers work through this process so that instruction is presented in a seamless and explicit way. Scaffold instruction to help students work through their individual zones of proximal development, and use verbal instructions and explanations to help them make sense of fluency concepts so that nothing important is omitted. Even veteran teachers

Getting to Know English Learners
"i + l" is the equivalent to scaffolding in EL instruction. Originally coined by Stephen Krashen, "i + l" directs teachers to target instruction a level above "input."

who are new to fluency instruction should fully complete the explicit fluency instruction lesson template, since they are very often "first-time" teachers in the reading skill area of fluency. Once you get your "sea legs" with this model, lesson planning can become less detailed in terms of language, but the steps given should always be followed to ensure comprehensive instructional coverage of fluency elements and practice.

Each of the remaining parts of the lesson plan is briefly described in the sections that follow.

Lesson Part I: Passage Introduction and Sight Word Instruction

The Fluency Formula (R. Cooter & K. Cooter, 2002) begins in earnest with your introducing the selection to be read, much as you might for a book talk. Start by showing the book jacket and telling about the author. Explain why you chose this selection. Children should feel excited about hearing the selection.

Teach High-Frequency Sight Words. Words can be fluently recognized in one of two ways (Sadoski & Pavio, 2004). First, words can be recognized as wholes without analysis of the parts—this is called **logographic reading.** Second, words can be recognized through recoding each letter into a sound, holding the sounds in sequence in short-term memory, and then blending the sequenced sounds together. This is referred to as **phonological recoding.** Regardless of the way words are initially recognized, for mature readers, most words have become sight words through repetitive exposure (practice) and attention to visual (logographic) and/or letter-sound (phonological recoding) details.

When young children begin to read, they often try to memorize words as wholes to avoid the difficult task of learning letter–sound relationships and using these relationships to analyze unknown words. This is often characterized as an immature and inefficient way for children to learn to read (Chall, 1983). There is, however, a group of words that occur so frequently in written language that it is better if children are helped to remember these words logographically, or as wholes, without resorting to repetitive letter–sound analysis. These words, called *high-frequency words* or *sight words*, are words that teachers should help children recognize instantaneously.

Snow, Burns, and Griffin (1998) and Burns, Griffin, and Snow (1999) recommend that early reading instruction include the learning of sight words. How can teachers help young children learn a corpus of high-frequency words by sight? One of the most popular and pervasive practices in today's elementary classrooms for teaching sight words is the use of a **word wall.**

A word wall is a large visual display, usually posted on a wall of the classroom, featuring high-frequency words. Many teachers struggle with deciding how many high-frequency words should be displayed. We recommend that kindergarten children fluently recognize a core of up to 25 of the most-frequently occurring sight words as featured in the Thorndike-Lorge high-frequency word list shown in Table 5.1. We further recommend that first and second grade students fluently recognize a core of 107 high-frequency words as shown in the Zeno et al. (1995) word list contained in Table 5.2.

Word walls are usually organized in alphabetical order. High-frequency words are typically displayed underneath an alphabet letter category in the order in which they were introduced or taught. Some word walls use colored ink to help children distinguish one sight word from another. Still other word walls make use of word shapes to help children remember high-frequency words. These three practices,

Chunk cards are used to divide stories into meaningful phrases. Learn how to incorporate text phrasing into fluency instruction. Reference the *Reading Methods* link in the Teacher Prep Website (*www.prenhall.com/teacherprep*) and select the article titled "Language Experience Approach."

while intuitively appealing, often conflict with the goal of helping children learn high-frequency words by sight. Displaying words underneath a particular letter is not the problem; rather, leaving the words in fixed order for long periods of time may cause children to use order cues rather than careful examination of the word to remember it. For example, a child might remember the word *the* because it is the fourth word in the list under the letter T. We strongly recommend that the order of sight words within each alphabetical category be regularly altered so that a word's position does not replace looking at it to identify it.

We also caution teachers against the use of color cues for displaying sight words on the word wall. Young children often learn colors long before they recognize words. Here again, a kindergarten child may remember the word *the* as the "green" word on the word wall, memorizing its color rather than the word itself.

Finally, we recommend that teachers not use word shapes or configuration when displaying sight words. Research has shown that configuration is one of the least reliable and least relied-upon cues for recognizing high-frequency words among those available to children (Harris & Sipay, 1990). Imagine, for a moment, that a kindergarten child is viewing a word wall that displays the words in the same order all year, using different colored ink and the configuration (shape) of words. It is highly probable that such a child might know the word *the* because it is the fourth word under the letter T, it is green, and it has one hump at the beginning of the word. Instead, we recommend that teachers use light or white card stock cut in standard rectangular size, standard black ink, and familiar print styles when making a word wall. Of course, a word wall should be in a location that can be clearly seen by teacher and children from all angles. Print size should also be large enough to meet the same test.

We have also found that the effectiveness of a word wall is not found in *having* it, but rather in *using* it in daily reading and writing instruction and practice. As young children learn to recognize basic sight words, they benefit from three interrelated processes in remembering these words: recognition, searching, and writing. Each of the three should be used in conjunction with the others.

Recognition involves visually distinguishing one sight word from others. This is accomplished by simple, game-like practices using word wall words, such as matching pairs. Make two copies of the 25 sight words (50 total cards) in kindergarten or 107 (214 total cards) in first and second grades. Shuffle the deck of sight word cards. Lay them out on a table top in five rows of five (or ten rows of eleven). The first player turns over two cards and reads each sight word exposed. If the two cards match, the player takes the cards and gets another turn. If they do not match, the player must put them back face down in exactly the same place, and the next player gets a turn. Play continues until all card pairs have been matched. Students can review the words after the game.

Searching for sight words is another process that may be used to aid retention. Look for sight words in easy books or other printed text like magazine or newspaper pages. Use highlighter tape or highlighter pens, or place a clear overhead transparency over the pages of the text selected. Give students one to three sight words to search for and a specific time frame (such as three minutes) to circle or cover with tape as many of those sight words as they can. Using a transparency and an overhead marker does not damage the book or text; the transparency can be cleaned repeatedly and used with other books or texts.

Writing sight words from teacher dictation leaves a more permanent "cognitive footprint" than do recognition or searching tasks. Children can be directed to quickly and accurately write the words dictated in a Beat-the-Clock format. This game requires that children have paper and pencil or, better yet, a gel board or white board and dry erase marker for writing. Set a timer for three minutes. Start by saying, "Go! Write the sight word *the*." Count ten seconds and say, "Write the sight word *me*." Proceed until three minutes have elapsed. Then ask children to show you their sight word dictation. Make quick notes about each student's performance on the dictation task. Then say, "Let's see if we can beat the clock." This time, only count to nine between each sight word dictated. This slightly faster pace challenges children to write their sight words as dictated more quickly, yet legibly and accurately. Using a simple graph for each child can also be used to help them beat their own best time.

Other questions related to the teaching of sight words relate to the pacing of sight word instruction and sight word review. We recommend teaching a new sight word each day in kindergarten and three sight words per day in first and second grade. Reviews of sight words already taught should occur using the "law of 10-20" recently researched by H. Pashler (2006). Sight word review cycles should take place between 10 and 20 percent of the time to be remembered. Hence six months is 183 days. The law of 10-20 suggests that a complete review of 25 kindergarten sight words should occur between every 18–36 days. Thus sight words, like other memory tasks, are best learned through distributed practice and review rather than from massed practice. Rather than teaching one to two sight words a week, these sight words should be taught quickly over time with spaced reviews. For example, the 25 sight words taught in kindergarten would take 5 weeks at one word per day, with seven review cycles occurring during the year. In first grade, the remaining 82 (of the 107) taught 3 per day would allow for seven review cycles during the school year in 1–2 grades.

Some children will struggle to remember specific sight words. If this is the case, we recommend using Cunningham's (1980) "drastic strategy." Although this strategy was intended to be used for teaching hard-to-remember "four-letter" function words, glue words, or structure words that do not have concrete meanings, the strategy is easily adapted for helping young children remember difficult-to-learn, high-frequency sight words.

You will need word cards, envelopes, markers, scissors, and classroom chalk or dry erase boards. Although the "drastic strategy" uses a six-step process, not all steps are always necessary. Carefully observe the progress of children to determine at which step the strategy has produced the desired memory for sight word learning. The six steps follow:

Step 1: Teacher Storytelling
Select a sight word and enlarge it on a card for each child in the class or group. Tell a story in which the displayed word—*the*—is used. Before you begin your story, tell students that they are to hold up their cards each time they hear the targeted word in your story. As you tell the story, pause briefly at those points where the word is used to "emphasize" it.

Step 2: Child Storytelling
Invite volunteers to tell a story in which the sight word displayed on the card is used. Tell students that both you and they will hold up the card containing the targeted sight word as it is used in the volunteer's story. Be an active listener and model for your students during this step.

Step 3: Scramble, Sort, and Find
Cut the targeted sight word into letters and scramble these letters on the student's table or desktop. The student's task is to unscramble the letters to create the word. Repeat the process three times.

Step 4: Take a Picture and Write It

Write the targeted word on the board. Ask children to pretend their eyes are the lens and shutter of a camera. Direct them to carefully look at the word on the board and close their eyes to take a picture of it in their minds. After several seconds, have them open their eyes to see if they correctly imaged the item in their minds. This can be repeated three times if necessary. Erase the word and have children write it on a card at their seats. Write the word on the board again for checking.

Step 5: Fill in the Blank

In a pocket chart, display several sentence strips containing a blank in the place of the word under study. Use sentences from previously read text in a big book or other enlarged text from shared reading. As you read the sentence strips and come to the missing word, invite a child to come forward and write the missing word on a card or strip and place it in the sentence strip at the correct location.

Step 6: New Text Close Reading

Using a new piece of enlarged text during shared reading, tell children to be on the lookout for the word under study. When they detect the word in the new text, they should make a signal or sound that the group predetermines before engaging in the shared reading.

Introduce Important Vocabulary. Introduce any new vocabulary that may not be familiar to students. There are three levels of vocabulary knowledge (National Reading Panel, 2000): unknown words, acquainted words, and established words. **Unknown words** are completely unfamiliar to students. **Acquainted words** are those students have some familiarity with, but which will require some kind of review. **Established words** are known to students when they hear them spoken or see them in print. Unknown and acquainted words that are important in the selection you plan to model are the ones you will need to introduce before reading aloud. In Chapter 6 dealing with vocabulary instruction, we go much more into detail on this point.

Introduce the Targeted Fluency Skill. Before reading the text, draw students' attention to the fluency skill you plan to emphasize. As noted earlier, the three main areas of fluency delineated in reading research are accuracy, rate, and expression. Name and describe the fluency skill you will be modeling, and then return to the skill after reading. Reread short portions of the selection, "thinking out loud" for students how you are using the fluency strategy. Thinking out loud (metacognition) is the essence of modeling and you should use many examples. Saturate students, if you will, with examples drawn from your reading.

One of the fluency skills you will want your students to develop is the ability to "chunk text"—read in meaningful phrases. **Scooping** (Hook & Jones, 2002) is a strategy useful in chunking phrases (see Figure 5.8).

Lesson Part II: Guided Oral Reading Practice

This part of the Fluency Formula provides students with repeated and monitored oral reading experiences. These **guided oral reading** sessions are at the heart of the Fluency Formula and are based on the very best reading research. The National Reading Panel (2000) noted:

> [Guided oral reading] encourages students to read passages orally with system- atic and explicit guidance and feedback from the teacher. . . . Guided repeated

Figure 5.8 Scooping*

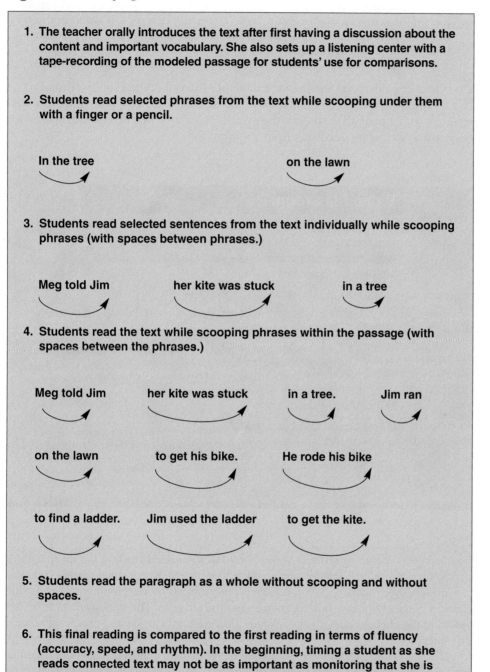

1. The teacher orally introduces the text after first having a discussion about the content and important vocabulary. She also sets up a listening center with a tape-recording of the modeled passage for students' use for comparisons.

2. Students read selected phrases from the text while scooping under them with a finger or a pencil.

   In the tree   on the lawn

3. Students read selected sentences from the text individually while scooping phrases (with spaces between phrases.)

   Meg told Jim   her kite was stuck   in a tree

4. Students read the text while scooping phrases within the passage (with spaces between the phrases.)

   Meg told Jim   her kite was stuck   in a tree.   Jim ran

   on the lawn   to get his bike.   He rode his bike

   to find a ladder. Jim used the ladder   to get the kite.

5. Students read the paragraph as a whole without scooping and without spaces.

6. This final reading is compared to the first reading in terms of fluency (accuracy, speed, and rhythm). In the beginning, timing a student as she reads connected text may not be as important as monitoring that she is applying prosodic features and chunking the text into syntactic units. Timing may be incorporated once rhythm has been clearly established.

Adapted from Hook P. E., & Jones, S. (2002). The importance of automaticity and fluency for efficient reading comprehension. *Perspectives, 28*(1), 9–14.

oral reading procedures that included guidance from teachers, peers, or parents had a significant and positive impact on word recognition, fluency, and comprehension across a range of grade levels. These studies were conducted in a variety of classrooms in both regular and special education settings with teachers using widely available instructional materials. . . . These results . . . apply to all students—good readers as well as those experiencing reading difficulties. (p. 12)

Two kinds of guided oral reading are called for in Step II of the Fluency Formula. The first is done with the aid and guidance of the teacher. The second involves repeated readings with a peer. In each case, the student has ample practice rereading texts for fluency and for getting feedback from a more fluent reader.

Video Classroom

Choral Readings Build Fluency.

Visit the *Video Classroom* on the Teacher Prep Website (*www.prenhall.com/teacherprep*) to View "The Second Rereading Multilingual Classroom".

As you view this clip, relate the descriptions of fluency to the choral reading.

- Accuracy and ease of decoding (automaticity)
- An age or grade level appropriate reading speed or rate
- Appropriate use of volume, pitch, juncture, and stress (prosadic features) in one's voice
- Appropriate text phrasing or "chunking"

Differentiating Instruction

How are choral readings multi-level?

What would be the benefits of this approach for struggling readers and second language learners?

Guided Oral Reading with Teacher Feedback. Guided reading is one means of providing oral reading practice that is guided by the teacher in small groups (Fountas & Pinnell, 1996; Mooney, 1990). Children are grouped by developmental levels that reflect a range of competencies, experiences, and interests. The strategy centers on developing the child's ability to successfully process text with limited teacher guidance and interaction.

Guided reading groups are composed of six to eight children who work together for a period of time under the direct guidance of the teacher. It is important to note that the membership in guided reading groups should change as children progress during the year. This is a crucial concern. Failure to modify groups as students progress can result in static ability groups much like the "Eagles, Bluebirds, and Buzzards" of earlier days. The static nature of ability groups in the past—particularly those comprised of struggling readers left in the "lower" developmental groups—caused children to suffer damage to their self-esteem and lowered academic expectations for them.

Getting to Know English Learners
Grouping for ELs must be modified during the year, too. Groups with same-language speakers who are more fluent readers are helpful, as our groups where English-speaking peers model read-alouds.

Success in fluency instruction during guided reading hinges on children working with texts appropriate to their reading level. Thus, the notion of **leveled books**—books categorized according to their difficulty so that they can be matched to students reading at that level—is an important one for fluency instruction. Before a guided reading group is begun, the teacher must take great care to match the level of text to the identified needs of a group of children to ensure that the group can enjoy and control the story throughout the first reading. Texts chosen for each leveled group should present children with a reasonable challenge, but also with a high degree of potential success.

Here is a listing of criteria typically used for leveling books for guided reading instruction (see Table 5.4).

Table 5.4   General Explanation of Criteria for Determining the Reading Levels of Texts

Levels 1–20 (A–K)

Levels 1–4 (A–D)

- Language patterns are repeated.
- Illustrations match and explain most of the text. Actions are clearly presented without much in the way of extraneous detail that might confuse the reader.
- The text is likely to match the experiences and conceptual knowledge common to most beginning readers.
- The language of the text developmentally matches the syntax and organization of most young children's speech.
- The sentences and books themselves are comparatively short (e.g., 10–60 words).
- Print is carefully laid out so that it consistently appears on the same place on the page throughout each book.

Assumption at this level: When students encounter an unknown word in print, they can easily use context from known words and illustrations along with language pattern cues and early word analysis skills for successful decoding.

Levels 5–8 (D–E)

- Reader often sees predictable, repetitive language patterns; however, the same pattern does not dominate the entire text.
- There is greater variation in language patterns, as opposed to one or two word changes.
- Words and phrases may express different meanings through varying sentence structures.
- By the end of these stages, the syntax is more typical of written or "book" language.
- Illustrations provide minimal support for readers' determination of exact language.

Levels 9–12 (E–G)

- Variation in sentence patterns is now the norm.
- There are longer sentences with less predictable text.
- Written language styles and genre become more prominent, including the use of some verb forms not often used by young children in oral settings.
- The average sentence length in text increases (double that found in levels 5–8).
- Events in a story may continue over several pages.
- Illustrations provide only moderate support to the meaning of the stories.

Levels 13–15* (G–H)

(*Consider these characteristics as enhancements to the description for levels 9–12.)
- There is a greater variety of words and the inclusion of more specialized vocabulary.
- Pictures provide some support for the overall meaning of the story, but cannot be used by the reader to interpret the precise message.

Levels 16–20 (I–K)

- Stories or sequences of events are longer.
- Story events are developed more fully than those in texts at lower levels.
- Vocabulary is progressively richer and more varied.
- Illustrations are used to help to create atmosphere and setting rather than to specifically depict content of the text.
- Full pages of print are now the norm.

Table 5.5 Guided Reading Leveling Comparisons

Here is a handy guide to help you translate books from publishers using Guided Reading ratings to leveling systems common in one-to-one tutorial programs (i.e., Reading Recovery, Cooter & Cooter's *BLAST* program, etc.).

Grade Level (Basal)	Guided Reading Level (Fountas-Pinnell)	One-to-One Tutoring Level	Stages of Reading
Kindergarten	A B	A 1 2	Emergent
Pre-Primer	C D E	3 4 6–8	Early
Primer	F G	10 12	
1st Grade	H I	14 16	Transitional
2nd Grade	J–K L–M	18–20 24–28	
3rd Grade	N O–P	30 34–38	Fluent/Extending
4th Grade	Q–R	40	
5th Grade	—	44	
6th Grade	—	—	

In Table 5.5 we include a useful reading level cross-referencing guide comparing grade levels to guided reading levels, and then to Reading Recovery levels (a popular remedial reading program for first grade students), and then the stages of reading.

Lesson Planning for Guided Reading. The basic lesson pattern employed in guided reading lessons consists of seven phases, which are listed and explained in Figure 5.9.

Teacher Feedback During Instruction. Understanding the nature, quantity, and quality of teacher feedback during guided oral reading, as well as in other "coaching" situations, is a crucial part of helping students become fluent readers. The following self-assessment questions for teachers are provided to assist in this process.

1. Am I more often telling the word than providing a clue?
2. What is the average self-correction rate of my students?
3. Do I assist poor readers with unknown words more often than good readers? If so, why?
4. Am I correcting miscues even when they do not alter the meaning of the text? If so, why?

Figure 5.9   Guided Reading Lesson Overview

Picture Talk • Walk through a new book by looking at the pictures. Ask children, "What do you see?"

First Reading • Depending on the students' developmental levels, the first reading is initially done by the teacher with children following the lead. Later, the teacher gradually releases responsibility for the first reading to the children by sharing the reading role and then fading into one who encourages children to try it on their own.

Language Play • In this phase of the guided reading lesson, the teacher carefully analyzes the text to find specific elements associated with written language to teach children how language works. For early emergent readers, this may mean letter identification, punctuation, or directionality. In the fluency stage, children might identify text genre or compound words.

Rereading • Children read the text again with the assistance of the teacher, a peer, or a mechanical device such as a computer or tape. Novice readers are encouraged to point to the text as they read, whereas fluent readers are encouraged to "read the text with your eyes" or silently.

Retelling • Children retell what they have read to their teacher or to their peers. Typically we say, "Can you tell me what you've read?" Sometimes we probe children's retellings with other questions to prompt recall.

Follow-up • The most effective follow-up activity to a guided reading lesson is to invite children to take guided reading books home for demonstrating their ability to parents and siblings. This provides needed practice time and promotes increased confidence and self-esteem among young readers.

Extensions • Extending books through performances, murals, artwork, and even music helps children deepen their understandings and increase their interpretations of text.

Source: Adapted from "Teacher Interruptions During Oral Reading Instruction: Self-Monitoring as an Impetus for Change in Corrective Feedback," by M. Shake, *Remedial and Special Education,* 7(5), pp. 18–24.

5. Does one reading group tend to engage in more self-correction than other groups? If so, why?
6. Does one reading group have more miscues that go unaddressed than other groups?
7. What types of cues for oral reading errors do I provide and why?
8. What is my ultimate goal in reading instruction?
9. How do I handle interruptions from other students during oral reading? Do I practice what I preach?
10. How does my feedback influence the self-correction behavior of students?
11. Does my feedback differ across reader groups? If so, how and why?
12. Would students benefit more from a form of feedback different from that which I normally offer?
13. Am I allowing students time to self-correct (3–5 seconds)?
14. Am I further confusing students with my feedback?
15. Do I digress into "mini-lessons" mid-sentence when students make a mistake? If so, why?
16. Do I analyze miscues to gain information about the reading strategies students employ?
17. Does the feedback I offer aid students in becoming independent, self-monitoring readers? If so, how?
18. Do I encourage students to ask themselves, "Did that make sense?" when they are reading both orally and silently? If not, why not?
19. Do students need the kind of feedback I am offering them?

Adapted from Shake, M. (1986). Teacher interruptions during oral reading instruction: Self-monitoring as an impetus for change in corrective feedback. *Remedial and Special Education,* 7(5), 18–24.

Hope Madden/Merrill.

Choral Reading. **Choral readings** of text can be done in at least three ways. Wood (1983) recommends **unison reading** and **echo reading.** In unison reading, everyone reads together. During echo (sometimes called *echoic*) reading, the teacher or a student reads a passage aloud, and then everyone else "echoes" by repeating it. A third method we have found useful is **antiphonal reading.** Derived from ancient monastic traditions, antiphonal reading involves two groups. The first reading group reads a passage aloud (usually a sentence or two), and the second group echoes the reading.

Getting to Know English Learners
Choral reading is a tried and true method of ELL instruction.

Student-Assisted Fluency-Building Strategies.
Partner or Paired Reading. **Partner** or **paired reading** ("buddy" reading) has a student reading aloud with a more fluent partner or one of equal fluency. The partner models fluent reading in place of the teacher, provides useful feedback, and helps with word recognition.

Usually partners take turns reading aloud an assigned passage to one another, with the more developed reader reading first, thus providing the model for fluent reading. The second reader then reads the passage in the same way as the first. The more fluent reader offers feedback on how his partner can read the passage more fluently, and the less fluent reader rereads the passage until he can do so independently.

Readers of about the same ability are sometimes paired for this exercise. The difference is that both readers first hear the teacher reading the passage as the model, then the two "buddies" take turns reading to each other and offering feedback until they can each read the passage fluently.

The Neurological Impress Method. The **neurological impress method** (NIM) involves the student and a more fluent reader in reading the same text aloud simultaneously (Heckelman, 1966, 1969). Unlike partner reading examples described earlier, NIM has the student and more fluent model reading in unison at the same volume at first. The model's voice gradually fades as the student becomes more confident.

The use of multiple sensory systems during NIM is thought to "impress" upon the student the fluent reading patterns of the teacher through direct modeling. It is assumed that exposing students to numerous examples of texts (read in a more sophisticated way than struggling readers could achieve on their own) will enable them to achieve automaticity in word recognition more naturally. This assumption stands to reason when viewed in light of more recent advances in learning theory, especially those espoused by Vygotsky (1978).

Each NIM session is aimed at reading as much material as possible in 10 minutes. Reading material selected for the first few sessions should be easy, predictable, and make sense for the reader. However, other more challenging materials that are on the student's normal guided reading level can eventually be used.

To use NIM, the student sits slightly in front and to one side of his or her partner as they hold the text. The more fluent reader moves her finger beneath the words as both partners read in near-unison fashion. Both try to maintain a comfortably brisk and continuous rate of oral reading. The more fluent reader's role is to keep the pace when the less-proficient student starts to slow down. Pausing for analyzing unknown words is not permitted. The more fluent reader's voice is directed at her partner's ear so that words are seen, heard, and spoken simultaneously.

Because many struggling readers have not read at an accelerated pace before, their first efforts often sound like mumbling. Most less-fluent readers typically take some time to adjust to NIM; however, within a few sessions they start to feel more at ease. Many struggling readers say they enjoy NIM because it allows them to read more challenging and interesting material like "good" readers.

At first, the more fluent reader's voice will dominate oral reading, but in later sessions it should be reduced gradually. This will allow the less-fluent student to assume the vocal lead naturally. Usually three sessions per week are sufficient to obtain noticeable results. This routine should be followed for a minimum of 10 consecutive weeks (Henk, 1983).

NIM can also be adapted for group use (Hollingsworth, 1970, 1978). Here the teacher tape-records 10 minutes of his or her own oral reading in advance. Individual students can read along with the tape while following the text independently, or the tape can be used in a listening center to permit the teacher to spend individual time with each student as others read with the tape. Despite the convenience of the prerecorded tape format, teachers' and more fluent peers' one-to-one interactions with individual students result in a better instructional experience.

Technology-Assisted Reading Strategies: Read-Along Audio Cassettes and CDs. In technology-assisted reading, children read a book with the assistance of a fluently read model on an audiotape or a computer. Technology-assisted reading for fluency development is a solution to the problem teachers experience in arranging one-to-one learning activities for students.

During a first reading using an audiotape, children follow along in their own copy of the text. They are instructed to point to each word as the fluent reading model says it on the audiotape. Younger children reading short books then read aloud with the tape three to five times or until they can read the text fluently. Students who are reading longer texts listen to the entire piece once, and then select a passage (usually 150–300 words) for repeated practice. Once they have read the passage repeatedly (3–5 times), they read the passage to the teacher.

Teacher management of technology-assisted fluency centers is of great importance. For some students, listening to a tape presents an opportunity to engage in off-task behaviors—looking like readers but not engaging (Stahl, 2004).

In recent years, a number of computer-based programs such as *Read Naturally* (Ihnot & Ihnot, 1996) at *http://www.readnaturally.com/* and *Insights: Reading Fluency* (Adams, 2005) at *http://www.charlesbridge-fluency.com/* have been developed to provide students with repeated reading practice. Generally speaking, most of these computer programs use speech recognition software and immediate feedback as students read text aloud as it is presented on the computer screen. Computer-assisted reading has been found to be effective in improving fluency across a range of grade levels (National Reading Panel, 2000).

Lesson Part III: Independent Fluency Practice

A teacher who develops fluent readers is like a coach who develops Olympic swimmers. Numerous skills must be taught until the learner reaches the point of automaticity. If the student, or swimmer, is to become proficient, he or she must put in many hours of practice. You might say, then, that guided and independent reading practice opportunities are intended to develop Olympic readers—strong, capable, and fluent.

Three of the more productive strategies for independent practice are repeated readings (Dowhower, 1991; Samuels, 1979), wide oral reading (Kuhn, 2005b; Kuhn & Schwanenflugel, 2006) and modified sustained silent reading (Reutzel & Smith, in preparation).

Repeated Readings. **Repeated readings** engage students in reading interesting passages orally over and over again to enhance their reading fluency (Dowhower, 1987; Samuels, 1979). Although it might seem that reading a text again and again leads to boredom, it can actually have just the opposite effect.

In the beginning, texts selected for repeated readings should be short, predictable, and easy. When students attain adequate speed and accuracy with easy selections, the length and difficulty of texts can gradually be increased.

Repeated readings help students by expanding the total number of words they can recognize instantaneously. They also help improve students' comprehension and oral elocution (performance) with each succeeding attempt. Improved performance quickly leads students to improved confidence regarding reading aloud and positive attitudes toward the act of reading. Additionally, because high-frequency words (e.g., *the, and, but, was,* etc.) occur in literally all reading situations, the increase in automatic sight word knowledge developed through repeated readings transfers far beyond the practiced texts.

Research indicates that repeated readings are most effective when students are supported during independent reading. Audiotapes, tutors, or peer feedback are supports shown to be most effective during repeated reading practice sessions (National Reading Panel, 2000). For example, try providing a tape-recorded version of the story or poem to be practiced. Students can read along with an audiocassette tape to develop fluency similar to the model's. Also, students can tape record their oral reading for immediate feedback. If two audiocassette tape players are available, have the student listen and read along with the taped version of the text using headphones. At the same time, use the second recorder for recording the student's oral reading. The student can then replay his version simultaneously with the teacher-recorded version to compare, or simply listen to his own rendition alone. Either way, feedback can be both instant and effective.

You may use taped recordings of repeated readings for further analysis of each reader's improvement in fluency and comprehension. Also, using a tape recorder frees you to work with other students, thereby conserving precious instructional time and leaving behind an audit trail of student readings for later assessment and documentation. On occasion, listen to tapes with the reader present. During this time, you and your students can discuss effective ways of reducing word recognition errors and increasing reading rate.

Several excellent technology-based software packages are available to augment classroom fluency practice and assessment. These rely heavily on repeated oral readings. We recommend that teachers examine *Insights Reading Fluency* RFCL 3 Workstation License at *www.charlesbridge.com* and *Read Naturally* at *www.readnaturally.com.* Both of these software packages are research-based.

Wide Oral Reading. Wide oral reading involves students in reading different text types (narrative, expository, and poetic) across a range of genres (fantasy, fairy tales, myths, science fiction, historical fiction, series books, autobiographies, diaries, journals, logs, essays, encyclopedia entries, information books) rather than reading the same book or passage over and over again. To assure that students read widely, many teachers find a reading genre wheel useful. See Figure 5.10.

Children are required to read one of each type of genre represented on the wheel during a specified period of time determined by the teacher. Children usually color in each part of the genre wheel as they complete it. In wide oral reading, children read aloud and receive support, guidance, feedback, and monitoring from a peer, a tutor, or the teacher. Some teachers encourage children to read aloud quietly, using a PVC-pipe-constructed fluency phone (pictured earlier in this chapter).

Recent research studies conducted by Stahl, Bradley, Smith, Kuhn, Schwanenglugel & Meisinger (2003) and Kuhn (2005a & 2005b) suggest wide readings of different texts rather than repeated readings of the same text may be as effective or more so for second grade readers. Stahl et al. (2003) found that a wide-reading group significantly outperformed a repeated-reading group. In a separate study of small-group fluency instruction focused on struggling second grade readers, Kuhn (2005a & 2005b) found that wide oral reading of different titles and genres compared with repeated oral reading resulted in equivalent gains in fluency using several measures that included number of words read in isolation, correct words per minute in context, and expressive reading measures. In addition, the wide oral reading group performed better on answering text-implicit and -explicit questions to assess comprehension than did the oral repeated reading group.

Figure 5.10   Reading Genre Wheel

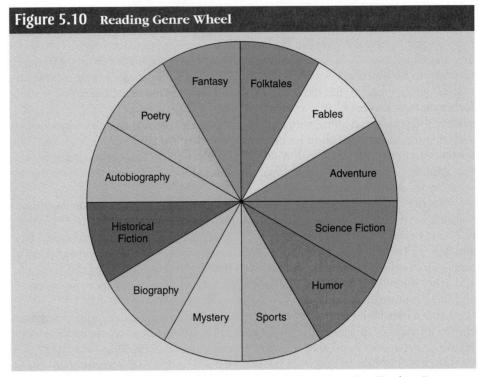

From D. R. Reutzel & P. C. Fawson. *Your Classroom Library: Ways to Give It More Teaching Power.* New York: Scholastic Professional Books.

Scaffolded Silent Reading (ScSR). Silent sustained reading (SSR) or some related form of silent, independent reading practice such as DEAR time (Drop Everything and Read) is a very popular method of independent reading practice in our schools. However, educators have discovered that simply providing all students the time to self-select their own books and read silently does not guarantee that they will actually engage in silent reading practice. In fact, it is quite possible that such practices allow many children (and some teachers) time to take an "in-the-room field trip" using a book as a prop!

Advocates of SSR suggest that allowing students time for unfettered, self-selected silent reading practice will lead to increases in motivation and engagement as compared with other less-motivating reading practices such as round-robin oral reading and/or the writing of book reports. Despite these claims, there is growing recognition among classroom practitioners and in the reading research community that some students derive little benefit from, or fail to make good use of, independent silent reading time (Gambrell, 1978; Lee-Daniels & Murray, 2000; Moore et al., 1980; Robertson et al., 1996). In fact, some elementary and secondary schools have experienced so many challenges implementing SSR over the long term that they have decided to discontinue the program (Halpern, 1981; Moore et al., 1980). Another problem with SSR is that some children become bored with the routine (Gambrell, 1978; Lee-Daniels & Murray, 2000). Other children, particularly younger or struggling readers, find it difficult to conform to the requirement of staying quiet, prompting some early grade teachers to modify the SSR acronym from "silent sustained reading" to "self-selected reading" (Reutzel & Cooter, 2000). Often, these younger, not-yet-independent students are in need of more—not less—assistance, guidance, and scaffolding to stay on task and to benefit from time allocated to reading practice (Robertson et al., 1996). Despite SSR's acceptance among some teachers, students, and reading researchers, many other educators and researchers, including members of the National Reading Panel, steadfastly maintain that more research needs to be conducted into the value of SSR and at what levels of reading development it may or may not be effective (Efta, 1984; Manning & Manning, 1984; Moore et al., 1980; National Reading Panel, 2000; Robertson et al., 1996).

One well-known concern associated with the implementation of SSR as described in the literature and as implemented in many classrooms across the nation is the conspicuous absence of interaction around the reading of texts or any accountability for whether or not students actually read during this allocated time.

It can be argued, and often has been argued, that teachers who themselves read silently during SSR time are, in fact, *teaching* by modeling the behaviors of a silent, engaged "reader." But no research has ever established the effect of teachers serving as "silent reading models" on either the achievement or the engagement of elementary-aged students. Conversely, we argue that modeling silent reading behaviors *without* discussion, interaction, and teacher explanation is often so transparent for many young students that it is entirely overlooked. Along this same line of criticism, Stahl (2004) notes that, "Many SSR advocates do not allow teachers to check up on children or recommend that teachers read their own books during this time to be a model of a reader. . . . One failing of SSR is that teachers may not monitor their children's reading . . . (p. 206). As a result, reading practice as found in the implementation of SSR may or may not be useful for children, but it is highly unlikely to be effective without the active monitoring, interaction, and guidance of a concerned teacher.

Recent research (Bryan, Fawson, & Reutzel, 2003) demonstrated that when classroom teachers randomly monitored their students during SSR through brief interactions and accountability conferences, even the most disengaged students in the class remained on task for up to three weeks without additional random monitoring visits. These findings seem to suggest that rather than reading silently to themselves, teachers ought to jettison the traditional SSR practice of modeling reading and instead engage in random monitoring of students' reading during SSR. Furthermore, the National Reading Panel (2000) asserted from their review of forms of reading practice that one prominent feature of effective time spent in reading practice was receiving feedback about one's reading. In this particular respect, the National Reading Panel (2000) also endorsed the need for teachers, and others, to monitor and interact with students around their reading. It is clear from these findings and criticisms that, without monitoring, teachers cannot be assured that children are in fact reading during traditional SSR time at all! As a result, we have designed and researched a modified silent sustained reading process that has been shown to equal the effects of the National Reading Panel's (2000) recommended approach of oral repeated readings (guided oral reading) with feedback among third grade students.

The way Scaffolded silent reading (ScSR) works is simple. Students are encouraged to read widely from across a variety of genres using a reading genre wheel like that shown in Figure 5.10. Students are asked to read one self-selected book from each slice of the reading genre wheel before selecting another book from that genre to read. This approach assures that students are reading widely. Next, students self-select an independent-level book of interest to them from a collection of leveled books displayed by genre in the classroom library. For example,

Figure 5.11   Rule-of-Thumb Strategy for Choosing "Just Right" Books

1. Choose a book that looks interesting.
2. Open the book to any page that has lots of words on it.
3. Begin reading aloud or silently. When you come to a word you do not know, hold up your small finger.
4. If you come to another word you do not know, hold up your next finger. If you use up all of your fingers on one hand (and come to your thumb) on one page, then the book is too hard and you should put it back. Find another book you like just as well and repeat the ROT exercise to make sure it is just right for you.

students wanting to read a fairy tale will go to the fairy tale section of the classroom library and select a book at their level by looking at the back of the book for a colored dot that indicates a match with their independent reading level. Alternatively, children can make sure the book they select will not be too hard for them using a strategy known as "Rule-of-Thumb," or ROT, that is taught to them by the teacher (see Figure 5.11). Many teachers like to use the chart below that shows the steps in (ROT).

Once students have chosen their books, they are ready to read. The goal is for students to read a total of 20 minutes per day in a self-selected book chosen from among various genres. Younger students may need to have two 10-minute periods of ScSR time. Teachers often set a timer for the amount of ScSR time they have allocated; the children read while the teacher circulates among them, randomly stopping and asking students to read aloud the book they have chosen. The teacher may ask the student some questions to measure comprehension, or talk with the student about her or his goal for reading in the next few days. The teacher also discusses with each student monitored a way that she or he can share with others what she or he has been reading, including posters, oral or written book reports, sharing a favorite part of the book through a read-aloud performance, or other form of expression. Teachers often give prompts like the following.

> "I'd like you to draw me a picture of your favorite character when you finish reading this story."

> "Find five ____ (e.g., color, describing, number, etc.) words for me as you read."

> "I will want you to act out one of the characters when you finish and I'll see if I can guess which one it is!"

After completing the reading of a book, students color in the appropriate genre in their reading genre wheel and tell the teacher they are ready to share their book. (In Chapter 11, we discuss several ways of sharing a book response with the group or the teacher). Stahl (2004) has indicated that for ScSR to be effective, student reading practice must be monitored by the teacher regularly!

Step IV: Performance Reading for Fluency Assessment

Performance reading has students reading aloud for the teacher and/or an audience so that the teacher can monitor fluency growth. Students prepare for the exercise, regardless of format, by orally rereading the text to be performed until they can read it with maximum fluency. There are several ways this can be done that have found support in evidence-based research. Before we get to those, we will examine a very well-known approach that you should *not* use—round-robin reading.

Long ago, teachers commonly relied on round-robin reading as a means for listening to students read orally. Students would sit in a circle, and the teacher would call on a student to begin reading orally from a story in the basal reader while the other students would follow along. After the first student read a paragraph or two, the teacher would stop him or her and call on the next student to continue reading. This process was repeated until every child in the circle had a chance to read aloud.

Though the simplicity of round-robin is very appealing, research has revealed it to be far less effective than other available strategies for monitoring fluency development. The process can even have a negative impact on some children (Eldredge, Reutzel, & Hollingsworth, 1996). Round-robin fails to give children adequate opportunities for repeated readings before performing, defeats comprehension (i.e., when a student realizes the paragraph he'll be asked to read is three ahead of the current student in the "hot seat," he'll tend to look ahead and start silently reading his passage feverishly, hoping he won't "mess up" when it's his turn), and causes some students embarrassment when they are unable to read their paragraph fluently. Our advice? Do not use round-robin in your classroom; there are better alternatives that will help you monitor fluency development, improve comprehension, and protect fragile egos in the process. Following are several activities that can be used for performance reading found to be effective in classrooms.

Readers' Theatre. Perhaps the most successful performance reading strategy, in terms of the research (Sloyer, 1982; National Reading Panel, 2000, Griffith & Rasinski, 2004) is readers' theatre. **Readers' theatre** involves rehearsing and performing before an audience a script that is rich with dialogue. The script itself may be one from a book or, in the upper elementary or middle school grades, could be developed by a group of students working in collaboration as part of a literature response activity (Cooter & Griffith, 1989).

Stayter and Allington (1991) tell about a readers' theatre activity for which a group of heterogeneously grouped seventh graders spent five days reading, rehearsing, and performing short dramas. After a first reading, students began to negotiate about which role they would read. More hesitant students were permitted to opt for smaller parts, but everyone was required to participate. As time passed, students critiqued each others' readings and made suggestions as to how they should sound (e.g., "You should sound like a snob"). The most common response in this experience was how repeated readings through drama helped them better understand the text. One student said,

> The first time I read to know what the words are. Then I read to know what the words *say* and later as I read I thought about how to say the words. . . . As I got to know the character better, I put more feeling in my voice. (Stayter & Allington, 1991, p. 145)

Texts selected for readers' theatre are often drawn from oral traditions, poetry, or quality picture books designed to be read aloud by children. However, nonfiction passages can also be adapted for presentation. Selections should, whenever possible, be packed with action, have an element of suspense, and comprise an entire, meaningful story or nonfiction text. Also, texts selected for use in readers' theatre should contain sufficient dialogue to make reading and preparing the text a challenge as well as necessitate the involvement of several children as characters. Narrative texts we have seen used in readers' theatre include Martin and Archambault's *Knots on a Counting Rope* (1987), Viorst's *Alexander and the Terrible, Horrible, No Good, Very Bad Day* (1972), and Barbara Robinson's *The Best Christmas Pagent Ever* (1972).

Here is an easy procedure to follow. If a story is selected for reading, students should be assigned to read characters' parts. If poems are selected, students may read alternating lines or groups of lines. Readers' theatre in-the-round, where readers stand around the perimeter of the room surrounding their audience, is a fun and interesting variation for both performers and audience.

Students will often benefit from a discussion prior to reading a readers' theatre script for the first time. This discussion helps students make connections between their background experiences and the text to be read. Also, struggling readers usually benefit from listening to a previously recorded performance of the text as a model prior to their initial attempts at reading the script.

Hennings (1974) described a simplified procedure for preparing readers' theatre scripts for classroom performance. First, the text to be performed is read silently by individual students. Second, the text is read again orally, sometimes using choral reading in a group. After the second reading, readers either choose their parts, or the teacher assigns parts to them. We suggest that students be allowed to select their three most desired parts, write these choices on a slip of paper, and submit it to the teacher. Teachers should do everything possible to assign one of these three choices. The third reading is also an oral reading with students reading their parts with scripts in hand. There may be several rehearsal readings as students prepare for the final reading or performance in front of the class or other audience.

Connect fluency to content areas through the use of technology. Read "State History Bites in the Morning News" on the Teacher Prep Website (*www.prenhall.com/teacherprep*). Visit *Content Area Reading* to learn how groups work cooperatively to research, write, and produce a video. How does this approach relate to each of the Five Pillars? (Teacher Knowledge, Classroom Assessment, Effective Instruction, Differentiating Instruction, and Family/Community Connections)

Readers' theatre offers students a unique opportunity to participate in reading along with other, perhaps more-skilled readers. Participating in the mainstream classroom with better readers helps students having reading problems feel a part of their peer group, provides them with ready models of good reading, and demonstrates how good readers, through practice, become even better readers. Working together with other readers fosters a sense of teamwork, support, and pride in personal and group accomplishment.

Radio Reading. **Radio reading** possesses all of the effective elements of practice in developing fluency we have just discussed. Radio reading (Greene, 1979; Optiz & Rasinski, 1998; Rasinski, 2003; Searfoss, 1975) is a variation on repeated reading and reader's theatre. We have found radio reading to be most

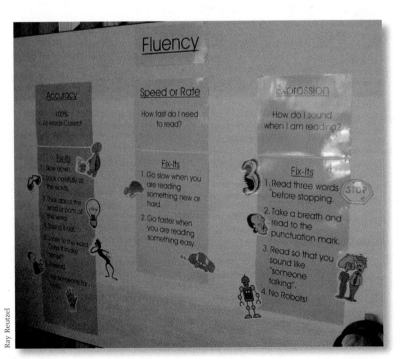

Ray Reutzel

effective with short selections from information texts threaded together into a single news broadcast performance script.

In radio reading, each student is given a script to read aloud. Selections can be drawn from any print media, such as newspapers, magazines, or any print source that can be converted into a news story, such as short selections from articles or sections in information books. One student acts as the news anchor, while other students act in the roles of various reporters presenting the weather, sports, breaking news, and so on. Only the radio readers and the teacher have copies of the scripts. Because other students have no script to follow, minor word recognition errors will go unnoticed if the text is well presented. Struggling students enjoy radio reading from *Know Your World*. This publication is well-suited for use in radio reading activities because the content and level of difficulty make it possible for older readers with fluency problems to read with ease and enjoyment. Short selections from information books on weather, volcanoes, spiders, sports figures, or any other topic can be presented as short reports by various reporters during the news broadcast. An example of a radio reading script is found in Figure 5.12 titled, "Mummies Made in Egypt." A script for the anchor may need to be written by students with help from the teacher to thread the various news reports together in a cohesive fashion. Once students have the radio reading script prepared for rehearsal, they gather materials for sound effects (police whistles, doors opening or shutting, people screaming, and others).

Before performing a radio reading for an audience, students should rehearse their parts with a partner or the teacher until they gain confidence and can read the script with proper volume, accuracy, rate, phrasing, and expression. Emphasis is first placed on the meaning of the text segments so that the students can paraphrase any difficult portions of the text if needed during the presentation. Students are encouraged to keep ideas flowing in the same way a reporter or anchor person does. After thorough rehearsal of the script with sound effects, the radio play is taped on cassette recorder and played over the school's public address system into other classrooms.

Step V: Goal Setting and Monitoring Student Progress

To conclude the Fluency Formula, students are taught to self-assess their fluency after reading using a simple assessment rubric containing the elements of oral reading fluency shown in Figure 5.13. Once students have self-assessed and identified areas of strength and weakness, they are taught to select an appropriate fluency "fix-up" strategy (see Figure 5.14) and apply this strategy in improving their fluency in future practice sessions.

Finally, children read aloud the passage or book they have been practicing for one minute for the teacher. After completing the one-minute sample, the teacher charts or graphs the words correct per minute (wcpm) for younger children. For children in grades 2–3 they chart or graph the number of words read correct per minute. Students set reasonable goals, usually two to four more words read correctly per minute the next week, trying to better their own reading rate and cut down on errors with each successive assessment. Also, students are encouraged to improve their prosody or vocal inflections, as fluent reading is not strictly confined to reading rate and accuracy (Dowhower, 1987; Hudson, Lane, & Pullen, 2005; Rasinski, 2006; Reutzel & Hollingsworth, 1993). Figure 5.15 illustrates a tracking graph for charting a student's progress across several one-minute reading samples.

Create a Reader's Theatre lesson plan through the Teacher Prep Website.

- You will be guided through the alignment of standards, lesson objectives, your introduction, planning for and sequencing lesson activities and procedures, planning for ongoing assessment throughout the lesson, and planning end of lesson assessment. You will also choose and list lesson materials/resources and create adapted instruction to meet all needs of students.

- This lesson can be sent to your instructor through this link.

- Review information provided in this chapter and in links to the *Reading Online-IRA* and *The National Council of Teachers of English* (NCTE) websites. You will find a plethora of articles relating to Readers' Theatre and lesson plans relating to reading fluency. These websites may be accessed through the *Internet Links* on the accompanying CD.

- As you reach the assessment portion of your plan, you may look ahead to *Step V: Goal Setting and Monitoring Student Progress* to learn about student self-assessment and fix up strategies for oral reading fluency.

Figure 5.12   Mummies Made in Egypt by Aliki

Radio reading script by
Dr. John A. Smith
Department of Elementary Education
Utah State University

Performers: Radio Newsperson #1 and Radio Newsperson #2

Radio Newsperson #1	We are here to report some very important information about mummies.
Radio Newsperson #2	We have learned that ancient Egyptians believed that a person would start a new life after he died. They believed that the person's soul would travel back and forth to a new world.
Radio Newsperson #1	They believed that the person's soul needed his body to come back to. That is why Egyptians preserved dead bodies as mummies.
Radio Newsperson #2	A mummy is a dead body, or corpse, that has been dried out so it will not decay. The earliest mummies were dried out naturally in the hot, dry sands of Egypt's deserts.
Radio Newsperson #1	Later, the Egyptians wrapped the mummies in cloth and buried them in wooden coffins or put them in tombs made of brick and stone.
Radio Newsperson #2	It took 70 days to prepare a mummy. First they took out the dead person's inner organs. They cut a hole in the mummy's side to remove the intestines. They pulled the dead person's brains out through the nose with metal hooks.
Radio Newsperson #1	The inner organs were kept in jars with a chemical called *natron* that dried out the body parts. After the inner organs were removed, embalmers also put natron inside the body to dry it out.
Radio Newsperson #2	After 40 days, the natron was removed from the body, and the body was cleaned with oils and spices.
Radio Newsperson #1	The body was packed with new chemicals to keep it dry. The mummy's eyes were closed, and the nose was stuffed with wax.
Radio Newsperson #2	The hole in the mummy's side was sewn up and the mummy was carefully wrapped with long strips of cloth.
Radio Newsperson #1	After the embalmers finished wrapping the mummy, they painted it to look like the person and then covered it with resin, a sticky substance that dried into a hard covering.
Radio Newsperson #2	When the mummy was finished, they made a coffin to put the mummy in for burial. The coffin was decorated with pictures of gods and magic spells to protect it. Jewels and other treasures were also put into the coffin.
Radio Newsperson #1	Finally, the mummy and its coffin were placed in a tomb made of brick and stone. The Egyptian pyramids are large tombs that are burial places for powerful Egyptian rulers.
Radio Newsperson #2	There would be an elaborate funeral parade. The mummy would be placed in the tomb, sometimes in a secret chamber. Then the tomb would be sealed shut for the mummy's eternal resting place.
Radio Newsperson #1	Thank you very much, and now back to our teacher.

Figure 5.13 Assessment Rubric of the Elements of Oral Reading Fluency

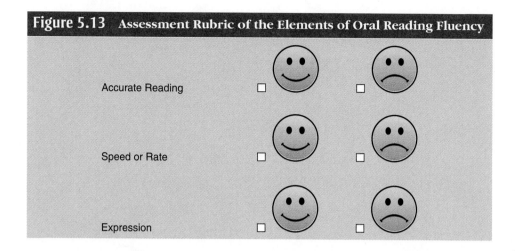

Accurate Reading

Speed or Rate

Expression

Figure 5.14 Fluency Fix-Up Strategies for Oral Reading Fluency Elements

Accuracy

1. Slow down your reading speed.

2. Look carefully at the words and the letters in the words you didn't read correctly on the page.

3. Think about if you know this word or parts of this word. Try saying the word or word parts.

4. Make the sound of each letter from left to right and blend the sounds together quickly to say the word.

5. Listen carefully to see if the word you said makes sense.

6. Try rereading the word in the sentence again.

7. After saying the word, use pictures to help you make sure you have the right word.

8. If the word still doesn't make sense, ask someone to help you.

Rate

1. Adjust your reading speed to go slower when the text is difficult or unfamiliar, or you need to read to get detailed information.

2. Adjust your reading speed to go faster when the text is easy or familiar, or you are reading to just enjoy the book.

Expression

1. Try to read three or more words together before pausing, stopping, or taking a breath.

2. Take a big breath and try to read to the comma or end punctuation without stopping for another breath.

3. Be sure to raise or lower your pitch when you see punctuation marks at the end of sentences.

Figure 5.15 One-Minute Reading Rate Tracking Graph

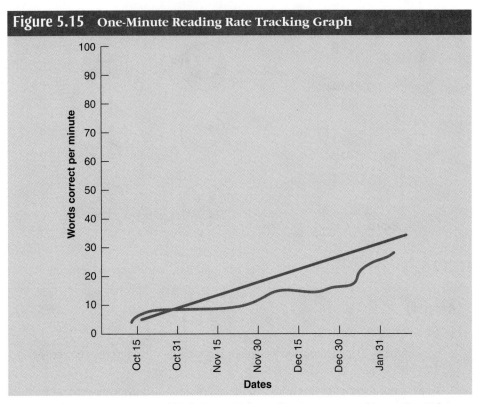

From Reutzel, D. R., & Cooter, R.B. (2007). *Strategies for reading assessment and instruction: Helping every child succeed,* 3rd edition. Upper Saddle River, NJ: Merrill/Prentice-Hall.

Some teachers draw a blue line indicating the number of wcpm needed to maintain grade level reading rates and use red lines to indicate the student's actual performances. As an illustration of the power of graphing progress, one second grade student recently remarked when he absorbed the fact that his red line was above the blue line: "Oh, I better slow down; I've gone over the blue line!" All students, especially struggling readers, find it greatly reinforcing to see visible evidence of their reading fluency improvement.

How Can Reading Fluency Instruction Be Adapted to Meet Diverse Student Needs?

Fluency Oriented Reading Instruction (FORI), based on repeated reading research, is an integrated lesson framework for providing differentiated instruction and practice in fluency (Stahl, Heubach, & Cramond, 1997; Kuhn & Schwanenflugel, 2006; Stahl 2004). FORI consists of three interlocking instructional steps: (1) a redesigned basal or core reading program lesson; (2) a free-reading period at school; and (3) a home reading program. Recent research on the effects of FORI showed that children receiving FORI instruction significantly outperformed a control group

(Stahl, et al., 2003). To provide a FORI lesson, teachers need a core reading or basal reading program text, an adequately appointed classroom library for free reading at school and home, extension activities drawn from the core or basal reading program text, a teacher-prepared graphic organizer of the text in the core or basal program, and a teacher-prepared audiotape for tape-assisted reading practice.

> **Getting to Know English Learners**
> Reading at home also helps parents of ELs who may not yet be fluent in English.

On the first day of a FORI reading lesson, the teacher begins by reading the core reading program story or text aloud to the class. Following the reading by the teacher, the students and teacher interactively discuss the text to place reading comprehension upfront as an important goal to be achieved in reading any text. Following this discussion, the teacher teaches vocabulary words and uses graphic organizers and other comprehension activities focused around the story or text.

On the second day of a FORI reading lesson, teachers can choose to have students echo read the core reading program text with the teacher or have children read only a part of the story repeatedly for practice with a partner or with the teacher. Following this practice session on the second day, the core reading program story is sent home for the child to read with his/her parents, with older siblings, or with other caregivers.

On the third and fourth day of a FORI lesson, children receive additional practice as well as participate in vocabulary and comprehension exercises based on the story read in the core reading program. On these two days, children are also given decoding instruction on difficult words in the core reading story or text.

On the fifth and final day of the FORI lesson, children are asked to generate a written response to the story to cement their comprehension of the text.

In addition to the basal or core reading program instruction to develop fluency found in the FORI framework, the teachers provide additional in-school free reading practice with instructional level books that are read alone or with a partner for between 15 and 30 minutes per day. At the beginning of the year, the time allocated to this portion of a FORI lesson is closer to 15 minutes; as the year progresses, it increases to 30 minutes. As a part of their homework assignment in the FORI framework, children are expected to read at home 15 minutes a day at least four days per week. This outside reading is monitored through the use of weekly reading logs turned in to the teacher (Stahl, 2004).

What Can Families and Communities Do to Develop Children's Reading Fluency?

One very effective way to connect fluency practice from the school to the home is to recommend to parents to use closed-caption television (Koskinen, Wilson, & Jensema, 1985; Neuman & Koskinen, 1992). Closed-caption TV has been found to be a particularly effective tool for motivating students who are learning English as a second language to improve reading fluency. Closed-caption television, which uses written subtitles, provides students with meaningful and motivating reading material. Parents should carefully select high-interest television programs. They may even want to record and preview programs before making final selections for captioned TV practice at home (Koskinen et al., 1985).

TEACHER PREP — Fluency can be practiced through the use of Language Experience Stories (LEA). Read how these stories benefit bilingual students as their entries are written in both first and second languages. Extending fluency practice from the school to the home provides opportunities for student engagement in generous amounts of daily reading/rereading practice. Visit the Teacher Prep Website (*www.prenhall.com/teacherprep*) and click on *Reading Methods* to read the article titled "Collecting Individual Dictation and Group Experiences."

One advantage of captioned TV fluency practice is that it does not require busy parents to sit and read daily with their children at home. However, if parents want to increase their involvement in captioned TV fluency practice, they can engage in a couple of different activities. First, parents and children can record and watch a part of the captioned TV program together. Then parents can stop the program and ask the child to predict what will happen next. They continue viewing the program so that the child can check his/her predictions. Second, after watching a closed-caption TV program, children can practice reading aloud along with the captions. If necessary, both the auditory portion and the closed captioning can be played simultaneously to provide children with support. At some later point, children should be allowed to practice reading the captioning without the auditory portion of the program. Koskinen et al. (1985) does "not recommend that the sound be turned off if this, in effect, turns off the children. The major advantage for using captioned television as fluency practice is the multisensory stimulation of viewing the drama, hearing the sound, and seeing the captions" (p. 6).

Summary

Fluency is the ability to read a text accurately, with appropriate intonation and phrasing, and at an age-appropriate speed. Fluency instruction, because it helps readers achieve automatic decoding, provides the opportunity for readers to turn more of their mental energies toward comprehending the message of text. Reading fluency can be developed through explicit teacher-led instruction, teacher modeling of fluency skills, and by having students participate in guided oral repeated reading sessions. Fluency is further strengthened by engaging children in generous amounts of daily reading practice. Struggling readers and, in fact, all others benefit most from practice reading that provides feedback and monitoring in appropriately challenging texts. Monitoring and assessing children's development of oral reading fluency is important in effecting needed improvements. Careful tracking of students' oral reading progress should lead to goal-setting, which in turn leads to incremental improvements in students' oral reading fluency.

Classroom Applications

1. In groups of four, perform the following tasks regarding a selected grade level.
   a. Identify your state's standards for fluency instruction for the selected grade level. These can usually be located on the state's department of education Web site.
   b. For each element of reading fluency (accuracy, rate, expression, and phrasing), determine which are addressed in the state standards and which are not.

c. Outline the strategies named in this chapter that would be appropriate for improving reading fluency at this level, and match each to one of the state standards.

d. If you are using this book as part of a college course, present your findings to the whole class. Be sure to provide your classmates with a copy of your findings for future reference.

e. If you are a small group of teachers from a school working through this exercise, share your findings with another grade-level team and your principal. Determine together whether a renewed emphasis on reading fluency is warranted in your school based on current classroom practices.

Recommended Readings

Brown, K. J. (1999). What kind of text—for whom and when? Textual scaffolding for beginning readers. *The Reading Teacher, 53*(4), 292–307.

Dowhower, S. L. (1989). Repeated reading: Research into practice. *The Reading Teacher, 42*(7), 502–507.

Opitz, M. F., & Rasinski, T. V. (1998). *Good-bye round robin: 25 effective oral reading strategies*. Portsmouth, NH: Heinemann.

Osborn, J., Lehr, F., & Hiebert, E. H. (2003). *Focus on fluency*. Available at *www.prel.org*. Honolulu, HI: Pacific Resources for Education and Learning (PREL).

Raskinski, T. V. (2003). *The fluent reader: Oral reading strategies for building word recognition, fluency, and comprehension*. NY: Scholastic, Inc.

Rasinski, T. V., Blachowicz, C., & Lems, K. (2006). *Fluency instruction: Research-based best practices*. New York: Guilford Press.

Stahl, S. (2004). What do we know about fluency? In P. McCardle & V. Chhabra (Eds.), *The voice of evidence in reading research*, (pp. 187–211). Baltimore, MD: Paul H. Brookes.

chapter 6

Increasing Reading Vocabulary

Chapter Questions

1. What does research tell us about vocabulary learning?

2. How can teachers effectively assess students' vocabulary knowledge?

3. What evidence-based strategies are used in vocabulary instruction?

4. What can be done to assist students with special needs in vocabulary learning?

5. How can "reading backpacks" be used to involve parents in their child's vocabulary learning?

Can You Hear Me Now?

(Authors' Note: Learn more about how to teach using Joint Productive Activities (JPA) and other innovative instructional techniques from the Center for Research on Education, Diversity & Excellence (CREDE) *free online at: http://crede.berkeley.edu/standards/standards.html.)*

It is November, and Becky just arrived at Hillview School a week ago from Pennsylvania. She likes living on the west coast and has made a new friend, Katy. Katy has been asked to be Becky's personal fourth grade *docent* for a few weeks by their teacher, Mr. Garcia, to help Becky feel comfortable in her new surroundings. Today is a great day for Katy-the-docent for two reasons. For one thing it is a stormy day.

"I positively *love* a good gulley-washer!" says Katy to Becky rather theatrically. Not only that, today Mr. Garcia is having the students work in groups of four on a "joint productive activity" or JPA during science. Katy enjoys JPAs because she gets to work with a small group and they have a chance to solve a kind of puzzle as a team. When they finish, the group always gets to post their "findings" on chart paper for a Gallery Walk and see how the other students did the same task. Since Katy is Becky's docent they get to be in the same group. Katy and Becky are assigned to work with Alfred and Walker in their JPA group. Their task sheet is on the following page.

After their group work and Gallery Walk were finished and they were at lunch, Katy asked Becky what she liked best about the JPA.

"I have never done anything like it," replied Becky. "I'm not used to being allowed to *talk* in class like that. It was pretty great! I liked how we were able to decide together how to fill out the grid. Raymond had some ideas about cell phones I *never* would have thought of on my own. Also, Walker did a great job being our champion for the Gallery Walk. I think I'd like to try being champion sometime."

"No problem," said Katy. "Mr. Garcia makes sure everyone gets a turn. Just let the rest of the group know when you want to try it. We'll all help you!"

Joint Productive Activity

Can you hear me now?
Comparing and Contrasting Hi-Tech Vocabulary

Time Allowed: 45 minutes

Your Group's Task: Scan the article we have been reading together, "The Cell Phone Revolution," from *Invention & Technology* magazine to complete the "semantic feature analysis grid" below. In this chart you will compare and contrast the important ideas and characteristics of the words listed in the left-hand column. This activity should be done in the same way I modeled the example yesterday when we compared insects and animals.

Important things to remember from past JPAs:
1. All group members must agree on answers.
2. You should appoint a timekeeper to keep things moving. You will only have 45 minutes to complete this task. No exceptions.
3. Use a "six-inch voice" when you talk so you don't disturb the other groups.
4. No "side bar" conversations. Listen as each person talks; you might learn something!
5. Observe "equity of voice"; let everyone talk at least two times.

When your work is done, copy your semantic feature analysis grid onto the chart paper provided using the colored markers at your table. Vote for one of your group members to be the "champion" for the group to do a one-minute presentation at the beginning of the Gallery Walk to explain your answers. If someone hasn't been champion for a group before, let them give it a go if they are ready.

Here is the semantic feature analysis grid for you to complete.

The Cell Phone Revolution

	Wireless	Makes this tool work	Early communications technology	People who use or have used this	Tool for two-way communication technology
cellular phone tower					
mobile phone					
transistor radio					
antenna					
silicon chip					
subscriber					
BlackBerry					
walkie-talkie					

Directions: After checking for the meanings of the vocabulary words in the left-hand column against the magazine article, "The Cell Phone Revolution," put a "0" in the appropriate box if the word and description do NOT go together, a "1" if the word partly matches, and a "2" if they go together well. If you have disagreement in your group, vote for a majority opinion before marking your response.

What Does Research Tell Us About Vocabulary Learning?

Understanding word meanings are essential to reading success. Indeed, unless students are able to understand the meanings of words as they read, the process is reduced to mindless decoding (Fountas & Pinnell, 1996). Children who come to school with thousands of words "in their head"—words they can hear, understand, and use in their daily lives—are already on the path to reading success (Allington & Cunningham, 1996). Conversely, children who have small listening, speaking, and reading vocabularies— who are from what could be termed "language-deprived backgrounds"—must receive immediate attention if they are to have any real chance at reading success (National Research Council, 1998; Johnson, 2001).

> Words are the symbols we use to express ideas—*captions,* you might say, that describe our life experiences (Reutzel & Cooter, 2007). Vocabulary development is a process that goes on throughout life and can be enhanced in the classroom through enticing learning experiences. Except for the economically deprived or children with learning disabilities, most acquire a vocabulary of over 10,000 words during the first five years of their lives (Smith, 1987). Most school children will learn between 2,000 and 3,600 words per year, though estimates vary from 1,500 to more than 8,000 (Clark, 1993; Johnson, 2001; Nagy, Herman, & Anderson, 1985).

How Do Students Acquire New Vocabulary?

Truth is, there are many sources for learning new words. Some of them may surprise you—at least, just a bit. Students learn a great deal of their new vocabulary from conversations, independent reading, and even from the media. However, they do not learn new words from each source equally. To illustrate this point, Table 6.1 presents selected statistics revealing the sources of rare words (i.e., new or unfamiliar words) found in various language and text sources that are commonly accessed by children and adults (Cunningham & Stanovich, 1998; Rasinski, 1998).

Were you surprised by any of these findings? How about the number of rare words used by college graduates in their conversations with friends compared to the

Table 6.1   Sources of Rare Words in Children's and Adults' Vocabulary Acquisition

Source	Number of Rare (Uncommon) Words per 1,000
Adult speech (expert testimony)	28.4
Adult speech (college graduates to friends)	17.3
Prime time adult television	22.7
Mister Rogers and *Sesame Street*	2.0
Children's books—preschool	16.3
Children's books—elementary	30.9
Comic books	53.5
Popular magazines	66.7
Newspapers	68.3
Adult books	52.7
Scientific article abstracts	128.0

number commonly found in comic books!? Or, for that matter, the number of un-common words found in comic books compared to elementary children's books? Perhaps there is a case to be made for daily reading for children in self-selected books—including comics and popular magazines!

In this section, we take a careful look—an *evidence-based* look—at how children learn new words and at the kinds of vocabulary they should learn.

Research on Vocabulary Learning

In reviewing recent research on vocabulary learning and its role in reading, one conclusion becomes crystal clear: Reading and writing activities are dependent on words. Indeed, all good readers have a large store of high-frequency words they can read and spell instantly and automatically (Allington & Cunningham, 1996). So what do we know about vocabulary learning? To partially answer this question, we discuss in the following section key findings supported by recent research (e.g., Adams, 1990; Burns, Griffin, & Snow, 1999; Guthrie, 1982; Krashen, 1993; Johnson, 2001; McKeown, Beck, Omanson, & Pople, 1985; Nagy, Herman, & Anderson, 1985; National Reading Panel, 2000; National Research Council, 1998; Stahl, Hare, Sinatra, & Gregory, 1991; Templeton, 1997).

Getting to Know English Learners
Language acquisition is innate, but social interaction with adult caretakers is crucial for this acquisition to take place.

Vocabulary Is Built Through Language Interactions

Children who are exposed to vocabulary through conversations learn words they will need to recognize and comprehend while reading (K. Cooter, 2006). Burns, Griffin, and Snow (1999) explain early language acquisition this way:

Hope Madden/Merrill

> Vocalization in the crib gives way to play with rhyming language and nonsense words. Toddlers find that the words they use in conversation and the objects they represent are depicted in books—that the picture is a symbol for the real object and that the writing represents spoken language. In addition to listening to stories, children label the objects in books, comment on the characters, and request that an adult read to them. In their third and fourth years, children use new vocabulary and grammatical constructions in their own speech. Talking to adults is children's best source of exposure to new vocabulary and ideas. (p. 19)

Reading and being read to also increase vocabulary learning. Books give us challenging concepts, colorful description, and new knowledge and information about the world in which we live. Children whose backgrounds are language-rich come to school with relatively expansive vocabularies that are fertile ground for beginning reading instruction. Conversely, children who come to school with limited vocabularies as a result of either second language learning or the effects of poverty (Cooter, 2003) struggle to take even their first steps in reading and understanding texts. Burns, Griffin, and Snow (1999) ask, "How can they understand a science book about *volcanoes, silkworms,* or *Inuits?* What if they know nothing of *mountains, caterpillars,* or *snow* and *cold climates?*" (p. 70). As teachers, we must make sure that no child is left behind because of inadequate vocabulary development.

Research Findings by the National Reading Panel. To determine how vocabulary can best be taught and related to the reading comprehension process, the National Reading Panel (NRP) examined more than 20,000 research studies identified through electronic and manual literature searches. The studies reviewed suggest that vocabulary instruction does not necessarily lead to gains in comprehension *unless the methods used are appropriate to the age and ability of the reader.* Several studies found that the use of computers in vocabulary instruction was more effective than some traditional methods, indicating that software programs are emerging as potentially valuable aids to classroom teachers in the area of vocabulary instruction.

Vocabulary also can be learned incidentally in the context of storybook reading or in listening to others read. Learning words before reading a text is also helpful. The technique of **repeated exposure** (having the student encounter words in various contexts) appears to enhance vocabulary development.

The Four Types of Vocabulary

Although we often speak of vocabulary as if it were a single entity, it is not. Human beings acquire *four* types of vocabulary. They are, in descending order according to size, listening, speaking, reading, and writing vocabularies. **Listening vocabulary,** the largest, is made up of words we can hear and understand. All other vocabularies are subsets of our listening vocabulary. The second-largest vocabulary, **speaking vocabulary,** is comprised of words we use when we speak. Next is our **reading vocabulary,** those words we can identify and understand when we read. The smallest vocabulary is our **writing vocabulary**—words we use in writing. These four vocabularies are continually nurtured in the effective teacher's classroom.

Levels of Vocabulary Knowledge

As with most new learning, new vocabulary words and concepts are mastered by degree. The Partnership for Reading (2001) described three levels of word knowledge, or degree of familiarity with words: in relation almost *unknown, acquainted,* and *established.* Definitions for these levels are presented in Table 6.2. Bear in mind that these levels of vocabulary knowledge apply to each of the four vocabularies: listening, speaking, reading, and writing; thus, helping children build strong reading and writing vocabularies can sometimes be a formidable task indeed.

We sometimes learn new meanings to words that are already known to us. The word *race,* for example, has many different meanings (to move with great speed, a group of people, a political campaign). One of the most challenging tasks for students can be learning the meaning of a new word representing an unknown concept. According to research, much of learning in the content areas involves this type of word learning. As students learn about *deserts, hurricanes,* and *immigrants,*

Students use designated vocabulary words within written context. Visit the Teacher Prep Website (*www.prenhall.com/teacherprep*) and select "The Ghost of Count Dracula" in *Artifacts—Reading Methods/Vocabulary.* Respond to the accompanying questions that can be printed or sent directly to your instructor.

Go to the National Reading Panel Website at *www.nationalreadingpanel.org* to learn about their conclusions.

Table 6.2 Levels of Vocabulary Learning (Partnership for Reading, 2001)

Level of Word Knowledge	Definition
Unknown	The word is completely unfamiliar and its meaning is unknown.
Acquainted	The word is somewhat familiar; the student has some idea of its basic meaning.
Established	The word is very familiar; the student can immediately understand its meaning and use it correctly.

they may be learning both new concepts and new words. Learning words and concepts in science, social studies, and mathematics is even more challenging because each major concept often is associated with many other new concepts. For example, the concept *deserts* is often associated with other concepts that may be unfamiliar, such as *cactus, plateau,* and *mesa.* (Partnership for Reading, 2001, p. 43)

Grand Conversations provide opportunities for students to apply text vocabulary as they share interpretations and reflect feelings. Read "Grand Conversations" to learn more about "talking about text" in *Strategies and Lessons—Language Arts Methods/Talking* in the Teacher Prep Website (*www.prehnall.com/teacherprep*)

What Research Tells Us About Teaching Vocabulary

Most vocabulary is learned indirectly, but some vocabulary *must* be taught directly. The following conclusions about indirect vocabulary learning and direct vocabulary instruction are of particular interest and value to classroom teachers (National Reading Panel, 2000):

- *Children learn the meanings of most words indirectly, through everyday experiences with oral and written language.* Typically, children learn vocabulary indirectly in three ways. First, they participate in oral language every day. Children learn word meanings through conversations with other people; as they participate in conversations, they often hear words repeated several times. The more conversations children have, the more words they learn!

  Another indirect way children learn words is by being read to. Reading aloud is especially powerful when the reader pauses to define an unfamiliar word and, after reading, engages the child in a conversation about the book using the word. Conversations about books help children to learn new words and concepts and to relate them to their prior knowledge and experience (Partnership for Reading, 2001).

  The third way children learn new words indirectly is through their own reading. This is one of the reasons why many teachers believe that daily, independent reading practice sessions of 10–20 minutes are so critical (Krashen, 1993). Put simply, the more children read, the more words they'll learn. There is a caveat to mention on this point, however. Struggling readers are often incapable of sitting and reading on their own for extended periods of time. For best results, many readers get much more from their practice reading when working with a "buddy" who has greater ability.

- *Students learn vocabulary when they are taught individual words and word-learning strategies directly.* Direct instruction helps students learn difficult words (Johnson, 2001), such as those that represent complex concepts that are not part of students' everyday experiences (National Reading Panel, 2000).

We also know that when teachers preteach new words that are associated with a text students are about to read, better reading comprehension results.

- *Developing word consciousness can boost vocabulary learning.* **Word consciousness** learning activities stimulate an awareness of and interest in words, their meanings, and their power. Word-conscious students enjoy words and are zealous about learning them. In addition, they have been taught how to learn new and interesting words.

The keys to maximizing word consciousness are wide reading and use of the writing process. When reading a new book aloud to students, call their attention to the way the author chooses her words to convey particular meanings. Imagine the fun you can have discussing some of the intense words used by Gary Paulsen (1987) in his novel *Hatchet*, Shel Silverstein's (1974) clever use of rhyming words in his book of poetry *Where the Sidewalk Ends,* or the downright magical word selection employed by J. K. Rowling (1997) in *Harry Potter and the Sorcerer's Stone.* Encourage your students to play with words, by constructing puns or raps. Help them research a word's history and find examples of a word's usage in their everyday lives.

Written vocabulary is reflected in personal journals as thinking and experiences are recorded. Access the Teacher Prep Website *(www.prenhall.com/teacherprep)* and go to *Strategies and Lessons—Language Arts Methods/Writing* to find "Personal Journals."

Which Words Should Be Taught?

McKeown and Beck (1988) have addressed an important issue in their research: Which vocabulary should be taught in elementary classrooms? They point out that one problem with traditional vocabulary instruction in basal readers has been the equal treatment of all categories of words. For example, a mythology selection in a basal reader about Arachne, who loved to weave, gives the word *loom* as much attention as the word *agreement.* McKeown and Beck point out that although the word *loom* may be helpful in understanding more about spinning, it is a word of relatively low use compared to the word *agreement,* which is key to understanding the story and of much higher utility as students move into adult life.

Not all words are created equal, especially in terms of difficulty in elementary classrooms. As McKeown and Beck (1988) explain:

> The choice of which words to teach and what kind of attention to give them depends on a variety of factors, such as importance of the words for understanding the selection, relationship to specific domains of knowledge, general utility, and relationship to other lessons and classroom events. (p. 45)

Why You Shouldn't Try to Teach *All* Unknown Words

There are several good reasons why you should not try to directly teach all unknown words. For one thing, the text may have far too many words that are unknown to students for direct instruction. Limit vocabulary teaching time to not more than 5 to 10 minutes so that students can spend the bulk of their time actually reading. Most students will be able to comprehend a fair number of new words, up to 5 percent, simply by using context clues in the passage. Students need many opportunities to practice and use the word-learning strategies you are teaching them for learning unknown words on their own.

Words You *Should* Teach

Realistically, you will probably be able to teach *thoroughly* only a few new words (eight to ten) per week, so you need to choose the words you teach carefully. Focus

Video Classroom

Visit a primary grades classroom to view vocabulary instruction

Refer to our Teacher Prep Website (*www.prenhall.com/ teacherprep*) **for a link to Video Classroom. Select Reading Methods to view "Introducing Words to Young Readers—Vocabulary.**

As you view the clip, note how the teacher introduces the vocabulary words in this lesson.

- Why might the teacher select the words "she" and "inside" to introduce for the story of "Hermit Crab"?
- What word learning techniques are utilized? Why are they powerful?
- What other alternate forms might be used for vocabulary introduction?

Video Classroom

Observe the introduction of tricky words, phrases, and word features to learn how readers make associations with them for accurate, future recall. View an example on the accompanying **CD** for this text. Click on *Guided Reading in Second Grade* to view the second clip titled *"2nd Book Introduction."*

- During the clip, notice how "windows" are created with fingers, how they find "what is different" about a word and how the phonics is incorporated, as they look closer at tricky words.
- Following viewing of the video, read the "Teacher" comments and list the items that she has considered in selecting the text and planning the introduction. A thorough book introduction is reflected in a successful first reading for a child.
- To enhance your understanding of powerful book introductions, read comments from "experts," "literature," and "students."

your energy on high-utility words and words that are important to the meaning of the selections you will be reading in class.

Sight Words. **Sight words** occur frequently in most texts and account for the majority of written words. Understanding text relies, in part, on the immediate recognition of these high-frequency words. Studies of print have found that just 109 words account for upwards of 50 percent of all words in student textbooks, and a total of only 5,000 words accounts for about 90 percent of the words in student texts (Adams 1990b; Carroll, Davies, & Richman, 1971). Knowledge of high-frequency sight words can help readers manage text in a more fluent way. Many of these words, such as *the, from, but, because, that,* and *this,* sometimes called **structure words,** carry little meaning but do affect the flow and coherence of the text being read. The actual meaning of the text depends on the ready knowledge of less-frequent, or **lexical words,** such as *automobile, aristocrat, pulley, streetcar, Martin, Luther, King,* and *phantom.* Adams and her colleagues (1991) concluded that

. . . while the cohesion and connectivity of English text is owed most to its frequent words (e.g., *it, that, this, and, because, when, while*), its meaning depends disproportionately on its less-frequent words (e.g., *doctor, fever, infection, medicine, penicillin, Alexander, Fleming, melon, mold, poison, bacteria, antibiotic, protect, germs, disease*). (p. 394)

Because it is critical that all students learn to instantly recognize sight words, the teacher should have a reliable list of these words as a resource. Figure 6.1 presents the Fry (1999) list of the 300 most common words in print. The Fry list is widely regarded as the best-researched list of sight words in the English language.

Sight Words for Bilingual Classrooms (Spanish). Just as the most common sight words have been identified in English, high-frequency words have also been identified for Spanish (Cornejo, 1972). This popular word list is divided by grade and presented in Figure 6.2.

Key Vocabulary. Silvia Ashton-Warner, in her classic book *Teacher* (1963), described **key vocabulary** as "organic," or lexical words that emerge from the child's experiences. Ashton-Warner describes key vocabulary words as "captions" for important events in the child's life.

Children can be taught key vocabulary through a variety of direct instructional strategies. One such strategy is described here: The student meets with the teacher individually at an appointed time, or during a group experience, and indicates which words he or she would like to learn. The teacher might prompt: "What word would you like to learn today?" The child responds with a lexical word—*police, ghost, sing*. The teacher writes the word on an index card or a small piece of tagboard using a dark marker. The teacher directs the student to share the word with as many people as possible during the day. After the child has done so, the word is added to his or her writing folder or word bank for future use in writing.

Ashton-Warner found that the most common categories of key vocabulary children wanted to learn were (1) fear words *(dog, bull, kill, police);* (2) sex (as she called them) or affection words *(love, kiss, sing, darling);* (3) *locomotion words (bus, car, truck, jet);* and (4) a miscellaneous category that generally reflects cultural and other considerations *(socks, frog, beer, Disneyland, Dallas Cowboys).*

Ashton-Warner (1963) referred to key vocabulary as "one-look words" because one look is usually all that is required for permanent learning to take place. The reason that these words seem so easy for children to learn is that they usually carry strong emotional significance and, once seen, are almost never forgotten.

Discovery Words. During the course of a typical school day, students are exposed to many new words. These words are often discovered as a result of studies in the content areas. Words such as *experiment, algebra, social, enterprise, conquest, Bengal tiger, spider,* and *cocoon* find their way into students' listening and speaking vocabularies. Every effort should be made to add these **discovery words** to the word bank as they are discussed in their natural context. Such words often appear in student compositions. Developing vocabulary in content areas can help children discover words in their natural context.

Which Words Are the Most Difficult to Learn? Some words (or phrases) can be especially difficult for students to learn (National Reading Panel, 2000).

- **Words with multiple meanings** are quite challenging for students. They sometimes have trouble understanding that words with the same spelling and/or

Figure 6.1 Fry New Instant Word List

First Hundred				Second Hundred				Third Hundred			
1–25	26–50	51–75	76–100	101–125	126–150	151–175	176–200	201–225	226–250	251–275	276–300
the	or	will	number	over	say	set	try	high	saw	important	miss
of	one	up	no	new	great	put	kind	every	left	until	idea
and	had	other	way	sound	where	end	hand	near	don't	children	enough
a	by	about	could	take	help	does	picture	add	few	side	eat
to	words	out	people	only	through	another	again	food	while	feet	face
in	but	many	my	little	much	well	change	between	along	car	watch
is	not	then	than	work	before	large	off	own	might	mile	far
you	what	them	first	know	line	must	play	below	close	night	Indian
that	all	these	water	place	right	big	spell	country	something	walk	really
it	were	so	been	year	too	even	air	plant	seem	white	almost
he	we	some	call	live	mean	such	away	last	next	sea	let
was	when	her	who	me	old	because	animal	school	hard	began	above
for	your	would	am	back	any	turn	house	father	open	grow	girl
on	can	make	its	give	same	here	point	keep	example	took	sometimes
are	said	like	now	most	tell	why	page	tree	begin	river	mountain
as	there	him	find	very	boy	ask	letter	never	life	four	cut
with	use	into	long	after	follow	went	mother	start	always	carry	young
his	an	time	down	thing	came	men	answer	city	those	state	talk
they	each	has	day	our	want	read	found	earth	both	once	soon
I	which	look	did	just	show	need	study	eye	paper	book	list
at	she	two	get	name	also	land	still	light	together	hear	song
be	do	more	come	good	around	different	learn	thought	got	stop	being
this	how	write	made	sentence	farm	home	should	head	group	without	leave
have	their	go	may	man	three	us	America	under	often	second	family
from	if	see	part	think	small	move	world	story	run	later	it's

Source: Fry, Edward. (2000). *1000 Instant Words*. Westminster, CA: Teacher Created Materials.

Figure 6.2 Cornejo's High-Frequency Word List for Spanish (Graded)

Pre-Primer	Primer	1st	2nd	3rd	4th	5th
a	alto	bonita	ayer	amar	árbol	amistad
azul	flor	arriba	aqui	aquí	bandera	azucar
bajo	blusa	fruta	año	debajo	abeja	contento
mi	ella	globo	cerca	familia	escuela	corazón
mesa	ir	estar	desde	fiesta	fácil	compleaños
pan	leche	café	donde	grande	fuego	edad
mamá	más	letra	hacer	hermana	hacia	escribir
lado	niño	luna	hasta	jueves	idea	felicidad
la	padre	luz	hijo	lápiz	jardín	guitarra
papá	por	muy	hoy	miércoles	llegar	estrella
me	si	noche	leer	once	manzana	igual
no	tan	nombre	libro	quince	muñeca	invierno
esa	sobre	nosotros	martes	sábado	naranja	orquesta
el	sin	nunca	mejor	semana	saludar	primavera
en	tras	ojo	mucho	silla	sueño	recordar
cuna	color	pelota	oir	sobrino	señorita	respeto
dos	al	porque	papel	vivir	tierra	tijeras
mi	día	rojo	paz	zapato	traer	último
de	bien	té	quien	tarde	ventana	querer
los	chico	taza	usted	traje	queso	otoño

From Cornejo, R. (1972). *Spanish High-Frequency Word List*. Austin, TX: Southwestern Educational Development Laboratory.

pronunciation can have different meanings, depending on their context. For example, note the different uses of *run* in the following sentences:

Molly complained when she found a *run* in her hose.

Jeff Johnston plans to *run* for Congress.

Also note the different uses and pronunciations of the word *read* in the following sentences:

I will *read* the story later today.

I *read* the story yesterday.

For some students, choosing a context-specific definition from a list of possible definitions in a dictionary can be daunting.

• **Idiomatic expressions** are combinations of words that has a meaning that is different from the meanings of the individual words. These can be especially problematical for language-deficient students and for students who are English language learners (ELL) (Cooter, 2003). Because idiomatic expressions do not convey the literal meanings of the words used, you may need to explain to students expressions such as "apple of my eye," "hell in a handbasket," or "like a chicken with its head cut off." A great book to use as a catalyst for discussing idioms is Fred Gwynne's (1976) *A Chocolate Moose for Dinner.*

Getting to Know English Learners
While urban students may have their own idiomatic expressions, or "slang" (that many "mainstream" students emulate and adapt), depending on one's culture and language, some idioms may be very foreign indeed!

How Can Teachers Effectively Assess Students' Vocabulary Knowledge?

As a teacher, you must consider ways of assessing reading vocabulary knowledge to plan and evaluate instruction (Blachowicz & Fisher, 2006). While everyone would surely agree that vocabulary knowledge is important to reading success, attempting to measure the extent of student vocabulary acquisition can be problematic. Dale Johnson (2001), a prominent researcher in the area of vocabulary learning, explains three problem areas: (1) choosing *which* words to test, (2) determining what it means for a student to actually "know" a word, and (3) deciding how to reliably test vocabulary knowledge. In this section, we take a look at ways classroom teachers can construct useful vocabulary assessments. We also examine commercially available assessment instruments sometimes used for diagnostic purposes.

Word Maps for Assessment and Teaching

A **word map** (Schwartz & Raphael, 1985) is a graphic rendering—a sketch—of a word's meaning. It answers three important questions about the word: What is it? What is it like? What are some examples? Answers to these questions are extremely valuable because they help children link the new word or concept to their prior knowledge and world experiences, a process known to have an effect on reading comprehension (Stahl et al., 1991). For this reason, word mapping can be used as an assessment tool to measure the depth of a student's understanding of a word. Mapping can also be used during instruction to help children construct new understandings of a word or concept. An example of a word map is shown in Figure 6.3.

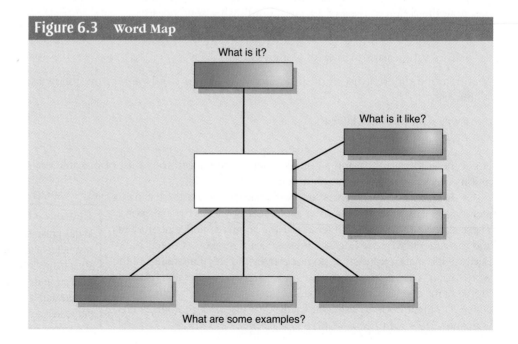

Figure 6.3 Word Map

What is it?

What is it like?

What are some examples?

Introducing this vocabulary assessment to students is a relatively easy task. First, the teacher presents the idea of using this kind of graphic organizer to understand new word meanings and models the word map with examples and think-alouds. Next, students work with the teacher using word maps featuring the target word(s) to be evaluated using the three key questions indicated earlier.

Simple concepts should be used in teacher modeling exercises to help students learn how to map. A practice map might be constructed using the word *car*. Answers for each of the word map questions that might be offered by elementary students follow:

Word: *car*

What is it? (Something that moves people and things from one place to another.)

What is it like? (It has four wheels, metal, glass, lights, seats, and a steering wheel.)

What are some examples? (Honda, station wagon, Thunderbird, convertible)

After working through several examples of word maps with the class, the teacher should give students opportunities to practice using the map before moving on to assessing word knowledge.

Before-and-After Word Knowledge Self-Ratings

Blachowicz and Fisher (2006) recommend the **before-and-after word knowledge self-rating** as an efficient way to survey student vocabulary knowledge. In introducing students to a new text, the teacher lists important vocabulary-building words in that text along the left-hand side of a before-and-after word knowledge self-rating form and distributes a copy of the form to students. Using the three-level self-rating on the form, students indicate whether they do not know a word (level 1), have heard the word (level 2), or can define and use the word (level 3). This rating system is congruent with research findings of the Partnership for Reading (2001) (alluded to earlier in this chapter) and the National Reading Panel (2000), which describe the three levels of vocabulary learning: unknown, acquainted, and established. Figure 6.4 features a completed before-and-after word knowledge self-rating form completed by a student before and after reading a text on the theme of transportation.

Teacher-Constructed Vocabulary Tests

Johnson (2001) summarized the common ways teachers construct effective vocabulary tests to fit their curriculum and students' learning needs. You can have students do one or more of the following:

- ✓ Read a target word in isolation (by itself) and select a picture that matches.
- ✓ Look at a picture and find the matching word.
- ✓ Read a target word in isolation and match it to its definition.
- ✓ Read a target word in isolation and find its synonym in a list.
- ✓ Read a target word in isolation and find its opposite (antonym) in a list.
- ✓ Read a target word in the context of a sentence or short paragraph and find a definition, synonym, or antonym in a list.

Figure 6.4 Before-and-After Word Knowledge Self-Rating Form

Before-Reading Word Knowledge			
Key Terms	I can define and use this word in a sentence. *(Established)* 3	I have heard this word before. *(Acquainted)* 2	I don't know this word. *(Unknown)* 1
mileage	X		
freight		X	
GPS		X	
passenger	X		
fossil fuel			X
ethanol			X
route			X
express		X	
destination		X	
ETA			X
alternative fuels			X

After-Reading Word Knowledge				
Key Terms	Self-Rating (3, 2, 1)	Define	Use in a Sentence	Questions I Still Have About This Term
mileage	3	How far it is to a place you're going	The mileage from Salt Lake City to Provo is about 50 miles.	
freight	3	Things that are being shipped by a truck or by another way	Boxes on a truck are called freight.	
GPS	2	A kind of compass	A GPS can help me find my way home.	I can't remember what GPS means.
passenger	3	A person going somewhere in a vehicle	I was once a passenger in an airplane.	
fossil fuel	2	Makes a car run	Cars use fossil fuels to run the engine.	I don't know what *fossil* means.
ethanol	1			I can't remember anything about this. Did we really learn this?
route	3	How you are getting to a destination	I took a northern route to get to Canada.	
express	3	Getting something or someone to their destination quickly	I sent my package by FedEx overnight express.	
destination	3	Where you are going	My destination on my next trip is Boston.	
ETA	3	When you are getting somewhere	My estimated time of arrival or ETA is 9 A.M.	
alternative fuels	2	Like gas and diesel fuel	Some cars run on gas; others use diesel.	I think there may be other kinds, but I'm not sure.

✓ Read a sentence that has a target word left out. Fill in the blank with the missing word.

✓ Read a sentence and supply the missing target word orally.

✓ Read the target word and draw a picture of it. (Best used with young children.)

✓ Read the target word and place it in a category.

Modified Cloze Passages

Cloze passages, from the word *closure*, are short passages from books commonly used in the classroom in which certain words have been deleted (usually every fifth word) and replaced with a blank. For vocabulary assessment, teachers often use a **modified cloze passage** in which targeted vocabulary words have been deleted. Students are asked to read the cloze passages and fill in the missing words based on what they believe makes sense using context clues. In the modified cloze example (Figure 6.5), we have supplied in parentheses the target words selected by the teacher for this partial passage.

Cloze tests require that students use their background knowledge of a subject, their understanding of basic syntax (word order relationships), and their word and sentence meaning (semantics) knowledge to guess what a word missing from print might be (Cooter & Flynt, 1996). If students know the word and are reading effectively and with adequate comprehension, they are usually able to accurately guess the missing word—or, at least, a word of the same part of speech. This helps the teacher know whether the student has sufficient background knowledge and vocabulary to cope with a particular text. Materials needed to complete a cloze test include the textbook, a computer and word-processing program, and means by which to copy the cloze passage for students.

Maze Passages

The **maze passage** (Guthrie, Seifert, Burnham, & Caplan, 1974) is a modification of the cloze passage. Maze passages tend to be less frustrating to students than cloze passages because they are provided three possible answers to choose from in filling in the blank. Thus, students tend to get a greater percentage of items correct. The purpose and structure of maze passages are otherwise identical to those of cloze passages. You will need the textbook, a computer and word-processing program, and means by which to create the passage for students. Figure 6.6 features a partial maze passage.

Figure 6.5   Cloze Passage

There exists an old American Indian legend about an eagle that thought it was a chicken. It happens that a *(Hopi)* farmer and his only son decided to go to a nearby mountain to find an eagle's nest. The *(journey)* would take them all day so they brought along some *(rations)* and water for the trip. The man and the boy hiked the *(enormous)* fields of *(maize)* and beans into the day. Soon thereafter they were on the mountain and the climb became *(rigorous)* and hazardous. They eventually looked back toward their village and at the *(panoramic)* view of the entire valley.

Figure 6.6 Maze Passage

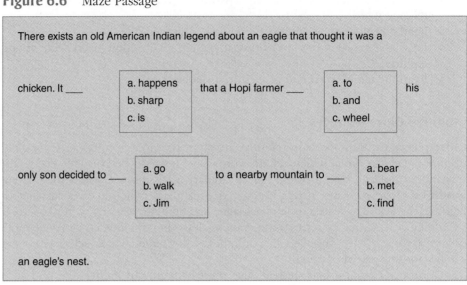

Vocabulary Flash Cards

A traditional way to conduct a quick assessment of a student's vocabulary knowledge uses flash cards. High-frequency words (those appearing most often in print) as well as other high-utility and specialized words for content instruction are printed individually in bold marker on flash cards and displayed to students for them to identify. Flash cards can also be produced with the computer and a word-processing program.

For recording purposes, you will also need a master list of the words to record each student's responses.

"Flash" each card to the student, one at a time, and ask him to name the word. Allow about five seconds for the student to respond. Circle any words that the student does not know or that he mispronounces on the student's record form.

This technique can be used to quickly assess vocabulary knowledge of an entire class. After you have shown the flash cards to all students, compile a list of troublesome words for whole-class or small-group instruction.

Published Diagnostic Vocabulary Tests

Several commercially published vocabulary tests are available. These are typically used by Title I reading specialists and special education faculty, but can be used by teachers who have appropriate training. We recommend three tests for assessing a student's word knowledge or **receptive vocabulary.** One is intended for native English speakers, and the other two are for students who speak Spanish as their first language and are learning to speak and read in English.

- *Peabody Picture Vocabulary Test, Third Edition* (PPVT–III) (Dunn & Dunn, 1997). The PPVT–III is a quickly administered instrument (11–12 minutes) that indicates how strong a student's vocabulary knowledge is compared to other students of the same age nationally. Results can help the teacher better understand the needs of students in terms of formal and informal vocabulary instruction.

- *Test de Vocabulario en Imágenes Peabody* (TVIP) (Dunn, Lugo, Padilla, & Dunn, 1986). This test is an adaptation of an early version of the previously described *Peabody Picture Vocabulary Test* for native Spanish speakers. It takes about 10 to 15 minutes to administer and measures Spanish vocabulary knowledge.
- *Woodcock–Muñoz Language Survey* (WMLS), English and Spanish Forms (Woodcock & Muñoz-Sandoval, 1993). Teachers, particularly in urban centers, often have a large number of students who are learning English as a second language (ESL). The extent to which students have acquired a listening and speaking vocabulary in English is an important factor in reading instruction because reading (a) is a language skill, and (b) depends on learners having a fairly strong English vocabulary. The WMLS is a widely respected instrument used throughout the United States. It takes about 20 minutes to administer. It features two subtests: Oral Language and Reading/Writing.

Another test used widely in schools for special diagnoses of reading ability, the *Woodcock Reading Mastery Tests–Revised* (Woodcock et al., 1997), includes a norm-referenced word identification subtest among its battery of six individually administered subtests. These subtests measure reading abilities from kindergarten through adult levels, and cover visual-auditory learning, letter identification, word identification, word attack, word comprehension, and passage comprehension. The Woodcock's design reveals a skills perspective of reading, and divides assessment into two segments according to age and ability levels: readiness and reading achievement. The WRMT–R/NU reports norm-referenced data for both of its forms and offers suggestions for remediation. Results may be calculated either manually or by using the convenient scoring program developed for personal computers.

Vocabulary can be taught within context to a whole group using the cloze exercises. Go to the Teacher Prep Website (*www.prenhall/teacherprep*) and link to *Strategies and Lessons*. Select *Reading Methods/ Vocabulary* and read "Speedy Cloze Words."

What Are Examples of Research-Proven Strategies Used in Vocabulary Instruction?

An important question for teachers is this: How can we help students increase their vocabulary knowledge? In this section we present some of the most successful methods.

Principles of Effective Vocabulary Instruction

From the research cited previously, as well as that conducted by Stahl (1986) and Rasinski (1998), we have developed a list of principles for effective vocabulary instruction.

Principle 1: Vocabulary is learned best through explicit, *systematic instruction.* Context helps readers choose the correct meaning for multiple-meaning words. The old adage that "experience is the best teacher" is certainly true in vocabulary learning. The next best way to learn new vocabulary is through indirect, vicarious experience through daily reading in interesting and varied texts (Rasinski, 1998). Marilyn Jager Adams (1990) put it this way:

The best way to build children's visual vocabulary is to have them read meaningful words in meaningful contexts. The more meaningful reading that children do, the larger will be their repertoires of meanings, the greater their sensitivity to orthographic structure, and the stronger, better refined, and more productive will be their associations between words and meanings. (p. 156)

Principle 2: Teachers should offer both definitions *and* context *during vocabulary instruction.* Children learn new words in two ways. First, they learn basic definitions or information that helps them connect the new word to known words (i.e., elaboration). This step can be accomplished by simply providing the definition, by building with students semantic maps linking the known with the new, and through examining the target word in terms of its synonym, antonym, classification, root, and affixes.

Context, which is the second foundation for building word knowledge, has to do with knowing the core definition of a word and understanding how that definition varies in different texts. For example, the word *run* is generally thought of as a verb meaning "to move swiftly." When looking for this simple word in the dictionary, one quickly realizes that the word *run* has approximately 50 definitions! Context helps the reader know which definition the author intends. In fact, without context, it is impossible to ascertain which meaning of a particular word is intended. Thus, it is important for teachers to help students understand both the definitional and contextual relations of words. Vocabulary instruction should include both aspects if reading comprehension is to benefit.

Principle 3: Effective vocabulary instruction must include depth of learning as well as breadth of word knowledge. Deep processing connects new vocabulary with students' background knowledge. Depth of learning, or **deep processing** of vocabulary, has two potential meanings: relating the word to information the student already knows (elaboration), and spending time on the task of learning new words (expansion). Stahl (1986) defines three levels of processing for vocabulary instruction:

1. *Association processing:* Students learn simple associations through synonyms and word associations.

2. *Comprehension processing:* Students move beyond simple associations by doing something with the association, such as fitting the word into a sentence blank, classifying the word with other words, or finding antonyms.

3. *Generation processing:* Students use the comprehended association to generate a new or novel product (sometimes called *generative comprehension*). This could be a restatement of the definition in the

student's own words, a novel sentence using the word correctly in a clear context, or a connection of the definition to the student's personal experiences. One caution relates to the generation of sentences by students: Sometimes students generate sentences without really processing the information deeply, as with students who begin each sentence with "This is a . . . ." (Pearson, 1985; Stahl, 1986).

Principle 4: Students need to have multiple exposures *to new reading vocabulary words.* Multiple exposures to new vocabulary improve comprehension. Vocabulary learning requires repetition. To learn words thoroughly, students need to see, hear, and use words many times in many contexts (Rasinski, 1998). Providing students with multiple exposures in varied contexts appears to significantly improve reading comprehension. The amount of time spent reading these new words also seems to be a relevant factor in improving comprehension.

> **Getting to Know English Learners**
> Remember, ELs may apply their knowledge of cognates when they come across unfamiliar vocabulary words. (Refer to Chapter 4.)

In the remainder of this section we discuss some of the strategies we have found effective in vocabulary instruction.

Word Banks

Word banks are used to help students collect and review sight words. They can also be used as personal dictionaries. A word bank is simply a student-constructed box, file, or notebook in which newly discovered words are stored. Students review the words in their bank for use in their writing. In the early grades, teachers often collect small shoeboxes from local stores for this purpose. Students decorate the boxes to make them their own. In the upper grades, more formal-looking word banks—notebooks or recipe boxes—are used to give an "adult" appearance.

Alphabetic dividers can be used at all levels to facilitate the quick location of word bank words. Alphabetic dividers in the early grades help students rehearse and reinforce knowledge of alphabetical order. Figure 6.7 shows a sample word bank.

Specific Word Instruction

Specific word instruction can deepen students' knowledge of word meanings and, in turn, help them understand what they are hearing or reading (Johnson, 2001). It also can help them use words accurately in speaking and writing. Three ways of providing specific word instruction have been drawn from research evidence (National Reading Panel, 2000; Partnership for Reading, 2001): preteaching vocabulary, extended instruction, and repeated exposures.

What Specific Word Instruction Looks Like in the Classroom. The Partnership for Reading, a federally funded collaborative effort of the National Institute for Literacy, the National Institute of Child Health and Human Development, and the U. S. Department of Education, published in 2001 a booklet titled *Put Reading First: The Research Building Blocks for Teaching Children to Read.* This document was compiled to help disseminate data from the 2000 report of the

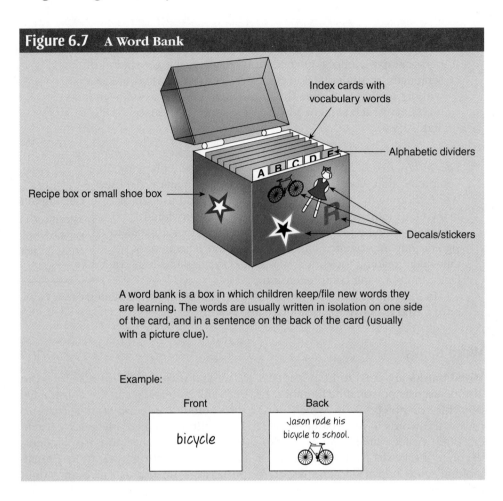

Figure 6.7 A Word Bank

A word bank is a box in which children keep/file new words they are learning. The words are usually written in isolation on one side of the card, and in a sentence on the back of the card (usually with a picture clue).

Example:

Front: bicycle

Back: Jason rode his bicycle to school.

You can order a free copy of *Put Reading First: The Research Building Blocks for Teaching Children to Read* (2001) online at *www.nifl.gov*. The report of the National Reading Panel titled *Teaching Children to Read: An Evidence-Based Assessment of the Scientific Research Literature on Reading and Its Implications for Reading Instruction* is also available at *www.nationalreadingpanel.org*.

National Reading Panel, and covers the topics of phonemic awareness instruction, phonics instruction, fluency instruction, vocabulary instruction, and text comprehension instruction. In order to help you better understand what each of the three specific word instruction components might look like in the classroom, we include examples after each definition borrowed from the *Put Reading First* booklet.

Preteaching Vocabulary. Teaching new vocabulary prior to students' reading of a text helps students learn new words and comprehend what they read.

AN EXAMPLE OF CLASSROOM INSTRUCTION

Preteaching Vocabulary*

A teacher plans to have his third grade class read the novel *Stone Fox,* by John Reynolds Gardiner. In this novel, a young boy enters a dogsled race in hope of winning prize money to pay the taxes on his grandfather's farm. The teacher knows that understanding the concept of taxes is important to understanding the novel's plot. Therefore, before his students begin reading the novel, the teacher may do several things to make sure that they understand what the concept means and why it is important to the story. For example, the teacher may:

- engage students in a discussion of the concept of taxes
- read a sentence from the book that contains the word *taxes* and ask students to use context and their prior knowledge to try to figure out what it means.

To solidify their understanding of the word, the teacher might ask students to use taxes in their own sentences.

*From *Put Reading First: The Research Building Blocks for Teaching Children to Read* (2001). Non-copyrighted material published by the National Institute for Literacy. Available online at *www.nifl.gov.*

Extended Instruction.   Students should be saturated (marinated!) with word-learning activities spread over an extended period of time. These should be activities that actively engage students as opposed to passive learning tasks.

AN EXAMPLE OF CLASSROOM INSTRUCTION

Extended Instruction*

A first grade teacher wants to help her students understand the concept of jobs, which is part of her social studies curriculum. Over a period of time, the teacher engages students in exercises in which they work repeatedly with the concept of jobs. Students have many opportunities to see and actively use the word *jobs* in various contexts that reinforce its meaning.

The teacher begins by asking students what they already know about jobs and by having them give examples of jobs their parents have. The class also has a discussion about the jobs of different people who work at the school.

The teacher then reads the class a simple book about jobs. The book introduces the idea that different jobs help people meet their needs, and that jobs provide either goods or services. The book does not use the words *goods* and *services;* rather, it uses the verbs *makes* and *helps*.

The teacher then asks students to make up sentences describing their parents' jobs using the verbs *makes* and *helps* (e.g., "My mother is a doctor. She helps sick people get well.").

Next, the teacher asks students to brainstorm other jobs. Together, they decide whether the jobs are "making jobs" or "helping jobs." The job names are placed under the appropriate headings on a bulletin board. Students might also suggest jobs that do not fit neatly into either category.

The teacher then asks students to share which kind of job—making or helping—they would like to have when they grow up.

The teacher also asks students to talk with their parents about jobs. She tells students to bring to class two new examples of jobs—one making job and one helping job.

As students come across different jobs throughout the year (for example, through reading books, on field trips, through classroom guests), they add the jobs to the appropriate categories on the bulletin board.

*From *Put Reading First: The Research Building Blocks for Teaching Children to Read* (2001). Non-copyrighted material published by the National Institute for Literacy. Available online at *www.nifl.gov.*

Repeated Exposures to Vocabulary.   You will find that the more students use new words in different contexts, the more likely they are to learn the words permanently. When children see, hear, and work with specific words, they seem to learn them better.

AN EXAMPLE OF CLASSROOM INSTRUCTION

Repeated Exposures to Vocabulary*

A second grade class is reading a biography of Benjamin Franklin. The biography discusses Franklin's important role as a scientist. The teacher wants to make sure that her students understand the meaning of the words *science* and *scientist,* both because the words are important to understanding the biography and because they are obviously very useful words to know in school and in everyday life.

At every opportunity, therefore, the teacher draws her students' attention to the words. She points out the words *science* and *scientist* in textbooks and reading selections, particularly in her science curriculum. She has students use the words in their own writing, especially during science instruction.

She also asks them to listen for and find in print the words as they are used outside of the classroom—in newspapers, magazines, at museums, in television shows or movies, or on the Internet.

Then, as they read the biography, she discusses with students ways in which Benjamin Franklin was a scientist and what science meant in his time.

*From *Put Reading First: The Research Building Blocks for Teaching Children to Read* (2001). Noncopyrighted material published by the National Institute for Literacy. Available online at *www.nifl.gov.*

Making Words

Making Words (Cunningham & Cunningham, 1992) is an excellent word-learning strategy that helps children improve their phonetic understanding of words through invented or "temporary spellings" while also increasing their repertoire of vocabulary words they can recognize in print (Reutzel & Cooter, 2007). Making Words will be a familiar strategy to anyone who has played the popular crossword board game Scrabble.

Students are given a number of specific letters with which to make words. They begin by making two- or three-letter words in a given amount of time; they then must increase the number of letters in each word they make until they arrive at a specific word that uses all the letters. This final word is usually the main word to be taught for the day. By manipulating the letters to make words using temporary or "transitional" spellings, students have an opportunity to practice their phonemic awareness skills. Making Words is recommended as a 15-minute activity for first and second graders. In Figures 6.8 and 6.9, we summarize and adapt the steps in planning and teaching a Making Words lesson suggested by Cunningham and Cunningham (1992).

Figure 6.10 features directions for two more lessons suggested by Cunningham and Cunningham (1992) that may be useful for helping students learn the Making Words procedure. Examples of Making Words activities and another Cunningham favorite, word walls, are discussed in Chapters 10 through 12.

Figure 6.8   Planning a Making Words Lesson

1. Choose a word to be the final word to be emphasized in the lesson. It should be a key word that is chosen from a fiction or nonfiction selection to be read by the class, or it may simply be of particular interest to the group. Be sure to select a word that has enough vowels and/or one that fits letter-sound patterns useful for most students at their developmental stage in reading and writing. For illustrative purposes, we will use the word *thunder*, as is suggested by Cunningham and Cunningham (1992).

2. Make a list of short words that can be spelled using the letters in the main word to be learned. From the word *thunder,* one could derive the following words: *red, Ted, Ned, den, end, her, net, hut, herd, nut, turn, hunt, hurt, under, hunted, turned, thunder.*

    From the words you were able to list, select 12 to 15 that represent a variety of characteristics of written language: (a) words that contain a certain pattern, (b) big and little words, (c) words that can be made with the same letters in different positions (as with *Ned, end, den*), (d) a proper noun, if possible, to remind students about using capital letters, and (e) words that students already have in their listening vocabularies.

3. Write each word on a large index card and order the words from smallest to largest. Also, write each of the individual letters found in the key word for the day on a large index card. Make two sets.

4. Reorder the words one more time to group them according to letter patterns and/or to demonstrate how shifting around letters can form new words. Store the two sets of large single-letter cards in two envelopes—one for the teacher and one for students participating in the modeling activity.

5. Store the word stacks in envelopes and note on the outside the words/patterns to be emphasized during the lesson. Also note clues you can use with students to help them discover the words you desire. For example, "See if you can make a three-letter word that is the name of the room in some people's homes where they like to watch television." *(den)*

Figure 6.9   Teaching a Making Words Lesson

1. Place the large single letters from the key word in the pocket chart or along the chalkboard ledge.

2. For modeling purposes the first time you use Making Words, select one student to be the "passer"; this student will pass the large single letters to other designated students.

3. Hold up and name each of the letter cards and have students selected to participate in the modeling exercise respond by holding up their matching card.

4. Write the numeral 2 (or 3, if there are no two-letter words in this lesson) on the board. Next, tell student volunteers the clue you developed for the desired word. Direct them to put together two (or three) of their letters to form the desired word.

5. Continue directing students to make more words using the clues provided until you have helped them discover all but the final key word (the one that uses all the letters). Ask student volunteers if they can guess what the key word is. If not, ask the remainder of the class if anyone can guess what it is. If no one is able to do so, offer a meaning clue (e.g., "I am thinking of a word with _____ letters that means . . .").

6. Repeat these steps the next day with the whole group as a guided practice activity using a new word.

Function ("Four-Letter") Words

Many words are very difficult for students to learn because their meanings are abstract rather than concrete. Referred to as *structure words* (also *functors, glue words,* and *four-letter words*), these words are perhaps the most difficult to teach because

Figure 6.10   Making Words: Additional Examples

Sample Making Words Lessons (Cunningham & Cunningham, 1992)

Lesson Using One Vowel

Letter cards: *u, k, n, r, s, t*

Words to make: *us, nut, rut, sun, sunk, runs, ruts, rust, tusk, stun, stunk, trunk, trunks* (the key word)

Sort for: rhymes, *s* pairs *(run, runs; rut, ruts; trunk, trunks)*

Lesson Using Big Words

Letter cards: *a, a, a, e, i, b, c, h, l, l, p, t*

Words to make: *itch, able, cable, table, batch, patch, pitch, petal, label, chapel, capital, capable, alphabet, alphabetical* (the key word)

Sort for: *el, le, al, -itch, -atch*

Reprinted by permission of the International Reading Association.

---

they express concepts, functions, and relationships. Imagine trying to define or draw a picture of the word *what!*

Patricia Cunningham (1980) developed the **drastic strategy** to help teachers solve this difficult instructional problem. Here is her six-step process:

Step 1: Select a function word and write it on a vocabulary card for each child. Locate a story for storytelling, or spontaneously create a story, that features multiple repetitions of the word. Before you begin your story, ask students to hold up their card every time they hear the word printed on it. As you tell the story, pause briefly each time you come to the targeted word in the text.

Step 2: Ask for volunteers to make up a story using the word on their card. Listeners should hold up their card each time they hear their classmate use the function word.

Step 3: Have students study the word on their card. Go around to each child and cut the word into letters (or allow students to do it for themselves). Direct students to arrange the letters to make the word. Check each student's attempt for accuracy. Have students repeat this process several times before moving on to the next step. Put the letters into an envelope and write the word on the outside. Encourage students to practice making the word during their free time.

Step 4: Write the word on the chalkboard. Have students pretend their eyes are like a camera and to take a picture of the word and put it in their mind. Have them close their eyes and try to see the word in their mind. Next, have them open their eyes and check the board to see if they correctly imagined the word. Have them repeat this process three times. Finally, have them write the word from memory after the chalkboard has been erased, then check their spelling when it is rewritten on the chalkboard. This should be done three times.

Step 5: Write several sentences on the board containing a blank in the place of the word under study. Read each aloud. As you come to the missing word in the sentences, invite a student to come to the board and write the word in the blank.

The drastic strategy is useful for teaching "function words," those having little meaning.

Step 6: Give students real books or text in which the function word appears. Have them read the story, and whenever they find the word being studied, lightly underline (in pencil) the new word. When they have done this, read the text to them, and pause each time you come to the word so students can read it chorally.

We recommend adding one final step to the drastic strategy: Deposit the word under study to students' word banks for future use in writing.

There is one drawback to the drastic strategy: time. It is not always necessary to teach every step in the drastic strategy for all words. A careful assessment of your students' vocabulary knowledge and needs, coupled with years of classroom experience, will help you decide when certain steps can be omitted.

Teaching Word Functions and Changes

Synonyms **Synonyms** are words that have similar, but not exactly the same, meaning (Johnson & Pearson, 1984). No two words carry exactly the same meaning in all contexts. Thus, when teaching new words and their synonyms, teachers should provide numerous opportunities for students to see differences as well as similarities. As with all reading strategies, this is best done within the natural context of real books and authentic writing experiences.

> **Getting to Know English Learners**
> English is a very rich language as it has borrowed vocabulary from many languages, so synonym games are very useful in helping students see these relationships.

One very productive way to get students interested in synonyms in the upper elementary grades is to teach them how to use a thesaurus to add variety and flavor to their writing. This tool is best used during the revising and editing stages of the writing process when students sometimes have problems coming up with descriptive language. For example, let's say a character in their story was tortured by hostile savages (sorry to be so violent in our example!), but the child writes that the victim felt "bad." If this word is targeted for thesaurus research, then the student might come up with synonyms for *bad* such as *in pain, anguished, in misery, depressed,* or *desperate.*

Following are several common words that students overuse and their synonyms as listed in a thesaurus.

good	big	thing
pleasant	vast	object
glorious	grand	item
wonderful	enormous	gadget
delightful	huge	organism

One way to stimulate students' interest in synonyms is to develop a modified cloze passage using an excerpt from a favorite book. In preparing the passage, leave out targeted words. Have students fill in the blanks with synonyms for the words contained in the original text. The following excerpt from Eric Carle's *The Grouchy Ladybug* (1986) is well-suited to this strategy.

"Good morning," said the friendly ladybug.
"Go away!" shouted the grouchy ladybug. "I want those aphids."
"We can share them," suggested the friendly ladybug.
"No. They're mine, all mine," screamed the grouchy ladybug.
"Or do you want to fight me for them?"*

*From *The Grouchy Ladybug* by E. Carle, 1977, 1986. New York: HarperCollins. Reprinted by permission.

The teacher might delete the words *said, shouted, suggested,* and *screamed* and list them on the chalkboard along with possible synonyms, such as *hinted, greeted, growled, yelled, reminded, mentioned, pointed out,* and *offered.* Student rewrites might look something like the following:

"Good morning," *greeted* the friendly ladybug.
"Go away!" *growled* the grouchy ladybug. "I want those aphids."
"We can share them," *hinted* the friendly ladybug.
"No. They're mine, all mine," *yelled* the grouchy ladybug.
"Or do you want to fight me for them?"

Class discussions might relate to how the use of different synonyms can alter meaning significantly, thus showing how synonyms have similar meanings, but not the exact same meanings. For example, if we took the sentence

"Go away!" *shouted* the grouchy ladybug.

and changed it to read

"Go away!" *hinted* the grouchy ladybug.

it would be easy for children to understand how the author's message had been softened considerably. This "cross-training" with reading and writing experiences helps synonyms take on new relevance as a literacy tool in the hands of students.

Antonyms. **Antonyms** are word opposites or near opposites. *Hard–soft, dark–light, big–small* are examples of antonym pairs. Like synonyms, antonyms help students gain insights into word meanings. When searching for ideal antonym examples, teachers should try to identify word sets that are mutually exclusive or that completely contradict each other.

Several classes of antonyms have been identified (Johnson & Pearson, 1984) that may be useful in instruction. One class is referred to as *relative pairs* or *counterparts* because one term implies the other. Examples include *mother–father, sister–brother, uncle–aunt,* and *writer–reader.* Other antonyms reflect a complete opposite or reversal of meaning, such as *fast–slow, stop–go,* and *give–take.* Complementary antonyms tend to lead from one to another, such as *give–take, friend–foe,* and *hot–cold.*

Antonym activities, as with all language-learning activities, should be drawn from the context of familiar books and student writing samples. Interacting with familiar text and clear meanings, children can easily see the full impact and flavor of different word meanings. Remember, in classroom instruction involving mini-lessons, teaching from whole text to parts (antonyms in this case) is key. Thus, if the teacher decides to develop an antonym worksheet for students, it should be drawn from a book that has already been shared (or will be shared) with the whole class or group. A fun book for this exercise is *Weird Parents* by Audrey Wood (1990), which could yield sentences like the following for which students supply antonyms for the underlined words.

1. There once was a boy who had <u>weird</u> (   ) parents.
2. In the <u>morning</u> (   ), the weird mother always walked the boy to his bus stop.
3. At twelve o'clock when the boy <u>opened</u> (   ) his lunchbox, he'd always have a weird surprise.

Another activity providing practice with antonyms is to ask students to find words in their writing or reading for which they can think of antonyms. A student in sixth grade who reads *A Wrinkle in Time* (L'Engle, 1962) might create the following list of words from the novel and their antonyms.

Wrinkle **Words**	**Antonyms**
punishment	reward
hesitant	eager
frightening	pleasant

A student in third grade who writes a story about his new baby sister, might select antonyms for some of the words he uses in his account.

Baby Story Words	**Opposites**
asleep	awake
cry	laugh
wet	dry

One way to assess students' ability to recognize antonyms is through multiple-choice and cloze exercises. The teacher should extract sentences from familiar text and have students select the correct antonym for a targeted word from among three choices. These choices might be (1) a synonym of the targeted word, (2) an unrelated word, and (3) the appropriate antonym. Following are two examples of this assessment technique that are based on *The Glorious Flight* (Provensen & Provensen, 1983).

1. Like a great swan, the *beautiful* (attractive, *homely*, shoots) glider rises into the air. . . .
2. Papa is getting *lots* (*limited,* from, loads) of practice.

Of many possible classroom activities, the most profitable will probably be those in which students are required to generate their own responses. Simple recognition items, as with multiple-choice measures, do not require students to think critically in arriving at a correct response.

Euphemisms. According to Tompkins and Hoskisson (1991, p. 122), **euphemisms** are words or phrases that are used to soften language to avoid harsh or distasteful realities, usually out of concern for people's feelings. Euphemisms are certainly worth some attention in reading instruction that focuses on building vocabulary because interpreting them correctly contributes to reading comprehension.

Euphemisms can be *inflated* or *deceptive.* Inflated euphemisms tend to make something sound greater or more sophisticated than it is. For example, *sanitation engineer* is an inflated euphemism for *garbage collector*. Deceptive euphemisms are words and phrases intended to misrepresent. Students should learn that this language often is used in advertisements to persuade an uninformed public to purchase a good or service. Several examples of euphemisms based on the work of Lutz (cited in Tompkins & Hoskisson, 1991, p. 122) follow:

Euphemism	**Real Meaning**
dentures	false teeth
expecting	pregnant

funeral director	undertaker
passed away	died
previously owned	used
senior citizen	old person
terminally ill	dying

Onomatopoeia and Creative Words. **Onomatopoeia** is the imitation of a sound in a word (*buzz, whir, vrooom*). Some authors such as Dr. Seuss and Shel Silverstein have made regular use of onomatopoeia and other creative words in their writing. One instance of onomatopoeia may be found in Dr. Seuss's *Horton Hears a Who!* (1954) in the sentence, "On clarinets, *oom-pahs* and *boom-pahs* and flutes." A wonderful example of creative language is found in Silverstein's (1974) poem "Sarah Cynthia Sylvia Stout Would Not Take the Garbage Out" in the phrase "Rubbery *blubbery* macaroni. . . ."

Students can be shown many interesting examples of onomatopoeia and creative words from the world of great children's literature. The natural extension to their own writing comes swiftly. Students may want to add a special section to their word banks for onomatopoeic and creative words to enhance their self-generated writing.

Shared Reading Experiences and Vocabulary Learning

Senechal and Cornell (1993) studied ways vocabulary knowledge can be increased through shared reading experiences—when adults and children read stories together. Methods investigated included reading the story verbatim (read-alouds), asking questions, repeating sentences containing new vocabulary words, and what has been referred to as "recasting" new vocabulary introduced in the selection.

Recasts build directly on sentences just read that contain a new word the teacher (or parent) may want to teach the child. The sentence is recast (changed) in some way to focus attention on a targeted word. For example, if a child says or reads, "Look at the *snake,*" the adult may recast the statement by replying, "It is a large, striped *snake.*" In this example, adjectives were added to enhance the learner's understanding of the word *snake.*

Interestingly, Senechal and Cornell concluded that teacher questioning and recasts were about as effective as reading a book aloud to a child as a word-learning tool. Thus, reading passages aloud to students can often be just as potent as direct teaching strategies. We need to do both: read aloud regularly *and* discuss passages containing new vocabulary with students in challenging ways.

Helping Students Acquire New Vocabulary Independently

The ultimate task for teachers is to help students become independent learners. The ongoing learning of new vocabulary throughout life is unquestionably a key to continued self-education. In this section, we feature ways students can become independent learners of new words.

Word-Learning Strategies

Students must determine the meaning of words that are new to them when these words are discovered in their reading. The teacher must help them develop effective **word-learning strategies** such as how to use dictionaries and other reference aids, how to use information about word parts to figure out the meanings of words in text, and how to use context clues to determine word meanings.

Using Dictionaries and Other Reference Aids. Students must learn how to use dictionaries, glossaries, and thesauruses to help broaden and deepen their knowledge of words. In preparation for using these tools, students must learn alphabetical order, ordinal language (i.e., first, second, third), and the function of guide words. The most helpful dictionaries and reference aids include sentences providing clear examples of word meanings in context.

Using Information About Word Parts. Structural analysis involves the use of word parts, such as affixes (prefixes and suffixes) and base words, to decode new words in print. Students can also use structural analysis independently as a meaning-based, word-learning tool. For example, learning the four most common prefixes in English *(un-, re-, in-, dis-)* can provide helpful meaning clues for about two-thirds of all English words having prefixes. Prefixes are relatively easy to learn because they have clear meanings (for example, *un-* means "not" and *re-* means "again") and they are usually spelled the same way from word to word. Suffixes can often be a bit more challenging to learn than prefixes. For one thing, quite a few suffixes have confusing meanings (e.g., the suffix *-ness,* meaning "the state of" is not all that helpful in figuring out the meaning of *tenderness*).

Students should also learn about **word roots.** About 60 percent of all English words have Latin or Greek origins (Partnership for Reading, 2001). Latin and Greek word roots are common to the subjects of science and social studies, and also form a large share of the new words for students in their content-area textbooks. Teachers should teach the highest-frequency word roots as they occur in the texts students read.

Using Context Clues to Determine Word Meanings. **Context clues** are meaning cues found in the words, phrases, and sentences that surround an unknown word. It is not an overstatement to say that the ability to use context clues is fundamental to reading success. This is because most word meanings will be learned indirectly from context. Following is another classroom example from the publication, *Put Reading First* (2001), this time demonstrating the use of context clues as a word-learning strategy.

AN EXAMPLE OF CLASSROOM INSTRUCTION

Using Context Clues*

In a third grade class, the teacher models how to use context clues to determine word meanings as follows:

Word Webs can be used for instruction with prefixes, suffixes, or common Greek and Latin roots. Learn more by visiting the Teacher Prep Website *(www.prenhall. teacherprep)*. Select *Strategies and Lessons* to access *Reading Methods/Vocabulary*—"Word Webs."

Getting to Know English Learners
Native-language dictionaries are very helpful for ELs as well, and are often permitted for use during certain statewide assessments as an ESL accommodation.

Getting to Know English Learners
English is a Germanic language in origin, but because of various influences, including the Battle of Hastings in 1066, most of our English vocabulary is indeed Latin in origin—stemming mainly from the Romance language of French.

The four most common prefixes in English, *un-, re-, in-,* and *dis-,* provide helpful meaning clues for about two-thirds of all words having prefixes.

Student *(reading the text):* When the cat pounced on the dog, the dog jumped up, yelping, and knocked over a lamp, which crashed to the floor. The animals ran past Tonia, tripping her. She fell to the floor and began sobbing. Tonia's brother Felix yelled at the animals to stop. As the noise and confusion mounted, Mother hollered upstairs, "What's all that commotion?"

Teacher: The context of the paragraph helps us determine what *commotion* means. There's yelping and crashing and sobbing and yelling. And then the last sentence says, "as the noise and confusion mounted." The author's use of the words *noise* and *confusion* gives us a very strong clue as to what *commotion* means. In fact, the author is really giving us a definition there, because *commotion* means something that's noisy and confusing—a disturbance. Mother was right; there was definitely a commotion!

*From *Put Reading First: The Research Building Blocks for Teaching Children to Read* (2001). Noncopyrighted material published by the National Institute for Literacy. Available online at *www.nifl.gov.*

Encouraging Wide Reading

> Wide reading is a powerful way for students to build vocabulary knowledge independently.

Reading involves cognitive skill development that in some ways mirrors physical skill development. As with physical skills, the more one practices reading, the more his or her reading ability increases. Over the years in our work with at-risk students, we have come to realize that if we can simply get children to read every day for at least 15 to 20 minutes, their reading ability will improve dramatically. In one study, Reutzel and Hollingsworth (1991c) discovered that allowing children to read self-selected books 30 minutes every day resulted in significantly improved scores on reading comprehension tests. These children performed as well as students who had received 30 minutes of direct instruction on the tested reading comprehension skills. Their results suggest that regular daily reading is probably at least as effective as formal reading instruction, and the students can do it on their own! Encouraging students to read books that match their interests can motivate them to read widely and independently, thereby nurturing vocabulary growth.

Scott Cunningham/Merrill

What Are Some Ways Teachers Can Encourage Wide Reading? How can teachers encourage students to read independently on a regular basis? The answer lies in helping students become aware of their interests and in finding books they can read. The interest issue can be resolved in two steps. First, the teacher can administer an **interest inventory** to the class at the beginning of the year (see Chapter 9 for ways of assessing student interest) to determine what types of books are indicated for classroom instruction. These results can be taken a little further. As the second step, we suggest that the teacher start an **individual interest sheet** (IIS) for each student based on inventory results. Students can review their IIS with the teacher during individual reading conferences (discussed more in later chapters). Besides listing topics that appear to be of interest to the student, the IIS can suggest books available in the school library that relate to those topics. Over time, students can list additional topics they discover to be of interest and can look for books in those areas. Figure 6.11 shows a sample IIS, with new interests written in by the student. A useful reference for teachers attempting to match students' interests with quality literature is Donna Norton's (1999) *Through the Eyes of a Child: An Introduction to Children's Literature*. Most high-interest topic areas are discussed in this text and are matched to several possible book titles. Book suggestions include brief descriptions of the main story line to help in the decision-making process.

> Surveying student interests with an Individual Interest Sheet (IIS) helps teachers select free-reading materials.

> Describe two ways teachers can enhance vocabulary learning.

Computer-Assisted Vocabulary Learning

As computers become more accessible to students and teachers, the question arises: Can innovative computer applications help students learn new vocabulary? Reinking and Rickman (1990) studied the vocabulary growth of sixth grade students who had computer-assisted programs available to them. They compared students who read passages on printed pages accompanied by either a standard dictionary or glossary (the traditional classroom situation) with students who read passages on a computer screen. These computer-assisted programs provided either optional assistance (on command) for specific vocabulary words or mandatory (automatic) assistance. Two very interesting things were learned from their research. First, students reading passages with computer assistance performed significantly better on vocabulary tests that focused on the words emphasized than did students in traditional reading groups. Second, students receiving automatic computer assistance with the passages also outperformed the more traditional reading group on a passage comprehension test relating to information read in the experiment. These results suggest that computer programs that offer students passages to read with vocabulary assistance can be helpful. Further, they suggest to

> Computer-assisted vocabulary instruction can provide highly motivating word-learning instruction in a classroom learning center.

Figure 6.11   Sample Individual Interest Sheet (IIS)

Individual Interest Sheet

Mrs. Harbor's Sixth Grade

Sunnydale School

Name: Holly Ambrose

Things I am interested in knowing more about, or topics that I like . . .

Topics	Books to consider from our library
horses	*The Red Pony* (J. Steinbeck)
getting along with friends	*Afternoon of the Elves* (J. Lisle)
romantic stories	*The Witch of Blackbird Pond* (E. Speare)
one-parent families	*The Moonlight Man* (P. Fox)

us another possible advantage of the computer: teaching students to use what might be termed a "vocabulary enhancer," such as a thesaurus program, with their writing, which could help students discover on their own new synonyms and antonyms for commonly used words. Most word processing programs, such as Microsoft Word, include a thesaurus.

Vocabulary Overview

Vocabulary overviews help students decide which words they will learn. In classroom settings, teachers can usually anticipate vocabulary that may be troublesome during reading and teach these words through brief mini-lessons. But when children read independently, they need to find ways to learn new words on their own. One activity that serves this purpose is the vocabulary overview. **Vocabulary overviews** help students select unfamiliar words in print and then use context clues and their background knowledge to determine word meaning.

One way of helping students develop their own vocabulary overviews is Haggard's (1986) **vocabulary self-selection strategy** (VSS). Our version of the VSS begins with a small-group mini-lesson during which the teacher explains the process. Students are asked to find at least one word they feel the class should learn. Next, they define the word to the best of their ability based on context clues and their background knowledge. On the day the words are presented for whole-class study, each student takes turns explaining (a) where he or she found his or her word, (b) his or her context-determined definition of the word, and (c) reasons why the class should learn the word.

TEACHER PREP

Create a lesson through the Teacher Prep Website.

- You will be guided through the alignment of standards, lesson objectives, your introduction, planning for and sequencing lesson activities and procedures, planning for ongoing assessment throughout the lesson and planning end of lesson assessment. You will also choose and list lesson materials/resources and create adapted instruction to meet all needs of students.
- This lesson can be sent to your instructor through this link.
- Select a children's book and plan an effective vocabulary lesson. You may consider ideas provided within this chapter.
- Assessment drives our instruction. Plan to incorporate before and after word knowledge self-rating forms.

What Can Be Done to Assist Students with Special Needs in Vocabulary Learning?

Students sometimes have particular needs in vocabulary learning. Students growing up in poverty circumstances and English language learners (ELL) are two key groups who may need special adaptations in vocabulary instruction to ensure learning. These two groups can benefit from many of the same instructional adaptations.

Peregoy and Boyle (2001), in their book *Reading, Writing, & Learning in ESL,* suggest guidelines for vocabulary development.

- Select words that you consider important to comprehending each assigned passage.
- Create several sentences loaded with context using these target words. This will give students an opportunity to use context to predict the meaning of the target words.
- Model prediction strategies using context.
- Follow modeling and guided practice sessions with discussion using excerpts from the text students will be assigned in which the target words appear.

Two vocabulary development activities are highly recommended for English learners (May & Rizzardi, 2002; Peregoy & Boyle, 2001; Reutzel & Cooter, 2003) that can also be helpful to children whose vocabularies are underdeveloped: the vocabulary cluster strategy and semantic maps.

The Vocabulary Cluster Strategy

It is especially important that students who struggle with reading use the context of the passage, their background knowledge, and the vocabulary they know to understand new words in print. This is true whether English is their second language or their first (as is the case with students from language-deprived backgrounds). With the vocabulary cluster strategy, students are helped to read a passage, gather context clues, and then predict the meaning of a new word targeted for learning. Here's how it works.

You will need multiple copies of the text students are to read, an overhead transparency and projector, and erasable marking pens for transparencies. Select vocabulary you want to teach from the text you will use; this text could be a poem, song, excerpt from a chapter book (novel), or nonfiction. Prepare a transparency containing an excerpt from this text with sufficient context to help students predict what the unknown word might be. Delete the target word(s) and replace them with a blank line, much the same as you would with a cloze passage. Figure 6.12 illustrates a passage prepared in this way along with a vocabulary cluster supporting the new word to be learned. This example is based on the book *Honey Baby Sugar Child*.

Through discussion, lead students into predicting what the unknown word might be. If the word is not already in students' listening vocabulary, you will be able to introduce the new word quite easily and effectively using the context and synonyms provided in the vocabulary cluster.

Semantic Maps

A **semantic map** is essentially a kind of blueprint in which students sketch out or map what is stored in their brain about a topic. Semantic maps help students relate new information to schemata and vocabulary already in the brain, integrate new information, and restructure existing information for greater clarity (Yopp & Yopp, 1996). Students who struggle with reading can use semantic maps prior to the act of reading to promote better recall (Sinatra, Stahl-Gemake, & Berg, 1984).

There are many ways to introduce semantic mapping to students, but the first time around it is best to use direct instruction followed up with a lot of teacher modeling and guided and independent practice.

The actual map is a form of graphic organizer in which a topic under discussion forms the center of a network of descriptors, concepts, and related categories. In introducing the process of mapping, begin with a topic familiar to the entire class, such as a state that is being studied. Write the topic on the board or an overhead transparency. Have students brainstorm categories of descriptors and concepts related to the topic. Record these. Connect these categories to the topic visually using bold or double lines. Then have students brainstorm details that relate to these major categories. Connect details to categories with single lines. Figure 6.13 shows a semantic map for the topic "Tennessee."

Semantic maps (also called webs) can also relate to a story or chapter book students are reading. Figure 6.14 features an example (Reutzel & Cooter, 2007) of a semantic map from a story in the book *Golden Tales: Myths, Legends, and Folktales from Latin America* (Delacre, 1996).

Any of the strategies found in this chapter can be adapted for struggling readers as long as you are direct and explicit in your teaching. Direct instruction helps

Semantic maps are useful in connecting new vocabulary with prior knowledge and related terms (Johnson & Pearson, 1984; Monroe, 1998; Reutzel & Cooter, 2003).

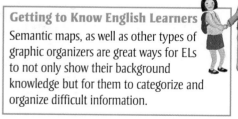

Getting to Know English Learners
Semantic maps, as well as other types of graphic organizers are great ways for ELs to not only show their background knowledge but for them to categorize and organize difficult information.

Figure 6.12   Vocabulary Cluster Based on *Honey Baby Sugar Child* (Duncan, 2005): largen word "twirl"

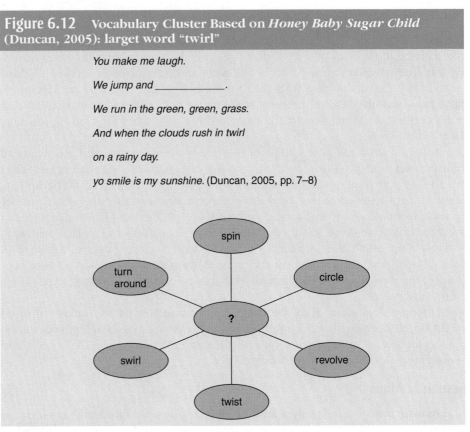

You make me laugh.

We jump and _____.

We run in the green, green, grass.

And when the clouds rush in twirl

on a rainy day.

yo smile is my sunshine. (Duncan, 2005, pp. 7–8)

Source: Honey Baby Sugar Child by A. F. Duncan and illustrated by S. Keeter, 2005, New York, Simon & Schuster Children's Publishing. Used with permission.

Figure 6.13   Tennessee Semantic Web

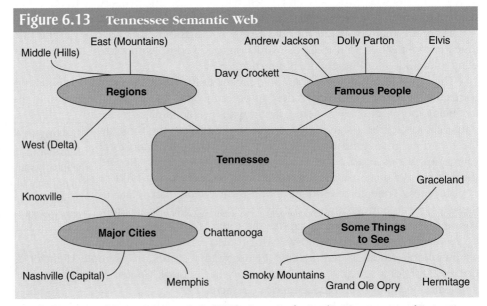

Source: From Reutzel, D. R., & Cooter, R. B. (2007). *Strategies for Reading Assessment and Instruction: Helping Every Child Succeed,* 3rd ed. Upper Saddle River, NJ: Merrill/Prentice-Hall.

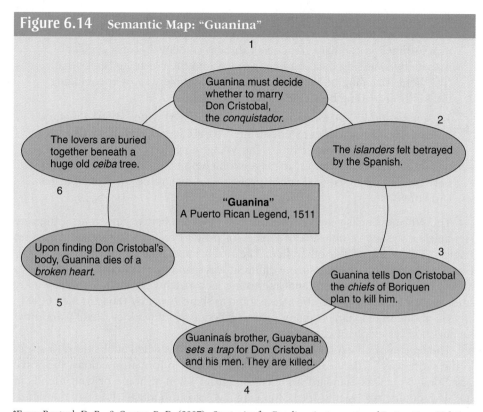

Figure 6.14   Semantic Map: "Guanina"

1

Guanina must decide whether to marry Don Cristobal, the *conquistador.*

2

The *islanders* felt betrayed by the Spanish.

The lovers are buried together beneath a huge old *ceiba* tree.

6

"Guanina"
A Puerto Rican Legend, 1511

Upon finding Don Cristobal's body, Guanina dies of a *broken heart.*

5

3

Guanina tells Don Cristobal the *chiefs* of Boriquen plan to kill him.

Guanina's brother, Guaybana, *sets a trap* for Don Cristobal and his men. They are killed.

4

*From Reutzel, D. R., & Cooter, R. B. (2007). *Strategies for Reading Assessment and Instruction: Helping Every Child Succeed,* 3rd ed. Upper Saddle River, NJ: Merrill/Prentice-Hall. Used with permission.

less-proficient readers create mental scaffolding for support of new vocabulary and concepts.

Linking Multicultural Experiences with Vocabulary Development

Vocabulary development in spoken and written English is at the heart of literacy learning (Wheatley, Muller, & Miller, 1993). Because of the rich diversity found in U.S. classrooms, teachers need to consider ways of adapting the curriculum so that all students can learn to recognize and use appropriate and varied vocabulary. In this section, we consider three possible avenues proven to be successful in multicultural settings.

Link vocabulary studies to a broad topic or novel. We know that there is a limit to the number of words that can be taught directly and in isolation. Au (1993) tells us that students in multicultural settings learn vocabulary best if the new words are related to a broader topic. Working on vocabulary development in connection with students' exploration of content area topics is a natural and connected way to learn new words and explore their various meanings.

Semantic Maps can be used to activate prior knowledge and preview new vocabulary. Refer to the Teacher Prep Website (*www.prenhall.com/teacherprep*) and select *Strategies and Lessons—Reading Methods.* "Semantic Maps" is located in the *Vocabulary* module.

Getting to Know English Learners
Every human being actually speaks several dialects—depending on situation and audience, for example, and all of us has our own dialect or "idiolect" which is thought to be as unique as our own fingerprints!

Encourage wide reading at independent levels as a vehicle for vocabulary development. Reading for enjoyment on a daily basis helps students increase their vocabulary. Teachers can help students become regular readers by assessing their reading interests and then locating books that "fit" them. Matching books with students is a simple way of encouraging the kinds of reading behaviors that pay dividends.

Implement the Village English activity. Delpit (1988) writes about a method of teaching Native Alaskan students new vocabulary that works well in many other multicultural settings. The Village English activity respects and encourages students' home language while helping them see relationships between language use and social/professional realities in the United States (Au, 1993).

The Village English activity begins with the teacher writing "Our Language Heritage" at the top of one side of a piece of poster board and "Standard American English" at the top of the other side. The teacher explains to students that in the United States people speak in many different ways, and that this variety of languages makes our nation as colorful and interesting as a patchwork quilt. For elementary students, we think this would be a good time to share *Elmer* by David McKee (1990), a book about an elephant of many colors (called a "patchwork elephant") and how he enriched his elephant culture.

The teacher then explains that there are many times when adults need to speak in the same way so they can be understood, usually in formal situations. In formal situations, we speak Standard American English. When at home or with friends in our community, we usually speak the language of our heritage. It is like the difference between a picnic compared to a "dressed-up" formal dinner. The teacher writes phrases used in students' native dialect under the heading "Our Language Heritage," and notes and discusses comparative translations on the side labeled "Standard American English." These comparisons can be noted in an ongoing way throughout the year as part of a special word wall. The Village English activity can be an engaging way to increase vocabulary knowledge while demonstrating appreciation for language differences.

TEACHER PREP

"Spotlight on English Learners: Generating Stories" describes wordless picture books and their use for linguistically different readers. Experiences with them are beneficial for the development of vocabulary. Visit the Teacher Prep Website (*www.prenhall.com/teacherprep*) and select *Strategies and Lessons—Language Arts Methods/Talking.*

How Can Reading Backpacks Be Used to Involve Parents in Their Child's Vocabulary Learning?

During our respective careers, we have gone back and forth between teaching in the elementary classroom and in teacher education programs. Some may think we have suffered a series of identity crises (especially our spouses), but we never tire of working with children and their families. Because our better halves are teachers themselves, they humor us. Teaching is the greatest profession on earth!

One of the mainstays of our instruction is the **reading backpack** strategy (Cooter et al., 1999; Reutzel & Cooter, 2007; Reutzel & Fawson, 1990). The technique is straightforward: Have available a number of backpacks, perhaps with your school's name and mascot emblazoned on them, that you send home at least once a week containing reading or writing activities that can be completed by the child and his or her parent. Many homes are without printed text of any sort, and reading backpacks can bring fresh opportunities for enjoyment and learning into the family's evening. They can also help parents in their efforts to do something constructive for their child's literacy development. We have used backpacks to send home a supply of trade books on a variety of topics on different reading levels matching the child's ability (in both English and Spanish), easy activities written on laminated card stock so they can be reused, and materials for written responses to books (e.g., markers, colored paper, scissors, tape, etc.). Sometimes, if parents themselves are not literate, we have sent books accompanied by tape recordings and a tape player. Teacher-produced videotapes or DVDs demonstrating educational games parents can play with their children can be sent home for special occasions.

> **Getting to Know English Learners**
> Well over 150 different languages are spoken in the New York City schools, for example—languages such as Quechua, Ndebele, and Pashto—making finding trade books in all these languages a challenge indeed!

In this section, we share a few backpack ideas you might consider for drawing families into the circle for developing reading vocabulary. In most cases these ideas are easy and inexpensive.

Newspaper Word Race. In the backpack, send home:

- ✓ two out-of-date newspapers
- ✓ two copies of a list of target words you want the child to practice seeing and saying
- ✓ an egg timer
- ✓ two highlighting markers
- ✓ directions explaining the task

On a laminated instruction card to the parents, explain that they are to sit down at a table with their child and take one newspaper and highlighter for themselves and give one of each to the child. They should set the egg timer for one minute, and then have a race to see how many of the target words they can find and circle in the newspaper with their highlighter. When they are finished, they should share with each other the words they found and read the sentence in which they appear. For beginning readers, the parent will sometimes need to read the sentence to the child for words located by the student, then explain what the sentence means. This process encourages meaningful verbal interaction between parent and child—*very powerful!*

Garage Sale Books. If you enjoy garage sales (and many teachers do), look for bargain books having lots of pictures that seem to tell a story. Children's books are best. Cut out pictures from books you find, arrange them on card stock, and laminate them into place so they can be reused. Send these story cards home in the backpack with directions that the parent and child are to write a story that goes along with the pictures. Child and parent can rename the picture so that the character or depiction is in their family or a familiar environment. For instance, the odd-looking little puppy could be one the child found at the park across from her apartment. Be sure to include a word card with target vocabulary to be used in the student's story. Sometimes parents are willing to come to school and share with the class the story they have written with their student. This will often inspire other students to do the same with their parents when you send the backpack home with them. For this backpack strategy you will need to send home only a handful of supplies:

✓ a story card
✓ writing materials (pencils, paper)
✓ target words card
✓ directions explaining the task

Barbie and G.I. Joe. We know of a teacher who purchased old Barbie dolls at (where else?) a garage sale for pennies on the dollar. In her center, this teacher placed catalogs where the little girls in her class could select clothes for Barbie and write about them. She also found a Barbie car and had students write about places she traveled. The center became so popular with the girls that boys complained that they wanted something similar—an argument for equity?! So, she went garage saling again, bought G.I. Joe action figures for the boys, and set up similar centers.

We recommend Barbie and G.I. Joe backpack activities in which you include:

✓ a doll or action figure that is appropriate to the child's gender
✓ a target words vocabulary card with words to be used in writing
✓ a catalog, map of the country, or other stimulus that may be used for inspiring joint writing between the child and parent
✓ directions explaining the task
✓ writing supplies (paper, pencils)

Catalog Interviews. In this backpack activity, the parent is given an imaginary $5,000 to spend in a shopping spree. The student interviews the parent about what she or he will purchase and why. After the interview, the student should write a short summary of what he or she learned from the interview.

This activity can also be carried out by supplying the student with a large, artificial "million dollar bill." The student is to interview family members to find out what they would do with such a fantastic sum. The student then writes about their responses.

The point here is to inspire real dialog between the parent and student in which words are exchanged and discussed. As we saw earlier in this chapter, students add words to their listening and speaking vocabularies when they are engaged in two-way discussions (K. Cooter, 2006), and this activity helps make that happen. For this backpack activity you will need:

✓ a target words vocabulary card with words to be used in writing
✓ a catalog that may be used for inspiring joint writing between student and parent
✓ directions explaining the task
✓ writing supplies (paper, pencils)

Mona Lisa. In this backpack strategy, the teacher sends home a photocopy of a famous painting or some other work of art. Abstract art works well for this activity. In your directions, ask the parent and student to describe what is going on in the painting or piece of art. For example, if you send home a copy of DaVinci's *Mona Lisa,* you might ask, "What do you suppose the young woman in Da Vinci's painting is smiling about?" This activity is especially powerful when you send along a list of target words that must be used in the written summary the student and parent co-produce (e.g., descriptive words, artistic terms the children may be learning, etc.). For this backpack activity you will need:

✓ a picture of a work of art (color is best)
✓ a target words vocabulary card with words to be used in writing
✓ directions explaining the task
✓ writing supplies (paper, pencils)

Scrabble. If you are lucky in your garage sale junkets you may come across an old edition of the perennial favorite *Scrabble* for your reading backpacks. This is the quintessential vocabulary game, of course, and having students play Scrabble with their family will provide a splendid opportunity for word talk. A variation would be to send home with the board game a target words vocabulary card and indicate that every target word used by anyone playing the game earns an extra five points. For this backpack activity you will need:

✓ a Scrabble game
✓ a target words vocabulary card with words to be used for bonus credit
✓ directions explaining the task

Summary

Dale Johnson (2001, pp. 41–48), an eminent researcher in the field of vocabulary development, provided valuable insights in his book entitled *Vocabulary in the Elementary and Middle School.* He wonderfully encapsulates information presented in this chapter. First, we know that word knowledge is essential for reading comprehension. Evidenced-based research tells us that vocabulary instruction should utilize activities (like the ones found in this chapter) that link word learning to concept and schema development. We should also teach specific word learning strategies to our students, as well as strategies they can use on their own to understand unfamiliar words in print.

Wide reading should be encouraged and made possible in the classroom. Literally thousands of words are learned through regular and sustained reading. Time should be set aside each day for this crucial learning activity. As an example, Johnson (2001) advocated the use of a program called "Read-a-Million-Minutes" which was designed to foster wide reading throughout Iowa. All students set their own in-school and out-of-school reading goal that contributes to the school's goal.

Direct instruction should be used to teach words that are necessary for passage comprehension. Considering how critical some words are for comprehending a new passage, teachers should not leave vocabulary learning to incidental encounters, but rather plan regular direct instruction lessons to make sure that essential words are learned. Active learning activities yield the best results. According to research conducted by Stahl (1986), vocabulary instruction that provided only definitional information (i.e., dictionary activities) failed to significantly improve comprehension. Active learning opportunities; such as creation of word webs, playing word games, and discussing new words in reading groups or literature circles, are far more effective in cementing new knowledge and improving comprehension.

We also know that students require a good bit of repetition to learn new words and integrate them into existing knowledge (schemas). In some cases, students may require as many as forty encounters to fully learn new vocabulary. To know a word well means knowing what it means, how to pronounce it, and how its meaning changes in different contexts. Repeated exposures to the word in different contexts is the key to successful learning.

Students should be helped to develop their own strategies for word learning from written and oral contexts. This includes the use of context clues, structural analysis (word roots, prefixes, suffixes), and research skills (use of the dictionary, thesaurus, etc.).

Finally, parents can help their children succeed in expanding concept and vocabulary knowledge by exposing them to new experiences and helping them to read about and discuss new ideas in the home.

In this chapter we have gained some important insights into ways children can be helped to expand their vocabulary knowledge. First, we know that word knowledge is essential for reading comprehension. Evidence-based research tells us that vocabulary instruction should utilize activities (like the ones found in this chapter) that link word learning to concept and schema development. We should also teach specific word learning strategies to our students as well as strategies they can use on their own to understand unfamiliar words in print.

Wide reading should be encouraged and made possible in the classroom. Literally thousands of words are learned through regular and sustained reading. Time should be set aside each day for this crucial learning activity. As an example, Johnson (2001) advocated the use of a program called Read-a-Million-Minutes, which was designed to foster wide reading throughout Iowa. All students set their own in-school and out-of-school reading goal that contributes to the school's goal.

Classroom Applications

1. Design a lesson plan introducing a word-learning strategy to third grade students. Be certain that the lesson includes rich literature examples, teacher-student interaction, student-student interaction, modeling, and ample guided practice.

2. Review a local school district's curriculum guide (or curriculum map) for a specific grade level, and select two topics or themes of study in either science or social studies. Locate in the college or university's curriculum library the textbook adopted by the school for that grade level for the selected subject area(s). With a partner, construct a before-and-after word knowledge self-rating form for each topic you selected. Present your form to your class or group. Use the suggested vocabulary words in the curriculum guide as a start, but consider the typical background knowledge of your learners as well in your thinking.

3. Prepare a lesson plan for second-year (not the same as second grade) EL students introducing one of the vocabulary learning strategies discussed in this chapter. Identify the age of the students as well as their first language, and consider the background knowledge they might have to help them use the new strategy. As always, be certain that the lesson includes rich literature examples, extensive dialogue, teacher modeling, and ample guided practice for students. Remember that children need to interact with the teacher or with each other using language to truly make it their own.

4. Conduct an interest inventory with five students at a local elementary school. Next, prepare an IIS that matches at least four of their interests to popular children's literature. Books might be recommended by the school librarian or

drawn from D. Norton's (2007) *Through the Eyes of a Child: An Introduction to Children's Literature* (7th ed.). Finally, present the IIS forms to the students and explain how they are to be used. Turn a copy of both forms in to your instructor, along with a journal entry explaining how each child reacted.

5. Prepare and teach a mini-lesson demonstrating the VSS for diverse classrooms. Develop a simple handout for students containing helpful hints about collecting new words for investigation.

6. With two partners, fully develop five reading backpack family activities. Work with your cooperating classroom teacher to distribute your backpacks to five students. Once the backpacks return, interview the students to discover what happened at home and what they thought of the backpack activity. Send home a brief survey to parents as well if time permits.

Recommended Readings

Blachowicz, C., & Fisher, P. J. (2006). *Teaching vocabulary in all classrooms* (3rd ed.). Upper Saddle River, NJ: Pearson/Merrill/Prentice Hall.

Cooter, K. S. (2006). When mama can't read: Counteracting intergenerational illiteracy. *The Reading Teacher, 59*(7), 698–702.

Cunningham, P. M., & Cunningham, J. (1992). Making words: Enhancing the invented spelling–decoding connection. *The Reading Teacher, 46*(2), 106–116.

Fry, E. B., Kress, J. E., & Fountoukidis, D. L. (1993). *The reading teacher's book of lists* (3rd ed.). Paramis, NJ: Prentice Hall.

Johnson, D. D. (2001). *Vocabulary in the elementary and middle school.* Boston, MA: Allyn and Bacon.

Peregoy, S. F., & Boyle, O. F. (2001). *Reading, writing, & learning in ESL.* New York: Longman.

Norton, D. (2007). *Through the eyes of a child: An introduction to children's literature* (7th ed.). Upper Saddle River, NJ: Pearson/Merrill/Prentice Hall.

Teaching Reading Comprehension

Chapter Questions

1. What is reading comprehension?

2. How do children develop reading comprehension?

3. What does research say about reading comprehension instruction?

4. How is reading comprehension assessed effectively?

5. What are evidence-based instructional practices or strategies for developing reading comprehension?

6. How can comprehension instruction be adapted to meet the needs of diverse learners?

7. How can can families and communities support children's reading comprehension development?

Breakthroughs to Comprehension

Since the beginning of the school year, Ms. Dewey has taught seven comprehension strategies to her students. She has taught these strategies one at a time, using clear explanations and think-aloud modeling, and has scaffolded her instruction so each student can use the strategies independently. But now, after the winter holiday break, Ms. Dewey decides to teach her second graders how to use the seven comprehension strategies altogether—as a "strategy family"—while reading and discussing texts. To start this process, she produces seven posters, one for each strategy in the set of seven. She refers to these posters when she models for her students how to select comprehension strategies and use them during reading. Her posters are shown in the photo on the next page.

Ms. Dewey loves to read science books with her students, especially big books. And her students particularly enjoy reading science big books and participating in lessons using the "family" of seven comprehension strategies.

One day while videotaping a lesson for later review, Ms. Dewey records one little boy, Juan, saying enthusiastically, "I just love this stuff!" The class is reading a book about different frogs.

It has taken several years for Ms. Dewey to reshape comprehension instruction in her classroom and to see students achieve on much higher levels. In fact, she is always making adjustments to her teaching as she learns more about comprehension instruction and, most importantly, her students. As she listens to Juan's excited pronouncement, she echoes it, whispering to herself, "I love this stuff, too!"

Comprehension is the very heart and soul of reading. Although learning to translate letters into words is extremely important, teachers must never lose sight of the ultimate goal of reading instruction—comprehending text! From the very beginning, teachers should help students apply meaning to print by providing effective comprehension instruction in listening and reading. But what is it that teachers like Ms. Dewey know that help them to provide students with reading comprehension instruction that is effective?

What Is Reading Comprehension?

Research on reading comprehension has been carefully summarized by two major "blue ribbon" panels, the National Reading Panel (2000) and the Rand Reading Study Group (2001). The National Reading Panel (NRP) (2000, pp. 4–5) described reading comprehension as follows:

> Comprehension is a complex process . . . often viewed as 'the essence of reading.' Reading comprehension is . . . *intentional thinking* [emphasis added] during which meaning is constructed through interactions between text and reader. Meaning resides in the intentional, problem-solving, thinking processes of the reader that occur during an interchange with a text. The content of meaning is influenced by the text and by the reader's prior knowledge and experience that are brought to bear on it.

Similarly, the Rand Reading Study Group (2001) described reading comprehension (Sweet & Snow, 2003, p. 1) as "the process of simultaneously extracting and constructing meaning." This process of comprehending entails four essential components: (1) the reader, (2) the text, (3) the activity, and (4) the situational context. The first three essential components of reading comprehension, the reader, the text, and the task, occur within the fourth essential component of reading comprehension, the situational context. Obviously, the reader is the one doing the comprehending in reading, and the text is the reading material (e.g., fiction/narrative text, nonfiction/expository text) the reader is approaching. The "activity" refers to what kind of comprehension task the reader is attempting. The National Reading Panel (2000) recommended eight comprehension strategies that provide a firm scientific basis for instruction:

1. comprehension monitoring
2. cooperative learning
3. graphic organizers
4. question answering
5. question generating
6. story structure/text structure
7. summarizing
8. multiple-strategy instruction

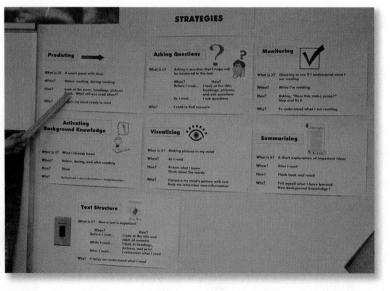

Ray Reutzel

The situational context of reading comprehension can be thought of in at least two ways. First, there is the actual location or setting in which the reading of a text occurs—the home, the school classroom, the library, a church, under a blanket at bedtime, and so on. There is little doubt that one's purpose for reading a text is influenced by the setting in which one reads.

Second, there is a social context associated with reading comprehension. In some cases, reading comprehension is a solitary activity in which the reader constructs meaning using the author's ideas in the text. This is, of course, a very limited social setting. In other cases, however, reading comprehension can be a vibrant social activity in which people—teachers, parents, and children—read a text together and jointly construct meaning through discussion.

The *Report of the National Reading Panel* (2000) found that lively discussion about a text in the company of others seems to be the optimal situational context to enhance students' reading comprehension. Classroom discussion, then, seems to provide the best context for children to improve their reading comprehension.

How Do Children Develop Reading Comprehension?

Research occurring in the past 25 to 30 years has contributed greatly to our collective understanding of the cognitive processes involved in reading comprehension, but little or no research has focused on the development of young children's comprehension (National Reading Panel, 2000; Reutzel, Smith, & Fawson, 2005). Pressley (2000) described the development of reading comprehension as a two-stage process. Reading comprehension begins with lower processes focused at the word level—word recognition (phonics, sight words), fluency (rate, accuracy, and expression), and vocabulary (word meanings). Several previous chapters in this book have focused on efficient and effective processing of text at the word level; thus, our focus in this chapter will be on how higher-order reading comprehension processes develop.

> **Getting to Know English Learners**
> Of course, ELs have their own sets of schemata, or background knowledge, matched to their unique, perhaps, language, cultural, and background experiences.

The second stage of reading comprehension development focuses on higher-order processing—activating and relating prior knowledge to text content, and consciously learning, selecting, and controlling the use of several cognitive strategies to assure remembering and learning from text. Reading comprehension research has been profoundly influenced in the past by **schema theory,** a theory that explains how information we have stored in our minds helps us gain new knowledge.

A **schema** (the plural is *schemata* or *schemas*) can be thought of as a kind of file cabinet of information in our brains containing related (1) concepts (chairs, birds, ships), (2) events (weddings, birthdays, school experiences), (3) emotions (anger, frustration, joy, pleasure), and (4) roles (parent, judge, teacher) drawn from our life experiences (Anderson & Pearson, 1984; Rumelhart, 1981). Researchers have represented the total collection of our schemas as neural networks (i.e., "brain networks") of connected associated meanings (Collins & Quillian, 1969; Lindsay & Norman, 1977). Each schema is connected to other related schemas, forming a vast, interconnected network of knowledge and experiences. The size and content of one's schemas are influenced by one's experiences, both direct and vicarious. Thus, younger children typically possess fewer, less well-developed schemas about a great many things than do mature adults.

One of the most important findings from the past three decades of comprehension research, from our point of view, is that readers can *remember* a text without *learning* from it. For instance, a reader might remember learning the definition of *photosynthesis* in a biology class. He might be able to recite the definition, but have no under-standing of a related concept, *semipermeable membrane,* which is important to a full understanding of photosynthesis.

Perhaps even more importantly, readers can *learn* from a text without *remembering* much of what they learned for a very long time (Kintsch, 1998). When readers successfully comprehend what they read, they construct meaning that is interrelated, establishing a logical, integrated understanding that they can draw from memory in the future to help them understand and learn from reading new texts.

Kintsch (1998) developed **construction-integration theory** to explain the complex cognitive processes used by readers to successfully comprehend a text. We will briefly illustrate how this construction-integration process works using the story *The Carrot Seed* by Ruth Krauss (1945). We begin with a familiar series of statements from the text:

> A little boy planted a carrot seed.
> His mother said, "I'm afraid it won't come up."
> His father said, "I'm afraid it won't come up."
> His big brother said, "It won't come up."
>
> © 1945 by Ruth Krauss. Used by permission of HarperCollins Publishers.

To understand these lines, we draw from our previous experiences with family members—parents and siblings. We also call up our specific situational recollections for planting seeds or growing a garden. Next we read:

> Every day the little boy pulled up the weeds around
> the seed and sprinkled the ground with water.

At this point, we focus in on the meaning of the actions taken by the little boy: pulling weeds and sprinkling the ground with water. This connects with our previous experiences of planting seeds and growing things. Next we read:

> But nothing came up.
> And nothing came up.

These two sentences lead us to make the prediction that, in this case, the outcome of planting a seed might be different than expected. Our motivation is to find out why, in this story, the seed is not coming up—or to think, "Maybe it will."

The **surface code,** or printed text as shown above, preserves in the reader's memory for an extremely short period of time the exact letters, words, and grammar or syntax of the text. This image is like the one you see quickly fading after turning off a television in a dark room. Once the text information is registered, it is quickly moved from a mental picture or *iconic* memory and processed through short-term or *working* memory in the brain. In long-term working memory in the brain, the image is transformed, using one or more strategies, into a text base that preserves the meaning of the text. A text base in long-term working memory might include connective inferences, for example, the inference that sometimes when seeds are planted, they do not grow (the microstructure). A text base in long-term working memory might also include important or gist ideas such as the fact that the little boy has done everything he can to get the seed to grow (the macrostructure). A constructed text base in long-term working memory is usually retained for several hours, but may also be forgotten in a few days. As a text base is formed and placed into long-term memory, these same memory processes and strategies are employed to integrate the details of the text base to form a situation model.

The **situation model,** according to Kintsch (1998), is what the text is really all about: ideas, people, objects, processes, or world events. And it is the situation model that is remembered longest—days, months, or even years. In the case of *The Carrot Seed,* the process of planting, nurturing, and harvesting as well as persevering in the face of doubt are the information and messages that are stored as the situation model(s) for this story.

Processing of a text by a reader occurs in cycles, usually clause by clause (just as we presented and discussed the story of *The Carrot Seed*), and it involves multiple, simultaneous cognitive processes. The cognitive processes involved in eventually creating a situation model are influenced by (a) the reader's knowledge about the text topic or message, (b) the reader's goals and motivations, (c) the reader's strategy selection and use, (d) the genre, type, and difficulty of the text, (e) the processing constraints of the reader's memory (Kintsch, 1998; van Dijk, 1999), and (f) the reader's ability to learn in and from a sociocultural context (group, classroom) if it is available when a text is processed.

Two phases of mental processing occur, then, for each clause the reader encounters in a text: (1) a construction phase and (2) an integration phase. In the construction phase, lower-level processes, such as activating prior knowledge and experiences, retrieving words meanings, examining the surface and grammatical structure of the printed text, and analyzing each clause into idea units called propositions occur. Propositions include text elements, connecting inferences, and generalizations, which are formed into a coherent network of connected meanings. For example, a sentence like "The student placed a tack on the teacher's chair" could be reduced in memory to a generalization that the student played a prank on his teacher (Zwann, 1999). In the construction phase of processing, other closely associated ideas also are activated, including irrelevant and even contradictory ideas. All of these activated elements are initially part of the coherence network of meaning under construction.

During the second phase of processing meaning, the integration phase, the ideas from the text that are strongly interconnected with our prior knowledge are strengthened; those associated concepts that do not fit with the meaning context of the story or text are deactivated and deleted from the network of integrated knowledge.

From this two-phase process, one first constructs meaning from text and then integrates it with prior knowledge to make what Kintsch (1998) calls the "situational model" that is stored in and retrieved from long-term memory. In the case of Krauss's (1945) *The Carrot Seed,* the situational model categorizes this story as being about how to grow things and how perseverance in the face of doubts expressed by others can lead to success. It is this situation model that is stored with other such instances in long-term memory.

What Does Research Say About Reading Comprehension Instruction?

During the late 1960s and throughout the 1970s, reading comprehension was largely taught by asking students questions following reading, or by assigning skill sheets as practice for reading comprehension skills such as getting the main idea, determining the sequence, following directions, noting details, and recognizing cause and effect relationships. In 1978, Dolores Durkin reported findings from reading comprehension studies conducted in public school classrooms. After observing a variety of "expert" teachers engaged in reading instruction in both reading and social studies classrooms, Durkin concluded that these teachers spent very little time actually teaching children how to understand text. *In fact, less than 1 percent of total reading or social studies instructional time was devoted to the teaching of reading comprehension.* Unfortunately, many researchers have concluded that the situation in today's schools has not improved appreciably over the past 25 years (Collins-Block, Gambrell, & Pressley, 2002). Durkin (1978) also suggested that effective comprehension instruction includes such teacher behaviors as helping, assisting, defining, demonstrating, modeling, describing, explaining, providing feedback, thinking aloud, and guiding students through learning activities. Simply asking students to respond to a worksheet or to answer a list of comprehension questions is not teaching and does nothing to develop comprehension strategies, concepts, or skills.

Getting to Know English Learners

Research among ELs indicates that a combination of activities or connecting to prior knowledge by the use of graphic organizers are effective strategies in EL instruction.

Past early literacy research has been directed toward the issues of word identification, particularly phonemic awareness and phonics instruction (National Reading Panel, 2000; RAND Reading Study Group Report, 2001; Snow, Burns, & Griffin, 1998). This is so much the case that "the terms *comprehension instruction* and *primary grades* do not often appear in the same sentence" (Pearson & Duke, 2002, p. 247). More recently, leading reading authorities, corporately sponsored study groups (RAND Reading Study Group), and federal government agencies have concluded that young children can and should be taught reading comprehension strategies from the onset of reading instruction.

As a result of this research, teachers are increasingly aware that they need to explicitly teach comprehension strategies to children (Pressley, 2000). Research has shown that reading comprehension improves most when teachers provide explicit comprehension strategy instruction to children (Bauman & Bergeron, 1993; Brown, Pressley, Van Meter, & Schuder, 1996; Dole, Brown, & Trathen, 1996; Morrow, 1985; National Reading Panel, 2000). From the work of the National Reading Panel, the evidence base supports the effectiveness of teaching the following reading comprehension strategies: (1) graphic organizers, (2) comprehension monitoring, (3) answering questions, (4) generating questions, (5) story structure, and (6) summarization. The National Reading Panel (2000) also examined the evidence for teaching the following comprehension strategies, but did not find sufficient numbers of studies disclosing the same findings: (1) activating or connecting to prior knowledge, (2) inferences, (3) visual imagery, and (4) listening actively. These findings do not imply that teachers should stop teaching these comprehension strategies, but rather suggest that more research is needed before we can know how effective these strategies are when taught. We suggest that teachers continue to include these latter strategies in their repertoire for comprehension strategy instruction, but give special emphasis to those that have proven their effectiveness. The National Reading Panel also found that comprehension instruction is most effective when there is a great deal of text-focused talk set in vibrantly interactive and collaborative classroom contexts (National Reading Panel, 2000; Pressley, 2006). And finally, research as reported by the National Reading Panel (2000) indicates that teaching children how to coordinate the use of a set or package of comprehension strategies as they read and discuss what they've learned with peers and with teacher support yields particularly strong results for improving children's reading comprehension. Examples of multiple-comprehension-strategy instruction include Palincsar and Brown's (1984) *Reciprocal Teaching* and Pressley's (2002) *Transactional Strategies Instruction.* When teaching multiple comprehension strategies, the goal is to teach children a "routine" for working through texts using a set of comprehension strategies. Recent research has also determined that teaching a combination of comprehension strategies as a set is, in some ways, preferable to teaching a series of single strategies one at a time (Reutzel, Smith, & Fawson, 2005).

Paris, Carpenter, Paris, and Hamilton (2005) have carefully examined correlates (things that seem to be related) of children's reading comprehension. They found that some correlates or relationships between reading comprehension and other variables are spurious (false) while other relationships are genuine. For example, oral reading fluency and print awareness are highly correlated with reading comprehension among very young readers. However, the relationship between oral reading fluency, print awareness, and reading comprehension is transitory in that it decreases with age and ability. Thus, oral reading fluency and print awareness are regarded as spurious or false correlates with comprehension because they do not continue to hold up over time. On the other hand, there are genuine correlates of children's reading comprehension, including (a) general oral language, (b) vocabulary, and (c) narrative text structure awareness. These correlates remain highly related with reading comprehension regardless of the age or experience of the reader. Implications for teaching reading comprehension from this research is that building children's understanding of text structure and store of word meanings is strongly predictive of the ability to comprehend text at all points of a child's reading development.

Other research evidence points clearly to the need for teachers to support students' ability to use comprehension strategies when reading a variety of text types (narrative and expository) and genres (fairy tales, realistic fiction, almanacs, encyclopedias, etc.) (Donovan & Smolkin, 2002; Duke, 2000). The key to successful reading comprehension instruction is for teachers to design and deliver carefully structured learning activities that support children while they are developing the ability to become self-regulated readers who can use multiple comprehension strategies to understand what they read (Pressley, 2006).

A Sequence for Reading Comprehension Instruction in Grades K–3

It is important that teachers know and understand the minimum expected outcomes, or **benchmark standards,** for comprehension development at each grade level, especially in the early years. This information becomes an essential roadmap for teachers to use in assessing each student's level of comprehension development. With this knowledge, you can plan instruction that best fits the needs of every child and that lays the groundwork for appropriate "next steps" in comprehension development. Of course, in the classroom you will discover students are at different places in their comprehension development, and you will need to plan small-group sessions each day for students having common needs. In this way, you can help all students continue learning in a systematic fashion.

Figure 7.1 lists the benchmark standards for reading comprehension for grades K through 3 (Cooter, 2004).

Figure 7.1   End-of-Year Reading Comprehension Benchmarks: K–3

Kindergarten End-of-Year Benchmarks
- ✓ Uses new vocabulary and language in own speech
- ✓ Distinguishes whether simple sentences do or don't make sense
- ✓ Connects information and events in text to life experiences
- ✓ Uses graphic organizers to comprehend text with guidance
- ✓ Retells stories or parts of stories
- ✓ Understands and follows oral directions
- ✓ Distinguishes fantasy from realistic text
- ✓ Demonstrates familiarity with a number of books and selections
- ✓ Explains concepts from nonfiction text

First Grade End-of-Year Benchmarks
- ✓ Reads and comprehends fiction and nonfiction that is appropriate for the second half of grade one
- ✓ Notices difficulties in understanding text
- ✓ Connects information and events in text to life experiences
- ✓ Reads and understands simple written directions
- ✓ Predicts and justifies what will happen next in stories
- ✓ Discusses how, why, and what-if questions in sharing nonfiction text
- ✓ Describes new information in own words
- ✓ Distinguishes whether simple sentences are incomplete or don't make sense
- ✓ Expands sentences in response to what, when, where, and how questions
- ✓ Uses new vocabulary and language in own speech and writing
- ✓ Demonstrates familiarity with a number of read-aloud and independent reading selections including nonfiction
- ✓ Demonstrates familiarity with a number of types or genres of text like storybooks, poems, newspapers, phone books, and everyday print such as signs, notices, and labels
- ✓ Summarizes the main points of a story

Second Grade End-of-Year Benchmarks
- ✓ Reads and comprehends both fiction and nonfiction that is appropriate for the second half of grade two
- ✓ Rereads sentences when meaning is not clear
- ✓ Interprets information from diagrams, charts, and graphs
- ✓ Recalls facts and details of text
- ✓ Reads nonfiction materials for answers to specific questions
- ✓ Develops literary awareness of character traits, point of view, setting, problem, solution, and outcome
- ✓ Connects and compares information across nonfiction selections
- ✓ Poses possible answers to how, why, and what-if questions in interpreting nonfiction text
- ✓ Explains and describes new concepts and information in own words
- ✓ Identifies part of speech for concrete nouns, active verbs, adjectives, and adverbs
- ✓ Uses new vocabulary and language in own speech and writing
- ✓ Demonstrates familiarity with a number of read-aloud and independent reading selections including nonfiction
- ✓ Recognizes a variety of print resources and knows their contents like joke books, chapter books, dictionaries, atlases, weather reports, *TV Guide,* etc.
- ✓ Connects a variety of texts to literature and life experiences (language to literacy)
- ✓ Summarizes a story including the stated main idea

Third Grade End-of-Year Benchmarks
- ✓ Reads and comprehends both fiction and nonfiction that is appropriate for grade three
- ✓ Reads chapter books independently
- ✓ Identifies specific words or wordings that are causing comprehension difficulties
- ✓ Summarizes major points from fiction and nonfiction text

Figure 7.1   (Continued)

> ✓ Discusses similarities in characters and events across stories
> ✓ Discusses underlying theme or message when interpreting fiction
> ✓ Distinguishes between cause and effect, fact and opinion, and main idea and supporting details when interpreting nonfiction text
> ✓ Asks how, why, and what-if questions when interpreting nonfiction text
> ✓ Uses information and reasoning to examine bases of hypotheses and opinions
> ✓ Infers word meaning from roots, prefixes, and suffixes that have been taught
> ✓ Uses dictionary to determine meanings and usage of unknown words
> ✓ Uses new vocabulary and language in own speech and writing
> ✓ Uses parts of speech correctly in independent writing (nouns, verbs, adjectives, and adverbs)
> ✓ Shows familiarity with a number of read-aloud and independent reading selections, including nonfiction
> ✓ Uses multiple sources to locate information (tables of contents, indexes, available technology)
> ✓ Connects a variety of literary texts with life experiences (language to literacy)

How Is Reading Comprehension Assessed?

Reading comprehension assessment is currently a topic of focused debate and some concern (Paris & Stahl, 2005). Reading comprehension, as we have already learned, is composed of several essential components: the reader, the text, the activity, and the social context. Because reading comprehension is multifaceted, it cannot be adequately measured with any single approach, process, or test (Paris & Stahl, 2005). However, one of the most effective processes for finding out if children understand what they read is to ask them to retell what they have read (Brown & Cambourne, 1987; Gambrell, Pfeiffer, & Wilson, 1985; Morrow, 1985; Morrow, Gambrell, Kapinus, Koskinen, Marshall, & Mitchell, 1986). Asking children to retell a story or information text involves reconstructing the entire text structure, including the major elements, details, and sequence. In stories, children retell using story structure, including the story sequence and the important elements of the plot; in addition, they make inferences and note relevant details. Retelling can be used to assess children's memory for story and information text.

You will need the following supplies for capturing students' oral retellings of texts they have read:

- blank audiotape
- portable audiocassette recorder with internal microphone
- brief story or information text

Because the processes for eliciting and scoring oral retellings are different for narrative and expository text types, we will discuss each separately.

Eliciting and Scoring Narrative Oral Retellings

For the sake of example, let us assume that we selected *The Carrot Seed* by Ruth Krauss (1945) as a story text for oral retelling. Type the text of the story onto a

Figure 7.2   Story Grammar Parsing of *The Carrot Seed*

Setting

A little boy planted a carrot seed.

Problem (getting the seed to grow)

His mother said, "I'm afraid it won't come up."

His father said, "I'm afraid it won't come up."

And his big brother said, "It won't come up."

Events

Every day the little boy pulled up the weeds around the seed and sprinkled the ground with water.

But nothing came up.

And nothing came up.

Everyone kept saying it wouldn't come up.

But he still pulled up the weeds around it every day and sprinkled the ground with water.

Resolution

And then, one day, a carrot came up just as the little boy had known it would.

Cultural dolls are used for retelling of stories that have been read and reread numerous times. Learn more about the "Cultural Character Concept" on the Teacher Prep Website (*www.prenhall.com/ teacherprep*) in *Strategies and Lessons—Language Arts Methods/Reading.*

separate piece of paper for parsing. Parsing, in this instance, refers to dividing a story into four major and somewhat simplified story grammar categories: setting, problem, events, and resolution. These are shown in Figure 7.2.

Oral story retellings may be elicited from children in a number of ways. One way involves the use of pictures or verbal prompts related to the story. As pictures of the story are flashed sequentially, the child is asked to retell the story as remembered from listening or reading. Morrow (1985, 2005) suggested that teachers prompt children to begin story retellings with a statement such as: "A little while ago, we read a story called [name of story]. Retell the story as if you were telling it to a friend who has never heard it before." Other prompts during the oral story retelling may be framed as questions:

- "How does the story begin?" Or, "Once upon a time. . . ."
- "What happens next?"
- "What happened to [the main character] when . . . ?"
- "Where did the story take place?"
- "When did the story take place?"
- "How did the main character solve the problem in the story?"
- "How did the story end?"

Getting to Know English Learners

Because beginning language learning is receptive, and not necessarily productive, it may make sense to elicit oral story retellings from ELs by assigning a more capable peer who can translate the EL's understandings into English.

Morrow (2005) recommends that teachers offer only general prompts such as those listed previously rather than ask about specific details, ideas, or a sequence of events from the story. Remember that when asking questions such as those previously listed, you are moving from free recall of text to a form of assisted recall of text information. Incidentally, you should know that assisted recall of story text information is especially useful with struggling readers.

Figure 7.3 Oral Story Retelling Coding Form

Student's name: _____ Grade: _____

Title of story: _____ Date: _____

General directions: Give 1 point for each element included, as well as for "gist." Give 1 point for each character named, as well as for such words as *boy, girl,* or *dog.* Credit plurals (*friends,* for instance) with 2 points under characters.

Setting

    a. Begins with an introduction   _____

    b. Indicates main character   _____

    c. Names other characters   _____

    d. Includes statement about time or place   _____

Objective

    a. Refers to main character's goal or problem to be solved   _____

Events

    a. Number of events recalled   _____

    b. Number of events in story   _____

    c. Score for "events" (a/b)   _____

Resolution

    a. Tells how main character resolves the story problem   _____

Sequence

    Summarizes story in order: setting, objective, episodes, and resolution. (Score 2 for correct order, 1 for partial order, 0 for no sequence.)   _____

Possible score: _____   **Student's score:** _____

Reutzel, D. Ray; Cooter, Robert B. *Strategies for Reading Assessment and Instruction: Helping Every Child Succeed,* 3rd Edition, © 2007. Reprinted by permission of Pearson Education, Inc.

A second way to elicit oral story retellings from students is to use unaided recall, in which students retell the story without picture or verbal prompts. Asking the child to tell the story "as if she were telling it to someone who had never heard or read the story before" begins an unaided oral story retelling. To record critical elements of the story structure included in the child's oral story retelling, use an audiotape recording and oral story retelling coding sheet like the one shown in Figure 7.3.

The information gleaned from an oral story retelling may be used to help you, the teacher, focus future instruction on enhancing students' understanding of narrative parts or story structure.

Children find cultural dolls helpful as they retell/re-enact favorite stories. Read "Retelling Stories with Cultural Character Dolls" by selecting *Strategies and Lessons—Language Arts Methods/Reading* on the Teacher Prep Website (*www.prenhall.com/teacherprep*)

Eliciting and Scoring Expository Oral Retellings

Several researchers have found that children in the elementary grades are aware of and can be taught to recognize expository text structures (McGee, 1982; Williams, 2005). One of the most effective ways to find out if a child understands expository text is to use oral retellings (Duke & Bennett-Armistead, 2003). Asking children to

"Monitoring Reading Progress," *found in Strategies and Lessons— Language Arts Methods/Reading* on the Teacher Prep Website (*www.prenhall.com/teacherprep*), helps you understand on-going progress monitoring through observational checklists, anecdotal notes, student reading logs, and self-assessments.

Learn how to assess motivation, comprehension strategy use and vocabulary knowledge as you read "Assessing Literature-Based Instruction" in *Strategies and Lessons— Language Arts Methods/Reading* on the Teacher Prep Website (*www.prenhall.com/teacherprep*).

retell an expository text involves reconstructing the contents of the expository text into its major, main, or superordinate ideas and its minor or subordinate details, both within the underlying organization of the text (compare/contrast, cause-effect, description, list, enumeration, etc.) Thus, oral expository text retellings assess both content comprehension and text structure knowledge in holistic, sequenced, and organized ways.

Begin an expository text oral retelling by selecting a brief, information trade book or textbook chapter for students to listen to or to read either aloud or silently, depending on the grade level and development of the student. We recommend that children in grades K–1 listen to the text read aloud, that children in grades 2–3 read aloud, and that students in grade 4 and beyond read silently. *Is It a Fish?* by Cutting and Cutting (2002) from the *Wright Group Science Collection* might be selected for the assessment. The teacher should type the text onto a separate piece of paper for parsing. Parsing, in this instance, refers to dividing a text into main or superordinate ideas and subordinate ideas as shown in Figure 7.4, *Oral Expository Text Retelling Coding Form.*

Expository text oral retellings may be elicited from children in a number of ways. One way involves the use of pictures or verbal prompts from the text. As pictures in the text are flashed sequentially, students are asked to retell what they remember from listening or reading about this picture. This approach is modeled after the work of Beaver (1997) in the *Developmental Reading Assessment* and the work of Leslie and Caldwell (2001) in the *Qualitative Reading Inventory–3.* Morrow (1985, 2005) suggests that teachers prompt children to begin oral retellings with a statement such as: "A little while ago, we read a book or text called [name the text or book]. Retell the text or book as if you were telling it to a friend who has never heard about it before." Other prompts during the recall may include the following:

- Tell me more about. . . .
- You said _____. Is there anything else you can tell me about. . . .
- Tell me about gills.
- Tell me about fins.
- Tell me how fish move, look, or breathe.

Asking students to retell what they remember using these types of prompts is a form of assisted recall and, as previously mentioned, may be especially useful with struggling readers.

A second way to elicit expository text oral retellings from students is to use unaided recall, in which students retell the content and order of the content in a book or text structure without pictures or verbal prompts. Asking the student to retell the information read "as if she were telling it to someone who had never heard or read the content of the book or text before" is used to begin an unaided expository text oral retelling. To record critical elements of the expository text oral retelling included in the child's oral retelling, use an audiotape recording. To make judgments about the quality of an unaided expository text oral retelling you might use a rating guide sheet like the one shown in Figure 7.5, which is based on the work of Moss (1997).

As you develop the ability to listen to expository text oral retellings, you may no longer need to use an audio recording and may simply make notes on the scoring sheet as to the features you hear the child include in his or her oral retelling.

Figure 7.4   Oral Expository Text Retelling Coding Form

**Put a check mark by everything the child retells
from his or her reading of the text.**

_____ **Big Idea: A fish is an animal.**

_____ Detail: It has a backbone (skeleton inside).
_____ Detail: Most fish have scales.
_____ Detail: It is cold-blooded.

_____ **Big Idea: All fish live in water.**

_____ Detail: Some live in salt water.
_____ Detail: Some live in fresh water.
_____ Detail: Salmon and eels live in salt and fresh water.
_____ Detail: Salmon leave the sea to lay eggs in the river.

_____ **Big Idea: All fish breathe with gills.**

_____ Detail: All animals breathe oxygen.
_____ Detail: Some get oxygen from the air.
_____ Detail: Fish get oxygen from the water.
_____ Detail: A shark is a fish.
_____ Detail: Gills look like slits.
_____ Detail: A ray's gills are on the underside of its body.
_____ Detail: Rays breathe through holes on top of their head when they rest.

_____ **Big Idea: Most fish have fins to help them swim.**

_____ Detail: A sailfish has a huge fin that looks like a snail on its back.
_____ Detail: A (sting) ray waves its pectoral fin up and down.

Scoring:

**Tally the marks for the big ideas and details. Place the total number in the
blanks shown below.**

Big Ideas _____ /4   Details: _____ /16   # of Prompts _____

Sequentially Retold (Circle One):   Yes   No

Other ideas recalled including inferences: _____

The information gleaned from an expository text oral retelling may be used to help you, the teacher, focus instruction on enhancing students' understanding of expository text structures. It will also be useful as you teach students strategies for sorting out the main ideas from details, sequencing, and summarizing information.

Figure 7.5 A Qualitative Assessment of Student Expository Text Oral Retellings*

Rating Level	Criteria for Establishing a Level
5	Student includes all main ideas and supporting details, sequences properly, infers beyond the text, relates text to own life, understands text organization, summarizes, gives opinion and justifies it, and may ask additional questions. The retelling is complete and cohesive.
4	Student includes most main ideas and supporting details, sequences properly, relates text to own life, understands text organization, summarizes, and gives opinion. The retelling is fairly complete.
3	Student includes some main ideas and details, sequences most material, understands text organization, and gives opinion. The retelling is fairly complete.
2	Student includes a few main ideas and details, has some difficulty sequencing, may give irrelevant information, and gives opinion. The retelling is fairly incomplete.
1	Student gives details only, has poor sequencing, gives irrelevant information. The retelling is very incomplete.

*Moss, B. (1997). A qualitative assessment of first graders' retelling of expository text. *Reading Research and Instruction, 37*(1), 1–13.

What Are the Characteristics of Effective Comprehension Instruction?

Review a week's plans for reading through text introductions, re-reading, word studies, partner reading, and retellings. Visit the Teacher Prep Website (*www.prenhall. com/teacherprep*) and select *Strategies and Lessons— Language Arts Methods/Reading* and read "First Grade Shared Reading Lesson Plan."

Pressley (2000) is quick to remind us that reading comprehension instruction begins with teaching decoding skills. Research shows there is a strong predictive relationship between well-developed word recognition skills and reading comprehension. Both the ability to decode unfamiliar words and recognize a core group of words by sight in the primary grades predicts good comprehension in the later elementary grades (Juel, 1988). Once students can recognize a word, they should be taught to use context—the surrounding print meaning or pictures—to evaluate whether the word has been properly recognized.

Students should be taught word meaning (vocabulary) if we are serious about improving their reading comprehension. This is especially true when students are taught word meanings that are related to reading selections (Beck, Perfetti, & McKeown, 1982; McKeown, 1985). As a part of extending children's vocabulary development and reading fluency, research clearly recommends extensive reading of a wide range of reading materials (National Reading Panel, 2000; Pressley, 2000; Stahl & Nagy, 2006). Within this environment of extensive reading of a variety of texts, children must be taught to activate their relevant background knowledge to understand and remember texts (Pearson & Anderson, 1984). They must also be explicitly taught comprehension strategies (National Reading Panel, 2000; Pressley, 2000). Teaching what comprehension strategies are and how to use each one independently is necessary; however, they are insufficient for effective, evidence-based comprehension strategy instruction. Children need to be taught how to orchestrate or self-regulate their selection and use of multiple comprehension strategies to remember and learn from text (Kintsch, 1998, 2004; National Reading Panel, 2000; Reutzel, Smith, & Fawson, 2005).

Another characteristic of evidence-based reading comprehension strategy instruction is assuring that students are guided to practice the application of comprehension strategies across a variety of text types—narrative and expository—as there is some indication that students do not spontaneously transfer their ability to select and use comprehension strategies across these text types (Donovan & Smolkin, 2002; Duke, 2000). Finally, students need to receive teacher-guided practice and feedback in using comprehension strategies in collaborative, highly interactive settings that stress student motivation and collaboration (National Reading Panel, 2000).

In summary, effective, evidence-based reading comprehension instruction recognizes the early need for children to learn to efficiently, effortlessly, and fluently recognize words. Children need to read extensively and receive expert and explicit reading comprehension instruction from teachers that is focused on vocabulary (see Chapter 6) and comprehension strategy acquisition. At some point, children need to be helped, through teacher-guided instruction, to select and use multiple comprehension strategies to process a variety of texts (National Reading Panel, 2000; Pressley, 2000). And finally, the conditions that support effective classroom comprehension instruction include rich interactions and collaborations among teachers and children around a variety of interesting texts (National Reading Panel, 2000; Pressley, 2000).

What Are Effective Reading Comprehension Strategies We Should Teach?

The answer to this question is organized around the four essential components of the Rand Reading Study Group's (2002) description of reading comprehension: (1) the reader, (2) the text, (3) the activities or strategies, and (4) the situational context. We begin our discussion of effective reading comprehension strategies with a focus on helping the reader prepare for and succeed in reading comprehension.

> **Getting to Know English Learners**
> Activating background knowledge for ELs follow the same rules—storytelling, particularly in the form of fairy tales or fables, is a universal, cross-cultural phenomenon.

The Reader

Activating Student Background Knowledge: Theme or Topic? Activating students' background knowledge in preparation for reading is critical for promoting reading comprehension. Many core reading program or basal reader teacher's guides contain a section titled "Building Background for the Story," or "Building Background Knowledge." Unfortunately, the guidance offered in many core reading program teacher's editions for building students' background knowledge is often misleading.

> Analyses of several basal teachers' manuals show instances of problems in the pre-reading component. Some manuals suggest that teachers focus on tangential concepts that are irrelevant to the upcoming selection; sometimes the suggestion for presenting the concepts would encourage far-ranging discussions that could distract children

from what is important. Even under the best conditions, the teacher's manuals may suggest concepts inappropriate for a specific group of children. (Beck, 1986, p. 15)

Some teacher's manuals make no distinction between activating students' prior knowledge for story texts as compared with information texts. For example, in presenting the story *The Ugly Duckling,* one teacher's manual focused background knowledge activation on a discussion of the differences between ducks and swans. Although such a concept may be appropriate for an information text dealing with the topic of ducks and swans, it was totally misdirected for the story *The Ugly Duckling.* Background knowledge activation for stories should focus discussion on the message or theme rather than on a topic. For example, one might ask students to respond to the question, "Have any of you ever experienced what it feels like to have someone not want to play with you? How did you feel when you were left out of a game?" These questions would be much more likely to evoke the necessary background knowledge to guide the interpretation of the story of the ugly duckling than would a study of the difference between ducks and swans. If the teacher determines the text is story (fiction or narrative), background knowledge activation should focus on evoking knowledge related to the theme or message of the story, e.g., exclusion or being left out because you are different.

On the other hand, if the text is informational (nonfiction or expository), background knowledge activation should focus on evoking knowledge from the particular domain or topic associated with the content of the text, e.g., migratory waterfowl or land formations.

Activating Student Background Knowledge: K-W-L. One well-known, highly-used-but-inadequately-researched strategy for activating background knowledge is called K-W-L (Ogle, 1986; Stahl, 2004). Although this strategy may in fact be useful, it can be misused in light of what we have just discussed about activating students' background knowledge. Before using this strategy, teachers must determine the type of text to be read and then shape the questions to guide the K-W-L process so that the appropriate knowledge is activated to act as the interpretive framework for reading the text. Ogle (1986), the originator of K-W-L, asserts that this strategy is best suited for use with information texts, although with appropriate guidance and questioning, teachers can adapt K-W-L for use with narratives as well.

Step K: What I Know. K-W-L strategy lessons begin with step K, *What I Know.* This step is composed of two levels of accessing prior knowledge: (a) brainstorming and (b) categorizing information. Ask children to brainstorm about a particular topic (in the case of a narrative, brainstorm a particular theme or message). For instance, you might ask children what they know about bats. A list of associations is formed through brainstorming. When students make a contribution, Ogle (1986) suggests asking them where or how they got their information to challenge them to use higher levels of thinking.

Next, ask students to look for ways in which the brainstorming list can be reorganized into categories of information. For example, you may notice that the brainstorming list shows three related pieces of information about how bats navigate. These can be reorganized into a "navigation" category. Encourage students to look at the list and think about other categories represented in the brainstorming list.

Step W: What Do I Want to Learn? During step W, students recognize gaps, inaccuracies, and disagreements in their prior knowledge to decide what they want to learn. You, the teacher, can play a central role in pointing out these problems and helping students frame questions for which they would like to have answers.

Grand Conversations allow students to explore interpretations and reflect on their feelings of a text. Select *Strategies and Lessons-Reading Methods/Comprehension* on the Teacher Prep Website (*www.prenhall.com/teacherprep*) and learn to implement "Grand Conversations."

Questions can be framed by using the stem "I wonder." After children generate a series of questions to be answered from the reading, they are to write down questions for which they would like answers. These are often selected from those questions generated by the group.

Step L: What I Learned. After reading, ask students to write down what they learned. This can take the form of answers to specific questions they asked or a concise written summary of their learning. These questions and answers may be discussed as a group or shared between pairs of students. In this way, other students benefit from the learning of their peers as well as from their own learning.

In summary, K-W-L has been shown to be effective in improving reading comprehension by causing students to activate, think about, and organize their prior knowledge as an aid to reading comprehension (DeWitz & Carr, 1987).

Motivation and Engagement

Turner & Paris (1995) discuss six "C's" of motivation that promote student engagement in the act of reading and comprehending a text: (1) choice, (2) challenge, (3) control, (4) collaboration, (5) constructing meaning, and (6) consequences. Choice does not mean that students are free to select any text or to make up what they have read when asked about it. Choices are never unlimited; instead they are bounded or limited. To offer choice may mean choosing to read from two different information books on rocks and rock formations. However, when children have the sense that they can make some choices about what to read and for which purposes, they are more willing to persist and remain intellectually engaged while reading.

Challenge is the second way in which we can encourage increased reading motivation and engagement to increase reading comprehension. Turner & Paris (1995) suggest that the common wisdom that children like "easy" reading texts and tasks more than more difficult or challenging reading texts or tasks is not supported by research. In fact, students enjoy challenge. Of course, here again the level of challenge associated with the text or task must not become excessive to the point of frustration. But giving children appropriately challenging texts and tasks has been shown to positively impact reader motivation to read for comprehension.

Control is the third motivational factor associated with increasing students' reading comprehension. Sharing the control of texts and tasks in the classroom with the teacher or other students is associated with greater engagement while reading. Students need to feel that they have an integral role to play while reading a text in order to take sufficient control of their own thinking processes to be successful in reading for comprehension.

Collaboration has been shown to be one of eight comprehension strategies for which there is sufficient scientific evidence of efficacy. The National Reading Panel (2000) recommends collaboration for implementation into classroom practice to improve students' reading comprehension. Collaboration requires that students discuss, interact, and work together with each other and their teachers to construct the meaning of texts. Collaboration results in students obtaining greater insights into the thinking processes of others around a text. Collaborative discussions and interactions also elaborate the outcomes of the reading comprehension process by adding to one another's memories for and meanings constructed from the reading of a text.

Constructing meaning is the very essence of reading comprehension instruction. This requires the conscious selection, control, and use of various cognitive comprehension strategies while engaged in reading text.

Help children to understand appropriate social behaviors during Grand Conversations as you model "good" and "bad" examples. In "Mrs. Shapiro Teaches Her Second Graders About Sustaining Conversations," children share strengths and weaknesses of their observations. Select *Strategies and Lessons—Language Arts Methods/Talking* on the Teacher Prep Website (*www.prenhall.com/teacherprep*) to learn more.

Getting to Know English Learners
Collaboration is also key to language acquisition as students discuss, share, listen to, and negotiate with language.

Consequences are the final factor that leads students to increased motivation and reading comprehension. This concept refers to the nature of the outcomes expected when comprehending. If the outcome expected is completing or participating in an open-ended rather than a closed-ended task, such as contributing to a discussion rather than getting the "right" answers to questions on a worksheet, students interpret their failures in comprehension differently. When seeking correct or "right" answers, they often feel that they just do not have enough ability (Turner & Paris, 1995). On the other hand, if through discussion they detect that they failed to pick up on some element in the text, they often view this failure as the result of insufficiently or improperly selecting or applying effective comprehension strategies rather than just that they are not "smart enough" or "don't have the ability."

In conclusion, when preparing to teach reading comprehension, teachers must carefully consider how they can increase students' motivation to actively engage in and take control of their own thinking processes while reading texts. The six Cs mentioned earlier—choice, challenge, control, collaboration, constructing meaning, and consequences—can be considered when building motivation.

The Text

The quality of the text examples children experience in the books or texts we use in teaching comprehension is a consideration of principal importance. Text that is well-presented, well-written, and well-organized has been shown by many researchers to have a positive impact on all students' comprehension (Donovan & Smolkin, 2002; McKeown, Beck, & Worthy, 1993; Seidenberg, 1989). As a teacher, you must select and use those texts that provide clear examples of the text features and structures you are intent upon teaching children to recognize and use to improve their comprehension.

Text Structure and Using Graphic Organizers. A model for teaching children to use text structure is found in Figure 7.6.

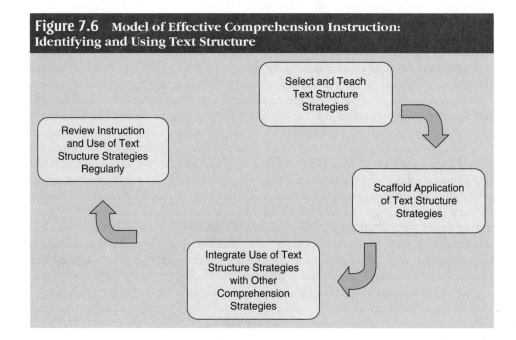

Figure 7.6 **Model of Effective Comprehension Instruction: Identifying and Using Text Structure**

To begin, text structure instruction should focus on the physical features that help students understand the way that an author has organized a text including the table of contents, chapter headings and subheadings, paragraph organization such as topic sentence location and signal words, typographic and spacing features, and visual insets or aids. Next, students can be helped to recognize and use the way the author has organized the text. For narrative texts, this means teaching explicitly the parts of a narrative or story structure (NRP, 2000). For young children, this may begin with the concepts of story to include *beginning, middle,* and *end.* Older children should be taught that a story has prototypical parts organized in a predictable sequence, including the *setting, problem, goal, events,* and *resolution.* Because our lives are stories, stories mirror lived experiences for which we all eventually acquire an internal context into which we can place story structure. Young children are relatively adept at working with and understanding narrative text structures.

Teaching the organization or structure of expository texts means explicitly teaching different text structures of time order, cause and effect, problem and solution, comparison, simple listing/enumeration, and descriptions. Among information texts, it appears that sequence text structures are the easiest for younger students to understand. Examples of sequence text structures include counting books, days of the week, months of the year, step-by-step instruction, seasons, and so on. These books typically follow an established order or sequence familiar to younger children from their everyday lives. Another sequence text structure is the question–answer format. In these types of expository structures, authors typically ask a question and then proceed immediately to answer the question in the very next sentence, paragraph, or page. After this type of text structure, in a developmental progression of difficulty, come information books that describe single topics such as frogs, sand, or chocolate. Another information book structure that is closely aligned with descriptive structures enumerates or lists a category of related concepts or objects for description such as reptiles, dogs, or information about the Pueblo Indians. In listing/enumerative text structures, different types, examples, and aspects of a category are described as a collection. Compare and contrast or cause-effect expository text structures are the most challenging for young readers.

Effective text structure instruction requires that teachers provide short, frequent review opportunities for application of the text structure strategies taught. We have listed the characteristics of effective text structure instruction in Figure 7.7.

We have chosen two types of text structures, narrative and expository, as examples to illustrate the kind of effective text structure instruction we describe in Figure 7.7. We begin by focusing on effective text structure instruction with a selected narrative text.

Effective Narrative Text Structure Instruction. We begin by selecting an excellent example of a narrative text.

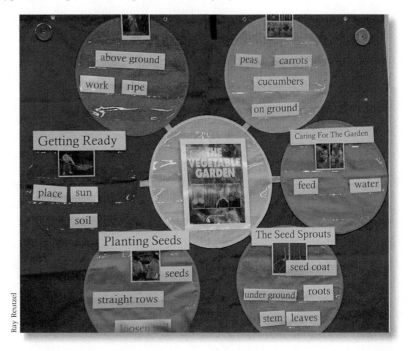
Ray Reutzel

Figure 7.7 Characteristics of Effective Text Structure Instruction

- Select exemplars of varying text types.
- Focus initial instruction on physical features of text that help students understand organization:
  - table of contents
  - chapter headings
  - subheadings
  - paragraph organization
    - main idea and topic sentence location
    - signal words
    - typographic features
    - spacing features
    - visual insets
- Teach children how to determine the way the author has organized or structured the text.
- Teach children how to think about and visually represent the way the author has implicitly organized the text using graphic organizers.
- Provide scaffolding or gradual release.
- Activate and use text feature and text structure knowledge in regular review cycles.

This means we want to find a story text that exemplifies the clear and traditional use of story structure. For a text to qualify for selection, it must possess the traditional elements and follow the traditional sequence of elements in a story grammar: setting, characters, problem, goal, events, and resolution. The familiar story *The Tale of Peter Rabbit* (Beatrix Potter, 1986) is well-suited to our purpose.

Next, we carefully examine the physical features of our text. We note several important physical features in *The Tale of Peter Rabbit* that we make a point of showing and discussing with students: the title, the author, the illustrator, the title page, and how many stories begins with "Once upon a time" and end with "The End." Although not as rich in physical features as some narrative texts, *The Tale of Peter Rabbit* does evidence clear paragraph structure. For example, when Peter saw Mr. McGregor, he was very frightened and the details of the paragraph clearly relate to actions and events that would support this major idea—the character's rushing all over, forgetting his way out, losing something in the tussle, and so on. This storybook also makes use of a great many signal words: *first, after, after a time, presently, suddenly,* and *at last.* The book also makes good use of spacing and print arrangements. On the first page, ONCE UPON A TIME is printed in all capitals, as is THE END. Also on the first page, the four little rabbits' names—Flopsy, Mopsy, Cottontail, and Peter—are printed one name to a line with an increasing paragraph indent as each name is added to the list, resulting in a four-stair, step-shaped list. This print arrangement is used several times throughout the book as a visual indicator of a list.

The Tale of Peter Rabbit is a narrative with traditional story structure. The setting is clearly stated in this story, including mention of the characters of Flopsy, Mopsy, Cottontail, Peter, and Mother. The problem is described when Mother Rabbit tells the children to stay away from Mr. McGregor's garden because their father had been caught and ended up in Mr. McGregor's pie. Peter, of course, decides he will test fate by straying away from his siblings into Mr. McGregor's garden. Once Peter has eaten his fill, he is spotted by Mr. McGregor. The story chronicles Peter's many close calls and his multiple attempts to escape Mr. McGregor. In the process, Peter loses his coat and his shoes. The resolution occurs when Peter escapes from Mr. McGregor and goes home to his waiting Mother, who gives him chamomile tea to settle his upset stomach.

For younger children, a simple graphic organizer with beginning, middle, and end of story components can be used to convey implicit story structure. Older students can be presented with a more complex graphic organizer that includes setting, characters, location, time, problem, goals, events, and resolution. Two examples of graphic organizers are shown in Figures 7.8 and 7.9. Figure 7.8 shows *The Tale of Peter Rabbit* graphic organizer for teaching younger children story structure. Figure 7.9 shows *The Tale of Peter Rabbit* graphic organizer for teaching older students story structure.

Once story structure is explicitly and thoroughly explained and modeled by the teacher, we turn our attention to the issue of scaffolding narrative text structure instruction effectively in the classroom. *Scaffolding* refers to the gradual release of control and responsibility for selecting and using text structure comprehension strategies like graphic organizers, beginning with high teacher control and involvement, moving to shared control and involvement between teachers and students, and finally to students' independent control over strategy selection and use. This release requires multiple lessons such as the one just described, perhaps using a variety of storybooks such as *The Little Red Hen, The Three Pigs,* or *Jack and the Beanstalk.*

In the first lesson, the teacher would do most of the explaining, thinking aloud, and representing of the elements of story structure in the graphic organizer. In the

Figure 7.8   Simple Story Structure Graphic Organizer

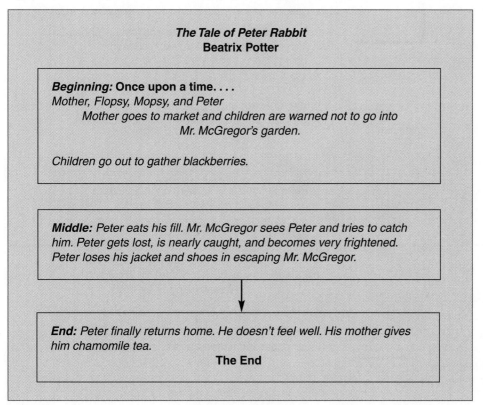

Figure 7.9   Complex Story Structure Graphic Organizer

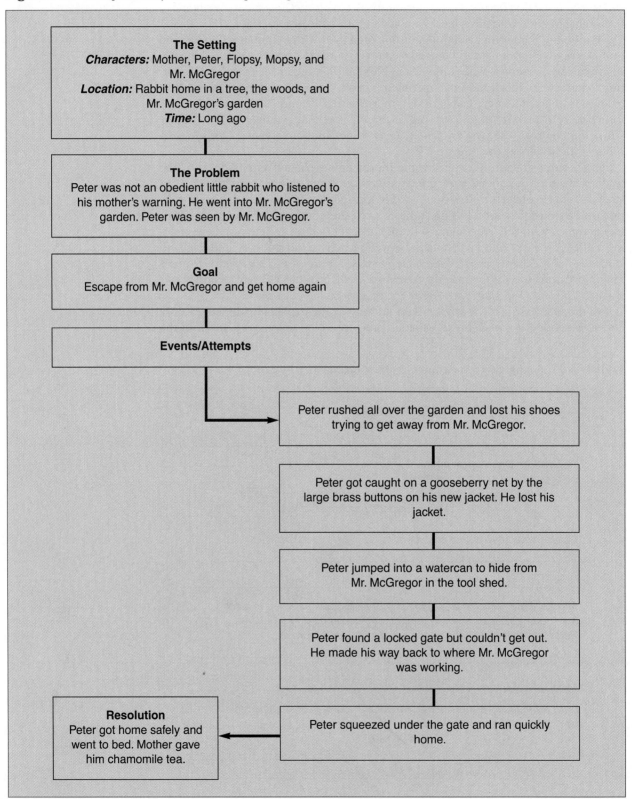

second and third lessons, the teacher might share the explaining of story structure, thinking aloud, and representing of the elements of story structure in the graphic organizer with students. Finally, in remaining lessons, students would do most of the explaining, thinking aloud, and representing of the elements of story structure in the graphic organizer with the expert guidance of the teacher. Later on, students would be encouraged to make and use graphic organizers of story structure independently to help them understand and remember the narrative texts with which they engage.

Effective Expository Text Structure Instruction. Here again, we begin by selecting an exemplary expository text, perhaps one within the information text genre. This means we want to find an expository text that exemplifies the clear and simple use of only one of the many expository text structures, such as problem–solution or question–answer. For a text to qualify for selection, it must utilize one and only one expository text structure throughout rather than a mix or variety of expository text structures, as many do. A simple information text, *Sand* (Clyne & Griffiths, 2005), serves as our example. This information book is published by Dorling-Kindersley/Celebration Press, part of the Pearson Education Group, and is found in the *I Openers* information text series. This book features an attractive appearance, clear layout, and interesting content for younger and even some older children.

To begin, we consider carefully the physical features of this expository text. We note several important physical features that we make a point of showing to and discussing with children, namely the title, the author, and post-reading follow-up questions at the end of the book. Although not as rich in physical features as some expository books, *Sand* does evidence the use of a single text structure—question–answer—throughout. For example, the book begins with the question "What is sand?" The book also makes good use of spacing, print arrangements, and typographic features. "What is sand?" is printed on a single line at the top of the first page in bold typeface. The answer to the question is at the bottom of the page in regular typeface.

Every question in *Sand* appears at the top of the page in isolation in bold typeface. Answers are all placed on the bottom of the page in regular typeface and relate to an illustrative photograph that helps answer the question. The book also uses black versus white type, depending on the background, color of the page. This use of color leads readers' attention to the answers to the questions in physically obvious ways.

For younger children, a simple graphic organizer using icons along with print can be helpful. For older students, a more complex graphic organizer may include student-generated questions for which they will seek and retrieve answers through reading across a variety of other information texts on the topic of sand, rocks, and soil. Two examples of question–answer graphic organizers for the book *Sand* are shown in Figures 7.10 and 7.11. Figure 7.10 shows a *Sand* graphic organizer for teaching younger students this expository text structure. Figure 7.11 shows a *Sand* graphic organizer for teaching older students about question-answer expository text structure.

Similar to our narrative example, we turn our attention to the issue of scaffolding expository text structure instruction effectively in the classroom. As mentioned earlier, scaffolding refers to gradually releasing the control and responsibility for selecting and using text structure comprehension strategies, beginning with high teacher control and involvement, moving to shared control and involvement between teachers and students, and finally relinquishing to students' independent control over strategy selection and use. This would require multiple lessons such as the one just described using a variety of expository books that implement question–answer text structure, such as *Bridges* (Ring, 2003), *How Do Spiders Live?* (Biddulph & Biddulph, 1992), and others. In the first

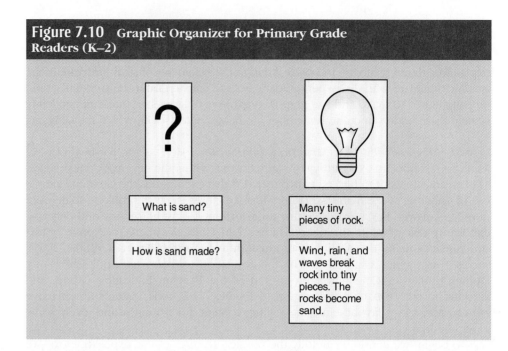

Figure 7.10 Graphic Organizer for Primary Grade Readers (K–2)

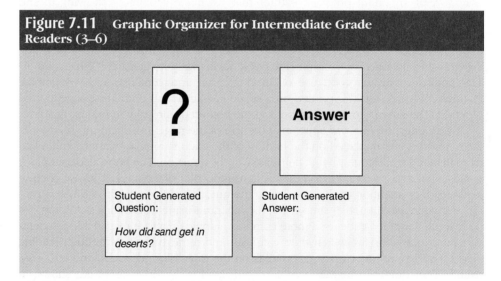

Figure 7.11 Graphic Organizer for Intermediate Grade Readers (3–6)

lesson, the teacher would do most of the explaining, thinking aloud, and representing of the elements of question–answer structure in the graphic organizer. In the second and third lessons, the teacher might share the explaining of question–answer expository text structure, the thinking aloud, and the representing of the elements of question–answer expository text structure in the graphic organizer with students. In subsequent lessons, students would do most of the explaining, thinking aloud, and representing of the elements of question–answer expository text structure in the graphic organizer with the expert guidance of the teacher. Later on, students would be encouraged to make and use graphic organizers of question–answer expository texts independently to help them understand and remember the expository texts they read.

The Activity or Strategies

The third essential component in the Rand Reading Study Group's (2002) definition of reading comprehension is the activity. One of the chief comprehension activities for young readers is learning how to use comprehension strategies to improve their understanding and memory for text. We begin our discussion of comprehension strategies by focusing on one strategy that has long been a mainstay in elementary school classrooms: question asking and answering.

Questions are an integral part of life both in and out of school. From birth, we learn about our world by asking and answering questions. In school, teachers ask questions to guide and motivate children's reading comprehension and to assess the quality of their reading comprehension after reading. Because questions are so much a part of teaching reading comprehension successfully, all teachers must know how to use questioning effectively. We begin with some basic information about the levels of thought required by different kinds of questions.

Asking Questions at Differing Levels of Thinking

During the past several decades, a variety of questioning taxonomies—ordered lists of questions that tap different levels of human thought, such as Bloom's (1956), Barrett's (1972), and Taba's (1975) taxonomies—were published along with impassioned appeals for teachers to ask students more higher-level questions. Figure 7.12 illustrates Bloom's taxonomy.

In addition to simplifying the task of teaching reading comprehension to the act of asking questions at differing levels of thinking, taxonomies were thought to help teachers develop sensitivity to the levels of thinking students would need to use to answer the questions they ask of students.

Visual imagery, along with higher-level thinking, can enhance text comprehension. Access *Student and Teacher Artifacts/Reading Methods* on the Teacher Prep Website (*www.prenhall.com/ teacherprep*) to view "Journal Assignment." Review the examples of multiple texts as you respond to the accompanying questions. These can be printed or sent directly to your instructor.

Others have challenged the idea that asking higher-level questions leads to higher-level thinking abilities (Gall et al., 1975). While much can be and will be argued about asking higher-level questions for some time into the future, the fact is that students will need to answer a great many questions throughout their school life and beyond. Unfortunately, many students are not helped to develop effective strategies for answering or asking their own questions to improve their reading comprehension. Raphael and Pearson (1985) developed a strategy for teaching students how to answer questions asked of them called **Question–Answer Relationships** (Raphael, 1982).

Question–Answer Relationships

Raphael (1982, 1986) and Raphael and Au (2005) describe four question-answer relationships (QARs) that help children identify the connection between the type of question asked and the information sources necessary and available for answering it: (a) right there, (b) think and search, (c) author and you, and (d) on my own.

Instruction using QARs begins by explaining that when students answer questions about reading, there are basically two places they can look for information: in the book and in their head. This concept should be practiced with students by reading aloud a text, asking questions, and having students explain or show where they would look to find their answers. Once students understand the two-category approach, expand the *in the book* category to include *right there* and *think and search*. The distinction between these two categories should be practiced under the guidance of the teacher using several texts and gradually releasing responsibility to students.

Rubrics can be helpful to guide students as they create a "Science Fiction Book Project." Learn to use Bloom's Taxonomy as you view examples of the project in *Student and Teacher Artifacts/Reading Methods* on the Teacher Prep Website (*www.prenhall.com/teacherprep*). Your responses can be printed or sent directly to your instructor.

Figure 7.12   Bloom's Taxonomy

LITERAL (LOW LEVEL)

KNOWLEDGE – Identification and recall of information

Who, what, when, where, how?
Describe . . .

COMPREHENSION – Organization and selection of facts and ideas.

Retell _____ in your own words.
What is the main idea of _____?

INFERENTIAL LEVEL (HIGHER ORDER THINKING)

APPLICATION – use of facts, rules, principles

How is _____ an example of _____?
How is _____ related to _____?
Why is _____ significant?

ANALYSIS – Separation of a whole into component parts

What are the parts or features of _____?
Classify _____ according to _____.
Outline/diagram/web _____.
How does _____ compare/contrast with _____?
What evidence can you list for _____?

SYNTHESIS – Combinations of ideas to form a new whole

What would you predict/infer from _____?
How would you create/design a new _____?
What might happen if you combined _____ with _____?
What solutions would you suggest for _____?

EVALUATIVE LEVEL (HIGHER ORDER THINKING)

EVALUATION – Development of opinions, judgments, or decisions

Do you agree _____?
What do you think about _____?
What is the most important _____?
How would you prioritize _____?
How would you decide about _____?
What criteria would you use to assess _____?

Raphael (1986) suggests that older students be shown specific strategies for locating the answers to *right there* questions. These include looking in a single sentence or looking in two sentences connected by a pronoun. For *think and search* questions, students can be asked to focus their attention on the structure of the text (cause–effect, problem–solution, listing–example, comparison–contrast, and explanation).

Next, instruction is directed toward two subcategories in the *in my head* category: (a) *author and me,* and (b) *on my own.* Here again, these categories can be practiced as a group by reading a text aloud, answering the questions, and discussing the sources of information. To expand this training, students can be asked to identify the types of questions asked in their basal readers, workbooks, content area texts, and tests as well as to determine the sources of information needed to answer these questions.

Students may be informed that certain types of questions are asked before and after reading a text. For example, questions asked before reading typically require that students activate their own knowledge. Therefore, questions asked before reading will usually be *on my own* questions. However, questions asked after reading will make use of information found in the text. Therefore, questions asked after reading will typically focus on the *think and search* and *author and me* types of questions.

Using the QAR's question–answering training strategy is useful for at least two other purposes. First, it can help teachers examine their own questioning with respect to the types of questions and the information sources students need to use to answer their questions. Second, some teachers may find that by using QARs to monitor their own questioning behaviors, they are asking only *right there* types of questions. This discovery should lead teachers to ask questions that require the use of other information sources.

Students can use QARs to initiate self-questioning before and after reading. They may be asked to write questions for each of the QAR categories and answer these questions. Finally, posters displaying the information in Figure 7.13 can heighten children's and teachers' awareness of the types of questions asked and the information sources available for answering those questions.

Raphael and Pearson (1982) provided evidence that training students to recognize these question–answer relationships resulted in improved comprehension and question–answering behavior. In addition, evidence also shows that teachers find the QAR strategies productive for improving their own questioning behaviors. More recently, Raphael and Au (2005) have shown that training in QARs can have positive effects on students' performance on a variety of local, state, and national reading assessments.

Questioning the Author

Research has shown that many students construct very little meaning from the information they read in expository books and textbooks. Several features in expository texts

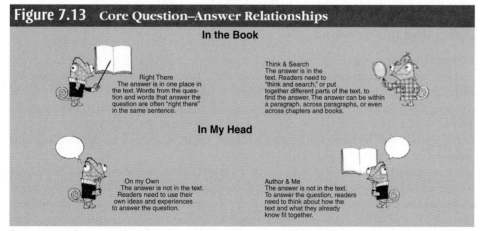

Figure 7.13   Core Question–Answer Relationships

In the Book

Right There
The answer is in one place in the text. Words from the question and words that answer the question are often "right there" in the same sentence.

Think & Search
The answer is in the text. Readers need to "think and search," or put together different parts of the text, to find the answer. The answer can be within a paragraph, across paragraphs, or even across chapters and books.

In My Head

On my Own
The answer is not in the text. Readers need to use their own ideas and experiences to answer the question.

Author & Me
The answer is not in the text. To answer the question, readers need to think about how the text and what they already know fit together.

From "QAR Enhancing comprehension and test taking across grades and content areas" by T.E. Raphael and K.H. Au. *The Reading Teachers,* 59(3), pp. 206–221. Used by permission of the publisher, McGraw-Hill/Wright Group.

Reading teachers model strategies by explaining their thinking as they read to children. Visit the Teacher Prep Website (*www.prenhall. com/teacherprep*) and select *Strategies and Lessons—Reading Methods/Comprehension*. Read, "Tips for Effective Think-Alouds" as you utilize this powerful teaching strategy.

combine to create a number of obstacles for young readers' comprehension of information text. These include (1) incoherence, (2) lack of clear descriptions and explanations, (3) assumption of an unrealistic level of background knowledge, (4) the objective nature of the language used, and (5) the "authority" that places it above criticism (McKeown, Beck, & Worthy, 1993). These "inconsiderate" features of a textbook's organization and content inhibit comprehension, and the textbook's authority causes students to attribute their difficulty in understanding text to their own inadequacies. As a result, some students are reluctant to persist in using their natural problem-solving abilities in the face of these perceptions (Anderson, 1991; Schunk & Zimmerman,1997).

Questioning the author lessons attempt, in a sense, to "'depose' the authority of the book or textbook through actualizing the presence of an author" (McKeown, Beck, & Worthy, 1993, p. 561). Recent research has shown that questioning the author results in increased length and complexity of recalled ideas from text and answers comprehension questions as compared with other forms of book discussions (Sandora, Beck, & McKeown, 1999).

To begin, students are shown examples in information books and textbooks where someone's ideas may not be written as well or as clearly as they might be. Next, the teacher prompts students as they read a book or textbook using a series of questions like the following:

- What is the author trying to tell you?
- Why is the author telling you that?
- Is it said so that you can understand it?

Asking children to search out answers to these questions encourages them to actively engage with the ideas in the text. As children encounter difficulties in understanding the text they are encouraged, again through teacher questioning, to recast the author's ideas in clearer language. Questions used for this purpose include:

- How could the author have said the ideas to make them easier to understand?
- What would you say instead?

Asking children to restate the author's ideas causes them to grapple with the ideas and problems in a text. In this way, children engage with text in ways that successful readers use to make sense of complex ideas presented in texts.

Elaborative Interrogation

Elaborative interrogation is a student-generated questioning intervention. It is especially well-suited to generating and answering questions in information texts. By helping students generate their own "why" questions, active processing of factual reading materials is promoted (National Reading Panel, 2000; Wood, Pressley, & Winne, 1990). By asking and answering their own questions, students link information together into a network of relationships improving both understanding and memory for text information.

It is important that "why" questions be asked about the text in such as way as to orient students to search their prior knowledge for supporting the facts they need to learn—otherwise such questions will not enhance comprehension and memory for text. We apply the elaborative interrogation student-generated questioning strategy to a trade book titled *Ways of Measuring: Then and Now* (Shulman, 2001), in the model lesson shown in Figure 7.14.

Figure 7.14 Example of an Elaborative Interrogation Lesson

Purpose for Learning the Strategy: This strategy will help students relate their own experiences and knowledge to what they read in information texts. By using this strategy, they will improve their understanding of and memory for text information.

Objective: To learn to respond to statements in text as if they were stated as "why" questions.

Teacher Explanation and Modeling: This strategy is begun by the teacher reading a section of text aloud and modeling. The teacher reads the title of the book: *Ways of Measuring: Then and Now.* She asks herself: "Why are ways of measuring today different than in the past?" Her answer might include ideas about in the past people not having scales, rulers, and measuring cups. Next, she reads the sentence: "Long ago, people used their bodies to measure the length of things." She asks herself the "why" question: "Why did people use their bodies to measure things instead of something else?" She reads on: *"Arms and hands were always around when you needed them, and they couldn't get lost. But you can't weigh flour with a hand span, or measure oil with a cubit. For thousands of years, people used stones to weigh things. They used hollow gourds and shells to measure out amounts."* She asks herself: "Why did people in the old days use stones and gourds to measure?"

Guided Application: The teacher says: "Now let's use this strategy together. Manny, please read this statement aloud for the class." Manny reads: "'The old ways of measuring had some problems.'" The teacher forms a "why" question based on the statement. Then she says, "Mariann, please read this statement." Mariann reads: "'The metric system is used almost everywhere in the world except in the United States.'" The teacher generates a "why" question based on the statement: "Why doesn't the United States use the metric system?" She then invites students to use their background knowledge to respond to her question. The teacher says: "Now let's reverse roles." She reads aloud the next statement from the text. "'Using these measurement systems solves a lot of problems.'" Who can put together a good "why" question based on this statement?" Benji raises his hand. He asks, "Why do measurement systems solve problems?" Discussion ensues.

Individual Application: The teacher says: "I want you to read the rest of this book. When you get to the end of each page, pick one statement and write a "why" question about it in your notebooks. See if you can answer the question from your own knowledge or experiences. If not, try using the book to answer your question. If neither source can answer your question, save it for our discussion of the book when we are all finished reading. Now, go ahead and read. If you forget what I want you to do, look at this poster for step-by-step directions." The teacher points to the poster at the front on the room on the board.

Using the Elaborative Interrogation Strategy

- Read each page carefully.
- Stop at the end of each page and pick a statement.
- Write a "why" question for the statement you pick in your reading notebooks.
- Think about an answer to the "why" question using your own knowledge and experiences.
- If you can, write an answer to your "why" question.
- Read the pages again looking for an answer. Read on to another page to look for the answer.
- If you can, write an answer to your "why" question.
- If you can't write an answer to your "why" question, save it for our group discussion after reading.

(continued)

Figure 7.14 (Continued)

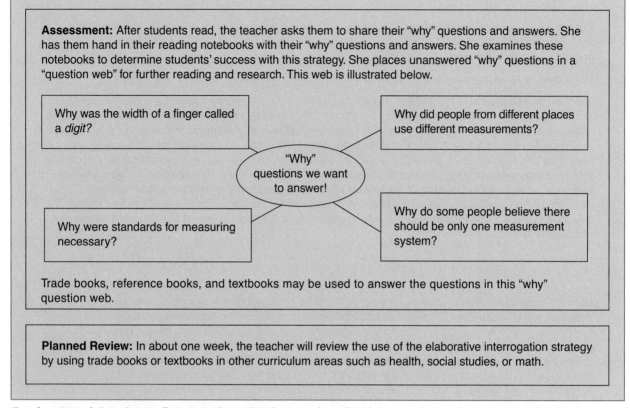

Assessment: After students read, the teacher asks them to share their "why" questions and answers. She has them hand in their reading notebooks with their "why" questions and answers. She examines these notebooks to determine students' success with this strategy. She places unanswered "why" questions in a "question web" for further reading and research. This web is illustrated below.

Why was the width of a finger called a *digit*?

Why did people from different places use different measurements?

"Why" questions we want to answer!

Why were standards for measuring necessary?

Why do some people believe there should be only one measurement system?

Trade books, reference books, and textbooks may be used to answer the questions in this "why" question web.

Planned Review: In about one week, the teacher will review the use of the elaborative interrogation strategy by using trade books or textbooks in other curriculum areas such as health, social studies, or math.

*Based on: Reutzel, D.R., Camperell, K., & Smith, J.A. (2002). Hitting the wall: Helping struggling readers comprehend (pp. 321–353). In C. Collins-Block, L. B. Gambrell, & M. Pressley (Eds.) *Improving comprehension instruction: Advances in research, theory, and classroom practice.* San Francisco, CA: Jossey-Bass.

Menke and Pressley (1994) state that, "answering 'why' questions is as good as constructing images to boost memory for facts, providing the questions are well focused" (p. 644). The elaborative interrogation strategy has been shown to improve readers' comprehension of factual material ranging from elementary school ages to adult. It is recommended that teachers use elaborative interrogation to train students to begin asking their own questions to guide their search for and construction of meaning from information and other expository texts and textbooks.

Comprehension Monitoring and Fix-Ups

The National Reading Panel (2000) found that teaching students to monitor the status of their own ongoing comprehension to determine when it breaks down is one of a handful of scientifically supported, evidence-based comprehension instructional strategies. The act of monitoring one's unfolding comprehension of text is called **metacognition,** or sometimes **metacomprehension.** The ability to plan, check, monitor, revise, and evaluate one's unfolding comprehension is of particular importance in reading. If a reader fails to detect comprehension breakdowns, then she or he will take no action to correct misinterpretations of the text. However, if a reader model for students how you would use the five summary rules in Figure 7.14 to produce a summary. After modeling, direct students to finish reading the entire text. Divide the chalkboard into four sections. For example, if you are learning about an animal (say, alligators), your subcategories might be "Description," "Food," "Home," and "Interesting Facts." As the groups read, have students write facts on the chalkboard in each of the four sections.

Next, organize students into groups of five to work on summarizing together. Each student in the group is assigned to take charge of one of the five summary-writing rules shown in Figure 7.15. Circulate around the classroom to assist groups as needed. After reading the selection and working in their groups, students responsible for the topic statement rule in each group should read their topic statement aloud to the other students in the group. Next, have students discuss the facts they have listed at the board, erase duplicates, and restate the remaining main ideas and detail facts in complete sentences. You may want to have students use different colored transparency pens for each of the five summary rules to record their work in the groups. For example, green may be used for lists, red for eliminating unnecessary details, and so on. Share each group's summarizing processes and their summary statement(s) with the entire class on the overhead projector. Be sure to provide additional practice on summarizing throughout the year with other books and gradually release the task of summarizing using all five rules to students for independent use.

If students encounter difficulties initially using the five rules in Figure 7.16, we have found the following procedure by Noyce and Christie (1989) to be helpful. The teacher will need to model this process and then guide students as they apply it in their work. Noyce and Christie (1989) use the four easy steps listed here.

> **Step 1:** Write a topic sentence, that is, one that summarizes the content in general terms. You need to either select one that the author has written or write your own.

> **Step 2:** Delete all unnecessary or irrelevant sentences, words, and other information from the entire passage.

> **Step 3:** After sorting all terms into categories, think of a collective term(s) for those things that fall into the same category.

> **Step 4:** Collapse paragraphs on the same subject down to one when they are largely redundant.

Strategy instruction on how to summarize text has been reported by the National Reading Panel (2000) to be highly effective in promoting children's reading comprehension and as such should be a part of regular comprehension strategy instruction in classrooms from kindergarten on.

The Situational Context

The National Reading Panel (2000) found four conditions that support effective comprehension instruction. First, when teachers provide explicit comprehension strategy instruction by explaining, modeling, guiding, and scaffolding, students are helped toward independence and self-regulated use of comprehension strategies. Research has shown for nearly three decades that explicit or formal comprehension strategy instruction has led to improved student understanding of text and use of information. Second, comprehension strategy instruction works well when readers work together to learn strategies in the context of reading, discussion, and interaction around a variety of text types and genres. Third, children comprehend text more readily when they are motivated to engage in reading. Finally, research indicates that comprehension strategy instruction is optimally effective when readers are taught to orchestrate or coordinate the use of a "set" or "family" of several reading comprehension strategies in interaction with the teacher over multiple texts over extended periods of time. In what follows, we discuss each of the three conditions of effective comprehension instruction.

Explicit Comprehension Strategy Instruction

The primary purpose of an explicit comprehension strategy lesson on comprehension monitoring is twofold: (1) to teach students to clearly understand what is meant by *comprehension monitoring,* and (2) to teach students, through guidance and practice, how to self-monitor, evaluate, self-regulate, and otherwise independently "fix up" their own comprehension problems.

> Some students struggle with reading because they lack information about what they are trying to do and how to do it. They look around at their fellow students who are learning to read [fluently and well] and say to themselves, 'How are they doing that?' In short they are mystified about how to do what other students seem to do with ease (Duffy, 2003, p. 9).

It is typically very difficult for teachers to provide explicit cognitive comprehension strategy explanations on how to monitor one's own construction of meaning from a text. To do so, teachers must become aware of the processes *they* use to monitor their own reading comprehension processes. However, because teachers are already readers who comprehend what they read, they often do not think deeply or systematically about the processes they use to do so (Duffy, 2003). Both information and story texts should be selected for providing explicit comprehension strategy instruction on comprehension monitoring. It is best if books can also be selected that can be read and discussed in a single sitting.

To teach an explicit comprehension strategy lesson such as comprehension monitoring, a framework lesson plan template is needed. Reutzel and Cooter (2007) have developed an explicit lesson framework called **EMS—*Explanation, Model, Scaffold.*** Explanations include what is to be learned, where and when it is to be used, and why it is important. Modeling requires teachers to demonstrate, often through think-alouds with a text, how an aspect of comprehension monitoring, like using fix-ups, is to be done. Finally, teachers gradually release through a series of guided practice experiences the reading of a text to individual student application through a process we call "Me (teacher model)—You and Me (teacher and student share the monitoring task, reading with the whole class or with partners)—and Me (student monitors reading comprehension independently)." A template explicit cognitive comprehension strategy lesson on comprehension monitoring is found in Figure 7.16. This model demonstrates each of the parts of the EMS explicit cognitive comprehension strategy lesson.

Remember, as unpopular as what we are about to say is with many teachers, to begin the process of becoming an explicit comprehension strategy teacher one must write out a lesson plan. In fact, this is the *only* way for you to become an explicit comprehension strategy teacher! Doing so helps you in at least three different ways. Writing a lesson plan helps you to (1) think through what to say and how to say it, (2) internalize the lesson template for explicit instruction, and (3) internalize the language necessary for explicit instruction.

Cooperative/Interactive Comprehension Discussions. Research reported by the National Reading Panel (2000) found that cooperative, collaborative, and highly

Create a lesson through TEACHER PREP the Teacher Prep Website.

- You will be guided through the alignment of standards, lesson objectives, your introduction, planning for and sequencing lesson activities and procedures, planning for ongoing assessment throughout the lesson, and planning end of lesson assessment. You will also choose and list lesson materials/resources and create adapted instruction to meet all needs of students.
- This lesson can be sent to your instructor through this link.
- Select a children's text to use as you create an explicit comprehension monitoring strategy lesson plan. Refer to Figure 7.16 to create a plan within the EMS-Explanation, Model, and Scaffold framework.
- The review of "Tips for Effective Think-Alouds" may be helpful, as you prepare your lesson.
- Implementation of your lesson with a group of children/peers, would provide you with the opportunity to practice these teaching strategies.

Figure 7.16 Explicit Comprehension Monitoring Strategy Lesson Plan Template

Objective *Children will monitor their own comprehension processes and use fix-up strategies to repair broken comprehension processes when necessary.*

Supplies
  • Exemplary story or information text

Explain

What
  • Today, boys and girls, we are going to be learning about how to monitor or check our understanding or comprehension as we read. The first step in learning to monitor our understanding or comprehension as we read is to learn to stop periodically and ask ourselves a few simple questions like "Is this making sense? Am I getting it? Do I understand what this is about?"

Why
  • We need to monitor our comprehension or understanding when we read because what we read should make sense to us. If it doesn't make sense, there is no point in continuing to read. Monitoring our comprehension while reading helps us to be aware of whether or not we understand or are making sense of what we read. We can just keep on reading if we understand, or stop and do something to help us understand if the text is not making sense to us.

When/Where
  • Whenever we read, we should monitor or think about whether or not we are understanding or comprehending what we are reading.

Model
  • I am going to read aloud the first two pages of our book *Volcano!* (Jewell Hunt, 2004). After reading the first two pages, I am going to stop and monitor my comprehension. I will think out loud about the questions I should ask when I stop to monitor my comprehension: "Is this making sense? Am I getting it? Do I understand what this is about?" I've written these monitoring steps (stop and question) on a poster to help me remember. I have also written the three comprehension-monitoring questions on the poster to help me remember. After thinking about these questions for a minute, I will answer the question with a yes or no. If my answer is yes, I will continue to read. If my answer is no, I will have to stop for now because I don't yet know what I should do when it doesn't make sense to me. Notice that I have also put YES and NO on our poster to help me know what to do when I answer yes or no to the three comprehension-monitoring questions. Okay. Here I go.

Volcano!*
There are many volcanoes in the world.
About 1,500 of them are active.
That means that they are erupting, or they might erupt someday.
An erupting volcano is quite a sight!
Rocks and ash shoot up.
Lava races down.
Smelly gases fill the air.
(STOP!)

"Am I getting it? Is it making sense? Do I understand what this is about?" Yes, I think I do. There are loads of volcanoes all over. Some of them are active, meaning they might erupt. An example of an active volcano is Mt. Etna. When volcanoes erupt they send rocks, ash, lava, and gases into the air. So, if what I have read makes sense and I answer yes, I just keep on reading. After I read a few more pages, I should STOP to monitor my comprehension again.

   (Repeat this cycle with a few more pages and one or two more stopping points for modeling.)

(continued)

Figure 7.16   (Continued)

Scaffolding (ME, YOU & ME, YOU)

Whole Group (Me & You)

- Now that I have shown you how I STOP and monitor my comprehension, I want to share this task with you. Let's read three more pages. At the end of the three pages, I want you to call out, "STOP!" After I stop, I want you to ask me the three monitoring questions on our poster: "Is this making sense? Am I getting it? Do I understand what this is about?" I will answer YES or NO. If I answer yes, tell me what to do. If I answer no, then tell me I will have to quit reading until we learn what to do tomorrow. Okay. Here we go.

Volcanoes come in different sizes and shapes. Some volcanoes have steep sides. They rise high above
the land around them.
Other volcanoes are very wide.
Their sides are not so steep.
This type of volcano may look like a regular mountain. But it isn't!
(STOP!)

Small Group/ Partners/Teams (Me & You)

- Now that we have shared the process of STOPPING and monitoring our comprehension as a group when we read, I want you to share this monitoring process with a partner. I am going to give you either the number 1 or the number 2. Remember your number. (Count heads by one and two.) We are going to read three more pages in our story. At the end of the three pages, I want partner #1 to call out, "STOP!" Then I want partner #2 to ask partner #1 the three monitoring questions on our poster: "Is this making sense? Am I getting it? Do I understand what this is about?" Then partner #1 will answer the questions asked by partner #2 with a yes or no. If partner #1 answers yes, partner #2 tells him/her to keep on reading. If partner #1 answers no, then partner #2 tells him/her to quit reading until we learn what to do tomorrow. Okay, ready.

Volcanoes can change the land quickly.
In 1980, a volcano in the state of Washington erupted. Its top blew off with a roar.
Mud raced down its sides.
Trees crashed, and animals fled.
But the land was not bare for long.
The ash from volcanoes helps things grow.
Today, Mount St. Helens is full of new life.
(STOP!)

Individual (You)
- Today we have learned that when we read we should STOP every few pages and monitor our comprehension or understanding by asking ourselves three questions. Today, during small-group reading or in paired reading, I would like for you to practice monitoring comprehension with a friend and/or by yourself as you read. STOP every few pages and ask yourself the three questions on our poster. Then decide if you should keep on reading or quit reading and wait until tomorrow, when we will learn about what to do when what you read isn't making sense.

Assess
- Pass out a bookmark that reminds students to stop every few pages while reading and ask the three questions. List the three questions on the bookmark to remind students about them.

Reflect
- What went well in the lesson?
- How would you change the lesson?

* Excerpted with permission from *Volcano!* from Reading Power Works by Sundance/Newbridge Educational Publishers, L.L.C.

interactive discussions where readers work together to learn comprehension strategies while interacting with each other and the teacher around a variety of texts is highly effective. There are multiple ways to create and sustain a cooperative and interactive classroom conducive to discussing texts. One effective approach for carrying on cooperative, collaborative, and highly interactive discussions of text to support reading comprehension instruction is called *text talk*.

Text Talk. Effective reading comprehension instruction, at least in the primary grades, is also dependent upon developing younger children's oral language vocabularies and language structures. Beck and McKeown (2001) have adapted their questioning-the-author strategy for intermediate grades for use in the early grades. They refer to this adaptation for simultaneously developing younger children's reading comprehension and oral language as **text talk.** Beck and McKeown (2001) recommend that teachers of younger students read aloud books that have stimulating and intellectually challenging content. Doing so allows younger students to grapple with difficult and complex ideas, situations, and concepts in text even when their word recognition abilities are quite limited. Talk around texts should give students a chance to reflect, think, and respond beyond simple answers to simple questions. Talk should be analytic, requiring that students think deeply about the content of the text and the language (Dickinson & Smith, 1994).

When they observed children talking about texts read aloud to them, Beck and McKeown (2001) found that children often talked about the pictures or related something from their background knowledge rather than focusing their attention and talk on the content of the text or the language in the text. Similarly, teachers' talk during read-aloud experiences in the classroom often focused on clarifying unfamiliar vocabulary by asking a question such as, "Does anyone know what a tsunami is?" The other practice among teachers talking with children about text was to ask a question directly from the language, such as, "When the little red hen asked the goose, the dog, and the cat for help, what did they say?" These types of interactions constrain children's construction of meaning for the whole text to local issues of understanding. Text talk was developed to help teachers further students' comprehension as well as to promote greater use of oral language in elaborated responses to text during discussion.

Text talk has six components: (1) selection of texts, (2) initial questions, (3) follow-up questions, (4) pictures, (5) background knowledge, and (6) vocabulary. For our discussion here, we will use the book *White Socks Only* by Evelyn Coleman (1996). This book has a challenging story line that centers on the theme of racial discrimination. When reading this book, we can focus on several important text-related concepts, including fairness, equality, and social justice. To begin our text talk, we will construct a series of open-ended questions that we can use to initiate discussion with students at several points in the story:

- When Grandma was telling her story, she said, "I had two eggs hid in my pockets. Not to eat mind you. But to see if what folk said was true." What do you think she was going to do with those eggs in her pocket?
- What is a "chicken man" in this story?
- When Grandma got to the courthouse, she broke the egg against the horse's leg. Why do you think she did this?
- What do you think "frying an egg on cement" means?

- There was a sign on the water fountain that read, "Whites only." What do you think Grandma thought this sign meant?

Next, we need to think of a few follow-up questions that will help children elaborate on their answers to our initial, open-ended questions:

- Grandma couldn't understand why the white man pushed her away from the water fountain and asked her if she couldn't read. After all, she was wearing her white socks when she stepped up to the fountain to get a drink. Why was the white man mad at Grandma?
- What does "whites only" mean?
- Why did people move aside when the chicken man came into town?
- What was the fight about between the white man and the black people in the town?

After reading each page in the book displaying the drinking fountain with the sign "Whites Only," we would draw students' attention to the picture on these pages, asking them to explain what the sign means. We might ask questions like: Why were the black people in this story ignoring the sign and stepping up to the drinking fountain to take a drink? Why did the white man whip the black people with his belt? What happened to Grandma when the chicken man showed up? Why did they take the sign "Whites Only" down? Remember that rich, text-related discussions occur *before* showing pictures in text talks. Seeing the pictures after reading and discussing the text will take some getting used to for younger children, but they will soon come to expect it and pay greater attention to the linguistic and meaning content of the text.

When children bring up their background knowledge in response to questions, teachers have found it best to acknowledge their comments by repeating back or re-phrasing what the child has said, and then moving discussion back to the text content. For example, a child might respond to the question "What does 'whites only' mean" with the comment "My grandpa says he eats only the whites from the eggs because it's better for his heart." The teacher might say, "Yes, I have heard that eating egg whites can be better for your heart. But why do you think they would put a sign that reads, "Whites Only" on a drinking fountain in the middle of town?"

An integral part of an effective text talk lesson is developing children's oral language vocabulary. Beck and McKeown (2001) recommend that vocabulary words be selected from the text that seem likely to be unfamiliar to young readers but that represent concepts they can identify with and use in normal conversation (p. 18). Words from our story, *White Socks Only,* that meet these criteria include *slinking, prancing, bandanna, fumbled,* and *snorted.* What seems to work best for vocabulary instruction is to create a chart of the words from the story along with their meanings, examples, and attributes. Then the teacher can keep track of the times during the day students read, say, or hear the words on the chart. Points can be awarded to individual students or teams for finding, saying, or hearing the words on the chart to create motivation for learning and using new vocabulary.

In summary, the keys to a successful text talk lesson are to (1) keep important ideas in the text as the focus of the discussion, (2) monitor length and quality of students's responses during the discussion, (3) scaffold the ideas of students toward constructing the meaning of the whole text, and (4) encourage students to extend their use of oral language to express the meanings they have gained from the read-aloud experience. Reading aloud can be done by most literate adults, but taking full advantage of the read-aloud experience to develop children's comprehension and use of language is demanding and complex. We have found that it is best to write out a lesson plan for initial text talk lessons. After writing and implementing several lessons, the format, content, and questioning routines will become a more natural and regular part of your teaching repertoire.

Affective Responses: Interpreting and Elaborating Meaning

Discussion and dialog are critical aspects of effective comprehension instruction (Gambrell & Almasi, 1996). One widely recognized and recommended approach to discussion of and dialog about text is called **reader response** which invites students to take a much more active role (Bleich, 1978; Rosenblatt, 1978, 1989, 2004). Reader response theories suggest there are many possible meanings in a text, depending on the reader's background and interpretation of that text. Rosenblatt's (1978) transactional theory describes reading as a carefully orchestrated relationship between the reader and the text.

Rosenblatt (1978) also described two stances readers may choose in focusing their attention during reading: efferent and aesthetic. When readers focus their attention on information to be remembered from reading a text, they are taking an efferent stance. When readers adopt an aesthetic stance, they draw on past experiences, connect these experiences to the text, often savor the beauty of the literary art form, and become an integral participant in the unfolding events of the text.

Discussion of or dialog about texts in small groups often takes place in **literature circles** or **book clubs** that lead students into **grand conversations** about books (Daniels, 1994; McMahon & Raphael, 1997; Peterson & Eeds, 1990; Tompkins, 2006). Grand conversations about books motivate students to extend, clarify, and elaborate their own interpretations of the text as well as to consider alternative interpretations offered by peers.

> **Getting to Know English Learners**
> Reader response techniques along with literature circles and other "alternative" ways of interpreting and elaborating meaning give ELs a chance to express their understandings in unique ways, such as making a "wanted poster" or "illustrating a book."

To initiate a literature circle, begin by selecting four or five books that will engender interest and discussion among students. Next, give a book talk on each of the four or five titles selected, enthusiastically presenting and describing each book to the students. Then, ask students to individually select their top three book choices they want to read. Give each student her first choice. If too many students want the same title, go to each student's second choice as you compile the assignments list. This system works well, because students always know that they get to read a book of their own choosing. After books are distributed the next day, give the students a large block of uninterrupted reading time in class to read. At the beginning of the year, students can read about 20 minutes without undue restlessness. However, later in the year children can often sustain free reading for up to one full hour.

As students complete several hours of independent reading, each literature circle meets on a rotating basis for about 20 minutes with the teacher. Group members discuss and share their initial reactions to the book. We have found that meeting with one to two literature circles per day—with a maximum of two days independent reading between meetings—works quite well.

Based on the group discussion, an assignment is given to the group to extend the discussion of the book into their interpretive media (i.e., writing, art, drama, and so on). Each member of the literature circle works on this assignment before returning to the group for a second meeting. This sequence of reading and working on an extension response assignment repeats until the entire book is completed. We recommend that the first extension assignment focus on personal responses and connections with the book. Subsequent assignments can focus on understanding literary elements (i.e., characterization, point of view, story elements, role of the narrator, and so on). At the conclusion of the book, the literature circle meets to determine a culminating project (Reutzel & Cooter, 2000; Zarillo, 1989). This project captures the group's interpretation and feelings about the entire book as demonstrated in a mural, story map, diorama, character wanted posters, and so on.

There are many ways to invite students to respond to texts they read. One of the most common is to ask children to write in a response journal (Parsons, 1990). We have developed a listing of affective responses to text that represent both aesthetic and efferent stances as described by Rosenblatt (1978) in Figure 7.17.

Figure 7.17   Alternative Affective Responses to Books

1. Prepare a condensed or simplified version of the text to read aloud to younger readers.
2. Draw a map of the journey of characters in a story.
3. Talk to your teacher or a peer about the book.
4. Make a "Wanted" poster for a character in the text.
5. Make a poster based on an information book.
6. Select a part of the book to read aloud to others.
7. Send a letter to your parents, a friend, or your teacher telling about a book and why they should read it.
8. Write a classified newspaper ad for a book.
9. Rewrite a story or part of a story as a Reader's Theater.
10. Make overhead transparencies about the story to use on the overhead projector.
11. Make a PowerPoint slide computer presentation about an information book.
12. Make a character report card on your favorite character.
13. Make a passport application as your favorite character.
14. Write a "Dear Abby" column as your favorite character.
15. Write a missing persons report about a story character.
16. Draw a part of the book and ask others to tell about what part of the story is illustrated.
17. Write a newspaper headline for a book or story.
18. Write a newspaper report for a story character or about information you have learned in an information book.
19. Write to the author to describe your responses to a book.
20. Illustrate a book using a variety of art media or techniques.
21. Write a letter to the librarian suggesting why he or she should or should not recommend a book to someone.
22. Study about the author and write a brief biography.
23. Compose a telegram about the book to tell someone why he or she must read this book.
24. Write a TV commercial and videotape it.
25. Plan a storytelling session for kindergarten children.
26. Interview a story character and write the interview.
27. Compare and contrast characters, settings, or facts in a book using a Venn diagram.
28. Construct a game of Trivial Pursuit using facts in an information book.
29. Construct a game of Password using clues about characters or events in a story.
30. Compose an imaginary diary that might be kept by a book character.

Multiple-Strategies Reading Comprehension Instruction

Although teaching comprehension strategies one at a time explicitly to students has been shown to be effective (Duffy, 2003; National Reading Panel, 2000), students also need to learn how to effectively orchestrate, coordinate, and self-regulate the application of many comprehension strategies to construct meaning when reading a variety of texts (El-Dinary, 2002; National Reading Panel, 2000; Pressley, 2002; Reutzel, Smith, & Fawson, 2005). Real readers do not use comprehension strategies one at a time; they do not use a single strategy for weeks at a time, as these are sometimes taught to students, and they do not apply a single comprehension strategy while reading an entire text. Teaching children to self-regulate their comprehension through the coordination and use of multiple comprehension strategies is exceedingly rare in U.S. classrooms, especially in the primary grades (El-Dinary, 2002; Pearson & Duke, 2002; Stahl, 2004). The rarity of collaborative multiple-strategies-comprehension instruction is largely the result of the difficulty and complexity of providing such instruction. Descriptive research by El-Dinary (2002) and Pressley et al. (1991) showed that acquiring the ability to teach the simultaneous use of multiple comprehension strategies required up to three years of practice before competency was achieved. Regardless of when or where teachers help students to self-regulate the application of multiple comprehension strategies during reading and discussion of texts, there are three important conditions that need to be in place (El-Dinary, 2002; Palincsar, 2003).

> **Getting to Know English Learners**
> Again, a highly interactive setting in the classroom is an ideal place for ELs to acquire language.

First, teaching for self-regulation requires teachers to gradually scaffold the responsibility and authority for determining what is worth knowing in a text or how the text might be interpreted, starting with the teacher's total control, moving to a shared control between teacher and students, and finally progressing to students' independent control. Second, multiple-comprehension-strategies instruction focuses on the *process* of constructing meaning from text rather than on the *product* of that construction. This means that teachers make explicit for students, usually through using think-aloud modeling, how one goes about making decisions about what is worth knowing in a text or how a text might be interpreted. The teacher must then make sure that students actually begin to adopt, adapt, and apply these reading comprehension strategies in their own reading. Finally, teachers must model for students in a collaborative, highly interactive setting how to strategically orchestrate, coordinate, and apply a collection of reading comprehension strategies to the comprehension of text. It is important for teachers to understand and convey to students that learning reading comprehension strategies is a means to an end and not an end in and of itself. Reading comprehension strategies are essential tools for constructing meaning with text, checking on one's own understanding, and prompting one to take certain actions when experiencing difficulty in understanding a text (Palincsar, 2003). In summary, teaching multiple reading comprehension strategies requires a highly interactive, collaborative social setting for discussing text. Teachers need to promote independence through explicitly showing students how to select and apply each and every reading comprehension strategy in the set of multiple strategies. This means starting by teaching each strategy explicitly and then quickly moving to combine the use of the entire set of strategies when reading a text. This means that teachers need to explicitly and interactively model how to strategically coordinate multiple strategies while interacting around texts over time. And finally, teachers gradually release the responsibility and authority for using multiple strategies in collaborative settings to the students themselves while interacting over texts (El-Dinary, 2002; Palincsar, 2003).

In order to illustrate how to teach multiple reading comprehension strategies, let us consider the case of Mr. Summo, a fifth grade teacher, who has taught for seven years in a low-achieving, low-income school in a southeastern city using reciprocal teaching.

Reciprocal Teaching. In 1984, Palincsar and Brown designed an instructional procedure called **reciprocal teaching (RT)** for students who struggled with comprehending text. RT makes use of a set of four reading comprehension strategies to enhance students' reading comprehension. The RT instructional process typically involves teachers and students in a discussion or dialog about text. The purpose of the discussion is for teachers and students to work together to co-construct the meaning of the text (Palincsar, 2003). Any discussion between teachers and students is supported by the consistent application of the four RT comprehension strategies: (1) predicting, (2) question generating, (3) clarifying, and (4) summarizing. When first using RT in the classroom, teachers explain and model the application of the four RT comprehension strategies while reading and thinking aloud over small text segments, usually paragraphs. Over time, however, teachers gradually progress to larger units of text and release the responsibility for using the four RT strategies independently to students. Prior to providing a classroom example of reciprocal teaching, we describe in a bit more detail the four RT strategies.

Predicting requires that students hypothesize or make a "best guess" based on their background knowledge of the topic, theme, text type, or other cursory information available to them from previewing a text. This information includes such variables as reading headings, chapter titles, pictures, or illustrations, boxed items, and so on. When predicting, students usually anticipate what might happen next, the order that events may take, or even the knowledge or information they expect to be able to learn from reading a text. Using a graphic organizer to facilitate predictions has also been shown to have positive effects on students' predictions and comprehension of text (Meyers, 2006; Oczkus, 2003, Reutzel & Fawson, 1989, 1991).

Question generating reinforces the summarizing strategy, according to one of RT's authors (Palincsar, 2003). Formulating appropriate questions is difficult, as we have previously discussed.

Clarifying, according to Palincsar (2003), is a particularly important strategy for working with children who have come to believe that reading is all about saying the words correctly and who do not monitor their understanding of text. When children are taught to clarify the meaning of text, their attention is directed toward unknown vocabulary words, unclear referent terms, and unfamiliar concepts or text organizations. When they encounter difficulty understanding a text or term, they are taught to identify what is causing the problem and take affirmative steps to "fix up" their comprehension difficulties.

Summarizing involves students in identifying, in proper sequence, the important ideas found within a text. They are asked to sort through many details and come up with the most important ideas through paraphrasing and integrating important ideas in sentences, paragraphs, and across the entire text. For example, if students have read a narrative text, they may summarize it by using story structure—setting, problem, events, and resolution. On the other hand, if students have read an expository text, they may summarize the important ideas by using headings, subheadings, and important related details in the proper sequence. Students need to pay attention to the most important ideas in the text as well as the order in which those ideas are presented. Research by Rinehart, Stahl, and Erickson (1986) has shown that summarizing improves students' reading comprehension of fiction and nonfiction texts.

Figure 7.18 Wall Poster Display of the Four RT Comprehension Strategies

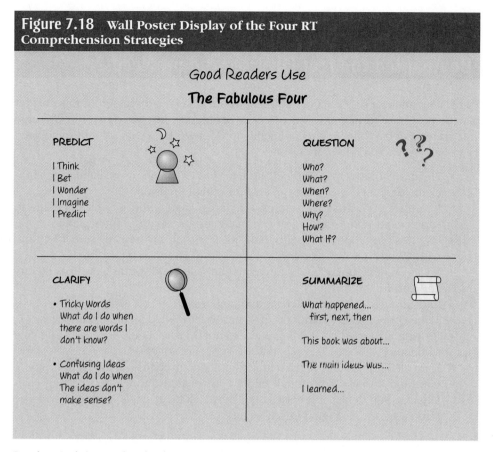

Good Readers Use
The Fabulous Four

PREDICT

I Think
I Bet
I Wonder
I Imagine
I Predict

QUESTION

Who?
What?
When?
Where?
Why?
How?
What If?

CLARIFY

• Tricky Words
  What do I do when
  there are words I
  don't know?

• Confusing Ideas
  What do I do when
  The ideas don't
  make sense?

SUMMARIZE

What happened...
   first, next, then

This book was about...

The main idea was...

I learned...

Based on Oczkus, L. D. (2003). *The Four Reciprocal Teaching Strategies.* In Reciprocal Teaching at work (pp. 13–28). Newark, DE: *International Reading Association.*

We recommend that a poster or wall chart be produced and displayed showing the four RT comprehension strategies. (See Figure 7.18).

Research on the effects of using reciprocal teaching has been summarized in a meta-analysis by Rosenshine and Meister (1994). These researchers analyzed 16 studies where RT was compared with traditional basal reader instruction, explicit instruction in reading comprehension, and reading to answer questions. These researchers found that using RT produced generally superior outcomes when compared to the other comprehension or reading instructional conditions. Effects favoring RT ranged from about 10 percent to 30 percent difference in students' comprehension performance. They also determined that neither the number of RT sessions nor the number of students in the groups seemed to significantly affect the positive outcomes of using RT on students' reading comprehension performance. And finally, Palincsar and Brown (1984) found that the collection of four strategies improved students' comprehension more than the use of any single strategy selected and used in isolation from among the four RT strategies. Hence the collection or set of four RT comprehension strategies taught was more powerful than teaching any single strategy drawn from among the four RT comprehension strategies for the same length of time.

TEACHER PREP Students may be grouped according to interests, learning styles, social needs, instructional needs, and goals. These groups change as opposed to "set" ability groupings. Find out more about "Flexible Learning Groups" on the Teacher Prep Website (*www.prenhall.com/teacherprep*). *Select Strategies and Lessons—Language Arts/Reading.*

TEACHER PREP Visualization can be a powerful comprehension strategy for all levels of readers. Access the Teacher Prep Website (*www.prenhall.com/ teacherprep*) and select *Strategies and Lessons—Reading Methods/Comprehension* to find "Mrs. Armstrong Teaches Visualizing to her Fourth Graders" to read about her "mind pictures."

How Can Reading Comprehension Instruction Be Adapted to Meet Diverse Student Needs?

Some adaptation of the reading comprehension strategies discussed in this chapter may be necessary to meet the varied needs of students in your classroom. We urge you to consider the following recommendations for working with students who need extra help in reading comprehension:

- Ensure that students can read the text fluently to allow availability of sufficient cognitive processing capacity for comprehension.
- Use dialog, discussion, pictures, diagrams, charts, and graphics liberally to supplement understanding of text materials and strategy applications.
- Use flexible, cooperative grouping to allow all children to learn from and with others.
- Focus on developing deep conceptual knowledge domains as well as literary appreciation.
- Capitalize on students' interests and abilities.
- Make connections to students' background knowledge and experiences.
- Provide increased scaffolding and extended instructional time for struggling students.
- Help all readers achieve self-regulation of comprehension, motivation, strategies, and knowledge through explicit instruction, modeling, selecting challenging but achievable tasks and texts, setting goals and performance standards, and engaging in self-evaluation.

What Can Families and Communities Do to Develop Children's Reading Comprehension?

Getting to Know English Learners
Where possible, provide the letter in multiple languages to meet the needs of EL's parents.

Although families usually do not have the expertise to provide explicit reading comprehension strategies instruction and guided practice, they can do a great deal to facilitate children's reading comprehension. For years now, Allington (2006) has insisted that children need to read a lot to get good at reading! Families are in an ideal position to facilitate wide reading and discussion of text. As teachers, we can provide families with both access to reading materials and structure for facilitating discussion and interaction around texts.

Richgels and Wold (1998) have designed the *Three for the Road* program to involve parents in choosing one or more books to read and discuss with their children at home from among three "leveled" books. These leveled books are placed in a backpack that is sent home to parents with their children. The three books selected in each backpack represent a variety of themes, including fantasy, comedy, math mania, adventure, ABCs, and sing-along. The three levels of books included in each backpack are at the "easiest," "in-between," and "most challenging" levels for the student's grade level. The backpack includes a letter to parents as shown in Figure 7.19. This letter may be easily adapted to suit the needs of parents and children in grades other than first.

TEACHER PREP Parents can learn more about motivating their child to read. Locate *Strategies and Lessons—Language Arts/Reading* on the Teacher Prep Website (*www.prenhall.com/teacherprep*) to read "Ways to Stimulate Reading in Young Children."

Figure 7.19 Parent Letter from Three for the Road

Dear First Grade Parents,

Beginning next week, the first graders will be taking home our "Three for the Road" backpacks. The packs are designed to foster enjoyment of children's literature and to nurture lifelong reading habits. We encourage your partnership in reading by sharing these stories and your responses together.

During the year, the A-B-C Pack, Adventure Pack, Comedy Pack, Fantasy Pack, Math Mania Pack, and Sing-Along Pack will rotate in the first grades. Your child will take a pack home once in the next 4 to 5 weeks. Please return the pack to school the next morning after you have helped your child recheck all of the contents on the inside pocket list. In this way, every child will have a chance to take home a class pack once each month.

Since your child may choose to read all or only some of the books included, please try to set aside a special reading time. First graders love to make choices about their reading and may ask a parent to read aloud, to read along with them, or to listen to them read alone. A black journal is also included for students' and parents' written comments and illustrations about meaningful characters or preferred story parts. Check the inside cover of the journal for parent and child response ideas. You may also choose how you would like to respond. Sock puppets are furnished to support language and literacy development. To encourage story responses, you may consider asking, "Which character seems most like the purple puppet?" Or your child may want to "role play" a favorite person or animal by making the puppet "talk" like the story character.

Whatever activities you choose, make this a relaxed and enjoyable experience in reading, from parent read-alouds to rereading children's favorite parts.

We thank you for your support and hope you enjoy our Three for the Road packs!

Your Partners in Reading at _____ School.

Printed with Permission. Richgels, D. J., & Wold, L. S. (1998). Literacy on the road: Backpacking partnerships between school and home. *The Reading Teacher, 52*(1), pp. 18–29.

Parents are given several ways to respond to and discuss the books with their children within each themed backpack. Child responses include writing or drawing about (1) whatever they wanted in relation to the book, (2) their favorite part, (3) how the book reminded them of something else, and (4) how these three books were alike or different. Parents can also respond by writing and drawing about (1) something of interest to them in the books, and (2) something they learned with their child from this activity.

The *Three for the Road* parent involvement program as described by Richgel and Wold is an easy-to-implement approach to extending students' opportunities to read widely, to interact meaningfully with their parents or caregivers, and to choose how many books to read and how to respond at home. When put into use in one Illinois school, the *Three for the Road* program was widely accepted and used by parents to partner with schools and teachers in providing reading materials and text talk in the home.

Summary

Comprehension is intentional thinking during which meaning is constructed through interactions between texts and readers. Comprehending a text involves two phases, a construction and an integration phase. In phase one of this process, one constructs meaning from text and in the second phase one integrates this newly constructed knowledge into the existing prior knowledge network. Monitoring and assessing children's development of comprehension is an important activity to help you, the teacher, select appropriate comprehension strategy instruction and other comprehension instructional supports. Reading comprehension is developed through activating and adding to students' background knowledge, explicit teacher-led comprehension strategy instruction, and by helping students coordinate a set or family of comprehension strategies to construct meaning through rich discussions and interactions around a variety of text structures and genres. Struggling readers and, in fact, all young readers benefit from increased scaffolding to support comprehension development including demonstrations, pictures, diagrams, charts, collaborating with other students, deepening students' breadth and depth of conceptual knowledge, and capitalizing on students' interests and motivations. Finally, families and communities can read and discuss appropriately challenging, themed books of interest as found in the *Three for the Road* program to add to children's background knowledge and develop their abilities to think and talk about a variety of texts.

Classroom Applications

1. Make a poster showing steps students can take to produce a text summary.
2. Select a popular children's story. Parse the story into its story structure parts: setting, characters, problem, goal, events, and resolution. Make a story map like the one shown in this chapter.
3. Summarize the Report of the National Reading Panel (2000) describing their findings on text comprehension. Make a poster displaying these major findings.
4. In small groups, examine several narrative and expository texts. With your peers, discuss how to activate or build students' background knowledge before reading these texts.
5. Organize into literature circle groups. Examine a set of children's books to read as a group. Use reciprocal teaching strategies to discuss one chapter of the book during class.

Recommended Readings

Almasi, J. F. (2003). *Teaching strategic processes in reading*. New York: Guildford Press.

Blachowicz, C., & Ogle, D. (2001). *Reading comprehension: Strategies for independent learners*. New York: Guildford Press.

Boyles, N. N. (2004). *Constructing meaning through kid-friendly comprehension strategy instruction*. Gainesville, FL: Maupin House.

Bransford, J. D., Brown, A. L., & Cocking, R. R. (2000). *How people learn: Brain, mind, experience, and school*. Washington, DC: National Academy Press.

Carr, E., Aldinger, L., & Patberg, J. (2004). *Teaching comprehension: A systematic and practical framework with lessons and strategies*. New York: Scholastic, Inc.

Collins-Block, C., Rodgers, L. L., & Johnson, R. B. (2004). *Comprehension process instruction: Creating reading success in grades K–3*. New York: Guilford Press.

Israel, S. E., Collins-Block, C., Bauserman, K. L., & Kinnucan-Welsch, K. (2005). *Metacognition in literacy learning: Theory, assessment, instruction, and professional development*. Mahwah, NJ: Lawrence Erlbaum Associates.

McLaughlin, M. (2003). *Guided comprehension in primary grades*. Newark, DE: International Reading Association.

Ockzus, L. (2004). *Super 6 comprehension strategies: 35 lessons and more for reading success*. Norwood, MA: Christopher-Gordon.

Owocki, G. (2003). *Comprehension: Strategic instruction for K–3 students*. Portsmouth, NH: Heinemann.

Paris, S. G., & Stahl, S. A. (2005). *Children's reading comprehension and assessment*. Mahwah, NJ: Lawrence Erlbaum Associates.

Pinnell, G. S., & Scharer, P. L. (2003). *Teaching for comprehension in reading: Grades K–2*. New York: Scholastic, Inc.

McLaughlin, M., & Allen, J. B. (2002). *Guided comprehension: A teaching model for grades 3–8*. Newark, DE: International Reading Association.

Spiegel, D. L. (2005). *Classroom discussion*. New York: Scholastic, Inc.

Sweet, A. P., & Snow, C. E. (2003). *Rethinking reading comprehension*. New York: Guilford Press.

chapter 8

Writing

Chapter Questions

1. How is reading related to writing?

2. How does writing develop?

3. How is writing development evaluated?

4. How is the writing process taught?

5. How can we adapt writing instruction to meet the needs of all learners?

6. What is a proven strategy for involving parents in writing instruction?

It Begins

Three-year-old Laura sat quietly on the living room couch next to her parents as they visited with a neighbor. In her hands were four unlined index cards and an old, tooth-marked pencil. After several minutes, she slipped down from the couch and timidly approached the visitor clutching one index card behind her back. Impulsively she thrust the card into the waiting hand of the visitor. He studied the marks she had made on the card. "Wow, Laura!" he exclaimed. "You are writing!" Laura's smile stretched from ear to ear. "I really writed, didn't I!"

Since the earliest days of humanity, people have had a strong desire to share their thoughts in writing. The written word is a potential time machine where one's ideas and experiences can be shared virtually forever. We see written time machines in the drawings of cave dwellers many millennia ago, in the Egyptian hieroglyphs of 3100 B.C.E., in the Declaration of Independence, or in an e-mail record submitted as evidence in a court of law. In all cases, writing is pointless without a *reader* to receive the message. Thus, writing and reading are complementary and essential processes of communication.

Writing surely must have been invented *before* reading. Perhaps it began like this: One of our forebears decided to record his thoughts about something important on a stone wall for another person's use. Perhaps the message had to do with a food source or a danger in the environment. The creator of the message had to somehow **encode** it into print—that is, generate a written symbol that represented the idea. When the intended recipient of the message came along later, he would need to be able to **decode** it, or translate the written symbols into language or thought.

As it happens, learning to write helps children become better readers (Tierney & Shanahan, 1996). A number of years ago, each of the authors of this text decided to leave college teaching and return to public schools as first grade teachers. It was the first time either of us had established writing as a key part of our reading program. Of course, we had included writing in our previous curricula, but not the full writing process as described by early leaders in the field such as Donald Graves (1983) and Lucy Calkins (1986). In a word, this addition to our instructional programs was powerful! Our students learned to write with excitement and passion, and their reading development was greatly accelerated (Reutzel & Cooter, 1990). So, if you are wondering why we include a chapter on writing in a reading methods textbook . . . well, research and our own first-hand experience have convinced us that writing and reading are reciprocal processes that simply *must* be taught together (Shanahan, 2006).

How Is Reading Related to Writing?

Reading and writing are often thought of as mirror images of each other (Reutzel & Cooter, 2007). Walter Loban (1964) once said that the relationship between reading and writing is "so striking to be beyond question" (p. 212). It happens that reading and writing share a number of traits or underlying processes (Tierney & Shanahan, 1996), but they also have some unique qualities as well. As Shanahan (2006) noted, they have somewhat different cognitive "footprints." Let's take a brief look at ways reading and writing are close cousins.

In the *Handbook of Writing Research,* Shanahan (2006) explains that " . . . reading and writing are dependent upon shared cognitive abilities (e.g., visual, phonological, and semantic systems or short- and long-term memory), and anything that improves these abilities may have implications for both reading and writing development. . . ." (p. 174). Shanahan's review of the research concluded that readers and writers rely on four common knowledge bases:

Getting to Know English Learners

Writing, highly valued as a sign of an educated person in the West, is no less important in Asian countries, for example, yet, as in many other parts of the world, writing may serve different purposes for different groups of people. Chinese students, for example, learn to write using a complex symbol system that takes many, many years to learn fully.

1. Content knowledge, because writing has to be about *something*.
2. Metaknowledge, which is knowing about the functions of reading and writing, that readers and writers interact, and that monitoring one's own meaning-making while writing or reading is critical. New learning often happens through examining and reexamining information from a variety of perspectives, and reading and writing provide alternate perspectives (Rijlaarsdam & van den Bergh, 2006; Shanahan, 2006). A person's culture, by the way, can have an impact—positive or negative—on how well the functions of reading and writing are understood. For example, a second language learner from an Asian country may not have the same understanding of how writing is understood in the United States compared to a native-born North American citizen.
3. Knowledge of specific components of written language that underlie reading and writing, such as phonemic (speech sounds) and orthographic (spelling) knowledge.
4. Procedural knowledge about how to access, use, and generate information during reading and writing (Mason, Herman, & Au, 1991). This includes an awareness of strategies intentionally used in reading and writing, such as predicting, questioning, and summarizing.

Figure 8.1 Laura's Scribbles

How Writing Develops

Young children discover early in life that writing is the sharing of ideas. In our opening vignette, Laura demonstrated her growing understanding that writing can be a tool for recording thoughts on paper to share with others. She came to this understanding without formal spelling and writing instruction. After carefully observing others in her environment, Laura risked acting like a skilled writer and tried out her hypothesis about how printed language functions.

Many of us have seen children attempting to solve the printed language puzzle through drawing and scribbling. One may be tempted to dismiss these early attempts at writing as cute, but certainly not *real* writing (see Figure 8.1). This judgment may be as misguided as concluding that a flower in its early stages of development is not truly a flower because it does not resemble a full-blown bloom.

Through careful study over a period of decades, researchers have discovered that young children pass through certain developmental stages in their writing and spelling similar to those discussed with respect to oral language and reading development. An understanding of these stages helps teachers recognize the roots of writing and spelling development and enables them to nurture the roots of scribbling and drawing into the flower of writing.

Scribbling and Drawing Stage. When young children first take a pencil or crayon in hand, they use this instrument to explore the vast empty space on a blank sheet of paper. In its earliest stages, children's writing is often referred to by adult observers as *scribbling* (Bear, Invernizzi, Templeton, & Johnston, 2000; Clay, 1987; Temple, Nathan, Burris, & Temple, 1993).

These random marks are the wellsprings of writing discovery. As shown in Figure 8.1, Laura's scribbles appear to be the result of acting on the paper just to see what happens, perhaps without any particular intent. Her scribbles do not demonstrate much of what adults normally consider to be conventional or even purposeful writing. In Figure 8.2, Laura's scribbles begin to reveal an exploration of alternative forms when compared to her previous markings. Circles, curved lines, and letterlike forms begin to appear as part of Laura's writing exploration.

Some time later, Laura's scribbles begin to look more and more like adult cursive writing. Note in Figure 8.3 that the marks have become linear, moving from left to right.

When questioned, Laura could tell what she meant by each of the scribbles reproduced in Figure 8.3. Unlike her marks in Figure 8.1, Laura's later scribbling represented her meaning in a more conventional way. Laura revealed that these later scribbles represented a "Christmas wish list." Often, letter-like writing or shapes, as

Figure 8.2   **Laura's Scribbles as Exploration**

Figure 8.3 Laura's Scribble Cursive Writing: Christmas List

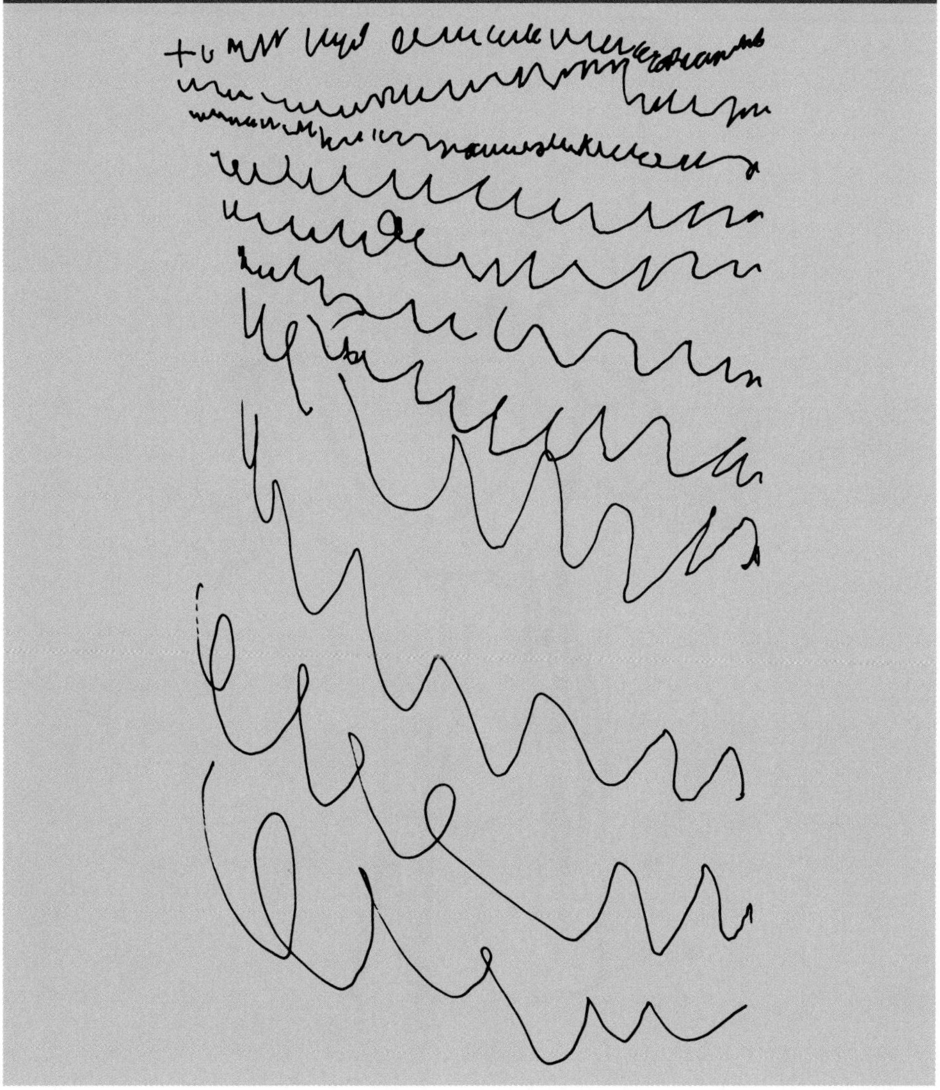

shown in Laura's Christmas list, are used repeatedly in early writing attempts. Clay (1987) calls the tendency to reuse and repeat certain scribblings and drawings **recursive writing.** The purpose for recursive writing seems to be the need for comfort and familiarity as children prepare to move into the next levels of writing development.

Weeks later, Laura produced the writing found in Figure 8.4. Note in this example that she uses drawings to carry part of her intended message. In addition, directly above the head of Laura's drawing of a young girl, one can detect the emergence of letter-like forms etched in broken detail. When queried about the intent of these letter-like forms, Laura responded, "That says 'Laura!'" Evidently, Laura had discovered at this point in her development as a writer that drawings can supplement a message and that writing is different from drawing.

Figure 8.4 Laura's Self-Portrait

In another example, Toby, a four-year-old, produced the writing found in Figure 8.5. Toby uses humanlike forms to represent members of his family in his thank-you letter. One sees the use of letter-like symbols randomly scattered about the page. Near the center, Toby signed his name. By looking carefully, one can see the upside-down letter *b* and what looks like a letter *y*, which Toby chose to represent his name. Thus, one can see that during this initial stage of writing development, Laura and Toby used scribbling, drawing, and disconnected letter-like forms to explore and record their meaning on paper. These children had discovered that writing can be used to communicate meaning, and that although drawing and writing are complementary processes, they are not the same.

Prephonemic Stage. The next stage of writing and spelling development among young children is often called the **prephonemic stage** (Temple et al., 1993). At this stage, children begin to use real letters—usually capitals—to represent

Figure 8.5   Toby's Thank-You Letter

meaning. Letters do not represent their phonemic or sound values; rather, they are used as placeholders for meaning, representing anything from a syllable to an entire thought. Chaundra, a kindergartener, produced the writing in Figure 8.6. Note Chaundra's use of letters to represent meaning. Only by asking the child to explain the meaning can one readily discern that she used letters as meaning placeholders and not as representations of phonemic values.

Clay (1975) points out that children in the prephonemic stage of writing development will usually produce a string of letters and proudly display their work to a parent while asking, "What does this say?" or "What did I write?" In many families today, children do this with magnetic letters on refrigerator doors: they meticulously arrange a string of letters and then ask what they have written.

Early Phonemic Stage.   During the next stage of writing development, the **early phonemic stage** (Temple et al., 1993), children begin to use letters—usually capitalized consonants—to represent words. Children at this stage of writing development have discovered that letters represent sound values. They write words represented by one or two consonant letters—usually the beginning or ending sounds of the word. In Figure 8.7, Samantha uses only consonants to represent the word *house* in her message.

Temple et al. (1993) suspect that the tendency for children in the early phonemic stage to represent a word with only one or two letters is the result of an inability to "hold words still in their minds" while they examine them for phonemes and match these to known letters (p. 101). Although this may be true, it is also possible that children at this stage are continuing to learn certain letters of the alphabet. It

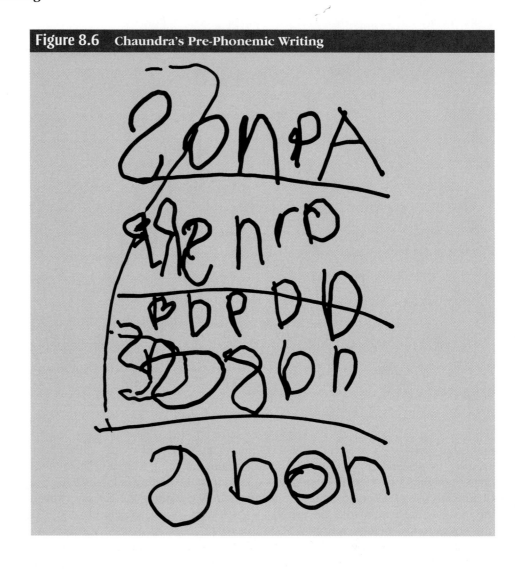

Figure 8.6   Chaundra's Pre-Phonemic Writing

may also be true that writers in this stage of development have not developed the ability to segment more than the initial or final sounds in a word. Certainly any of these possibilities would lead to the incomplete representation of words as found in the early phonemic stage of writing development. This is an area needing much more investigation (Teale, 1987; Templeton, 1995).

Getting to Know English Learners

Not all students' first languages use the same alphabetic system as English; directionality (both horizontally and vertically) may also be different, causing English Learners' first attempts with writing in English very challenging indeed!

Letter-Naming Stage. The **letter-naming stage** of writing development is a small but important jump from the early phonemic stage. This stage is characterized by the use of more than one or two consonants with at least one vowel to represent the spelling of words (Temple et al., 1988). Chris, a kindergartener, produced an example of the letter-naming stage of writing in response to his teacher's urging him to write about the rainbow he had seen the day before (see Figure 8.8).

Figure 8.7   Samantha's Early Phonemic Writing: A House

Although Chris continues to use capital letters exclusively, vowels have begun to appear in his writing. He has clearly discovered that words are made up of phonemes, both vowels and consonants; that these phonemes occur in an auditory sequence; and that these phonemes are properly represented in printed form from left to right. Although Chris does not yet read independently, he has made important discoveries about print that have nurtured his acquisition of reading, and his acquisition of reading will inform his acquisition of conventional spellings. With continued experiences in reading, Chris's writing will rapidly become more closely aligned with standard spelling and lead to the final stage of writing development, the transitional stage.

Transitional Stage

Figures 8.9 and 8.10 illustrate the **transitional stage** of writing and spelling. Writing produced by youngsters in this stage looks like English, but words are a mix of phonetic and conventional spellings. Typically, these writers neglect or overgeneralize certain spelling patterns. For example, the final silent *e* is sometimes omitted by these writers, familiar phonic elements are substituted for less familiar phonic elements, and double consonants are typically neglected.

"The Bear and the Horse" is a story summarization written in the transitional writing stage. View the edited example in the *Artifacts—Reading Methods/Writing* of the Teacher Prep Website (*www.prenhall.com/teacherprep*). Respond to the accompanying questions that can be printed or sent directly to your instructor.

Think about conferencing with a student as you view "We Clied" in *Artifacts—Language Arts/Writing* in the Teacher Prep Website (*www.prenhall.com/teacherprep*). Discuss or respond to questions about feedback, modeling and instruction and share them with your instructor.

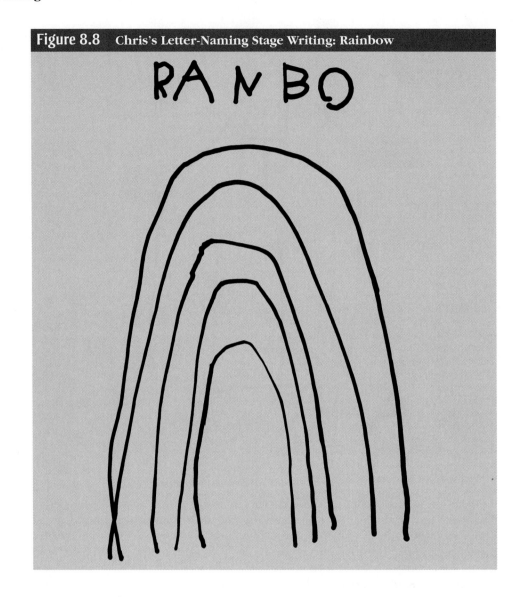

Figure 8.8　Chris's Letter-Naming Stage Writing: Rainbow

Devin, a first grader, wrote the story shown in Figure 8.9 during October. He demonstrates not only some of the substitutions and omissions mentioned previously, but also a top-to-bottom arrangement for his story.

Figure 8.10 shows a note that Candice wrote to her parents during the fall of her second-grade year. Notice the spellings of *parents, hurting, guys,* and *special.* Some of the spellings are unconventional, but the writing of this child looks very much like English and communicates the message well. Candice's writing is also a good example of the characteristics of transitional writing mentioned previously—the mix of standard and nonstandard spellings. Note also that transitional writers have discovered the use of other features of standard writing such as possessives, punctuation, and the standard letter- or note-writing format.

These examples demonstrate the progression of children's writing along a developmental continuum, originating with their early attempts to make meaning on

Figure 8.9 Devin's Halloween Story

paper through scribbling and drawing to later refinements including the use of conventional spelling, grammar, and mechanics.

One note of caution should be sounded at this point: Although we may discuss oral language, writing, and reading development in terms of stages through which children pass, we want to emphasize to teachers that they should not use this information to try to hasten development or expect that children will—or even should—pass through each stage of development in the order described. Rather, teachers should use this information as a basis for understanding and supporting children's language learning by providing an environment rich in print and print use, gentle guidance, and enthusiastic encouragement as children struggle to solve the language and literacy puzzle. Just as children learned to speak within a nurturing home environment filled with supportive oral language users, they will develop into readers and writers within print-rich school and home environments filled with the support and encouragement of other competent and caring readers and writers. Figure 8.11 integrates information about oral language, reading, and writing development to show that these modes of language learning are developmentally similar.

Figure 8.10   Candice's Note to Her Parents

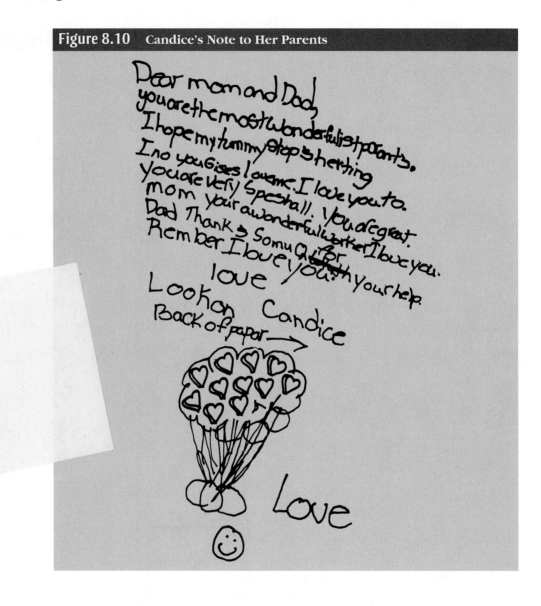

Unique Writing Patterns Used by Authors

Narrative texts (fiction) are organized in a story grammar scheme using such common elements as setting, theme, characterization, plot, and resolution. Expository text (nonfiction), however, is quite different: Its structure tends to be much more compact, detailed, and explanatory (Heilman et al., 2001). Five common expository text structures have been described (Meyer & Freedle, 1984; Williams, 2005): description, collection, causation, problem/solution, and comparison. When preparing to teach units in the content areas, teachers need to establish which expository text structures are used and organize for instruction accordingly. Here are the five expository text patterns identified earlier along with examples taken from content textbooks.

Description: Explains something about a topic or presents a characteristic or setting for a topic.

Figure 8.11   Development Across the Language Modes of Oral Language, Reading, and Writing

Oral Language Acquisition	Reading Development Stages	Writing Development Stages
Sounds, cooing, babbling	Picture-governed attempts: Story not formed	Scribbling and drawing
Holophrases and telegraphic speech	Picture-governed attempts: Story formed	Prephonemic
Vocabulary growth and negation language structures	Picture-governed attempts: Written language like—print not watched	Early phonemic
Vocabulary growth and interrogative structures	Print-governed attempts: Print watched	Letter-naming
Vocabulary growth, analogical substitutions, and passive language structures	Print-governed attempts: Strategies imbalanced	Transitional
Adult-like language structures, continuing vocabulary growth, and the ability to articulate all the sounds of the language	Print-governed attempts: Independent reading	Conventional

Decimals are another way to write fractions when the denominators are 10, 100, and so on.

(from *Merrill Mathematics [Grade 5]*, 1985, p. 247)

Collection: A number of descriptions (specifics, characteristics, or settings) presented together.

Water Habitats

Freshwater habitats are found in ponds, bogs, swamps, lakes, and rivers. Each freshwater habitat has special kinds of plants and animals that live there. Some plants and animals live in waters that are very cold. Others live in waters that are warm. Some plants and animals adapt to waters that flow fast. Others adapt to still water.

(from *Merrill Science [Grade 3]*, 1989, p. 226)

Causation: Elements grouped according to time sequence with a cause–effect relationship specified.

America Enters the War

On Sunday, December 7, 1941, World War II came to the United States. At 7:55 A.M. Japanese warplanes swooped through the clouds above Pearl Harbor. Pearl Harbor was the American naval base in the Hawaiian Islands. A deadly load of bombs was dropped on the American ships and airfield. It was a day, Roosevelt said, that would "live in infamy." *Infamy* (IN. fuh. mee) means "remembered for being evil."

The United States had been attacked. That meant war.

(from *The United States: Its History and Neighbors [Grade 5]*, Harcourt Brace Jovanovich, 1985, p. 493)

Problem/Solution: Includes a relationship (between a problem and its possible cause[s]) and a set of solution possibilities, one of which can break the link between the problem and its cause.

Agreement by Compromise (Events That Led to the Civil War)

For a while there was an equal number of Southern and Northern states. That meant that there were just as many Senators in Congress from slave states as from free states. Neither had more votes in the Senate, so they usually reached agreement on new laws by compromise.

(from *The United States and the Other Americas [Grade 5]*, Macmillan, 1980, p. 190)

Comparison: Organizes factors on the basis of differences and similarities. Comparison does not contain elements of sequence or causality.

Segregation

Segregation laws said that blacks had to live separate, or apart, from whites. Like whites, during segregation blacks had their own parks, hospitals, and swimming pools. Theaters, buses, and trains were segregated.

Many people said that the segregation laws were unfair. But in 1896, the Supreme Court ruled segregation legal if the separate facilities for blacks were equal to those for whites. "Separate but equal" became the law in many parts of the country.

But separate was not equal. . . . One of the most serious problems was education. Black parents felt that their students were not receiving an equal education in segregated schools. Sometimes the segregated schools had teachers who were not as well educated as teachers in the white schools. Textbooks were often very old and out-of-date, if they had any books at all. But in many of the white schools the books were the newest ones. Without a good education, the blacks argued, their students would not be able to get good jobs as adults.

Finally in 1954, the Supreme Court changed the law.

(Adapted from *The American People [Grade 6]*, American Book Company, 1982, p. 364)

What Are the Writing Skills to Be Learned at Each Grade Level (K–6)?

Burns, Griffin, and Snow (1999), in their book *Starting Out Right,* summarize the skills to be learned in writing for grades K through 3 according to scientific research. These should be viewed as "end-of-year benchmark skills," or targets for every child to attain by the end of the school year in order to be on track in his or her development.

Kindergarten
- Writes uppercase and lowercase letters
- Writes own name
- Uses invented spellings to express meaning
- Uses invented spellings to write teacher-dictated words
- Is becoming aware of the differences between kid writing and conventional writing

First Grade
- Spells three- and four-letter short vowel words conventionally
- Writes texts for others to read
- Writes independently using a mix of invented and conventional spellings
- Uses basic or terminal punctuation (periods, question marks, exclamation points) and capitalization
- Produces a variety of types of compositions and texts (e.g., stories, information texts, poems, notes, recipes, journal entries)

Second Grade
- Correctly spells previously studied words and spelling patterns in own writing
- Represents the complete sound of the word when spelling independently (invented spellings)
- Writes using formal language patterns rather than oral language patterns at appropriate places in own writing
- Makes reasonable judgments about what to include in own writing
- Can discuss productively ways to improve own writing and that of others
- Is able to use, with assistance, conferencing, revision, and editing processes to improve the quality of own writing
- Writes informative, well-structured reports with assistance
- Attends to spelling, mechanics, and presentation for final products
- Produces a variety of types of compositions

Third Grade
- Begins to incorporate literary words, language patterns, figures of speech, and elaborate descriptions in own writing
- Correctly spells previously studied words and spelling patterns in own writing
- Combines information from multiple sources in writing reports
- Productively discusses ways to clarify own writing and that of others
- Uses conferencing, revision, and editing processes to improve the quality of own writing
- Independently reviews work for spelling, mechanics, and presentation
- Produces a variety of written work in various formats including multimedia forms

Source: Adapted from pp. 85, 107, 118–119 of Starting Out Right: A Guide to Promoting Children's Reading Success by the National Research Council. Copyright 1999 by the National Academy of Science. Washington, D.C.: National Academies Press. Used with permission.

Teachers in grades 4–6 must also have a clear understanding of the writing skills expected of normally developing students. In this section, we provide you with our adaptation of the grade-level goals and accompanying performance objectives developed by the state of California. Because they are founded on evidence-based reading research, the California standards essentially mirror those developed by the other states (see Figure 8.12).

Figure 8.12   Writing Standards for Grades 4–6

STANDARD 1: WRITING STRATEGIES*

***Coding System**
First numeral = Grade level expectation
Second numeral = Standard
Third numeral = Skill number
Example: 5.2.3 = Fifth grade expectation, Standard 2 (Writing Applications), Skill #3
(Write research reports about important ideas, issues, or events . . .)

Standards 1: Grades 4–6

Grade 4: Students write clear, coherent sentences and paragraphs that develop a central idea. Their writing shows they consider the audience and purpose. Students progress through the stages of the writing process (e.g., prewriting, drafting, revising, editing successive versions).

Grade 5: Students write clear, coherent, and focused essays. The writing exhibits the students' awareness of the audience and purpose. Essays contain formal introductions, supporting evidence, and conclusions. Students progress through the stages of the writing process as needed.

Grade 6: Students write clear, coherent, and focused essays. The writing exhibits students' awareness of the audience and purpose. Essays contain formal introductions, supporting evidence, and conclusions. Students progress through the stages of the writing process as needed.

Performance Objectives: Grades 4–6

Organization and Focus
- 4.1.1 Select a focus, an organizational structure, and a point of view based upon purpose, audience, length, and format requirements.
- 4.1.2 Create multiple-paragraph compositions:
  a. Provide an introductory paragraph.
  b. Establish and support a central idea with a topic sentence at or near the beginning of the first paragraph.
  c. Include supporting paragraphs with simple facts, details, and explanations.
  d. Conclude with a paragraph that summarizes the points.
  e. Use correct indention.
- 4.1.3 Use traditional structures for conveying information (e.g., chronological order, cause and effect, similarity and difference, and posing and answering a question).
- 5.1.1 Create multiple-paragraph narrative compositions:
  a. Establish and develop a situation or plot.
  b. Describe the setting.
  c. Present an ending.
- 5.1.2 Create multiple-paragraph expository compositions:
  a. Establish a topic, important ideas, or events in sequence or chronological order.
  b. Provide details and transitional expressions that link one paragraph to another in a clear line of thought.
  c. Offer a concluding paragraph that summarizes important ideas and details.
- 6.1.1 Choose the form of writing (e.g., personal letter, letter to the editor, review, poem, report, narrative) that best suits the intended purpose.
- 6.1.2 Create multiple-paragraph expository compositions:
  a. Engage the interest of the reader and state a clear purpose.
  b. Develop the topic with supporting details and precise verbs, nouns, and adjectives to paint a visual image in the mind of the reader.
  c. Conclude with a detailed summary linked to the purpose of the composition.

Figure 8.12 (Continued)

- 6.1.3 Use a variety of effective and coherent organizational patterns, including comparison and contrast; organization by categories; and arrangement by spatial order, order of importance, or climactic order.

Penmanship
- 4.1.4 Write fluidly and legibly in cursive or joined italic.

Research and Technology
- 4.1.5 Quote or paraphrase information sources, citing them appropriately.
- 4.1.6 Locate information in reference texts by using organizational features (e.g., prefaces, appendixes).
- 4.1.7 Use various reference materials (e.g., dictionary, thesaurus, card catalog, encyclopedia, online information) as an aid to writing.
- 4.1.8 Understand the organization of almanacs, newspapers, and periodicals and how to use those print materials.
- 4.1.9 Demonstrate basic keyboarding skills and familiarity with computer terminology (e.g., cursor, software, memory, disk drive, hard drive).
- 5.1.3 Use organizational features of printed text (e.g., citations, end notes, bibliographic references) to locate relevant information.
- 5.1.4 Create simple documents by using electronic media and employing organizational features (e.g., passwords, entry and pull-down menus, word searches, the thesaurus, spell checks).
- 5.1.5 Use a thesaurus to identify alternative word choices and meanings.
- 6.1.4 Use organizational features of electronic text (e.g., bulletin boards, databases, keyword searches, e-mail addresses) to locate information.
- 6.1.5 Compose documents with appropriate formatting by using word-processing skills and principles of design (e.g., margins, tabs, spacing, columns, page orientation).

Evaluation and Revision
- 4.1.10 Edit and revise selected drafts to improve coherence and progression by adding, deleting, consolidating, and rearranging text.
- 5.1.6 Edit and revise manuscripts to improve the meaning and focus of writing by adding, deleting, consolidating, clarifying, and rearranging words and sentences.
- 6.1.6 Revise writing to improve the organization and consistency of ideas within and between paragraphs.

STANDARD 2: WRITING APPLICATIONS: GENRES AND THEIR CHARACTERISTICS
Standard 2: Grades 4–6

Grade 4: Students write compositions that describe and explain familiar objects, events, and experiences. Student writing demonstrates a command of standard American English and the drafting, research, and organizational strategies outlined in Writing Standard 1.0.

Grade 5: Students write narrative, expository, persuasive, and descriptive texts of at least 500 to 700 words in each genre. Student writing demonstrates a command of standard American English and the research, organizational, and drafting strategies outlined in Writing Standard 1.0.

Grade 6: Students write narrative, expository, persuasive, and descriptive texts of at least 500 to 700 words in each genre. Student writing demonstrates a command of standard American English and the research, organizational, and drafting strategies outlined in Writing Standard 1.0.

Using the outline in Writing Standard 1.0, students:
Write Narratives
- 4.2.1 *Write narratives:*
  a. Relate ideas, observations, or recollections of an event or experience.
  b. Provide a context to enable the reader to imagine the world of the event or experience.

(continued)

Figure 8.12   (Continued)

   c. Use concrete sensory details.

   d. Provide insight into why the selected event or experience is memorable.

- 5.2.1 Write narratives:

   a. Establish a plot, point of view, setting, and conflict.

   b. Show, rather than tell, the events of the story.

- 6.2.1 Write narratives:

   a. Establish and develop a plot and setting and present a point of view that is appropriate to the stories.

   b. Include sensory details and concrete language to develop plot and character.

   c. Use a range of narrative devices (e.g., dialogue, suspense).

Write Responses to Literature

- 4.2.2 Write responses to literature:

   a. Demonstrate an understanding of the literary work.

   b. Support judgments through references to both the text and prior knowledge.

- 5.2.2 Write responses to literature:

   a. Demonstrate an understanding of a literary work.

   b. Support judgments through references to the text and to prior knowledge.

   c. Develop interpretations that exhibit careful reading and understanding.

- 6.2.4 Write responses to literature:

   a. Develop an interpretation exhibiting careful reading, understanding, and insight.

   b. Organize the interpretation around several clear ideas, premises, or images.

   c. Develop and justify the interpretation through sustained use of examples and textual evidence.

Write Information/Research Reports

- 4.2.3 Write information reports:

   a. Frame a central question about an issue or situation.

   b. Include facts and details for focus.

   c. Draw from more than one source of information (e.g., speakers, books, newspapers, other media sources).

- 4.2.4 Write summaries that contain the main ideas of the reading selection and the most significant details.

- 5.2.3 Write research reports about important ideas, issues, or events by using the following guidelines:

   a. Frame questions that direct the investigation.

   b. Establish a controlling idea or topic.

   c. Develop the topic with simple facts, details, examples, and explanations.

- 6.2.3 Write research reports:

   a. Pose relevant questions with a scope narrow enough to be thoroughly covered.

   b. Support the main idea or ideas with facts, details, examples, and explanations from multiple authoritative sources (e.g., speakers, periodicals, online information searches).

   c. Include a bibliography.

Write Persuasive Letters or Compositions

- 5.2.4 Write persuasive letters or compositions:

   a. State a clear position in support of a proposal.

   b. Support a position with relevant evidence.

   c. Follow a simple organizational pattern.

   d. Address reader concerns.

- 6.2.2 Write expository compositions (e.g., description, explanation, comparison and contrast, problem and solution):

   a. State the thesis or purpose.

   b. Explain the situation.

   c. Follow an organizational pattern appropriate to the type of composition.

   d. Offer persuasive evidence to validate arguments and conclusions as needed.

Figure 8.12 (Continued)

- 6.2.5 Write persuasive compositions:
  a. State a clear position on a proposition or proposal.
  b. Support the position with organized and relevant evidence.
  c. Anticipate and address reader concerns and counterarguments.

STANDARD 3: WRITTEN AND ORAL ENGLISH LANGUAGE CONVENTIONS
Standard 3: Grades 4–6
Grade 4–6: Students write and speak with a command of standard English conventions appropriate to this grade level.

Performance Objectives: Grades 4–6
Sentence Structure
- 4.3.1 Use simple and compound sentences in writing and speaking.
- 4.3.2 Combine short, related sentences with appositives, participial phrases, adjectives, adverbs, and prepositional phrases.
- 5.3.1 Identify and correctly use prepositional phrases, appositives, and independent and dependent clauses; use transitions and conjunctions to connect ideas.
- 6.3.1 Use simple, compound, and compound-complex sentences; use effective coordination and subordination of ideas to express complete thoughts.

Grammar
- 4.3.3 Identify and use regular and irregular verbs, adverbs, prepositions, and coordinating conjunctions in writing and speaking.
- 5.3.2 Identify and correctly use verbs that are often misused (e.g., *lie/lay*, *sit/set*, *rise/raise*), modifiers, and pronouns.
- 6.3.2 Identify and properly use indefinite pronouns and present perfect, past perfect, and future perfect verb tenses; ensure that verbs agree with compound subjects.

Punctuation
- 4.3.4 Use parentheses, commas in direct quotations, and apostrophes in the possessive case of nouns and in contractions.
- 4.3.5 Use underlining, quotation marks, or italics to identify titles of documents.
- 5.3.3 Use a colon to separate hours and minutes and to introduce a list; use quotation marks around the exact words of a speaker and titles of poems, songs, short stories, and so forth.
- 6.3.3 Use colons after the salutation in business letters, semicolons to connect independent clauses, and commas when linking two clauses with a conjunction in compound sentences.

Capitalization
- 4.3.6 Capitalize names of magazines, newspapers, works of art, musical compositions, organizations, and the first word in quotations when appropriate.
- 5.3.4 Use correct capitalization.
- 6.3.4 Use correct capitalization.

Spelling
- 4.3.7 Spell correctly roots, inflections, suffixes and prefixes, and syllable constructions.
  5.3.5 Spell roots, suffixes, prefixes, contractions, and syllable constructions correctly.
  6.3.5 Spell frequently misspelled words correctly.

Source: http://www.cde.ca.gov/standards/
*Adapted from the California Department of Education English Language Arts Content Standards

How Is Writing Development Evaluated?

Two writing assessment perspectives are commonly thought of when analyzing student compositions (Moskal, 2003): *analytic scoring rubrics* and *holistic scoring rubrics*. A third assessment model that essentially combines holistic and analytic methods uses *trait rubrics* (Shermis et al., 2006). Each of these methods will be briefly described in this section. First, we take a look at some general guidelines for constructing writing rubrics.

Rubrics and Writing Assessment: Some Things to Remember

Moskal (2003) offers useful advice to teachers about implementing writing rubrics in their classrooms. This advice applies to all three types of writing assessment we will discuss in this chapter.

First, when developing scoring rubrics for writing, teachers should be certain that the assessment criteria are aligned with state requirements and objectives. Many states have their own rubrics and timelines for writing assessment, and students should be given ample opportunities to practice the kinds of writing on which they will be evaluated. The state of Florida has a very helpful Web site for teachers that provides this information (see the "Sunshine State Standards" online at *http://www.firn.edu/doe/ menu/sss.htm*).

Second, rubric criteria should be (1) expressed in terms of observable behaviors, (2) written in specific, clear, and meaningful language, and (3) designate clear distinctions between scoring levels. Third, rubric criteria should be explained to students prior to the writing experience. These criteria should be communicated to students in language that is easy for them to understand.

When conducting a writing assessment, teachers should ensure that students have easy access to appropriate writing tools (e.g. updated dictionaries, thesaurus, ample writing materials, computer access, etc.) that support the completion of assessment activities. Fourth, the rubric criteria should be fair and free from bias.

Analytic Scoring Rubrics

Analytic scoring rubrics divide writing performance into separate components. Each component is evaluated using a separate scale. The "Big Five" writing traits that are most often evaluated (Shermis et al., 2006) are:

- content
- creativity
- style
- mechanics
- organization

Because only one of the "Big Five" traits is examined in the analytical model of writing assessment, all that is required in the simplest kind of analytic scoring rubric is a place for the student's name, date, the specified trait, and a numerical scale (usually 1 to 5) for rating student performance. In group settings, we recommend that teachers read all student compositions once without grading to get a feel for the range of development in the class before assigning numerical values to each paper.

Figure 8.13 shows an example of a simple analytic scoring rubric for writing mechanics that have been studied in grade 4. This example uses criteria from *Tinkertoy Writing: A Systematic Approach for Grades K–5* (K. S. Cooter, 2006).

Figure 8.13   **A Grade 4 End-of-Year Analytic Scoring Rubric: Mechanics**

Name _____

Date _____

Trait: Mechanics of Writing

1. Three paragraphs with 12–15 sentences	1	2	3	4	5
2. Included 4Ws and an H in composition	1	2	3	4	5
3. Accurate spelling throughout	1	2	3	4	5
4. Completed composition in 30 minutes	1	2	3	4	5

Holistic Scoring Rubrics

Holistic scoring rubrics use a single scale to evaluate the larger writing process (Moskal, 2003). Put another way, holistic scoring has teachers evaluate a piece of writing for its overall quality (i.e., all of the traits that make up the writing task are evaluated in combination). This method is sometimes called **focused holistic scoring,** and teachers are encouraged not to become overly concerned with any one aspect of writing but to look at the composition as a whole.

Many states offer holistic scoring rubrics for teachers to use in preparing their students for high-stakes testing (i.e., testing linked to the *No Child Left Behind* federal legislation). Figure 8.14 features the rubric offered to Florida teachers for holistic scoring.

The Florida Department of Education also offers on its Web site descriptors for specific writing scores to assist in further interpreting the holistic scoring rubric (see Figure 8.15). We offer these as exemplars of interpretations of levels of achievement that align with numerical scores on the rubric.

The Six-Trait Model for Writing Assessment

In 1983, the Beaverton Oregon school district sought a means of assessing student writing that could lead to more effective writing instruction. The district examined research conducted by Paul Diederich (1974) featured in his book *Measuring Growth in English*. Diederich had assembled a group of writers, editors, attorneys, business executives, and English, natural science, and social science teachers and asked them to read student essays and rank order them into three groups: effective,

Video Classroom

Visit a 4th grade classroom working on voice in writing.

A mini-lesson on "Voice" in a 4th grade classroom can be viewed on the CD that accompanies this text. Select a mini-lesson on "Voice" in the *Writing Workshop-4th.*

- During the clip, think about why a teacher would select this topic for a meaning lesson.
- How are the examples powerful for helping the children understand the concept of "voice"?
- Children demonstrate that they understand the concept of voice. How?

Figure 8.14 Example of a Holistic Scoring Rubric

6 Points
The writing is focused, purposeful, and reflects insight into the writing situation. The paper conveys a sense of completeness and wholeness with adherence to the main idea, and its organizational pattern provides for a logical progression of ideas. The support is substantial, specific, relevant, concrete, and/or illustrative. The paper demonstrates a commitment to and an involvement with the subject, clarity in presentation of ideas, and may use creative writing strategies appropriate to the purpose of the paper. The writing demonstrates a mature command of language (word choice) with freshness of expression. Sentence structure is varied, and sentences are complete except when fragments are used purposefully. Few, if any, convention errors occur in mechanics, usage, and punctuation.

5 Points
The writing focuses on the topic, and its organizational pattern provides for a progression of ideas, although some lapses may occur. The paper conveys a sense of completeness or wholeness. The support is ample. The writing demonstrates a mature command of language, including precision in word choice. There is variation in sentence structure, and, with rare exceptions, sentences are complete except when fragments are used purposefully. The paper generally follows the conventions of mechanics, usage, and spelling.

4 Points
The writing is generally focused on the topic but may include extraneous or loosely related material. An organizational pattern is apparent, although some lapses may occur. The paper exhibits some sense of completeness or wholeness. The support, including word choice, is adequate, although development may be uneven. There is little variation in sentence structure, and most sentences are complete. The paper generally follows the conventions of mechanics, usage, and spelling.

3 Points
The writing is generally focused on the topic but may include extraneous or loosely related material. An organizational pattern has been attempted, but the paper may lack a sense of completeness or wholeness. Some support is included, but development is erratic. Word choice is adequate but may be limited, predictable, or occasionally vague. There is little, if any, variation in sentence structure. Knowledge of the conventions of mechanics and usage is usually demonstrated, and commonly used words are usually spelled correctly.

2 Points
The writing is related to the topic but include extraneous or loosely related material. Little evidence of an organizational pattern may be demonstrated, and the paper may lack a sense of completeness or wholeness. Development of support is inadequate or illogical. Word choice is limited, inappropriate or vague. There is little, if any, variation in sentence structure, and gross errors in sentence structure may occur. Errors in basic conventions of mechanics and usage may occur, and commonly used words may be misspelled.

1 Point
The writing may only minimally address the topic. The paper is a fragmentary or incoherent listing of related ideas or sentences or both. Little, if any, development of support or an organizational pattern or both is apparent. Limited or inappropriate word choice may obscure meaning. Gross errors in sentence structure and usage may impede communication. Frequent and blatant errors may occur in the basic conventions of mechanics and usage, and commonly used words may be misspelled.
Unscorable
The paper is unscorable because

- the response is not related to what the prompt requested the student to do.
- the response is simply a rewording of the prompt.
- the response is a copy of a published work.
- the student refused to write.
- the response is illegible.
- the response is incomprehensible (words are arranged in such a way that no meaning is conveyed).
- the response contains an insufficient amount of writing to determine if the student was attempting to address the prompt.
- the writing folder is blank.

Source: Florida Writing Assessment Program-FLORIDA WRITES! *(http://www.firn.edu/doe/sas/fw/fwaprubr.htm).* Example of a Holistic Scoring Rubric appears by permission of the Florida Department of Education, Assessment and School Performance Office, Tallahassee, Florida 32399-0400.

Figure 8.15 Description of Writing Scores for a Holistic Rubric (Florida)

For the Florida Writing Assessment, students are given 45 minutes to read their assigned topic, plan what to write, and then write their responses. The descriptions of eleven possible scores from 6.0–1.0 are given below.

Score 6.0:
The writing focuses on the topic, is logically organized, and includes ample development of supporting ideas or examples. It demonstrates a mature command of language, including precision in word choice. Sentences vary in structure. Punctuation, capitalization, and spelling are generally correct.

Score 5.5:
The writing was given a 5 by one reader and 6 by the other reader.

Score 5.0:
The writing focuses on the topic with adequate development of supporting ideas or examples. It has an organizational pattern, though lapses may occur. Word choice is adequate. Sentences vary in structure. Punctuation, capitalization, and spelling are generally correct.

Score 4.5:
The writing was given a 4 by one reader and a 5 by the other reader.

Score 4.0:
The writing focuses on the topic, though it may contain extraneous information. An organizational pattern is evident, but lapses may occur. Some supporting ideas contain specifics and details, but others are not developed. Word choice is adequate. Sentences vary somewhat in structure, though many are simple. Punctuation and capitalization are sometimes incorrect, but most commonly used words are spelled correctly.

Score 3.5:
The writing was given a 3 by one reader and a 4 by the other reader.

Score 3.0:
The writing generally focuses on the topic, though it may contain extraneous information. An organizational pattern has been attempted, but lapses may occur. Some of the supporting ideas or examples may not be developed. Word choice is adequate. Sentences vary somewhat in structure, though many are simple. Punctuation and capitalization are sometimes incorrect, but most commonly used words are spelled correctly.

Score 2.5:
The writing was given a 2 by one reader and a 3 by the other reader.

Score 2.0:
The writing may be slightly related to the topic or offer little relevant information and few supporting ideas or examples. There is little evidence of an organizational pattern. Word choice may be limited or immature. Sentences may be limited to simple constructions. Frequent errors may occur in punctuation, capitalization, and spelling.

Score 1.5:
The writing was given a 1 by one reader and a 2 by the other reader.

Score 1.0:
The writing may only minimally address the topic because there is little or no development of supporting ideas or examples. No organizational pattern is evident. Ideas are provided through lists, and word choice is limited or immature. Unrelated information may be included. Frequent errors in punctuation, capitalization, and spelling may impede communication.

Source: Florida Writing Assessment Program-FLORIDA WRITES! *(http://www.firn.edu/doe/sas/fw/fwapscor.htm).* "Description of Writing Scores for a Holistic Rubric" appears by permission of the Florida Department of Education, Assessment and School Performance Office, Tallahassee, Florida 32399-0400.

somewhat effective, and problematic. The group was also asked to discuss why they had ranked the papers as they had. Interestingly, Diederich found that the various members of the group described virtually the same qualities in the writing samples, including ideas and content, organizational structure, voice, and mechanics.

Beaverton teachers decided to repeat Diederich's study with a group of 17 teachers and a writing consultant. They read, rank ordered, and took notes on hundreds of student papers and found that they largely agreed with Diederich's conclusions. The Beaverton teachers' notes were eventually condensed into a six-trait scoring guide. This six-trait model was adopted by the Oregon Department of Education for use in its statewide writing assessment. The ODE continued to develop and refine the six-trait scoring guide, which has become quite popular in school districts across the United States. Oregon currently uses a six-point scale for measuring performance on each writing trait. In the next section, we describe the six traits and scoring guidelines used by the ODE.

Describing the Six Traits of Writing. Here is a brief description of the six traits for scoring student writing samples drawn from the Oregon Department of Education's Web site at *www.ode.state.or.us*. The ODE criteria for evaluating the traits are also included.

1. *Ideas and content.* This trait refers to the writer's main ideas, purpose for writing, and supporting details. It focuses on how well the writer communicates and supports his or her ideas through the provision of examples, facts, anecdotes, and details appropriate to the target audience. ODE criterion: *The ideas are clear, focused, complete, and well-developed with specific details.*

2. *Organization.* This trait has to do with the structure of a written composition, including the writer's ability to hold the central meaning throughout the document. It focuses on how well the writer is able to organize information in a clear sequence and make connections and transitions among ideas, sentences, and paragraphs. ODE criterion: *The paper moves naturally from one idea to the next, with a strong beginning and ending.*

3. *Voice.* Here the writer demonstrates his or her unique quality of expression. Voice is closely allied to style, which is the manner in which the author expresses himself or herself. Style can be formal, casual, academic, or anecdotal. ODE criterion: *The writing style is lively and interesting and is appropriate to the audience and topic.*

4. *Word choice.* Mark Twain once said that the difference between a word and just the right word is like the difference between *lightning* and *lightning bug.* In relation to this trait, we evaluate the writer's use of words that are appropriate to the topic and audience, as well as her or his ability to convey the intended message and emotion. ODE criterion: *Words are carefully selected to convey precise meaning, images, and tone.*

5. *Sentence fluency.* This trait relates to the writer's understanding and application of the underlying structures of language. When read aloud, the writing should create a natural flow of language. ODE criterion: *Sentences are smooth, varied, and carefully constructed.*

6. *Conventions.* The sixth trait focuses on the writer's knowledge of spelling, grammar, punctuation, capitalization, and penmanship—the mechanics of writing. ODE criterion: *Correct spelling, grammar, usage, punctuation, capitalization, and paragraphing are used throughout the paper.*

Rubrics for Evaluation of the Six Traits. Over the years, six trait scoring has been revised and marketed by various consultants and companies, each evidencing a unique twist on the popular model. Some evaluate each trait using a three-point, five-point, or six-point scale. We share with you in Figure 8.16 a six-point rubric derived from the one used by the Oregon Department of Education (n.d.).

Scoring six traits on six levels can be time-consuming for busy classroom teachers, so we have crafted an alternative three-level scoring for your consideration (see Figure 8.17).

Figure 8.16 Scoring Rubric for the Six Traits

Score	Evaluation	Description
6	Exemplary	The paper showed **outstanding performance and exceptional control** in this trait of writing.
5	Strong	The paper showed **many strengths,** and the writer seemed to be perfecting control of the writing.
4	Proficient	The paper showed **more strengths than weaknesses,** and the writer seemed to be gaining control of the writing.
3	Developing	The paper **needs further development in this trait** because the writer seemed only partially in control of the writing.
2	Emerging	The paper **needs quite a bit more development,** but the writer is addressing this writing trait.
1	Beginning	The paper needs significant development and **represents a very beginning effort.**

Figure 8.17 An Alternate Three-Level Scoring Rubric for the Six Traits

Score	Evaluation	Description
3	Proficient/Exemplary	Outstanding performance and exceptional control in this trait of writing.
2	Developing	Some evidence of the trait, but further development is needed.
1	Emergent	Represents little or no evidence of this trait.

How Is the Writing Process Taught?

Understanding the Writing Process

Writing process instruction teaches the kinds of thinking processes skilled writers use in producing different forms of text. As authors themselves, children are better able to learn from models of good writing how skillful writers paint pictures with words, how they choose words that convey just the right meaning, and craft sentences that grab the attention of readers. Through writing process instruction, children become wordsmiths and begin to enjoy the works of other authors on new and higher levels.

Writing instruction has changed significantly in recent years. Teachers once assigned students writing tasks such as preparing essays, reports, or research papers, expected students to submit one draft of their work, and then moved on to the next focus of study. Based on this "one-draft mentality" (Calkins, 1986), students learned that writing was a one-phase process that resulted in either success or failure. In recent years, researcher-practitioners like Donald Graves (1983) and his protégé Lucy Calkins (1994) have helped teachers (and students) understand that writing is a *process* rather than a one-time, "quick-and-dirty" project. Children are taught to understand and use the phases of authorship.

Video Classroom

Visit an intermediate classroom beginning the writing process.

Observe 6th grade students as they begin the prewriting stage of the writing process. Access *Language Arts Videos-Video 1* in the Teacher Prep Website *(www.prenhall.com/teacherprep)*. You may respond to accompanying questions that can be printed or sent directly to your instructor.

- As you view the clip, note the kinds of references available in the classroom and determine what types of reference material a teacher can expect students to use independently.
- How does the teacher review these process steps with them? What examples indicate independent application by the students?
- Do these references lead a writer toward opportunities for critical thinking and reflection? If so, how?

Writers do not move rigidly from one stage of writing to another. They sometimes move back and forth from one phase to another, or even quit in the middle of one writing project to start another.

It can be very instructive to examine the various stages through which writers progress in producing text. These stages have been identified as prewriting, drafting, revising and editing, and publishing. As teachers, we are in a position to help students learn these stages through our modeling, mini-lessons, and practice sessions.

Prewriting Stage. **Prewriting** is the getting-ready-to-write stage (Tompkins, 2004). Writing begins with an idea or message the writer wants to express. Many teachers help students begin the writing process by asking them to brainstorm a list of topics they might be interested in writing about at some point in the future. These should be topics that generate a certain amount of emotion in the student, as it is this emotional engagement that helps drive the entire writing process through to completion.

Donald Graves, in his classic *Writing: Teachers and Children at Work* (1983), suggests that teachers model each of the stages in the writing process to help students see adult examples. For this first step of brainstorming, the teacher might list at the overhead projector or chalkboard several topics that he or she is interested in writing about—sailing, collecting antiques, attending wrestling matches, or traveling to South Pacific islands. It is important that teachers explain to the class *why* each topic is appealing to them. A brainstorming session sometimes helps children who are having difficulty discovering topics of interest. The key to success is helping students find topics that generate emotion, which helps drive the entire writing process through to completion.

After students have selected an interesting topic, they gather information. This information-gathering may be simply recalling a special event in their life, or thinking about a favorite place, or trying to imagine what life might have been like before television. Depending on their purpose for writing, students may need to go to the library to gather information, surf the Internet for the latest news on their subject, interview people in their family or community, or write to local, state, or federal agencies.

"Kids in the News," explains how students in grades 5–8 research and write scripts for a school news program. Access the Teacher Prep Website *(www.prenhall.com/teacherprep)* *Strategies and Lessons— Language Arts Methods/Writing.*

Cooperative Groups research and write about a state history project to present in a newscast. Visit the Teacher Prep Website *(www.prenhall.com/teacherprep)* and select *Strategies and Lessons— Language Arts Methods/Writing* to read "State History Bites in the Morning News."

Once the student-writer has settled on a topic and collected useful support information, he or she is ready to begin organizing ideas for presentation—in short, to develop a plan for writing of some kind. This plan's form is relatively unimportant, but the writer should have some kind of organizational scheme for the composition. This step helps make the piece clear, concise, and thorough. Several formats depicting the story theme "My Birthday Trip to Universal Studios," written by an intermediate student named Jina, are presented as examples in Figures 8.18 and 8.19.

Sometimes children have a difficult time getting started with their composition, or even coming up with an idea compelling enough to commit to paper. In this situation, it is usually helpful to engage in free writing. During **free writing,**

"Quick Writes and Quick Draws" provide students the opportunity to respond to literature in an impromptu setting. Learn more in *Strategies and Lessons—Reading Methods/Writing* at the Teacher Prep Website (*www.prenhall.com/teacherprep*).

Figure 8.18 Semantic Web

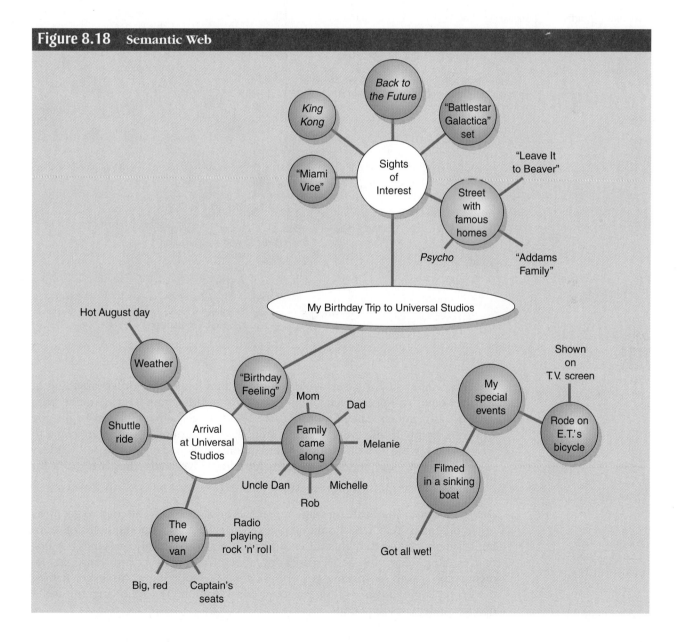

Figure 8.19 Structured Overview

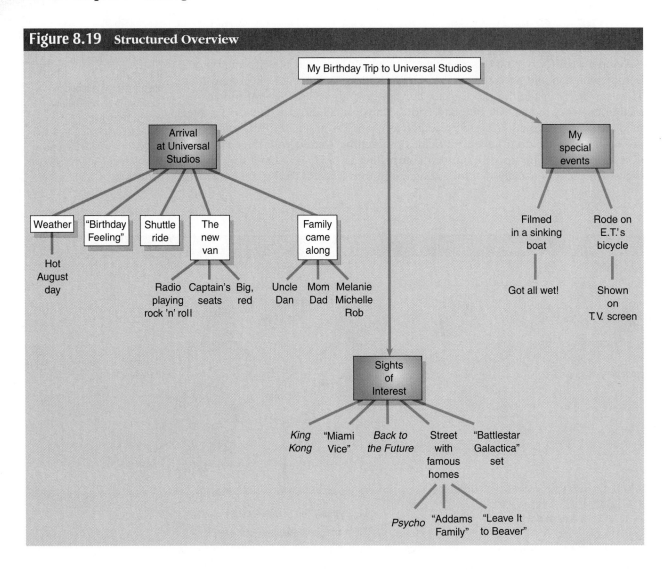

students simply sit for a sustained period of time and write down anything at all that comes to mind. What often emerges is a rather rambling narrative with many idea fragments. Lucy Calkins (1986, 1994) suggests that children begin free writes by simply listing things in their immediate environment until they come to an idea they wish to write about. After students have an organized set of ideas about which to write and have constructed alternative leads, they are ready for the drafting stage.

Drafting Stage. The **drafting stage** represents an author's first attempt to get ideas down on paper. Teachers should emphasize that the most important part of drafting is simply getting thoughts down on paper, not mechanical correctness. A first draft is often referred to as "sloppy copy." Such fine points as verb tense, agreement, subject-verb or spelling correctness are *not* important at this stage. Rather, the expression of *ideas* is the paramount consideration. The following are useful tips for students as they draft:

- Write as though you were telling a story to an interested friend.
- Use your own "voice" instead of trying to sound like your favorite author.
- Use words that create a picture in the reader's mind. Your words should be descriptive and clear.
- Be sure to describe sights, sounds, smells, and other sensory images that are important parts of the story you want to tell.
- Say what you want to say directly. (*More* is not necessarily *better*. Sometimes *less* is *more* if words are chosen well.)

During the drafting process, the writer can create several opening sentences or *alternative leads* for his or her piece. Having an interesting beginning, one that grabs the reader, helps create a successful composition. For example, Jina might have begun her story like this:

> On my birthday my family and I went to Universal Studios. It was a very fun day that I will never forget.

Ellen B. Senisi/Ellen Senisi

On the other hand, if Jina wrote several alternative leads, then picked the most exciting one to begin her story, perhaps she would come up with an introduction like this:

> Imagine a birthday party with King Kong, E.T., and the stars from Miami Vice as your guests! That's exactly what happened to me on my 13th birthday. If you think that's something, hold on to your seat while I tell you the rest of my story.

Struggling students may have difficulty getting their ideas down on paper the first time they attempt to draft. Frequently their handwriting ability impedes the flow of their ideas. One solution is to have students dictate their story into a tape recorder and then transcribe the story onto paper later. This solution helps keep struggling students from becoming frustrated and improves their ability to transcribe a composition to paper. Another option is to allow students to dictate their story to an older student or a peer tutor. The advantage here is that the storyteller can get valuable and immediate feedback from the peer tutor, aiding in the clarity of the composition.

Video Classroom

Visit a 4th grade classroom to see independent writing.

An independent writing area can be viewed on the accompanying CD to this text. Click on *Writing Workshop/4th* to view "Independent Writing," a writing workshop in action.

- Observe arrangements in the classroom, access to materials and references as you watch this video segment.
- Generate a list of ideas that you could use as you set up a writing workshop in your classroom.

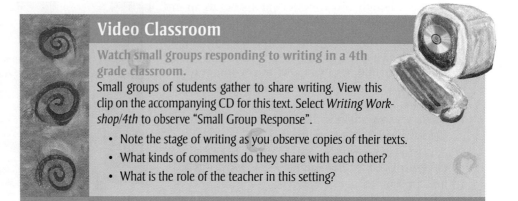

Video Classroom

Watch small groups responding to writing in a 4th grade classroom.

Small groups of students gather to share writing. View this clip on the accompanying CD for this text. Select *Writing Workshop/4th* to observe "Small Group Response".

- Note the stage of writing as you observe copies of their texts.
- What kinds of comments do they share with each other?
- What is the role of the teacher in this setting?

Revising and Editing. Once the draft has been completed, the author is ready to begin the stages of revising and editing. **Revising,** or "re-visioning" (taking a second look), is changing the first draft to include new ideas—or perhaps to rearrange current ideas—to improve it. **Editing** is rereading the manuscript to find errors and omissions. This phase of the writing process is often a joint effort between the author and peer editors—often classmates—who offer constructive criticism.

The revision process can begin in many ways. Perhaps the most traditional method is the student–teacher writing conference, in which students meet with the teacher after she has read the composition. The teacher asks questions and offers suggestions for revisions. Some teachers like to use a form for recording their comments (see Figure 8.20).

Another option for helping students improve their compositions is **peer editing.** Many students prefer to get suggestions from their peers before the final publishing stage. Peer editing allows students to help each other in a collaborative and risk-free

Figure 8.20   Writing Evaluation Form

Writing Evaluation Form

Student Name _____   Date _____

Title of Composition _____

Overall Evaluation of the Composition:

——▶

Underdeveloped   Partially Ready   Advanced   Excellent

Areas Needing Further Development

_____ Character development   _____ Spelling

_____ Setting   _____ Grammar

_____ Conflict description   _____ Punctuation

_____ Conflict resolution   _____ Capitalization

_____ Story closure

Video Classroom

Watch how an editing conference with a teacher works.

Visit a video classroom in the *Reading Methods Section/Writing* of the Teacher Prep Website *(www.prenhall.com/teacherprep)* to observe an "Editing Conference With the Teacher". This video can also be accessed on the CD that accompanies this text in *Writing Workshop/4th*. Select "Individual Edit." Responses to the video classroom prompts may be printed or sent directly to your instructor.

- Observe a conference between a teacher and student and the use of an editing checklist.
- What indicators do you note that demonstrate how this conference is customized to match the student's level of writing development?

Video Classroom

See how peer editing works in the 6th grade.

Students work together in a 6th grade classroom to peer edit. Access *Video Classroom* on the Teacher Prep Website *(www.prenhall.com/teacherprep)* and select *Language Arts/Writing* to view "Peer Editing." Responses to questions may be printed or sent directly to your instructor.

- How does peer editing support the idea of writing being a social activity?
- Why is peer editing helpful prior to meeting for an editing conference with the teacher?
- Based on your observations, think about the instruction that had to precede this lesson and which should follow.

environment. Though some students are able to work one-on-one with their peers successfully, peer editing is often more effective in small groups known as **teacherless writing teams** or **peer editing conferences.** Three to four students work together to produce their best work. At each stage of the writing process, students share their work with their team, and team members question the author and offer suggestions for improvement.

During the editing process, students check compositions for misspelled words, usage errors, poor sentence construction, missing topic sentences, awkward language, and coherence. Many teachers encourage students to use word banks (key word lists on the subject), a thesaurus, and a dictionary or the spelling and grammar checking features on word processing programs. Although some advocate the use of reference tools during the drafting stage, Calkins (1986, 1994) recommends reserving them for these final stages of the writing process.

Figure 8.21 Proofreaders' Marks

Text with Proofreader Markings	Explanation
injured Jamie carried the ⋀ puppy home.	⋀ is for inserting missing words
Let's go (to Mark's house over.)	∩ for moving text
Let's go to Mark's house over.	ℓ for marking out text

During the editing stage, writers use **proofreaders' marks.** These are notations that an author uses to add, delete, or rearrange information on manuscripts. Figure 8.21 features several examples of proofreaders's marks teachers might consider demonstrating to young writers.

Many schools now provide students with personal computers (PCs) for writing projects. These make the editing process both quick and relatively painless, but students must first learn keyboarding skills. Selected computer applications for assisting writing development are discussed in greater detail later in this chapter.

Publishing. A natural desire for most authors, young or seasoned, is to share their composition with an audience. For children, publishing can take many exciting forms. One publishing experience common in elementary classrooms is called the **author's chair.** Each day at a designated time, young authors who have completed a composition can sign up to share their most recent compositions in the author's chair. When the appointed time arrives, students take turns reading their creations to the class, answering questions about their story, and reaping generous applause. Other forms of publishing include letter writing to pen pals, school officials, favorite authors, and media stars, or making stories into classroom books, newspapers, and yearbooks. The key to success in publishing is that students feel their writing projects have an audience.

Video Classroom

Watch more of the writing process as students share from the author's chair.

View students sharing writing with their classmates on the accompanying CD. Select *Writing Workshop/4th* to observe "Share For Class" where students share writing from the author's chair, before the final stage of publishing.

- Note the kinds of creations that are shared along with questions asked about the story.
- Why is this an important part of the writing process?

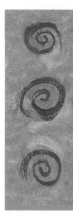

How Do *Interactive Writing* Procedures Help Learners Acquire New Writing Skills?

In this section we discuss ideas that may be called **interactive writing** (Gipe, 2006). The idea is for the teacher to demonstrate new ideas about writing for learners in their zones of proximal development—ideas that bridge the reading and writing processes and help students grow in each language area. We begin with a very flexible method of writing instruction known as Writing Aloud, Writing To, followed by activities that fit nicely into this paradigm. Later, we describe other activities that make writing connections with books and other texts for students, followed by book-making ideas.

Writing Aloud, Writing To: A Way of Structuring Your Teaching

In read-aloud activities, teachers share books orally with students and model such reading essentials as comprehension strategies and decoding skills. *Writing Aloud, Writing To* (Cooter, 2002; Gunning, 2006) is an adaptation of Routman's (1995) technique for getting students' attention and demonstrating various aspects of the writing process. *Writing Aloud, Writing To* has been used with great success in the Dallas Reading Plan, a massive teacher-education project in Texas, which resulted in significant improvement in student writing and reading achievement levels. The Writing To part of *Writing Aloud, Writing To* comes from the notion of writing to, with, and by: in a balanced program of writing instruction, teachers should engage daily in writing *to* students (demonstrations and mini-lessons), writing *with* students (guided practice sessions where students implement new writing skills with the help of the teacher or a more skilled peer), and writing *by* students (independent writing sessions where they practice their newly acquired skills).

The materials you will use depend greatly on the kinds of writing strategies you plan to model. In general, we like to use an overhead projector, transparencies, and erasable markers or a large tablet on an easel for writing demonstrations with groups. If the demonstration involves a computer, it is usually best to conduct *Writing Aloud, Writing To* sessions in small groups unless you have access to a computer projection system.

As with materials, the strategies you will employ will be based on the writing/ reading connections you choose to emphasize. Routman (1995) and Cooter (2002) do, however, provide us with some useful tips.

- In *Writing Aloud, Writing To,* the teacher thinks aloud while writing in front of the students.
- Students watch the teacher as he writes and sometimes read aloud with the teacher as he says explicitly what he is doing. This may include the writer's thinking processes, format that has been chosen and why, layout of the piece, spacing, handwriting, spelling, punctuation, and discussion of vocabulary.
- Teachers help students relate the spoken word to the written word at all times.
- The teacher often asks questions that relate to the conventions of writing or features of text.

A graphic was prepared for the Dallas Reading Academy (Cooter, 2002) that summarizes key elements of *Writing Aloud, Writing To* based on the work of Regie Routman (1995). It is shown in Figure 8.22.

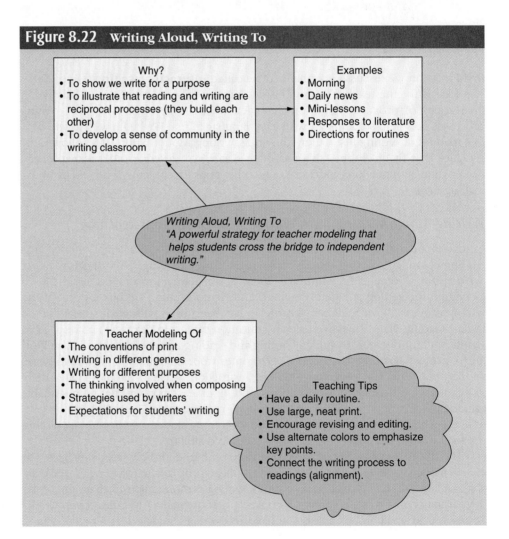

Figure 8.22   Writing Aloud, Writing To

Why?
- To show we write for a purpose
- To illustrate that reading and writing are reciprocal processes (they build each other)
- To develop a sense of community in the writing classroom

Examples
- Morning
- Daily news
- Mini-lessons
- Responses to literature
- Directions for routines

Writing Aloud, Writing To
"A powerful strategy for teacher modeling that helps students cross the bridge to independent writing."

Teacher Modeling Of
- The conventions of print
- Writing in different genres
- Writing for different purposes
- The thinking involved when composing
- Strategies used by writers
- Expectations for students' writing

Teaching Tips
- Have a daily routine.
- Use large, neat print.
- Encourage revising and editing.
- Use alternate colors to emphasize key points.
- Connect the writing process to readings (alignment).

Shared Writing. **Shared writing** is an opportunity for teachers and students to share the act of composing a piece of writing. Let's take a look at some highly effective ways teachers can "share the pencil" with children.

Morning Message. A morning message is brief, no more than two to six sentences on the level of students' ability to attend to and produce print (Payne & Schulman, 1998). Topics for the morning message are based on recent or upcoming school or class events and ideas or experiences individual students want to share. Typically, you, the teacher, will write the first sentence of the morning message. It might read, "Good morning, first grade! Today is ____" or "Wow! Yesterday was really special because ____." Leads such as this get students reading and thinking to start the day.

Next, read the first sentence of the morning message aloud to students. Then, while pointing, have students read it with you. Ask students if they have anything they would like to write to fill in the next part of the morning message. As children offer suggestions, ask them questions like, "What will we write first?" or "How many sounds do we hear in the first word? Let's clap and count the sounds." Sharing the pen with students, write two to six sentences to complete the morning message.

In kindergarten and early first grade, some teachers prepare pictures to be used in place of words to keep the writing of the morning message moving along more rapidly. But by grades 2–3, most students will be able to write their message quite rapidly. Keep the editing tape handy so that you can fix mistakes in spelling, punctuation, and capitalization as you talk about them. Morning message provides a nice means of sharing the responsibilities for writing between students and teacher and is an ideal segue into interactive writing.

Interactive Writing. An **interactive writing** session focuses on the teacher writing *with* children—what is sometimes called "sharing the pen" (McCarrier, Pinnell, & Fountas, 1999). Teachers use interactive writing to:

- Connect reading and writing by using literature as a take-off point for writing reproductions, innovations, and new texts
- Help students develop increasingly sophisticated writing skills
- Demonstrate saying words slowly and connecting sounds in words to letters and letter combinations
- Expand students' repertoire of writing genres and forms
- Help children learn how the spelling process works

The subject and form of interactive writing may vary greatly depending on the developmental levels of the students and the context of experiences in the classroom. Typically in the early years, the teacher helps students write simple sentences. As students learn more about the writing process and different types of writing forms and genres, the teacher structures writing activities that become more complex.

Conducting an Interactive Writing Lesson. There is no one correct way to teach an interactive writing lesson, but based on the writings of McCarrier, Pinnell, & Fountas (1999), we recommend the following approaches:

1. In the early stages of writing, the teacher should help students compose a simple message drawn from literature or from the group's experiences. For example, consider this line from *The Very Hungry Caterpillar* (Carle, 1981):

"On Monday, he ate through one apple." If the teacher asked children to innovate on what the caterpillar ate on Monday, a child might offer the following: "On Monday, he ate through one tomato." As the teacher asks students to replace text with new words, as she did in the example above, the entire message is reread from the beginning to help students remember how composing proceeds.

2. Teacher and students share the pen as a message is written word by word. When new words are added to a line of text, the children reread the line up to the added word. In the earliest stages of writing development, the teacher may write the word for students. With time and development, the teacher shares the pen, inviting children to contribute a letter, several letters, or an entire word.

3. Where appropriate, the teacher encourages the child to stretch the word and say it slowly to predict the letters by analyzing the sounds (see "word rubberbanding" in Chapter 4). Children may attempt any letter in the word in any order. Working within the child's zone of proximal development a la Vygotsky (1962), the teacher fills in those letters that the child is unable to analyze on his own.

4. The teacher can construct a word wall, like that recommended by Cunningham (2000), which might be used as a writing resource for students. Words can be listed on the wall as "Words We Know and Can Write," "Words We Almost Know," and "Words We Need to Analyze and Write with Help."

5. As teachers and children write interactively, the teacher helps children learn directionality, punctuation, spaces, features of print, and capitalization. In this fashion, children learn the mechanics and the authoring processes necessary to produce high-quality writing products.

Interactive writing sessions typically last from 5 to 15 minutes, depending on the nature of the text to be produced. The goal of interactive writing is neat, legible, and sensible text.

Organizing for Instruction: The Writing Workshop

The **writing workshop** is an organizational structure for teaching composition skills that can be modified as needed. Instruction can be organized into five phases: teacher sharing time, mini-lesson, state of the class, workshop activities, and student sharing time. Figure 8.23 depicts the organizational scheme for the writing workshop.

Phase 1: Teacher Sharing Time (5 to 10 minutes): The purpose of teacher sharing time is to present students with language and experiences through writing that stimulate the natural energies of thinking (Holdaway, 1984). The substance of these teacher-led presentations is usually an assortment of brain-enticing poems, songs, stories, and exposition written by the teacher. The goal is to inspire students to strike out on new adventures in writing. This phase should be brief, perhaps 5 to 10 minutes, and should serve as a stimulating introduction to the rest of the writing period.

Phase 2: Mini-Lesson (5 to 10 minutes): The mini-lesson (Calkins, 1986, 1994), as is its counterpart in the reading workshop, is a brief time for teaching skills. Class discussions about such topics as selecting good ideas to write about, gathering reference materials, conducting interviews,

Figure 8.23   The Writing Workshop

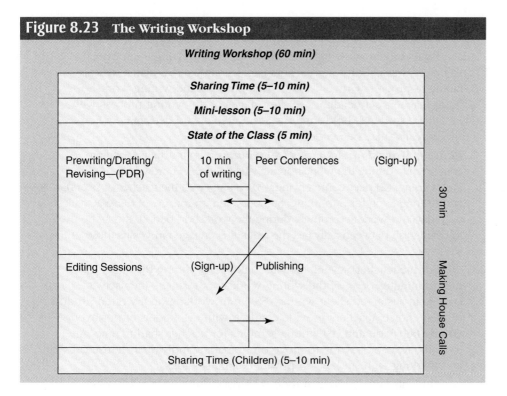

organizing information, and publishing are all viable. Some examples of common mini-lesson topics suggested by Atwell (1987) are:

illustrations	narrative leads
essay writing	spelling
form	writing good fiction
mythology (Greek and Roman)	the dictionary
resumé writing	genre
writing conferences with yourself	job applications
correspondence	punctuation
focus	style
	writing short stories

Teachers usually share examples from their own writing or those volunteered by students during mini-lessons. The main focus of the mini-lesson at all grade levels is helping students write with quality at their stage of development.

Phase 3: State of the Class (5 minutes): The state-of-the-class phase of the writing workshop takes the same form as it does in the reading workshop: The teacher simply lists each student's name on the left side of a chart and students fill in the blanks for each day, indicating what they will be doing (e.g., drafting, peer conferencing, editing, publishing). Sometimes writing instructors, like Atwell, prefer to complete the state-of-the-class chart in the whole-class setting:

> I think the [state-of-the-class] conference is worth three minutes of the whole class's time. I can't begin to know all the ways my students find ideas for writing, but I do know that eavesdropping is right up

there. When they make their plans public, writers naturally teach each other about new options for topic and genre. (Atwell, 1987, p. 90)

By recording students' plans for writing and saving them over the weeks of the school year, teachers can see almost at a glance who is failing to progress (Atwell, 1987). This phase of the writing workshop helps teachers set deadlines for key stages of the writing process with individual students, hold students accountable, and determine when "house calls" may be needed.

Phase 4: Workshop Activities (30 minutes): Four activities operate concurrently during the workshop activities phase: (1) prewriting, drafting, and revising; (2) peer conferencing; (3) editing (with the teacher or peers); and (4) preparing for publishing. Students sign up for one of these activities each day and work accordingly during the workshop period. It may be useful to distinguish between activities the teacher is engaged in versus those of the students.

For the teacher, several activities take place during this time. In the first 10 minutes or so of the writing workshop, teachers themselves engage in sustained silent writing (SSW). In working on a written product of their choice, teachers provide children with (a) models of positive writing behavior, and (b) writing samples for teacher sharing time. After SSW, the teacher is ready to move on to making individual "house calls" and working with students in private editing sessions.

Students largely move at their own pace during Writing Workshop activities and select from the four tasks identified earlier. If they choose to prewrite, draft, or revise, student might choose topics for narratives, gather resources and references, conduct interviews, create an outline for organizing their document, and eventually produce a draft.

Once students finish their first drafts, they are ready to sign up for a peer conference. During peer conferencing, small groups of students, usually three or four, read each other's first drafts and make recommendations for revisions. Peer conferences are sometimes known as "teacherless writing groups" because the teacher is not involved during this analysis phase unless invited by the group for consulting purposes.

Teachers have told us that some students learning the writing workshop system want to peer conference almost all the time. This can be problematic because a goal of comprehensive writing instruction is to promote peer collaboration and cooperation. One solution is to establish guidelines differentiating peer conferences from what might be termed "one-minute conferences." When students need a quick opinion about their composition, they can usually arrange a one-minute conference with a peer. Students should not require more than three one-minute conferences during a writing workshop session.

Group etiquette rules for student interactions should be established early in the school year to ensure maximum productivity and to minimize conflicts. Role-playing is one way to form group-developed rules. (Remember the teachers who made a videotape acting out positive and negative group behavior in the reading workshop section.) Students themselves also have no problem coming up with a list of their own group etiquette rules, which are applicable in all group experiences.

TEACHER PREP

View an example of published writing in *Language Arts Artifacts—Module 2* on the Teacher Prep Website (*www.prenhall.com/teacherprep*). Select "Song of Myself" to learn more. You may respond to your instructor through this site.

- Think about how this artifact illustrates careful prewriting and brainstorming.
- How could this be used to model organizational structure and audience awareness?
- How does this artifact reflect the teacher's attention to self-esteem and motivation to write?

A word regarding classroom noise levels seems warranted. Whenever teachers begin to experiment with modes of instruction that allow students to work on their own or in small groups, the noise level will invariably go up. This may be distressing at first for some teachers, but this issue can be addressed. If the class becomes unruly, then appropriate steps must be taken to maintain class control. More often than not, however, the increase in classroom noise should be viewed as the sound of learning and creative interaction. Silvia Ashton-Warner (1963) refers to this kind of classroom hubbub as "peaceful noise" (p. 86).

Once the peer conference group meets and considers each students' manuscript, members make suggestions for improvement. Of course, authors are free to accept or reject their peers' suggestions. Manuscript revisions follow the peer conference, paving the way for an editing session with the teacher.

Editing sessions are special times for students to meet with the teacher to discuss their writing project and receive independent skill instruction or coaching. To take part in an editing session, students sign up the day before the conference and submit a copy of their writing project. This allows teachers time to read the composition and prepare notes for the student. Teachers should avoid writing directly on the composition. Instead, remarks should be made on a separate sheet of paper or a stick-on note to prevent defacing the project. When examining some narrative compositions, it may be a good idea to refer to a story grammar outline to make sure all-important elements have been included. Semantic and syntactic considerations should also be discussed.

After the editing session, students frequently need to edit or revise further before publishing. It may be desirable for the student and teacher to have an additional editing session to go over modifications before publishing. A visit to the publishing center to put the writing project into final form is the last stop.

One final point: Publishing does not necessarily happen with every writing project. Sometimes a student will say to the teacher, "I'm running out of interest for this story. May I work on another one?" Most writers occasionally run out of gas during a project and start a new one. Some may have several projects in process. It is not the number of publications a student produces during a given period that is important, but the process itself. Although it is desirable that students reach closure on a regular basis with writing projects, it does not have to happen every time.

Phase 5: Sharing Time (5 to 10 minutes): The Writing Workshop concludes with student sharing time or publishing. This period is for sharing and publishing completed writing projects. Students proceed to sharing time only with the approval of the teacher after an editing session.

Even students who may be publishing their writing project outside of class (e.g., putting their book in the school library or submitting their work to a children's magazine) should take part in sharing time. This allows other students to see and enjoy their finished product. The most common format for sharing time is the author's chair experience, where students sit before the group and share their composition.

Organizing for Instruction: The Writing Center

Find out how the use of computer clip art motivates struggling readers along with providing them opportunities to use the computer. Access *Strategies and Lessons—Reading Methods/ Writing* on the Teacher Prep Website *(www.prenhall. com/teacherprep)* to read "Literacy and Computers."

The **writing center** is an integral part of the Writing Workshop approach in the K–3 classroom. Because of the nature of the multiple activities occurring in the writing center, it should be located away from the quiet areas designated for silent sustained writing.

The writing center (see Figure 8.24) often includes three smaller integrated areas:

- Work area for collaborative writing projects, conferences, and editing
- Quiet area for silent sustained writing
- Publishing area with necessary supplies

As part of the writing area, a space for collaborative writing is designated for children to interact with teachers and peers about their writing projects—projects that may have been authored by individuals or groups or that may have been coauthored. A conference area with table and chairs or just a quiet carpeted corner can function as a location for conducting peer–student or teacher–student conferences about developing writing projects. An editing area can be located at a desk or table near the conference area. An older student, the teacher, or an adult volunteer can function as an editor for student-authored works in the classroom. An editor's visor, printer's apron, various writing and marking media, and a poster displaying editorial marks can be located here for the editor's use. The publishing area should be stocked with pencils, pens, markers, staplers, and paper of various colors and sizes for covers. Materials also should be available for students to bind or publish their final writing products in a variety of ways. The location for each of the many supplies in this area can be indicated by a printed label or an outline of the object; doing so makes it easier for students to help in keeping the publishing area neat and tidy. Student works published in this area may take the form of big books, shape books, micro-books, accordion books, letters, notes, lists, posters, bulletin boards, and murals.

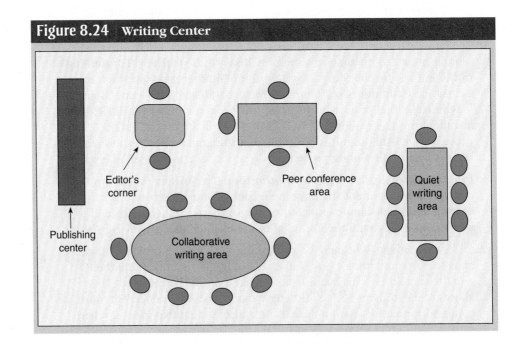

Figure 8.24 Writing Center

Editor's corner

Peer conference area

Quiet writing area

Publishing center

Collaborative writing area

Classroom Computers and Writing Development

When teachers think of computers, word processing often comes to mind. **Word processing** is a general term that refers to the use of software programs that permit someone to write, edit, store, and print text (Strickland, Feeley, & Wepner, 1987, p. 13). In addition to standard word processing packages for elementary and upper elementary-age students, other related computer software programs are available that help students develop as writers.

Because computer software programs come and go so rapidly, it is very difficult to make specific recommendations. Professional publications in the literacy field, such as *The Reading Teacher, Reading Research and Instruction,* and *Language Arts* and product journals like *MacWorld* frequently feature product reviews that can help guide purchasing decisions. We offer only a brief sampling of writing programs that help students develop and extend their authoring abilities. *Bank Street Writer* is a pioneering effort that is both easy to use and affordable. It is suggested for grade 3 and up. *MacWrite* is the oldest text-processing program for the Macintosh computer and remains one that all Macs can open. Version 4.6 (or even 5), bundled with Mac computers to model SE, remains a very useful format, even with its size limit (*MacWrite 4.6* files cannot exceed 64 KB).

IBM's *Writing to Read 2000*. *Writing to Read 2000* is the next generation of IBM's landmark product, *Writing to Read*. It is a beginning reading–writing program based on a modified alphabet idea (one symbol for each of 42 language sounds) for kindergarten and first grade. It was developed by John Henry Martin, a retired teacher and school administrator. The typical routine, usually 30 to 40 minutes per day, takes children through a five-station rotation in a special computer lab. Students begin with the computer station, where they are taught to type 42 phonemes (representing English language sounds) using color images and synthesized speech. These lessons are repeated in a work journal. Then students listen to a tape-recorded story while following along in a book in the listening library. These activities are followed by a session in the typing–writing center, during which students can write compositions of their own choosing. The final center, where other reinforcement activities are practiced, is called "Make Words."

Writing to Read 2000 includes a component called the "Computer Center," where "cycle words" teach young children sound/letter relationships. Four other centers support and encourage children to practice these associations using a variety of activities, including work journals, manipulatives, books, and writing. Other components of the new program follow:

- a writing/typing center program called *Write Along*
- graphical menus, audio support, and mouse, enabling easy and independent navigation for young students
- context rhymes that introduce "cycle words"
- teacher options, which include bookmaking, partner support, student management, and reporting information
- a *Writing to Read 2000* Game Board and assortment of games, puzzles, and manipulatives
- a collection of 23 age-appropriate children's literature books, 16 accompanied by natural, expressive voice cassette recordings
- a teacher's guide that provides cross-curricular connections, curriculum integration, and thematic unit suggestions

The First Six Weeks of Writing Instruction

From the first day of school, you must show students that you consider them to be competent writers (albeit, at their own stage of development). In this section, we offer some general guidelines for structuring writing instruction for the first six weeks of school.

Week 1. Writing and reading are reciprocal processes and should be started at the same time. In order to get a sense of momentum established right away, do the following.

- Introduce writing mini-lessons working with the whole group. Mini-lessons could focus on selecting appropriate topics, using graphic organizers, crafting opening sentences (leads), and learning the conventions of writing.
- Make in-class writing assignments to help you begin the assessment process.
- Introduce students to the writing center, the variety of tools available there, and their purposes/correct uses.
- Introduce students to the writer's notebook concept and have them begin making entries.

Weeks 2 and 3

- Introduce students to the notion of using a "writer's notebook" for gathering such things as brainstorming ideas, completed graphic organizers, "sloppy copy" first drafts, and so forth. This can take the form of a pocket folder, a file folder kept in an easily-accessible storage unit, or a tabbed three-ring binder.
- Explain how student writing folders are to be used to store work.
- Introduce the rudiments of letter writing and have students use that format to write a letter to a friend or family member.

Weeks 4 Through 6

- Conduct mini-lessons in small- and large-group settings, focusing primarily on revising and editing fundamentals.
- Post and discuss numerous writing models for each stage of the writing process that meet curriculum or state assessment requirements for best-quality work. Students need to see examples of competent work to understand the expectations.
- Conference with two to three students per day about the progress of their work using work samples in their writing folders.
- Conduct small- and whole-group guided writing sessions.
- Introduce writing backpacks as homework assignments that involve parents.
- If adult volunteers are available, begin to assign them to struggling writers to assist in specific areas of need. You must first train the volunteers on writing activities they can deliver, then match them to students having that particular need.

Getting to Know English Learners

During the first week of writing instruction with your ELs, try to get a writing sample from each student. Here are a few questions that will guide your assessment and help you to know whether or not you need to seek outside assistance.

1. What is EL's native language?
2. Does your EL student's language use the Greek alphabet like English or another system? How is that system different?
3. Does your EL student read in her first language? Does she write in her first language?
4. Can your EL student write in English?
5. If not, can your EL student dictate in English so you may write for her?
6. If not, can your EL student draw a picture to accompany a story you read aloud to the class or one she prefers to "talk about."

Now, if necessary, you can work with your school's ESL or English Language Arts teacher and capable peer reading/writing buddies to modify your writing instruction for your ELs.

Primary children prepare to write written descriptions and they plan through webbing. Read more in "Writing Through Webbing for Elementary Students" on the Teacher Prep Website (www.prenhall.com/teacherprep) in *Strategies and Lessons—Reading Methods/Writing.*

How Can We Adapt Writing Instruction to Meet the Needs of All Learners?

We have recently discovered two novel approaches for helping struggling readers and writers. The first is a revision of the K-W-L strategy by Ogle (1986), and the second has to do with online technologies.

Reading and Analyzing Nonfiction (RAN) Strategy

Tony Stead (2001, 2006), an Australian teacher, points out that some 85 percent of all reading that we do as adults is nonfiction or informative in nature, but most of what we deal with in K–3 classrooms is personal narrative or fiction. We strongly believe that all learners, and especially struggling readers and writers, can benefit from an increased diet of nonfiction reading and writing activities. Not only that, children truly enjoy expository texts! These activities can help children do the following:

- ✓ Increase their concept knowledge and vocabulary
- ✓ Learn important research skills using a variety of tools
- ✓ Develop cooperative learning abilities
- ✓ Learn the writing patterns and styles used by authors in constructing informational texts

Stead (2006) explains that good learning with expository/informational texts has students talking, listening, seeing, exploring, questioning, observing, and sharing. In the **reading and analyzing nonfiction strategy (RAN),** Stead has produced innovations on the popular K-W-L strategy (Ogle, 1986) to promote small group, interactive learning. Featured in Figure 8.25 is an example of our interpretation of Stead's RAN model completed by a group of students beginning a study of *arachnids* (spiders).

With the RAN strategy learners begin by working with a team of students to list what they *think* they know about the subject. This creates an implicit understanding in the learner's mind that some of what they think they know may not be true, and that it is okay to have some knowledge that is not accurate.

The second part of RAN has students looking for information about the subject—researching. Stead (2006) explains that information resources must be pre-selected by the teacher to ensure that students do not become frustrated in trying to locate information or lose precious time reading unrelated or unreliable sources. After the team's research is completed, they compile what they have learned in the columns labeled "Information We Have Confirmed" and "New Information and Facts We Have Learned." In doing this, students give evidence that they recognize the validity of some of their previous knowledge and can articulate their new knowledge. In the next column of the summary form, students list misconceptions about the topic they have debunked as a result of their research.

The final column of the RAN Team Learning Form is directed toward what the learners still wonder about. For the topic of spiders, learners may wonder how they can tell which spiders are poisonous, or which spiders can be found in their home town. If they are learning about zebras, they might wonder if the stripes are as different as fingerprints in humans. This "wondering" column is driven by students' research, and frequently results in higher levels of learning and comprehension.

Using RAN to Help Students Transition to Written Summaries. RAN can be quite useful as a Prewriting tool. To help students use RAN to move into the Drafting stage of writing, teachers must provide direct and explicit modeling examples.

For teacher "think-aloud" modeling, it may be helpful to use a graphic organizer like the one recommended in the *Memphis Striving Readers Project* called **Structure**

English Learners can use wordless picture books to help them predict and develop vocabulary. They can "read" the book in their own languages and then create a story. Read more in "Generating Stories" in *Language Arts Methods/Writing* on the Teacher Prep Website (*www.prenhall.com/teacherprep*)

Children can write their own nursery rhymes individually or as a group in inclusive classrooms. Visit the Teacher Prep Website (*www.prenhall.com/teacherprep*) and select *Strategies and Methods—Language Arts Methods/Writing* to read "Rhyming Time" for grades K–4 & L.D. students.

Scott Cunningham/Merrill

Figure 8.25   Reading and Analyzing Nonfiction (RAN) Team Learning Form: *Arachnids* Example

What We *Think* We Know About This Topic	Information We Have *Confirmed*	*New Information and Facts We Have Learned*	Some *Misconceptions* We Have Learned About This Topic	We *Now* Wonder . . .
They're scary We think there is a song about an Eensy Weensy spider My cousin says to stay away from them 'cause they'll hurt you They kill people every now and then All spiders are poisonous The biggest spider is as big as a cat	Songs about spiders we found in the Internet: Eensy Weensy Spider Spider Dance Busy Spider Four Little Spiders Most spiders carry venom to stun or kill creatures they want to eat, not to hurt humans. Of all spiders only about 25 are thought to have venom that can hurt humans. Not all spiders are poisonous. Two venomous spiders in the U.S. are the black widow and brown recluse—but they have not been proven to kill people in more than 20 years. The biggest spider is the Goliath birdeater tarantula. It is found in the rain forests of northeastern South America, and can be as big as a dinner plate. It can grab birds from their nests! The smallest spider is from Borneo and is the size of a pinhead.	The scientific name for spiders is arachnids. There are 37,000 species of arachnids. Some spiders eat insects we don't like such as flies and mosquitoes. Others eat frogs, fish, lizards, and snakes.	Some people think spiders have hair, so they must be mammals. Spiders are not mammals, they are insects. Some think spiders kill people, but no one has died from a spider bite in 20 years. All spiders eat bugs—not true. Some eat animals. Some people think there are spiders that are as big as a cat, or even bigger. This is not true since the biggest spider is the size of a dinner plate.	What is the biggest spider in North America, since we live there? What is the strongest kind of silk made by spiders? Can you make clothes out of spider silk? Do any spiders live under water? Where did the name "arachnid" come from?

Free Online Sources for Teachers and Children:
*Adapted from *National Geographic News. Spider Sense: Fast Facts on Extreme Arachnids.* (n.d.). Retrieved March 31. 2007, from *http://news.nationalgeographic.com/news/2004/06/0623_040623_spiderfacts.html.*
**Titles from Music & Rhyme Station: Spider songs and rhymes. (n.d.). Retrieved March 31, 2007, from *http://www.preschoolexpress.com/ music_station03/music_station_oct03.shtml.* Full text and tunes listed.

for Written Retellings or **SWR** (K. S. Cooter, 2006) as seen in Figure 8.26. A completed version of the SWR is shown in Figure 8.27 in which the teacher has demonstrated how information gathered using RAN could be transposed onto the Structure for Written Retellings (SWR) graphic organizer to create a first draft of a summary paper. (Note: In modeling, teachers should use alternative examples of previously learned material cast in the RAN format since it is the *process*, not the content, that is being emphasized.) Some Internet sites related to writing you and your young techno-experts might investigate follow:

Wikipedia	*http://en.wikipedia.org/wiki/Main_Page*
National Geographic's	*http://news.nationalgeographic.com/kids/*
Kids News	

Figure 8.26 **Structure for Written Retellings (K. S. Cooter, 2007)**

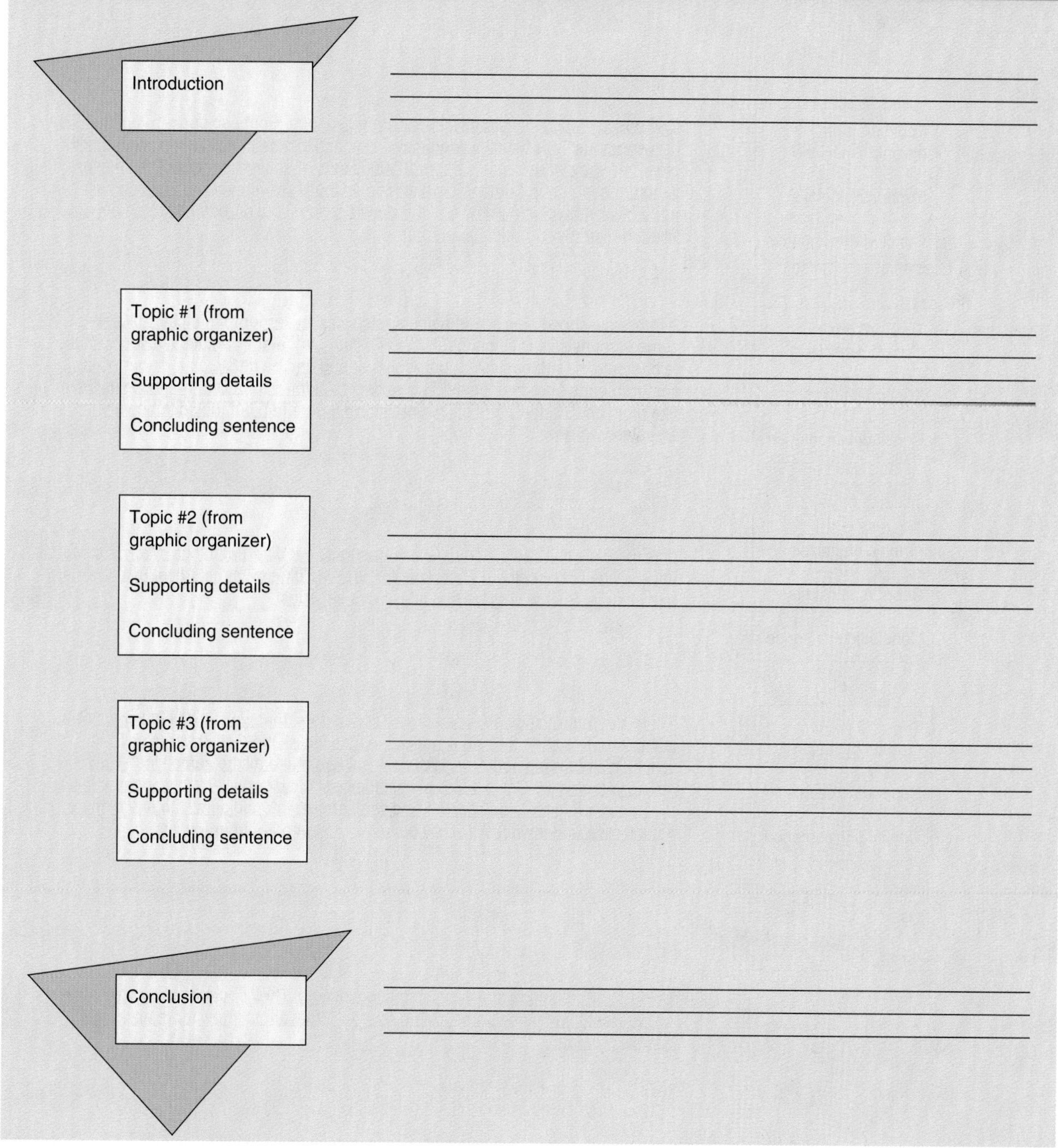

Introduction

_____
_____
_____

Topic #1 (from graphic organizer)

Supporting details

Concluding sentence

_____
_____
_____

Topic #2 (from graphic organizer)

Supporting details

Concluding sentence

_____
_____
_____

Topic #3 (from graphic organizer)

Supporting details

Concluding sentence

_____
_____
_____

Conclusion

_____
_____
_____

Figure 8.27   Example of a Completed Structure for Written Retellings on *Arachnids*

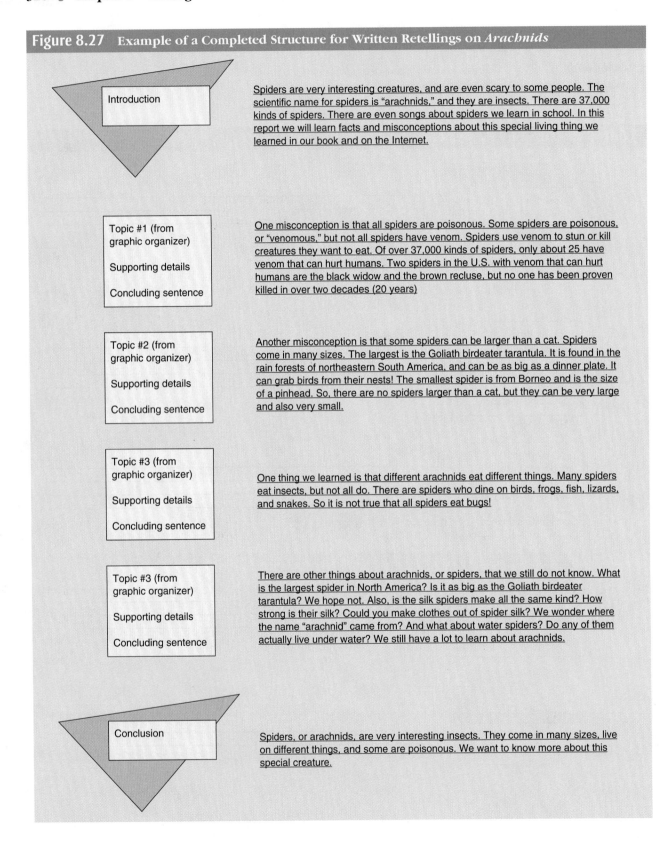

Introduction

Spiders are very interesting creatures, and are even scary to some people. The scientific name for spiders is "arachnids," and they are insects. There are 37,000 kinds of spiders. There are even songs about spiders we learn in school. In this report we will learn facts and misconceptions about this special living thing we learned in our book and on the Internet.

Topic #1 (from graphic organizer)

Supporting details

Concluding sentence

One misconception is that all spiders are poisonous. Some spiders are poisonous, or "venomous," but not all spiders have venom. Spiders use venom to stun or kill creatures they want to eat. Of over 37,000 kinds of spiders, only about 25 have venom that can hurt humans. Two spiders in the U.S. with venom that can hurt humans are the black widow and the brown recluse, but no one has been proven killed in over two decades (20 years)

Topic #2 (from graphic organizer)

Supporting details

Concluding sentence

Another misconception is that some spiders can be larger than a cat. Spiders come in many sizes. The largest is the Goliath birdeater tarantula. It is found in the rain forests of northeastern South America, and can be as big as a dinner plate. It can grab birds from their nests! The smallest spider is from Borneo and is the size of a pinhead. So, there are no spiders larger than a cat, but they can be very large and also very small.

Topic #3 (from graphic organizer)

Supporting details

Concluding sentence

One thing we learned is that different arachnids eat different things. Many spiders eat insects, but not all do. There are spiders who dine on birds, frogs, fish, lizards, and snakes. So it is not true that all spiders eat bugs!

Topic #3 (from graphic organizer)

Supporting details

Concluding sentence

There are other things about arachnids, or spiders, that we still do not know. What is the largest spider in North America? Is it as big as the Goliath birdeater tarantula? We hope not. Also, is the silk spiders make all the same kind? How strong is their silk? Could you make clothes out of spider silk? We wonder where the name "arachnid" came from? And what about water spiders? Do any of them actually live under water? We still have a lot to learn about arachnids.

Conclusion

Spiders, or arachnids, are very interesting insects. They come in many sizes, live on different things, and some are poisonous. We want to know more about this special creature.

USGS Learning Web   *http://interactive2.usgs.gov/learningweb/students/*
Smithsonian Education *http://www.smithsonianeducation.org/*
PBS Kids   *http://pbskids.org/*
Oz Projects   *http://www.ozprojects.edna.edu.au/sibling/home*
Grassroots   *http://www.schoolnet.ca/grassroots/e/home/index.asp*
Starfall   *http://www.starfall.com/*
Funbrain   *http://www.funbrain.com/*

What Is a Proven Strategy for Involving Parents in Writing Instruction?

Traveling Tales Backpack

We have used the **traveling tales backpack** (Reutzel & Fawson, 1990; Reutzel & Fawson, 1998; Yellin & Blake, 1994) strategy to involve parents and children in collaborative writing projects. A traveling tales backpack (see Figure 8.28) is filled with writing media and guidelines for parents to work with their children at home in producing a self-selected writing project.

The backpack is sent home with the student for two nights. To maximize involvement and success, parents are contacted by phone or note before the backpack is sent home. Parents and children can choose a variety of ways to respond to their favorite book: They can write shape stories, pocketbooks, accordion books, or cards. Included in the traveling tales backpack is a letter (Figure 8.29) to parents with guidelines on how to engage their child in the writing process.

After completing the writing project together, parent and child are invited to share their work with the class in the author's chair at school. After sharing, the written product is placed on display for students to read and enjoy.

"Plentiful Penguins," located in the Teacher Prep Website *(www.prenhall.com/ teacherprep)* will provide you with ideas for including parents in your units. Find out more in *Strategies and Methods— Language Arts Methods/Writing.*

Figure 8.28   **Traveling Tales Backpack**

Figure 8.29 Traveling Tales Parent Letter

Dear Parent(s):

Writing activities provided at home can have a great influence on your child's reading and writing development. Traveling Tales is a backpack that includes a variety of writing materials for use by you and your child. As per our conversation, we encourage you to work together cooperatively with your child to create a story that will be shared at school. *Please avoid competition or trying to outdo others.*

Your child has been given this backpack for two nights. If you need more time, please call us at XXX–XXXX. Otherwise, we will be looking forward to you and your child returning the Traveling Tales backpack in two days.

We would like to suggest some guidelines that may help you have a successful and enjoyable Traveling Tales experience with your child.

1. Help your child brainstorm a list of ideas or topics by asking questions that will invite him or her to express ideas, interests, feelings, etc., about which he or she may wish to write. Stories about personal experiences (factual or fictional), information stories that tell of an area that your child finds interesting, biographies of family members or others, and stories of science or history are possible topics.

2. After selecting a topic, help your child decide which of the writing materials included in the Traveling Tales backpack he or she will need to use to create his or her story. Suggest that the story may take several different forms. Some ideas include (1) poetry, (2) fold-out books, (3) puppet plays, (4) pocket books, (5) backward books, and (6) shape books.

3. Help your child think through or rehearse the story before beginning writing. You may wish to write down some of the ideas your child expresses for him or her to use in writing the first draft.

4. Remember, your child's first draft is a rough draft. It may contain misspellings, poor handwriting, and incomplete ideas. This should be expected. Be available to answer questions as your child works on the first draft. Be careful to encourage him or her to keep writing and not worry about spelling, punctuation, etc. Tell him or her to just do his or her best and both of you can work on correctness later. *This is the idea development stage of writing.*

5. Once the first draft is completed, try to involve others in the household by asking them to listen to the first draft read aloud. Reading one's writing aloud helps writers determine the sensibleness of the message. Be sure to tell those who are invited to listen to be encouraging rather than critical. Ask questions about ideas that were unclear or were poorly developed. Questions help a writer think about his or her writing without feeling defensive.

6. Write down the questions and suggestions made by the home audience. Talk with your child about how a second draft could use these suggestions to make the story easier to understand or more exciting. Remember to be supportive and encouraging! Offer your help, but encourage your child to make his or her best efforts first.

7. After the second draft is completed, your child may wish to read his or her writing to the family group again. If so, encourage it. If not, it is time to edit the writing. Now is the time to correct spellings, punctuation, etc. Praise your child for his or her attempts and tell him or her you want to help make his or her writing the best it can be. Show your child which words are misspelled and why. Do the same with punctuation and capitalization.

8. With the editing complete, the writing is ready to be revised for the final time. When your child writes the final draft, encourage him or her to use neat handwriting as a courtesy to the reader. Feel free to help your child at any point as he or she makes final revisions.

9. Once finished, encourage the members of your family or household to listen to the final story. This practice will instill confidence in your child as he or she shares his or her writing at school.

10. We cordially invite you to come to school with your child, if possible, to share the writing you have done together. Your child will appreciate the support, and we would like to talk with you.

Thank you for your help. We appreciate your involvement. If you have an interesting or special experience and are unable to come to school with your child, we would appreciate hearing about these. Please call us or send a note with your child. We will be glad to call back or visit with you. Thanks again for your support. We hope you enjoyed your experiences!

Summary

Writing instruction is an essential part of a comprehensive literacy program. Among numerous benefits, writing shares the same cognitive processes as reading (Shanahan, 2006), helps children crystallize their understanding of important reading skills such as phonics and other word recognition skills (Juel & Minden-Cupp, 2004), and has great power in helping students' deepen procedural knowledge about how to access, use, and generate information (Mason, Herman, & Au, 1991).

In this chapter we saw how writing develops progressing from scribbles and drawing in the early stages to transitional and fluent written communications. Comprehensive writing instruction insures that students learn logical stages of the writing process, and involves both the construction of narrative writing and expository passages in various forms. Thus, students learn the logic of writing conventions used by myriad writers—they become "insiders" in the world of authoring texts. Over time, student-writers begin to read in order to learn how their *author-peers* maneuver the English language to tell a story or expound upon ideas to guide the construction of their own compositions.

Part of our journey through this chapter involved an exploration of the specific writing skills to be learned at each level, and how to assess student knowledge in a real-world classroom. Tools added to our assessment toolboxes included the use of story grammars, rubrics, and the six-trait scoring assessment paradigm. These tools help us to monitor student progress, differentiate instruction by forming small groups according to student needs, and plan "next steps" in instruction.

Once we have gathered initial assessment data on student knowledge in writing the teacher is ready to begin instruction. We learned about the basic stages of the writing process that may be used to author everything from poetry to biographies. We also saw how critical the teacher's role is in modeling the writing process, and in establishing collaborative writing activities such as *Writing Aloud, Writing To; Shared Writing; Interactive Writing Lessons;* and the *Writing Workshop.*

Differentiating instruction is critical if we are to meet the needs of every learner. We saw how Ogle's (1986) popular K-W-L strategy can be modified to better suit content learning through Stead's (2001, 2006) *Reading and Analyzing Nonfiction Strategy* or RAN. Appropriate uses of technology for reaching students with special needs were also explored.

Families also have an important role to play in student learning, as we saw in this chapter on writing. One of the most powerful strategies we have used ourselves, *Traveling Tales Backpacks* (Reutzel & Fawson, 1990; Reutzel & Fawson, 1998; Yellin & Blake, 1994), was described in some detail for your use. Using this and the other evidence-based ideas presented in this chapter can help you create a community of writers in your own classroom!

Classroom Applications

1. This activity is intended for those who are practicing teachers, or teacher education students working closely with a teacher in a practicum experience. We call this activity **"The Investigator."** Assume the role of an investigator to discover and describe resources that are available to teachers for teaching writing at your school. Complete a summary chart for your **investigator's notebook** (it can take any form) showing specific materials of any type (i.e., books, non-print materials, computer-related, etc.) available to *supplement* your writing curriculum. You should search for the following resources that may be available at your school:

    *   Resources available in your **school library**
    *   Resources for accommodating struggling readers and writers
    *   **Graphic organizer** resources
    *   **Computer resources** (hardware and software, as well as on the internet)
    *   Resources to help student with their **written retellings** about new subject-related information.

    Using your summary chart/reporter's notebook, write a brief news article (2–3 double-spaced pages) reporting on what you found. Be sure to include a statement of needs that your principal should consider to help you do your job as a core content teacher. Note: Be sure to attach your summary chart with your news article as backup support.

2. This is an activity for teacher education students OR practicing teachers we call **"Sage on the Stage."** It may be done as a small group activity or individually. Assume the role of a master teacher who is now touring the country conducting three-day seminars for elementary or middle school teachers (you decide). Your task is to develop "real world classroom examples" to illustrate proven assessment OR teaching writing strategies. Do the following:

    a. **Select four writing assessment and/or teaching strategies for your workshop.** These must come from this chapter.
    b. Develop **model examples** you can share with the teachers attending your seminar. Be sure to identify key textbook readings and any supplemental materials you might use.
    c. Create a **list of resources for writing instruction** you could use based on what is available at YOUR school (if you already a teacher) or with a partner school (if you are a teacher education student). This will help you to have an authentic presentation even though school resources may vary.
    d. Develop a **lesson plan or handout** showing how you would implement these strategies in your school day. State clearly *which* writing assessment or teaching strategy you would use and the procedure. Remember, this will be new information for teachers in your seminar, so they will need for you to be *very* specific.

Recommended Readings

Jancoloa, L. (n.d.). *Six-Trait writing*. Retrieved November 3, 2006, from *http://www.kent.k12. wa.us/staff/LindaJancola/6Trait/6-trait.html*

Stead, T. (2001). *Is that a fact? Teaching nonfiction writing K–3*. Portland, ME: Stenhouse.

Online Tool for Teachers

Read Write Think   *http://www.readwritethink.org/*

chapter 9

Assessment

Chapter Questions

1. What are the principles of effective classroom reading assessment?

2. What are the four purposes of classroom reading assessment? What is an example of each?

3. What commercial reading tests are available for classroom use?

4. What is *student* and *classroom profiling*? How is profiling used to form needs-based reading groups?

5. What is meant by "IF–THEN Thinking"?

Great Teaching Begins with Assessment!

When I was in my second year of teaching, I moved to a new school in order to teach third grade—my dream job. The other three third grade teachers at Mt. Juliet Elementary School were smart and welcoming as we began planning for our new year. One problem, they explained, was that we would have almost 120 students and little, if any, assessment information about our students' reading abilities and needs. One teacher asked, "Bob, since you're still fresh from college, what did they teach you about beginning-of-the-year reading assessment?"

I broke into a cold sweat as I wracked my brain for some semblance of an intelligent thought. Then I remembered something. "One thing I have used is an informal reading inventory. It's a published reading test that teachers can use to determine students' overall reading level, how well they comprehend what they read, and how well they deal with phonics and other word attack skills."

"Have you got one with you?" asked Ms. Holden, a veteran teacher whom everyone seemed to admire.

"Yes," I responded, "and I had a chance to use it with quite a few of my fourth grade children last year, and during summer school."

That did it. Before I knew it, my colleagues had elected me to screen *all* third graders at Mt. Juliet Elementary using my trusty informal reading inventory and chart their strengths and needs so that we could plan small-group instruction. (They agreed, as their part of the bargain, to take my students into their classes mornings of the first week of school so that I could test each child one at a time.)

In the end, the plan worked as a starting point for our reading instruction. The data from my initial screening helped us group children according to their reading needs *across* all of our classrooms. This experience was an epiphany for me. I saw first-hand the power assessment gives us to provide every child, from the first days of school, the reading instruction he or she needs.

—RBC

Reading assessment is the tool that informs your teaching. In Chapter 1 we identify classroom reading assessment as one of the "pillars" of effective reading programs. In Chapters 2 through 8 we explain how key assessment strategies are used to plan instruction in such areas as oral language development, phonics, reading comprehension, fluency, and so forth. These assessment strategies help teachers know which reading skills each child already has and which he or she has yet to develop. Assessment happens in effective classrooms before, during, and after instruction has taken place. It is essential for making sure every student receives appropriate instruction, and then verifying that learning has taken place. With the array of data teachers are able to assemble through classroom reading assessment, they are able to analyze and plan "just-in-time" instruction that meets the need of every student.

In this chapter, we add to what you have learned about classroom reading assessment in earlier chapters. The focus here is on the guiding principles of effective reading assessment, school-wide assessment concerns, important assessment terminology for teachers to know, and national issues surrounding reading assessment. We also provide wide-ranging assessment strategies not discussed in earlier chapters, but that are quite useful. Let's begin at the beginning with a brief summary of the governing principles and fundamental purposes of reading assessment.

Principles and Purposes of Reading Assessment

The following **principles of classroom assessment** are intended to help teachers decide which strategies should be adopted to improve their classroom instruction. They are based on our own classroom experiences, current research in the field, and expert opinions expressed to us by successful classroom teachers.

Principle 1: Assessment should inform and improve teaching. When considering whether or not to perform any sort of reading assessment, the teacher should ask, "Will this procedure help me make important instructional decisions regarding my students' reading needs?" The procedure should yield rich insights as to materials and ways of offering instruction (e. g., skills to be learned next, grouping based on student needs, etc.) that can positively affect students' reading growth. The process begins with an understanding of required state standards, and careful survey of what is known about students using available information (home surveys, cumulative records, informal assessments, student self-assessments, and the like).

Next, the teacher forms hypotheses about where each student is in his or her reading development (Bintz, 1991; Flippo, 2003; McKenna & Stahl, 2003; Rathvon, 2004). The task is to select assessment procedures that will help the teacher better understand student abilities and confirm or reject earlier hypotheses. Armed with information obtained from these processes, the teacher teaches lessons aimed at helping the student improve in reading proficiency. Figure 9.1 depicts this assessment–teaching process.

Principle 2: Assessment procedures should help teachers discover what children can *do, not just what they cannot do.* Rather than spending

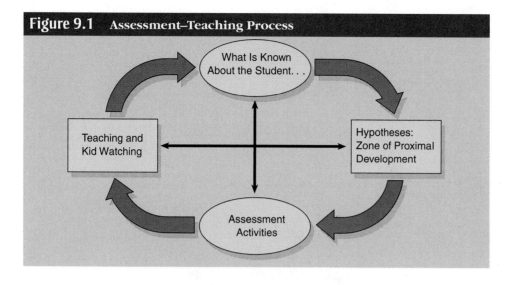

Figure 9.1   Assessment–Teaching Process

precious classroom time trying to identify the myriad skills students *do not* possess, many teachers focus on determining the skills they *do* possess, and then deciding what students are ready for next in reading development, i.e., building on students strengths to help them develop new skills. Once teachers understand student strengths in reading, it becomes much easier to decide which learning experiences should be offered to help them develop further.

Principle 3: Every assessment procedure should have a specific purpose. Sometimes we can fall into the habit of giving reading tests just because they are our "standard operating procedure" rather than selecting assessment activities as an integral part of providing high-quality instruction. For instance, it is common practice in many schools for students identified by their teacher as having reading problems to be given a "battery" of tests (i.e., a preselected set of tests) to discover what the problem seems to be. This one-size-fits-all approach fails to take into account what is already known about the student's reading ability, and the specific *purpose* of the assessment experience (e.g., for diagnosis, for provision of data for progress reports, for information to be given to parents, etc.). We need to enter into student assessment with a clear purpose.

There are Four Purposes of Reading Assessment

Because reading assessment removes children from precious instructional time in the classroom, we should be mindful of the **four purposes of reading assessment.** These purposes, by the way, are embedded in the federal Reading First and No Child Left Behind legislation and are built on principles of valid and reliable measurement (see principle 7 in this list). These purposes are depicted metaphorically in Figure 9.2 as a chalice.

At the open end or broadest part of the chalice, since it involves the whole class, is **outcome assessment.** Outcomes are the results of our reading program in terms

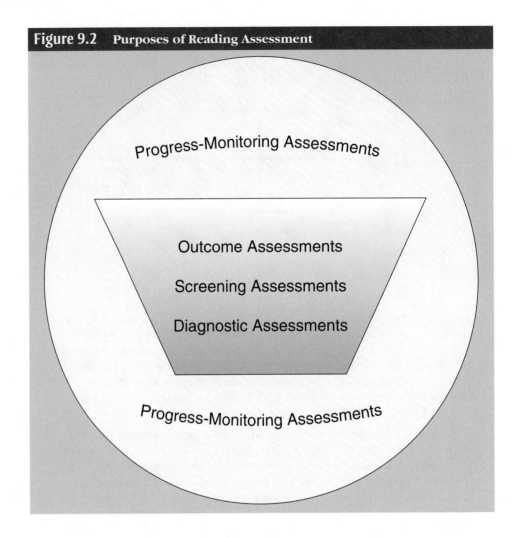

Figure 9.2   Purposes of Reading Assessment

Progress-Monitoring Assessments

Outcome Assessments

Screening Assessments

Diagnostic Assessments

Progress-Monitoring Assessments

of student test scores and other hard data. The main purpose of outcome assessment is to survey the reading achievement of the class as a whole. It provides a snapshot of the reading program's effectiveness when compared to established end-of-year reading benchmarks (standards) for each grade level.

In order for differentiated instruction to occur, the focus of assessment shifts to individual students. **Screening assessments** provide initial information about students' reading development. These assessments should be quick but also provide reliable and valid data. These assessments should help teachers place students into preliminary instructional groups based on their general reading abilities and needs. They provide an especially critical "first look" at students who may be at-risk and in need of special instructional services.

Invariably, teachers notice that some students are having unusual difficulty with tasks during small-group instruction. Parents also might bring their child's reading problem to the teacher's attention. **Diagnostic assessments** provide in-depth information about each student's particular strengths and needs. These assessments are a bit more involved and take longer to administer. Sometimes an educational psychologist, a certified diagnostician, or a bilingual specialist may be needed to administer a diagnostic test because of the time investment involved or because special training is needed. Students requiring special education or who are enrolled in Title I programs for reading often undergo diagnostic testing for initial placement or for retention in the program.

Encircling the chalice in Figure 9.2 are **progress-monitoring assessments.** These are an essential part of every reading teacher's daily plan, which is why they surround all other assessments (and students) represented in the chalice. Progress-monitoring assessments provide ongoing and timely feedback as to how well individual students are responding to teaching, referred to today as **Response to Intervention,** or **RtI.** This allows the teacher to continually reevaluate her or his instruction and make adjustments as needed.

Principle 4: Classroom assessment should be linked to accountability standards *and provide insights into the* process *of reading.* Passage of the No Child Left Behind Act and other state and federal legislation in reading has generated a pervasive emphasis on classroom assessment. **Accountability standards** established by the individual states and professional organizations, such as the International Reading Association (IRA) and the National Council of Teachers of English (NCTE), describe evidence-based reading skills that are typically mastered by the end of each school year. These **benchmark skills** (as they are often referred to) should be monitored on a regular basis.

Principle 5: Assessment procedures should help identify zones of proximal development. In Chapter 2, we discuss Vygotsky's (1962, 1978) notion of a zone of proximal development, or the area of potential growth in reading that can occur with appropriate instruction. To identify students' zones of proximal development, teachers need to determine accurately what children can already do, and thus, which new skills they may be ready to learn next. For example, in a kindergarten or first grade classroom, children who can create story lines for wordless picture books and who have been doing so for some time should be ready for books containing simple and predictable text.

David Mager/Pearson Learning Photo Studio

Principle 6: Assessment should not supplant instruction. State and locally mandated testing sometimes seems to overwhelm teachers and take over the classroom. In Texas, for example, a state that has had high-stakes testing since the early 1980s, many principals complained to us that some teachers virtually stop teaching from January until April in order to drill students on practice tests. If a teacher loses sight of the purpose of classroom assessment—to inform and influence instruction—then he or she may well move into the role of teacher as manager rather than teacher as teacher (Pearson, 1985). The assessment program should complement the instructional program and grow naturally from it.

Principle 7: Effective classroom assessment makes use of both valid and reliable *instruments.* Although master teachers are comfortable using many informal assessment processes to gather information about students' reading progress, instruments that possess validity and reliability evidence are sometimes necessary. These assessment tools give teachers consistent and trustworthy feedback for adapting or modifying their teaching to meet individual needs.

Reliability evidence demonstrates whether student performance will be measured in a stable and consistent manner (Jennings, Caldwell, & Lerner, 2006). In other words, a reliable test is one that provides the same results for the same children with repeated testing no matter who administered the test. Reliability is reported numerically with a coefficient (a perfect reliability score for a test would be 1.0). Salvia and Ysseldyke (2004) believe that if a test is used for screening it should have a reliability of 0.80 or better. If a test is to be used for decisions about individual students, such as placement in Title I or special education, the test's reliability should be 0.90 or higher.

Measures of **validity** indicate the degree to which tests measure what their developers claim they measure (Jennings, Caldwell, & Lerner, 2006). If a test measures reading, then it should measure the complete reading act, or at least the area of reading specified by the test-makers (e.g., phonics, reading comprehension), not some other skill, ability, or construct.

The Reliability-Validity Caveat

Though the selection of reading tests that are both reliable and valid is our goal, finding one that meets our highest standards in each category is problematic. There is an important caveat commonly understood in assessment circles (Cooter, 1990): *As test reliability increases, validity usually decreases, and vice versa.* For example, informal reading inventories (IRIs) are widely used and respected as *valid* measures of reading ability, but they are also notorious for being rather unreliable (i.e., two teachers giving an IRI to the same child can come to substantially different conclusions about the student's reading needs). Conversely, the *Stanford Diagnostic Reading Test* (SDRT) is considered to be a very reliable test, but not very valid (i.e., the multiple-choice format for measuring reading comprehension is very *unlike* normal reading behavior). A number of tests are now available that report both validity and reliability estimates, but you will discover that the validity-reliability caveat is evident: if the test is high in reliability, it is probably weak in the validity department, or vice versa.

How does a teacher overcome the validity-reliability caveat? You will need to develop a *comprehensive* approach to reading assessment, one that includes some tests and procedures that are extremely valid and others that are highly reliable.

Where Do We Begin? A Classroom Teacher's Perspective

In the remainder of this chapter we take a closer look at reading assessment, adding special reading assessment strategies to those presented in Chapters 2 through 8. It seems logical to us that we should start with the kinds of assessments you might use every day. Screening assessments useful for the first days and weeks of school and progress-monitoring assessments used daily to check the effectiveness of your teaching are the daily bread and butter assessment tasks you will use to validate teaching and learning. Because these assessments—screening and progress-monitoring—may be used more or less interchangeably, we group them together in the upcoming sections. How will you know which assessment tool is best for screening or progress-monitoring? Not to worry. Early in the next section we provide you with a handy chart that helps you decide.

Screening and Progress-Monitoring Assessments

Screening Assessments

The first day of school is always magical. It is a day filled with hope, expectation, and, for some, even fear. Your young charges walk slowly into your classroom— some tall and gangly, some short, some smiling, some moving very cautiously. It is the day when you begin to establish classroom management routines and get to know each student a little. It is also the day they begin to form opinions about *you!*

The first week of school should include a basketweave of assessment activities that are quick and efficient and that yield a lot of important information about reading. They should also be pleasant and nonthreatening, since some of your students will have had repeated experience with failure and you don't want to lose them.

It is essential to use screening assessments during the first days of school, or for students who come to you after the school year has begun. These assessments are easy to administer and yield extremely useful information. You may actually decide to use many of these same tools for progress-monitoring.

> **Getting to Know English Learners**
> Often, necessary screening assessments are conducted for you by the ESL teacher in your school or district, as required by law. ELs, unlike students with special needs, do not have IEPs, so be prepared to ask your ESL teacher to help plan an appropriate reading/writing program for your ELs.

Progress-Monitoring in the Reading Classroom

Progress-monitoring is an essential part of teaching. As you learn more about your students, you plan instruction that you believe will best meet their needs. In essence, you try to find the zone of proximal development for each reading skill area for each student—not a simple task. Thus, as you offer targeted instruction in small groups, you constantly reassess each student's growth to see if learning is occurring and then tailor your instruction based on what you discover.

So, how do you decide which of the tests or strategies that follow in this section should be used, either for screening or progress-monitoring? In Figure 9.3 we offer a kind of "IF–THEN" chart to help you choose. IF–THEN Thinking works like this: IF you have a particular need that is represented by one of the assessments listed along the left-hand column, THEN you determine the particular test or assessment

Teachers can use checklists to document observations in oral and silent reading. Find examples as you visit the Teacher Prep Website (www.prenhall.com/teacherprep) in *Strategies and Lessons— Reading Methods/Reading Assessment*. Read "Diagnostic Checklists".

Figure 9.3 Selected Screening and Progress-Monitoring Assessment Strategies

	Appropriate for SCREENING? (First days/weeks)	Appropriate for PROGRESS-MONITORING?
CATEGORY: Interests and Self-Perception		
Comprehensive Reading Inventory	YES	NO
Burke Interview	YES	YES
Self-Rating Scale–Subject Areas	YES	YES
Background Knowledge	YES	YES
Family Survey	YES	NO
Kid-Watching	NO	YES
Screening Checklists	YES	YES
Concepts About Print	YES	YES (for emergent readers only)
CATEGORY: Phonemic Awareness (PA) and Alphabet Knowledge (AK)		
PA- Recogn. Rhyming Words	YES (in small groups)	YES
PA- Oddity Task	YES (in small groups)	YES
PA- Same-Different Word Pairs	YES (in small groups)	YES
PA- Syllables and Counting Syll.	YES (in small groups)	YES
PA- Auditory Sound Blending	YES (in small groups)	YES
PA- Segmenting Sounds	YES (in small groups)	YES
AK- Alphabet Identification	YES (in small groups)	YES
AK- Letter Production	YES (in small groups)	YES
CATEGORY: Decoding and Word Attack		
Running Records	YES (first three weeks)	YES
CATEGORY: Vocabulary		
Oral Reading Assessment	NO	YES
Vocabulary Flash Cards	YES	YES
CATEGORY: Comprehension		
Questioning (Bloom)	YES	YES (use mainly higher levels)
Retelling–Story Grammars (Oral)	YES (in small groups)	YES
Retelling–Using Graphic Organizers	YES (in small groups)	YES
Retelling–Written Summaries	NO	YES
Expository Text Frames	YES (in small groups)	YES
Cloze	YES	YES
Maze	YES	YES
Content Area Reading Inventory (CARI)	YES (in small groups)	YES
CATEGORY: Fluency		
Multidimensional Fluency Scale (MFS)	YES (in small groups)	YES
Rubric for evaluation	NO	YES
CATEGORY: Commercial Tools		
Informal reading inventories	YES (in first three weeks)	YES (quarterly)
Curriculum-based measurements (CBM)	YES (in first month)	YES (quarterly)

strategy that is appropriate for screening or progress-monitoring by checking the appropriate row to the right. Following Figure 9.3 is a detailed description of many of these strategies (others may be found in Chapters 2–8). Let's get started!

Kid Watching

For many teachers, the most basic assessment strategy is systematic observation of children engaged in the reading act, or **kid watching.** Clay, in her classic book *The Early Detection of Reading Difficulties* (1985), explains her philosophy concerning observations:

> I am looking for movement in appropriate directions. . . . For if I do not watch what [the student] is doing, and if I do not capture what is happening in records of some kind, Johnny, who never gets under my feet and who never comes really into a situation where I can truly see what he is doing, may, in fact, for six months or even a year, practice behaviours that will handicap him in reading. (p. 49)

Observation and systematic data collection during observation are critical tool at the teacher's disposal for the early assessment of students and their abilities.

But Do You Know **What** *to Look For?* One semester a young student teacher was busily making anecdotal notes on a clipboard as she watched second graders working away. The students were engaged in activities such as reading, planning writing projects, working at a computer station, listening to books on tape while following along in small books, and several other reading-learning tasks. When the student teacher was asked by the visiting college supervisor what she was working on, she said, "I'm trying to figure out where the children are in their reading development." The supervisor responded, "That's great! How do you know what to watch for?" The student teacher appeared bewildered, so the supervisor said, "If you have time later, I'd like to share with you information about reading milestones. They are observable learning stages that can be noted as part of your assessment profiling system." The student teacher quickly accepted the offer and welcomed the information enthusiastically.

To be an effective "kid watcher," you must gain an understanding of end-of-year benchmark reading skills (Cooter, 2003), or the reading milestones through which children grow. Knowing which of these skills students have and have not acquired will help you construct a classroom profile and plan whole-class, small-group, and individualized instruction. We have provided benchmark skills by grade level in Chapters 2 through 8 in the sections titled "Classroom Assessment" to assist you with your kid-watching. Most state departments of education also have a listing of reading and language arts skills that should be learned by grade level. The effective teacher will have a copy of his or her state's reading standards (benchmarks) and use it to monitor the full range of readers he or she is likely to have in his or her classroom. (Note: State standards are provided online on the Web page for each state's department of education. You can link to your own state's standards from the Teacher Prep site that accompanies this text.)

Assessing Reading Interests and Self-Perception

On the most basic level, we need to know what kinds of books and materials will be of interest to our students. This helps us choose (or avoid) certain topics of interest for small-group instruction, as interest can have a powerful effect on student reading performance (Guthrie, Hoa, Wigfield, Tonks, & Perencevich, 2006). We also want to be sure and ask the obvious question: Are you a good reader? Why?

Students and teachers monitor reading progress through the use of observation checklists. Read "Monitoring Reading Progress" on the Teacher Prep Website (*www.prenhall.com/teacherprep*). Select *Strategies and Lessons—Reading Methods/Reading Assessment* to access this article with examples.

Video Classroom

Look at Classroom Assessment

Observe a teacher initiating teaching strategies that allow her to assess comprehension on the CD that accompanies this text. View this example by selecting *Guided Reading in Second Grade* to select "Repeat Patterns," "Summarize-Understand" and "Real World Connections." Be sure to read the comments shared beneath the video box. The "Teacher" comments provide an explanation of her teaching and organizational strategies.

- As you view each segment, watch for examples where the teacher is informally assessing individual and class understanding of the big book and real world connections.
- "Think-Pair-Share," small groups, and a "T-Party" allow students to actively engage in conversation. How do these provide her with opportunities to assess?
- Find an example of student self-assessment as you view the segments.
- How is the use of graphic organizers used to inform her of student comprehension?

In this section, we share some essential tools for screening students in the areas of interest and self-perception.

Attitude/Interest Inventories. Getting to know students is critical if the teacher is to have insights into their background knowledge and oral language abilities. It is also useful in selecting reading materials that will be of interest to students. An interest inventory that is administered either one-to-one or in small groups is a great tool for getting to know students. However, there are many inventories from which you can choose, and all interest inventories are not created equally. Further, not all questions on the inventory can tell you what is helpful in choosing appropriate reading materials for instruction.

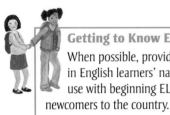

Getting to Know English Learners

When possible, provide all these forms in English learners' native languages for use with beginning EL students and newcomers to the country.

Figures 9.4 and 9.5 feature two interest inventories developed by Flynt and Cooter (2004) that we find to be helpful. The primary form is appropriate for students in kindergarten through grade 2, and the upper-level form is to be used with students from grade 3 and above.

The Burke Reading Interview. The *Burke Reading Interview* (Burke, 1987) provides some initial insights into how students see themselves as readers and the reading task in general. The following questions have been adapted from the Burke procedure:

1. When you are reading and come to a word you don't know, what do you do? What else can you do?
2. Which of your friends is a good reader? What makes him/her a good reader?
3. Do you think your teacher ever comes to a word she doesn't know when reading? What do you think she does when that happens?
4. If you knew that one of your friends was having problems with his or her reading, what could you tell your friend that would help?

Figure 9.4 The Flynt–Cooter Interest Inventory: Primary Form

PRIMARY FORM

Student's Name _____ Age _____

Date _____ Examiner _____

Introductory Statement: *[Student's name], before you read some stories for me, I would like to ask you some questions.*

Home Life

1. Where do you live? Do you know your address? What is it?

2. Who lives in your house with you?

3. What kinds of jobs do you have at home?

4. What is one thing that you really like to do at home?

5. Do you ever read at home? [*If yes, ask:*] When do you read and what was the last thing you read? [*If no, ask:*] Does anyone ever read to you? [*If so, ask:*] Who, and how often?

6. Do you have a bedtime on school nights? [*If no, ask:*] When do you go to bed?

7. Do you have a TV in your room? How much TV do you watch every day? What are your favorite shows?

8. What do you like to do with your friends?

9. Do you have any pets? Do you collect things? Do you take any kinds of lessons?

10. When you make a new friend, what is something that your friend ought to know about you?

School Life

1. Besides recess and lunch, what do you like about school?

2. Do you get to read much in school?

3. Are you a good reader or a not-so-good reader?

   [*If a good reader, ask:*] What makes a person a good reader?

   [*If a not-so-good reader, ask:*] What causes a person to not be a good reader?

4. If you could pick any book to read, what would the book be about?

5. Do you like to write? What kind of writing do you do in school? What is the favorite thing you have written about?

6. Who has helped you the most in school? How did that person help you?

7. Do you have a place at home to study?

8. Do you get help with your homework? Who helps you?

9. What was the last book you read for school?

10. If you were helping someone learn to read, what could you do to help that person?

Figure 9.5 The Flynt–Cooter Interest Inventory: Upper Level Form*

UPPER LEVEL FORM

Student's Name _____ Age _____

Date _____ Examiner _____

Introductory Statement: *[Student's name], before you read some stories for me, I would like to ask you some questions.*

Home Life

1. How many people are there in your family?

2. Do you have your own room or do you share a room? [*Ask this only if it is apparent that the student has siblings.*]

3. Do your parent(s) work? What kinds of jobs do they have?

4. Do you have jobs around the house? What are they?

5. What do you usually do after school?

6. Do you have a TV in your room? How much time do you spend watching TV each day? What are your favorite shows?

7. Do you have a bedtime during the week? What time do you usually go to bed on a school night?

8. Do you get an allowance? How much?

9. Do you belong to any clubs at school or outside school? What are they?

10. What are some things that you really like to do? Do you collect things, have any hobbies, or take lessons outside school?

School Environment

1. Do you like school? What is your favorite class? Your least favorite class?

2. Do you have a special place to study at home?

3. How much homework do you have on a typical school night? Does anyone help you with your homework? Who?

4. Do you consider yourself a good reader or a not-so-good reader?

   [*If a good reader, ask:*] What has helped you most to become a good reader?

   [*If a not-so-good reader, ask:*] What causes someone to be a not-so-good reader?

5. If I gave you the choice of selecting a book about any topic, what would you choose to read about?

6. What is one thing you can think of that would help you become a better reader? Is there anything else?

7. Do you like to write? What kind of writing assignments do you like best?

8. If you went to a new school, what is one thing that you would want the teachers to know about you as a student?

9. If you were helping someone learn to read, what would be the most important thing you could do to help that person?

10. How will knowing how to read help you in the future?

*From: Flynt, E. S., & Cooter, R. B. (2004). *The Flynt/Cooter Reading Inventory for the Classroom* (5th ed). Upper Saddle River, NJ: Merrill/Prentice Hall. ISBN: 0-13-112106-5. Used with permission.

Table 9.1 Class Interests Profile Sorting Table

Student Names	Q1	Q2						

5. How would a teacher help your friend with reading problems?
6. How do you think you learned to read?
7. Are you a good reader?
8. What would you like to be able to do better as a reader?

Sorting Out Student Interests. After you have collected student responses to the *Flynt/Cooter Interest Inventory,* create a grid for your class like the one shown in Table 9.1. List student names along the left hand column, and question numbers along the top row (i.e., "Q1" for question number 1, "Q2" for question number 2, and so on). You may decide that some questions provide more information than others; if so, only list the numbers you plan to survey.

After the entire class has been surveyed, compile the individual responses into a class profile. Record abbreviated answers to each question for each student in the class interests profile. Look over the responses to each question by all of the children for categories of interests to be observed in your teaching and for choosing reading materials. Make any changes on the class profile sheet you discover throughout the year. This updated information about your students' reading interests will help you adjust your selection of topics and reading materials as the year progresses.

Self-Rating Scales for Subject Area Reading

No one knows better than the reader how he or she is doing in reading. A teacher carrying out an assessment agenda should never overlook the obvious: Ask kids how they're doing! Although this is best achieved in a one-to-one discussion setting, large class sizes frequently make it a prohibitive practice. A good alternative to one-to-one interviews for older elementary children is a student self-rating scale, in which students complete a questionnaire tailored to obtain specific information about the reader from the reader's point of view. One example is illustrated in Figure 9.6 for a teacher interested in reading and study strategies used with social studies readings. Whichever reading skills are to be surveyed, remember to keep self-rating scales focused and brief.

Assessing Background Knowledge

Children's background knowledge and experiences are among the most important contributors (or inhibitors) of comprehension. Researchers have determined that students who possess a great deal of background information about a subject tend to recall greater amounts of information more accurately from reading than do students with little or no background knowledge (Carr & Thompson, 1996; Pearson, Hansen, & Gordon,

Self-assessment, of appropriate work habits, helps students to monitor themselves. An example is shown on the Teacher Prep Website (*www.prenhall. com/teacherprep*) under *Artifacts*. Select *Assessment—Informal Classroom Assessment* to find "Work Habits Ratings." You may respond to the accompanying questions and print or send them directly to your instructor.

Results of formal and informal assessments can be shared with parents. View an example of a report in the *Artifacts* section of the Teacher Prep Website (*www. prenhall.com/teacherprep*). Select *Assessment—Informal Classroom Assessment* for review and response to "Group Participation and Work Habits." A copy of your responses may be printed or sent to your instructor.

Figure 9.6   Self-Rating Scale: Reading Social Studies

Reading Social Studies

Name _____ Date _____

1. The first three things I usually do when I begin reading a chapter in social studies are (number 1, 2, 3):

   _____ Look at the pictures.

   _____ Read the chapter through one time silently.

   _____ Look at the new terms and definitions.

   _____ Read the questions at the end of the chapter.

   _____ Read the first paragraph or introduction.

   _____ Skip around and read the most interesting parts.

   _____ Skim the chapter.

   _____ Preview the chapter.

2. What is hardest for me about social studies is . . .

3. The easiest thing about social studies is . . .

4. The thing(s) I like best about reading social studies is (are) . . .

Getting to Know English Learners
Background knowledge and experience may vary widely with an EL's linguistic and cultural background and may include often overlooked important facts like whether or not the EL came from a rural or urban setting.

1979; Pressley, 2000). It is also a well-known fact that well-developed background information can inhibit the comprehension of new information that conflicts with or refutes prior knowledge and assumptions about a specific topic. Thus, knowing how much knowledge a reader has about a concept or topic can help teachers better prepare students to read and comprehend successfully. One way that teachers can assess background knowledge and experience is to use a procedure developed by Langer (1982) for assessing the amount and content of students' background knowledge about selected topics, themes, concepts, and events.

Here's the procedure you will follow. Select a story for students to read. Construct a list of specific vocabulary terms or story concepts related to the topic, message, theme, or events to be experienced in reading the story. For example, you might have students read the story *Stone Fox* by John R. Gardiner (1980), which is about a boy named Willy who saves his grandfather's farm from the tax collector. Construct a list of five to ten specific vocabulary terms or concepts related to the story, such as those presented here:

broke

taxes

tax collector

dogsled race

samoyeds

Figure 9.7 Checklist of Levels of Prior Knowledge

Phrase 1   What comes to mind when . . . ?
Phrase 2   What made you think of . . . ?
Phrase 3   Have you any new ideas about . . . ?

Stimulus used to elicit student background knowledge _____
(Picture, word, or phrase etc.)

Much (3)	Some (2)	Little (1)
category labels	examples	personal associations
definitions	attributes	morphemes
analogies	defining characteristics	sound alikes
relationships		personal experiences

Student name

Maria		X	
Jawan	X		

Source: Reutzel, D. R., & Cooter, R. B. (2007). *Strategies for Reading Assessment and Instruction: Helping Every Child Succeed,* (3rd ed.). Upper Saddle River, NJ: Merrill/Prentice Hall. Used with permission.

Ask students to respond to each of these terms in writing or through discussion. This is accomplished by using one of several stem statements (see Figure 9.7) such as, "What comes to mind when you think of paying bills and you hear the word *broke?* Once students have responded to each of the terms, score responses to survey the class's knowledge (Figure 9.7). Assign the number of points that most closely represents the level of prior knowledge in the response is used to score each item. Divide the total score by the number of terms or concepts in the list to determine the average knowledge level of individual students. Compare these average scores against the Checklist of Levels of Prior Knowledge in Figure 9.7 for each student. By scanning the Xs in the checklist, you can get a sense of the entire class's overall level of prior knowledge. You can easily use information thus gathered to inform both the content and nature of your whole-group comprehension instruction.

Family Surveys of Reading Habits

We recently observed a friend of ours who has a heart condition going through his normal daily activities with a small radio-like device attached to his belt. When asked what this gadget was, he indicated that it was a heart monitor. He went on to say that the device constantly measured his heart rate for an entire day to provide the doctor with a reliable account of his normal heart rhythms in the real world of daily activity.

Traditional reading assessment has often failed to give teachers such a "real-world" look at students' reading ability by restricting the assessment to school settings. So the question posed here is, "How do we acquire information about a student's reading habits and abilities

Getting to Know English Learners
Again, where possible, provide the family surveys in the native language of the ELs' parents or have local translators help you make phone calls to the home where you can then conduct the home survey information orally.

Figure 9.8   Family Survey

September 6, 200____

Dear Adult Family Member:

    As we begin the new school year, I would like to know a little more about your child's reading habits at home. This information will help me provide the best possible learning plan for your child this year. Please take a few minutes to answer the questions below and return in the self-addressed stamped envelope provided. Should you have any questions, feel free to phone me at XXX–XXXX.

Cordially,

Mrs. Shelley

_____

1. My child likes to read the following at least once a week (check all that apply):

Comic books _____   Sports page _____

Magazines (example: *Highlights*) _____   Library books _____

Cereal boxes _____   Cooking recipes _____

T.V. Guide _____   Funny papers _____

Others (please name):

2. Have you noticed your child having any reading problems? If so, please explain briefly.

3. What are some of your child's favorite books?

4. If you would like a conference to discuss your child's reading ability, please indicate which days and times (after school) would be most convenient.

away from the somewhat artificial environment of the school?" One way is to assess what is happening in the home using family surveys.

    Family surveys are brief questionnaires (too long and they'll never be answered!) sent to adult family members periodically to maintain communication between the home and school. They also remind parents of the importance of reading in the home to support and encourage reading growth. When taken into consideration with other assessment evidence from the classroom, family surveys enable teachers to develop a more accurate profile of the child's reading ability. An example of a family survey is provided in Figure 9.8.

Screening Checklists and Scales

Teachers often create their own screening checklists using the reading benchmarks for their grade level. Lamme and Hysmith (1991) developed a scale that can be used to identify key developmental behaviors in emergent readers. It describes 11 levels often seen in the elementary school and can be used in tandem with the much more comprehensive reading benchmarks previously discussed. Following is an adaptation of that scale:

Level 11: The student can read fluently from books and other reading materials.

Level 10: The student seeks out new sources of information. He or she volunteers to share information from books with other children.

Level 9: The student has developed the ability to independently use context clues, sentence structure, structural analysis, and phonic analysis to read new passages.

Level 8: The student reads unfamiliar stories haltingly (not fluently), but requires little adult assistance.

Level 7: The student reads familiar stories fluently.

Level 6: The student reads word-by-word. He or she recognizes words in a new context.

Level 5: The student memorizes text and can pretend to "read" a story.

Level 4: The student participates in reading by doing such things as supplying words that rhyme and predictable text.

Level 3: The student talks about or describes pictures. He or she pretends to read (storytelling). He or she makes up words that go along with pictures.

Level 2: The student watches pictures as an adult reads a story.

Level 1: The student listens to a story but does not look at the pictures.

Many teachers find that checklists that include a **Likert scale** (a five-point scale) can be useful in student portfolios because many reading behaviors become more fluent over time. One example, developed by Deborah Diffily (1994), is shown in Figure 9.9.

Assessing Students' Reading of Nonfiction Texts

The key to effective expository (i.e., nonfiction) text instruction lies in the accurate identification of the types of nonfiction texts that students are able to read effectively, as well as the forms of expository writing that are difficult for them to comprehend. We have discovered that several rather common forms of reading assessment are easily adaptable to expository texts and can help teachers plan instruction. Offered in this section are some examples of each for your consideration.

Expository Text Frames. **Expository text frames** are useful in identifying types of expository text patterns that may be troublesome for students. Based on the "story frames" concept (Fowler, 1982; Nichols, 1980), expository text frames are completed by the student after reading an expository passage. Instruction can be focused much more precisely, based on student needs, as a result of this procedure.

To develop your own expository text frames for classroom assessment, you will need a reading selection from the adopted content textbook, a personal

Figure 9.9   Diffily's Classroom Observation Checklist

Student's Name _____   Date _____

Literacy Development Checklist

	Seldom				Often
Chooses books for personal enjoyment	1	2	3	4	5
Knows print/picture difference	1	2	3	4	5
Knows print is read from left to right	1	2	3	4	5
Asks to be read to	1	2	3	4	5
Asks that story be read again	1	2	3	4	5
Listens attentively during story time	1	2	3	4	5
Knows what a title is	1	2	3	4	5
Knows what an author is	1	2	3	4	5
Knows what an illustrator is	1	2	3	4	5
In retellings, repeats 2+ details	1	2	3	4	5
Tells beginning, middle, end	1	2	3	4	5
Can read logos	1	2	3	4	5
Uses text in functional ways	1	2	3	4	5
"Reads" familiar books to self/others	1	2	3	4	5
Can read personal words	1	2	3	4	5
Can read sight words from books	1	2	3	4	5
Willing to "write"	1	2	3	4	5
Willing to "read" personal story	1	2	3	4	5
Willing to dictate story to adult	1	2	3	4	5

Gratefully used by the authors with the permission of Deborah Diffily, Ph.D., Alice Carlson, Applied Learning Center, Ft. Worth, TX.

Figure 9.10   Expository Text Frames: Description

Decimals are another way to write fractions when _____
_____
_____
_____

Source: Reutzel, D. Ray; & Cooter, R. B. (2007). *Strategies for Reading Assessment and Instruction: Helping Every Child Succeed,* (3rd ed.). Upper Saddle River, NJ: Merrill/Prentice Hall. Used with permission.

computer, and a printer or photocopier. Abbreviated examples of expository text frames for each of the primary expository text patterns are shown in Figures 9.10 through 9.14.

Before asking students to read the targeted selection, list the major vocabulary and concepts. Discuss what students already know about the topic and display it on the chalkboard or on chart paper. Next, have students read an expository selection

Figure 9.11   Expository Text Frames: Collection*

Water Habitats

Freshwater habitats are found in _____, _____, _____, and rivers. Each freshwater habitat has special kinds of _____ and _____ that live there. Some plants and animals live in waters that are very _____. Others live in waters that are _____. Some plants and animals adapt to waters that flow _____.

Figure 9.12   Expository Text Frames: Causation*

America Enters the War

On Sunday, December 7, 1941, World War II came to the United States. The entry of the United States into World War II was triggered by _____. Roosevelt said that it was a day that would "live in Infamy." *Infamy* (IN·fuh·mee) means remembered for being evil.

Figure 9.13   Expository Text Frames: Problem/Solution*

Agreement by Compromise
Events that led to the Civil War

For a while there were an equal number of Southern and Northern states. That meant that there were just as many senators in Congress from slave states as from free states. Neither had more votes in the Senate, so they usually reached agreement on new laws by compromise. One way that the balance of power was maintained in Congress was _____

_____.

Figure 9.14   Expository Text Frames: Comparison*

Segregation

Many people said that the segregation laws were unfair. But in 1896, the Supreme Court ruled segregation legal if _____

_____. "Separate but equal" became the law in many parts of the country.

But separate was not equal. One of the most serious problems was education. Black parents felt _____

_____. Sometimes the segregated schools had teachers who were not _____ as teachers in the white schools. Textbooks were often _____ if they had any books at all. But in many of the white schools the books were _____. Without a good education the blacks argued their children would not be able to get good jobs as adults.

* *Source:* Reutzel, D. Ray; & Cooter, R. B. (2007). *Strategies for Reading Assessment and Instruction: Helping Every Child Succeed,* (3rd ed.). Upper Saddle River, NJ: Merrill/Prentice Hall. Used with permission.

similar to the one you will ask them to read in class. Once the passage has been read, model the process for completing expository text frames using examples. Finally, have students read the actual selection for the unit of study and complete the expository text frame(s) you have prepared for this passage.

Content Area Reading Inventory (CARI). A **content area reading inventory (CARI)** (Farr, Tully, & Pritchard, 1989; Readence, Bean, & Baldwin, 1992) is a teacher-made informal reading inventory used to assess whether students have learned sufficient reading/study strategies to succeed with content materials. Constructing a CARI can be quite time consuming, but is well worth the effort.

A CARI can be administered to groups of students, and typically includes three major sections (Farr et al., 1989) that assess the following:

- Student knowledge of and ability to use common textbook components (i.e., table of contents, glossary, index) and supplemental research aids (card catalog, reference books, periodicals)
- Student knowledge of important vocabulary and skills such as context clues
- Comprehension skills important to understanding expository texts

For the last two sections of a CARI assessment, students are asked to read a selection from the adopted text. Readence et al. (1992) suggest contents of a CARI assessment.

Suggestions for Content in a CARI

Part I: Textual Reading/Study Aids

1. Internal aids
2. Table of contents
3. Index
4. Glossary
5. Chapter introduction/summary
6. Information from pictures
7. Other aids included in the text
8. Supplemental research aids
9. Online card catalog searches
10. Periodicals
11. Encyclopedias
12. Other relevant resources that lead students to access additional information related to the content (e.g., online search engines like Google.com, video libraries, online university periodicals)

Part II: Vocabulary Knowledge

1. Knowledge and recall of relevant vocabulary
2. Use of context clues

Part III: Comprehension Skills and Strategies

1. Text-explicit (literal) information
2. Text-implicit (inferred) information
3. Knowledge of text structures and related strategies

To develop a CARI, follow this process.

Step 1: Choose a passage of at least three to four pages from the textbook(s) to be used. The passage selected should represent the typical writing style of the author.

Step 2: Construct about 20 questions related to the text. Readence et al. (1992) recommend eight to ten questions for Part I, four to six questions for Part II, and seven to nine questions for Part III. We urge the use of questions based on writing patterns used in the sample selection; they should reflect the facts, concepts, and generalizations in the selection.

Step 3: Explain to students that the CARI is not used for grading purposes, but is useful for planning teaching activities that will help them succeed. Be sure to walk students through the different sections of the CARI and model appropriate responses.

Step 4: Administer Part I first, then Parts II and III on separate day(s). It may take several sessions to work through a CARI. We recommend devoting only about 20 minutes per day to administering parts of a CARI so that other class needs are not ignored during the assessment phase.

Readence et al. (1992) suggest the following criteria for assessing the CARI.

Percent Correct	**Text Difficulty**
86%–100%	Easy reading
64%–85%	Adequate for instruction
63% or below	Too difficult

From careful analysis of this assessment, teachers can plan special lessons to help students cope with difficult readings and internalize important information. Students can be grouped according to need for these lessons and practice strategies leading to success.

Published Reading Tests for Screening and Progress-Monitoring Assessments

A number of products are available commercially to help teachers survey their students. While these may be helpful, they can also be somewhat expensive. In this section, we present products that have been useful in our own classroom practices and meet with our general approval. We begin with the most valid of them all, informal reading inventories, or IRIs.

Informal Reading Inventory

The **informal reading inventory** (IRI) is an individually administered test (though some can be given to groups of children), and often has graded word lists and story passages. The IRI is one of the best tools for observing and analyzing reading performance and for gathering information about how a student uses a wide range of reading strategies (Jennings, Caldwell, & Lerner, 2006). Emmett A. Betts is generally considered to be the first developer of the IRI; however, several other individuals contributed to its development as far back as the early 1900s (Johns & Lunn, 1983).

The Teacher's Guide to Reading Tests (Cooter, 1990) lists several advantages and unique features of IRIs that help explain why teachers continue to find them useful.

One benefit is IRIs provide authentic assessments of the reading act: (i.e., an IRI more closely resembles real reading). Students are better able to "put it all together" by reading whole stories or passages. Another advantage of IRIs is that they usually provide a systematic procedure for studying student miscues or reading errors.

IRIs are rather unusual when compared to other commercial reading tests. First, because they are "informal" most IRIs do not offer norms, reliability data, or validity information, though a few have begun offering validation information in recent years (see *The Comprehensive Reading Inventory* later in this chapter). Second, IRIs are unusual (in a positive way) because they provide a great deal of information that is helpful to teachers in making curricular decisions, especially teachers who place students into needs-based or guided reading groups (Fountas & Pinnell, 1996). IRIs supply an estimate of each child's ability in graded or "leveled" reading materials, such as basal readers and books used for guided reading. IRIs usually offer student performance data in several key areas of reading: word identification via a running record (see Chapter 4 for details about running records), passage comprehension, and reading fluency.

IRIs tend to be somewhat different from each other. Beyond the usual graded word lists and reading passages, IRIs vary a great deal in the subtests offered (e.g., silent reading passages, phonics, interest inventories, concepts about print, phonemic awareness, auditory discrimination) and in the scoring criteria used to interpret reading miscues. Some argue (us included) that the best IRIs are those constructed by classroom teachers themselves using reading materials from their own classrooms. Several examples of IRIs now used in many school systems follow:

- *The Comprehensive Reading Inventory: Measuring Reading Development in Regular and Special Education Classrooms (CRI)* (R. Cooter, Flynt, E.S., & Cooter, K.S., 2007) is a modern version of the traditional IRI concept, and has both English and Spanish forms under one cover. The authors apply National Reading Panel (2000) and other more recent research on "alphabetics" (i. e., phonemic awareness, letter-naming, phonics, etc.), vocabulary knowledge, comprehension processes, running records, fluency, and miscue analysis into an effective authentic reading assessment.

  Unlike most commercial IRIs on the market today, the *CRI* also includes validity and reliability data, a feature required by many states for tax-supported adoption by school districts. The authors include such research-based procedures as unaided/aided recall and story grammar comprehension evaluation, high-interest selections, appropriate length passages, both expository and narrative passages, and a time-efficient miscue grid system for quick analyses of running records.

- *Developmental Reading Assessment (DRA)* (Beaver, 2001). An informal reading inventory offering graded reading passages for students to read, rubrics for evaluating students' oral reading, and a handy box in which to store student portfolios.

- *The English * Español Reading Inventory* (Flynt & Cooter, 1999). This easy-to-use tool offers complete informal reading inventories for pre-kindergarten through grade 12 students in both Spanish and English. The Spanish passages were carefully developed and field-tested with the aid of native Spanish-speaking teacher-researchers from the United States, Mexico, and Central and South America to avoid problems with dialect differences and to maximize their usefulness in United States classrooms.

Curriculum-Based Measurement

Curriculum-based measurement (CBM) is a tool for measuring student skill development in the areas of reading fluency, spelling, math, and written language. CBM uses "probes" developed from each school district's curriculum; thus, it measures what students are taught.

Curriculum-based measurement looks at three different areas that pertain to reading.

- Reading fluency measures how many words a student correctly reads in one minute. In practice, three reading probes are given and the middle or median score is reported.
- The spelling measure presents 10 words (at first grade) or 17 words (second through fifth grades). Spelling lists are scored for words spelled correctly.
- For the written expression task, students are presented with a story starter and given three minutes to write a story. Student work is scored for total words written, words spelled correctly, and correct writing sequences.

CBM procedures are usually used to screen for students who may be at risk for reading difficulty and to monitor student progress and response to instructional interventions. Screenings are conducted three times each year in many school districts for all students: fall, winter, and spring. If a student receives additional support in reading, CBM might be administered several times weekly to evaluate the effects of the intervention. Similarly, CBM is often used for decision making when determining if a student should receive special education services.

Outcome Assessments

Outcome assessments help us determine how effective our reading program and our teaching is in helping students attain grade level standards or benchmarks. These kinds of tests are usually given to whole groups of students at once, but may be given individually when necessary. The following two measures are used nationally and are considered to be exemplars in this emerging area of reading assessment.

Dynamic Indicators of Basic Early Literacy Skills (DIBELS)

The *Dynamic Indicators of Basic Early Literacy Skills* or DIBELS are a set of four standardized, individually-administered measures of early literacy development. DIBELS was specifically designed to assess three of the "Five Big Ideas" of early literacy development: phonological awareness, alphabetic principle, and oral reading fluency (measured as a corrected reading rate) with connected text. Another test not directly linked to the 3 of 5 Big Ideas in early literacy but used as a risk indicator is the *Letter Naming Fluency* (LNF) measure. These short, efficient, and highly predictive measures are designed to be one minute, timed indicators used to regularly monitor the development of pre-reading and early reading skills. A full description was presented in Chapter 4.

Texas Primary Reading Inventory (TPRI)

The *Texas Primary Reading Inventory* or TPRI is an assessment tool that provides a picture of a student's reading progress in kindergarten, first, and second grades. Originally developed to help teachers in Texas in measuring the state's "essential knowledge and skills" in reading, this instrument is suitable for outcome assessment as well as for screening and progress-monitoring assessment purposes. A quick screening section is designed to work together with a more detailed inventory section to help teachers identify strengths and problem areas as well as to monitor students' progress.

TPRI covers all five of the "big ideas" in early reading development: phonemic awareness, phonics, fluency, vocabulary, and comprehension strategies. The TPRI also provides an *Interventions Activities Guide* directly linked to students' performance of each on the parts of TPRI.

The TPRI is administered individually by the classroom teacher. In the screening section of the TPRI, three assessment measures are provided: (1) graphophonemic knowledge, (2) phonemic awareness, and (3) word reading. In the graphophonemic measure, students are assessed on their ability to recognize letters of the alphabet and their understanding of sound-to-symbol relationships. In the phonemic awareness measure, students are assessed on their ability to identify and manipulate individual sounds within spoken words so that letters can be linked to sounds. In the word reading measure of the screening portion of the TPRI, students are asked to identify a list of high-frequency words.

In the inventory section of the TPRI, students are assessed across seven measures: (1) book and print knowledge, (2) phonemic awareness, (3) listening comprehension, (4) graphophonemic knowledge, (5) reading accuracy, (6) reading fluency, and (7) reading comprehension. The TPRI, unlike the DIBELS, addresses the important role of concepts about print in the development of early reading.

The TPRI is based on longitudinal data on over 900 English-speaking students. More recently, the TPRI has also become available in Spanish, which, like DIBELS, has yet to be shown to be a valid and reliable indicator of reading development in this population. For a more extensive review of the TPRI, we recommend that you consult: *www.tpri.org*.

Diagnostic Assessments

Diagnostic assessments are used to gather in-depth information about students' particular strengths and needs and are typically used for struggling readers. Diagnostic assessments probe deeper than other assessments and take extra time to conduct. An educational psychologist, certified diagnostician, or a bilingual specialist is sometimes needed to administer certain tests due to time constraints or required special training. Students in special education or Title I programs for reading often require diagnostic testing.

Diagnosing Vocabulary Knowledge

When teachers notice students who seem to struggle with reading, it is logical for them to want to know the extent to which these students' vocabulary has developed. We recommend three tests for assessing a student's word knowledge or **receptive vocabulary.** One is intended for native English speakers, and the other two are for students who speak Spanish as their first language and are learning to speak and read in English.

- *Peabody Picture Vocabulary Test, Third Edition* (PPVT-III) (Dunn & Dunn, 1997). The PPVT-III is a quickly administered test (11–12 minutes) that indicates how strong a student's vocabulary knowledge is compared to other students of the same age nationally. Results can help the teacher better understand the needs of students in terms of formal and informal vocabulary instruction.
- *Test de Vocabulario en Imágenes Peabody* (TVIP), (Dunn, Lugo, Padilla, & Dunn, 1986). This test is an adaptation of an early version of the previously described *Peabody Picture Vocabulary Test* for native Spanish speakers. It takes about 10 to 15 minutes to administer and measures Spanish vocabulary knowledge.
- *Woodcock-Muñoz Language Survey* (WMLS), English and Spanish Forms (Woodcock & Muñoz-Sandoval, 1993). Teachers, particularly in urban centers, often have a large number of students who are learning English as a second language (ESL). The extent to which students have acquired a listening and speaking vocabulary in English is an important factor in reading instruction because reading (a) is a language skill, and (b) depends on learners having a fairly strong English vocabulary. The WMLS is a widely used instrument used throughout the United States (García, McKoon, & August, 2006) that takes about 20 minutes to administer. It features two subtests: Oral Language and Reading/Writing.

Individual Diagnostic Reading Tests

Teachers sometimes believe it necessary to assess an individual student's reading ability using norm-referenced measures. This often happens when new students move into a school district without their permanent records, or when struggling readers are being considered for extra assistance programs such as Title 1 or special education services provided in inclusive classrooms. Following is an example of a commonly used test:

- *Woodcock Reading Mastery Tests—Revised* (Woodcock et al., 1987, 1997). The Woodcock Reading Mastery Tests—Revised (WRMT-R/NU) is a battery of six individually administered subtests intended to measure reading abilities from kindergarten through adult levels. Subtests cover visual-auditory learning, letter identification, word identification, word attack, word comprehension, and passage comprehension. Its design reveals a skills perspective of reading, and divides the assessment into two sections according to age and ability levels: *readiness* and *reading achievement*. The WRMT-R/NU reports norm-referenced data for both of its forms, as well as insights into remediation. Results may be calculated either manually or using the convenient scoring program developed for personal computers (PCs). This WRMT-R/NU is frequently used by teachers in special education and Chapter 1 reading programs.

Individually Administered Achievement Tests

It can be informative to know how well a student has developed over a wide range of academic subjects. Achievement tests are often given to whole groups of students at scheduled grade levels, but you may need this information right away to better understand a troubled reader's knowledge and abilities. Following is a description of our preferred wide range achievement test that can be individually administered as a diagnostic tool.

"Review of Reading Tests" on the Teacher Prep Website (www.prenhall.com/teacherprep) will provide you with names, types, purposes and descriptions of reading tests. Select *Strategies and Lessons—Reading Methods* to locate this article.

- *Kaufman Test of Educational Achievement* (K-TEA/NU) (Kaufman & Kaufman, 1997). Sometimes teachers require norm-referenced data to determine how a child is progressing compared to other children nationally, such as when teachers are working with a population of students who are performing at atypically high or low levels. That is, working with either struggling readers or gifted students over a long period of time may give teachers a distorted view of what "normal" achievement looks like. The Kaufman Test of Educational Achievement (K-TEA/NU), available in both English and Spanish forms, can provide useful insights in these situations.

The K-TEA/NU is a norm-referenced test yielding information in the areas of reading, mathematics, and spelling. Intended for students in grades 1 to 12, the K-TEA/NU is available in a brief form for quick assessments (when only standardized data are needed) and a comprehensive form, which provides both standardized data and insights into classroom remediation. Alternate forms are not available, but the authors suggest that the two versions may be used as pretest–posttest measures.

Getting Organized: Profiling Your Class

The assessment ideas presented in this chapter and in the classroom assessment section in Chapters 2 through 8 provide a means of measuring the development of various reading skills. But that is only one part of the reading teacher's job. Organizing and analyzing the assessment data—first for each child individually and then for the entire class—constitute an extremely important next step in instructional planning. Charting the reading skills students have learned and still need to acquire, both individually and as a class, is what we refer to as **profiling.**

Valerie Schultz/Merrill

Two Documents Needed for Profiling

Teachers need two profiling documents: a **student profile document** to record individual strengths and needs in some detail, and a **class profile document** to help organize the entire class's data for the formation of needs-based reading groups. A profiling system should be driven either by the state's reading standards or the school district's scope and sequence skills list. These are usually provided in a curriculum guide to all teachers upon assignment to a school.

Student Profiling Document. In Figure 9.15 you will find a partially completed student profiling document. Note that each skill has a blank space to note

Figure 9.15 A Partially Completed Student Profile Form (Fall, 3rd Grade)

STUDENT PROFILE FORM—READING

Student: Molly H.

Teacher: Ms. K. Spencer

KEY: Reading Skill Development Rating

E = Emergent (not observed)
D = Developing (some evidence, but not fully competent)
P = Proficient (fully competent)

Date of Observation	Category	Benchmark Skill	Student Skill Level
October 14	**Phonics**	Uses phonic knowledge and structural analysis to decode words.	Proficient
December 5	**Fluency**	Reads aloud with fluency any text that is appropriately designed for grade level.	Developing (Molly read at 71 WCPM)
September 12	**Comprehension**	Summarizes major points from fiction and nonfiction texts.	Fiction—Proficient
	Comprehension	Summarizes major points from fiction and nonfiction texts.	
August 15	**Comprehension**	Discusses similarities in characters and events across stories.	Proficient
	Comprehension	Discusses underlying theme or message when interpreting fiction.	

(a) the date the teacher observed the student performing the specified skill, and (b) the degree (rating) to which the student was able to demonstrate the skill. For the latter, a three-point rubric is provided: "E" for students who are just *emerging* with an awareness of the skill or who have not demonstrated any competency with the skill; "D" for students who are in the midst of *developing* competency in the skill; and "P" for students who have attained *proficiency* (i.e., mastery) of the skill. These designations are important because they help the teacher differentiate the needs of students in the class. The designations can also be useful for informing parents about how their child is developing as a reader.

Note that in the example provided in Figure 9.15, the child has skills at each level of development, as well as some with no designation at all. (This means that the child has not been tested for the skill.)

Class Profiling Document

Accompanying the student profile is the class profile. (Always have both.) This document lists the same reading standards as the student profile only in abbreviated form. Figure 9.16 features a partial classroom reading profile for third grade. Notice that the skills listed match those found in the individual student profile.

To demonstrate how individual student data can be collated into a class profile, we provide an example in Figure 9.17. This example is for decoding and word recognition, as well as spelling and writing skills assessment. It is easy to see how the teacher can begin forming reading groups based on student needs. For instance, the teacher not only might form a group of students who need to develop revising and editing skills, but also recognize that two groups are actually needed—one for those who are emerging in this ability (E-level students), and another for those who are a little further along, or developing (D-level students).

IF–THEN Thinking

An absolutely essential key to success in reading instruction is the teacher's ability to analyze reading assessment data and translate this information to a plan for instruction to meet students' learning needs. Earlier in this chapter, we referred to "IF–THEN" reasoning in analyzing reading data. IF–THEN Thinking (Flynt & Cooter, 2004; Reutzel & Cooter, 2007; R. Cooter, Flynt, & K. S. Cooter, 2007) works like this in relation to student and classroom assessment data:

> **If** you have identified specific learning needs in reading for a student(s), **then** which reading skills and strategies are appropriate to offer the student(s) next in your classroom instruction?

Said another way by Cooter and his colleagues (2007), the teacher must first collect a good bit of information through valid classroom assessments that begin to paint a picture of where the student is in his or her reading development. Once that picture begins to take shape and the teacher has an educated impression of what the student is able to do independently in reading and what the student needs to learn, then she might think . . .

> **If** the student has this reading need, **then** I should teach the reading skill _____ using the _____ teaching strategy.

R. Cooter et al. (2007), in order to guide your instruction in using IF–THEN Thinking, have offered examples of which we provide two in Tables 9.2 through 9.4 on the following pages. They describe a few common reading needs along with selected instructional strategies from a variety of sources.

Figure 9.16   Partial Class Profiling Instrument

CLASS PROFILE (BLAST™): THIRD GRADE LITERACY MILESTONES

Teacher: _____   **Date/Grading Period Completed:** _____

Instructions: Record the degree to which each milestone skill has been achieved by each student (**E** = Emergent, **D** = Developing Skill, **P** = Proficient) in each box corresponding to the student and skill in the grid.

Decoding and Word Recognition

3.D.1   Context clues, phonic knowledge, and structural analysis

Spelling and Writing

3.SW.1   Uses studied words and spelling patterns

3.SW.2   Uses the dictionary to check spelling

3.SW.3   Uses these aspects of the writing process:

   3.SW.3.1   Combines information/multiple sources

   3.SW.3.2   Revises and edits

   3.SW.3.3   Variety of written work

   3.SW.3.4   Graphic organizational tools

   3.SW.3.5   Descriptions and figurative language

   3.SW.3.6   Variety of formal sentence structures

3.SW.4.S.1   Orthographic patterns and rules (Spanish only)

3.SW.5.S.2   Spells words with three or more syllables using

   silent letters, dieresis marks, accents, verbs (Spanish only)

Oral Reading

3.OR.1   Reads aloud with fluency

(continued)

Figure 9.16 (Continued)

Reading Fluency										
3.F.1	Very few word-by-word interruptions									
3.F.2	Reads mostly in larger meaningful phrases									
3.F.3	Reads with expression									
3.F.4	Attends consistently to punctuation									
3.F.5	Rereads to clarify or problem-solve									
3.F.6	Reads sixty (60) words per minute (minimum)									
Language Comprehension and Response to Text										
3.C.1	Comprehends both fiction and nonfiction on level									
3.C.2	Reads chapter books independently									
3.C.3	Identifies problem words or phrases									
3.C.4	Summarizes fiction and nonfiction text									
3.C.5	Similarities: characters/events across stories									
3.C.6	Theme or message: interpreting fiction									
3.C.7	Nonfiction:									
	3.C.7.1 Cause/effect									
	3.C.7.2 Fact/opinion									
	3.C.7.3 Main idea/details									
3.C.8	Evaluation: Uses information/reasoning									
3.C.9	Word meaning from roots and affixes									
3.C.10	Dictionary: Determine meanings/usage									
3.C.11	Uses new vocabulary in own speech and writing									
3.C.12	Writing: Basic grammar/parts of speech									
3.C.13	Familiar w/read-aloud, indep. reading, nonfiction									
3.C.14	Locates information using:									
	3.C.14.1 Tables of contents									
	3.C.14.2 Indexes									
	3.C.14.3 Internet search engines									
3.C.15	Connects literary texts with life experiences									

Figure 9.17   Needs-Based Groups

CLASS PROFILE (BLAST™): THIRD GRADE LITERACY MILESTONES

Teacher: *K. Spencer*   Date/Grading Period Completed: ___12 – 14___

Instructions: Record the degree to which each milestone skill has been achieved by each student (**E** = Emergent, **D** = Developing Skill, **P** = Proficient) in each box corresponding to the student and skill in the grid.

Decoding and Word Recognition

Skill		Dora	Paula	Ameenah	Jason	Rosa Maria	Harry	James	Dirk	Syoria	Alicia	Johnny	Anna
3.D.1	Context clues, phonic knowledge, and structural analysis	P	P	P	D	D	P	P	D	P	D	P	P

Spelling and Writing

Skill		Dora	Paula	Ameenah	Jason	Rosa Maria	Harry	James	Dirk	Syoria	Alicia	Johnny	Anna
3.SW.1	Uses studied words and spelling patterns	D	D	E	E	D	D	E	D	P	E	E	P
3.SW.2	Uses the dictionary to check spelling	D	D	D	D	D	D	P	D	D	D	E	P
3.SW.3	Uses these aspects of the writing process:												
3.SW.3.1	Combines information/multiple sources	E	E	E	E	E	E	E	E	E	E	E	E
3.SW.3.2	Revises and edits	D	D	D	E	E	E	E	E	D	E	E	P
3.SW.3.3	Variety of written work	E	D	P	E	E	P	E	D	E	E	E	P
3.SW.3.4	Graphic organizational tools	E	D	E	D	E	D	D	P	P	E	P	D
3.SW.3.5	Descriptions and figurative language	E	E	E	P	E	D	D	P	D	E	E	P
3.SW.3.6	Variety of formal sentence structures	D	D	D	D	E	D	D	D	E	D	D	P
3.SW.4.S.1	Orthographic patterns and rules (Spanish only)	D	P		D	D	D						
3.SW.5.S.2	Spells words with three or more syllables using silent letters, dieresis marks, accents, verbs (Spanish only)	P	P		P	P		D					

363

Table 9.2   IF–THEN Chart for Phonemic Awareness (PA)

IF a Student Has This Learning Need . . .	THEN Try Using a Strategy Like . . .	Resources for These and Other Strategies
Initial Sounds	• Word families (same/different beginning sounds) • Songs and poetry • Word rubber-banding • Tongue twisters	***Selected Internet Resources*** *http://www.songsforteaching.com* *http://www.literacyconnections.com* *http://www.nifl.gov/partnershipforreading/* *http://www.readingrockets.org* *http://reading.uoregon.edu/pa/pa_features.php* ***Books*** Blevins, W. (1999). *Phonemic Awareness Songs and Rhymes* (Grades PreK-2). New York: Scholastic.
Phonemic Segmentation of Spoken Words	• Word rubber-banding • Add/take a sound from spoken words • Environmental print/logos • Songs, chants, raps, poetry	Opitz, M. (2000). *Rhymes and Reasons: Literature and Language Play for Phonological Awareness.* Portsmouth, NH: Heinemann.
Blending Sounds Into Spoken Words	• Add/take a sound • Word rubber-banding • Environmental print/logos • Songs, chants, raps, poetry • Odd word out	Reutzel, D. R., & Cooter, R. B. (2007). *Strategies for Reading Assessment and Instruction* (3rd ed.). Upper Saddle River, NJ: Merrill/Prentice-Hall.
Rhyming	• Songs, chants, raps, poetry • Alphabet books • Tongue twisters	

Table 9.3   IF–THEN Chart for Phonics and Other Word Attack Skills

IF a Student Has This Learning Need . . .	THEN Try Using a Strategy Like . . .	Resources for These and Other Strategies
Letter Sounds	• Explicit phonics instruction • Word boxes • Tongue twisters • Letter–sound cards • Making words • Nonsense words	Selected Internet Resources "Between the Lions" (PBS)-*http://pbskids.org/lions/games/* "BBC Schools" *http://www.bbc.co.uk/schools/wordsandpictures/index.shtml* *http://www.adrianbruce.com/reading/* *http://cwx.prenhall.com/bookbind/pubbooks/literacy-cluster/* *http://toread.com/*

Table 9.3   (Continued)

IF a Student Has This Learning Need . . .	THEN Try Using a Strategy Like . . .	Resources for These and Other Strategies
"C" Rule	• Explicit phonics instruction • Word boxes • Letter–sound cards • Making words • Nonsense words	**Books** Rycik, M., & Rycik, J. (2007). *Phonics and Word Identification: Instruction and Intervention K-8:1/e.* Upper Saddle River, NJ: Merrill/Prentice-Hall. Lucht, L. (2006). *The Wonder of Word Study: Lessons and Activities to Create Independent Readers, Writers, and Spellers.* Portsmouth, NH: Heinemann.
"G" Rule	• Explicit phonics instruction • Word boxes • Letter–sound cards • Making words • Nonsense words	Cunningham, P. (2005). *Phonics They Use* (4th ed.). Boston: AB/Longman. Reutzel, D. R., & Cooter, R. B. (2007). *Strategies for Reading Assessment and Instruction* (3rd ed.). Upper Saddle River, NJ: Merrill/Prentice-Hall.

Table 9.4   If–Then Chart for Reading Fluency

IF a Student Has This Learning Need . . .	THEN Try Using a Strategy Like . . .	Resources for These and Other Strategies
Reading Rate	• Repeated readings • Choral reading • Buddy reading • Reading television captions	**Selected Internet Resources** *http://pbskids.org/readingrainbow/*
Reading Accuracy/Automaticity	• Oral recitation lesson • Assisted reading • Guided oral reading	**Books** Opitz, M., & Rasinski, T. (1998). *Good-bye Round Robin: Effective Oral Reading Strategies.* Portsmouth, NH: Heinemann.
Quality/Prosody	• Repeated readings • Choral reading • Guided oral reading • Oral recitation lesson	Reutzel, D. R., & Cooter, R. B. (in press). *Strategies for Reading Assessment and Instruction* (3rd ed.). Upper Saddle River, NJ: Merrill/Prentice-Hall.

Summary

Assessment exists to inform and improve classroom teaching. When employed properly, assessments help teachers chart individual students' learning and proficiency with essential reading skills. Put another way, assessment helps teachers understand what each child *can* do in reading, and what they are ready to learn next. Once teachers know where students are in their reading development they are able to plan appropriate "next steps" in instruction, select appropriate reading materials with which to teach, and plan small group instruction according to the mutual needs of students.

Four purposes of reading assessment have been described that are derived from two federal initiatives: the *No Child Left Behind* initiative, and *Reading First. Outcome assessments* are intended to survey the reading achievement of teacher's class as a whole and provide a kind of snapshot of the reading program's effectiveness. *Screening assessments* provide initial (beginning of the year, or the beginning of a new part of the reading curriculum) or "first look" information about each student's ability. *Diagnostic assessments* provide more in-depth information about students' individual strengths and needs. *Progress-monitoring assessments* are an extremely valuable tool for teachers as they provide ongoing and timely feedback as to how well individual students are responding to instruction currently in motion—"real time" feedback. Examples of commonly used assessment tools and strategies for each of these assessment purposes were described in some detail to augment other strategies shared throughout our text.

A number of commercially published reading assessments commonly used in schools were presented. We grouped these according to the four purposes just summarized for your convenience. These included informal reading inventories, curriculum-based measurements (CBM), DIBELS, the *Woodcock Reading Mastery Tests Revised,* and many more. While a school psychologist often administers some of these tests, all may be given by classroom teachers with minimal training.

Once student data has been gathered, the next phase of reading assessment requires interpretation of results. We described ways teachers can create student and classroom profiling documents to sort data and make decisions about small group instruction. We also shared a way of selecting evidence-based teaching strategies that meet each students' needs called "IF – THEN Thinking." This is a classroom proven methods that is both quick and effective in selecting best teaching practices. In this way we can insure that every child receives the reading instruction needed.

Classroom Applications

1. With a partner (or two), conduct a library search of professional journals (e.g., *Educational Leadership, Phi Delta Kappan*) and education periodicals (e.g., *Education Week*) and prepare a response to this question: What are some of the issues regarding reading assessment? Be sure to take a look at the literature relating to No Child Left Behind and Reading First legislation.

Start with the year 2000 to get a good chronology of issues. Present a poster session of your findings to your classmates.

2. Develop a schedule for your classroom (name the grade level) that includes time for the daily assessment of at least four students. What will be the typical assessment tools you will probably use during this time period? (Identify at least four.) Justify your choices.

3. Develop three evaluation checklist forms that could be used in your classroom or a grade level you specify for reading comprehension, word identification, and content reading strategies. Include a suggested rubric with a rationale for each item.

Recommended Readings

Cooter, R. B., Flynt, E. S., & Cooter, K. S. (2007). *The comprehensive reading inventory.* Upper Saddle River, NJ: Merrill/Prentice Hall.

Dunn, L., & Dunn, L. M. (1997). *Peabody Picture Vocabulary Test–Third Edition* (PPVT-III). Circle Pines, MN: American Guidance Service.

Dunn, L., Lugo, D. E., Padilla, E. R., & Dunn, L. M. (1986). *Test de Vocabulario en Imágenes Peabody* (TVIP). Circle Pines, MN: American Guidance Service.

Reutzel, D. R., & Cooter, R. B. (2007). *Strategies for reading assessment and instruction: Helping every child succeed* (3rd ed.). Upper Saddle River, NJ: Merrill/Prentice Hall.

chapter 10

Programs and Standards for Reading Instruction

Chapter Questions

1. What is meant by "standards" for reading instruction?

2. What is a core reading program?

3. What are the supplemental reading programs for helping struggling readers succeed?

4. Which reading programs have been shown to be effective with English learners (ELs)?

5. How can teachers help parents and interested stakeholders better understand reading standards?

Which Reading Program Is Best?

It's Friday morning, 8:00 a.m. You are attending a meeting of the new Textbook Adoption Committee for your school district. The committee's task is to choose a new reading program. Just one month into your first year as a teacher, you and your teammates must review a plethora of basal reading programs, supplemental materials for reading instruction, and sundry other kits and manipulatives. The 40' by 40' conference room is absolutely packed with the latest offerings from major- and minor-league publishers, and properly coiffed sales representatives are waiting in the hallway like obedient soldiers to retrieve any needed information at a moment's notice. Great food and beverages are provided. The state's reading standards have been made available for your convenience as you match required skills to appropriate materials.

It all sounds straightforward, but where do you begin? Some of your colleagues feel strongly that a program that best matches the state standards should be selected. Others think that materials that supposedly help teachers teach to the state test are imperative. Still others like the programs with lots of "free stuff," like classroom libraries and technology support. As a new teacher, this latter option is especially appealing; you don't have much to work with beyond the relatively few supplies and materials you inherited from your predecessor. However, you admit that the other arguments may make better sense. After all, you will be judged by how well your students perform on the state standards and test.

But you also know that you are there to represent those who have no voice—the students. What should you do?

Many programs for reading instruction are available to teachers. While many publishers claim to offer comprehensive curriculums, in our view, no reading instructional program has ever been designed—or ever will be designed—that meets the needs of all learners. Therefore, it is important for teachers to know their learners' current developmental levels, the fundamentals of reading instruction, state reading standards, and reading instruction programs and materials that meet the needs of their students.

Our focus, as we discuss reading instruction standards and reading instruction programs, are the "Big Five" instructional strands drawn from the report of the National Reading Panel (2000): phonemic awareness, phonics, vocabulary, comprehension, and fluency. In this chapter, we look at how each of the Big Five is treated at each grade and developmental level of literacy learning according to scientifically-based reading research (SBRR).

First, we want to acquaint you with a summary of the standards-based movement in the United States and how it has impacted the development of reading programs.

What Is Meant by "Standards" for Reading Instruction?

In our opening vignette, our new teacher was caught between the horns of a dilemma: how to balance her need for high-quality books and materials with state demands for standards-based teaching and the omnipresent high stakes tests. In the past decade or so, standards-based curriculums and assessments have been prescribed as a cure for the poor performance and accountability of many public schools (Watt, 2005; Zuzovsky & Libman, 2006). Billions of dollars have been spent on programs and state tests, in part so that federal and state agencies can rank schools in terms of student achievement (Baines & Stanley, 2006).

Overview of the Standards-Based Movement

Read more about No Child Left Behind legislation on the accompanying CD to this text. Select the *Internet* connection, locating the link to the *International Reading Association*. Search for "NCLB" to locate a plethora of documentation.

Additional information about No Child Left Behind legislation is available on the CD that accompanies this text. Access the *Internet* and visit the *National Council of Teachers of English* website to search for NCLB.

According to Watt (2005), the **standards-based movement** in the United States began as an outgrowth of a growing public debate on the rather tepid performance of school children on measures of reading, not to mention in other academic areas like mathematics and science. Concern for the effectiveness of U.S. education was heightened following the release of a number of national studies in the 1980s, most especially the report of the National Commission on Excellence in Education in 1983. In general, these reports sparked calls for the reform of public education by either decentralizing authority to local communities or, conversely, by giving more authority to state and federal agencies.

In 1989, then-governor George W. Bush convened the Charlottesville Education Summit involving President Clinton and the nation's fifty governors. The goal was to identify ways to make the U.S. more internationally competitive by 2000. Watt (2005, pp. 3–4) described the outcome thus:

> They reached agreement to establish a process for setting national education goals, seeking greater flexibility and accountability in using federal resources to meet the goals, undertaking a state-by-state effort to restructure the education system, and reporting annually on progress in achieving the goals (Vinovskis, 1999). . . . The six National Education Goals became the foundation for America 2000 and later

Goals 2000, and provided the impetus for defining national standards based in academic disciplines.

A multiplicity of trends in U.S. education had concurred [sic] by this time leading conservatives and liberals to forge a consensus about focusing on what students should know and be able to do. Policy-makers set nationally recognized groups in key disciplines [with] the task of developing national standards consisting of content, performance, and opportunity-to-learn standards. **Content standards** refer to broad descriptions of knowledge and skills that students should achieve in particular subject areas. **Performance standards** are examples and definitions of knowledge and skills in which students need to demonstrate proficiency. **Opportunity-to-learn standards,** which address conditions necessary at each level of the education system to provide all students with opportunities to master content standards and meet performance standards, provide criteria covering six elements. These elements refer to the quality and availability of curricula, materials and technology, the capability of teachers to meet learning needs, the availability of professional development, the alignment of the curriculum to content standards, the adequacy of school facilities for learning, and the application of non-discriminatory policies.

It seems fair to conclude that when Bush was elected president in 2000 he used the outcomes generated by the Charlottesville Education Summit to form the basis of the No Child Left Behind (NCLB) legislation. Approved by Congress with near-unanimous support, NCLB in effect federalized the standards-based movement and required all states to conform or risk losing tax dollars. NCLB also caused the producers of reading programs, tests, and support materials to conform to mandated "evidence-based" standards. If they did not do so, then their products would likely not be adopted by state or local education agencies. Regardless of where one stands on the philosophy of the standards-based movement and its implementation, it is nevertheless a matter of current law that dramatically influences the types and quality of reading instruction materials available.

Where Can I Find My State's Reading Standards and the Tools to Assess Them?

In Chapters 3 through 8, we present evidence-based standards for each skill area of reading. These are based on the most comprehensive and scientific research studies available, and make up the skeletal framework for most state standards in reading. But don't stop there. You should also seek out the specific standards articulated by your own state department of education and the state-mandated tests for measuring their acquisition by students. This information is available to teachers online. For your convenience, we present a listing of all state agencies that provide this important information.

In the next section, we turn our attention to the most prevalent type of reading materials. These are basal reading programs, also known as core reading programs.

Getting to Know English Learners
The standards for ELs are produced by the Teachers of English to Speakers of Other Languages (TESOL) based in Washington, DC. Its mission is to advocate for the education of ELs and for the profession of teaching ELs. Its standards may be found on their website: *http://www.tesol.org*

Locate your state
TEACHER PREP standards through the
CD that accompanies
this text, or on the Teacher Prep
website. Select the *Internet
connection* to "State by State
Standards" and click on your
state on the CD. On the website,
visit *Getting Your License and
Beginning Your Career* and click
on *State Licensure Standards*.

What Are Basal or Core Reading Programs?

Basal readers in one form or another have played an integral role in U.S. reading instruction for centuries and are likely to continue to do so well into the future (Giordano, 2001; Hoffman, 2001; McCallum, 1988; Reutzel, 1991; Robinson, in press). According to *The Literacy Dictionary,* a **basal reading program** is "a collection of student texts and workbooks, teachers' manuals, and supplemental materials for developmental reading and sometimes writing instruction, used chiefly in the elementary and middle school grades" (Harris & Hodges, 1995, p. 18). Simmons and Kame'enui (2003) explain that basal reading programs are the primary instructional tool that teachers use to teach children to learn to read and to ensure that they reach reading levels that meet or exceed grade-level standards. Historically, these programs have been termed "basal" because they serve as the "base" for reading instruction. These programs are also referred to as **core reading programs;** however, for our purposes, we will use the term "basal reader."

Understanding the Basal Reader

Research indicates that basal readers are used daily in 92 to 98 percent of primary classrooms in the United States (Flood & Lapp, 1986; Goodman, 1989; Wade & Moje, 2000). Recent data suggest that 85 percent of intermediate grade classrooms continue to rely on basal reader instruction to some degree (Shannon & Goodman, 1994; Wade & Moje, 2000).

Anatomy of the Basal Reading Approach

Basal readers are typically composed of a set of foundation materials. These include: (1) the student text, (2) the teacher's edition (TE), (3) student workbooks, (4) a teacher's edition workbook, (5) supplemental practice exercises, (6) enrichment activities (usually the latter two are in the form of masters that can be duplicated), (7) big books, (8) leveled readers, (9) phonic or decodable readers, and (10) end-of-unit and end-of-book tests. Other supplemental materials can be acquired at additional cost: picture cards, picture-with-letter cards, letter cards, word cards for display on word walls, pocket charts, classroom trade-book libraries, big books, and

technology resources such as videotapes, CDs, DVDs, and publisher World Wide Web sites on the Internet. In addition, many basal reading series provide a system for record keeping, management of the reading skills taught and mastered, and assessments. Because many teachers will employ a basal series in a school reading program, we will describe each of the most basic basal components and provide examples.

The Basal Teacher's Edition (TE). For teachers, perhaps the most important part of the basal reading program is the **teacher's edition** or **TE** because it

© Ellen B. Senisi/Ellen Senisi

contains instructional guidance and support (see Figure 10.1). For many new teachers, the TE is an important resource for initial professional development.

Within the pages of the teacher's edition, one usually finds three important features: (a) the scope and sequence chart of the particular skills taught in the basal reading program, (b) a reduced version or facsimile of the student text, and (c) recommended lesson plans (see Figures 10.2 and 10.3). A **scope and sequence chart** describes in great detail the *range* of skills and or concepts to be taught in a basal program as well as the *sequence* in which these are to be presented during the school year. The entire student text, shown as a reduced facsimile, is included for convenience in the teacher's edition. Lesson plans in the basal reader are included to save the teacher preparation time. Current basal readers typically design reading lessons around a modified sequence of the directed reading thinking activity (Stauffer, 1969).

It is important that teachers and administrators understand that the teacher's edition (TE) is a resource to be used discriminately—not a script to be followed rigidly. Teachers and administrators should not allow the basal teacher's edition

Figure 10.1 **Example of a 2000 Teacher's Edition for** *Scott Foresman Reading* **Basal Series**

From *Scott Foresman Reading: Take Me There* (Teacher's ed., Grade 1, Volume 5), Glenview, IL: Scott Foresman Company. Copyright 2000 by Scott Foresman Company. Reprinted by permission.

Figure 10.2   A Scope and Sequence Chart Showing the Range of Skills to Be Taught in a Basal Program

Left page (p. 228):

Phonics, Word Analysis, Spelling, Vocabulary, and Fluency *Continued*	K	1	2	3	4	5	6
Understand easily confused words and idioms			•	•	•	•	•
Understand connotation and denotation				•T	•T	•T	•T
Use etymologies for meaning (including Greek and Latin roots and affixes)					•	•	•
Develop vocabulary through listening and discussing	•	•	•	•	•	•	•
Develop vocabulary through meaningful and concrete experiences	•	•	•	•	•	•	•
Develop vocabulary through reading	•	•	•	•	•	•	•
Develop vocabulary through the use of grade-appropriate reference materials	•	•	•	•	•	•	•
Recognize words in the environment	•						
Recognize regular and irregular high-frequency words	•	•T	•T				
Understand selection vocabulary	•	•T	•T	•T	•T	•T	•T
Understand content-area vocabulary					•T	•T	•T
Make analogies						•	•T

Comprehension	K	1	2	3	4	5	6
Comprehension strategy: Know and use the reading process; preview and activate prior knowledge, predict, read, self-monitor, use fix-up strategies, summarize, reflect and respond	•	•	•	•	•	•	•
Comprehension strategy: Construct meaning using all possible avenues: text, knowledge of selection and topic, illustrations, text features, other print and technological/software resources, resource people	•	•	•	•	•	•	•
Formal assessment strategy: Develop test-taking strategies and answer test-like questions (multiple choice, true/false, short answer)		•	•	•	•	•	•

Strategies and Skills	K	1	2	3	4	5	6
Activate prior knowledge and preview	•	•	•	•	•	•	•
Self-question to assess overall understanding		•	•	•	•	•	•
Self-monitor and use fix-up strategies		•	•	•	•	•	•
Recognize author's possible viewpoint/bias				•	•	•T	•T
Understand author's purpose (e.g., inform, entertain, persuade, express)	•	•T	•T	•T	•T	•T	•T
Recognize cause and effect	•T	•T	•T	•T	•T	•T	•T
Classify/categorize	•T	•T	•T	•	•	•	•
Compare and contrast	•	•T	•T	•T	•T	•T	•T
Use context clues for understanding words, phrases, and word referents		•T	•T	•T	•T	•T	•T
Draw conclusions	•T	•T	•T	•T	•T	•T	•T
Recognize statements of fact and opinion			•T	•T	•T	•T	•T
Generalize	•	•	•	•T	•T	•T	•T
Understand graphic sources (e.g., charts, maps, lists, pictures, etc.)	•	•	•	•T	•T	•T	•T
Make judgments about ideas and text			•T	•T	•T	•T	•T
Infer main idea or main idea with supporting details					•T	•T	•T
Paraphrase					•T	•T	•T
Recognize persuasive devices and propaganda							•T
Predict and verify or refine predictions	•T	•T	•T	•T	•T	•T	•T
Distinguish realism/fantasy or fact/nonfact/fantasy	•	•T	•T	•T	•		
Recall and retell	•T	•T	•	•	•	•	•
Identify sequence of events	•	•T	•T	•T	•T	•	•
Identify steps in a process			•T	•T	•T	•T	•T
Recognize story elements							
Character	•T	•T	•T	•T	•T	•T	•T
Plot and plot structure	•	•T	•T	•T	•T	•T	•T
Setting	•	•T	•T	•T	•T	•T	•T
Theme		•	•T	•T	•T	•T	•T
Summarize	•	•	•T	•T	•T	•T	•T
Identify text structure or method of presenting information					•T	•T	•T
Visualize		•	•	•T	•T	•T	•T

• = instructional opportunity   T = tested in standardized test format

228   Scope and Sequence

Right page (p. 229):

Comprehension *Continued*	K	1	2	3	4	5	6
Critical Thinking							
Infer		•T	•T	•T	•T	•T	•T
Analyze		•T	•T	•T	•T	•T	•T
Organize ideas and information		•	•T	•T	•T	•T	•T
Make judgments		•T	•T	•T	•T	•T	•T
Hypothesize		•	•	•	•	•	•T
Synthesize ideas within a text	•	•T	•T	•T	•T	•T	•T
Synthesize ideas from different texts and media	•	•	•T	•T	•T	•T	•T
Compare and contrast across selections, genres, and cultures (intertextuality)	•	•	•T	•T	•T	•T	•T
Evaluate and critique ideas and text			•	•T	•T	•T	•T
Make analogies		•	•	•	•	•	•T

Literature

Genres and Literary Craft	K	1	2	3	4	5	6
Genres							
Fiction							
Animal fantasy	•	•	•	•	•		
Drama/play	•	•	•	•T	•T	•T	•T
Fantasy	•	•	•	•T	•T	•T	•T
Historical fiction			•	•T	•T	•T	•T
Humorous fiction	•		•	•	•	•	•
Mystery				•	•	•	•
Picture book	•	•	•				
Realistic fiction	•	•	•	•T	•T	•T	•T
Science fiction					•		•T
Short story					•	•	•
Traditional stories: fable, fairy tale, folk tale, tall tale, legend, myth	•	•	•	•T	•T	•T	•T
Nonfiction							
Almanac entry					•	•	•
Biography/autobiography	•	•	•	•T	•T	•T	•T
Diary/journal					•	•	•
Encyclopedia article (print or CD-ROM)					•	•	•
Expository article	•	•	•	•T	•T	•T	•T
How-to article		•	•	•	•	•	•
Internet article				•	•	•	•
Interview			•				
Magazine article				•	•	•	•
Narrative writing		•	•	•T	•T	•T	•T
Newsletter		•	•				
Newspaper article				•	•	•	•
Personal essay				•	•	•	•
Persuasive essay							•
Photo essay				•	•	•	•
Textbook				•	•	•	•
Poetry and Song	•	•	•	•	•	•	•

• = instructional opportunity   T = tested in standardized test format

Scope and Sequence   229

From *Scott Foresman Reading, Take Me There* (Teacher's ed., Grade 1, Volume 5, pp. 228–229), 2000, Glenview, IL: Scott Foresman Company. Copyright 2000 by Scott Foresman Company. Reprinted by permission.

Figure 10.3   Example of the Internal Pages from a 2002 Teacher's Edition for *SRA Open Court Reading* Basal Series

Preparing to Read — On the Go — Theme: Animals

Reading a Decodable Book

Core Set, Book 41: *Chuck's Chest*
Phonics Focus: /ch/ Spelled *ch*

High-Frequency Words
- No high-frequency words are introduced in this book.
- Follow the procedure used on T196 to guide you through this part of the lesson.

Reading Recommendations
- The nondecodable words in this book are *I'll, park, switch,* and *toss.*
- Follow the procedure used on T196 to guide you through the lesson.

Responding
- Invite the students to discuss any hard words they encountered in *Chuck's Chest* and how they figured out these words. Have volunteers retell the story.
- Follow the procedure used on T197 to guide you through this lesson.
  - Who does the chest belong to? (*Chuck*)
  - How much cash does Chad find in the chest? (*There is not much.*)
  - What else is in the chest? (*Chuck's lunch is in the chest.*)

MEETING INDIVIDUAL NEEDS
ELL Tip
PREREAD Preread the story with the English-language learners. Have the students sit in a semicircle around you as you read the story. Point out each word as you read. Ask them to repeat each sentence as you point to the words. Make sure that they understand the meanings of the words by asking them to define them. Call on different students to define words or to read a sentence as you point to the letters. Make sure that they understand the meaning of the story.

Informal Assessment
READING PROGRESS While the students are reading to each other, invite several individuals to read with you so that you can assess their reading growth.

T222   Unit 3 Lesson 11

Decodable Book 41
Chuck's Chest

Decodable Book 42
Patch Gets the Ball

Reading a Decodable Book

Core Set, Book 42: *Patch Gets the Ball*
Phonics Focus: /ch/ Spelled ■tch

High-Frequency Words
- No high-frequency words are introduced in this book.
- Follow the procedure used on T196 to guide you through the lesson.

Reading Recommendations
- The nondecodable words in this book are *I'll, park, switch,* and *tossed.* See page T196 for the Reading Recommendations procedures.

Responding
- Invite the students to discuss any hard words they encountered in *Chuck's Chest* and how they figured out these words. Call on volunteers to retell the story.
- Refer back to page T197 as a guide for this portion of the lesson.
  - Who met at Chestnut Ridge Ball Park? (*Lil, Midge, and Chuck met at Chestnut Ridge Ball Park.*)
  - Where did Midge hit the pitched ball to? (*The ball went past Chuck, past tall grass, past plants, and landed in a ditch.*)
  - What kind of buzz is it? (*It is a big buzz.*)
  - What did Midge tell Patch to do? ("*Fetch the ball, Patch!*")

Building Fluency
Encourage partners to build fluency by rereading *Decodable Books 41* and *42* of the Core Set. After the second reading, the partners should read *Decodable Books 32, Lunch on the Porch,* and *33, Patch Helps,* of the Practice Set.

Teacher Tip   DECODABLE TAKEHOME BOOKS It is recommended that you send a story home after it has been read several times in class. Stories are available in the *Decodable Takehome Books.*

Routine Card
Refer to Routine 5 for the reading a Decodable Book procedure.

Unit 3 Lesson 11   T223

From *SRA Open Court Reading: Things That Go* (Teacher's ed., Level 1, Unit 3), 2002, Columbus, OH: SRA/McGraw-Hill. Copyright 2002 by SRA/McGraw-Hill. Reprinted by permission.

to dictate the reading program. Rather, teachers should be encouraged to decide what is and what is not appropriate in the TE for use with a particular group of children.

The Student Basal Text. The student basal text is an anthology of original contemporary and classic stories, poems, news clips, and expository text selections. Some reading selections have been created expressly for inclusion in the student basal reader. Other selections have been adapted from contemporary and classic children's literature or trade books. High-quality artwork generally accompanies the selections. Interspersed throughout the student text, one may also find poems, jokes, riddles, puzzles, informational essays, and special skill and/or concept lessons. Some basal student texts contain questions children should be able to answer after reading the selections. Upper-level basal readers often contain a glossary of words that students can refer to when decoding new words or that they can use to determine the meaning of unfamiliar or new words found in the text.

Changes in basal student texts have resulted in a "more engaging basal" than those of two decades ago as judged by students, teachers, and reading experts (Hoffman et al., 1994; McCarthey et al., 1994).

Inclusion of Authentic Trade Literature. A close examination of quality children's literature included in the more recent basal reader revisions reveals few, if any, alterations of the authors' language or word choice. However, one disturbing publishing practice relates to cropping or cutting original artwork in children's picture book stories. Because of costs involved in the reproduction and permission for use of original artwork, basal publishers have sometimes cut the beautiful artwork that supports and sustains the text in many children's books (Reutzel & Larsen, 1995). The practice of cropping or cutting support artwork may be even more damaging than altering the text for young, emergent readers who may rely more heavily on the pictures for support throughout their initial readings of a new or unfamiliar text.

Information Texts. **Information texts,** those that are factual or nonfiction in nature, are important for helping children increase their vocabulary and concept knowledge—much more so than fiction texts (i.e., stories). Duke (2000) explains that information texts have several distinct features: (a) a function to communicate information about the social or natural world; (b) factual content; (c) technical vocabulary; (d) classificatory or definitional material; (e) graphic elements like maps, graphs, and diagrams; (f) varying text structures (e.g., cause and effect, problem and solution, compare and contrast, etc.); and (g) repetition of topical themes. Duke (2000) reviewed the reading experiences offered to children in 20 first grade classrooms selected from very low and very high socioeconomic status school districts with reading information texts. She found a scarcity of informational texts available in these classrooms—particularly in low socioeconomic status schools. To compound the scarcity of information texts found in the classrooms, there were relatively few informational texts available in school libraries and on classroom walls and other display surfaces in the schools. As a result, young children in low socioeconomic classrooms read information texts only 3.6 minutes per day on average.

In a more recent study, Moss and Newton (2001) investigated the amount of information text available in current 2nd, 4th, and 6th grade basal reading series.

Getting to Know English Learners
The five general TESOL standards are a blend of many disciplines and include wording on the necessity for ELs to engage successfully with informational texts across disciplines such as math, science, and social studies.

These researchers found that only 16–20 percent of all selections in current basal readers could be classified as information texts. The preponderance of selections found in current basal readers continues to be narrative or fictional (66 percent). Thus, one shortcoming of many basal programs is a lack of informational texts necessary for increasing student word knowledge and vocabulary. It is critical that you ensure that all students are exposed to a great deal of informational text, even if that means supplementing heavily your core or basal reading program. At least one-half of the reading curriculum, if not more, should involve informational texts.

Beginning Reading Texts

Controlling Word Difficulty and Frequency. Control over word difficulty in beginning reading texts presumably allows for the systematic introduction of a predetermined number of unfamiliar words in each story (Hiebert, 1999; Hoffman, 2000). Control of word difficulty is typically achieved by using simpler words or words with fewer syllables in place of longer words and by shortening sentences. Basal publishers have for many years controlled the language of beginning reading texts by using simple, one-syllable words. Town and Holbrook (1856), in the *Progressive Reading* basal reading series, are perhaps the earliest educators to explain the use of controlled texts in beginning reading materials:

> The authors, satisfied that the most simple language is best adapted to the class of pupils for whom this Reader is designed, have adhered, as strictly as possible, to the one-syllable system. They have departed from it only when necessary to avoid any stiffness of style, or weakness of expression, which might arise from too closely following it in every instance.

Compare the text from the following 1865 and 2000 basal readers beginning text.

1865

John stands by his father.
"I will be a good boy, father."

2000

Bob went to the barn for Dad.
Dad asked Bob to feed the pigs.

Controlling the difficulty of words encountered in basal reader stories supposedly renders text less difficult to read. However, research by Pearson (1974) challenged the idea that shorter sentences are easier to read. Pearson found that short, choppy sentences are actually more difficult to read because explicit connecting or sequencing words such as *because, and, so, then, before,* and *after* are deleted from the text and consequently must be inferred by the reader in order for her or him to comprehend the text.

Controlling Decoding Difficulty. In some basal reader programs, the earliest books, or **primers,** often contain reading selections known as **decodable text** (Adams, 1990; Beck, 1997; Foorman, Francis, Fletcher, Schatschneider, & Mehta, 1998; Grossen, 1997; Hiebert, 1999). Decodable texts are designed to reinforce the teaching of particular phonic elements, such as short *a,* by using highly controlled vocabulary in their selections (e.g., *Nan* and *Dan*). Decodable texts are frequently sold as supplemental books to school districts to augment basal reader instruction.

A decodable text example is shown in the following excerpt (*Scholastic,* Book 14, Phonics Readers, pp. 2–7; Schreiber & Tuchman, 1997).

The Big Hit

Who hid? Pig.
Who had a mitt? Pig.
Who did not sit?
Who did hit?
Up. Up. Up.
Who had a big hit? Pig.
Who slid? Pig did!

From SCHOLASTIC PHONICS READERS, Book 14 by Schreiber and Tuchman. Copyright © 1997 by Scholastic Inc. Reprinted by permission of Scholastic Inc.

Although decodable texts can be useful for teaching phonics, children seldom encounter such contrived texts outside of school. As a consequence, the practice of controlling vocabulary to this extent continues to be questioned on the grounds that it tends to result in senseless or "inconsiderate" texts, and tends to cause children to think that reading is primarily a decoding task rather than a search for meaning (Allington, 1997; Armbruster, 1984; Hiebert & Martin, 2001). The lack of real content or a discernable story line in these decodable texts—particularly if they are over-used—is suspected to cause children to quickly lose interest in reading.

Controlling Language Patterns in Texts. Predictable texts are characterized by the repetition of a syntactic unit that can range from a phrase to a group of sentences, e.g., "Run, run, as fast as you can. You can't catch me, I'm the Gingerbread Man." Perhaps one of the best-known examples of patterned trade books are those authored and advocated by Bill Martin (1967), such as *Brown Bear, Brown Bear, What Do You See?* These books have been found to decrease the control over new or unique words and feature engaging illustrations. Other patterned books have been published as part of a total reading program. For example, those published by Wendy Pye Publishing that began in New Zealand have been well accepted in the United States (Literacy 2000). Books in the *Sunshine Series* begin with simple repetitious phrases accompanied by strong picture or illustration supports such as is found in the story titled "*Look.*"

Look said the birds, cats.
Look said the birds, dogs.
Look said the birds, bread.
Look said the birds, children.

From *Look* from the Sunshine Series. Wendy Pye Publishing. Used with permission.

You can clearly see that the difficulty of the language found in patterned beginning readers is still controlled as in the past. The major difference is that the control is exerted at larger levels of text—phrases and sentences. This approach to beginning reading has produced some interesting research findings. Children who read patterned texts learned a group of sight words as quickly as children who read controlled word difficulty and frequency texts (Bridge, Winograd, & Haley, 1983). However, more recently, Johnston (1998) found that learning new words in first grade was improved when words were learned separate from the text than in the context of predictable texts. It seems that controlling text patterns also presents some limitations in providing the texts needed for effective beginning reading instruction.

The Workbook

In years past, the most used part of any basal reading series was the workbook (Osborn, 1985). In fact, if any part of the basal reading lesson was neglected, it was seldom the workbook pages (Durkin, 1984; Mason, 1983). Although clearly less frequently the case today, workbook exercises remain firmly entrenched in many classrooms. It appears that some teachers, administrators, and publishers, as evidenced by their continued inclusion of workbook pages or worksheets as part and parcel of basal reading series, still see seatwork as the real "work" of the school literacy program (Allington & Cunningham, 1996). (See Figure 10.4.)

Workbook exercises are not intended to supplant time for structured, well-planned reading instruction or independent reading. Rather, workbook exercises are intended for use by students to independently practice skills, strategies, and literary understandings previously taught by the teacher. Also, workbook exercises are often used as a type of formative or on-going "paper-and-pencil" assessment. In addition to these twin purposes, many teachers also use workbook exercises to manage, direct, or focus student activity in independent learning centers when the teacher is actively working with small groups of children in teacher-guided reading groups. Used in these ways, workbook exercises play at least three distinct roles in classrooms: practice, assessment, and management.

Research has revealed that primary grade students spend up to 70 percent of the time allocated for reading instruction—or 49 minutes per day—in independent practice or completion of worksheets, whereas less than 10 percent of total reading instructional time—or about 7 to 8 minutes per day—is devoted to silent reading. In fact, publishers indicate that there is an insatiable demand for worksheets (Anderson, Hiebert, Scott, & Wilkinson, 1985). Other studies (Knapp, 1991) indicate that many teachers assign or provide time for only small amounts of real reading and writing—in some cases less than 5 minutes per day! Jachym, Allington, and Broikou (1989) and Allington and Cunningham (1996) reported that seatwork (independent completion of worksheets) is displacing many of the more important aspects of reading instruction, such as the acquisition of good books and time spent in actual reading. Based on these findings, it seems obvious that workbooks have been misused and overused. However, when teachers judiciously select workbook exercises to support and reinforce concepts and skills provided during teacher-guided instruction, students benefit from valuable practice and feedback on their progress in relation to specific reading skills, strategies, and literary understandings. Dole, Osborn, and Lehr (1990, pp. 8–15) provide six guidelines for assessing the worth of workbook and worksheet-type reading tasks in the Workbooks subtext for the Basal Reading Programs: Adoption Guidelines project.

Standards and Guidelines for Analyzing Workbook Tasks

1. When analyzing the content of workbook tasks, look for tasks that
   - Are integrated with the lessons in the teacher's manual and with the student textbook
   - Relate to the most important (and workbook-appropriate) instruction in the lessons
   - Are based on the reading selections
   - Use vocabulary that is from current or previous lessons
   - Increase in difficulty as grade level increases

Figure 10.4 Many Basal Reading Programs Still Integrate Workbook, Seatwork, and Practice Sheets Devoted to Skill Practice into the Basal Reading Program

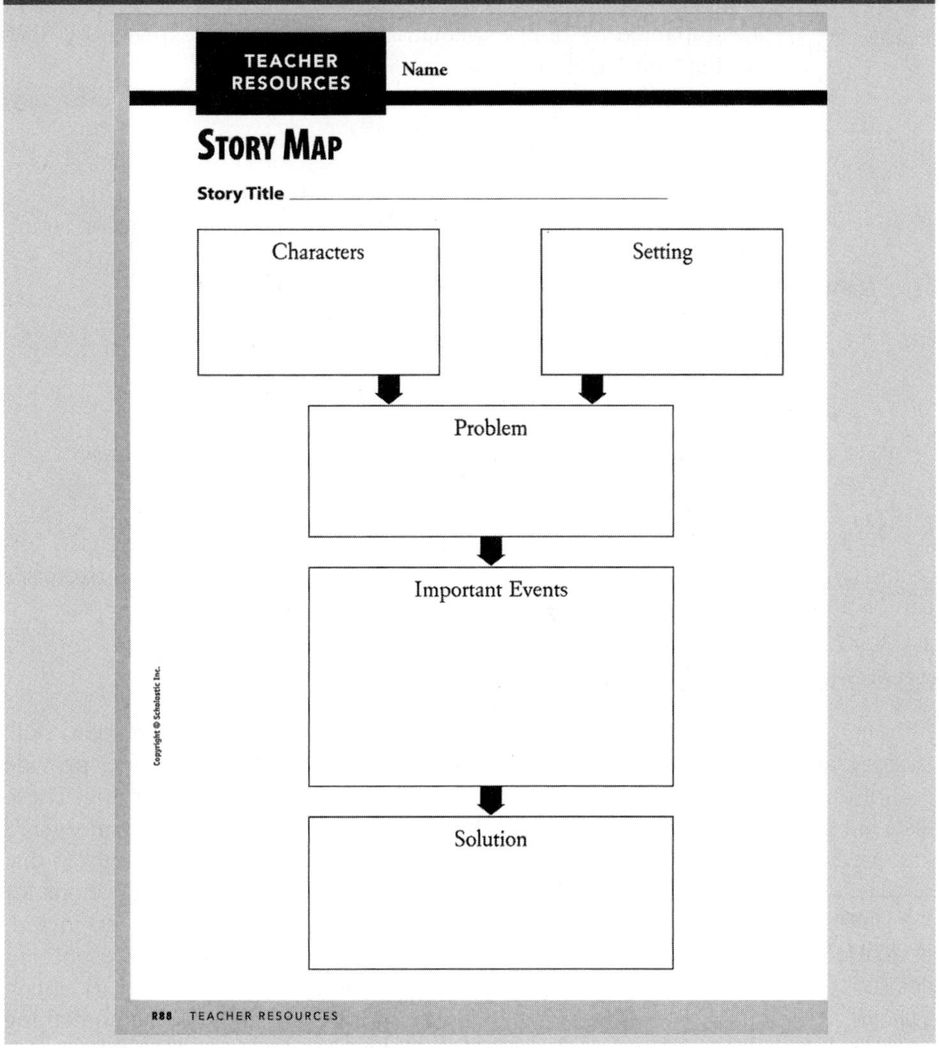

TEACHER RESOURCES   Name

STORY MAP

Story Title _____

Characters

Setting

Problem

Important Events

Solution

Copyright © Scholastic Inc.

R88   TEACHER RESOURCES

From *Scholastic Literacy Place: Problem Patrol* (p. R88), 2000, New York: Scholastic. Copyright 2000 by Scholastic, Inc. Reprinted by permission.

2. When analyzing the content of workbook task design, look for tasks for which
   - The student must read all of the possible choices before selecting an answer
   - Student responses can be judged correct or incorrect
   - Student responses indicate to the teacher what the student knows
   - Students can successfully complete part two of the task without successfully completing part one
3. When analyzing the practice and review tasks, look for tasks that provide
   - Sufficient practice
   - Independent practice

- Extra practice
- Systematic review

4. When analyzing instructional language, look for tasks that
   - Use language consistent with the rest of the program
   - Are accompanied by brief explanations of purpose or explanatory titles that students understand
   - Have clear and easy-to-follow instruction, with attention to consistency, sentence length, and directional steps

5. When evaluating reading and writing responses, look for tasks that
   - Provide opportunities for students to respond in their own words
   - Provide opportunities for students to apply several comprehension strategies or decoding skills in one task

6. When evaluating the considerateness to students, look for
   - Repeated use of task formats
   - Consistent responses
   - Occasional tasks that are fun
   - Few or no nonfunctional tasks

From Dole, J. A., Osborn, J., & Lehr, F. (1990). *A guide to selecting basal reading programs.* Urbana, IL: Center for the Study of Reading.

Workbooks can be a valuable resource for teachers and students when used correctly. On the other hand, when they are misused or overused, workbook exercises can be a debilitating deterrent to students' reading progress.

Assessment

Although workbook exercises can be used for formative assessment of reading skill, strategy, and literary understandings development, most basal reading series provide end-of-unit or end-of-book tests for summative evaluation of student learning. These tests are generally criterion-referenced tests, which means that the items measured are directly related to the specific skills, strategies, or literary concepts taught in that unit, level, or book. Most basal readers now provide suggestions for designing individual assessment portfolios for each student, including the use of running records. Teachers who want to present students' reading demonstrations to their parents will need to obtain audiotapes of students' reading and analyze them using something like running records analysis (see Chapter 4 for details about running records). As the stakes are raised higher and higher in terms of standardized assessment measures, many basal readers are correlating skills, strategies, and literary understandings with nationally published standardized tests (See Figure 10.5).

Getting to Know English Learners

Workbooks can be a valuable tool for ELs especially if they include visual learning aids such as maps, photos, pictures, diagrams, graphs, and/or tables.

Just as workbook exercises can be abused, so can tests. Tests should provide teachers with information about the quantity and quality of children's literacy learning to inform, shape, and direct future instructional choices and selection of interventions. Test results should not be used to label children or embarrass teachers. Two poignant examples of the misuse of test data are found in the books *First Grade Takes a Test* (Cohen, 1980) and *Testing Miss Malarkey* (Finch, 2000). No single test score should ever form the basis for making important decisions about children's learning or their teachers' competence. Administrators and teachers must be extremely cautious in the use and interpretation of single literacy (reading and writing) test scores.

Figure 10.5 Many Basal Teacher's Editions Show How Program Elements Correspond with Nationally Published Standardized Tests

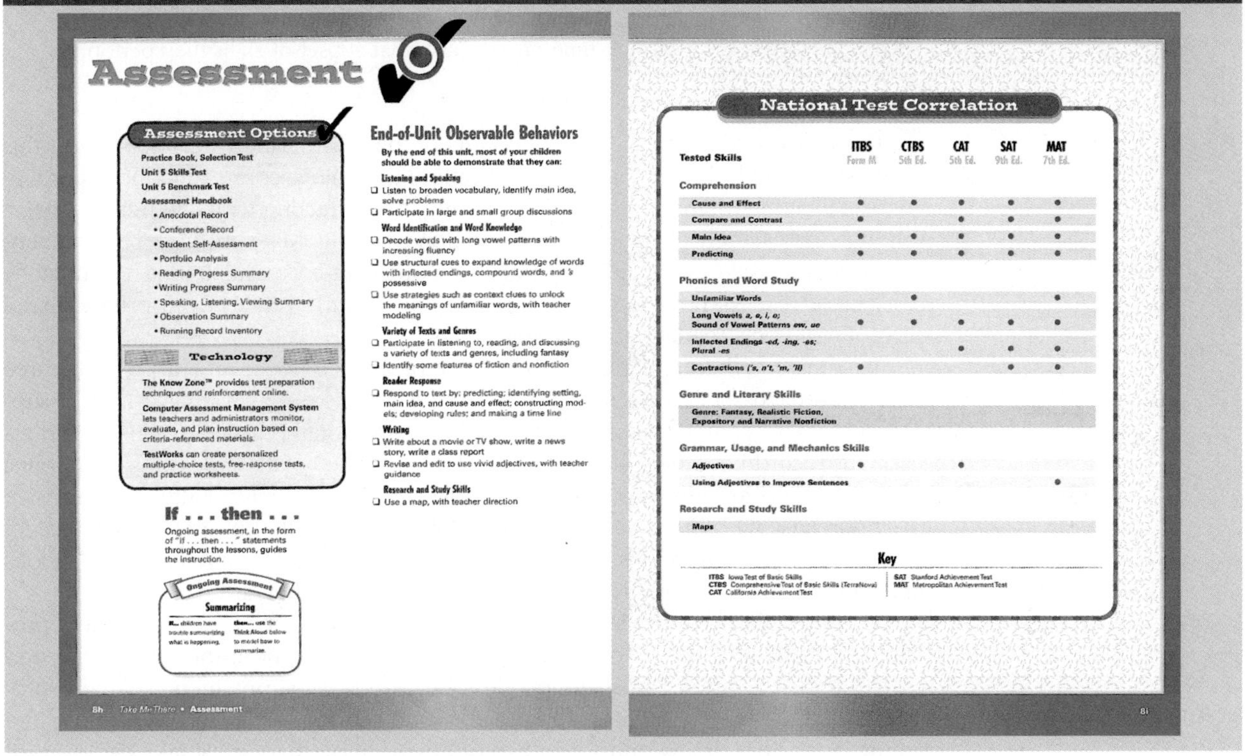

Assessment

Assessment Options

Practice Book, Selection Test
Unit 5 Skills Test
Unit 5 Benchmark Test
Assessment Handbook
- Anecdotal Record
- Conference Record
- Student Self-Assessment
- Portfolio Analysis
- Reading Progress Summary
- Writing Progress Summary
- Speaking, Listening, Viewing Summary
- Observation Summary
- Running Record Inventory

Technology

The Know Zone™ provides test preparation techniques and reinforcement online.

Computer Assessment Management System lets teachers and administrators monitor, evaluate, and plan instruction based on criteria-referenced materials.

TestWorks can create personalized multiple-choice tests, free-response tests, and practice worksheets.

If . . . then . . .

Ongoing assessment, in the form of "If . . . then . . ." statements throughout the lessons, guides the instruction.

Ongoing Assessment

Summarizing

If... children have trouble summarizing what is happening,	**then...** use the **Think Aloud** below to model how to summarize.

End-of-Unit Observable Behaviors

By the end of this unit, most of your children should be able to demonstrate that they can:

Listening and Speaking
- ❑ Listen to broaden vocabulary, identify main idea, solve problems
- ❑ Participate in large and small group discussions

Word Identification and Word Knowledge
- ❑ Decode words with long vowel patterns with increasing fluency
- ❑ Use structural cues to expand knowledge of words with inflected endings, compound words, and *'s* possessive
- ❑ Use strategies such as context clues to unlock the meanings of unfamiliar words, with teacher modeling

Variety of Texts and Genres
- ❑ Participate in listening to, reading, and discussing a variety of texts and genres, including fantasy
- ❑ Identify some features of fiction and nonfiction

Reader Response
- ❑ Respond to text by: predicting; identifying setting, main idea, and cause and effect; constructing models; developing rules; and making a time line

Writing
- ❑ Write about a movie or TV show, write a news story, write a class report
- ❑ Revise and edit to use vivid adjectives, with teacher guidance

Research and Study Skills
- ❑ Use a map, with teacher direction

8h *Take Me There* • **Assessment**

National Test Correlation

Tested Skills	ITBS Form M	CTBS 5th Ed.	CAT 5th Ed.	SAT 9th Ed.	MAT 7th Ed.
Comprehension					
Cause and Effect	•	•	•	•	•
Compare and Contrast	•		•	•	•
Main Idea	•	•	•	•	•
Predicting	•	•	•	•	•
Phonics and Word Study					
Unfamiliar Words		•			•
Long Vowels *a, e, i, o*; Sound of Vowel Patterns *ew, ue*	•	•	•	•	•
Inflected Endings *-ed, -ing, -es*; Plural *-es*			•	•	•
Contractions (*'s, n't, 'm, 'll*)	•			•	•
Genre and Literary Skills					
Genre: Fantasy, Realistic Fiction, Expository and Narrative Nonfiction					
Grammar, Usage, and Mechanics Skills					
Adjectives	•		•		
Using Adjectives to Improve Sentences					•
Research and Study Skills					
Maps					

Key

ITBS Iowa Test of Basic Skills
CTBS Comprehensive Test of Basic Skills (TerraNova)
CAT California Achievement Test
SAT Stanford Achievement Test
MAT Metropolitan Achievement Test

8i

From *Scott Foresman Reading: Take Me There* 2000, (Teacher's ed., Grade 1, Volume 5, pp. 8h–8i), Glenview, IL: Scott Foresman Company. Copyright 2000 by Scott Foresman Company. Reprinted by permission.

Record Keeping

An **instructional management system** allows teachers to keep accurate records from year to year regarding each child's progress through the adopted basal reading program's scope and sequence of skills. Maintaining records to document teaching and learning is an important part of accountability. Most basal reading series provide a means for keeping records on children's progress through the skills outlined in the scope and sequence chart of the basal. Most often, the methods of assessment specified are paper-and-pencil testing or worksheet administration. The scores obtained on these exercises are entered into a master list or record available today in CD-ROM form, which follows students throughout their elementary years.

Unfortunately, some teachers spend inordinate amounts of time keeping records of this kind, which leads to a most undesirable condition as captured by Pearson in 1985 when he stated:

> The model implicit in the practices of [this teacher] was that of a manager—[a] person who arranged materials, texts, and the classroom environment so learning could occur. But the critical test of whether learning did occur was left up to the child as s/he interacted with the materials.

Children practiced applying skills; if they learned them, fine; we always had more skills for them to practice; if they did not, fine; we always had more worksheets and duplicating sheets for the same skill. And the most important rule in such a mastery role was that practice makes perfect, leading to the ironic condition that children spent most of their time on precisely that subset of skills they performed least well. (p. 736)

To this we would like to add the comment that, disturbingly, teachers under this model spent the bulk of their time duplicating, assigning, correcting, and recording worksheets rather than guiding, demonstrating, or interacting with children or books. Although increasingly elegant with the addition of CD-ROM technology, record keeping should go well beyond keeping track of worksheet-type evaluations. Fortunately, many basal readers now recognize this fact and include process and product measures of children's reading and reading habits.

In summary, basal reading series are typically composed of a core of three elements—teacher's edition, student text, and workbooks—as well as a host of supplementary kits, charts, cards, tests, technology, additional practice exercises, and assessment/record-keeping systems. In an effort to compete with trade book publishers, basal publishers are also producing big books to complement the already expansive list of purchasable options listed previously. Teachers should be careful not to accept these new "basal" big books without careful examination. In some cases, big books published by basal companies are not big books at all—they are big basals!

Although the basal reader approach offers a resource for helping teachers provide systematic and sequenced reading instruction throughout the elementary and middle grades, teachers must nonetheless be careful to supplement this core program with trade books, silent reading time, group sharing, extensions of reading into writing, speaking, drama, music, and so on. In addition, they must take care to provide individual assessment of children's reading progress, behaviors, and attitudes. When this goal is understood and achieved, basal readers are valuable literacy tools and resources for schools, administrators, teachers, and children. In addition, basals provide a safety net for many teachers, novice and experienced, because they help teachers make personal and professional growth toward implementing balanced, comprehensive reading instruction.

Production and Organization of Basal Readers

Basal reading series are owned by large, diversified corporations and are produced by a variety of publishing houses from coast to coast. A chief editor oversees the production of a basal reader with the assistance of a senior author team, a group of individuals in the field of reading who are known and respected as experts.

Basal reading programs are often recognized and known by the name of the publishing houses that produce them. Over the past twenty years, the number of basal publishing companies that have survived intense competition, demanding and sometimes invasive state standards, and the vicissitudes of change has dwindled from over twenty to a half dozen or fewer.

Harcourt

Houghton Mifflin

National Geographic School Publishing

SRA/McGraw Hill

Scholastic

Scott Foresman

Minor revisions of basal readers occur every few years; major revision cycles occur every 5 or 6 years. Major revisions are usually slated for completion during the same year Texas and California consider basal readers for statewide adoption. Consequently, the "Texas and California" effect is known to exert considerable influence on the content and quality of new basal readers (Farr, Tulley, & Powell, 1987; Keith, 1981). In reading circles, one often hears the axiom, "As Texas and California go, so goes the nation."

Organization of the Basal Reader

Basal readers are designed to take children through a series of books, experiences, and activities toward increasingly sophisticated reading behaviors. Each basal series typically provides several readers or books of reading selections at each level. For example, the *Scott Foresman: Reading (2000)* basal provides the following books organized by theme for each grade level:

Grade 1

Good Times We Share
Take a Closer Look
Let's Learn Together
Favorite Things Old and New
Take Me There
Surprise Me!

Grade 2

You + Me = Special
Zoom In!
Side by Side
Ties Through Time
All Aboard!
Just Imagine

Grade 3

Finding My Place
The Whole Wide World
Getting the Job Done
From Past to Present
Are We There Yet?
Imagination.kids

Grade 4

Focus on Family
A Wider View
Keys to Success
Timeless Stories
Other Times, Other Places
Express Yourself!

Grade 5

Relating to Others
My World and Yours
A Job Well Done
Time and Time Again
Traveling On
Think of It!

Grade 6

Discovering Ourselves
The Living Earth
Goals Great and Small
The Way We Were—The Way We Are
Into the Unknown
I've Got It!

Important features to be found in current teacher's editions include (1) philosophical statements, (2) a skills overview for each unit, (3) classroom routines, (4) suggestions for accommodating special needs, (5) assessment ties to national standards and tests, (6) technology information, (7) themes, (8) projects, (9) assessment benchmarks, (10) a glossary, (11) a bibliography, and (12) a scope and sequence chart. The scope and sequence chart is a year-by-year curricular plan, usually in chart form, that includes the instructional objectives and skills associated with a specific basal reading program. Objectives and skills are arranged in the scope and sequence chart by categories and grade levels. It is in the scope and sequence chart that teachers learn about the objectives of the basal program and the sequence of lessons designed to accomplish the objectives.

Most contemporary basal readers are organized into **themed units,** with several selections organized around a selected theme or topic; still others are organized into arbitrarily divided units of instruction. Most basal readers follow a somewhat modified version of the directed reading thinking activity (DRTA) format developed by Stauffer in 1969. This format can be represented in nine discrete parts or steps in the lesson.

1. Activating prior knowledge and building background
2. Delivering skill lessons in phonics, spelling, vocabulary, and comprehension
3. Previewing and predicting
4. Setting the purpose
5. Guiding the reading
6. Confirming predictions
7. Responding to comprehension discussion questions
8. Providing skill instruction and practice in oral language, writing, grammar, phonics, handwriting, comprehension, and fluency
9. Ideas and projects for enrichment

Lessons are arranged for teachers into a daily planner. It is intended that teachers will not use all of the resources of the basal reader teacher's edition, but rather will select those resources on a daily basis that best suit the needs of the students in the classroom. We remind our readers emphatically that basal teachers' editions are resources to augment the teacher's knowledge of the reading process and the needs of his or her students. They are not scripts to be followed without judgment, skill, and decision making.

Standards for Evaluating and Adopting Basal Readers

Few professional decisions deserve more careful attention than evaluating and adopting a basal reading series for a school district. Because you will probably be asked to evaluate one or more basal reading series during your professional career, you need to understand how to evaluate and select basal reading programs effectively. Learning about this process will also empower you to help reform, restructure, and strengthen future revisions, editions, and basal reading adoption processes.

Ways of Evaluating Basal Readers

Only after teachers are sufficiently well informed about the characteristics of effective basal reader programs can they act to correct or adjust the use of the basal to benefit their students. Dole, Rogers, and Osborn (1987) recommend that the evaluation of basal readers should focus on the following:

1. Identify the facets of effective reading instruction to be identified in each program.
2. Delineate criteria related to effective reading instruction to be analyzed in the basal readers.
3. Provide a means for carefully recording how well basal readers measure up to the established criteria.

Because many reading teachers are concerned with curriculum changes that reflect a decided move toward evidence-based comprehensive reading instructional practices in basal readers, we strongly recommend that classroom professionals obtain the materials, worksheets, and procedures found in Dole, Osborn, and Lehr's "Adoption Guidelines Project" (*A Guide to Selecting Basal Reading Programs*). These can be obtained by sending requests to the Center for the Study of Reading, University of Illinois-Guide, P.O. Box 2121, Station A, Champaign, IL 61825-2121.

A Consumer's Guide to Evaluating a Core Reading Program

Recently, Simmons and Kame'enui (2003) developed an instrument to help educators evaluate basal reading programs called *A Consumer's Guide to Evaluating a Core Reading Program*. It particularly focuses on grades K through 3 and offers guidelines for evaluating the Big Five in reading instruction: phonemic awareness, phonics, vocabulary, comprehension, and fluency. You can obtain *A Consumer's Guide to Evaluating a Core Reading Program* free online at *http://reading.uoregon.edu/ curricula/con_guide.php*. Figure 10.6 features several excerpts from *A Consumer's Guide to Evaluating a Core Reading Program* at the grade 1 level. Many other states have also developed core reading program evaluation instruments as part of justifying reading interventions for the Reading First legislation. Kentucky and Ohio are two that provide good examples available on the Internet. To see Ohio's basal evaluation instrument online, go to *http://www.readingfirstohio.org/assets/pdf/ Eval_Guide_for_Supplemental_&_Intervention.pdf*.

Figure 10.6 Excerpts from A Consumer's Guide to Evaluating a Core Reading Program

Phonemic Awareness is the ability to hear and manipulate the sound structure of language. It is a strong predictor of reading success. Phonemic awareness is an auditory skill and consists of multiple components.

High Priority Items—Phonemic Awareness Instruction

Rating	Criterion	Initial Instruction	Evidence	
			Week ____	Week ____
○○●	1. Allocates appropriate amount of daily time to blending, segmenting, and manipulating tasks until proficient. *(w)* [NRP, pg. 2–41]			
○○●	2. Incorporates letters into phonemic awareness activities. *(w)* [NRP, pg. 2–41]			

First Grade Phonemic Awareness Instruction—High Priority
Tally the number of elements with each rating.

● ____   ○ ____   ○ ____

High Priority Items—Phonics Instruction

Rating	Criterion	Initial Instruction	Evidence	
			Week ____	Week ____
○○●	1. Progresses systematically from simple word types (e.g., consonant-vowel-consonant) and word lengths (e.g., number of phonemes) and word complexity (e.g., phonemes in the word, position of blends, stop sounds) to more complex words. *(ss)* [NRP, pg. 2–132]			
○○●	2. Models instruction at each of the fundamental stages (e.g., letter–sound correspondences, blending, reading whole words). *(w)* and *(ss)*			

Simmons, D.C. & Kame'enui, E.J. (2003). *A Consumer's Guide to Evaluating a Core Reading Program* & Corales K.J.: *A Critical Elements Analysis* Eugene, OR: University of Oregon.

Figure 10.6 Continued

High Priority Items—Phonics Instruction

Rating	Criterion	Evidence		
		Initial Instruction	Week ___	Week ___
○○●	3. Provides teacher-guided practice in controlled word lists and connected text in which students can apply their newly learned skills successfully. *(w)*			
○○●	4. Includes repeated opportunities to read words in contexts in which students can apply their knowledge of letter–sound correspondences. *(w)* and *(ss)* [NRP, pg. 3–28]			
○○●	5. Uses decodable text based on specific phonics lessons in the early part of the first grade as an intervening step between explicit skill acquisition and the students' ability to read quality trade books. Decodable texts should contain the phonics elements and sight words that students have been taught. *(w)* and *(ss)*			

First Grade Phonics and Instruction—High Priority
Tally the number of elements with each rating.

●———○———○

High Priority Items—Connected Text and Fluency Instruction

Rating	Criterion	Evidence		
		Initial Instruction	Week ___	Week ___
○○●	1. Introduces passage reading soon after students can read a sufficient number of words accurately. *(w)*			

(continued)

Figure 10.6 Continued

High Priority Items—Connected Text and Fluency Instruction

Rating	Criterion	Initial Instruction	Evidence	
			Week ___	Week ___
○○●	2. Contains regular words comprised of letter-sounds and word types that have been taught. *(w)* and *(ss)*			
○○●	3. Contains only high-frequency irregular words that have been previously taught. *(ss)*			
○○●	4. Uses initial stories/passages composed of a high percentage of regular words (minimum of 75–80% decodable words). *(w)*			
○○●	5. Builds toward a 60-word-per-minute fluency goal by end of grade. *(ss)* [NRP, pg. 3–4]			
○○●	6. Includes sufficient independent practice materials of appropriate difficulty for students to develop fluency. *(w)* and *(ss)* [NRP, pg. 3–28]			

First Grade Connected Text and Fluency Instruction—High Priority
Tally the number of elements with each rating.   ● ___ ○ ___ ○ ___

High Priority Items—Vocabulary Instruction

Rating	Criterion	Initial Instruction	Evidence	
			Week ___	Week ___
●○○	1. Provides direct instruction of specific concepts and vocabulary. *(w)*			

Figure 10.6 Continued

High Priority Items—Vocabulary Instruction

Rating	Criterion	Initial Instruction	Evidence	
			Week _____	Week _____
○ ○ ●	2. Provides repeated and multiple exposures to critical vocabulary. (w) and (st)			
○ ○ ●	3. Integrates words into sentences and asks students to tell the meaning of the word in the sentence and to use it in a variety of contexts. (w)			

First Grade Vocabulary Instruction—High Priority
Tally the number of elements with each rating.
● _____ ○ _____ ○ _____

High Priority Items—Reading Comprehension Instruction

Rating	Criterion	Initial Instruction	Evidence	
			Week _____	Week _____
○ ○ ●	1. Guides students through sample text in which teachers think out loud as they identify the components of story structure. (w) [NRP, pg. 4–122]			
○ ○ ●	2. Provides plentiful opportunities to listen to and explore narrative and expository text forms and to engage in interactive discussion of the messages and meanings of the text. (ss) [NRP, pg. 4–109]			
○ ○ ●	3. Explicitly teaches critical comprehension strategy (e.g., main idea, literal, inferential, retell, prediction). (w) and (ss)			

First Grade Reading Comprehension Instruction—Discretionary
Tally the number of elements with each rating.
● _____ ○ _____ ○ _____

(continued)

Figure 10.6 Continued

Summary of First Grade Ratings

High Priority Items

	●	○	○
Phonemic Awareness Instruction (2)	●	○	
Phonics Instruction (5)	●	○	
Irregular Words Instruction (2)	●	○	
Connected Text and Fluency Instruction (6)	●	○	
Vocabulary Development (3)	●	○	
Reading Comprehension Instruction (3)	●	○	

First Grade High Priority Totals   ●   ○

Discretionary Items

	●	○	○
Phonemic Awareness Instruction (5)	●	○	○
Phonics Instruction (4)	●	○	
Irregular Words Instruction (2)	●	○	
Connected Text and Fluency Instruction (2)	●	○	
Vocabulary Development (3)	●	○	
Reading Comprehension Instruction (3)	●	○	

First Grade Discretionary Totals   ●   ○

First Grade Design Features

● ○	1. Aligns and coordinates the words used in phonics/word recognition activities with those used in fluency building.
● ○	2. Provides ample practice on high-priority skills.
● ○	3. Provides explicit and systematic instruction.
● ○	4. Includes systematic and cumulative review of high priority skills.
● ○	5. Demonstrates and builds relationships between fundamental skills leading to higher order skills.

Additional Comments

Table 10.1 The Oregon Reading First Center (ORFC) Review of Reading Programs in the Areas of Phonemic Awareness, Phonics, and Fluency*

Basal/Core Program	Ranking: Phonemic Awareness Instruction	Ranking: Phonics Instruction	Ranking: Fluency	Overall Ranking
Houghton Mifflin	1	1	2	1
Open Court (McGraw Hill)	4	4	1	2
Harcourt	2	2	3	2
Scott Foresman	5	3	4	4
Macmillan (McGraw Hill)	3	5	5	5
Wright Group	6	6	6	6
Rigby	7	7	7	6

*Retrieved from *http:reading.uoregon.edu/curricula/or_rfc_review.php*

Recent Evaluations of Basal (Core) Reading Programs: Phonemic Awareness, Phonics, and Fluency

A number of evaluations of prominent basal/core reading programs and supplemental reading programs have been conducted in recent years by various state departments of education (SDE). Florida, Oregon, Maryland, Indiana, Ohio, Kentucky, California, Utah, and Texas are just a few of the states conducting such reviews in connection with Reading First funding. In many cases, the SDEs have opted to use Simmons and Kame'enui's (2003) *A Consumer's Guide to Evaluating a Core Reading Program* to aid them in this process.

One such evaluation that seems to reflect a consensus of findings on basal reader effectiveness is the *Oregon Reading First Center (ORFC): Review of Comprehensive Programs* (ORFC Curriculum Review Panel, 2004). Two rather severe limitations of the report is that it only considers reading programs for grades K–3, and only three of the Big Five areas of reading: phonemic awareness, phonics, and fluency. Reading comprehension and vocabulary development are ignored. Nevertheless, the report is very useful indeed for examining the strengths of each program in the three areas of reading considered. In Table 10.1 we offer a summary of the reading programs reviewed and their relative rating in each of the three areas reviewed. Our rankings summary from the ORFC reflects the mean score on "high priority" skills for all grade levels reviewed. Also, please note that we are only including the ORFC findings for what we consider to be basal/core reading programs. We will examine their findings for two other supplemental reading programs *(Reading Mastery, Success for All)* later in this chapter.

What Programs Are Available for the Struggling Reader?

In 1998, Pikulski reviewed the effectiveness of several national reading programs designed to prevent reading failure. Later, similar reviews of the effectiveness of supplemental programs were published by other researchers, committees, and state departments of education (e.g., St. John & Loescher, 2001; ORFC Curriculum Review Panel, 2004; Maryland Evaluation Committee, 2006) to help us better understand their relative merits. Although basal readers remain the predominant form of reading instruction in most classrooms, several of these national programs are worth noting.

Reading Recovery

Reading Recovery, developed by clinical child psychologist Marie Clay, is an early intervention program designed to reduce reading failure in the first grade for the lowest performing 20 percent of students. The aim of the program is to help low-achieving children catch up to the level of their age-related peers. Reading Recovery was imported to the United States by faculty at the Ohio State University (Allington, 1992). Reading Recovery (RR) trained teachers enroll in a yearlong course of graduate studies with regular follow-up professional development seminars to keep one's training current and approved (Lyons & Beaver, 1995). Teachers trained in RR must receive training from an approved RR teacher trainer and at one of several approved sites throughout the nation.

> **Getting to Know English Learners**
>
> ELs always benefit from programs such as Reading Recovery, Success For All, and Early Steps because of the one-to-one intensive daily reading instruction and individual tutoring sessions. Providing bilingual or culturally-different basal textbooks as well as picture and trade books will also help ELs feel welcome and succeed more quickly.

The average RR student is recovered from below-grade-level performance in an average of 12 to 14 weeks. Discontinued children show normal development after release from the program. Students in New Zealand and in the United States demonstrate the substantial positive effects this invention has on young children's reading and writing development (Clay, 1990; DeFord, Lyons, & Pinnell, 1991; Pinnell, DeFord, & Lyons, 1994).

Children selected for the RR program receive one-to-one, intensive, daily reading instruction for 30 minutes. During this instructional period, teachers and children engage in five major activities in a sequenced and structured format. The first activity is the rereading of at least two familiar books or "familiar rereads" of books students have read previously with the assistance and guidance of the RR teacher taking a daily "running record" of the student's oral reading. During a running record, the teacher notes which words are read accurately or inaccurately and analyzes the inaccuracies for the cue system the student used or neglected to use to inform upcoming instructional emphasis and planning. Third, teacher and students work with letters and words. A typical activity is word-making using plastic magnetic letters on a cookie sheet. The teacher might show a child the word *ran* and ask him or her to blend the sounds to pronounce the word. Then the teacher might remove the *r*, substitute *f*, and ask the child to blend the new sound to get the word *fan*. In the fourth activity, the child dictates a sentence or two; this is called a "story" in RR terminology. The teacher helps the child write the "story" by stretching words with the child, encouraging him or her to write the letter for each sound to form each word. After each word is written, the teacher asks the student to reread the word(s) until the entire sentence is written. After reading the entire sentence, the teacher cuts the sentence into words strips and asks the student to re-order the word strips into the sentence. The fifth and final activity in an RR lesson is the introduction of a new story. The teacher has pre-read the story and noted challenges and obstacles the child might face in his or her reading. The teacher walks the student through the "pictures," introducing new vocabulary, sounding out "tricky" words with the student (often using a small, white board and marker), and discussing any unfamiliar concepts or language. Then the child reads the book with careful guidance, support, and feedback from the teacher.

Some educators have suggested that RR may be too expensive to realistically implement on a wide scale in the United States, where the reading failure rate exceeds 20 percent. However, with over 80 percent of children in RR moving to discontinuance and grade level performance in less than a semester of intensive instruction and continuing to make acceptable progress, it seems that RR is substantially more cost effective than are many of the commonly tried remedial options, including special education, for addressing the needs of low-performing children (Dyer, 1992).

In their 2007 review of the Reading Recovery Program, the What Works Clearing house (WWC) rated it as highly effective in assisting struggling readers in improving general reading achievement. Reading Recovery received their highest or next to highest ratings for alphabetic (phonics and word attack skills), reading fluency and comprehension.

Success for All

Success for All (SFA) is a total school reform program for grades K–3. Originally developed for struggling readers, the goal of the SFA program is to have all children reading on grade level by third grade, with no retentions and referrals to special education for reading problems. Robert Slavin, Director of the Center for Research and Effective Schooling for Disadvantaged Students at Johns Hopkins University, and his colleagues developed the SFA program. The SFA program is grounded on three premises. First, the primary-grade classroom is the best place to work on ensuring children's school success. Second, additional instruction should be provided to students as soon as they are identified as needing it. Third, educators need to think creatively about the use of school resources, personnel, and instructional time.

SFA focuses on providing quality reading instruction in grades K–3 as well as providing supplementary support in the form of individual tutoring sessions. Students are placed into heterogeneous classroom groupings for most of the day, but when the 90-minute reading instructional block is begun, children are regrouped into "ability" groups of 15 to 20 students across the three grade levels 1–3. Regrouping according to reading levels allows whole group, direct instruction of children and is intended to eliminate the over reliance on seatwork and worksheets found in many classrooms.

For students who are not responsive to whole class instruction in their reading groups, supplementary individual tutoring for 20 minutes per day is provided in the SFA program. Tutoring sessions focus on the same strategies and skills taught in the whole class sessions and, whenever possible, the classroom teacher is freed up by the use of classroom aides to provide the tutoring sessions. SFA also recommends that children attend half-day preschool and full-day kindergarten to accelerate progress in learning to read successfully. Multiple evaluations have shown that SFA is an effective program for reducing referrals to special education and grade-level retentions. However, studies indicate that SFA has not achieved its stated goal of helping every child read on grade level by the end of third grade (Slavin et al., 1990, 1992, 1996).

In the report *Oregon Reading First Center (ORFC): Review of Comprehensive Programs* (ORFC Curriculum Review Panel, 2004), SFA was fairly weak in the areas of phonemic awareness (6th), phonics (7th), and fluency (6th) when compared to eight other leading core programs.

Four Blocks

The **Four Blocks (FB)** program implemented in Winston-Salem, North Carolina by P. Cunningham is a program of first grade reading instruction. The FB program organizes daily reading instruction around four 30-minute blocks of instruction: (1) Basal Block, (2) Writing Block, (3) Working with Words Block, and (4) Self-Selected Reading Block. During Basal Block, the teacher and students selectively use materials and suggestions provided in the school's or district's adopted basal reading program. This means that students read stories, essays, articles, and other text found in the anthology (student's text) of the basal reader program. The activities found in the basal reader are used during this instructional time block.

During Writing Block, the teacher typically begins with a five- to ten-minute mini-lesson on a writing convention, style, or genre. Following this mini-lesson, students engage in individually selected writing projects, taking these projects through the typical stages and activities of a writer's workshop—drafting, revising, editing, and publishing. The Working with Words Block of instructional time consists of reading words from the word wall and making words. Word wall words are high-frequency, phonically irregular words posted on a wall that students learn to read and spell by sight rather than through pattern analysis or decoding. The word-making activities consist of using groups of letters to make as many words as possible. The teacher usually issues a clue as to the words that can be made by using two or more letters in various combinations. This activity concludes with students using all of the letters in the group to make a single word known as the "secret" word. During the final 30-minutes time block, Self-Selected Reading, students read books of their own choosing. They complete projects and responses to the books they read to share their experiences and knowledge with other children. Results reported by Cunningham, Hall, and Defee (1998) indicate that the program has been successful with students of a wide range of literacy levels without the use of ability or leveled grouping.

Early Steps

Early Steps (ES) developed by Darrell Morris (Morris, Shaw, & Perney, 1990), is an early intervention program designed to reduce reading failure in the early years. Children selected for the ES program receive one-to-one, intensive, daily reading instruction for 30 minutes. During this 30-minute daily instructional period, teacher and students engage in four major activities in a sequenced and structured format. To begin a lesson, students reread familiar leveled books for 8 to 10 minutes. In the second activity, the teacher takes the student through a series of word sort activities for 5 to 6 minutes. The teacher places three words (for example, *hat, man, cap*) horizontally across the table or desktop. After watching the teacher demonstrate the task of sorting the words that remain in the deck, the student completes the task. Sorting tasks focus initially on sorting words according to phonograms, word families, or rimes. For the next 5 to 8 minutes of the lesson, the child writes a sentence from his or her own experience. After a short dialogue with the teacher, the student writes while saying aloud each word, stretching the word, and recoding the letter for each sound segmented from the stretched word. After the student is finished writing, the teacher writes the sentence on a sentence strip and cuts it apart for the student to put together and reread. The fourth and final step in the ES lesson is the introduction of a new book the child is expected to read the next day without much help. Books are selected in ascending levels of difficulty, thus pushing the student's reading progress forward. Before reading, the teacher helps the student look at the pictures, talk about the unfamiliar vocabulary words, and situate the book in a meaningful frame of reference. During the reading, the teacher coaches the student to use strategies and self-correct. When the student finishes this book, it is used the next day for familiar rereading.

In many ways, Early Steps is very much like Reading Recovery, only with a more systematic approach to the teaching of phonic decoding strategies. Research by Santa and Hoien (1999) showed Early Steps intervention in grades 1 and 2 helped the most at-risk students to approach the average performance level of their peers within one academic year of instruction. Early Steps boosted scores in decoding, spelling, word recognition, and reading comprehension.

Reading Mastery

Reading Mastery is a supplemental reading program best suited to students having severe reading problems, and for whom traditional programs and methods have failed. It may also be useful as a supplemental reading program for students at high risk of reading failure, and or for English language learners (Gunn, Biglan, Smolkowski, & Ary, 2000; Gunn, Smolkowski, Biglan, & Black, 2002). The What Works Clearinghouse (WWC) (see WWC online at: *http://www.whatworks.ed.gov/*) describes the program as follows:

> Reading Mastery is a direct instruction program designed to provide explicit, systematic instruction in English language reading. Reading Mastery is available in two versions, Reading Mastery Classic levels I and II (for use in grades K–3) and Reading Mastery Plus, an integrated reading-language program for grades K–6. The program begins by teaching phonemic awareness and sound-letter correspondence and moves into word and passage reading, vocabulary development, comprehension, and building oral reading fluency. Later lessons continue to emphasize accurate and fluent decoding while teaching students the skills necessary to read and comprehend and to learn from expository text. Lessons are designed to be fast-paced and interactive. Students are grouped by similar reading level, based on program placement tests. The program includes placement assessments and a continuous monitoring system.

Reading Mastery was originally developed by Siegfried Engelmann under the title *Distar® Reading* for use in Project Follow Through as part of the direct instruction teaching model, and is marketed by SRA/McGraw-Hill.

In the report *Oregon Reading First Center (ORFC): Review of Comprehensive Programs* (ORFC Curriculum Review Panel, 2004), Reading Mastery ranked highest in high-priority standards of all nine programs reviewed in the areas of phonemic awareness, phonics, and fluency. There is no extant impartial evidence we can find as to Reading Mastery's benefits to vocabulary learning or comprehension development. The What Works Clearinghouse rated Reading Mastery as having "potentially positive effects," though this evaluation is based on only one recorded study with English learners.

Reading Expeditions: Language, Literacy, & Vocabulary!

The National Geographic Society, a nonprofit organization famous for high-quality publications, has introduced a new informational text series called ***Language, Literacy, & Vocabulary!*** **(LLV).** The Reading Expeditions component of *Language, Literacy,*

& *Vocabulary!* for students in grades 3 through 8 uses a powerful "sheltered-instruction approach" that combines essential science and social studies content with nonfiction reading skills and strategies. This affordable program features the following:

- 48 high-interest, age-appropriate science and social studies titles
- Key vocabulary repeated and applied in different contexts
- Content broken down into manageable units
- Limited text loads; simple text layouts and sentence patterns
- Academic vocabulary with on-page definitions
- Comprehension strategies and fluency practice
- Research and writing opportunities
- Rich instructional support and tools based on latest research
- Differentiated instruction for various stages of English language proficiency and reading development
- Alignment with national and state standards

McNabb (2006) summarized a recent study of the effectiveness of *Language, Literacy, & Vocabulary!* as follows:

> The study was conducted in urban Illinois public schools with 259 students in 4 schools, 90 students in the treatment groups and 169 students in the control groups. . . . A thorough analysis of the data collected indicates that the students in treatment groups made statistically significant gains in their content area literacy development compared with students who did not use the *Language, Literacy, & Vocabulary!* curriculum. In each curriculum group, the mean improvement from pretest to posttest was substantially higher for the students in the treatment groups.

Language, Literacy, & Vocabulary! has been adopted as a key supplemental program in the Memphis research study in the federal Striving Readers project because of its infusion of scientifically-based reading research (SBRR) in an appealing informational text format. For online information about this innovative product, go to *www.ngschoolpub.org.*

Waterford Early Reading Program

The Florida Center for Reading Research (online at *www.fcrr.org*) describes the **Waterford Early Reading Program** as

> a comprehensive early intervention curriculum designed to develop literacy for kindergarten through third grade students. The three levels of the program are for emerging, developing, and fluent readers and include multimedia technology to provide daily, research-based, individualized instruction for every student in the classroom. Each of the three levels contains one school year's worth of instructional material so students work at their instructional level regardless of the grade level in which they are placed. Waterford provides all the materials necessary for implementation including the teacher guides (teacher-led or center-based off-line activities), CDs, videotapes, audiotapes, student materials, parent resources, hardware, software (curriculum that students engage in on the computer), and earphones with microphones. The computers can be in a lab setting or at a center in the classroom that contains three to four computers. Guidelines for teachers to follow in order to place students at appropriate levels of the program are also delineated in the Waterford "Getting Started Guide." For the software component, engaging tutorials regarding how to use the mouse are available for young children.

The only independent scientific-based reading research study available at this point on Waterford seems to be one showing disappointing results with an urban population. Paterson and colleagues (2003) conducted a one-year study of the effectiveness of the Waterford Early Reading Program on kindergarten and first grade children in a large urban school district. They concluded that Waterford classrooms failed to outperform non-Waterford classrooms in part because the program did not encourage the social interactions necessary for growth in early emergent reading and writing.

Supplementing Your Reading Program with Leveled Books

There is no such thing as a "one-size-fits-all" reading program. Any program will need to be supplemented if the needs of all learners are to be met. Sometimes a program lacks strength in one or more of the Big Five areas. Other times the core program, as we have seen, may lack sufficient nonfiction/informational reading selections. A common solution is to supplement the reading program with trade books. The problem here is knowing the reading level (difficulty level) of the different selections to be used; this is critical knowledge for matching "just right" books to each learner.

Fountas and Pinnell (1999), in their book *Matching Books to Readers: Using Leveled Books in Guided Reading, K–3,* describe a way to "level" reading materials in the classroom. Reutzel and Cooter (2007) have summarized key attributes of the Fountas and Pinnell leveling system for books as well other comparison information. We share this in Figure 10.7.

Many teachers in the primary grades rely heavily on a system for leveling books to match students with texts that meet their instructional needs. Although leveled books can be an enormously helpful tool in beginning reading instruction, Szymusiak and Sibberson (2001) in their book *Beyond Leveled Books: Supporting Transitional Readers in Grades 2–5,* warn against the dangers of a "steady diet" of reading in leveled books. They state:

> When students' reading diet is exclusively a leveled one, their purpose for reading disappears. They read for us. They become eager to reach the next level instead of being eager to earn more from what they are reading. (pp. 15–16)

We know the leveling mania has gone too far when students must read only from leveled materials, when teachers will only purchase materials for reading based on levels, and when students and teachers no longer seek the goal of independence in reading through instruction in self-selection of appropriately challenging and interesting reading materials!

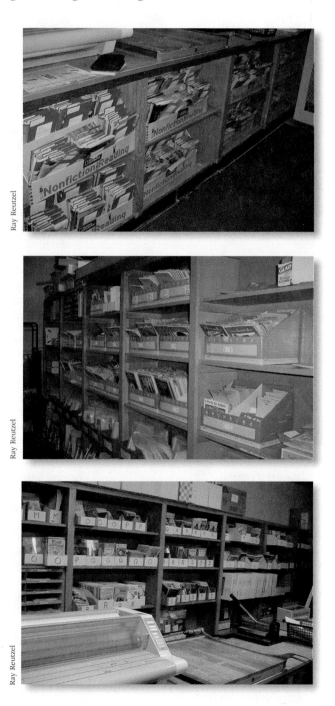

Figure 10.7 Reading Level Translations

Reading Levels (traditional designations)	Guided Reading (GR) Levels (Extrapolated from Fountas & Pinnell, 1996, 2001)	Common Text Attributes	Exemplars Books and Publishers (using GR levels)	Approximate Level of Reading Development
Preschool-Kindergarten (Readiness)	A	Wordless picture books	A = *Dog Day!* (Rigby)	Emergent
	B	Repeated phrases; text-picture matching; experiences common to readers; short (10–60 words)	B = *Fun with Hats* (Mondo)	
PP (preprimer)	C D E	Same as above for B, but repeating phrases don't dominate the book; more language variation; by level E, syntax becomes more like regular "book language"	C = *Brown Bear, Brown Bear* (Holt) D = *The Storm* (Wright Group) E = *The Big Toe* (Wright Group)	Emergent → Early
P (primer)	F G	Longer sentences/less predictable text; new verb forms appear; story grammar elements continue over multiple pages; pictures provide only a little support.	F = *A Moose Is Loose* (Houghton Mifflin) G = *More Spaghetti I Say* (Scholastic)	Early
Grade 2 (early) Grade 2 Grade 2 (late)	J K L M	Longer stories with more complicated story grammar elements; varied vocabulary with rich meanings; common to have whole pages of text; more content (nonfiction) selections are in evidence	J = *The Boy Who Cried Wolf* (Scholastic) K = *Amelia Bedelia* (Harper & Row) L = *Cam Jansen and the Mystery of the Monster Movie* (Puffin) M = *How to Eat Fried Worms* (Dell)	Transitional → Fluent

(continued)

Figure 10.7   (Continued)

Grade 3	N–P	Fewer illustrations; more complex nonfiction; complex sentences and challenging vocabulary; higher order thinking begins here	**N** = *Pioneer Cat* (Random House) **O** = *Whipping Boy* (Troll) **P** = *Amelia Earhart* (Dell)	**Fluent (Basic)**
Grade 4	Q–S	Few illustrations; more complex language and concept load; higher order thinking is deepened; appearance of metaphor; topics are farther from student experiences; historical fiction is common; complex ideas are presented	**Q** = *Pony Pals: A Pony for Keeps* (Scholastic) **R** = *Hatchet* (Simon & Schuster) **S** = *Story of Harriet Tubman, Conductor of the Underground Railroad* (Scholastic)	**Fluent → Extending to Content Texts**

From D. R. Reutzel & R. B. Cooter. (2007). *Strategies for Reading Assessment and Instruction: Helping Every Child Succeed* (3rd ed.). Upper Saddle River, NJ: Pearson Merrill Prentice Hall. Reprinted by permission.

On the other hand, to abandon some controls on text difficulty seems to be, as Holdaway (1979) puts it, "sheer madness." Holdaway reminds us that many children continue to struggle to read authentic texts that are far too difficult for them to handle independently. It is clear that basal readers need to provide a balance of text types, including decodable, leveled, patterned, informational, and authentic story texts in quantities that allow teachers to choose what works best with each child at various levels of reading development. Hiebert (1999) makes an impassioned call for authors to produce a new kind of beginning reading text modeled after the creations of Dr. Seuss in books such as *Green Eggs and Ham*. She states:

> Over a decade ago, Anderson, et al. (1985) called for inventive writers to use Dr. Seuss as a model for creating engaging texts for beginning readers. This call needs to be extended again but, this time, with a clearer mandate—one that derives from a strong vision of what beginning readers need to learn. Such texts require thought to word density ratios and to the repetitions across as well as within texts of words that share phonetic elements (p. 565).

Finding Leveled Books. Many Web sites provide information about leveled books using the Fountas and Pinnell (1999) and Pinnell and Fountas (2002) A–Z leveling approach. Some of these are listed here:

http://www.fountasandpinnellleveledbooks.com/
http://registration.beavton.k12.or.us/lbdb/
http://www.pps.k12.or.us/curriculum/literacy/leveled_books/
http://www.leveledbooks.com/
http://www.readinga-z.com/
http://www.readinglady.com/gr/Leveled_Books/leveled_books.html

The Internet site *www.readinga-z.com* provides many choices—at our last count, 1,300 downloadable leveled books—that can be easily used as "benchmark books" for assessment purposes.

How Can Basal Reading Programs Be Adapted to Assist the Struggling Reader?

Historically, the basal reader has not served very successfully as a tool for assisting struggling readers. There are several reasons for this situation. First, some teachers find the stories in basal readers to be bland and uninviting, especially for problem readers. What is needed most is literature that "turns on" the "turned-off" learner—an order too tall for many basals to fill. Second, if a student is failing to achieve success using one approach to reading instruction, in this case the basal reader, then common sense tells us that what is needed is an alternative strategy—not just more of the same. Finally, basal reader systems frequently do not allow students enough time for real reading. The multifarious collection of skill sheets and workbook pages tends to be so time-consuming that little time is left for actual reading. In Chapter 1, we discuss principles for encouraging literacy, some of which are most pertinent when using basal readers to help students with special needs. Three direct applications of these principles follow.

Reading the Basal Straight Through

Teachers working with special needs students recognize that what these children need most is regular and sustained reading. We suggest that skill sheets and workbook pages be used judiciously, or even avoided, to allow for more time spent reading. Students should be allowed to read basals straight through as an anthology of children's stories. The teacher may wish to skip stories that offer little to the reader in this setting.

Repeated Readings

In repeated readings, the teacher typically introduces the story as a shared book or story experience, then students attempt to read the book alone or with a friend (Routman, 1988). If the story has rhyme or a regular pattern, it may be sung or chanted. Repeated readings of stories help children achieve a sense of accomplishment, improve comprehension, and build fluency.

Supported, or Buddy, Reading

Many times, at-risk readers are very reluctant to become risk takers. Teachers simply must find ways of breaking the ice for them and create classroom safety nets.

Supported, or "buddy," reading allows students to read aloud basal stories together, either taking turns or in unison. By rereading these supported selections, students' fluency and comprehension improve. Another variation is for teacher–student combinations to read together. Similar to the procedure known as *neurological impress* (Hollingsworth, 1978), the student and teacher read aloud in unison at a comfortable rate. For first readings, the teacher usually assumes the lead in terms of volume and pace. In subsequent repeated readings, the student is encouraged to assume the lead.

Chapter 11 provides more insights into how teachers can enhance the reading and writing environment as they begin making the transition from basal-only teaching to more balanced literacy perspectives and practices. In the process, teachers discover numerous opportunities for assisting students with special needs within the elementary classroom.

Grand Conversations, prediction relays, partner retellings, and text extension activities are some of the differentiation ideas found in "General Strategies for Promoting Reading Development". Visit the Teacher Prep Website (*www.prenhall.com/teacherprep*) and go to *Strategies and Lessons—Reading Methods/Instructional Approaches* to select this link.

What Programs Are Available for Helping Students with Diverse Cultural or Language Needs Succeed?

Students who do not possess reading and writing ability in a first language should be taught to read and write in their native or first language to support and validate them as worthwhile individuals. In addition, reading instruction in the first language helps students capitalize on what they already know about their primary language and culture to build concepts that can facilitate the acquisition of English (Freeman & Freeman, 1992; Krashen & Biber, 1988). In any case, teachers must be sensitive to these students' special needs, which include (a) a need for safety and security, (b) a need to belong and be accepted, and (c) a need to feel self-esteem (Peregoy & Boyle, 1993).

Teachers should help English as a second language (ESL) or English learners (EL) feel at ease when they arrive in the classroom by assigning them a "personal buddy" who, if possible, speaks the language of the newcomer. This buddy is assigned to help the new student through the school day, routines, and so on. Another approach is to avoid changes in the classroom schedule by following a regular and predictable routine each day, which creates a sense of security. To create a sense of belonging, assign the student to a home group for an extended period of time. A home group provides a small social unit of concern focused on helping the newcomer adapt to everyday life. Finally, self-esteem is enhanced when an individual's worth is affirmed. Opportunities for the newcomer to share her or his language and culture during daily events in the classroom provide a useful way to integrate her or him into the ongoing classroom culture.

To help ESL or ELL students succeed in classrooms where basal readers are the core of instruction, Law and Eckes (1990, p. 92) recommend the following:

- Supplement the basal as much as possible with language experience stories.
- Encourage extensive reading. Gather basal textbooks from as many different levels as possible. Also acquire easier textbooks in content areas as well as trade books to provide a wide range of reading topics.
- Expose children to the many different types of reading available in the "real" world (magazines, *TV Guide,* newspapers, product labels, signs, etc.).

How Can Teachers Help Parents Better Understand Reading Standards?

Many parents and interested stakeholders are aware of the standards-based movement in education as a result of its politicization and publicity surrounding state testing and the No Child Left Behind (NCLB) legislation. However, most people who are not educators, and probably some who are, find standards-based education to be confusing at best. Fortunately, there are free resources available that you can use to explain reading standards to parents and others. Here are three splendid resources to get you started.

- *Big Dreams: A Family Book About Reading*. Available free online from the National Institute for Literacy at *http://www.nifl.gov/partnershipforreading/publications/pdf/big_dreams.pdf* or order by telephone by calling 1-800-228-8813.
- *Put Reading First: Helping Your Child Learn to Read—A Parent Guide*. Available free online from the National Institute for Literacy at *http://www.nifl.gov/partnershipforreading/publications/Parent_br.pdf* or order by telephone by calling 1-800-228-8813.
- *A Child Becomes a Reader*. Available free online from the National Institute for Literacy at *http://www.nifl.gov/partnershipforreading/publications/reading_pre.pdf* or order by telephone by calling 1-800-228-8813.

Summary

For reading instruction to be effective, teachers must first be aware of the development and sequence of reading skills to the learned. Thus, we began this important chapter with a discussion of the evidence-based skills and related curriculum "standards" for reading instruction. Reading curriculum standards help us understand the progresion of reading development in five essential areas of reading instruction: phonemic awarenes, phonics, vocabulary, comprehension, and fluency.

In the past decade or so, standards-based curriculums and assessments have been prescribed as a cure for the poor performance and accountability of many public schools (Watt, 2005; Zuzovsky & Libman, 2006). Literally billions of dollars have been spent on programs and state tests, in part so that federal and state agencies can rank schools in terms of student achievement. Indeed, the *No Child Left Behind* (NCLB) legislation grew directly out of the standards-based movement. An understanding of the most essential skills adopted by state and other governmental agencies help teachers plan for classroom assessments and subsequent instruction tied to evidence-based research.

Core reading programs, also known as *basal* programs, are a collection of student texts and workbooks, teachers' manuals, and supplemental materials for teaching reading and sometimes writing instruction. Core reading programs are used primarily in the elementary and middle school grades as a foundation for consistent, basic instruction. We learned about a valuable resource in selecting core reading programs known as *A Consumer's Guide to Evaluating a Core Reading Program* which offers evidence as to the effectiveness of different core programs. In the end, core reading programs provide teachers with one of many tools for meeting the reading needs of every child.

When core reading programs are not effective for some learners, there are supplemental reading programs for struggling readers teachers can consider. An online tool to help teachers select programs and other resources is the What Works Clearinghouse *(www.whatworks.ed.gov)*. For example, in 2007 the What Works Clearinghouse identified *Reading Recovery* as an effective supplemental program for meeting the needs of struggling readers in first grade. Other popular supplemental programs we learned about included *Four Blocks,* and *Reading Mastery*. However, it is not always necessary to turn to commercial programs for helping struggling readers achieve success. Many teachers use leveled books as one part of guided oral reading instruction, repeated readings to improve reading fluency, and other research-supported practices.

At this point in time, there are few reading programs for English learners (EL) that have been shown effective through rigorous scientific research. However, in this chapter we did learn about some promising practices that may be used to supplement instruction for this growing population. In general, the most logical approach is for teachers to supplement their instruction with strategies proven to be effective with "English-only" students as identified throughout this book in the areas of phonemeic awareness, phonics, reading vocabulary, comprehension, and fluency.

It is important that we help parents understand reading standards and find practical ways to help their children become literate. Parents are the first and often the best teachers. We learned about free, research-supported tools we can use to educate parents about reading standards and home supports. One of these tools we can access is *Put Reading First: Helping Your Child Learn to Read–A Parent Guide*. This booklet is a good place to start and several others were provided to help every child become a successful reader.

Classroom Applications

1. Go to your local school district or university curriculum materials library. Select a leading basal reading series. Locate the following items in the teacher's edition: (a) the scope and sequence chart, (b) the parts of a directed reading lesson, (c) the skill lessons, (d) the workbooks, and (e) the book tests or assessment materials. Use *A Consumer's Guide to evaluating a Core Reading Program, Grades K–3: A Critical Elements Analysis* by Simmons and Kame'enui (2003) to evaluate the program. Report your results to your class.

2. Plan Block 1 in the Four-Block Reading Program using a basal reader. Determine how you would use the basal for 30 minutes per day for a week of instruction.

3. Select a leveled book. Go through the parts of a Reading Recovery lesson and write a plan about how you would introduce this as a new book to a struggling reader.

4. Interview a teacher in the field about the strengths and weaknesses of the basal. Find out why this teacher uses or does not use the basal. Find out how he or she supplement reading instruction with other materials to meet the needs of all students.

5. Visit a classroom in a local elementary school where Success for All is used. Observe a teacher teaching reading. Which parts of the SFA program did the teacher use? Which parts did the teacher omit? Write an essay about your observations.

6. Prepare a basal reading lesson to be taught in the schools. Secure permission to teach this lesson in a local grade-level appropriate classroom. Write a reflective essay about your experience detailing successes, failures, and necessary changes.

Recommended Readings

Baines, L. A., & Stanley, G. K. (2006). *Clearinghouse: A Journal of Educational Strategies, Issues and Ideas, 79* (3), 119–123.

Dole, J. A., Osborn, J., & Lehr, F. (1990). *A guide to selecting basal reading programs.* Urbana, IL: Center for the Study of Reading.

Duke, N. K. (2000). 3.6 minutes per day: The scarcity of informational texts in first grade. *Reading Research Quarterly, 35*(2), 202–224.

Fountas, I. C., & Pinnell, G. S. (1999). *Matching books to readers: Using leveled books in guided reading, K–3.* Portsmouth, NH: Heinemann.

Hiebert, E. H. (1999). Text matters in learning to read. *The Reading Teacher, 52*(6), 552–566.

Reutzel, D. R., & Larsen, N. S. (1995). Look what they've done to real children's books in the new basal readers. *Language Arts, 72*(7), 495–507.

Simmons, D. C., & Kame'enui, E. J. (2003). *A consumer's guide to evaluating a core reading program, Grades K–3: A critical elements analysis.* Eugene, OR: University of Oregon.

Szymusiak, K., & Sibberson, F. (2001). *Beyond leveled books: Supporting transitional readers in grades 2–5.* Portland, ME: Stenhouse.

chapter

11

Effective Reading Instruction and Organization in Grades K–3

Chapter Questions

1. What do teachers need to know and do to provide effective K–3 reading instruction?

2. How do K–3 children develop as readers?

3. What does research say about the relationship between K–3 reading instruction and K–3 children's reading achievement?

4. What are the characteristics of effective K–3 reading instruction?

5. How can K–3 teachers differentiate K–3 reading instruction to meet diverse student needs?

6. How can K–3 teachers make connections with students' families and communities?

Looking in a Primary-Grade Classroom: Effective Reading Instruction at Work

It is a warm, summerlike day at Mission Elementary School. We scurry down the covered walkways shielding us from direct sunlight to observe Ms. Rivera's second grade class. As we enter Room #6, we are immediately struck with the "busy" noise we hear: Children are engaged in a variety of reading practice tasks in learning centers. We scan the room to locate Ms. Rivera. She is busily working with a small group of children.

"Please take out your white boards and markers." Ms. Rivera tells the students. "I think you can solve this problem, but we'll just have to wait and see. Here is the problem: Using the letters on our cookie sheet" she points to an *a, e, i,—c, h, l, m*— "make the word *him*. You may work together. After you have done your very best, I want you to hold up your white boards so that I can see how each of you did."

Ms. Rivera leaves her small group deeply engaged in their problem to greet us. She points out to us how she is working with this group of children to help them increase their ability to use phonics in reading and writing. Then pointing around the room, she shows us her other centers: a reading nook; an integrated curriculum center focused on science content where children are learning about how different kinds of weather affect rock; a listening center with small books, headphones, and a CD player; a comprehension strategy center where children are completing a categorization task using a graphic organizer of different kinds of soil for growing bean plants under the headings of *clay, loam,* and *sand*.

In this quick visit to Ms. Rivera's classroom, we find students busy speaking, reading, listening, and writing. We see them reading stories in the reading nook and focusing on the acquisition of content knowledge and new vocabulary. We see them using their acquired knowledge to carry out the many tasks that their teacher had organized and assigned. Ms. Rivera's room is a busy place where children learn new and interesting things. Most importantly, they are learning that reading, writing, speaking, and listening are important tools for getting smarter!

What Do Teachers Need to Know and Do to Provide Effective K–3 Reading Instruction?

In the past five years, several major research studies have been undertaken with the objective of describing the practices, beliefs, and knowledge of exemplary K–3 literacy teachers (Block, Oaker, & Hurt, 2002; Morrow, Tracey, Woo, & Pressley, 1999; Pressley, Allington, Wharton-McDonald, Block, and Morrow, 2001; Rogg, 2001; Taylor, Pearson, Clark, & Walpole, 1999; Taylor, Pearson, Peterson, & Rodriguez, 2005). Taken together, these research reports reveal identifiable characteristics of those teachers whose practices lead to exceptional reading achievement for their primary grade students. Highly effective primary grade reading teachers who make a difference in young children's reading achievement shared the characteristics listed in Figure 11.1.

Of course, to implement highly effective primary grade reading instruction, teachers must understand how young children develop as readers and writers.

How Do K–3 Children Develop as Readers?

You will recall from an earlier reading of Chapter 5 Jeanne Chall (1983) proposed that there are six stages for becoming a fluent, accomplished reader. We will briefly summarize this earlier information here, but refer you back to this chapter for greater detail and review of these stages of young children's reading development. In the first stage or Stage 0, children have not yet begun to pay much attention to the letters and words on the page. They ask for books to be read aloud repeatedly; rely rather heavily on the pictures, and often need someone to read to or with them in order to successfully navigate their way through text.

Once young children understand that reading requires more than listening to a story read aloud repeatedly and following along with the pictures, they focus their attention on the printed page. As they do so, they come to understand that reading involves looking at and processing the print on the page. In Stage 1 young children learn the way in which letters and sounds connect to form words that may be spoken. As young children's reading development progresses and they can more effortlessly assign sounds to letters and quickly blend these sounds together to form spoken words, they begin to return to a concern for not only how a word *looks* but also for what it *means*.

In Stage 2, children consolidate what they have about the connections between letters and sounds by reading easy books that are familiar or well known to gain a sense of fluency. Once children can read fluently or with *automaticity,* Chall (1983) indicates that reading development progresses into Stages 3–5. In Stage 3 children read for information; in Stage 4 children and adolescents read books that require dealing with more than one point of view; and in Stage 5 readers become self-directed having learned to read many genres of text and knowing what not to read as well as what to read.

In summary, as young children develop the ability to read, they seem to pass through a stage of acting like readers. Next, they realize that reading the story is

Figure 11.1 Characteristics of Exemplary Primary Grade Teachers

- *Instructional balance.* Teachers integrate explicit skills instruction seamlessly with authentic, connected text reading and writing practice and experiences.
- *Instructional density.* Teachers cover many more skills/concepts/strategies per hour of instruction. Every moment in the classroom is oriented toward the goal of promoting learning—even lining up for lunch or recess!
- *Instructional scaffolding.* Teachers provide sufficient support to help children independently perform literacy tasks.
- *Understanding and respects for developmental differences.* Teachers seek to determine each child's ZPD (zone of proximal development) through appropriate assessment prior to providing instruction and designing learning experiences.
- *Encouragement of self regulation.* Teachers structure the classroom environment and learning activities so that students understand expectations, behaviors, and outcomes. Independence, cooperation, and task completion are emphasized.
- *Integration of reading and writing.* Teachers structure learning so that reading and writing are used in mutually supportive ways. Children learn to "read what they write" and "write what they read."
- *High expectations.* Teachers expect all children to learn and meet high standards of performance.
- *Good classroom management.* The classroom is well organized with clear procedural training about the purposes and expectations for each area of classroom space. Instructional routines and procedures are clearly defined, well understood, conspicuously displayed, and consistently applied.
- *Skills/concepts/strategies explicitly taught.* Teachers teach reading skills through explanation, demonstration, modeling, and gradual release of responsibility to students. Teachers believe that reading and writing are "taught," not "caught."
- *Access to and emphasis upon books.* Teachers focus learning activities on a variety of real texts: poetry, songs, environmental print, stories, decodable books, pattern books, and information texts. Teachers also recognize the importance of providing access to a large quantity and variety of books of differing levels of challenge and using books as a primary means of scaffolding the acquisition of reading skills and strategies.
- *Volume of reading and writing.* Teachers structure classroom learning experiences so that every possible moment is focused on authentic reading and writing tasks rather than on completing "skill and drill" sheets.
- *Task difficulty matched to student competence.* Teachers make every effort to assess and monitor students to assure that the tasks assigned in reading and writing are of sufficient challenge to promote engagement and progress, but not to induce frustration and failure.
- *Connect literacy across the curriculum.* Teachers draw no stark boundaries between learning to read and write and reading and writing to learn. Teachers are as comfortable teaching content knowledge to children during reading and writing instruction as they are teaching reading and writing skills as tools for acquiring content knowledge.
- *Postive, personally reinforcing classroom environment.* Teachers create and maintain a classroom atmosphere of respect, support, and clear expectations. Children are taught to help, support, cooperate, and collaborate in the best interests of others as well as themselves.
- *Work is play in kindergarten.* Kindergarten teachers structure multiple play and exploration centers with literacy learning as the focus.
- *Multidimensional word recognition instruction.* Teachers teach children to use letter–sound information, word parts and patterns, and contextual information to identify unknown words.
- *Printed prompts prominently displayed.* Teachers recognize the human tendency to forget rules, routines, and procedures. Such critical information is conspicuously displayed in effective classrooms.
- *Teacher expectations.* Teachers hold high expectations for students to make substantial progress toward use of writing conventions (capitalization, spelling, handwriting, punctuation, form, and appearance) by year's end.
- *Daily allocated instruction and practice time.* Teachers engage children in a preponderance of reading and writing experiences and activities on a daily basis while allocating sufficient time daily for reading instruction and practice.

governed by the print on the page but they do not yet understand how to decode the print. At this stage, children focus intently on figuring out how to decode the print. As young children learn to decode the print with ease, they return to sounding like fluent, expressive readers.

What Does Research Say About the Relationship Between K–3 Reading Instruction and K–3 Children's Reading Achievement?

One clear and central theme emerges from historical and recent national and international reports about the relationship between K–3 reading instruction and K–3 children's reading achievement: *Teachers—their knowledge and instructional actions, not the method, materials or approach—make the critical difference in whether or not students will ultimately succeed in reading.* Linda Darling-Hammond, Executive Director of the National Commission on Teaching and America's Future, in a report titled *What Matters Most: Teaching for America's Future* (1996) asserted that, "What teachers know and do is the most important influence on what students learn. Competent and caring teaching should be a student right" (p. 6).

In *Becoming a Nation of Readers* (1985), experts concluded that teacher ability was at least five times more important than the adoption of newly published reading materials:

> An **indisputable** [emphasis added] conclusion of research is that the quality of teaching makes a considerable difference in children's learning. Studies indicate that about 15 percent of the variation among children in reading achievement at the end of the school year is attributable to factors that relate to the skill and effectiveness of the teacher. In contrast, the largest study ever done comparing approaches to beginning reading found that about 3 percent of the variation in reading achievement at the end of first grade was attributable to the overall approach of the program (Anderson, Scott, Hiebert, & Wilkinson, 1985, p. 85).

In the report *Preventing Reading Difficulties in Young Children,* a similar conclusion about the significant contribution of teacher competence and knowledge to children's achievement in reading was asserted (Snow, Burns, & Griffin, 1998). The National Education Association's Task Force on Reading 2000 summarized this critical point well and succinctly: "The teacher, not the method, makes the real difference in reading success" (p. 7).

Research suggests, then, that teachers influence student academic growth more than any other single factor, including families, neighborhoods, and the schools students attend (Sanders & Horn, 1994). Teachers' general instructional ability and knowledge are strongly related to student achievement (Greenwald, Hedges, & Laine, 1996). Successful schools that produce high student reading achievement test scores regardless of SES or the nature of reading instruction employ teachers who are knowledgeable and articulate about their work (McCardle & Chhabra, 2004; Mosenthal, Lipson, Torncello, Russ, & Mekkelsen, 2004). It is now accepted as nearly axiomatic that effective reading teachers must have knowledge specific to effective reading instruction and the young children they teach and actively apply this knowledge in their classroom instruction.

What Are the Characteristics of Effective K–3 Reading Instruction?

Do you recall the seven important characteristics of highly effective reading teachers we introduced in Chapter 1? We cannot emphasize strongly enough that it is a teacher's knowledge about effective reading instruction that makes the single greatest difference in whether or not every child will have an equal and effective opportunity to learn to read successfully in elementary school. In the balance of this chapter, you will learn about how to implement the principles of effective reading instruction and put them into practice in primary grade classrooms. As you read about planning for effective primary grade reading instruction, review the seven characteristics of highly effective teachers in, Chapter 1, and the observable characteristics of highly effective primary grade reading teachers shown in Figure 11.1, p. 409.

With the advent of each new school year, empty classroom walls and floors call out to the experienced and novice teacher alike, "Welcome back!" And each new year, you, the teacher are faced in late summer or early fall with the task of planning, organizing, and preparing a classroom soon to be occupied by lively, enthusiastic, and somewhat anxious young children. Planning the effective use of classroom space and literacy supplies and resources is the first challenge in teaching children to read.

Getting to Know English Learners
A teacher's general knowledge or understanding of language acquisition and the challenges ELs face also makes a huge difference in every learner's success.

First Steps: Preparing the Classroom Environment

The physical environment of a classroom exerts a powerful influence on teaching and learning behaviors related to reading (Loughlin & Martin, 1987; Reutzel & Wolfersberger, 1996; Roskos & Neuman, 2001; Smith, Dickinson, Sangeorge, & Anastasopoulos, 2002). Research has demonstrated a clear relationship between environments in classrooms, homes, and neighborhoods and the acquisition of reading and writing concepts, skills, and strategies (Morrow, Reutzel, & Casey, 2006; Roskos & Neuman, 2001).

Spending ample time and expending significant effort prior to the beginning of the school year in preparing the classroom for its eventual occupants—young children— will pay learning and management dividends all year. It is best if you can access literacy instructional materials, i.e., the basal or the core reading program teacher's edition, district curriculum guide, and other relevant materials provided by the school at least three months prior to the beginning of the school year. While you might not have this much lead time for planning, it is important that you begin thinking about designing the year's curriculum plan and daily lessons. It is also critical to get into your classroom at least one month prior to the beginning of the school year in order to prepare the environment, assess the adequacy of classroom supplies, and acquire additional supplies if necessary. Of course, each elementary school and school district will schedule different amounts of time for teachers' planning. You will need to check with your school principal or director to see what is possible.

Designing a Classroom Floor Plan

The major reason for carefully designing the physical environment of the classroom is to encourage children to learn from the environment and to interact

Video Classroom

Look at Valuable Classroom Environment Organizations

Visit a video classroom on our Teacher Prep Website (*www.prenhall.com/teacherprep*). Select *Classroom Management—Organizing Your Classroom and Supplies* to view "Arranging Furniture and Materials."

- Note how this teacher is helping to develop her students' confidence and self-direction.
- Explain how the readiness of materials on the students' desks promotes intrinsic motivation.
- Provide at least two examples of the teacher trying to teach her 2nd graders self-regulation. Why is this important? What might you try in your classroom?
- Note the classroom environment, including the physical and behavioral aspects, and how they might relate to teacher/student control and the presentation of content.

productively with you and with each other. It will also help you to more efficiently and effectively manage the environment while addressing the diverse learning needs of all the students in your care. Decisions about the classroom literacy environment generally focus on three major concerns: (1) how to structure the environment, (2) what to place into the environment, and (3) activities to be carried out in the environment.

Our best advice is to begin simply. You will want to plan a whole class instructional area along with a few small-group and/or individual learning areas or centers. As you feel able to manage a more complex classroom environment, you will most likely want to subdivide the classroom into additional, multipurpose learning and instructional spaces.

Start by drawing a classroom floor plan. Measure the width and length of your classroom and plot it onto a piece of graph paper. Using graph paper helps you maintain a sense of scale. Think about where and how you want to conduct whole-class instruction and learning activities in reading. Then, survey the remaining space for small-group reading instruction and reading practice areas; these are often referred to among practicing teachers as **learning centers.** Carefully plan where you will locate your learning centers to reinforce reading instruction and provide students opportunities to practice reading skills, strategies, concepts, and processes.

Planning Whole-Class Instructional Areas

A **whole-class instructional area** is logically located near chalkboards and well away from designated quiet areas in the classroom. A large piece of well-padded carpet can be used to comfortably seat an entire class of young children in this area. For management purposes, it is recommended that this carpet be divided into individual spaces or squares so each child has an assigned place during "rug time." Audiovisual equipment needs to be located near the whole-class sharing area. Audiovisual equipment may include a wall-mounted television, a video or DVD

Figure 11.2 Whole-Class Learning and Sharing Area

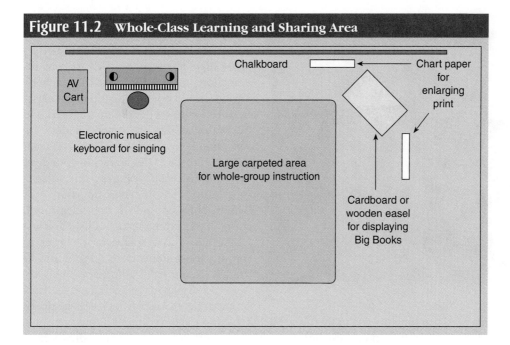

player, an computer projector, and overhead, an audio cassette or CD player, an easel for displaying enlarged print of stories, poems, riddles, songs, or group experience charts; an electronic keyboard for music accompaniment; and a display easel for reading commercial or child-produced big books. Although not all schools will have all of these audiovisual resources available, this certainly gives you a "wish list" for planning future classroom purchases to complete your reading instruction tool box. The whole-class instructional area should be clear of obstructions and may occupy up to 25 percent of the total space in the classroom (see Figure 11.2).

When planning the whole-class instructional area, consider two important questions: (1) Where is the best place in my classroom for the whole group to see and interact with me when I am demonstrating or modeling a literacy skill, concept, process, or strategy? and (2) How do I want my students to be seated during whole-group instruction—in their desks? On carpet squares on the floor? At tables? Once you have come to a decision about the design of your whole-class instructional space, draw it on your classroom floor plan in as much detail as possible. It is important to consider details, as you will want to think about your needs as a teacher as well. Where will you write during whole-class instruction—on the chalkboard? The dry erase whiteboard? A large chart paper tablet? A handheld chalkboard or dry erase board? An overhead projector? How will you share and display books, poems, song lyrics, and other text? Will you need a VHS or DVD player or a computer and monitor? Will you need access to a CD or tape player, or electronic keyboard or piano? Do you need an easel, a pointer, highlight tape, markers, chalk, editing tape, sticky notes? Think through the types of instruction and modeling you will offer in this area and make a list of supplies you will likely need. Plan a place for storage and display as well.

A next step in designing the classroom floor plan is carefully considering where and how to arrange your own workspace. In some schools and classrooms, you may have a walled-off space or office directly adjacent to the classroom. However, in

Ray Reutzel

most schools the teacher's workplace is integrated into the classroom, and for good reason: this arrangement encourages high levels of teacher–student interaction. Our advice is that the teacher's space should not be situated in the classroom so as to be the dominant focus. We recommend that the teacher's desk be "sidelined" in a corner of the classroom (see Figure 11.3). Avoid facing your desk toward the wall: doing so discourages you from spending time at your desk when children are in the classroom. Also, have your desk, bookshelf, files, computer, and displays in a corner to protect these items from damage resulting from normal traffic flow. With respect to displays, we encourage teachers to prominently display their college diplomas and teaching license in this area. Such a display speaks volumes about your professional preparation and qualifications as a teacher! Be sure to have a shelf where you can store and display professional books, journals, and reference materials. This, too, speaks to your professionalism! Having thought about your personal space in the classroom, draw your workspace into the classroom floor plan.

You are now ready to plan and design the number and variety of small-group instructional and reading practice areas you desire in your classroom. These are often called *learning centers*.

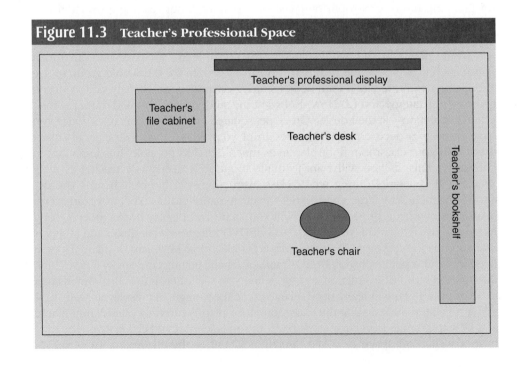

Figure 11.3   Teacher's Professional Space

Planning Small-Group Instruction and Learning Centers

When you plan learning centers in a classroom, there is much to contemplate. First, consider how many learning centers you can manage. If you are inexperienced as a teacher, have trouble with multitasking, or feel the need to have a more controlled environment to start the year, you may not want to have more than two or three learning centers. For most teachers, the process of planning learning centers starts by focusing on those centers that provide practice in the essential components of evidence-based reading instruction. An excellent source of information for designing effective literacy centers is found in Morrow's (2002) book, *The Literacy Center: Contexts for Reading and Writing,* 2nd edition. We describe essential reading centers first and then offer suggestions about additional learning centers. Please note that the writing center, which is essential, has already been described in Chapter 8.

Essential Center: The Word Work Center. A word work center serves a variety of purposes. For example, it may focus children's attention on learning sight words. If this is one of the purposes of the word work center, it should be located near and have an unobstructed view of the classroom word wall described in Chapter 5. If another purpose for this center is to accommodate children's practice with letters in making words, it should be stocked with magnetic letters, laminated letters, individual-sized dry erase or magnetic gel boards, markers, erasers, zip-lock packets, pictures for word or letter sorts, letter trays with plastic letters, and letter tiles. Computer (CD or DVD) programs that allow children to work with letters and words can be set up in this center as well. Word, letter, and picture sorts and word and letter games have a place in this center as well. (For a comprehensive treatment of working with words, we heartily recommend Bear, Templeton, Invernizzi, and Johnston's (2008) *Words Their Way: Word Study for Phonics, Vocabulary, and Spelling Instruction,* 4th edition.)

The word work center is expressly designed to directly reinforce and provide practice for whole-class, explicit, and systematic *previous* instruction in letters, phonemic awareness, spelling, phonics, and sight words. The word work center is a place for exploration of or activities involving letters, phonemic awareness, spelling, phonics, and sight words. Each day's word work activities ought to be designed to (a) reinforce instruction, and (b) provide accountablity through teacher-assigned word-work tasks to be completed by students working with others or alone independently. For example, if children are asked to make several words using a word tile containing the *ick* word family, they should be expected to write on paper the *ick* words they made to ensure that they have engaged in the assigned task. This also provides informal assessment feedback to the teacher regarding student progress for each assigned task.

Essential Center: Listening Comprehension Center. The **listening comprehension center** is a spot in the classroom where students listen to books read aloud. A table, chairs, a CD/tape player, books on tape or CD, and six to eight copies of each title are essential supplies for this center. If possible, the center should house multiple sets of headphones for listening. If this is not possible, we suggest that you find a way to mark the appropriate volume on the CD/tape player. You may want to use fingernail polish to draw a line on the volume dial of the tape player so that students can adjust the volume independently.

Directions for who is to distribute copies of books, insert the tape or CD, and operate the CD/tape player must be in place. It is also important that students be assigned

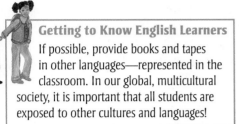

Getting to Know English Learners

If possible, provide books and tapes in other languages—represented in the classroom. In our global, multicultural society, it is important that all students are exposed to other cultures and languages!

several follow-up tasks to be completed after listening: You might have them sequence pictures to represent the order of the events in the story, write a summary, or orally retell the story to a partner. For very young readers, answers to comprehension questions can be "yes" or "no" or smiling or frowning faces. To encourage the development of listening comprehension, it is important that children should be held accountable for time spent in this center and that they listen and follow along in the book for a purpose. CD ROMs or DVD books can be easily used in listening comprehension centers. If a computer is the means of delivery in the listening comprehension center, no more than four children should be seated at a single unit to be able to effectively read along with the print.

Essential Center: Paired Reading Fluency Center. A paired reading fluency center contains a variety of reading tasks that can be pursued in pairs or with reading buddies. In terms of classroom space allocation, consider using the whole-class instructional area for the paired reading center, as these two activities typically do not occur simultaneously. You will need to provide a cassette tape recorder, individual tapes, or access to computers for students' recording of their reading of assigned texts. Large pointers and frames for use with big books should also be supplied. You may want to consider providing stopwatches or cooking timers for students to assess their reading rate.

In this center, students may read sight word cards, phrases containing sight words, poetry, stories, and information texts. Children should read quietly aloud together or to one another. Students can be taught to use various choral reading techniques such as unison readings, echo readings, and mumble readings. Students should also be taught how to give one another feedback as to how they might improve their reading fluency.

To hold children accountable for their time spent in this center, you might have them read an assigned list of sight words or a repeatedly practiced text onto a tape or computer audio file at prescribed intervals. You can then systematically check to see if students are indeed practicing and benefiting from their time spent in this center. These benefits should increase accuracy and rate of sight word recognition and improve fluency and expression in oral reading. We advise pairing students whose reading skills are slightly to moderately different; frustration results when students are partnered with a peer whose reading skills are widely discrepant from their own. Some research has indicated that allowing students to choose their own partners produces better results and fewer squabbles between partners (Meisinger, Schwenenflugel, Bradly, Kuhn, & Stahl, 2002).

Ray Reutzel

Essential Center: Vocabulary Center. Vocabulary acquisition consists of three integrated or interrelated dimensions: (a) incidental vocabulary learning through exposure to new words in spoken and written language; (b) explicit vocabulary instruction on words that students need to learn to acquire a mature adult vocabulary or words they need to learn to become knowledgeable in a domain of study or knowledge; and (c) self-directed vocabulary learning, which involves cultivating an awareness and love of words through word play and through acquiring word learning strategies. The vocabulary center should directly focus on helping children review and deepen their knowledge of previously taught words and on helping them develop a love of and respect for words through word play.

As you plan a vocabulary learning center, consider acquiring several important sources for word learning. These include dictionaries (especially picture dictionaries for younger children), a computer for searching word-learning sites, word study lists, a thesaurus, and a word history book, such as *Word Histories and Mysteries: From Abracadabra to Zeus,* by the editors of the American Heritage Dictionaries. You might also think about having available vocabulary games such as Taboo, Boggle, Apples to Apples, and so on. Other supplies might include a pocket chart for matching scrambled word meanings and words, "like-a-test" activities, a word wall of favorite new words and meanings, and the history of names such as *http://www.behindthename.com/.* This center is one that children should have opportunities to sort words into meanings, fill in word maps (see Chapter 6), and interact with other children to review and deepen their knowledge of new and interesting word meanings.

Suggested Center: Literacy-Enriched Play Centers (Kindergarten). Play, according to Vygotsky (1978), involves the child in behavior that creates a new relationship between the field of meaning and the visual field—that is, between situations in thought and real situations (p. 104). Play is the child's work. Through it children can learn how to engage in literacy tasks demanded in different situations in the real and imagined world and "try on" the language that people use in different places, situations, and vocations in life.

Grounded in the research of Neuman and Roskos (1992, 1997) as well as many other early childhood literacy educators (Morrow, 2005, 2002; Rogg, 2001), play centers are a significant part of effective early literacy classrooms. Neuman and Roskos (1992, 1997) found that enriching play centers with a variety of situation-specific literacy tools (artifacts) and materials (props) increased children's use of literacy as part of their imaginative play. In other words, children incorporated more literate acts and behaviors into their imaginative play when literacy tools were present than when they were not. Also, embedding literacy learning in play centers encourages children to interact and collaborate with peers using language and literacy as a medium during play. Observations of young children at play have shown that in the presence of literacy tools appropriate to the social situation in the play center, children will engage in attempted and conventional reading and writing acts in collaboration with other children more often (Morrow, 1990; Neuman & Roskos, 1990, 1992, 1997).

Potential play centers appropriate to be considered in K classrooms include the following.

- Offices—business offices, post offices, doctor's offices, newspaper offices
- Businesses—labs, restaurants, bakeries, carpentry shops, art galleries, grocery stores, auto mechanics and repair shops
- Travel—airports, airplanes, bus stations, buses, train stations, trains
- Home—kitchens, home offices, schoolrooms, playrooms
- Drama—plays, readers' theater, puppetry, creative movement

Play centers should be a feature of every K classroom.

Ray Reutzel

For play centers to effectively press children into literacy behaviors, literacy tools and materials need to meet certain criteria and be appropriately arranged. Play centers also need to be organized so that literacy interactions between students are encouraged and supported. The play center is typically not a quiet place, but rather a very busy place where language and literacy acts are "tried on" for fun and fit. Design principles for organizing literacy tools and materials in the classroom and play centers is discussed in a later section of this chapter.

Learn more about your role in conducting and developing learning centers. Access the Teacher Prep Website *(www.prenhall.com/ teacherprep)* and go to *Strategies and Lessons—Reading Methods/ Organizing for Reading Instruction* to find "Using Learning Centers."

Suggested Center: Integrated or Content Curriculum Learning Centers. A content learning center focuses learning on concepts or processes found in a single curriculum subject such as mathematics, science, art, music, or social studies. An integrated learning center integrates several subjects and literacy together into a single unit of exploration, discovery, or learning. In an integrated center, activity may initially focus on reading a particular book and following up with several projects, tasks, or assignments related to a particular topic. Or the center may involve children in several projects, tasks, or assignments initially and progress to reading books to answer questions or add new insights and understandings.

For example, children may begin their work in this center by reading the book *Corn: From Farm to Table* by William Anton (1999). During the planning of a project or inquiry center focused on life cycles, you might begin by identifying resources available for learning about corn as a part of a life cycles science curriculum. You might have children look at different kinds of corn seeds under a magnifying glass, or count how many corn kernels are in a row on a corncob, representing the numbers using Cuisenaire rods. Students might make popcorn using an air pop machine so they can see the popcorn popping open! They might create a semantic feature web (see Chapter 6 on vocabulary instruction) to compare corn with beans and peas in terms of features such as color, shape, taste, uses, and so on. For extended exploration, children could locate items at home that use corn or corn products and then write a brief report on their findings.

In these centers, the goal is to integrate literacy learning with another curricular area. In these centers, as in all others, it is critical to design accountability into the daily operation of the center. In the end, children might complete a series of brief assignments or tasks related to acquiring content knowledge or applying reading strategies.

Organizing Classroom Literacy Tools and Materials

Based on the literacy environmental research mentioned earlier, Reutzel and Wolfersberger (1996) describe six criteria for selecting and arranging literacy tools and materials in K–3 classrooms: (1) appropriateness, (2) authenticity, (3) utility, (4) proximity, (5) uses, and (6) change. We begin by considering the criterion of

Video Classroom

Look at the Ways Learning Centers Can Be of Value
Learning centers require careful planning and effective management. Hear a classroom teacher describe her centers on the accompanying CD for this text. Select *Guided Reading-2nd Grade* and view, the "Plan and Manage" clip. This clip may also be accessed through the Teacher Prep Website *(www.prenhall.com/teacherprep)* under Videos. Select "Organizing for Reading Instruction."

- Note the centers that she has functioning within her classroom.
- Compare the "Characteristics of Exemplary Primary Grade Teachers" (Figure 11.1) to the opportunities provided in centers described. How would these centers support exemplary reading achievement?

---

appropriateness. To determine the appropriateness of literacy tools or materials, ask yourself questions like the following: Are the literacy materials developmentally appropriate? Can students use these tools and materials safely? Can students use these tools and materials in purposeful ways? Can students use these tools and materials in socially meaningful ways to communicate and interact? Will these literacy tools or materials help students explore and develop early literacy skills, concepts, and strategies? If so, how?

> **Getting to Know English Learners**
> Tools and materials found in other cultures, like foreign language cookbooks, add a welcoming and multicultural touch to any classroom.

When selecting literacy tools and materials, you should also consider the criterion of *authenticity*. Ask: Are these tools and materials found and used in a variety of settings in school and out? For example, if you put a recipe box, cards, and cookbook, menu, or newspaper food advertisements into a housekeeping play center, would these literacy tools and materials be found in almost any household? Third, when selecting literacy materials determine if the literacy tools and materials fit the criterion of *utility*. In relation to this criterion ask: Do these literacy tools and materials serve useful literacy functions found in society? A partial listing of appropriate, authentic, and useful literacy tools and materials is found in Figure 11.4.

Include art, technology, living things, music, and food to present a varied approach to content. Read "Ideas for Enriching the Learning Environment" in the *Strategies and Lessons—Reading Methods/Organizing for Reading Instruction* section on the Teacher Prep Website *(www.prenhall.com/teacherprep)*.

In terms of arrangement and organization, literacy tools should be *proximal* to students and their activities. Children will not use literacy tools readily if they are stored in a location removed from the major area(s) of activity. Also, students must be able to easily access literacy tools and be able to return them to their proper place. It is important that the teacher carefully *suggest possible uses* for the literacy tools and materials supplied. For example, you might suggest that a message board in the classroom be used to post announcements, ask questions, or send personal communications. When used in a kitchen play center, a message board might be used to post a grocery list or telephone messages. In a science center, a message board might be used to list materials needed to conduct an experiment, to record the steps of the experiment, or to make a diagram for displaying the process or outcome of an experiment.

Finally, literacy tools and materials should be *regularly rotated* and/or replaced. Like adults, young students grow weary of the same old thing. You should add to, delete from, and rotate literacy tools and materials on a regular basis in your K–3 classroom.

Figure 11.4   Possible Literacy Props to Enrich Literacy Learning

Books, pamphlets, magazines	Posters of children's books	Appointment book
Ledger sheets	Small drawer trays	Signs (e.g., open/closed)
Cookbooks	Library book return cards	File folders
Labeled recipe boxes	A wide variety of children's books	In/out trays
Personal stationery	Telephone books	Business cards
Grocery store ads/fliers	A sign-in/sign-out sheet	Self-adhesive notes and address labels
Empty grocery containers	ABC index cards	Bookmarks
Note cards	Small plaques/decorative magnets	Post Office mailbox
Pens, pencils, markers	Assorted forms	Computer/address labels
Trays for holding items	Blank recipe cards	Calendars of various types
Message pads	Emergency number decals	Posters/signs about mailing
Envelopes of various sizes	Food coupons	Stamps for marking books
Racks for filing papers	Play money	Typewriter or computer keyboard
Index cards	Small message board	Telephone
Clipboards	Notepads of assorted sizes	Paper of assorted sizes
Stationery	Large plastic clips	
Stickers, stars, stamps, stamp pads		
A tote bag for mail		

Making the Most of Classroom Display Areas to Support Literacy Learning

Immerse K–3 students in an environment of interesting and functional print. Display areas can be located almost anywhere in the classroom—on walls, windows, floors, doors, and ceilings. Where possible, displays should be student-produced rather than teacher-produced. A message board for leaving notes is one means for teachers and students to communicate with each other. A sign-in board encourages even the very youngest children to write their names to begin the school day. Window writing using pens with water-soluble ink allows students to transcribe their stories, poems, jokes, riddles, and song lyrics onto the window glass. Windows are a fun and novel way to publish writing projects in classrooms or sign in at the beginning of the year. Many children are very intrigued by window-published writing projects.

A logo language wall or environmental print bulletin board can be devoted to print that children bring from home. Logo language is both fun and instructionally useful because it helps even the youngest children know they can already read. Children bring labels from cans, cereal boxes, old packages, bumper stickers, and newspaper advertisements to display on a logo language or environmental print wall. This wall can be a resource for guided reading lessons and whole-group instruction throughout the year. (Be sure to remind students that they must label the contents of a can from home if they take the label off before it is used!)

Informational displays should be located in prominent places in the classroom. These displays are used for posting rules, calendars, lunch menus, TV guides, and

posters. In addition, informational displays can be used to exhibit information about classroom routines, time schedules, hints on successful reading, the writing process, steps and media for publishing writing, lists of words the class knows, songs the class likes, favorite books, and so on.

Scheduling displays can be used for making appointments with peers and teachers for reading and writing conferences as well as editing sessions. Figure 11.5 shows an example of scheduling displays for these purposes.

Objects in the classroom may be labeled by even the youngest of students. Children may invent spellings for objects in the classroom and write these on cards.

Figure 11.5   Writing Peer Conference Sign-up Board

Monday—Date _____

8:00 A.M.

Name of Author _____ Names of Peers _____

_____

8:15 A.M.

Name of Author _____ Names of Peers _____

_____

8:30 A.M.

Name of Author _____ Names of Peers _____

_____

Tuesday—Date _____

8:00 A.M.

Name of Author _____ Names of Peers _____

_____

8:15 A.M.

Name of Author _____ Names of Peers _____

_____

8:30 A.M.

Name of Author _____ Names of Peers _____

_____

For example, we have seen the following object labels written by young children in kindergarten classrooms: *seling (ceiling), klok (clock), weindos (windows), dr (door), fs (fish),* and *srk (shark).* During language lessons, students can be alerted to look for these words in their reading and then alter these invented spellings. Many teachers find that within a matter of weeks, invented spellings used to label classroom objects will be revised to reflect conventional spellings (Calkins & Harwayne, 1987). Other areas in the classroom can be used to display helpful reference information such as numbers, colors, alphabet letters, lunchtime, and classroom helpers. Remember that all classroom displays should be neat and clear so as to set the standard for published works in the classroom.

Planning and Organizing Necessary Storage Spaces

Devote selected areas in the classroom to storage of classroom and student materials. A writing storage area for children's emerging writing products is a must. Neatly file authors' folders, response journals, and learning logs in corrugated cardboard file boxes. You may wish to store students' writing drafts in three-ring binders on a bookshelf or in another accessible location. A small tablet for recording spelling words can be inserted into the pocket or sleeve of this writing draft binder. Be sure to put each child's name on his/her writing draft binders!

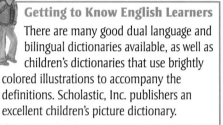

Getting to Know English Learners

There are many good dual language and bilingual dictionaries available, as well as children's dictionaries that use brightly colored illustrations to accompany the definitions. Scholastic, Inc. publishers an excellent children's picture dictionary.

Each child needs a personal storage area in the classroom. We recommend vinyl tubs for this purpose. These tubs can house children's personal writing materials, pencil boxes, and belongings. They can also double as post office boxes. Each tub can have a name and a P.O. box number written on the front. These tubs can be stored in specially constructed shelves, along coat racks, on the top of bookshelves, and on windowsills. Properly cleaned and covered with contact paper, two- to five-gallon ice cream buckets can be stacked along coat racks, cupboards, and windowsills for the same purposes without incurring the expense of purchasing tubs.

When you arrange staplers, paper punches, construction paper, and unlined paper for students' daily use, keep in mind easy accessibility and clean up. The proper location of each item in the publishing area needs to be labeled to facilitate cleanup and maintenance. We strongly suggest that each item in this center be labeled with both a word and a picture for younger children's use. Also be sure to properly label sorting baskets or bins to facilitate easy cleanup of this area and improve its appearance. The publishing storage area should be located near other busy and potentially noisy areas in the classroom. Book storage areas, such as the classroom library, need to be properly located to facilitate retrieval, reshelving, and accessibility. You will learn more about how to design an effective classroom library in the next section of this chapter.

Word cards can be stored in old, labeled shoeboxes on the bookshelves in this area. Child-authored books are to be afforded the same respect as commercially produced books. A library card pocket and a checkout card should be placed in each child-authored book. These books should have a section in the classroom library where they can be read, reread, and checked out. Child-authored big books and charts can be given a prominent display area and/or stored along with other commercially published big books. Plastic pants hangers with clothespins, hooks, or specially designed pocket charts can be used to store or display big books and chart tablets effectively.

Storage for reference materials such as dictionaries, atlases, *The Guinness Book of World Records,* encyclopedias, almanacs, and spellers should be placed near the editing area in the classroom but be accessible to students and editors. Writing media should be placed near where they are needed in the classroom. Plastic tubs or baskets, boxes, cut-down milk containers, and the like can be used for both storage and sorting of writing materials. Crayons, markers, pencils, pens, erasers, and chalk can be placed in individual containers for storage. In this way, children can easily sort and clean up writing materials scattered during busy writing output times. Other containers should be made available into which small quantities of writing media can be placed from large-capacity storage bins for transport to other classroom areas. These small transport containers can be taken to conference areas and collaborative project areas for use and returned and sorted for storage and cleanup.

Organizing Effective Storage: Planning an Effective Classroom Library. A classroom library is an important part of every classroom and is often where many literacy tools and materials are stored and displayed. Give careful thought to designing your classroom library. Reutzel and Fawson (2002) have written an accessible book titled *Your Clasroom Library: New Ways to Give It More Teaching Power* that details how to plan, organize, and use a classroom library to support an evidence-based, effective reading instructional program.

The classroom library is the place in the K–3 classroom where primary literacy tools and materials—books—and young children come together. Classroom libraries, like good restaurants, provide staple foods—a core book collection—along with exciting new recipes in the form of rotating books that come and go. Classroom libraries, like restaurants, also provide for dining in and for taking out. In most classroom libraries, take home, check out, book trading, and book-ordering processes are in place.

Classroom libraries should be more than mere haphazard collections of old books, donated books, books purchased at sheltered workshops and garage sales, and books obtained from class book order points. Well-designed classroom libraries serve five important functions (Reutzel & Fawson, 2002). These functions are: (1) to support instruction, (2) to facilitate learning about books, (3) to organize storage of classroom resources, (4) to provide resources for independent reading and curricular extensions, and (5) to provide a place for student talk and interaction about books.

The first function of a classroom library is to support reading instruction—in school and out. Include in your classroom library books and other media materials to support student learning in all curricular areas. Materials related to the content areas of science, health, mathematics, history, economics, geography, music, art, drama, dance, language, grammar, spelling, literature, and computers should be provided. Build an adequate collection of fiction and non-fiction materials at a variety of reading levels to accommodate the many interests and reading skill levels of students desiring to check out books for take-home reading.

A second function of an effective classroom library is for teaching children how to select appropriately challenging and interesting books. The

Ray Reutzel

classroom library is a place where children can learn about a variety of literary genres. It is also a place where they learn how to properly care for books. A book hospital with instructions on how to "operate" on torn pages, remove marks in the books, cover frayed edges, or fix broken bindings provides useful and relevant instruction for younger students.

A third function of a classroom library is to provide an organized, central storage location for classroom instructional resources. Classroom libraries can provide additional space for organizing science equipment, CD and tape players, VHS tapes and DVDs, computers wired to the Internet, games, magazines, and other materials that support learning. In this respect, the classroom library mirrors the organization of media centers at the school and district levels.

The fourth function of a classroom library is to be a resource—although not the only resource—of reading materials that support children's daily guided or independent reading. The classroom library provides students readily accessible information print materials, expository books, computer technology, and media for conducting research or completing thematic or research projects. It offers students the opportunity to browse and explore the world of print. It can also provide a setting for comfortably reading and talking about a book with a peer or the teacher. The classroom library often provides an ideal location for the teacher to sit down next to a reader and have him or her read aloud. In this way, the teacher can conduct an informal assessment of each student's reading, maintaining a running record to monitor progress.

This means that the classroom library should be organized to provide cues to appropriate levels and different types of materials for students and to facilitate easy clean-up and maintenance. Having a classroom library area is only the beginning. Making optimal use of the classroom library is the key to its effectiveness.

Grouping Students for Effective Reading Instruction

Grouping students for instruction is one of the ways in which teachers are able to address diverse learning needs and manage students' movement and activity when engaged in independent reading and learning center activities. Unlike instructional programs of the past that focused on grouping students by ability, today's delivery models make use of a wide variety of grouping plans. This practice is referred to as *flexible grouping*.

Flexible Learning Groups. In flexible grouping, students are placed into temporary groups based on their level of independence as learners and their personal interests. Optiz (1998) says that flexible groups allow "students to work in differently mixed ability groups depending upon the learning task at hand" (p. 10). There are several significant differences that separate ability groups from flexible groups as summarized in Table 11.1.

Flexible groups are established and reorganized on the basis of several well-articulated principles (Unsworth, 1984, p. 300):

Read more about flexible learning groups in *Strategies and Lessons—Reading Methods/Organizing for Reading Instruction* section of the Teacher Prep Website (*www.prenhall.com/teacherprep*). Select "Flexible Learning Groups."

- There are no permanent groups.
- Groups are periodically created, modified, or disbanded to meet new needs as they arise.
- At times there is only one group consisting of all pupils.
- Groups vary in size from 2 or 3 to 9 or 10, depending on the group's purpose.
- Group membership is not fixed; it varies according to needs and purposes.

Table 11.1 Understanding the Differences Between Ability Groups and Flexible Groups

Considerations for Grouping Decisions	Ability Groups	Flexible Groups
Assigning Students to Groups	Tests, informal reading inventories, and word list scores	Ability to read leveled books
Duration of Groups	Static; long-term	Dynamic; change regularly
Instructional Expectations	Dependent on level of students in the group, i.e., high, medium or low achievers	High expectations for all students regardless of achievement level
Forms of Reading Practice	Oral reading—barber shop or round robin reading	Guided oral and silent reading with feedback and discussion
Instructional Materials	Core reading program; selections determined by teacher	Core reading program; trade and leveled books chosen by teacher
Mode of Assessment	Criterion or norm-referenced assessment	Observations, running records, informal checklists, progress-monitoring, assessments

- Student commitment is enhanced when students know how the group's work relates to the overall program or task.
- Children are able to evaluate the progress of the group and the teacher's assessment of the group's work.
- There is a clear strategy for supervising the group's work.

Flexible-grouping strategies can also be used to accommodate student interests, learning styles, and social needs. The potential for unproductive chaos is high in flexible group arrangements if the teacher has not carefully prepared the learning tasks and the environment for success. For flexible grouping to function well in the classroom, the organization and purpose of tasks must be clearly understood; students must be well trained to handle the independence and collaboration inherent in the settings (i.e., independent literacy learning centers) for which flexible grouping is particularly well suited.

Getting Off to a Good Start: Planning the First Day of School in the K–3 Classroom

Planning for the first day of school is something that both excites and frightens every teacher every year no matter how many years they have taught. Wong and Wong (1998) point out that one of the most critical parts of a successful first day is establishing effective **classroom management.** Wang, Haertel, and Walberg (1994) examined 11,000 research reports to determine the factors that most influence student learning in school classrooms. They identified 28 factors, the most significant of which was classroom management. They concluded that a teacher who is "grossly inadequate in classroom management skills is probably not going to accomplish much" (Wong & Wong, 1998, p. 84).

What is classroom management? It is everything you do as a teacher to organize students, classroom resources, time, and classroom space so that effective instruction can take place. We have already discussed one issue that relates to effective classroom management: organizing classroom space and instructional tools and

Figure 11.6   Goals and Objectives to Begin the Year Successfully

- Send a letter home to parents *before* the year begins explaining how they can help their child succeed in early literacy instruction.
- Have classroom seating, learning centers, instructional spaces, materials, activities, and work planned and ready.
- Enthusiastically greet each child at the door, giving clear directions for what to do to find his or her place in the classroom.
- Prepare the classroom so that each child can find his or her place in the room (seating chart, nametags, labels) and be able to independently put away his or her things in an orderly manner.
- Introduce yourself to students.
- Get to know something about each child the first day.
- Discuss with students classroom rules and consequences.
- Establish a routine for getting the day started.
- Prepare a daily schedule and post it where students can see it.
- Encourage reading and writing from the first day—giving directions and receiving requests.
- Provide first-day literacy activities: interactive read-alouds, shared readings, and language experiences.

Getting to Know English Learners
Sending a letter home in the parents' native language is an especially welcoming touch.

materials. To bring off a successful first day of school, you must carefully consider the goals and objectives that need to be accomplished in a K–3 classroom on that first day and in that first week of school. We would like to suggest the goals and objectives featured in Figure 11.6.

Preparing Parents and Students for Success: Making Initial Contact with a Letter

Each year, at least one week before school begins, obtain a copy of your class list from your school principal. Along with this, request a list of parents' or caregivers' names and mailing addresses. Even better, if the school secretary can print mailing labels, request these. Compose one letter for parents and one for students. Letters should be welcoming, informative, and positive. A sample letter to a first grade student's parent is shown in Figure 11.7.

A similar letter to students can be included with your letter to parents. If at all possible, send students' letters in an individually addressed envelope. A sample letter to a kindergarten student is shown in Figure 11.8.

The First Day: First Impressions

Be sure to arrive early on the first day. Be available to students and parents as they arrive. Greet each child with a smile at the door of the classroom. Ask his or her name and pin a nametag on him or her that matches the one at his or her seat. Give each child simple directions for what to do after you greet him or her. We invite our first graders to sign their names on the classroom windows using a water-soluble

Figure 11.7   Sample Letter to a Parent

Dear Mr. and Mrs. _____,

   Welcome to first grade! I want to tell you how excited I am to have _____ in my first grade class this year. First grade is an extraordinary year for all students during which they will learn to read and write. Because I know how much you care about your child's success in school, I'd like to offer some simple suggestions.

- Please ask your child every day what he or she has learned at school. Don't accept the response, "Nothin'." I can assure you that there will never be a day this year when children will learn nothing!
- Make time each day to read with your child. Reading at home helps children succeed at school.
- Get books in your home for your child to read. If you need some suggestions, ask me. I would be glad to give you a short list of good books.
- Point out print and discuss reading in your daily living—breakfast cereal boxes, grocery stores, post office, hospital, bus stops, and so on.
- Get some magnetic letters for your refrigerator door. Talk about letters and the sounds these letters represent at home. Spell out your child's name on the refrigerator door. Scramble the letters and have your child make his or her name. Play games with these letters to make words.
- Get your child a library card and make a weekly visit to the public or school library together.
- Provide your child with a variety of writing materials including pencils, crayons, markers, paper, thank-you notes, stationery, recipe cards, and so on. You can store these materials where you have some control of their use, but making them handy for your child will encourage him or her to write.
- Encourage your child to read. You have a strong influence on your child's attitude about reading. If reading is important to you, it is likely to be important to your child.

   These are just a few things you can do to get your child off to a good start this year. Each week I will send home a report about what we will be learning in class in the week ahead as well as a summary of what we have learned during the past week. I will also include a couple of activities you can do with your child to (1) practice what he or she has learned this past week or (2) prepare him or her for what he or she will be learning the next week.
   I look forward to working with you and your child this year. I pledge to you my very best efforts in making this year a successful and learning-filled one for _____.

Warmest regards,

_____

Figure 11.8   Sample Letter to a Kindergarten Student

Dear _____,

   Hi! My name is _____. I will be your teacher this year in kindergarten. I am so excited that you will be in my class. I hope you are excited to come to school, too! We are going to have a wonderful time learning and playing together. I'll have a place ready for you to put your things when you arrive. I'll have a seat with your name on it and a nametag prepared for you. This way, we can get to know each other.
   I look forward to meeting you on the first day of school. I'll be at the door to meet you and to help you get settled.

Your teacher,

_____

transparency marker. Alternatively, have a card or sign-in board where children can see their name or write their name to register their presence.

Make sure that the room is completely ready for students. Have the classroom floor plan completed. Seating, storage, displays, and furnishings should all be arranged according to the floor plan. Learning areas, centers, and storage spaces should be clearly marked with signs, posters, and labels. Students' storage areas, seats, cubbies, and other areas should be labeled and ready. Wear a nametag similar to those you have prepared for students. Each child's seat or place at a table should have his or her nametag affixed. Arrange for something students can do at their seats as they arrive—a puzzle, a counting activity, or a reading or coloring activity.

Establishing a Routine for What to Do Before School Begins Each Day

Once the bell signals the beginning of the school day, you need to establish your opening routine. Taking attendance and lunch count are traditional activities at this time. An efficient way to take roll is to have an attendance board in your room: children take a card with their name on it and place it into a pocket that also has their name on it, indicating they are present.

Another wall chart can be used for children to indicate whether they are eating school lunch. A simple chart can feature a picture of a lunch pail or bag (Brought My Own Lunch) on one side and a picture of a food tray (Eat School Hot Lunch) on the other side. Children take a clothespin with their name on it and place it on either side of the chart to indicate if they are eating school lunch or one they brought from home.

We recommend having a message-of-the-day on a classroom message board posted by the door. We also encourage a classroom environmental print wall where students can bring examples of environmental print for posting. We also advise that, as students enter the room each day, they have at their seats a journal in which they can draw or write until instruction formally begins.

On the first day of school, tell, show, and select students to demonstrate your classroom routines. Post simple written directions near the classroom door to remind students about what they are to do upon entering the classroom each day.

Establishing a Morning Routine

We recommend beginning the school day with a song illustrated and displayed on large chart paper. In our own first grade classrooms, we sing "Good Morning, Says the Sun" to start our morning. Using a calendar chart, we review the day, the days of the week, the month, and the season of the year. We also review the weather for the day—sunny, partly cloudy, cloudy, foggy, rainy, or snowy. A school lunch chart displays the meal to be served that day. We display the daily schedule at the front of the room and review it each and every morning. We also make daily additions to and discuss our environmental print wall and our word wall. Finally, we provide time daily for students to orally share something about themselves or their families.

Although many teachers, parents, and administrators may question the value of "show-and-tell" (or as some call it, "bring-and-brag"), we find this time to be especially valuable in getting to know

Getting to Know English Learners

"Show and Tell" can really give ELs a chance to share their culture. You may even want to have your ELs bring in a parent or grandparent to share interesting facts from the home country.

Figure 11.9 A Suggested Morning Routine

- Sing a song together.
- Review the calendar and weather chart.
- Review the school lunch menu.
- Review the daily schedule posted in the pocket chart.
- Review environmental print words and/or word wall words.
- Provide time for guided oral sharing.

our students and in providing them with a comfortable setting in which they could use oral language. Typically we structure this time so as to establish parameters about what to bring and share rather than allowing children to bring just anything. For the first month of school, we invite one child per day to bring to school a box labeled "All About Me." In this box, students place three to five special items from home that revealed their interests, where they were born, their favorite food, and so on. We send home a note to parents telling them what items would be appropriate and meaningful for show-and-tell. We model showing and telling on the first day of school as a means of introducing ourselves to students.

Our morning routine is shown in Figure 11.9.

Making the Classroom Work: Rules and Consequences

Rules are expectations for appropriate student behavior in the classroom. Consequences are the rewards for choices made with respect to honoring the rules in a classroom. Classroom rules and consequences should be discussed on the first day of school. Teachers often solicit input from their students about rules that would help everyone talk, listen, and get along with each other in order to learn. It is important that even the youngest children have an opportunity to express their needs and ideas related to classroom rules and consequences. It is wise to keep rules to a minimum for very young children. In practical terms, this means no more than five classroom rules.

Discuss with students the consequences for both keeping and breaking classroom rules. These can be listed on chart paper or poster board and displayed in a prominent location. Many teachers encourage their students to suggest rewards and potential consequences, but retain the final say in these matters. Our classroom rules and consequences are shown in Figure 11.10.

"Steps in Developing the Discipline Plan" on the Teacher Prep Website (*www.prenhall.com/teacherprep*) will provide you with ideas to consider as you develop a plan in your future classroom. Select *Strategies and Lessons— Classroom Management/Getting Off to a Good Start* to find this article.

Reading from the Start: Getting Attention and Giving Directions

On the first day of school, we use written direction cue cards along with our oral directions. We tell students that we will not give oral directions after the first week of school; rather, we will use only cue cards. We produce on laminated poster board a series of cue cards that we place near a hotel register bell in the middle of the classroom. If we want students to line up, we ring the bell to get their attention. We then hold up a direction sign: "Please line up quietly at the door." If we want students to come to the front of the room for whole-group instruction, we ring the bell and hold up a card that reads, "Please sit down quietly on the carpet." This process creates an immediate need for students to focus their attention on print. It was clear from the

Figure 11.10　Classroom Rules and Consequences

- Raise your hand to ask to speak.
- Listen courteously when others are speaking.
- Keep hands, feet, and objects to yourself.
- Stop anything you are doing when you hear the signal to do so.
- Listen carefully to directions.

What Happens If You Choose to Break Our Classroom Rules

- 1st time—Verbal warning from the teacher
- 2nd time—Lose morning recess
- 3rd time—Lose morning and afternoon recesses
- 4th time—Call to parents
- 5th time—Go to principal and in-school discipline room

outset of the school year that reading is necessary to function well in our classroom environment!

Reading and Writing Activities on the First Day

Because we do not know a great deal on the first day about children's individual reading and writing development, activities should be done primarily in the large group. Our past experiences have shown that some of the best activities on the first day (and every day thereafter) include interactive read-alouds, shared reading, language experience activities, and interactive writing. "What Happens When _____?" is a good first day theme. Read-alouds and other activities can focus on this theme or a variation thereof. Figure 11.11 features sample first-day kindergarten and firstgrade literacy schedules.

Planning the First Week of K–3 Reading and Writing Instruction

Having survived the first day of school, we now turn our attention to planning the first full week of the new school year. The major goal of the first full week of school is to get to know the children and their individual learning needs. This means that you will need time to meet with individual children while managing the whole class. This is not easy and requires careful thought and planning.

Assessing Where Students Are

Because the goal is to get to know students' individual learning needs, an assessment plan for the beginning of the year should be a major part of your preplanning. Assessment of individual children is best carried out in a quiet area of the classroom. Lay out the assessment tools (inventories, forms, books, and records) that you will use to assess students in an assessment folder or portfolio.

Figure 11.11 Kindergarten and First Grade First Day Literacy Schedules

Half-Day Kindergarten (90 minutes literacy)

8:30–9:00 A.M.: Greet children and parents
9:00–9:10 A.M.: Morning routine (roll, lunch, weather, calendar)
9:10–9:20 A.M.: Sharing time
9:20–9:35 A.M.: Interactive read-aloud
9:35–10:05 A.M.: Shared reading of a big book
10:05–10:20 A.M.: Whole-class explicit lesson on letters and sight words
10:20–10:35 A.M.: Recess
10:35–10:45 A.M.: Science experiment: Magnets
10:45–11:00 A.M.: Shared writing/language experience chart
11:00–11:20 A.M.: Literacy-enriched dramatic play centers

First Grade (180 minutes literacy)

8:30–9:00 A.M.: Greet children and parents
9:00–9:10 A.M.: Morning routine (roll, lunch, weather, calendar)
9:10–9:20 A.M.: Sharing time—oral language
9:20–9:35 A.M.: Interactive read-aloud: story book
9:35–10:00 A.M.: Shared reading of enlarged text
10:00–10:30 A.M.: Whole-class science experiment: balloons, water, and baking soda
10:30–10:45 A.M.: Recess
10:45–11:15 A.M.: Writing: language experience chart about science experiment
11:15–11:30 A.M.: Word work—whiteboard letter/sight word dictation
11:30–11:45 A.M.: Word wall Bingo—high-frequency sight words
11:45–11:55 A.M.: Phonemic awareness—blending and segmenting to make words
12:00 Noon–12:45: Lunch
12:45–1:00 P.M.:—Interactive read-aloud: information book

You will need to call each child from independent or group work to the area of the classroom where you intend to conduct individual assessment. As you begin the assessment process, put the child at ease. Tell him or her that you want to learn about what he or she knows so that you can help him or her learn.

You will also need to provide meaningful independent seatwork and center work for the students you are not assessing. You might ask for parent volunteers to assist in the classroom during this first week to help with management, to read to students in small-group or whole-class sessions, and to interact with children in learning centers. It is important that you not plan to assess for more than one hour per day in kindergarten and two hours per day in first grade during the first week of the school year. We say this because your interaction with your students is of critical importance in establishing community in the classroom. We also say this because young children cannot sustain long periods of independent activity without teacher-guided, group interaction. The first week is also the ideal time to begin to train students in how to function in learning centers successfully and to practice how small groups will rotate through several learning centers each day.

Training Students to Effectively Use Learning Centers

For learning centers to be effective, their use must be carefully explained, highly structured with clearly defined rules, directions, and tasks to be completed, and

Video Classroom

View the Preparation That Makes Centers So Valuable to Literacy Learning

Children require teacher modeling and practice in learning how to use centers. Following this training, they can provide evidence of understanding through explanation. View and hear more on the CD that accompanies this textbook. Select *Guided Reading-2nd Grade* to view the "Centers Training" and "Centers Work" clips.

- How would you support children in your classroom as they begin to use centers more independently?
- Why would student journaling be helpful as you incorporate the inclusion of centers in your reading program?
- How could you use the children's explanations of "how the centers work" to enhance future introductions?

complemented by built-in accountability. To accomplish this necessary management task, you should plan on spending 4–6 weeks providing a series of procedural lessons on how to work effectively in learning centers.

During the first week of the school year, Reutzel and Morrow (2007) suggest ignoring learning centers and literacy materials placed in and around the room for students' eventual small-group and independent use. During the second week, mention to students that they will eventually be working in small groups and independently in the spaces designated around the classroom, but before they can do so, they will need to learn some skills and procedures. This heightens students' curiosity and motivation to learn the expectations and procedures to eventually enter and engage with these spaces and materials. Explain the purpose of each learning center: for listening, for paired reading, for alphabet and word work, for learning content, for writing, and so on. Explain the purpose of one or two centers per day during the second week, but do not let students enter these spaces or use these materials yet.

During the third week, fully explain and model how students are to use one or two of the learning centers. For example, on the first day of the third week you might model how students should go to the word work center in the classroom. You might show them how, before going to this space, they need to pick up their word work folders and quietly gather around the rules and the directions displayed for the day with other children in the word work center. On the second day of the third week, you might explain that you will appoint a team leader to lead the small group in a review of the rules and directions each day. You might model how this is to be accomplished through a quiet oral reading of the posted rules and the directions for working in the word work center that day. Be sure to model how the team leader is to ask if there are any questions and answer these when possible.

On the third day of the third week, you might model how students are to take their places in the word work center and wait for the team leader to distribute any needed materials for completing the displayed task for the day. On this same day, you might discuss with students your expectation that assigned tasks will be completed in the time allotted either independently or with others, depending on the directions for the day. You might also demonstrate for students how they are to seat themselves for independent work in the word work center.

On the fourth day of the third week of training, you might explicitly identify the consequences of failing to follow directions and obey the rules. You might direct children's attention to the posted consequences for failure to follow directions and behave appropriately in activity centers.

On the last day of the third week of training, you might model the clean-up process for the selected learning centers. A bell or other signaling device can alert children that time for using the center has ended. You might model how students are to "freeze" quietly in place while the team leader gathers up materials and returns them to their proper storage places. A second bell or signal can tell children they have 15–30 seconds to tidy up their own materials and seating area. A final bell or signal can direct children to move to another reading center or return to their own seats in the classroom.

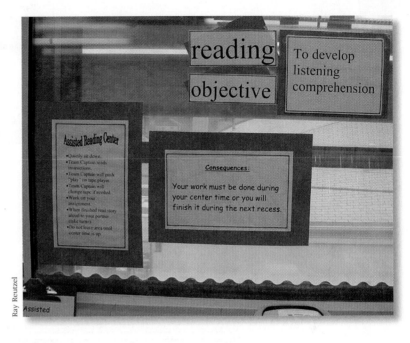

Training for using learning centers will likely require approximately 10 minutes per day for the entire third week of the school year. The process can be repeated at a slightly accelerated pace over the next two weeks with each of the remaining learning centers.

Role Playing the Use of Learning Centers in the Classroom. During the sixth and final week of training, teachers form small groups with team leaders for role playing the use of the learning centers and materials around the classroom. To begin the role play, students practice moving from their regular classroom seats to their first assigned learning center. Movement from one learning center to another using planned rotations during the literacy time block is also practiced. We show two possible approaches for managing learning center group rotations in Figure 11.12.

The wise teacher realizes that students must be able to role play these movements and behaviors to fully understand and internalize them.

During this role play, anyone who fails to follow directions exactly causes the entire group to stop and re-practice the movement and expected behaviors. Remaining firm about meeting expectations as children role play their use of these spaces and materials will save many management problems later on. Typically, ten minutes per day for one week is sufficient to prepare children. During this ten-minute role play, students should (a) move from their seats into the designated learning centers; (b) read as a small group the posted rules and daily task directions; (c) settle into proper seating arrangements based on posted task directions; (d) distribute reading tasks and materials; and (e) practice cleaning up the center space and materials.

Of course, children become excited, anxious, and motivated to enter these learning centers as they engage in their role playing. We have found that displaying digital photographs of children properly engaged in various center activities are helpful in encouraging children to behave appropriately during center work. One teacher we know simply asks her students if they look like the children in the picture. If not,

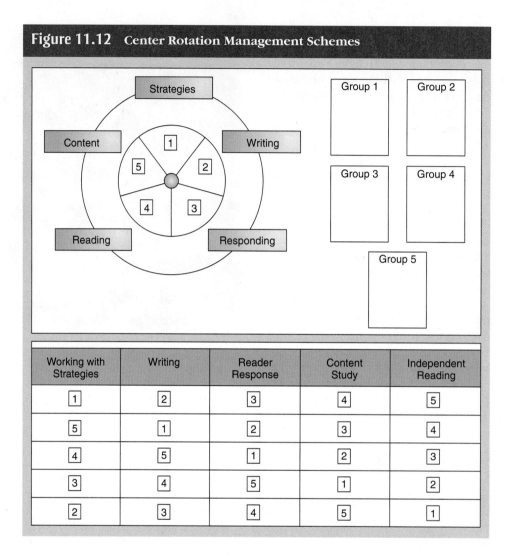

Figure 11.12   Center Rotation Management Schemes

Working with Strategies	Writing	Reader Response	Content Study	Independent Reading
1	2	3	4	5
5	1	2	3	4
4	5	1	2	3
3	4	5	1	2
2	3	4	5	1

she asks what they should do about their behavior to align it with the learning activity as shown in the example picture.

Minimizing Transition Times and Maximizing Reading and Writing Practice and Instruction. Training children for efficient movement between activities and into and out of various classroom literacy spaces is essential for minimizing transition times and maximizing literacy practice and instructional time. Here again, experience has taught us the value of using timers, stop watches, and other devices to motivate children to accomplish transition tasks briskly and without dallying. A worthwhile goal is to reduce transition times between activities and movements to other classroom spaces to only one minute so that the bulk of classroom time is spent on reading and writing practice and instruction. We use three steps to make this happen.

First, we use a consistent signal (ringing a hotel registration bell, turning off the lights, playing of a familiar song on tape) to alert students to stop what they are doing, freeze, and listen for directions. Second, we provide brief, well sequenced, and repetitive oral directions coupled with written directions displayed on cue cards.

Figure 11.13 Kindergarten and First Grade Daily Literacy Schedule

---

Half-Day Kindergarten (90 minutes literacy)

8:30–9:00 A.M.: Greet children and parents
9:00–9:10 A.M.: Morning routine (roll, lunch, weather, calendar)
9:10–9:20 A.M.: Sharing time
9:20–9:35 A.M.: Interactive read-aloud
9:35–10:05 A.M.: Shared reading
10:05–10:20 A.M.: Whole-class explicit lesson on letters and sight words
10:20–10:35 A.M.: Recess
10:35–10:45 A.M.: Science experiment: Magnets
10:45–11:00 A.M.: Shared writing/language experience chart
11:00–11:20 A.M.: Learning centers training—procedural lessons

First Grade (180 minutes literacy)

8:30–9:00 A.M.: Greet children and parents
9:00–9:10 A.M.: Morning routine (roll, lunch, weather, calendar)
9:10–9:20 A.M.: Sharing time—oral language
9:20–9:35 A.M.: Interactive read-aloud
9:35–10:00 A.M.: Shared reading
10:00–10:30 A.M.: Whole-class lesson on sight words or phonics
10:30–10:45 A.M.: Recess
10:45–11:15 A.M.: Writing
11:15–11:30 A.M.: Word work—whiteboard letter/word dictation
11:30–11:45 A.M.: Word wall Bingo
11:45–11:55 A.M.: Phonemic awareness—blending and segmenting to make words
12:00 Noon–12:45: Lunch
12:45–1:00 P.M.: Learning centers training—procedural lessons

---

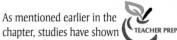

As mentioned earlier in the chapter, studies have shown that reading achievement is related to a teacher's skillful, effective instruction. "A First Grade Shared Reading Lesson Plan" will allow you to see five days of lessons as reflected in the "Characteristics of Exemplary Primary Grade Teachers." Visit our website (*www.prenhall.com/teacherprep*) and select *Strategies and Lessons—Language Arts Methods/Reading* to learn more.

Create a lesson through the Teacher Prep Website.

- You will be guided through the alignment of standards, lesson objectives, your introduction planning for and sequencing lesson activities and procedures, planning for ongoing assessment throughout the lesson and planning end of lesson assessment. You will also choose and list lesson materials/resources and create adapted instruction to meet all needs of students.

- This lesson can be sent to your instructor through this link.

- Select a K, 1, or 2 big book and plan a daily lesson plan. You may consider examples in this chapter.

- Use of a nonfiction book might provide the opportunity for the application of comprehension reading strategies with expository text.

Children must look, listen, and read to get the directions for what is to be done. Third, we use our signal devise once again to alert children to follow the oral and written directions to move to the next learning center. A sample daily schedule for the first few weeks of school is shown in Figure 11.13, including time for providing daily procedural learning center lessons.

Preparing Written Lesson Plans to Build Teacher Capacity for Explicit Instruction

The first week is also a good time to start the practice of writing daily lesson plans. It has been our experience that teachers who take the time to write and reflect on daily lesson plans provide higher quality instruction than those teachers who try to teach from a mere activity mentioned in a teacher's planning book block or those who simply "fly by the seat their pants." To put it bluntly, quality of outcomes in learning are directly related to the quality of the teacher's planning and delivery of instruction. To help you get a sense for the detail necessary in a daily lesson plan, a sample lesson plan for an oral guided reading of an information book in the second grade is featured in Figure 11.14.

Figure 11.14　Written Daily Lesson Plan—Second Grade

Title of Book　*Amazing Water*

Objective: Children will use several comprehension strategies to help them learn content knowledge from reading an information book.

Supplies Needed: *Amazing Water* big book, ice, water, different-shaped containers, hotplate, pan, mirror or piece of clear glass, word cards with pictures, graphic organizer

Step 1: Introduce the Book

Say: "This is an information book. An information book is different from a storybook. Let's talk for a moment about some of the differences. Information books give us facts, knowledge, and information about real things in our world like rocks, animals, or how to make chocolate! Storybooks are made up and are often not about real people or things in our world. Animals might talk, places might not really exist, and events might be imaginary."

Step 2: Activate Background Knowledge

Show students the different forms of water. Say: "Isn't water amazing!"
• Liquid—water in different-shaped containers
• Solid—ice cubes
• Gas—steam collected onto glass or mirror

Model by saying: "Before I read a book, I stop and think about what I know that connects to the book. If the book is about dogs, then I think about what I know about dogs. To become better readers, we need to stop and think about what we know about our book today. Now, stop and think about your own experiences with water. What do you think is "amazing" about water? If you have something to share, raise your hand and wait for your turn."

Step 3: Discuss the Author

Identify the author of the book. Point to his/her name on the book cover. Remind students that the author of a book is its writer.

Step 4: Table of Contents

Remind students that information books are different from storybooks. Information books have a table of contents at the beginning. The table of contents tells what is in the book and the order or sequence the author uses to organize the information he or she presents.

Step 5: Text Structure

Say: "Successful readers try to figure out how the author has put the book together. One of the ways authors put books together is to use a "book web." Let's look at the board. I have on the board a book web for our book today, *Amazing Water*. Here, in the center of the book web, I have written the title of our book, *Amazing Water*. You also see that I have other picture/word cards on the board. Do you notice that the book web looks kind of like a spider web? That's why we call it a 'web.'

"The author of our book is going to tell us about water by describing each of the things we see in our book web. Having this web helps us see how the author wants us to read the book and how he wants us to remember the information. Let's look at what the author is going to tell us about water and how he wants us to remember it. At the end of the first web strand, we have a picture/word card that says *liquid*. So the author is going to tell us about water as a liquid. What else is the author going to tell us? Let's look at the other web strands: *solid, gas, weather,* and *forms of water*. Remember, the book web is to help us notice and think about how the author is going to tell us the information in the book."

Step 6: Predicting

"Notice that I have put picture/word cards along the chalkboard tray. Each of these picture/word cards fits underneath one of the five web strands around the title of our book. Let me show you what I mean." Pick up one

Figure 11.14 (Continued)

picture/word card and think aloud about where and why this picture/word card goes here. Invite individual children to take each picture/word card and predict its place in the web.

Step 7: Question Generating

Say: "Before I read, I often think of some questions I'd like to answer as I read. Asking myself some questions helps me focus on important information and remember it. For example, I might want to ask, 'What makes water turn to ice?' Can you think of any questions you would like to ask before we read? Let's put a few up here."

Step 8: Read

Read aloud with the children the big book *Amazing Water* in a shared reading.

Step 9: Elaborative Interrogation

Stop at statements shown below. Mark points in the big book for turning statements into questions using sticky notes showing a question mark before the following statements:

Water is a liquid.
Ice is a solid.
Steam, or water vapor, is a gas.
Lots of different kinds of weather are forms of water.

Model for children how to turn the statement "Water is a liquid" into a question: "Why is water a liquid?" Write question on chart paper or whiteboard. Invite students to turn the other statements into questions.

Step 10: Monitoring

Stop at points with a "Stop Sign" on a sticky note to monitor comprehension. Tell children: "Let's review what we have learned so far to see if you are getting it. If you are getting it or it *clicks,* then read on. If you aren't getting it or it *clunks,* then we need to use some 'fix up' strategies." (See Chapter 7.)

Pages to stop for monitoring:

Page 9
Page 13

Step 11: Making Inferences and Confirming

After reading, have students respond to the following questions:

• What new things did you learn about water from this book?
• What things do you feel you didn't understand?
• How could the author have made these ideas clearer? Give the author some advice.
• Who can tell me three different forms of water?
• Let's look at the questions we asked before we read the book. Can we answer any of these? Discuss.
• Let's look at our predictions in the *Amazing Water* book web. How did we do? Let's look closely.

Step 12: Summarizing

Say: "We are going to make a summary. A summary helps us organize what we know using a few big ideas. We are going to make a summary web of what we have learned about "amazing water." I'm going to put up one sentence strip. It says, The Three Forms of Water. Can anyone tell me what the three forms of water are?" As students give the three forms of water, place three word cards—*liquid, solid,* and *gas*—around the sentence. Divide children into three groups. Give children word cards from the book containing terms like *rain, vapor, ice,* and others. Give each group three randomly selected word cards. Ask them to talk about each word and place it under the proper category of liquid, solid, or gas. Once they are finished, write one sentence to summarize the book: "Water is amazing because it can be a liquid, a solid, or a gas."

(continued)

Figure 11.14 (Continued)

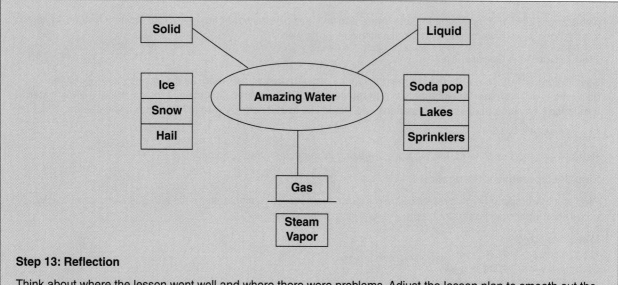

Step 13: Reflection

Think about where the lesson went well and where there were problems. Adjust the lesson plan to smooth out the problem spots.

Written lesson plans look like a great deal of work, and they are, but to carefully think through each lesson while planning the materials, information, modeling, explanations, questions, and so on, will result in greatly increased learning on the part of your students. Written lesson plans also give you the satisfaction of knowing you did your best to plan, instruct, reflect on, and improve your teaching. Written lesson plans need to be developed daily for each learning center as well as for small-group and whole-class instruction. Careful planning is often the difference between a well-managed classroom and chaos!

After writing daily lesson plans, schedule time for each literacy lesson and literacy learning center. This can be a rather simple listing of times when you will (1) teach a group literacy lesson, (2) assess individual children's literacy development and rotate groups through literacy and learning centers, and (3) provide group and independent seatwork. We suggest following a general daily schedule for literacy instruction and assessment during the first week of school in K–3 classrooms as found in Figure 11.13.

Designing a Year-Long Curriculum Plan

For most new teachers (and many experienced teachers as well), perhaps the most difficult thing to create is the annual curriculum plan. The literacy curriculum is defined as *a description of the reading and writing skills and strategies at a specific grade level*. To do this, some of the best sources to begin with are (1) the state's curriculum standards, (2) the school district curriculum guide, and (3) the district-adopted basal or core reading program's scope and sequence chart. When designing your curriculum plan, it is important to remember that the teaching of a reading or writing skill is not accomplished in one lesson. The curriculum plan also needs to include a schedule for reviewing previously taught lessons.

Because it would not be practical to describe the specifics of every state's standards, every basal reading program's scope and sequence, or every school district's curriculum guide, we use instead guidelines found in two prominent national reading research reports: *Starting Out Right: A Guide to Promoting Children's Reading Success* (Burns, Griffin, & Snow, 1999) and *Put Reading First: The Research Building Blocks for Teaching Children to Read, K–3* (Armbruster, Lehr, & Osborn, 2001). In Figure 11.15, we list the "evidenced-based" grade level accomplishments for K–3 students in reading. As you plan your curriculum, be sure to attend to each of these grade-level accomplishments.

Effective Reading and Writing Practices for All Year Long

Research consistently indicates that young children's reading and writing progress is most dramatically influenced by engaging them in substantial amounts of teacher-guided reading and writing practice (McCardle & Chhabra, 2004; National Reading Panel, 2000; Samuels & Farstrup, 2006; Stahl & McKenna, 2006; Tabors & Dickinson, 2001). The power of effective, evidence-based reading and writing instruction is truly realized when teachers guide students to apply their knowledge of reading and writing skills, strategies, and concepts during the actual reading and writing of a variety of texts for a variety of purposes. There are any number of ways to organize activities and schedule instruction for each school day. However, it is important that students experience a variety of interactive settings in which they are taught the essential components of reading and writing coupled with large amounts of time allocated for reading and writing practice. Groups for reading and writing interactions should be flexible, meet the needs of students, and involve best practices associated literacy instruction. In the next section, you will learn about several effective, evidence-based ways to engage young children in teacher guided reading and writing instruction and practice, including interactive read-aloud, shared reading, language experience approach, morning message, and interactive writing.

Interactive Read-Aloud. In Chapter 2, in the section on Making Family and Community Connections, we discussed how to conduct effective interactive read-alouds in homes and families. In this section, we discuss how to conduct effective classroom interactive read-alouds. In 1986, Teale and Martinez (1986) and Hoffman, Roser, and Battle (1993) summarized read-aloud research and proposed guidelines for reading aloud to children. We have provided a few of these guidelines in Figure 11.16.

Most reading aloud to children in school takes place with the entire class. Morrow (1988b) reminds teachers to take advantage of the benefits associated with reading aloud to smaller groups of young children and one-to-one with individuals. Children whose reading development lags behind that of their peers can be helped a great deal by teachers, volunteers, or older peers who take time to read to them in small-group or one-to-one settings. Children who are identified through early screening as lagging behind their peers can experience added benefits from read-aloud sessions when these are offered to them in small groups and individually.

Getting to Know English Learners
While ELs may not yet be productive in their language learning yet, they are receptive language learners. Read-Alouds therefore are appropriate for your ELs as they, too, will benefit from the rhythm and tone of the English language.

Figure 11.15 Expected Literacy Accomplishments for K–3 Students

Kindergarten

Reading

- Engages in language activities and games to develop phonological and phonemic awareness–an awareness of word parts (phonemes, onsets and rimes, etc., see Chapter 4)
- Understands basic book and print concepts
- Recognizes upper- and lowercase letters
- Makes connections between letters and sounds (alphabetic principle, see Chapter 4)
- Recognizes a few high frequency words by sight
- Reads simple emergent or beginning reader books (memorized and finger-point reading)
- Notices when oral or book language doesn't make sense
- Makes predictions while listening to stories read aloud

Writing

- Writes upper- and lowercase letters
- Writes own name
- Uses invented spellings to express own meaning
- Uses invented spellings when writing teacher dictated words
- Aware of the difference between "kid" writing and conventional writing

First Grade

Reading

- Makes transition from emergent (memorized and finger-point reading) to reading accurately what is recorded in the text.
- Decodes regularly spelled one-syllable words and nonsense words.
- Accurately reads and comprehends any text designed for first half of first grade.
- Uses letter–sound knowledge (phonics) to sound out unfamiliar words.
- Has a reading vocabulary of 300–500 sight words and easily sounded-out words.
- Monitors own reading and self-corrects using language sense and context when reading fails to make sense.
- Reads and comprehends story and information texts appropriate to the grade level.
- Reads and comprehends simple written instructions.
- Makes predictions and justifies predictions for stories.
- Activates background knowledge and uses it to understand new information.
- Can count the number of syllables and phonemes in one-syllable words.
- Can blend and segment the phonemes of one-syllable words.
- Can answer simple comprehension questions.
- Engages voluntarily in a variety of reading and writing activities.

Writing

- Spells three- and four-letter short vowel words conventionally.
- Writes texts for others to read.
- Writes independently using a mix of invented and conventional spellings.
- Uses basic or terminal punctuation (period, question marks, exclamation marks) and capitalization.
- Produces a variety of types of compositions and texts, i.e., stories, poems, notes, cards, recipes, journal entries, information texts, and so on.

Figure 11.15 (Continued)

Second Grade

Reading

- Reads and comprehends both fiction and nonfiction books at grade level.
- Accurately decodes regular, multisyllable words and nonsense words.
- Uses letter–sound knowledge to decode unknown words.
- Accurately decodes irregularly spelled words containing diphthongs, special vowel combinations, and common word endings.
- Reads voluntarily for interest and own purposes.
- Recalls facts and details.
- Reads nonfiction to answer specific questions or for specific details.
- Responds creatively to books through dramatizations, fantasy play, or oral presentations.
- Discusses similarities in characters and events across texts.
- Connects and compares information across texts.
- Poses answers to how, what, why, and what-if questions.

Writing

- Correctly spells previously studied words and spelling patterns in own writing.
- Represents the complete sound of a word when spelling independently.
- Writes using formal language patterns in place of oral language patterns at appropriate spots in own writing.
- Makes reasonable judgments about what to include in own writing.
- Productively discusses ways to clarify own writing and that of others.
- With assistance, uses conferencing, revision, and editing processes to increase quality of own writing.
- Given help, writes informative, well-structured reports.
- Attends to spelling, mechanics, and presentation for final products.
- Produces a variety of types of compositions.

*Based on grade level accomplishments found in Burns, M. S., Griffin, P., & Snow, C. E. (1999). *Starting out right: A guide to promoting children's reading success*. Washington, DC: National Research Council.

Figure 11.16 Interactive Read-Aloud Guidelines

- Designate a legitimate time and place in the daily curriculum for reading aloud.
- Select quality books.
- Select literature that relates to other literature.
- Prepare by previewing the book.
- Group children to maximize opportunities to respond.
- Provide a brief introduction.
- Read with expression.
- Discuss literature in lively, invitational, thought-provoking ways.
- Encourage children's responses to the book.
- Allow time for discussion and interaction about the book.

Based on Teale and Martinez, 1986; Hoffman, Roser, and Battle, 1993.

Shared Reading. In 1979, Don Holdaway described the reading of bedtime stories as one of the earliest and most significant practices supporting the reading development of young children. Shared reading, or what is sometimes called the shared book experience, is designed to be used with very young readers to model how readers look at, figure out, and operate on print. Shared reading experiences have been shown to be especially useful with young children in several scientific research studies (Eldredge, Reutzel, & Hollingsworth, 1996; Reutzel, Hollingsworth, & Eldredge, 1994; Reutzel & Hollingsworth, 1993).

During shared reading, teachers typically use an enlarged text called a **big book.** Big books permit teachers to demonstrate for students how to operate effectively on print (Barrett, 1982; Payne, 2005). When selecting big books for purchase, it is critical that teachers evaluate the size and legibility of the print from a distance of up to 15 feet away. Many publishers have simply enlarged the print found in traditionally sized books. The result can sometimes be print far too small to be effective with a group of children. The print in big books must be large enough so that the entire group of children can see it as easily as if they were sitting on your knee.

Shared reading books should have literary merit and engaging and meaningful content, and they should sustain high interest. Illustrations in shared reading books and stories must augment and expand upon the text (Payne, 2005). Pictures should tell or support the reading of the story in proper sequence. The proper selection of big books for shared reading experiences "hooks" children on the sounds and patterns of language, engages their minds with meaningful content and knowledge, and makes clear the multiple purposes of reading. Big books chosen for shared reading ought to put reasonable demands on younger readers' capabilities. The number of unknown words in relation to known words in a new book selected for shared reading should not overwhelm students. Big books selected for initial shared reading experiences should contain pictures that largely carry the storyline. Print in initial shared reading big books may amount to little more than a repeated line or two underneath the pictures, such as that found in the books *Brown Bear, Brown Bear What Do You See?* or *Polar Bear, Polar Bear What Do You Hear?* by Martin (1990, 1991). Print should occupy the same space on each page rather than move from place to place.

Conducting a Shared Book Experience. To begin a shared book experience, introduce the book to students. Begin by inviting them to look at the book cover with the prompt: "What do you see?" Allow children to talk about what they see. Ask them: "What do you think the print will tell you about the picture?" Let them study the title carefully and read the title with you. Talk about the front and back of the book and point out certain features of the cover and title page, such as the title, the author, and the illustrator. Next, read the book with "full dramatic punch, perhaps overdoing a little some of the best parts" (F. L. Barrett, 1982, p. 16). While reading the story, invite children to join in on any repeated or predictable phrases or words they recognize or predict. At key points during the shared reading, pause to encourage children to predict what is coming next in the story.

After reading, invite children to share their responses to the book. Ask them to talk about their favorite parts, connect the book to their experiences, as well as discuss how well they were able to predict and participate. The shared reading book is reread on subsequent days by using hand and body movements, simple props related to the book, or rhythm instruments are excellent ways to increase student involvement and activity in any rereading of a shared reading book.

Once a shared reading book has been reread twice, select something from the print in the book to examine in a "close reading." For example in the big book,

Video Classroom

Watch How Shared Reading Can Lead to Comprehension in a Second Grade Classroom.
Shared Reading experiences allow children of varying abilities to participate in the group. The CD that accompanies this text allows you to view a "Shared Reading" clip in *Comprehension Strategies-2nd Grade.*

- How does this approach support multi-level instruction as you think about vocabulary development, questioning and repeated readings?
- Listen for what the teacher mentions about "strategies that good readers use." Why is this a powerful, reinforcing approach as she works with the children?

The Three Billy Goats Gruff: A Norwegian Folktale (E. Appleby, 2001), the teacher may decide that students should begin to notice the sight word "the" in the text. To direct students' eyes to the word "the" in the text, the teacher takes stick, 'em notes from a pad and cuts several to the size necessary to cover or mask the word "the" in the text. As children and teacher engage in a "close reading" they note the masked words. The teacher unmasks the first "the" and asks students to look carefully at this word. What are the letters in the word? Invite a student to come up and copy the word from the book onto a large card. Each time the word "the" is encountered in the close read, it is unmasked and stressed aloud in the reading. After the close reading for "the" the teacher gives each child a "the" word card. The children are instructed to pick up a pair of scissors from the basket and return to their seats. While at their seats they cut the card into its three letters and scramble the letters. Each child unscrambles the letters to form the word "the" on their desktops. Each child is given a new index card to write the word "the" to keep in his/her own word collection. Interactive read alouds and shared reading experiences ought to be the primary focus of reading instruction during the first six months of Kindergarten and also during the first 4-6 weeks of first grade reading instruction! Shared reading is gradually replaced in Grade 2 with more work in Guided Reading Groups.

> **Getting to Know English Learners**
> The language experience approach is a tried-and-true ESL technique, stemming from the 1970s. In today's diverse classroom, you may have students from cultures that do not celebrate Christmas, but Hanukah and Kwanza for example. Excellent titles for these holidays include: Chanukah Lights Everywhere by Rosen & Iwai; Sammy Spider's 1st Hanukkah by Rouss & Kahn; My 1st Kwanzaa by Pinkney. Also, "Holiday Series Variety Pack" by Creative Teaching Press includes easy-to-read titles on a variety of American holidays.

Language Experience Approach. As young children are initially challenged by the transcription demands of writing, many teachers turn to a long-practiced and very useful early writing instructional approach called language experience. The essence of the **language experience approach** is to use students' talk about personal or vicarious experiences as the basis for creating a piece of writing they can read. In this approach, children dictate text and the teacher writes, resulting in the creation of a group language experience chart. This means, of course, that the entire class has shared an experience such as a field trip, a new book read aloud, or the visit of an outside guest. The typical sequence of events associated with the creation of a group language experience chart follows:

You will find instructions for a Language Experience lesson along with suggestions for modifications on the Teacher Prep Website *(www.prenhall. com/teacherprep).* Select *Strategies and Lessons—Reading Method/Emergent Literacy* to read "Language Experience Approach."

1. Students participate in a common experience.
2. Teacher and students discuss the common experience.

TEACHER PREP　Following the dictation of a Language Experience Story, students can revisit it during the week. Four days of plans can be accessed on the Teacher Prep Website *(www. prenhall.com/teacherprep)* in the *Strategies and Lessons—Reading Methods/Emergent Literacy* section. Read "Collecting Individual Dictation and Group Experience" to learn more about taking the text to fluency and how this approach can be powerful for bilingual students.

3. Students dictate the chart while the teacher transcribes the dictation.
4. Teacher and students share in reading the chart.
5. The chart is used to learn about words and other important language concepts such as punctuation, left-to-right orientation, and sight words.

The selection of an interesting and stimulating experience or topic for students largely determines the success or failure of any language experience activity. Topics and experiences simply must capture the interest of children to provide the necessary motivation. A few examples of ideas for supporting the creation of a group language experience chart include:

- Our mother hamster had babies last night.
- Writing a new version of *The Napping House* (A. Wood, 1984).
- What mountain men did in the old days.
- What we want for our birthdays.
- Planning our Valentine's Day party.
- What did Martin Luther King, Jr., do?
- Sometimes I have scary dreams. Once . . .
- Once I got into trouble for . . .
- A classmate is ill; make a get-well card from the class.
- What we want to tell our parents for the open house tomorrow night.

Discuss the experience carefully and completely. Help children assess what they have learned, help them make personal connections, and motivate them to share with others their knowledge, experiences, and personal connections. Be careful not to dominate the discussion. Ask many open ended questions to promote discussion. Do not make the mistake of beginning dictation too early in the discussion to prevent a dull, even robotic recounting of the experience.

A Language Experience Example Using-The Polar Express. Imagine reading aloud the book *The Polar Express* by Chris Van Allsburg (1985) a few weeks prior to Christmas in a first-grade classroom. After inviting children to discuss the book, ask, "If you had been chosen by Santa to receive the first gift of Christmas, what would you have chosen?" Call on individual children to give their ideas. After plenty of discussion, call on children to dictate aloud their best ideas for responding to this question. Record each child's dictation on the chart. With emergent readers, you may wish to record each child's dictation with different colored markers; the colors help children identify their own dictation more easily in the future. Later, you may write the children's names by their dictations. When the chart is complete, read the chart aloud to the children while pointing to each word. After reading the chart aloud, invite the children to read along a second time. Next, ask individual children to read their own responses aloud or invite volunteers to read aloud the responses of other children.

As the teacher, you may wish to read aloud a certain line from the chart and ask for a child to come up to the chart and point to the line you just read aloud. You may copy the lines of the chart on sentence strips and have children pick a sentence strip and match it to the line in the chart. Favorite words in the chart story can be copied onto word cards for matching activities as well. Thus, the text generated by the children for the chart story can be used in subsequent large- and small-group meetings to build the students' sight vocabulary of words in the chart, demonstrate word-recognition strategies, and even help children learn about letter sounds for decoding purposes. The chart also can be copied on to a regular sized sheet of paper and sent home with each child for individual reading practice.

Effective K–3 Classroom Reading Instruction: The Five-Block Reading Essentials Model

Children develop a sense of security when the events of the school day revolve around a predictable sequence of anticipated activities. Although variety is the spice of life for children, too, they find comfort in familiar instructional routines in a well-organized classroom (Holdaway, 1984). A tip for beginning teachers or veterans who may experience problems with behavior management: We highly recommend the book *The First Days of School* (Wong & Wong, 1998) as a resource. It's great for helping teachers get the school year off to a good start with very basic routines and expectations. See the reference at the end of this chapter.

One approach that is increasingly used to organize the school day is the five-block reading/writing essentials model. Although this organizational framework was originally proposed for all K–12 students in the public schools of Chicago by Dr. Timothy Shanahan, we have implemented it successfully in the elementary school (K–6). We have found this organizational framework for reading and writing instruction to be both effective and manageable for many classroom teachers of elementary and middle school-aged children.

The five-block reading/writing essentials model is a framework for scheduling and focusing daily reading and writing instruction so that all children receive daily instruction in the five essential components of reading: phonemic awareness, phonics, fluency, vocabulary, and comprehension strategies + writing. In the five-block reading/writing essentials model, it is expected that the literacy instructional block will be scheduled for a minimum of 180 minutes (3 hours) in length in grades 1 and 2 and for 90 minutes (1.5 hours) in half-day kindergarten settings. It is best if this time is uninterrupted by outside intrusions.

The 180 minutes of allocated literacy instruction time in the five-block reading/writing essentials model is divided into four 30-minute contiguous blocks of instructional time followed by a 60-minute block of small-group differentiated reading instruction with the teacher and paired or independent reading and writing practice time. Kindergarten teachers should divide the amounts in half for each block. The five-block reading/writing essentials model is shown in Figure 11.17.

Dr. Timothy Shanahan, a member of the National Reading Panel, reported that installing the five-block reading/writing essentials model of instructional time allocation for reading and writing instruction in the Chicago Public Schools led to significant improvements in K–12 student reading achievement scores in a single year

---

Figure 11.17 **The Five-Block Reading Essentials Instruction Model**

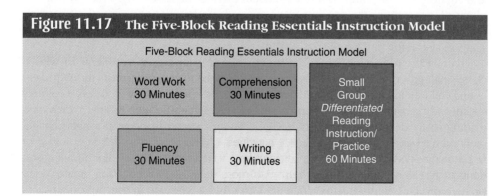

Five-Block Reading Essentials Instruction Model

| Word Work 30 Minutes | Comprehension 30 Minutes | Small Group *Differentiated* Reading Instruction/ Practice 60 Minutes |
| Fluency 30 Minutes | Writing 30 Minutes | |

(Shanahan, 2004). In addition to this endorsement of implementation efficacy, many Reading First schools across the nation are now using the five-block reading/writing essentials model as well. To give you, our reader, insight into how this model works in practice, we describe each of the five components in greater detail.

Word Work (30 Minutes). During this whole-group instructional time, teachers provide explicit instruction focused on learning to recognize and decode words, learning the structure of words, and learning the meaning of words. This time is devoted to (1) teaching younger students to recognize the alphabet letters (upper-case and lowercase); (2) training students to hear sounds in spoken words (phono-logical and phonemic awareness); (3) helping students learn to recognize and spell a body of high-frequency sight words; (4) teaching students to decode and spell simple CV, CVC, CVVC, CVCE words; (5) teaching students about prefixes, suffixes, word tense, and singular and plural, forms; and (6) providing vocabulary instruc-tion. In kindergarten and first grade, instruction during word work time is focused primarily on learning and writing the alphabet letters, recognizing and spelling sight words, and decoding and spelling simple two- or three-letter words. In the second and third grade years, the focus shifts from word recognition and spelling to understanding the structure and meaning of words. In the intermediate and mid-dle school years, the primary focus of word work is concentrated on acquiring a vast store of word meanings and increasing reading vocabularies.

Writing (30 Minutes). During this whole-group instructional time, teachers focus student attention on the core elements of the elementary school writing curriculum, on a variety of writing products, and on the various phases of the writing process within the context of a writer's workshop. With respect to the core elements of the writing curriculum, teachers explain and model word choice, organization, word and sentence fluency, ideas, conventions, voice, and presentation. Teachers also help children understand the various forms of writing such as narration, exposition, persuasion, and poetry. In addition, students are engaged in a variety of writing tasks as they produce letters, reports, recipes, poems, bumper stickers, newspaper headlines, riddles, and so on. All of this occurs within the supportive framework of the writer's workshop (Calkins, 1994), which provides students with teacher-modeled mini-lessons, drafting, conferencing, revising, editing, and publishing.

Fluency (30 Minutes). This 30-minute period is divided into two separate sets of activities for teacher and students: explicit fluency instruction with the whole class and small-group or paired fluency practice. During the first 8 to 10 minutes of this block of instruction, the teacher explains and models various aspects of reading fluency including accuracy, rate, and expression. For an explicit fluency lesson plan, please refer to Chapter 5.

During the remaining 20 to 22 minutes, the teacher engages students in whole-class, small-group, and oral repeated reading practice to build automaticity. With very young children in kindergarten and first grade, fluency practice may focus on accurately and quickly recognizing and writing alphabet letters, high-frequency sight words, and reading easily decodable words (CV, CVC). This practice can occur through engage-ment with a variety of fluency practice activities. Choral readings of texts in unison or in echo voices helps students get a sense of how to read with fluency. Encouraging stu-dents to reread a passage helps them read more fluently, thus enabling greater com-prehension. One very effective strategy is to engage students in the performance of

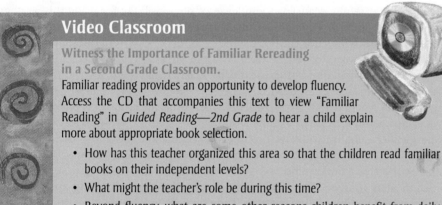

Video Classroom

Watch How New Vocabulary Is Introduced to Emergent Learners.

Observe children taking new words to fluency during small group instruction. Go to the Video section on the Teacher Prep Website *(www.prenhall.com/teacherprep)* and select *Reading Methods—Vocabulary* to view "Introducing Words to Young Readers."

- Why might the teacher select the words "she" and "inside" for instruction?
- Why does she redirect a student during the word learning activity?
- What other approaches might you include in centers to increase automaticity of these words in writing? How might the internalization of these words look as the child read?

Video Classroom

Witness the Importance of Familiar Rereading in a Second Grade Classroom.

Familiar reading provides an opportunity to develop fluency. Access the CD that accompanies this text to view "Familiar Reading" in *Guided Reading—2nd Grade* to hear a child explain more about appropriate book selection.

- How has this teacher organized this area so that the children read familiar books on their independent levels?
- What might the teacher's role be during this time?
- Beyond fluency, what are some other reasons children benefit from daily opportunities to read familiar text?

reader's theater productions. A range of reader's theater scripts can be obtained on the Internet at *http://www.aaronshep.com/rt/RTE.html, http://scriptsforschools.com/,* and *http://www.geocities.com/Athens/Thebes/9893/readerstheater.htm.*

Students who have achieved grade level **automaticity** can benefit from individual, wide oral, and silent, monitored reading (Reutzel, 2006; Stahl, 2004). This means that silent reading ranges across a prescribed set of genre types for a given period of time, say a nine-week quarter (fairy tales, biographies, information books, stories, etc.), and each student's silent reading is monitored periodically—often randomly—by the teacher. For the teacher, the bulk of this time is devoted to meeting individually with five to eight students, two minutes each, to hold individual fluency assessment conferences. Students sign up for a one-minute fluency assessment conference with the teacher. Students read a teacher-selected, grade- or instructional-level text for one minute while the teacher tracks errors, rate, and expression. Information yielded by these fluency assessment conferences is used to set student fluency goals and inform later fluency instruction.

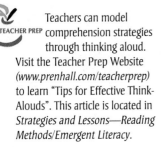

Teachers can model comprehension strategies through thinking aloud. Visit the Teacher Prep Website (*www.prenhall.com/teacherprep*) to learn "Tips for Effective Think-Alouds". This article is located in *Strategies and Lessons—Reading Methods/Emergent Literacy*.

Comprehension Strategy (30 Minutes). During this whole group instructional time, teachers provide explicit comprehension strategy instruction for all students, even for those in kindergarten and first grade. In these early grades, comprehension strategy instruction may take place through listening rather than reading. But for those students in second grade on up, daily attention to explicit comprehension strategy instruction is a critical part of a comprehensive, balanced reading program.

Teachers explain (1) which comprehension strategy is to be learned, (2) why it is important to learn, and (3) when and where the strategy can be applied with effectiveness. Next the teacher models how to use the strategy in connection with reading and discussing a text. Very often, this modeling includes the teacher using a think-aloud to help students get a toehold on the workings of the mind when it engages with text. During a think-aloud, the teacher shares her thoughts about the application of a comprehension strategy. Comprehension strategies include answering questions, generating questions to be answered, understanding narrative structure, using graphic organizers, monitoring one's own comprehension processes, summarizing, making inferences, visualizing imagery, predicting, and connecting text to one's background experiences. Once the teacher has modeled a comprehension strategy, she carefully scaffolds the release of responsibility for using this strategy to the individual student (Pearson & Gallagher, 1983). She accomplishes this by sharing parts of the task with students. For example, in responding to a question, the teacher may give the answer and ask students to offer support for it based on their knowledge or what is contained in the text. The teacher may then reverse these roles by having students answer a question while she offers supportive information. Following this, the teacher may have students work in small groups or pairs, sharing the task of answering questions as they assume roles such as question answerer and answer justifier. Finally, students practice answering and justifying their answers to questions independently. Daily comprehension strategy instruction should focus on using strategies to understand text—not on learning the strategy per se.

Allocating sufficient time to the essential elements of reading and writing instruction is of paramount importance. Time on task and academic learning time have long been shown to bear direct influence on children's reading and writing achievement. However, allocating more time without an appropriate instructional focus will yield little. Teachers must allocate sufficient time to the important components of reading and writing achievement. The Five-Block Reading/Writing Essentials Model helps teachers focus on important elements of reading and writing instruction and allocates sufficient amounts of time for that instruction.

Differentiating K–3 Instruction to Meet Diverse Student Needs

Recent research by Mathes et al. (2005) has shown that small-group differentiated reading instruction has significant positive effects on struggling young readers' achievement in reading. The structure that small-group, differentiated reading instruction takes does not seem to make much of a difference. What does seem to matter is that students with similar instructional needs are grouped together into clusters of 5 to 6 students for targeted and intensive reading instruction. Also, this small-group instruction must be focused on providing children instruction and practice in reading appropriately challenging and support texts while teaching them to apply their knowledge of the essentials of reading—phonemic awareness, letter name knowledge, phonics, fluency, vocabulary, and comprehension strategies.

Tyner (2003) describes excellent routines and processes for providing small-group, differentiated reading instruction in a book titled *Small-Group Reading Instruction: A Differentiated Teaching Model for Beginning and Struggling Readers.* Perhaps the most important thing that can be said about small-group, differentiated reading instruction is that teachers monitor students' progress regularly, group membership is changed regularly, and time spent is focused on teaching students the essentials of reading instruction drawn from scientific-based reading literature—phonemic awareness, phonics, fluency, vocabulary, and comprehension strategies.

Differentiated reading instruction small groups typically meet daily for 20 minutes. This allows the teacher to have at least three small groups for differentiated instruction. If more than three groups are necessary to meet diverse student needs, the teacher might meet only every other day with the more skilled students' small group. In order to support small-group, differentiated reading instruction, teachers need to provide for collaborative and independent practice of reading and writing skills, strategies, and concepts by other students in the classroom who are not involved in small-group instruction.

To begin, you may want to create only one learning center for a small group (five to six children) to visit daily for about 20 minutes. Other students—those not in small-group, differentiated reading instruction or who are not involved in learning center activities—remain in their seats, either working with cross-age peer tutors or in paired reading with another student in the classroom. Cross-age peer tutoring that involves trained, older students reading with younger, less experienced students and providing them feedback and paired-reading of peers within the classroom have long proven their worth in helping to provide effective reading practice (Labbo & Teale, 1990; Osborn, Lehr, & Hiebert, 2003). Another approach for providing these collaborative and independent practice settings, which we have discussed extensively earlier in this chapter, involves the establishment of collaborative or independent learning centers.

Getting to Know English Learners
Providing your EL students with a more capable "reading buddy" (whether in English or the EL's native language) is another approach for differentiated instruction.

Increase your knowledge of ideas and ways to work with a child on different instructional level. Go to the Teacher Prep Website (*www.prenhall.com/teacherprep*) and select *Strategies and Lessons—Reading Methods/Organizing for Reading Instruction.* Read the article "Individualization" to learn more about differentiation.

Making Family and Community Connections in the K–3 Years

Evidence continues to mount showing the indispensable nature of the partnership between parents and schools. In schools that serve disadvantaged children, where teachers are teaching and children are learning to read against the odds, a strong school-and-family partnership is cited as a chief ingredient in the success formula (Taylor, Pearson, Clark, & Walpole, 1999). It is never too late to start a school-family community partnership. The first step is to just start! Begin by identifying participants during parent-teacher conferences. Participants must include K–3 children's parents or caregivers and may include local businesses, government agencies, and senior citizen centers. These participants will provide tutoring, learning center supervision, and oral reading to or with young children.

"Ways to Stimulate Reading in Young Children" provides suggestions for teachers and parents to make connections with children so that they see how reading is used in their daily lives. Find out more about involving parents in your program. Go the Teacher Prep Website (*www.prehnall.com/teacherprep*) and visit *Strategies and Lessons—Reading Methods/Organizing for Reading Instruction* to locate this article.

Once a group of participants has been identified, determine the time and location of meetings. If you want to include all parents and other potential participants, it is important that you plan to provide child care, transportation, and other incentives (Vopat, 1994, 1998). We have found that providing a meal as a part of evening parent-and-community involvement meetings is a real hit, as are read-alouds and free take-home books. Parents, volunteers, tutors, businesses, and agencies need to be willing to sign a commitment form indicating that they are in the project for the duration. In many cases, it is a good idea to offer parent-and-community involvement workshops or seminars in multilingual formats to encourage broad participation.

Seminars or workshops are best based on involving parents and other participants in the ongoing aspects of the school's reading instruction program: thematic units, writing workshops, reading aloud books, and so on. Parents and other community partners want to experience the curriculum and learn ways to help children succeed in learning to read (Vopat, 1998). Although agendas should be planned for workshops or seminars, it is important that these be flexible so that participants can help in building or fleshing out projects based on their interests and desires. Starting a study group where participants read and discuss important documents, books, and materials together can be most helpful. Also, be sure to include at least one quality read-aloud book to be shared with participants for each seminar, session, or workshop. Vopat (1998) discusses using a "Roving Parent or Community Partner Journal," which is sent between home and school and in which teachers and parents or other community partners can communicate questions or issues of common concern.

Communicate your learning goals and curriculum clearly to parents, partners, and students. Neither the curriculum nor expected outcomes should be considered "classified" information. Projects that target how parents and other partners can help children learn the curriculum and achieve expected outcomes are usually well received. If the means you are using to communicate with parents and partners isn't working, don't give up. Try another method, such as phone calls, newsletters, telephone trees, and so on. It has also been useful to provide a place on regular grade reports for parents to write a response, question, or concern back to you, the teacher. Family histories also have been shown to be an effective way to get parents, community partners, and students involved in an initial activity that focuses on identify and roots. These need to be shared in subsequent parent-and-community involvement workshops and seminars as a regular part of the meeting. Remember: Most barriers to parent-and-community partner involvement are found within schools and school practices—not within parents or the community!

Start today. Start small or large or somewhere in between, but get started! Think of one thing you can do to connect your classroom and school with families and communities, whether it is your first year of teaching or your thirtieth. And don't forget to listen to parents and partners; they have much to share because of how much they care (Edwards, 1999).

Summary

In this chapter, we describe the characteristics of exemplary primary grade reading teachers from research. These characteristics included: instructional balance, density, and scaffolding; understanding young children's reading development; encouraging student self-regulation during reading instruction and practice; integrating reading and writing into other curriculum areas; holding high expectations for students to learn; engaging in good classroom management; explicitly teaching reading skills, concepts, and strategies; providing access to a variety of print materials; engaging students in authentic reading and writing practice; allocating sufficient instructional time to increase student achievement; displaying useful procedural and conceptual information in the classroom; providing positive, specific feedback to improve student performance; encouraging literacy enriched play in kindergarten; and offering multidimensional word recognition and word study instruction.

We briefly reviewed from Chapter 5 how young children develop from novice to fluent to critical readers based upon the stage theories of J. Chall (1983). We then turned our attention to hallmarks of effective reading instruction in the primary grades. First we described how to prepare a print rich classroom environment. This process included making a classroom floor plan and designing spaces within the classroom for whole and small group instruction and selected learning centers. Essential and suggested learning centers were described in detail including purpose for the center, contents, organization, and procedures. Planning and organizing classroom storage spaces to support a variety of reading and writing functions were detailed with special focus given to organizing the classroom library. We also briefly discussed different ways of grouping students for reading instruction to meet their individual learning needs.

Next, we provided detailed information about how to get reading instruction off to a good start from the first day, the first week, and planning for effective instruction across the entire year. We discussed the importance of writing lesson plans to support explicit instruction of skills, concepts and strategies during the school year. A sample explicit reading instruction lesson plan was provided followed by a listing of standards or accomplishments expected for students to achieve in grades K–3.

After this we described several excellent teaching practices that may be used to provide effective reading instruction and guided practice throughout the school year including interactively reading aloud, shared reading experiences, and the language experience approach. Scheduling the daily reading instructional routine made use of a *Five-Block Reading Essentials Models* that included daily instructional attention to and practice in word work, fluency, comprehension/vocabulary, writing, and teacher-directed, small group differentiated reading instruction and guided practice. Additional information about how to use small group differentiated reading instruction as a way to meet diverse student learning needs was provided. Finally, developing and implementing a parent involvement program was offered as a way to connect school-based, primary grade reading instruction to families and communities.

Classroom Applications

1. Draw a classroom floor plan illustrating how you will arrange and utilize your classroom space during your first year of teaching. Give a supporting rationale for the design you choose. (Keep in mind the idea of beginning with simple classroom arrangements!)
2. Prepare a letter to parents and students in which you introduce yourself and welcome them to your class. Discuss your letter with a parent you know. Ask him or her for feedback. How is your letter helpful? How might it be improved?

3. Make a schedule of literacy activities you plan to use on the first day of school. Then develop individual lesson plans like those in this chapter for each of the activities you scheduled.

4. Develop a first-week plan of literacy activities. Then structure individual lesson plans like those in this chapter for each of the activities you scheduled.

5. Develop a year-long plan to increase parental, family, and community involvement in your anticipated classroom. Go to the library and Internet to obtain copies of letters, training curricula, and communications ideas. Present your plan in the form of a tri-fold brochure to your classmates. Discuss and evaluate each other's work.

Recommended Readings

Campbell, R. (2001). *Read-alouds with young children*. Newark, DE: International Reading Association.

Diffily, D., & Sassman, C. (2004). *Teaching effective classroom routines: Establishing structure in the classroom to foster children's learning—from the first day of school and all through the year*. New York: Scholastic, Inc.

Dragan, P. B. (2001). *Literacy from day one*. Portsmouth, NH: Heinemann.

Drapeau, P. (2004). *Differentiated instruction: Making it work*. New York: Scholastic, Inc.

Gregory, G. H., & Chapman, C. (2002). *Differentiated instructional strategies: One size doesn't fit all*. Thousand Oaks, CA: Corwin Press.

Wong, H. K., & Wong, R. T. (1998). *The first days of school: How to be an effective teacher* (2nd ed.). Mountain View, CA: Harry K. Wong Publications.

chapter 12

Effective Reading Instruction and Organization in Grades 4–8

Chapter Questions

1. What does research tell us about the special challenges of informational texts?

2. How can teachers assess students' subject area knowledge?

3. How do teachers prepare to teach informational texts?

4. What are some successful ways to organize for instruction?

5. How can teachers use writing to improve learning?

6. What are some study strategies that can help students improve their reading comprehension?

7. What can be done to help struggling readers succeed?

8. How can we help English Learners (ELs) do well with content texts?

Holmes* and His Protégés Solve the "Acid Mystery"

Fred Holmes is teaching his eighth graders about acids and bases in his science class. Not only does he want to teach these fundamental scientific concepts, he hopes to help his students apply what they are learning to better understand the *acid rain* phenomenon as specified in the school curriculum. Fred has a personal experience with acid rain: he learned from the state's agricultural extension agent last spring that his cherished magnolia tree met an early and unexpected death due to acid rain! So Fred has declared war on this repugnant phenomenon and wants his students to join the fight. But first, he must make sure they have a solid grounding in facts about acids in the environment.

Mr. Holmes began planning for the acids and bases unit by first constructing a content analysis of the important facts, concepts, and generalizations to be learned. After picking apart the textbook chapter on this subject, as well as the supplemental readings he selected from other print and Internet sources, he constructed a simple graphic organizer showing the important information to be learned. From there he mapped out his entire unit over ten 50-minute class sessions using the lesson plan format adopted by the school district.

Holmes embedded key content literacy strategies in his acids and bases unit plan that would help all learners, including those reading two or more years below level, gain knowledge on high levels. In addition to a great deal of concept and vocabulary development, a fundamental strategy Holmes used throughout the unit was "three-level retelling" for better comprehension. First, students read and reread key information in groups of two or "buddy reading." This helped them gain reading fluency with the science texts while also providing multiple exposures to important information. After several readings, Holmes had students participate in a structured oral retelling exercise to help them realize what they had learned, and discover other information they needed to review.

The second phase of science retelling had students working in small groups to retell using a graphic organizer. This step moved students from oral retelling to retelling-using-words-and-phrases. Fitting the newly learned information into a graphic organizer also helped his students see relationships between new concepts about acids and bases.

In the third and final retelling stage, Fred Holmes taught his young *protégés* how to use a graphic organizer to construct written summaries about what they were learning. As part of his modeling, Holmes shared with his students this graphic that portrays his thinking on how to move information from a graphic organizer to paragraph form and then on again to a completed science paper summarizing what has been learned.

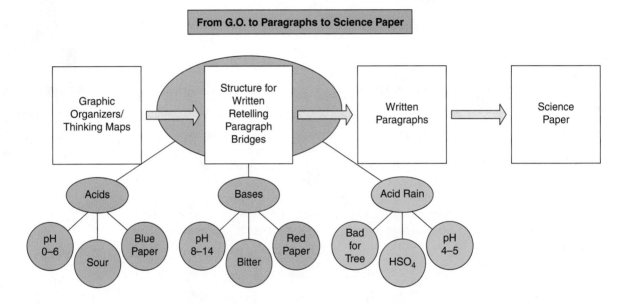

To make his modeling more concrete for his learners, Mr. Holmes presented a draft of what he called "Structure for Written Retelling Paragraph Bridges" based on the work of Kathleen S. Cooter. A completed *paragraph bridge* is shown on the next page. Armed with these new insights, Holmes's students were ready to begin trying their hands at moving information from their own graphic organizers into written summaries about acids and bases. When students completed this first study of acids and bases, they were prepared for the next stop on Mr. Holmes's unit: Acid Rain!

*Note: This vignette is closely based on the work of Mr. Fred Holmes, a science teacher in Memphis (TN). He is also a teacher-mentor on the federally funded Striving Readers project.

Structure for Written Retellings (A Model by K.S. Cooter)

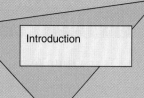

Introduction

Have you ever tasted something sour? Well, if you have, then you tasted an acid. I want to invite you on a trip with me in discovering three new and exciting concepts. We will discover new things about acids, bases, and how acids and bases are similar.

Paragraph Bridge 1

Topic #1 (Bubble Map of Acids)

Supporting details

Concluding sentence

An acid is a substance that donates hydrogen ions when dissolved in water. Did you know that the soft drink Sprite was an acid? Another example of an acid is a lemon. You can tell an acid in other ways besides its taste. One way is if the substance has a pH between 0 and 6, then it is an acid. Also, if a substance turns blue litmus paper red then it is an acid. Lastly, acids can be dangerous; however, you don't have to take my word for it. Just taste and see!

Paragraph Bridge 2

Topic #2 (Bubble Map of Bases)

Supporting details

Concluding sentence

A base is a substance that either contains hydroxide ions or reacts with water to form hydroxide ions. Foods that are bases tend to be bitter. Moreover, bases can be found in other places in the home such as common cleaning products like Pine Sol or Windex. Bases can be identified using red litmus paper and has a pH between 8 and 14. Finally, bases are very useful especially if you can't see the hummingbird outside your window.

Paragraph Bridge 3

Topic #3 (Acids & Bases Double Bubble Map)
Supporting details

Concluding sentence

Acids and bases are different in so many ways, but they share a few things in common. For example, some people think that acids can be harmful, but strong bases can be just as harmful. Also, both acids and bases can conduct electricity. In contrast, they have different tastes. Acids are sour and bases are bitter. The pH of an acid is between 0 and 6, but the pH of a base is between 8 and 14. Lastly, acids and bases are important to know because whenever your stomach aches you might just need a base to calm your acidic stomach down.

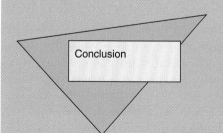

Conclusion

In conclusion, acids and bases are interesting. They share many things in common, but they have may differences as well. While this journey may be over, our next adventure will be discovering the exciting and often dangerous changes caused by acid rain.

What Does Research Tell Us About the Special Challenges of Content Reading Materials?

Changing Realities: Reading Instruction in the Transition Years

The years of learning at this level have rightly been referred to as the "transitional grades." Children in grades 4 through 8 can range widely in their reading ability. At one end of the continuum, students are still struggling to conquer basic reading and writing skills, and at the other end fluent readers are chomping at the bit for new challenges.

Master teachers in these grades have an understanding of reading and writing standards from the earliest stages through fluency. They also have a significant arsenal of strategies for teaching a wide range of literacy skills. Finally, they are able to establish effective and flexible classroom routines involving small- and large-group instruction, learning centers, and independent learning activities.

From our own experience, we can assure you that teaching at this level is as exciting as it is rewarding.

Keeping Our "Balance"

There can be a great deal of pressure at the intermediate and middle school levels to show significant literacy gains on state-mandated tests. Other academic pressures commonly occur during grades 4 through 8. We all remember being introduced as children to cursive writing, long division, and more in-depth studies of science, social studies, and the arts during our intermediate years. If we are not careful, we can lose our balance and forget to continue developing reading and writing skills in our students. As one teacher recently remarked to us,

> "I have come to understand that, in a very real way, children do not truly begin learning to *read* until the upper elementary years and beyond. Before that time, they are mostly learning to *decode*. Now they learn how to use those skills to understand their world."
>
> *(Earlene Mills-House)*

The Challenge of the Textbook Genre

Reading in grades 4 through 8 is a different ballgame for students. Here the student is asked to read and understand nonfiction or expository texts in science, mathematics, and the social studies almost exclusively. We agree with others (e.g., Brent, 1994; Kornblith & Lasser, 2005) that textbooks are so different from any other type of book—including the nonfiction found in libraries and bookstores—that they should be classified as a distinct genre. Textbook reading can be an especially formidable hurdle for the struggling reader. As one reading expert points out, reading problems in the upper elementary grades and middle school can become almost viral, attacking students' confidence and severely limiting academic progress (Cooter, 1999). In this era of high-stakes testing and No Child Left Behind legislation, the job of teaching reading becomes even more critical.

There can be negative consequences for students who cannot read and understand content area textbooks (Hall, 2004). These include (a) not learning the required content, (b) failing to pass high-stakes tests, (c) low self-efficacy, and (d) behavior problems. The critical question for us is this: How can we assist all learners by infusing content instruction with scientifically-*proven reading strategies?*

In this chapter, we look at ways teachers can help students succeed in reading and understanding subject area materials commonly found in the upper grades. We examine the unique ways in which textbooks are written and the reading demands placed on this group of youngsters. Before closing this final chapter of our book, we also consider ways to help struggling readers and involve families.

Textbook Reading Is Vastly Different from Story Reading

There are at least four different kinds of informational text commonly found in textbooks: *argumentation, description, exposition,* and *narration.* The majority of these readings are expository in nature. **Expository texts** are written to convey information about a topic (Gregg & Sekeres, 2006). Formal reading instruction in the upper grades focuses on successful strategies for reading and comprehending expository texts, study skills, and efficient, or "speed," reading strategies. The field that deals with applying reading skills to expository texts is known as **content area reading** (Cooter & Flynt, 1996).

Unlike the stories or **narrative texts** commonly used in beginning reading instruction, expository texts have unique organizational patterns. Explaining new ideas to others is a different form of language than storytelling, so different styles must be used to get important points across to the learner. Hence, different writing and reading techniques are employed in content area reading materials.

> **Getting to Know English Learners**
>
> In American schools, almost 90,000 word forms (e.g., history, historian, historical) occur in print from 1st through 12th grade (Nagy & Anderson, 1984) with the bulk of these word forms coming out of students' content area reading!

We begin with a discussion of the text demands that make reading subject area materials challenging for adolescent readers, such as increased concept load and readability considerations. We then examine the writing patterns or structures commonly used in expository texts.

Specialized Vocabulary and Concepts. A formidable task for every teacher of older students is helping them learn previously unknown concepts and vocabulary. As we see in Chapter 6, vocabulary knowledge is developmental and based on background experiences (Heilman, Blair, & Rupley, 2001). Vocabulary in expository texts and textbooks can be quite technical, specialized, and alien from students' experiences. Consider the kind of background building a teacher must construct for a science concept like *quarks* or a math concept like *variable.* Teachers, therefore, must scaffold instruction in order to somehow link what is known about students' worlds to the new information, vocabulary, and concepts found in textbooks (Gregg & Sekeres, 2006). This can be especialy challenging for teachers of English language learners (ELLs) and children with limited experience.

Students Need "Hands-On" Learning Experiences. The best way to teach students new ideas, vocabulary, and concepts is through concrete, or hands-on, experience. For example, if one wanted to teach students from rural Wyoming about life in New York City, the most effective way would be to take them there for a visit! Similarly, the very best way one could teach students about the space shuttle would be to put them through astronaut training and then fire them into space on a mission. Obviously, neither of these experiences is feasible, so we must seek the best concrete experiences within our reach as teachers.

Link vocabulary learning to student comprehension as you find procedures and extension activities for "Vocabulary Development in the Science Classroom." Visit the Teacher Prep Website (*www.prenhill.com/teacherprep*) accessing Strategies and Lessons–Reading Methods/ Comprehension.

"Concept-Oriented Reading Instruction" (CORI) provides the reader with procedures to demonstrate powerful connections of new knowledge to what is known. Assessment is also described as you read this article on the Teacher Prep Website (*www.prenhall.com/ teacherprep*). Select Strategies and Lessons–Reading Methods/ Comprehension to learn more.

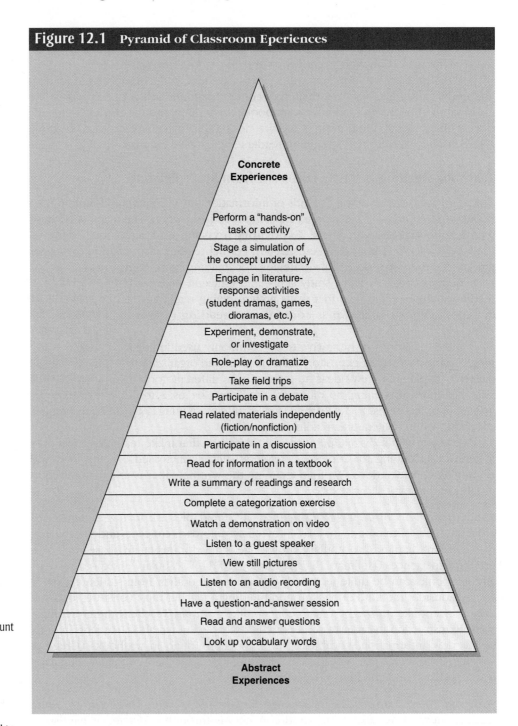

Figure 12.1   Pyramid of Classroom Eperiences

Concrete
Experiences

Perform a "hands-on"
task or activity

Stage a simulation of
the concept under study

Engage in literature-
response activities
(student dramas, games,
dioramas, etc.)

Experiment, demonstrate,
or investigate

Role-play or dramatize

Take field trips

Participate in a debate

Read related materials independently
(fiction/nonfiction)

Participate in a discussion

Read for information in a textbook

Write a summary of readings and research

Complete a categorization exercise

Watch a demonstration on video

Listen to a guest speaker

View still pictures

Listen to an audio recording

Have a question-and-answer session

Read and answer questions

Look up vocabulary words

Abstract
Experiences

"The Ghost of Count Dracula" is an artifact on the Teacher Prep Website *(www.prenhall.com/ teacherprep).* Visit *Artifacts–Reading Methods/Vocabulary.* Respond to the accompanying questions as students incorporate vocabulary words into creative text. Think about why this method might be more powerful than putting words in isolated sentences.

Some educators (Dale, 1969; Estes & Vaughan, 1978) have suggested hierarchies for typical classroom activities, ranging from concrete to abstract experiences. Such hierarchies help prospective teachers select concept and vocabulary development activities of a more concrete nature, and they help practicing teachers review their past practices for evaluative and curriculum redesign purposes. We have developed a composite version of these hierarchies, which we present in Figure 12.1. Notice that as one ascends to the top of the classroom experiences *pyramid,* activities become more concrete and thus easier for students to assimilate.

Increased Concept Load. **Concept load** (also called *concept density*) has to do with the number of new ideas and the amount of technical vocabulary introduced by an author (Singer & Donlan, 1989). Sentences of equal length may require very different comprehension skills from a reader. Expository reading materials found in textbooks are often much more difficult to understand than narrative/story readings because of greater concept load (Harris & Sipay, 1990). In story reading, elements such as setting, plot, and characterization are laced with information quite familiar to most readers. Expository writers, however, usually present new and abstract information unfamiliar to the reader, which requires the building of new *schemas* or memory structures in the brain. Authors who introduce several new concepts in a single sentence (high concept load) create a situation that is extremely difficult for all but the best readers. Consider the following passage about the history of Mesopotamia and an early hero. Words that carry rather deep meaning and require a good bit of vocabulary, background, and concept knowledge are underlined to emphasize concept load.

> **Getting to Know English Learners**
> Definition and understanding of concepts may vary from culture to culture—think of the concept, "democracy," making comprehension even more difficult for some ELs.

GILGAMESH

In early *Sumerian* history, *priests* were also the kings of the *city-states.* Gilgamesh was one of the most *heroic priest-kings* of this time. He was the priest-king of Uruk which was located on the *Euphrates River approximately* fifty miles northwest of *Ur.* The oldest written story in the world *delineates* Gilgamesh's *legendary deeds.* In the story, Gilgamesh is *characterized* as being both human and *divine.* Gilgamesh and his *companion,* Enkidu, *journey* the world *performing* heroic *acts.*

High concept load reading materials can create a major obstacle for readers lacking in background experiences and fluency. One way to supplement conceptually dense textbooks is to select several smaller books that concentrate on just a few topics and cover them in some depth. An excellent example is the *Reading Expeditions* series by National Geographic. You can see these materials online at *http://www.ngschoolpub.org.*

Readability Considerations. Another concern of teachers preparing content material for instruction is text difficulty or **readability.** Text difficulty is most often measured using a readability formula. The purpose of a readability formula is to assign a grade-level equivalent—or approximate difficulty level—to narrative or expository reading material used to teach children. Sentence length and complexity of vocabulary are two elements often measured in readability formulas.

A number of readability formulas are available for classroom use. The Fry (1977) readability formula (Figure 12.2), one of the more popular formulas available, bases its estimates on sentence and word length. Another formula that many regard as more user friendly (Baldwin & Kaufman, 1979) is the Raygor (1977) readability graph (Figure 12.3). Instead of having to count the number of syllables contained in a 100-word passage, teachers merely count the number of words having six or more letters. Readability software programs are also available.

Figure 12.2   The Fry Readability Formula

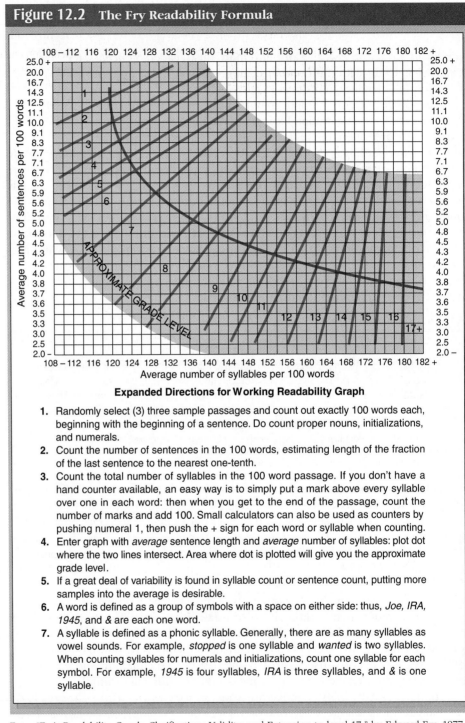

Expanded Directions for Working Readability Graph

1. Randomly select (3) three sample passages and count out exactly 100 words each, beginning with the beginning of a sentence. Do count proper nouns, initializations, and numerals.
2. Count the number of sentences in the 100 words, estimating length of the fraction of the last sentence to the nearest one-tenth.
3. Count the total number of syllables in the 100 word passage. If you don't have a hand counter available, an easy way is to simply put a mark above every syllable over one in each word: then when you get to the end of the passage, count the number of marks and add 100. Small calculators can also be used as counters by pushing numeral 1, then push the + sign for each word or syllable when counting.
4. Enter graph with *average* sentence length and *average* number of syllables: plot dot where the two lines intersect. Area where dot is plotted will give you the approximate grade level.
5. If a great deal of variability is found in syllable count or sentence count, putting more samples into the average is desirable.
6. A word is defined as a group of symbols with a space on either side: thus, *Joe, IRA, 1945,* and *&* are each one word.
7. A syllable is defined as a phonic syllable. Generally, there are as many syllables as vowel sounds. For example, *stopped* is one syllable and *wanted* is two syllables. When counting syllables for numerals and initializations, count one syllable for each symbol. For example, *1945* is four syllables, *IRA* is three syllables, and *&* is one syllable.

From "Fry's Readability Graph: Clarifications Validity, and Extension to level 17," by Edward Fry, 1977, *Journal of Reading, 21,* pp. 242–252.

Figure 12.3 The Raygor Readability Formula

1. Count out three 100-word passages at the beginning, middle, and end of a selection or book. Count proper nouns but not numerals.
2. Count sentences in each passage, estimating to the nearest tenth.
3. Count words with six or more letters.
4. Average the sentence length and word length over three samples, and plot the average on the graph.

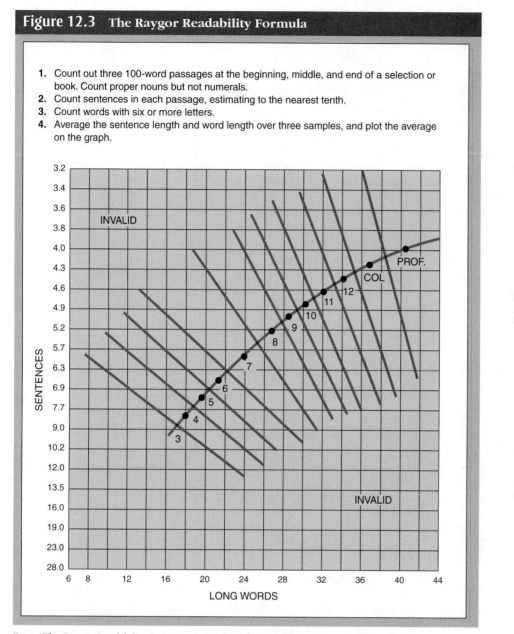

From "The Raygor Readability Estimate: A Quick and Easy Way to Determine Difficulty," by A. L. Raygor, in *Reading: Theory, Research and Practice. Twenty-Sixth Yearbook of the National Reading Conference* (pp. 259–263), edited by P. D. Pearson, 1977. Clemson, SC: National Reading Conference.

Unique Writing Patterns. Narrative texts are comprised of such elements as setting, theme, characterization, and plot. Expository texts, however, are quite different: their structure tends to be much more compact, detailed, and explanatory (Heilman et al., 2001). Five common writing patterns, or **expository text structures,** have been described by Cook and Mayer (1988): generalization, enumeration, sequence, classification, and comparison/contrast. Meyer and Freedle (1984) add a sixth: cause and effect. A description of each of these structures is provided in Figure 12.4 based on the work of Cook and Mayer (1988, p. 449) and Meyer and Freedle (1984).

Figure 12.4   Writing Patterns Found in Expository Texts

Generalization

Description
Passage always has a main idea. Most of the other sentences in the passage try to provide evidence for the main idea by either clarifying or extending. Some sentences explain the main idea by using examples or illustrations; these tend to *clarify* the main idea. Other sentences explain the main idea in more detail; these *extend* the main idea.

Example
Irritability is defined as an organism s capacity to respond to conditions outside itself, or an organism's response to a stimulus from the environment. The stimulus may be light, temperature, water, sound, the presence of a chemical substance, or a threat to life. The organism's response is the way it reacts to stimulus. For example, a plant may have a growth response. This happens when a root pushes toward water or a stem grows unevenly and bends toward light.

Enumeration

Description
Facts listed one after another. There are two general kinds of enumeration passages: specified, which lists facts by numbering them; and unspecified, which lists facts in paragraph form, with each fact stated in one or more sentences.

Example
There are four general properties of solids: (1) *Tenacity* is a measure of a solid's resistance to being pulled apart. (2) *Hardness* is a measure of a substance's ability to scratch another substance. (3) *Malleability* refers to a solid's ability to be hammered or rolled into thin sheets. (4) *Ductility* is the ability to be drawn out in the form of wires.

Sequence

Description
Describes a continuous and connected series of events or the steps in a process. Examples of sequences include changes as the result of growth, a biological process, steps in an experiment, or the evolution of some event.

Example
Hearing occurs in five separate stages. First, sound waves are captured by the external portion of the ear. The outer ear's function is to focus or concentrate these sound waves. During the second stage, the sound waves travel down the auditory canal (a tube embedded in the bones of the skull) and strike the tympanic membrane or eardrum. The third stage occurs when the vibrations of the eardrum begin a series of similar vibrations in several small bones. These vibrations are transmitted to the inner ear, called the *cochlea,* during the fourth stage. At this point, the vibrations are turned into neural impulses that are sent to the brain. The fifth and final stage of the hearing process is the brain's interpretation of the sound patterns.

Classification

Description
Groups or segregates material into classes or categories. Develops a classification system to be used in the future to classify items.

Example
Experimental variables can be grouped into one of two categories manipulated and controlled. A manipulated variable that can be acted on directly. The flow of steam into a room is an example of a manipulated variable, as it can be controlled directly. In contrast, a controlled variable, cannot be acted on directly. The temperature of a room is an example of a controlled variable because it must be achieved through manipulating another variable. In this case, it must be achieved through manipulating the flow of steam.

Comparison/Contrast

Description
Primary objective is to examine the relationship between two or more things. Comparison can analyze both similarities and differences, while contrast focuses only on differences.

Figure 12.4 (Continued)

Example
There are two different hypotheses for the origin of the earth. The nebular hypothesis maintains that our planet began in an aggregation of interstellar gas and dust. This theory is gaining more and more acceptance. In contrast, the comet-produced hypothesis states that the earth began as a piece of the sun that was ripped out by a comet. The first hypothesis assumes the earth began as small elements that combined into larger ones. The latter hypothesis asserts the earth was essentially already formed when it began taking on its present-day characteristics.

Cause/Effect

Description
The relationship between two things when one thing makes something else happen. Elements are usually grouped according to a time sequence, resulting in a cause–effect relationship.

Example
The North Pole has 24 hours of daylight on the first day of the summer because the sun never drops below the horizon on that day.

When preparing to teach units in the content areas, teachers need to establish which expository text structures are used and organize for instruction accordingly (Hall, 2004). According to Montelongo and colleagues (2006):

> Research has shown that reading comprehension and the recall of information are dependent on a student's ability to recognize organizational text structures (Cook & Mayer, 1988). The recognition of an organizational pattern enables the student to form a mental representation of the information and to see the logical relationships advanced by the author. Good readers use textbook structure to abstract main ideas and to help them remember propositions from their readings. (p. 29)

Suggestions for teaching textbook structure to students are included in the Effective Instruction section of this chapter.

Scientifically Based Reading Strategies

Scientifically-based reading research (SBRR) practices selected for your classroom should be those proven effective in rigorous research design trials and widely referenced in the professional literature. Cooter (2006) conducted an extensive review of the research to identify SBRR strategies that have been proven effective that could be applied to content reading instruction. Table 12.1 summarizes his research findings and recommendations for grades 4 through 8. You will note that some of the strategies have not been proven through rigorous research, though Cooter and his colleagues are currently engaged in a five-year study to do just that. The three areas deemed to be most important for improving content reading instruction, according to Cooter, are reading comprehension, vocabulary, and fluency.

In the next two sections of this chapter, we will take a look at instructional strategies consistent with the research findings discussed so far in this chapter.

Table 12.1 Scientifically Based Reading Research (SBRR) Practices Recommended for Grades 4–8

KEY: RC = Reading Comprehension, VL = Vocabulary Learning, RF = Reading Fluency, RF w/O = Reading Fluency with Oral Reading

Key SBRR Evidence	RC	VL	RF	RF w/O	Evidence of Effectiveness (*NRP Findings)
Graphic organizers (Baumann, 1984; Gordon & Rennie, 1987; Alvermann & Boothby, 1986; Armbruster & Anderson, 1991)	•	•			Two studies at grades 6–8 exist; both reported positive findings.
Comprehension monitoring (Capelli & Markman, 1982; Pressley et al., 1989; King 1992)	•	•			100% of the 16 SBRR studies showed positive results over control groups.
Question generation (Cohen, 1983; Rosenshine, Meister, & Chapman, 1996; NICHD, 2000)	•	•			Strong evidence (Rosenshine et al. (1996) meta-analyses effect sizes of .85–.95).
Multiple or "sets" of comprehension strategies embedded within highly interactive, collaborative setting (NICHD, 2000; Pearson & Duke, 2002; Pressley, 2002; Stahl, 2004; Reutzel et al., 2005)	•	•			Strong evidence of elaborated knowledge gains in science texts (Reutzel, et al., 2005), but only tested at 2nd grade level thus far.
Expository text structures (Carnine, Kame'enui, & Woolfson, 1982; Baumann, 1983; Berkowitz, 1986; Gordon & Rennie, 1987)	•	•			Three SBRR studies extant, all grade 6 or below; showing positive effects.
Cooperative learning (Stevens, Slavin, & Famish, 1991; Anderson & Riot, 1993; Bramlett, 1994; Klingner et al., 1998)	•	•	•	•	10 of 10 studies showed significant reading improvement in grade 2–6.
Guided, repeated oral reading (Thomas & Clapp, 1989; Rasinski, 1990; Van Wagernen, et al., 1994; Rasinski et al., 2005)	•	•	•	•	All interventions studied saw clear improvement with average effect size of 0.48, and a high of 1.48.
Modeling fluent reading (Bereiter & Bird, 1983; Baumann, et al., 1992; Opitz & Rasinski, 1998; Armbruster, Lehr, & Osborn, 2001; Rasinski et al., 2005)		•		•	No SBRR research exists at any level.
Repeated, multiple exposures to new vocabulary (Kame'enui, Carnine, & Freschi, 1982; Dole, Sloan, & Trathen, 1995)	•	•	•	•	Strongest evidence of success at PK–1, and effective in 2–6; no studies exist above grade 6
Direct, explicit instruction (Tomeson & Aarnouste, 1998; Rinalid, et al., 1997; Dole, Sloan, & Trather, 1995)	•	•	•	RF	Found to be "highly effective for vocabulary learning" by the NRP, but there is a small body of data.
Indirect instruction of vocabulary words (Kameenui, Carnine, & Freschi, 1982; Dole, Sloan, & Trathen, 1995; NICHD, 2000)	•	•			Significant learning is achieved for high risk students through read-alouds of content (NRP cites Stahl et al., 1991).
Pre-instruction of vocabulary words (Brady, 1990; Brett, Rothlein, & Hurley, 1996; Wixson, 1986)	•	•			Significant effect on retention of social studies vocabulary (e.g., Carney et al., 1984).

How Can Teachers Assess Critical Knowledge and Vocabulary to Be Learned in Order to Plan Effective Instruction?

Analyzing Texts: Performing a Content Analysis

One of the best ways to begin planning for content area instruction is to perform a **content analysis.** The purpose of a content analysis is to identify the important facts, concepts, and generalizations presented in a given unit of study. This is an essential process for establishing instructional objectives and structuring learning activities for students (Martorella, 2000). By carefully analyzing information to be presented and determining which skills are to be learned by students, the teacher arrives at important decisions about what he or she will teach, how he or she will teach it, how he or she will provide guided and independent practice, and how he or she will assess students' knowledge and skills. Effective content analysis, then, can be the springboard for the creation of a cohesive unit of study.

Facts are individual bits of information that are known to be true. In a science unit dealing with our solar system, some of the facts presented might have to do with atmosphere, satellites, and Saturn. In a history unit pertaining to the life and accomplishments of Dr. Martin Luther King, Jr., the teacher might focus on facts related to the March on Washington, sit-ins, the sanitation workers' strike in Memphis, and Civil Rights legislation.

Concepts are categories into which we group all facts or phenomena known through our experiences (Martorella, 2000). In the previous example of a unit about the solar system, *satellites* and *Saturn* could be grouped into the single concept *objects orbiting the sun.* Concepts are usually stated in a simple word, phrase, or sentence expressive of the characteristics shared by facts or phenomena.

A *generalization* is a principle or conclusion that applies to the entire class or sample being examined (Harris & Hodges, 1995). In the classroom, generalization is often teacher-generated, written in the language of students, and usually expressed in complete sentences. Generalizations organize and summarize a large amount of information, sometimes an entire unit. Here are two examples:

> There are many reasons why Harry Truman, perhaps an unlikely president, chose public life.

> Our solar system is made up of many satellites.

Once facts, concepts, and generalizations have been identified by the teacher as the focus of study, he or she organizes them into some form of graphic representation—a traditional outline, a semantic web, a structured overview, or some other graphic organizer. Arranging information in this way allows the teacher to make decisions about instructional content and delivery. One typical query follows.

Teachers sometimes discover that the textbook adopted by their district or school contains information that is not relevant to the major concepts they plan to structure a unit around, or that some material may actually obfuscate students' understanding and skill development. In this event, the teacher needs to determine if the information in question helps build students' background knowledge. If it does,

Accuracy, content, style, organization, illustrations, and format are evaluated as we look for appropriate informational text. Locate *Strategies and Lessons— Language Arts Methods/Viewing* to read "Guidelines for Choosing Literature" on the Teacher Prep Website (*www.prenhall. com/teacherprep*).

the information is useful, even though it may not be directly related to identified learning outcomes. However, if the information serves no real purpose, it should not be included in unit activities or discussion.

Figures 12.5 and 12.6 feature examples of partially finished content analysis graphic representations by two middle school teachers. Notice that they are essentially schema maps.

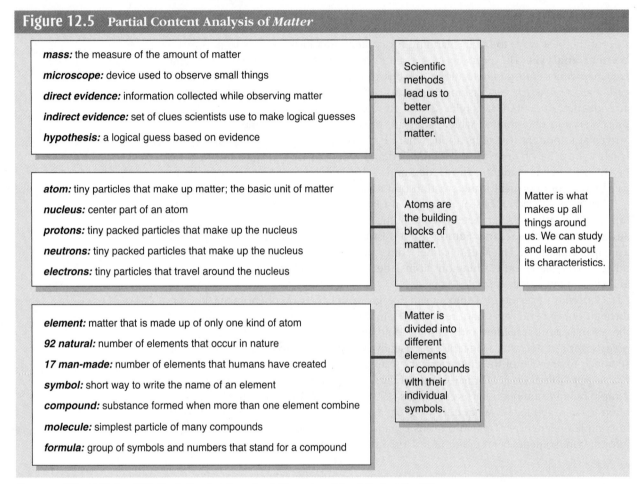

Figure 12.5 **Partial Content Analysis of *Matter***

mass: the measure of the amount of matter

microscope: device used to observe small things

direct evidence: information collected while observing matter

indirect evidence: set of clues scientists use to make logical guesses

hypothesis: a logical guess based on evidence

Scientific methods lead us to better understand matter.

atom: tiny particles that make up matter; the basic unit of matter

nucleus: center part of an atom

protons: tiny packed particles that make up the nucleus

neutrons: tiny packed particles that make up the nucleus

electrons: tiny particles that travel around the nucleus

Atoms are the building blocks of matter.

Matter is what makes up all things around us. We can study and learn about its characteristics.

element: matter that is made up of only one kind of atom

92 natural: number of elements that occur in nature

17 man-made: number of elements that humans have created

symbol: short way to write the name of an element

compound: substance formed when more than one element combine

molecule: simplest particle of many compounds

formula: group of symbols and numbers that stand for a compound

Matter is divided into different elements or compounds with their individual symbols.

Courtesy of David Harlan, Fifth Grade Teacher, Sage Creek Elementary School, Springville, UT.

Figure 12.6 Partial Content Analysis of Events Leading to the Civil War

Generalization

Differences between states in the North and South led to the Civil War.

Concept

The northern economy was based on industry; the southern economy was based on agriculture.

Facts

Samuel Slater built many factories in the North.

In these factories, Slater discovered that machines could be used instead of people to make things more quickly and cheaply.

Figure 12.6 (Continued)

> Soon, things made in northern factories were being sold to people living in southern states.
>
> Farmers discovered that cotton could be processed more quickly and easily with the cotton gin than by hand.
>
> Many southern farmers grew cotton and sold it to people living in northern states.
>
> Many immigrants became factory workers; many slaves were forced to work in cotton fields.
>
> *Concept*
>
> Both the North and the South fought for control of the government.
>
> *Facts*
>
> The North wanted laws favoring business and industry; the South wanted laws favoring farming and slavery.
>
> Northerners wanted any new states entering the Union to be free states.
>
> Southerners wanted any new states entering the Union to be slave states.
>
> In 1820, when Missouri asked to become a state, there were 11 free and 11 slave states in the Union.
>
> Northerners wanted Missouri to be a free state; Southerners wanted Missouri to be a slave state.

Courtesy of Laurie McNeal, Fifth Grade Unit, Brigham Young University.

How Do Teachers Assess Students' Reading Skills Using Content Area Materials?

The Comprehensive Reading Inventory

The Comprehensive Reading Inventory **(CRI)** (R. Cooter, Flynt, & K. Cooter, 2007) is an individually administered informal reading inventory (IRI) featuring alternate forms of expository reading passages through grade 12. The CRI also includes a Spanish version. This tool yields information about students' skills in reading comprehension, vocabulary/concept knowledge, word decoding skill, and fluency. Reliability and validity data on the CRI are included, which is not typically the case with commercial IRIs. The authors recommend that the CRI be reserved for assessing individuals who are thought to be struggling readers, but it could be group administered to assess silent reading ability with content texts. For more information about the CRI, go to www.prenhall.com/catalog/academic/product/0,1144,0131135600,00.html

Oral Retellings of Expository Texts

McGee (1982) found good readers in the elementary grades are aware of expository text structures. One of the most effective ways to find out if a child understands expository text is to use oral retellings (Duke & Bennett-Armistead, 2003; Moss, 2004). An oral retelling is a verbal recounting of a text that has been read either silently or orally. Asking children to retell an expository text involves describing the contents of the text including the main or super-ordinate ideas, the minor or subordinate details, and the underlying organization of the ideas in the text compare/contrast, cause-effect, description, *enumeration*, etc. Oral expository text retellings assess content comprehension and text structure knowledge in holistic, sequenced, and organized ways. In Chapter 7 we provide details on how teachers may use Oral Retellings with expository texts.

How Do Teachers Prepare to Teach Informational Texts?

Constructing Learning Tools for Students

Interesting and informative content area units do not come together by accident; they require deliberate planning and certain key ingredients, which can be drawn from the content analysis you have constructed. Instructional materials you can develop directly from your content analysis include graphic organizers, vocabulary and concept learning activities, *study guides,* and *expository text response activities.* You should also consider supplementing the textbook with relevant nonfiction trade books.

Using Trade Books as Supplements to Textbooks

Trade books (library books) can breathe life into content investigations while also providing needed background information for comprehension and schema building (Wepner & Feeley, 1993). They also help the teacher adjust instruction for students on a variety of reading levels. The key to success in weaving good literature into the content curriculum is remembering that books can be read for enjoyment or to learn new information (Cox & Zarillo, 1993). Both purposes are important in content learning.

A good beginning is for the teacher to read a relevant trade book daily to students for about 15 to 20 minutes (Brozo & Simpson, 1995). For example, if a study of Japan is underway and the teacher decides that some knowledge of Japanese feudal times is important, she might choose to read aloud *The Coming of the Bear* by Lensey Namioka (1992). In a science class focusing on robotics and mechanization, the teacher could select such traditional favorites as *Jed's Junior Space Patrol* (Marzollo & Marzollo, 1982), *The White Mountain* (Christopher, 1967), or Simon Watson's (1976) *No Man's Land.* Reading aloud great books such as these sparks interest in the subject matter and makes complex ideas more accessible to students. It is equally important that students be encouraged to independently read trade books pertaining to the subject under study.

There are a number of resources available in print and online to help you locate appropriate trade books for content classes. Here are just a few that we have found helpful.

- *The Reading Teacher.* International Reading Association (IRA). This professional journal for literacy educators has a very large readership and focuses mainly on instruction in early and elementary levels. *RT* publishes lists of popular books each year called "Children's Choices" (October) and "Teachers' Choices" (November). Summaries presented in these and other issues are helpful in planning instruction. The IRA Web site is at *http://www.reading.org.*

- *Journal of Adolescent and Adult Literacy.* International Reading Association (IRA). This is IRA's periodical for middle school and secondary teachers. It features a "Books for Adolescents" column and reviews of classroom materials. Substantial summaries presented in some issues are most helpful in planning units.

- *NAACP Image Awards.* Each year, the NAACP Image Awards honors authors of children's fiction and nonfiction books portraying African Americans in honest, historically accurate, and respectful ways. You can find winners by year online at *http://www.naacpimageawards.net.*

- *The Texas Bluebonnet Award (TBA).* One of our favorites, the TBA was established in 1979 to encourage children to read more books, to explore a variety of current books, to develop powers of discrimination, and to identify their favorite books. The award process provides librarians, teachers, parents, and writers with insight into young students' reading preferences. The TBA Web site is at *http://www.txla.org/groups/tba/index.html.*

- *The Newbery and Caldecott Awards: A Guide to Medal and Honor Books.* American Library Association. This publication provides helpful information regarding some of the most celebrated trade books available.

Using Graphic Organizers or GO! Charts

It has been demonstrated through research that student-generated drawings can improve learning from expository text (Van Meter, Aleksic, & Schwartz, 2006). Perhaps the most widely advocated method for encouraging student-generated drawings is **graphic organizers.** Sometimes referred to as "GO! charts," graphic organizers are maps, graphs, diagrams, or other visuals that summarize information to be learned and identify the relationships between ideas (Alvermann & Phelps, 2001; Barron, 1969). They provide a means for focusing on new vocabulary and its relationship to larger concepts and generalizations (Tierney, Readence, & Dishner, 1990; Wang & Dwyer, 2006). Graphic organizers are often used as a means of introducing a unit of study, are referred to regularly during the course of the unit, and may be used as a review instrument near the end of the unit.

Constructing a Graphic Organizer. Constructing a graphic organizer is a simple matter once a content analysis has been completed. Simplify or condense the facts, concepts, and generalizations in the unit by reducing each to a single word or

Video Classroom

Look into Mapping in Content Area Reading

"Mapping" is demonstrated as introductory instructional strategy on our Teacher Prep Website *(www.prenhall. com/teacherprep).* Select the link to *Video Classroom—Content Area Reading Methods/Comprehension Strategies* for viewing.

As you view the clip, note how the teacher utilizes small group discussion before the whole class shares ideas.

- Why did the teacher incorporate time for small group conversation into the lesson?
- What procedures need to be in place to make concept mapping effective?
- How does concept mapping foster student understanding of text?

phrase, then arrange them graphically in the same hierarchical pattern as the content analysis. If a thorough content analysis is not possible, the following steps can be used to develop a graphic organizer (adapted from Barron, 1969).

1. Identify all facts and vocabulary that are essential to understanding the unit under study, thus forming the bottom layer of information, or subordinate concepts (Thelen, 1984). For the sake of consistency with the content analysis idea discussed earlier in this chapter, we refer to these subordinate concepts as *facts*.
2. Group related facts into clusters. These clusters form a second layer of understanding in the unit we refer to as *concepts*.
3. Group concepts that relate to each other under the major heading for the unit we refer to as a *generalization*. Most often, the unit will have only a single generalization, but occasionally, two or more generalizations may be needed, especially for large or complex units.

Video Classroom

Watch How a Teacher Uses KWL Charts to Help Students Organize Literacy Learning in Content Areas

KWL Charts can be powerful graphic organizers in content areas. In "Building Background Knowledge," found on the Teacher Prep Website *(www.prenhall.com/teacherprep)*, you can view a teacher using this chart as a link between a magazine article and a story in reading. Select *Video Classroom—Content Area Reading Methods/Reading and Writing in Social Studies* to learn more.

- As you view the video, note what the teacher in the interview has to say about carefully picking out texts that provide the best examples.
- Note how conversation allows the students and teacher to bring up examples and then transfer what they know to other texts. Would you consider this a strong strategy for the teacher to employ? Why or why not?

Video Classroom

Watch How Think Alouds Are Valuable in Content Area Classrooms

The "Think Aloud Strategy" video provides a viewer with a model for incorporation in a future classroom. Visit the Teacher Prep Website *(www.prenhall.com/teacherprep)* and go to *Video Classroom—Content Area Reading Methods—Comprehension Strategies* to access this video.

- As you view the video, think about why the teacher relates the text he is reading to his own life?
- Why does the teacher pause so often to share?
- What strategy is the teacher using to ensure his students understand the text?

Video Classroom

Watch the Way a Teacher Uses a Think Aloud to Model Inferencing

Inferencing can be modeled through the think aloud strategy as you view "Reading for Information" on the Teacher Prep Website *(www.prenhall.com/teacherprep).* Select *Video Classroom— Content Area Reading Methods—Reading and Writing in Social Studies* to see how the teacher uses a graphic organizer with the core literature selection.

- Note the need to preview, predict, and set a purpose as the teacher instructs.
- Why is predicting what might come next in the text important?
- What does inferencing mean and why does it matter?
- How does this teacher encourage critical thinking?

Limit the Number of Graphic Organizers Used Each Year. Try to stick to using only two or three graphic organizers each year, but refer to them often. Many teachers throw too many formats at students, and thus students become experts at none. When using graphic organizers, teachers should be careful to select the appropriate GO! Chart format to re-represent the organizational or text structure of the content text to be read.

Several popular formats for graphic organizers to depict the hierarchical nature of the information in a text on the structure of American government are shown in Figures 12.7 through 12.10. There are many Web sites where teachers can find graphic organizers and related activities. Here are just a few we have used. (You can find dozens more through a Google search at *www.google.com*).

www.edhelper.com

www.eduplace.com/kids/hme/k_5/graphorg/

www.sdcoe.k12.ca.us/SCORE/actbank/torganiz.htm

Study Guides

Study guides (Manzo, Manzo, & Estes, 2000; Vacca & Vacca, 2001) are materials intended to help students move successfully through a unit of study. They can be used before, during, and/or after reading unit materials. Frequently, study guides consist of a series of key questions or problems for students to work through,

Figure 12.7   Traditional Outline

Structure of American Government

1. Constitution provides for three branches
   A. Executive Branch
      1. President
   B. Legislative Branch
      1. House of Representatives
      2. Senate
   C. Judicial Branch
      1. Supreme Court

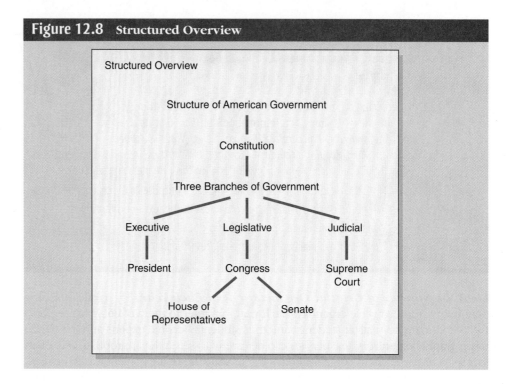

Figure 12.8   Structured Overview

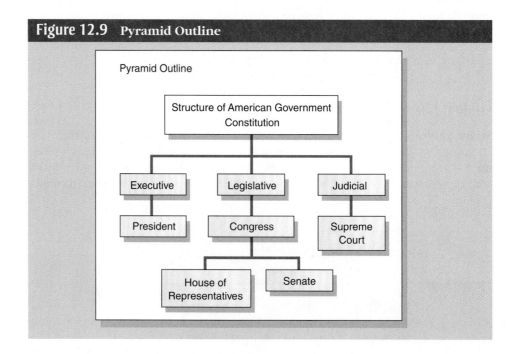

Figure 12.9   Pyramid Outline

Figure 12.10   Semantic Web

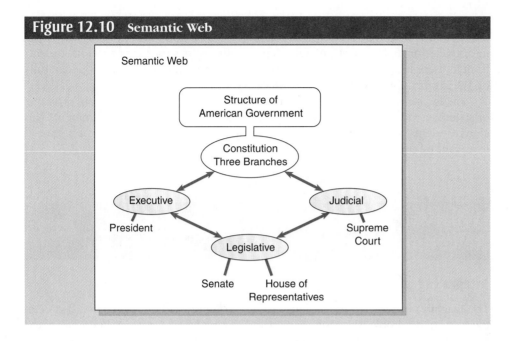

followed by page references to text materials used in the unit. Students use the references to seek answers to questions or other items and become familiar with the content. Some study guides accompany published materials; others are teacher-generated.

Three-Level Guide. A **three-level guide** (Herber, 1978) is a classic study guide in that it leads students from basic levels of comprehension to more advanced levels (Manzo, Manzo, & Estes, 2000). The first level (literal comprehension) helps students understand what the author said, the second level (interpretative comprehension) helps students understand what the author means, and the third level (applied comprehension) helps students understand how text information can be applied (Manzo, Manzo, & Estes, 2000). In constructing a three-level guide, we suggest the following guidelines adapted from Vacca and Vacca (2001).

1. Begin by constructing the study guide at the interpretative comprehension level by determining what the author means. Write inferences that make sense and that align with instructional objectives. Revise your statements so that they are simple and clear.
2. Search the text for explicit pieces of information (details, facts, and propositions) that are accessible at the literal level of the text and that support inferences chosen for the second part of the guide. Put these into statement, question, or problem form.
3. Develop statements, questions, or problems for the applied comprehension level of the guide. These should represent additional insights or principles that may be drawn when analyzing parts 1 and 2. Part 3 of the reading guide should help students connect what they already know with what they have learned from their study during the unit.

Be flexible when using a three-level guide. The format should be varied from unit to unit to help hold students' attention. It is also a good idea to occasionally put in distracter or "foil" items (i. e., false items); distracters sometimes prevent students from indiscriminately focusing on every item and cause them to focus more carefully on the information search (Vacca & Vacca, 1989).

Finally, include page numbers in parentheses following each question, problem, or statement indicating where answers can be found in the reading assignment. This alerts students to key ideas found on each page and enables them to screen out irrelevant information.

What Are Some Effective Ways to Organize for Instruction?

Integrating the Curriculum

The teaching of reading and writing using a comprehensive perspective has been the focus of this book. Although reading and writing have sometimes been presented as separate entities for the sake of clarity, effective reading teachers typically do not apply these literacy skills separately. Rather, they are integrated across the curriculum so that boundaries between reading and writing virtually cease to exist. In full curriculum integration, reading and writing become integral parts of subject area investigations and vice versa by way of interdisciplinary **themed studies.** A theme such as "Changes" or "Exploration" can become an exciting classroom experience involving social studies, the sciences, mathematics, literature, art, music, and other important areas of the curriculum.

The advantages of curriculum integration are numerous. Reading and writing skills are acquired and refined within a rich context of real world significance, which in turn inspires students to want to know more. Skills are no longer taught in isolation as rote drill but are learned as tools for communicating ideas. Integration of the curriculum results in a blend of instruction in literacy communication skills and content as well as the planting of seeds for future searches for new knowledge.

Guidelines for Conducting Themed Studies

Themed studies involve total curriculum integration. A brief summary of the essential components of themed studies—as identified from the work of Paradis (1984) and Gamberg et al. (1988)—follows.

• *Selecting a theme.*   Themes that meet the criteria previously described should be chosen.

• *Identifying resources.*   The teacher should identify and collect resources before beginning the unit. Examples of materials include nonfiction books, other pertinent print media (e. g., documents, travel brochures, and government publications); hands-on materials that pertain to the topic, nonprint media (videotapes, films, radio recordings), relevant basal stories; or literacy selections, and computer-related resources. Resources also include community members and the opportunities afforded by field trips.

- *Brainstorming.* Themed studies involve brainstorming on the part of both teacher and students. Teachers brainstorm as part of the planning process to anticipate ways that curriculums can be integrated into the unit and to assist in the selection of materials. Paradis (1984) offers a brainstorming web (Figure 12.11) to assist teachers in this process. Students are also encouraged to brainstorm as a way of becoming involved initially with the topic. Brainstorming helps students focus their thinking, articulate their interests and background knowledge, and develop an appreciation for the ideas of their peers. It also encourages collaboration—a highly prized skill in both school and the workplace.

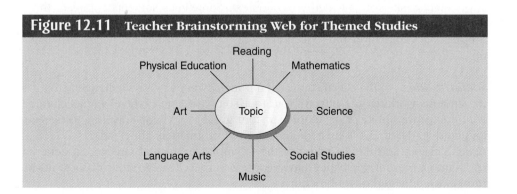

Getting to Know English Learners

Tapping into English learners' background knowledge, using a KWL for example, can greatly aid them (and you as the teacher) in preparing them for more difficult content area reading.

- *Demonstrating learning.* Students complete projects and tasks that demonstrate their newly acquired knowledge. Projects like those cited for themed literature units generally apply here. In addition, students may complete other products such as displays, speeches, demonstration fairs, and guided tours.

Teachers building themed studies search for ways to incorporate reading and other basic literacy skills into content subjects because they know that these processes help students deepen their knowledge of the wider world. The dynamic created in these cross-curricular units is quite powerful and spawns many positive outcomes in the classroom, including heightened interest in the subject matter and a sense of empowerment (Cox & Zarillo, 1993; Wepner & Feeley, 1993).

After many years of helping school districts around the United States build thematic units, we have discovered several practices that speed the process of curricular integration. The most efficient way to begin is by first constructing a themed literature unit using the process described in this chapter; this achieves full integration of the language arts within the context of great literature. Themed literature units also contain all the essential elements of a comprehensive reading program, such as daily reading and writing, the teaching of nonnegotiable skills, literature response, cooperative groups, opportunities to practice fluency, and student self-evaluation. Once teachers build themed literature units as the curriculum core it becomes a relatively simple matter to infuse the content areas. Finally, we have learned that once teachers go through the process of building thematic units we will describe, they better understand all the essential elements and can re-create the process in the future in their own way—keeping some elements and deleting others—to create a balanced learning system that meets the needs of their students.

Figure 12.11   **Teacher Brainstorming Web for Themed Studies**

Reading

Physical Education   Mathematics

Art —— Topic —— Science

Language Arts   Social Studies

Music

Planning thematic units involves five major phases that can be applied equally well in grades 5 through 8. These phases are theme selection, setting goals and objectives, webbing, choosing major activities and materials, and unit scaffolding.

Theme Selection. In many ways, the success of thematic units depends on the concept chosen to be the theme. It must be broad enough to accomplish linkage between the various content subjects, address local and state requirements listed in curriculum guides (Pappas, Kiefer, & Levstik, 1990), include quality nonfiction and fiction, and still be interesting to youngsters. Topics like "Our State's History" or "Nutrition" can be far too confining for the kinds of engaging learning experiences we hope to craft. There are a large number of possible topics, which might give teachers a good starting point; these include "Legends," "Survival," "Heroes," "Changes," "Seasons," and "Journeys." If the theme selected is broad enough, teachers will discover creative and enticing ways to weave various content subjects into the unit. To demonstrate more clearly ways thematic units can be constructed, we build on the themed literature unit called "Journeys."

Setting Goals and Objectives. Once the theme has been selected, teachers should consult the district curriculum guide and other available resources to determine possible goals and objectives. Some teachers prefer to do this step first because themes occasionally grow logically out of the required curriculum. Whether done as a first or second step, establishing goals and objectives must come early so that appropriate learning activities and materials can be chosen.

Webbing. The next step in planning thematic units is **webbing,** which is essentially the process of creating a schematic or schema map of the linkage between each aspect of the unit. By creating a web of the major aspects of the proposed unit, the teacher can gain a global view—the big picture. Webs can also be revised and adapted later to use as an advance organizer for students at the beginning of the thematic unit. In Figure 12.12, we see an initial (not fully developed) thematic unit web for the "Journeys" theme. The theme now spans three additional content areas: social studies, science, and mathematics. Major activities have also been suggested, which is the next topic we explore.

Choosing Major Activities and Materials. One of the joys of thematic units is that they infuse the curriculum with great ideas, activities, and materials that energize learners. What a great alternative this is for teachers ready for modest yet powerful change! Activities chosen for thematic units provide students with opportunities to apply literacy skills in a wider-world context. Sometimes students complete these activities independently, other times as part of a problem-solving team. Occasions for personal exploration and reflection are also seen as valuable aspects of thematic unit activities.

Social Studies. In the social studies component, the problem/challenge activity is for students working in groups of four to assume the role of travel agents charged with the responsibility of developing a "tour guide" for clients traveling to Greece. Required parts of the tourist guide involve information about ancient Greece, Greek cuisine, and the founding of the Olympics in ancient Greece. Students in each group present what they have learned to the class, or other classes, in the form of an enlarged travel brochure.

Reading "Guidelines for Interdisciplinary Planning" on the Teacher Prep Website (*www.prenhall.com/ teacherprep*) offers tips to as you develop thematic units. Select *General Methods—Unit and Lesson Planning* and find out more to help students discover relationships between disciplines.

Visit the Teacher Prep Website (*www.prenhall. com/teacherprep*) to read "Thematic Unit on Friendship for Middle School Students." Webbing is discussed and objectives, materials and activities are shared. Go to *Content Area Reading Methods—Vocabulary Strategies* to link to this article.

Figure 12.12 Initial Thematic Unit Web: Journeys

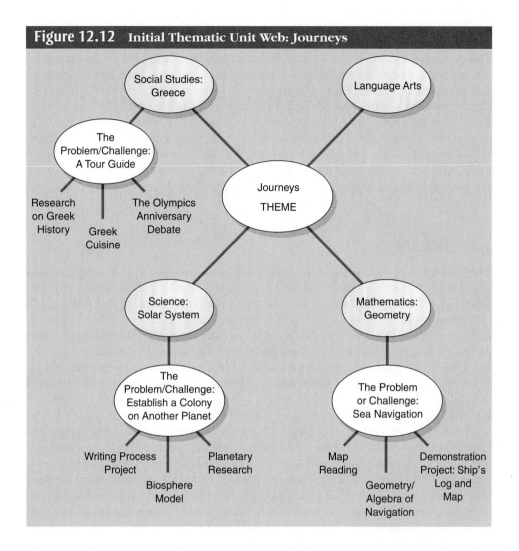

Science. The problem/challenge activity for science has student groups assume the role of astronauts aboard a space shuttle. Their mission is to travel to a planet of their choosing and establish a colony. This activity involves scientific research into such things as what humans need to sustain life, surface conditions on the selected planet, useful natural resources on the planet (if any), and information about the building of life-supporting human environments (biospheres). To present their findings, students in each group will draft a report in the form of a book using the writing process, and construct a model of the biosphere they propose to build on the planet surface.

Mathematics. The problem/challenge activity for mathematics is for students to assume the role of sea voyagers who must navigate their ship to Greece from the United States. This project can be completed by students independently or with a partner. Skills involved include basics in map reading, geometry as related to navigation, translation of miles per hour to knots, and journal writing. The product is a ship's log, which details daily destinations, map coordinates, travel times, and (if desired) some brief information about what students see at each port.

Thematic Unit Materials

The preceding examples clearly alert us to the fact that many and diverse materials are needed to create an engaging and relevant thematic unit. Both fiction and nonfiction materials are needed to plan rich and interesting activities. The core materials are books, lots of books of every kind. Pappas and colleagues (1990) got it just right when they said, "as with chocolate, you never have enough books!" Essential are reference materials, fiction books that awaken imaginations, and nonfiction books to read aloud. Teachers will also need to locate what are known by historians as "primary source materials"—original sources of information. Later in this chapter, we mention a number of time-saving resources for locating specialty books and other media.

Unit Scaffolding

"From To Be a Slave" describes a 5th Grade unit on the Southern Colonies. Find out more about the jigsaw model of cooperative learning through this lesson example on the Teacher Prep Website (*www.prenhall.com/teacherprep*). Click on *Strategies and Lessons—Teaching Methods/ Comprehension* to learn about to relating to diverse needs in the classroom.

The final stage of planning is unit scaffolding. At this point, the teacher determines just how long the unit should run and makes final decisions about which activities to include. Typically, thematic units last one to two weeks in grades 4 through 6 (Wiseman, 1992) and up to four or five weeks in the middle school. The teacher should resist the temptation to run units for months at a time; this usually becomes too much of a good thing and turns high student interest into boredom.

One of the decisions teachers must make is whether the unit is to be fully integrated and presented as a seamless curriculum. Some teachers in grades 4 through 6 in nondepartmentalized situations may operate a unit for a few days or a week. For example, in a "Journeys" unit, the teacher may focus almost exclusively on the social studies problem/challenge. When the social studies portion is concluded, the class may move on to the science problem/challenge, focusing on that aspect for entire days at a time. The mathematics problem/challenge may come next. The value of seamless integration is that students use critical thinking and problem-solving skills in much the same way as adults in the working world. They also use literacy skills throughout the day. A third advantage is that students move from one problem/challenge to another every few days, thus maintaining a higher level of interest. Unfortunately, seamless integration cannot be achieved very easily in departmentalized middle schools—self-contained classrooms are generally necessary.

Maintain a high level of interest with a "Cereal Box Unit." Visit *Language Arts Methods— Writing* to find out details on the Teacher Prep Website (*www.prenhall.com/ teacherprep*).

Another option for organizing thematic units that can be used in departmentalized situations is **segmented integration.** In segmented integration, each content area portion is developed concurrently by the core subject area teacher. A sample daily schedule depicting how this integration might occur in a departmentalized middle school setting is shown in Figure 12.13. Segmented integration permits teachers in fully departmentalized schools to develop thematic units collaboratively as faculty teams. Sometimes all teachers in a departmentalized team will choose to take part in the thematic unit; on other occasions, one or two teachers may work independently on a unit to satisfy district or state mandates.

We have found that planning daily activities is greatly facilitated by webbing each content component separately. Teachers should include in the web such information as key reference books, computer software, important questions to be answered, special activities, and demonstrations they may wish to perform. In Figure 12.14, we share a web used in the science portion of the "Journeys" theme.

Figure 12.13   Segmented Integration for Journeys Theme

8:30–9:30	**Language Arts:** Themed Literature Unit on Journeys
9:30–10:45	**Social Studies:** Greece/Tour Guide
10:55–11:30	Computer Lab
11:30–12:30	**Science:** Solar System/Biosphere Model
12:30–1:00	Lunch
1:00–2:15	**Specials:** Library, P.E.
2:30–3:25	**Mathematics:** Sea Navigation

Figure 12.14   Science Web for Journeys Theme

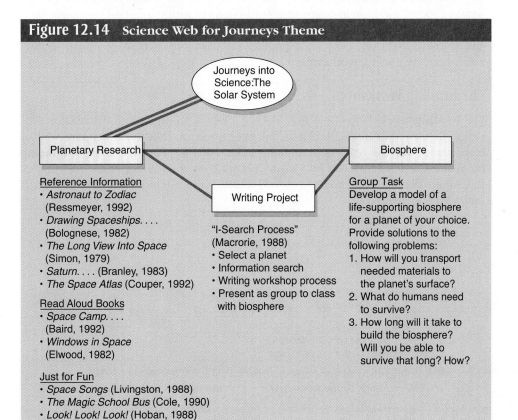

Journeys into Science:The Solar System

Planetary Research

Biosphere

Writing Project

Reference Information
• *Astronaut to Zodiac* (Ressmeyer, 1992)
• *Drawing Spaceships. . . .* (Bolognese, 1982)
• *The Long View Into Space* (Simon, 1979)
• *Saturn. . . .* (Branley, 1983)
• *The Space Atlas* (Couper, 1992)

Read Aloud Books
• *Space Camp. . . .* (Baird, 1992)
• *Windows in Space* (Elwood, 1982)

Just for Fun
• *Space Songs* (Livingston, 1988)
• *The Magic School Bus* (Cole, 1990)
• *Look! Look! Look!* (Hoban, 1988)

"I-Search Process" (Macrorie, 1988)
• Select a planet
• Information search
• Writing workshop process
• Present as group to class with biosphere

Group Task
Develop a model of a life-supporting biosphere for a planet of your choice. Provide solutions to the following problems:
1. How will you transport needed materials to the planet's surface?
2. What do humans need to survive?
3. How long will it take to build the biosphere? Will you be able to survive that long? How?

How Is Instruction in Reading and Writing Organized?

Developing Integrated Curriculums

In Chapter 11, we saw how emerging reading and writing skills are facilitated by literacy-learning events in the classroom. As children move into upper elementary and middle school, their teachers seek ways of facilitating and advancing their literacy development to inspire lifelong reading and writing activities. Because of the complementary benefits of reading and writing instruction (Shanahan, 1984; Squire, 1983), teachers frequently seek ways of involving the two simultaneously. An integrated curriculum is a powerful vehicle for merging reading and writing instruction, problem-solving skills, cooperative learning, and other desirable curricular elements in authentic learning situations. In Chapter 8 we took a detailed look at the basics of the writing process and how to organize instruction. Its inclusion is critical in content leaving in grades 4 through 8. Later in this section we expand our vision to encompass content learning. Next, we look at a popular organizational scheme for orchestrating instruction: the reading workshop.

The Reading Workshop

The **reading workshop** (Reutzel & Cooter, 1991) is an organizational scheme providing explicit skill instruction and full integration of children's literature and/or basal stories into the reading program. It is intended to provide flexible scaffolding for reading instruction. The five main components are sharing time, mini-lesson, state of the class, reading workshop, and sharing time. Each of these components is outlined in Figure 12.15.

Figure 12.15 The Reading Workshop

Reading Workshop (70 minutes)		
Sharing Time (Teacher) (5–10 min) **Mini-Lesson** (10–15 min) **State of the Class** (5 min)		
Self-Selected Reading (SSR), Small Group Work (SGW),& Independent Reading Conferences (35–45 minutes)		
SSR	**Small Group Work (SGW)**	**Individual Reading Conferences (IRC)**
1. Read a self-selected book (alone or with a "buddy") 2. Respond to text readings (10–30 min)	1. Guided oral reading 2. Buddy reading for fluency 3. Learning center activities 4. Group reading response activities (20–30 min)	Conduct 2–3 per day involving oral reading, comprehension checks, running records, reading nonfiction texts, vocabulary quiz, etc. (10–15 min)
Sharing Time (Students) (5–10 minutes)		

From "Organizing for Effective Instruction: The Reading Workshop" by D. R. Reutzel and R. B. Cooter, Jr., 1991, *The Reading Teacher,* *44* (8), pp. 548–555. Copyright 1991 by International Reading Association. Reprinted by permission.

Phase 1: Teacher sharing time (5 to 10 minutes). During sharing time, teachers read aloud myriad selections to spark interest in literature forms (e.g., nonfiction, biographies, folktales, short stories, poetry). The sharing time activity can serve as a catalyst for writing workshop projects (explained in Chapter 8) or as an introduction for the reading workshop mini-lesson.

Phase 2: Mini-Lesson (10 to 15 minutes). As teachers instruct students in reading content materials, they often note that a number of students are experiencing difficulties with a similar concept, skill, or procedure. When the teacher notes such shared difficulties, she may decide to form a temporary group to provide additional instruction related to a skill, strategy, concept, or procedure. This type of temporary grouping strategy is called **needs grouping.**

Mini-lessons are typically whole-class or small-group lessons that last approximately 10 to 15 minutes. Mini-lessons are used to teach reading and writing skills, literary response, or a necessary procedure (Hagerty, 1992; Strickland, 1998). Mini-lessons help teachers get to the point with their skill instruction and end the lesson before student attention fades. For example, a teacher wishes to teach a word identification or comprehension strategy, such as inferring character traits, a mini-lesson can be offered once each day until students learn the strategy.

Types of Mini-Lessons. Hagerty (1992) describes three types of mini-lessons: procedural, literary, and strategy/skill. A listing of possible mini-lesson topics is found in Table 12.2. A procedural mini-lesson might involve teaching students how to handle new classroom library acquisitions or how to repair worn books. The teacher might demonstrate how to break in a new book's binding by standing the book on its spine, opening a few pages on either side of the center of the book, and carefully pressing them down. Cellophane tape and staplers can be used to demonstrate how to repair tears in a book's pages or covers.

A literary mini-lesson for readers might result in a student presenting the teacher with a small booklet written at home in the shape of an ax blade that retells favorite parts from the book *Hatchet* (Paulsen, 1987). For a literary mini-lesson at the upper elementary level, a student may assemble a poster resembling the front page of a newspaper to show major events from a just-read novel, such as Betsy Byars's (1970) *The Summer of the Swans.*

A skills mini-lesson might cover a method of development used by nonfiction writers to make abstract information more easily understood (e.g., cause–effect, description, problem–solution, and comparisons). This mini-lesson could involve (a) identifying and describing the pattern used in a nonfiction text, (b) searching for other examples of that method of development in science, mathematics, and social studies materials, and then (c) having students write a paragraph in which they use the method of development in dealing with a topic of their choices.

Teaching Skills Using Mini-Lessons. Mini-lessons begin with engaging texts and work down to the essential strategy or skill to be developed. This process allows students to see the new strategy related to real reading tasks. There are three steps or phases to presenting a comprehensive mini-lesson:

- Skill introduct ion
- Guided practice
- Student performance

Following is a sample mini-lesson and accompanying explanation describing the three components of mini-lessons.

Table 12.2 Possible Mini-Lesson Topics

Procedural Mini-Lessons	Literary Mini-Lessons	Strategy/Skills Mini-Lessons
Where to sit during reading time	Differences between fiction and nonfiction books	How to choose a book
Giving a book talk		Selecting literature log topics
How to be a good listener in a sharing session	Learning from dedications	Connecting reading material to your own life
Appropriate noise level during reading time	Books that show emotion	Tips for reading aloud
	Books written in the first, second, or third person	Figuring out unknown words
What to do when you finish a book	Author studies	Using context
What kinds of questions to ask during a sharing session	How authors use quotations	Substituting
Running a small-group discussion	How the story setting fits the story	Using picture clues
Self-evaluation	Characteristics of different genres	Using the sounds of blends, vowels, contractions, etc.
Getting ready for a conference	Development of characters, plot, theme, mood	
How to have a peer conference	How leads hook us	Using Post-its to mark interesting parts
Where to sit during mini-lessons	How authors use the problem/event/solution pattern	Monitoring comprehension (does this make sense and sound right?)
Taking care of books	Differences between a picture book and a novel	Asking questions while reading
	Titles and their meanings	Making predictions
Keeping track of books read	Characters' points of view	Emergent strategies
Rules of the workshop	Examples of similes and metaphors	Concept of story
		Concept that print carries meaning
	Examples of foreshadowing	Making sense
	How authors use dialogue	Mapping a story
	Predictable and surprise endings	How to retell a story orally
	Use of descriptive words and phrases	Looking for relationships
	How illustrations enhance the story	Looking for important ideas
	Secrets in books	Making inferences
		Drawing conclusions
		Summarizing a story
		Distinguishing fact from opinion
		Emergent reader skills: directionality, concept of word, sound/symbol relationships

From *Readers' Workshop: Real Reading* (pp. 113–115), by P. Hagerty, 1992, Ontario, Canada: Scholastic Canada, Ltd. Copyright 1992 by Patricia Hagerty. Reprinted by permission.

MINI-LESSON SCHEDULE (WHOLE-TO-PARTS-TO-WHOLE)

Skill from the curriculum (6th grade level):* (6.3.2) Analyze the effect of the qualities of the character (e.g., courage or cowardice, ambition or laziness) on the plot and the resolution of the conflict.

Subskill to learn: Inferring character traits from accounts in the story.

Materials needed: Multiple copies of *Harry Potter and the Sorcerer's Stone* (Rowling, 1997).

*Adapted from the California Department of Education English-Language Arts Content Standards.

Step 1: Skill Introduction (within the context of a reading passage)

1. *Begin with a reading selection.* After having students read *Harry Potter and the Sorcerer's Stone,* discuss key points of the story with the group and list their favorite parts on chart paper (post in sequence using tape for each sheet of paper with individual points on each). This step provides a "whole text" context from which the new skill can be introduced.

2. *Teacher modeling.* The point of teacher modeling is to show students what the new skill to be learned "looks like" when a competent reader (the teacher) uses it. First, the teacher introduces the skill or "part" of reading to be learned. (In this case, we will emphasize a subskill of #6.3.2—"Inferring character traits from accounts in the story.") Modeling of the skill is essentially a "think aloud" activity in which the teacher talks through the thinking process used to apply the skill. In this instance, she may begin by explaining: "Sometimes we are able to learn a lot about a character by noting how he reacts to difficult situations in the story. I sometimes list things I remember the character did in the story to help me decide what kind of person he or she is." The teacher might then direct the class to reread key passages with a specific character in mind and list key events on chart paper. If Harry Potter were chosen by the teacher for modeling this thinking strategy, the resulting notes made on chart paper with the group may look something like the following.

CHARACTER: HARRY POTTER

Examples of Things That Happened:

Harry was patient and kind even though he was mistreated by the Dursleys (Chapter 1). Harry wanted to stay in the same house with his new friends at Hogwarts (Chapter 7).

Harry used the invisibility cloak to go into dangerous places (Chapter 12).

Character Traits We Can INFER:

Harry is kind, patient with others, loyal to friends, and brave.

Finally, the teacher discusses (thinks aloud) how all of the pieces of information, when taken together, paint a vivid picture of the character, so much so that it is not difficult to list his character traits. This process of (a) explaining the skill to be used, (b) thinking aloud while drawing relevant information clues from the text, and (c) demonstrating how the skill can be used in real reading situations are the key elements of the Skill Introduction phase of mini-lessons.

Step 2: Guided Practice

In the guided practice phase of mini-lessons, students develop a growing understanding of the new strategy to be learned; it begins to crystallize. To make this strategy their own they must practice it themselves repeatedly, but with assistance available when needed. Here's how.

1. First, choose an identical situation from the same text selection used during the Skill Introduction phase (with a different part of the story or character). In this example, the teacher might begin shifting responsibility for using the skill to the learners by selecting another character from *Harry Potter and the Sorcerer's Stone*

for a character trait analysis. Students could be asked to complete their analysis by first listing key events, then inferring character traits based on those events or facts. The students' predictions, as with those modeled by the teacher earlier, should be based on what is known about the character from earlier accounts in the book. In other words, during guided practice students try using the skill with support from the teacher or in collaboration with other more advanced readers. Again, notice that students typically use the same reading selection as that used by the teacher during the introduction phase. The difference is that a different character from another episode is used. For example, during guided practice you might spend some time outlining some of the character traits learned from *Harry Potter and the Sorcerer's Stone* about other characters and list them on chart paper, perhaps Draco Malfoy (Harry's not-so-nice rival), Ron (his red-headed friend), and Hermione (Harry's intelligent female friend). For Malfoy, a student may write the following.

CHARACTER: DRACO MALFOY

Examples of Things That Happened:

Malfoy's family were part of the evil group led by Voldemort (Chapter 6).

Malfoy was part of the rival house, Slytherin, at Hogarts (Chapter 7).

Malfoy and his friends made fun of Harry during potions class (Chapter 8).

Malfoy picked on weaker students at the lunch table, and took away Longbottom's gift from home saying, "It's that stupid thing Longbottom's gran sent him" (Chapter 9).

Character Traits We Can INFER:

Malfoy is selfish, mean, and possibly evil.

Support students as they work through numerous examples to gain skill and confidence. This is essential during guided practice. Sometimes students are assumed to have competence prematurely. If in doubt, over-practice the new skill until students are marinated in the new experience, and be there to lend assistance as needed. Be sure students can demonstrate their ability verbally, graphically, or in writing.

When you feel reasonably certain the new skill is "owned" by the student, move on to the last phase of the mini-lesson.

Step 3: Student Performance

The final mini-lesson stage involves students demonstrating their newly acquired skill in another text or reading situation. Unlike the guided practice phase where students have help available when they try out the new skill, in student performance students use the new skill independently. The length of the passage is not very important. Your goal is to make sure that the new skill has been learned permanently and that students can apply it in other reading situations. To demonstrate their competence using the skill of inferring character traits from events presented in the reading selection, you might use such fiction texts such as *The Lion, the Witch, and the Wardrobe* (Lewis, 1961), *Julie of the Wolves* (George, 1972), or nonfiction accounts of such figures as Christa MacAuliffe, Martin Luther King, Jr., Anne Frank, Barbara Jordan, or Winston Churchill.

In Figure 12.16 we share a simple mini-lesson planning guide.

 Five steps are described to teach three mini-lessons in "Strategy: Mini-Lessons" found on the Teacher Prep Website (*www.prenhall.com/ teacherprep*). Select *Strategies and Lessons— Reading Methods/ Comprehension* to locate the article to see an example and gain further ideas.

A student's writing gave the teacher an idea for a mini-unit. The article, "Chinese Writing," can be found on the Teacher Prep Website (*www.prenhall.com/teacherprep*). Click on *Reading Methods— Vocabulary* to locate this article and learn how this unit featured ELL learners in the classroom.

Figure 12.16   Mini-Lesson Planning Guide*

Mini-Lesson Planning Guide

PRE-PLANNING

Objective of the mini-lesson series (based on student need or curriculum requirements)

_____

_____

Materials Needed† for teacher modeling, guided practice, and student performance/assessment

_____

_____

_____

†Reading selections for upper elementary instruction may include narratives (stories), informational texts (expository), and/or bridging books (i.e., part story/part information).

STEP 1: SKILL INTRODUCTION

A. Reading & Discussion to Create a Context for Learning (Specify the task to be used.)

_____

_____

B. Skill Introduction and Teacher Modeling

- **Skill Introduction** (Write out the language you will use to introduce and explain the new skill to be learned using words students can understand.)

_____

- **Teacher Modeling** (Activities you will use to model the new skill for your reading novices. Remember the "think-aloud" aspect of modeling, and have multiple modeling experiences ready to help students fully understand what you expect them to do.)

Modeling Activity #1

_____

Modeling Activity #2

_____

Modeling Activity #3

_____

_____

STEP 2: GUIDED PRACTICE (*with* coaching/support)

Practice activities that will be used to help students learn the skill *thoroughly* (Note: Remember that the guided practice experiences should mirror those used by the teacher in modeling—same format, same text sources, if possible).

Guided Practice Activity #1

_____

_____

Coaching Resource (teacher, another student, or an adult volunteer):

Guided Practice Activity #2

_____

_____

(continued)

Figure 12.16   Continued

Coaching Resource (teacher, another student, or an adult volunteer) _____

Guided Practice Activity #3

_____

_____

Coaching Resource (teacher, another student, or an adult volunteer) _____

STEP 3: STUDENT PERFORMANCE

Explain how learning will be assessed. (Specific [quantifiable] criteria should be listed to objectively determine whether the student has mastered the new skill or strategy.)

_____

_____

_____

TEACHER PREP

Create a Lesson through the Teacher Prep Website.

- You will be guided through the alignment of standards, lesson objectives, your introduction, planning for ongoing assessment throughout the lesson, and planning end of lesson assessment. You will also choose and list lesson materials/resources and create adapted instruction to meet all needs of students.
- This can be sent to your instructor through this link.
- Select a text and strategy/skill and develop a mini-lesson plan. You might review standards for a grade level of interest and consider ideas provided within this chapter.

Phase 3: State of the Class (3 to 5 minutes). One of the management concerns for teachers using a reading workshop format is monitoring what students do during independent work periods. **State of the class** is a wonderful classroom management tool that informs teachers of student activities each day and reminds students of their responsibilities during the workshop period. Each day, students fill in a state-of-the-class chart like the one shown in Figure 12.17, explaining their major activities for the next day. Just before the SSR and response period begins (see next section), the teacher reviews the chart with students to help them remember what they are supposed to be doing and assigns deadlines. Some teachers, like Nancy Atwell (1987), prefer to complete the chart themselves with the whole class. Atwell describes state of the class as a brief (3 to 5 minutes) and effective way of "eavesdropping" on students' plans and activities during independent activity periods.

When problems are observed, such as a student's spending several days on one task with no apparent progress, then a "house call" or teacher-student conference is scheduled (see individual reading conferences in Figure 12.17). This simple process ensures that students having difficulty are not neglected and provides teachers with a daily audit trail of each student's work that can be referred to during conferences with parents and when planning mini-lessons.

Phase 4: Self-Selected Reading and Response (40 minutes). Self-selected reading and response (SSR&R) is the beginning of the reading period. It involves three student activities: SSR, literature response (LR), and individual reading conferences (IRC).

Self-Selected Reading. During SSR (also known as sustained silent reading (SSR) or Drop Every-thing and Read (DEAR)), students may become involved in one or more activities. To begin the workshop period, students and teachers engage in free reading of a book they have chosen for 10 to 20 minutes of SSR. Another

Figure 12.17 State of the Class Chart

State-of-the-Class Chart					
Student Name	M	T	W	TH	F
John	LR-GM	LR-GM			
Maria	LR-NM	IRC			
Jalissa	LR-NM	LR-GM			
Sue	IRC	LR-NM			
Miguel	SSR-LRG	SSR-LRG			
Yumiko	IRC	SSR-LRG			
Jamie Lee	LR-NM	LR-GM			
Seth	SSR-SSB	SSR-SSB			
Andrea	SSR-SSB	SSR-RL			
Martin	IRC	SSR-SSB			
Heather	SSR-SSB	SSR-SSB			
April	LR-NM	LR-GM			
Jason	ABSENT	SSR-SSB			
Malik	LR-GM	IRC			
Juanita	SSR-LRG	SSR-LRG			
J.T.	SSR-LRG	SSR-LRG			
Francesca	ABSENT	IRC			
Shelley	LR-NM	LR-GP			
Melanie	SSR-SSB	SSR-LRG			

Key
SSR: Self-selected reading
SSB: Self-selected book
LRG: Literature-response group goal pages
RL: Responding to literature
RK: Record keeping
LR: Literature-response group
GM: Group meeting for response
NM: New meeting
RM: Determining new response
IRC: Individual reading conference

From "Organizing for Effective Instruction: The Reading Workshop" by D. R. Reutzel and R. B. Cooter, Jr., 1991, *The Reading Teacher, 44*(8), pp. 548–555. Copyright 1991 by the International Reading Association. Reprinted by permission.

option is for students to read goal pages established by their LRG. These are daily reading goals established by students themselves.

Students who continue SSR while others rotate through the SGM activities may engage in four activities. First, they must complete their SSR goal pages. Next, they may work on literature response projects. Third, they update their reading records—filling in book time and title logs, updating their activities on the state-of-the-class chart, or signing up for an IRC with the teacher.

Small Group Work (SGW). After the initial 10 minutes of SSR, most students will be rotating through small group work (SGW) activities and spend about 20 minutes in each group. They will participate in guided oral reading for about 20 to 30 minutes, then rotate to one of the other activities. Here's how it works.

Student Small Group Assignments During SGW

- *Guided Oral Reading* As mentioned, most students will work with the teacher each day in a guided oral reading group to build reading fluency, vocabulary, and learn new skills and strategies (see Chapter 6).

- *Buddy Reading* Another group of students may be working in pairs on reading activities assigned by the teacher.

- *Learning Center Work* About one-third of the class should spend about 20 minutes in one of the learning centers. They will work in a different center each day according to a rotation schedule established by the teacher.

- *Group Literature Response* Some students may be working on a group literature response activity as part of a themed literature unit or core book activity.

- *Burgess Summary.* A kind of cloze passage, Burgess summaries (Johnson & Louis, 1987) are teacher constructed and use a summary of a selected passage. Instead of blanks representing selected missing words from the story, nonsense words replace the missing words. The ratio suggested for replacement words to regular text is about 1:12.

- *Clue Cards.* Clue cards (Johnson & Louis, 1987) are a relatively simple idea useful in developing vocabulary knowledge. The child draws cards from a deck specially prepared for a particular book. On the front of the card is a sentence summarizing or defining the target word using context from the story. The word being emphasized is printed on the back so that students can self-monitor their prediction. Figure 12.18 offers several examples drawn from *The Red Pony* by John Steinbeck (1937).

- *The Unknown Character.* The Unknown Character is an activity patterned after 20 Questions. The teacher assumes the role of one of the characters from a selection, perhaps a biography. Students ask questions that can be answered with a simple yes or no. Teachers find this activity a natural vehicle for teaching children about characterization and inferential comprehension.

- *Yakity-Yak.* Yakity-Yak is a reciprocal retelling procedure involving groups of two students. After the initial reading of the selection, each pair of students sits together with copies of the passage. Students take turns rereading sections, usually paragraphs, and then stop to retell their partner what they have just read. The process is repeated by the other student, using the next section of text. Yakity-Yak can be combined with Manzo's (1969) ReQuest procedure in upper elementary grades for comprehensive student analysis of the passage.

- *ReQuest.* ReQuest (Manzo, 1969) is also a reciprocal response procedure that follows an initial reading of the whole text. Typically, students working together in a one-to-one setting take turns silently rereading a portion of text. Next, one team member asks the other as many questions as possible about the portion of text just read. After the questioning is complete, the students continue reading the next unit of text and the second partner assumes the role of questioner. In Manzo's (1969) scheme, the selection is reread sentence by sentence, but larger units of text are often preferred.

Figure 12.18 Clue Cards for *The Red Pony* (Steinbeck, 1937)

Front of the card	Back of the card
Sometimes I had to talk to Jody as though I was his father.	**Billy Buck**
Sounded the triangle in the morning and said irritably, "Don't you go out until you get a good breakfast in you."	**Jody's mother**

Manzo also presents ReQuest as a procedure to be practiced between the teacher and one student, usually in a tutorial setting. However, questioning could easily be addressed in a whole-class mini-lesson, thus allowing students to work together.

Yakity-Yak and ReQuest could easily be combined in the following format.

1. Students read the entire selection or chapter independently.
2. Students form partnerships.
3. Students reread portions of the text. One partner (called the "listener") says, "Yakity-Yak!" indicating that the teller should retell the passage just read. After the retelling is complete, the "listener" asks his or her partner (the "teller") as many questions as possible related to story elements not mentioned.
4. The process is repeated over and over with students switching roles each time.

Newspaper Elements. Using various newspaper elements offers motivating ways to help students develop many important comprehension skills. Some of the formats that newspaper projects can follow are:

1. *Ads*
   Wanted—Time Traveler! Have mutant VCR capable of zapping people back in time. Need partner to help stop robbery and shooting of relative. No pay, just thrills. Phone Kelly at 293-4321. (Pfeffer, 1989)
2. Headlines
   Children Discover World through old Wardrobe
   Track Coach Resnick Says "Take a Long Jump"
   John Henry Beats Steam Hammer, Wins Race!
3. *Crossword:* Can be developed for *Henry and Beezus* (Cleary, 1952) using a Minnesota Educational Computing Consortium (MECC) computer program.
4. *Other:* Stimulating literature-response projects using the newspaper motif also include letters to the editor, Dear Gabby, editorials, sports, and cooking.

• *Individual Reading Conferences.*   During the last 10 to 15 minutes of each reading workshop, or whenever it is most appropriate, the teacher meets with two students for individual reading conferences (IRCs). Students make appointments on a sign-up board at least one day in advance, usually at the teacher's request, during the state of the class period; the advance notice gives the teacher enough lead time to review the student's reading profile (see Chapter 9) and decide what to assess. We

"Critics Corner via E-mail" provides you with an idea that may be helpful for students functioning below reading level. This article, found on the Teacher Prep Website (*www.prenhall.com/teacherprep*), will provide you with a unique idea. Select *Strategies and Lessons—Reading Methods/Comprehension* to learn more.

recommend as a goal three individual conferences per quarter (9 weeks) with each student. If students forget or avoid conferences, the teacher should inform them of their next appointment. During IRC time, students not involved return to the previously described activities. Assessment activities described later in this chapter for themed literature units work just as well for IRC time in the reading workshop. In Chapter 9, we also discussed in some detail additional assessment activities that could be selected for IRC time.

Phase 5: Student Sharing Time (5 to 10 minutes). As a daily closing activity in the reading workshop, we recommend that teachers and students come together for a few minutes to allow students to share with the group their written activities, books, and projects. Student groups might share progress reports on their literature-response projects, such as play practices, murals, or readers' theatre scripts. Some students may wish to share books they have been reading during SSR in the form of book talks. Others can share their responses to books discussed in their SGW. At times it may be difficult to restrict this second block of sharing time to the 10-minute time limit: students are generally enthusiastic about sharing their ideas, work, and discoveries!

Core Book Units

Core book units are four- to five-weeklong reading plans organized around a single book read by a small group of students or the entire class. When planning core book units, the teacher must gather enough books that each student has one. When used in conjunction with small-group skill instruction and writing activities, core book units can be powerful and enjoyable literacy experiences.

Teachers typically follow a pattern when planning a core book unit (Zarillo, 1989; Cox & Zarillo, 1993). First, they allow students to preselect books from an extensive list of popular literature. Be sure to consult such lists as "Children's Choices" and "Teachers' Choices" for the best new books being released; these are published annually by the International Reading Association in its journal *The Reading Teacher*. Teachers begin the unit by presenting the book selected to the class with enthusiasm and drama. Sometimes students are involved in introducing the book using a readers' theatre (play production) format. Teacher book talks and shared book experiences are also effective. Most important, successful teachers use the core book as a springboard for independent reading and writing activities.

Themed Literature Units

Themed literature units (Cooter & Griffith, 1989) organize reading and writing activities around a central concept or theme. They differ significantly from themed studies in that themed studies integrate content areas (e.g., science, mathematics, literature, and social studies) and integrate reading and writing into the prescribed content curriculum. Themed literature units, on the other hand, are intended to build reading skills and mainly involve reading fiction and nonfiction texts not necessarily connected to the other curricular areas.

With themed literature units, students are permitted to choose a book from a short list of book options selected by the teacher. After reading the book, **reader response groups** (also called **literature-response groups**), are formed to develop a project that demonstrates students' comprehension of the book.

TEACHER PREP

Students research and write news stories and commercials to videotape and present. Read more about this motivational opportunity to incorporate reading, writing, speaking, and listening. Access *Strategies and Lessons—Content Area Reading Methods/ Comprehension Strategies* on the Teacher Prep Website (*www.prenhall.com/ teacherprep*).

Research concerning themed literature units posits certain criteria that should be met if the unit is to be successful.

- Themes should be linked to high-quality literature and expository texts. Themes help teachers select from the vast numbers of quality children's literature and nonfiction books.
- A good theme is broad enough to allow the selection of books that accommodate a wide range of student interests and abilities, yet narrow enough to be manageable.
- Themes are not limited to fiction or narrative text, but often involve content in science, social studies, health, and other academic disciplines.

The theme of "Journeys," which we used earlier in this chapter in discussing themed studies, might also be used for a themed literature unit. In planning this unit, teachers would first brainstorm as many interpretations as possible for the theme and diagram them on paper in the form of a web (see the example in Figure 12.19). After identifying subtopics, teachers would search for popular children's books that might align with each subtheme.

For instance, in children's literature, characters are often seen going on long journeys to fantasy lands full of mystery and danger. *The Lion, the Witch, and the Wardrobe* (Lewis, 1961), *The Phantom Tollbooth* (Juster, 1961), *Charlie and the Chocolate Factory* (Dahl, 1964), or the old favorite by Frank Baum (1900/1972), *The Wizard of Oz,* all fit nicely into this interpretation of journeys. Figure 12.20 shows a completed web for the journeys theme with subtopics and possible literature selections.

Another popular theme is "Courage." This is a rich multifaceted theme that can be interpreted in many ways, yet allows teachers to choose literature from a manageable body. Again, teachers wishing to develop a themed literature unit using courage as the theme should begin by webbing out several interpretations or subtopics. For instance, the kind of courage demonstrated on a battlefield might be called "bravery in battle." The kind of courage exhibited by people having to cope with problems of the human condition might be called "overcoming adversity." Many times, young people have to display courage when dealing with peer relationships, showing "grace under pressure." Figure 12.21 shows a fully developed web with literature possibilities for a "Courage" theme for upper elementary students.

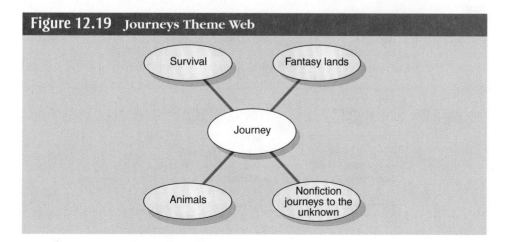

Figure 12.19 Journeys Theme Web

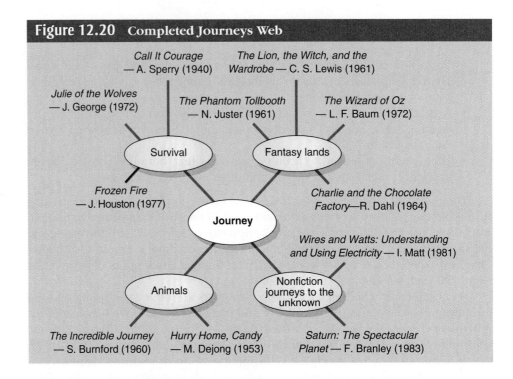

Figure 12.20   Completed Journeys Web

Call It Courage — A. Sperry (1940)

The Lion, the Witch, and the Wardrobe — C. S. Lewis (1961)

Julie of the Wolves — J. George (1972)

The Phantom Tollbooth — N. Juster (1961)

The Wizard of Oz — L. F. Baum (1972)

Survival

Fantasy lands

Frozen Fire — J. Houston (1977)

Charlie and the Chocolate Factory—R. Dahl (1964)

Journey

Wires and Watts: Understanding and Using Electricity — I. Matt (1981)

Animals

Nonfiction journeys to the unknown

The Incredible Journey — S. Burnford (1960)

Hurry Home, Candy — M. Dejong (1953)

Saturn: The Spectacular Planet — F. Branley (1983)

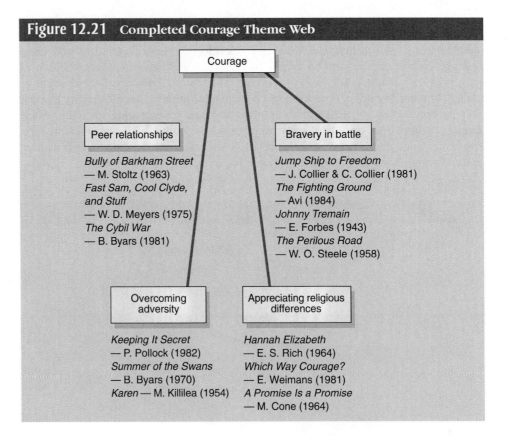

Figure 12.21   Completed Courage Theme Web

Courage

Peer relationships

Bully of Barkham Street — M. Stoltz (1963)
Fast Sam, Cool Clyde, and Stuff — W. D. Meyers (1975)
The Cybil War — B. Byars (1981)

Bravery in battle

Jump Ship to Freedom — J. Collier & C. Collier (1981)
The Fighting Ground — Avi (1984)
Johnny Tremain — E. Forbes (1943)
The Perilous Road — W. O. Steele (1958)

Overcoming adversity

Keeping It Secret — P. Pollock (1982)
Summer of the Swans — B. Byars (1970)
Karen — M. Killilea (1954)

Appreciating religious differences

Hannah Elizabeth — E. S. Rich (1964)
Which Way Courage? — E. Weimans (1981)
A Promise Is a Promise — M. Cone (1964)

To review, a good theme is broadly interpretable and can be linked to quality children's literature. When these criteria are met, planning a successful themed literature unit is possible. A number of viable themes collected from several school systems using themed literature units are included in the list in Figure 12.22. In-service teachers have classified them into specific grade levels. Students have the freedom to choose which books they wish to read. When possible, students should be permitted to select themes so as to enhance interest (Jacobs & Borland, 1986). Each theme should include a variety of choices that reflect the diversity of interests and ability levels in the classroom. This view of reading instruction is in sharp contrast to the over-structured "teacher as dictator" forms of teaching. After previewing each of the book choices through teacher book talks, students are able to make their selection.

Literature response allows students to demonstrate what they have learned. In addition to answering teacher-generated comprehension questions, students complete special projects pertaining to the book's content. These projects may take the form of student dramas, creative writing projects, or other creative responses.

Figure 12.22 Selected Themes by Grade Level: Prekindergarten Through Sixth Grade

Prekindergarten and Kindergarten	Giants	Tales–Tails
	Grandparents*	Wheels*
ABC	Native Americans*	
Color	Sea*	**Fifth Grade**
Community Helpers*	Space*	Cultures*
Dinosaurs*	Tall Tales	Fantasy–Fairy tales
Fairy tales	Weather*	Friends
Families*		Journeys
Friends	**Third Grade**	Little People–Giants
Holidays*	Adventure	Monsters
Monsters	Beasts/Creatures	Occupations*
Pets*	Biographies*	Prejudices*
School*	Culture*	Seasons of Life*
Seasons*	Folktales	Survival
	Legends	The Future*
First Grade	Magic	Transportation*
Animals*	Mystery	
Famous People*	Pioneers*	**Sixth Grade**
Feelings	Sports*	Adventure
Food*	War*	Animals*
Growing Up*	Western Stories	Cars and Motorcycles*
Insects*	Witches	Conflict*
Numbers		Family*
Poems	**Fourth Grade**	Ghosts
Travel*	Changes in Life*	Heroes*
	Explorers*	Humor
Second Grade	Geographical Regions*	Music*
Author (specific)*	Heroes*	Overcoming Adversity
Birthdays	Mysteries	Seasonal
Deserts*	Myths*	Sports*
Fable	Night Frights	Survival
Fairy Tales	Space*	

Note: Many of the themes could be used at different grade levels
*Nonfiction and/or expository text.

Team planning and collaboration help teachers efficiently develop themed literature units. These units are often developed by reading and language arts teachers at each grade level. This approach allows teachers to develop units more quickly and with greater depth. The old adage "two heads are better than one" definitely holds true here.

Teaching Themed Literature Units: The Nuts and Bolts

Gathering Learning Resources. Here is a list of items needed for themed literature units.

- Multiple copies of books selected (permanently bound books are preferred)
- Classroom library related to theme (textbooks, trade books from the school library, videos or DVDs, recordings, computer software programs)
- Art supplies for literature response projects (e.g., markers, scissors, tag board, rulers)
- Classroom computers
- Reference books (e.g., dictionaries, encyclopedias, thesauruses)

Themed Literature Unit Time Line: An Example. Themed literature units can be relatively short (one to two weeks) or last from four to six weeks. Factors such as grade or developmental level of the students, the nature of the theme itself, and school district curriculum requirements usually help teachers decide which time frame is best. For illustrative purposes, a five-week timeline for upper elementary students has been selected (see Figure 12.23).

Week 1: Introducing the Theme. Many teachers like to begin themed literature units with introductory activities of some sort. The purpose of these activities is to activate students' prior knowledge and generate motivation to explore the selected theme. Introductory activities might include a collage bulletin board depicting many interpretations of the new theme, role-playing, a guest speaker, or group participation activities.

One class about to begin work on a "Courage" unit reviewed a teacher-made collage bulletin board. The teacher had clipped pictures from magazines depicting several interpretations of the word *courage*—two police officers on patrol in their squad car, a young woman in a wheelchair, a young student making a speech, and

Figure 12.23   Themed Literature Unit Timeline for Fifth or Sixth Grade Students

WEEK 1:	Class introduction to the theme. Book talks and book selection. Self-selected reading (SSR).
WEEK 2:	Reading response groups are formed. Response projects approved by the teacher. Groups begin work on projects.
WEEKS 3 to 4:	Response project work continues. Teacher conducts mini-lessons (student performance objectives).
WEEK 5:	Students present response projects to class. Closure activities by the teacher and class.

a soldier on a battlefield. The teacher and class had a most productive discussion, and the stage was set for the introduction of the literature selections. A similar bulletin board could be constructed using jackets from the books to be introduced. Lines could spiral out from the theme word in a web format and connect to each book jacket, introducing the theme and book choices at once.

Many other theme introductions are possible. A guest speaker might visit the classroom. For the theme "Animals," a local veterinarian might speak to students about specific animals portrayed in the books selected. In one instance we observed, the presenter brought along some of the instruments used for administering medicine to animals, talked about some of the myths and facts about the animals under study, and answered questions from the class. This experience created strong interest in the theme and resulted in a great deal of recreational reading in the library and student writing in the form of language experience stories.

Other introductory activities might involve drama. Role-playing, readers' theatre, and even an occasional video production can be used for theme introduction. Once an anticipatory set has been created, the teacher is ready to introduce the books.

Book Talks. One of the most enjoyable parts of a themed literature unit, for both teacher and students, is the book talk (Fader, 1976). The object is to draw students into the texts selected for reading—in other words, to build motivation and purpose for reading. When a teacher-presented book talk is well executed, students often want to read several of the books mentioned. In fact, a little consternation may result as each student tries to choose the one book he or she most wants to read!

A book talk is easy to plan and deliver. First, the teacher finds an enticing section in each of the books used in the unit (about six titles for a class of 25, with five copies of each title available). We recommend that the excerpt take about 5 to 10 minutes to read and be taken from the first third of the book. Second, the teacher enthusiastically tells the class about each book, perhaps adding some background information about the author. The teacher then reads an exciting part of the book to the class. Naturally, the more drama and excitement a teacher puts into her book talk, the more likely she is to stimulate students' interest in reading. Third, the teacher should conclude her talk without giving away the ending to the story. In other words, the book talk should be a cliffhanger. After each book has been introduced, students are ready to make their selection.

Student Self-Selection. An important element of motivation in evidence-based, effective reading programs is for students to be given choices. In themed literature units, students should be allowed to choose which of the selected books they will read. As mentioned earlier, about six titles (five copies of each title) should be made available to a class of 25 students.

A good way to help students avoid peer pressure in selecting a book for reading is to have them choose by secret ballot. Have students write their names on a blank piece of paper, then list in order their first, second, and third choices. Inform them that they will be given one of their choices—if at all possible, their first choice.

During the teacher's planning period, he or she simply lists on a sheet of paper the title for each book and writes the numbers from one to five under each title (this corresponds to the multiple copies acquired for each title). Next, the teacher opens the ballots and gives each student his or her first choice. Should the teacher run out of a given title, he or she simply gives the student the second choice. Even if the teacher has to give students their second choice, they will feel they were given a book

Figure 12.24   Themed Literature Unit Book Assignment Chart

Themed Unit Title: "Courage"	
Book: *Fast Sam, Cool Clyde, and Stuff*	Book: *The Perilous Road*
1. Jason B.	1. Christen M.
2. Jina M.	2. Ramesh B.
3. Melanie C.	3. Michelle L.
4. Bill J.	4. Jason L.
5. Mark S.	5.
Book: *Summer of the Swans*	Book: *Which Way Courage?*
1. Austin K.	1. Skip C.
2. Sutton E.	2. Margarette S.
3. Jill E.	3. Julian G.
4. Emilio C.	4. Jason U.
5. Bruce W.	5.
Book: *Johnny Tremain*	Book: *The Cybil War*
1. Shelley P.	1. Toni G.
2. Jackson B.	2. Marion H.
3. Deb F.	3. Luis J.
4.	4. Jillian Y.
5.	5. Charesse D.

of their own choosing instead of one chosen by the teacher. Figure 12.24 illustrates a typical book assignment chart. Sometimes only one student chooses a given title. In this event, the student simply works through learning activities for that book independently. During the course of a school year, it may be desirable for all children to work independently at least once.

Self-Selected Reading (SSR). Once book assignments have been announced, students are ready to begin reading. It is recommended that the unit begin in earnest by allowing students uninterrupted time to read their books. We call this reading period **self-selected reading (SSR)** rather than sustained silent reading because readers may want to share an exciting reading discovery with a friend during the period. These positive encounters with books should be encouraged as long as class disruption does not become a factor.

The purpose of SSR in this situation is threefold. First, students are given time to read—an activity that improves reading skill over time. Second, students are allowed to get involved with their books, which creates a strong motivation to continue reading. Third, students who may have selected a book that is too difficult will have time to trade their book in for one of the remaining titles. Usually, a 24-hour grace period is allowed for exchanging books. The equivalent of two reading class periods on consecutive days is a good start for SSR.

Teachers frequently ask how long students should take to complete their books. Some teachers point out that when students are given a generous amounts of time to finish reading their books—say three to four weeks—they simply procrastinate until one or two days before deadline. The result is a not-so-pleasurable reading experience—the opposite of our intended purpose. To counteract this, some teachers prefer a shortened timetable, say five to seven days for a 120-page book. With this timetable comes a mild sense of urgency, a feeling on the part of the student that "I better get busy reading or I won't be finished in time."

Some books require more time to read than others because of length or complexity. Usually, the teacher can work out a formula to determine how many days should be allowed for each book. For instance, if the teacher believes that the average child can read 20 pages of a given book per night, then a 300-page book will require at least 15 days to read. Teachers should also consider such factors as print size, number of words per page, and the author's writing style when developing these formulas. Whatever the formula used, teachers should try to come up with reasonable limits that help students stay on task and enjoy the book.

Week 2: Beginning Literature-Response Projects. As teachers well know, sometimes students can be very reluctant readers. Literature-response activities are a wonderful vehicle for spurring interest in books and can create writing opportunities. During the second week, students begin work with their literature-response groups (LRGs). They are grouped by mutual interest, namely, which book they chose. This type of grouping capitalizes on students' intrinsic interests, needs, and motivations.

Students working in LRGs are required to conceive of a project that demonstrates their comprehension of their book. All project ideas should be subject to approval by the teacher, particularly when refinement is required. We observed one group that read Lewis's *The Lion, the Witch, and the Wardrobe* create a "Narnia game" fashioned after a popular trivia game. Contestants landing on certain spaces on the game board were required to answer questions related to the book. Because students in the LRG were required to write all questions and answers for the game (on a variety of comprehension levels), understanding of and appreciation for the book seemed to be deeper than that typically resulting from completing workbook exercises.

Several LRG project ideas have been particularly successful with themed literature units. Some are rather extensive and take considerable preparation, whereas others may be accomplished in just one or two sessions.

Student Dramas. Reenactment of major events in a book is a popular LRG activity for students in elementary through upper elementary grades. These student dramas foster deeper understanding of story structures and narrative competence (Martinez, 1993), facilitate content mastery, and provide a marvelous forum in which to display oral fluency skills. Only minimal props and costumes are needed to help students participate.

Students begin by choosing a favorite part of the book to retell through drama. Next, they develop a script based on a combination of actual dialogue in the book and narration. Usually the narration is delivered by a reader or narrator, who explains such story elements as setting, problem, and other pertinent information. Typically, the drama is presented as a one-act play and concludes in the same way as a book talk—it leaves the audience in suspense. This often makes the audience (other students in the class) want to select the book themselves for recreational reading.

Dialogue Retellings. Cudd and Roberts (1993) suggest another drama form using fables to help students better understand the importance of dialogue. First, the teacher selects a short fable having two characters and reads it to the class; Cudd and Roberts suggest Arnold Lobel's (1983) *Fables*. Second, the teacher chooses two students to retell the fable orally, each assuming the part of one character. The other students listen for story sequence and help supply any missing parts. The whole class has a discussion about how dialogue is important to story and character development. Third, the teacher provides each student with a copy of the fable for rereading and analysis of the dialogue mechanics in writing. Fourth, students working in pairs write a retelling of the fable from memory, with each student assuming one of the character roles. As they write/retell the dialogue and their character speaks, the paper used to create the draft should be physically handed to the appropriate person so that he or she is constantly reminded, for example, to indent. In the final stages of this activity, students share their dialogues with the class, then create their own original fables individually, in pairs, or in groups.

Radio Play. Developing a radio play involves virtually the same process as any other student drama, except that it involves a purely oral–aural (i.e., speaking--listening) delivery. Students first write a one-act play based on their book as described in the preceding section. Next, materials are gathered for the purpose of creating needed sound effects (police whistles, recorded train sound effects, door opening/closing, etc.), and different human sounds are practiced (such as a girl's or boy's scream, tongue clicking noise, and throat clearing). After thorough rehearsal of the script with sound effects, the radio play is taped on a cassette recorder and played over the school's public address system into the classroom.

Teachers may want to obtain recordings of old radio shows such as *The Shadow* to help students better understand the elements and characteristics of the radio play. Garrison Keillor's radio program, *A Prairie Home Companion,* which airs on National Public Radio stations, is another excellent model of radio programming students might enjoy.

Evening Newscast. Students enjoy acting out book summaries in the form of a nightly newscast, often titled something like "The Ten O'Clock Eyewitness Action News." Each student prepares a news story script (perhaps using the writing workshop method described later in this chapter) that retells an important event or piece of information in the book. After LRG members have helped each other refine their scripts, they dress up and rehearse as news reporters until the performance is ready for presentation to the class. The evening newscast can either be acted out live in front of the class or recorded on videotape and replayed to the class on television.

Novels in the News. Rice (1991) describes an activity called "Novels in the News," which has students learn to combine the journalistic style found in newspaper headlines with the story structure of novels. The idea is to reduce major events in the novel or nonfiction book to simplest terms, then display these mock headlines on a bulletin board. Thus, one might see such headlines as LOCAL SCARECROW SEEKS BRAIN IMPLANT for *The Wizard of Oz* (Baum, 1900/1972), COB STEALS TRUMPET FROM LOCAL MUSIC STORE for *The Trumpet of the Swan* (White, 1970), or LOCAL BOY BECOMES FOOTBALL HERO for *Forrest Gump* (Groom, 1986).

In a more advanced version, a mock newspaper front page is created. News stories are created with each LRG member acting as a writer/reporter. Stories are typed at the computer, printed out, then pasted onto a large piece of poster board using a newspaper front-page style. The front page is then displayed in a prominent place and presented to the class.

Formula Retelling. Many popular authors are formula writers; they have discovered a successful basic story line, which is altered in each book in terms of setting, characters, and problem. In formula retelling (Cooter, 1994), students in LRGs read two or three stories or books by the same author, chart the basic story line, then respond through group writing to create their own short story using the author's formula. For example, Donald Sobol, author of the popular *Encyclopedia Brown* series, appears to have used a formula in creating these detective stories. These titles are also excellent choices for a themed literature unit with young readers because of their high-interest content, easy readability, and avoidance of profanity and adult situations that might cause some parents to object. Group members (usually a group of five) begin by reading at least one story in an *Encyclopedia Brown* book, with all the chapters read by someone in the group. As the stories are read and the plots unfold, students begin a comparison grid detailing major points in the story. Eventually the stories are completed, as is the comparison grid. After carefully examining the comparison grid and discussing similarities, the final step is for students to create their own short story using common elements from the author's formula.

In Figure 12.25, a completed formula retelling comparison grid is shown depicting Sobol's formula for three stories in *Encyclopedia Brown Solves Them All*. Students' short stories can be presented to the class using a dramatic reading format, printed copies of the short story, a radio play, or a dramatic production. Teachers in middle elementary grades may want to consider works of such authors as E. B. White, C. S. Lewis, Beverly Cleary, and Betsy Byars for formula-retelling activities.

A Meeting of Minds. In the early days of television, Steve Allen hosted a program called *A Meeting of Minds*. Famous people of the past were played by actors who held high-level discussions about issues of their time and problems they were trying to solve. Peggy Lathlaen (1993) has adapted *A Meeting of Minds* in her classroom and found it especially useful with biographies.

> **Getting to Know English Learners**
> Encouraging all students to consider researching famous people from other countries has many benefits for your ELS, including self-esteem.

Students begin by thoroughly researching a famous person from the past so that they can later "become" this person before the class. This work involves careful reading of one or more books, constructing a timeline of this person's life (which is then compared to a general timeline recording significant inventions and world events at the time), researching costumes of the era, developing Venn diagrams comparing the person to others being researched in the LRGs, and searching *Bartlett's Familiar Quotations* for memorable quotes made by the individual. Reenactments of famous events and question–answer sessions are typical presentations made by students. Famous figures portrayed in Lathlaen's classroom include Thomas Jefferson, Queen Elizabeth I, Barbara Jordan, and George Bush.

Dioramas. A diorama is an important scene from the chosen book that is re-created for presentation. Students, usually working in pairs, often re-create the scene on a small scale using art materials. The diorama is presented to the class along with a prepared explanation of why this scene was deemed important to the book. Multiple dioramas can be presented to portray a visual sequence retelling key scenes in the book.

Big Book or Predictable Book with Captions. A popular response activity that can be constructed by individuals or groups is the creation of a big book or predictable book version of the novel or nonfiction book under study. Students create a simplified version of the book to be shared with kindergarten or first grade audiences. One upper elementary student adopting our themed literature unit's model decided to construct a multiple-page predictable book retelling the story line of *The Adventures of Huckleberry Finn*. After completion of his project, he shared his predictable book with first grade classes at the neighboring elementary school—a treat for the young children and the author alike!

Figure 12.25 Formula Retelling Comparison Grid (Plot Similarities Noted in Bold)

	The Case of the Missing Clues	*The Case of Sir Biscuit-Shooter*	*The Case of the Muscle Maker*	*Our Story*
The hero	**Encyclopedia Brown**	**Encyclopedia Brown**	**Encyclopedia Brown**	
Problem to solve	Is Bugs threatening Abner?	Who robbed Princess Marta?	Is the Hercules's Strength Tonic fake?	
How Encyclopedia gets involved	Abner **hires** him	Sally **asks him to help**	Cadmus **hires** him	
Villain	Bugs Meany	Kitty, the bareback rider	Wilford Wiggins	
What Encyclopedia does	**Listens** to Abner, examines clubhouse, **finds inconsistencies**	**Listens** to accusations against Barney, **finds inconsistencies**	**Listens** to Wilford's claims, **finds inconsistencies**	
Clues	Cherries	Noise of pots and pans	Suit coat	
In the end	**Encyclopedia proves Bugs lied**	**Encyclopedia proves Kitty lied**	**Encyclopedia proves Wilford lied**	
Results	Bugs repaid Abner	Kitty confessed	Wilford repaid Cadmus	

Stories from *Encyclopedia Brown Solves Them All* by Donald Sobol.

Discussion Webs. Discussion webs are a kind of graphic aid for teaching students to look at both sides of an issue before making final judgments (Alvermann, 1991). They may be useful with novels and other narrative selections, but we feel they are particularly effective with nonfiction. Adapted from the work of social studies teacher James Duthie (1986), there are five steps in using discussion webs. The first step is much like traditional reading activities in that a discussion is held to activate background knowledge, discuss new or challenging vocabulary, and provide a purpose for reading. Students then read, or begin reading, the selection. The second step is to state the central question to be considered and introduce the discussion web. Students complete both the *yes* and *no* columns individually, usually

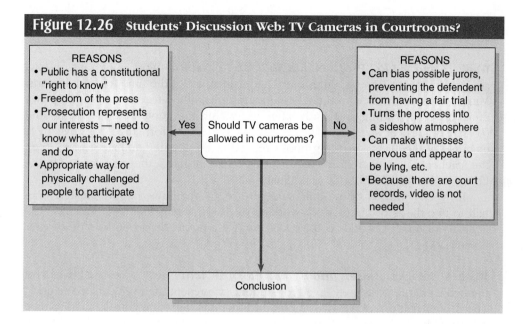

Figure 12.26   Students' Discussion Web: TV Cameras in Courtrooms?

REASONS
- Public has a constitutional "right to know"
- Freedom of the press
- Prosecution represents our interests — need to know what they say and do
- Appropriate way for physically challenged people to participate

Yes Should TV cameras be allowed in courtrooms? No

REASONS
- Can bias possible jurors, preventing the defendent from having a fair trial
- Turns the process into a sideshow atmosphere
- Can make witnesses nervous and appear to be lying, etc.
- Because there are court records, video is not needed

Conclusion

recording key thoughts as opposed to complete sentences. The third step is for students to be paired for comparing responses and beginning to work toward consensus. Later, two pairs work together for the purpose of further consensus building. In the fourth step, a group spokesperson reports to the whole class which of the reasons best reflects the consensus of the group; usually, a 3-minute period is allotted for reporting. The final step suggested is that students individually write a follow-up position paper about their judgment on the matter. In Figure 12.26, we present a discussion web completed by students researching whether television cameras should be permitted in courtrooms.

Homemade Filmstrip. Homemade filmstrips are an interesting way for students to retell the sequence of a story. Pictures are made with captions that retell important parts of the book. The pictures are then taped together in sequence and viewed with the aid of an opaque projector (if available). Filmstrips can be shared with the class or with other audiences.

Talk Show. Combining drama, action news, and *A Meeting of Minds,* students might write a script for a TV talk show. One student can be cast as the TV host or interviewer, while other team members portray characters from the book under study who are interviewed. The talk show can be acted out in front of the class and followed by a question-and-answer session, or videotaped and aired on television.

Giant Comic Strips. Similar to a mural in size, giant comic strips are made by students to re-create and retell the main story line of a book they've read. First, the group sketches out a comic strip having, typically, six to eight panels that retell an important part of a narrative or facts from a nonfiction book. Next, the teacher reviews the comic strip sketch for accuracy and approves it. The group then reproduces the comic strip on a large sheet of butcher paper and displays it on a wall in the classroom. Giant comic strips are helpful in assessing understanding of sequence.

Weeks 3 and 4: LRG Projects and Skill Mini-Lessons. Work continues on LRG projects in weeks 3 and 4, but the teacher claims part of the time for mini-lessons. Mini-lessons, as applied to themed literature units, allow teachers to (a) help students develop reading and study strategies within the context of the theme and (b) satisfy local or state mandates regarding student performance objectives. For example, if the class is reading books related to the theme "Animal Stories," then the teacher may prepare a related mini-lesson about using the card catalog in the library to locate other books on animals.

In weeks 3 and 4 of the unit, students should be allowed approximately one-half to two-thirds of the time for working on LRG projects and SSR. Students who need more time to work on their LRG projects should do so outside of class as homework.

Week 5: Project Presentations and Closure Activities. The final week of themed literature units is reserved for students to present their projects to the class. These presentations serve two important functions. First, they are a sharing time that provides LRGs with an opportunity to make public their efforts. Second, students in the class are reintroduced to the books they did not read, a process that often stimulates further recreational reading.

Themes should be concluded with some sort of closure activity that brings about a positive sense that the work is now complete and the class is ready to move on to something new. Closure activities might include a guest speaker, a field trip, or perhaps a film presentation related to the theme.

Writing to Deepen Learning: Having Students Create Their Own Expository Texts

Of the many ways to help readers succeed with content materials, teaching them to become authors of expository texts may be the most powerful. There is something about creating our own texts that clarifies and permanently embeds new concepts, facts, and vocabulary in our minds. It also appears that our interest in content information frequently increases as we gain mastery over it in writing. In this section, we suggest a few ways students create expository texts and, by doing so, become more competent and fluent readers.

Paraphrase Writing. Shelley M. Gahn (1989), an eighth grade language arts teacher in Ohio, recommends paraphrase writing as one way students can re-create content information found in textbooks. The basic idea is that students re-state information in their own words, which tends to keep the vocabulary simple and the resulting material brief. This strategy helps students to clarify their personal understanding of what has been studied.

Gahn suggests three types of paraphrase writing: rephrasing, summarizing, and elaborating. Rephrasing involves rewording relatively short paragraphs from content textbook chapters. Summarizing calls on students to identify the text's major points. Elaborating requires students to compare information in the new text to previous knowledge, sometimes using graphs, charts, or comparison grids. Paraphrase writing is often most effective when students write in small groups or pairs. It is also

"The State vs. The Big Bad Wolf" is a mock trial featured in a mini-unit titled "Fair Trials." Read more on the Teacher Prep Website (*www.prenhall.com/teacherprep*). Select *Strategies and Lessons—Reading Methods/Comprehension* to view the organizational framework and ideas for implementation.

Students develop a project to document and illustrate Native American legends. View "Multi-Media Descriptions of Native America Legends" (grades 5–12) on the Teacher Prep Website (*www.prenhall.com/teacherprep*). Select *Strategies and Lessons—Reading Methods/Organizing for Reading Instruction* to learn more.

crucial that teachers model each type of writing for students, showing examples of acceptable paraphrases and those that are flawed.

"Cubes." Gail Tompkins (2000) recommends "Cubes" as an expository writing activity. She explains that a cube has six sides, and in this activity, students review what they are learning about a topic from six sides, or perspectives, using the following strategies.

- They describe it.
- They compare it to other things they know about.
- They associate it with things it makes them think of.
- They analyze it to see what it is composed of.
- They apply it by explaining what they can do with it.
- They argue for or against it using reasons they have discovered through their investigation.

What Are Some Study Strategies That Can Help Students Improve Their Reading Comprehension?

Efficient (Speed Reading) Study Strategies

One of the characteristics of successful mature readers is that they read selectively instead of word by word. This means that efficient reading strategies are a conscious or unconscious search for meaning in the text, not a word-by-word, laborious process. Even though much of efficient reading is an unconscious process carried out automatically by the brain (LaBerge & Samuels, 1974), it is desirable for teachers to show students several efficient reading strategies that, when practiced, become internalized over time, resulting in improved reading fluency and comprehension.

Skimming and Scanning. **Skimming** is an easy-to-learn skill that is useful with a variety of reading materials. It is very helpful with periodicals, popular press materials, and most science and social studies textbooks. Skimming can be used to preview or review materials.

The object of skimming is quite straightforward: Students practice forcing their eyes to move quickly across each line of print. As they do so, they try to attend to a few key words from each line. Sometimes it is helpful for students to move their finger rapidly under each line of text, following the text with their eyes (this is called *pacing*). At first, comprehension will drop off dramatically because students are concentrating more on the physical movement of their eyes than on the meaning of the text. But over time and with practice, students are able to perform the skimming operation with as much or more comprehension.

The teacher should first lead the class through practice skimming exercises. Emphasis should be on the fact that the key words on each line will tend to be nouns, verbs, and adjectives—meaning-carrying words. Articles, conjunctions, and other function words in the sentence add little to the comprehension process and can essentially be ignored.

Scanning is another simple skill to teach and learn. The idea is to have students visually sweep or scan a page of text to locate specific information, such as an important date, a key term, or the answer to a question. Instead of attempting to comprehend all information on the page, the reader is simply trying to locate information "bits." Teachers should model the scanning process in teaching the skill.

Previewing. **Previewing** is an especially useful strategy for improving comprehension, of nonfiction text, in particular, textbooks. Previewing allows readers to cover material in a fraction of the time required for full reading with up to 50 percent comprehension. The process is simple to teach and learn, but students may need quite a bit of practice to achieve useful comprehension levels.

The first step in previewing text is to read the first two paragraphs of the selection. Most authors provide the reader with an overview of a chapter in the first couple of paragraphs, so reading every word of the first two paragraphs is important. In the second step of previewing, students read only the first sentence of each paragraph after the first two. Most writers of textbooks and nonfiction texts begin paragraphs with a topic sentence, which summarizes the main idea of each paragraph. Reading the first sentence in each paragraph will thus provide crucial information absent supporting details. In the final step of previewing, the student reads the last two paragraphs of the selection, which typically provide the reader with a summary of major points covered. If the final section is headed "Summary," "Conclusion," or the like, the student should read the entire segment.

Fluency: Adjusting Reading Rate to Match the Level of Difficulty of Text. Another important reading lesson focuses on varying reading rate. Reading rate is the speed at which readers attempt to process text. Different types of content require different reading speeds for optimal comprehension. For example, some students may be able to read a Hardy Boys mystery very quickly. After all, not every word is crucial to understanding the author's message in a book of this kind, and previewing or skimming may be sufficient for adequate comprehension. On the other hand, when students read a story problem in mathematics, they must read each word carefully at a much slower rate. Students must become aware of the need to consciously vary their reading rate to match the style and purpose of the text they are reading. This requires direct, explicit teaching.

Our Recommended Efficient Reading Strategy. After working with scores of middle school students, we have arrived at an efficient reading strategy that works with most expository and narrative materials. (The one exception is mathematics texts, which require more specialized strategies.) The procedure is a combination of previewing and skimming, as previously described. Here are the steps students should be taught to follow.

- Read the first two paragraphs of the selection to get an overview of the piece.
- Read the first sentence of each successive paragraph, then skim the remainder of the paragraph to extract important supporting details for each topic sentence.
- Read the final two paragraphs of the selection to review main ideas.

This procedure has yielded comprehension rates of up to 80 percent with fluent readers, but requires only about one-third the time of normal reading.

In addition to efficient reading strategies, evidence-based research supports the use of many other study skills. It seems that when students understand *what* to study, *how* to study quickly and efficiently, and *why* the information is pertinent to their world, classroom performance is improved.

SQ3R

Perhaps the most classic and widely used study system is **SQ3R** (Robinson, 1946), which is an acronym for *survey, question, read, recite, review*. Especially effective with expository texts, SQ3R lends itself to independent student use (Huber, 2004), and provides students with a step-by-step study method that ensures multiple exposures to the material to be learned. Many students also find that they can trim their study time using SQ3R and still earn better grades.

SQ3R is best taught through teacher modeling followed by a whole-class walk-through. Each step of SQ3R is explained here.

- *Survey.* To survey a chapter in a textbook, students read and think about the title, headings and subheadings, captions under any pictures, vocabulary in boldface type, side entries on each page (if there are any), and the summary.

- *Question.* Next, students use the survey information, particularly headings and subheadings, to write prediction questions about what they are about to read. The first few times they use SQ3R, students need teacher assistance in developing questions that will alert them to important concepts in the unit.

- *Read.* The third step is for students to read actively (Manzo & Manzo, 1990), looking for answers to their questions. They should also attend to boldface type, graphs, charts, and any other comprehension aid provided.

- *Recite.* Once the material has been read and the questions answered fully, the students should test themselves on the material. Anything difficult to remember should be rehearsed aloud or recited. This multisensory experience helps difficult material to move into short-term—and with practice, long-term—memory.

- *Review.* The final step is to periodically review the information learned. This can be done orally with a peer, through rewriting notes from memory and comparing to a master set of notes, or with mock quizzes developed by a peer or the teacher.

Learn more about the SQ3R strategy as you visit the Teacher Prep Website (www.prenhall.com/teacherprep). Select Strategies and Lessons—Reading Methods/Comprehension to find "Strategy: SQ3R Study Strategy."

Using Text Structures

Earlier in this chapter, we discussed expository text patterns (Cook & Mayer, 1988; Meyer & Freedle, 1984) frequently found in textbooks. Because these patterns can be difficult for many readers to comprehend, teaching students to write using expository text patterns can often lead to a wonderful breakthrough in understanding.

Teach Students to Identify Text Patterns. In a now-classic study, Cook and Mayer (1988) conducted extensive research on how to help students successfully identify expository text patterns found in science texts. They used three worksheets corresponding to one of three text structures to be emphasized: generalization, sequence, and enumeration (see Figure 12.27). Following are excerpts explaining how the teaching and learning process worked:

> On the worksheet for generalization passages, students wrote down the main idea (Step 1) and supporting evidence (Step 2). On the worksheet for enumeration passages, students wrote down the general topic (Step 1), listed a title for each subtopic (Step 2), and wrote a summary for each subtopic (Step 3). On the worksheet for

Students write using expository text patterns as they create a student video project. Visit Artifacts on the Teacher Prep Website (www.prenhall.com/teacherprep) and select Educational Technology/Video to locate "We Became a Country." Respond to the accompanying questions as you think about advantages of this creative product based on a piece of expository writing.

Figure 12.27   Three Text Structure Worksheets

GENERALIZATION

STEP ONE: Identify the generalization (main idea).

List and define key words in the generalization.
      Word   Definition

Restate the generalization in your own words.

STEP TWO: What kind of support is there for the generalization?
Does it use examples or illustrations? Does it extend or clarify the generalization?

     Supporting Evidence   Relation to Generalization

SEQUENCE

STEP ONE: Identify the topic of the passage.

STEP TWO: Name each step and outline the details in each.

Step 1
Step 2
Step 3
Step 4

STEP THREE: Discuss briefly what is different from one step to the next.

Step 1 to 2
Step 2 to 3
Step 3 to 4

ENUMERATION

STEP ONE: What is the general topic?

STEP TWO: Identify the subtopics.

A.
B.
C.
D.

STEP THREE: Organize and list the details in each subtopic. (Do one subtopic at a time, using your own words.)

A.
B.
C.
D.

Cook, L. K. & Mayer, R. E. (1988). Teaching readers about the nature of science text. *Journal of Educational Psychology, 80*(4): 448–456.

sequence passages, students wrote down the general topic (Step 1), wrote a name and description for each step (Step 2), and described the change that occurred between each successive pair of steps (Step 3). (p. 000)

To prepare students for using the worksheets for scaffolding new knowledge learning, the teacher provided 8 to 9 hours of training in how to identify and use expository structures. Each of the three text structures was then described separately, beginning with generalization and followed by enumeration and sequence.

> The instructor provided an initial overview of the structure and displayed a sample passage showing that structure on an overhead projector. All three sample passages were drawn from the chapter that the class had read the previous week. Reading strategies based on the work sheets described earlier were then carefully modeled for the students. For example, for the generalization passage, the instructor explicitly stated how to identify the generalization in the text, how to put the generalization in one's own words, how to identify and define the keywords in the generalization, and how to identify the supporting evidence.
>
> All subsequent training sessions were conducted individually; students attended an open lab at times that were convenient with their schedules. The instructor presented nine training passages from the student's [science] textbook; three of the passages corresponded to each of the three types of prose structures. The instructor explained that each training passage was an example of one of the structure types described in the first session. Then a training passage was selected for analysis. The student was asked to identify the type of text structure used in the passage and to complete the worksheet for that type of text structure. For example, completion of the worksheet for a generalization passage involved writing the main idea, listing and defining keywords in the main idea, restating the main idea, and listing the supporting evidence. When finished with each passage, the student brought the worksheet to the instructor, who then provided an evaluation of the student's work. If the student had not correctly followed directions, the instructor pointed out the errors; the student then worked independently to correct the errors and returned to the instructor for additional evaluation. (Cook & Mayer, 1988, pp. 452–453)

Note from the preceding extract that the teacher provided a good bit of direct instruction and guided practice with feedback. This is an approach that can be adapted and used to help students improve their comprehension of informational text.

What Can Be Done to Help Struggling Readers Succeed?

Problems for struggling readers can become acute during the upper elementary and middle school years. If not addressed, these problems often worsen and compound, resulting in students' frustration, discouragement, and declining achievement. Students not reading on or near grade level by the end of grade 3 typically do not close the performance gap. Indeed, the gap can widen and contribute to the drop-out crisis in grades 9 and 10. Thus, it is critical that struggling readers benefit from expert teaching in grades 4–6 and supplemental support from Title I or special education classes, if needed.

Good Decoding Is Not Sufficient for Comprehension Development

Getting to Know English Learners

ELs benefit greatly too by the use of graphic organizers. Use semantic webs and KWLs for getting at their background knowledge; sequence maps and cause and effect maps to help them chunk and categorize information; learning logs to help them wrestle with difficult vocabulary; and T-notes to aid them in highlighting important concepts.

A common pitfall facing reading teachers at this level—and their students—is the assumption that students who are good decoders will spontaneously develop higher order comprehension skills. Not so. Inferential and evaluative comprehension skills, commonly referred to as *higher order thinking,* require extensive and direct instruction in a variety of text genres.

Each student has his or her own zone of proximal development for the myriad higher order thinking skills he or she must develop; thus, careful assessment, needs-based grouping, and instruction using modeling and guided practice are required.

Commercial Programs for Low-Performing Readers

We believe the long-term solution to reading problems lies in improving teacher expertise and providing sufficient learning materials, appropriate and safe classroom environments, and proper support from family and community members. In the end, it really does take a village to properly raise a child.

Nevertheless, several research-proven commercial reading programs can be helpful as supplemental tools in a comprehensive reading instructional program. The following programs are useful with certain populations of students. Be aware, however, that one size does not fit all; use your informed discretion in selecting programs for supplementary purposes.

• *Boys Town Reading Program* (Omaha, NE: Boys Town) This is a four-course reading program for low-achieving readers developed at the world-famous Father Flanagan's Boys Town in Omaha, Nebraska. It features a diagnostic component for student placement into one of the four reading courses. The courses progress in difficulty from the first level, which is appropriate for students still learning basic reading skills, to a rather sophisticated level for advanced readers. The intent is for all middle schoolers to have an appropriate reading development course in which they can enroll.

• *Read 180* (New York: Scholastic) This is a computer-supported program developed at George Peabody College for Teachers of Vanderbilt University, then field tested in Orlando (Florida) and other school districts nationally. It appears to be quite motivating and effective with struggling readers in grades 5–8. One of the authors of this text is currently participating in a major study of Read 180 with inner-city middle school students.

Comprehension "Strategy Families"

Dana (1989) has grouped several effective reading comprehension strategies for readers with learning problems into what she refers to as **strategy families.** These strategies can be used with relative ease in minimal time, and they have similar or complementary functions in aiding comprehension. The first strategy family explained below, SIP (summarize, image, predict), helps students focus on content. The second strategy, EEEZ (take it easy, explain, explore, expand), is a set of elaborative strategies that can be used as a postreading experience to "help anchor the content in memory" (Dana, 1989, p. 32). The acronyms for these strategies remind students of important steps they are to follow.

SIP. The SIP set of strategies is reportedly consistent with Anderson's (1970) findings that students benefit from learning activities that require attention to content and active engagement in processing.

> **S** reminds students to *summarize* the content of each page or naturally divided section of the text. This summarization of text invites students to reflect on and interact with content.

> **I** represents the notion of *imaging*. This is a reminder that students should form an internal visual display of the content while reading, which provides a second imprint of the text's content.

> **P** reminds students to *predict* while reading. As each page or naturally divided section is read, students should pause to predict what they might learn next. While reading the section predicted, students verify, revise, or modify predictions according to what they learned. This process of predicting and verifying can carry students through entire selections and help hold their interest.

EEEZ. The second strategy gets students to elaborate mentally on new content to facilitate long-term retention. In her introduction to this strategy, Dana (1989) explains:

> After reading, it is recommended that students review what they have read in light of the purpose that was set for the reading assignment. Students are told that after reading they should "take it easy" (EEEZ) and make an attempt to explain (E) the content in a manner commensurate with the purpose set for reading. They might have to answer questions, generate questions, define a concept, or provide a summary. (p. 33)

The remaining strategies represented by the EEEZ acronym are:

> **E:** *Explore* the same content material as it has been described by other authors of different texts. These comparisons often help clarify important ideas.

> **E:** *Expand* the subject matter by reading other texts that go beyond the content covered by the original text.

After expanding, students should respond to the original purpose for reading the assignment and embellish their responses with additional content discovered during the EEEZ process.

Improving Fluency

All students, and especially struggling readers, should spend significant amounts of time—20 to 30 minutes per day—in the act of reading if they are to grow and progress. Krashen's (1992) research demonstrates that 20 minutes of daily sustained reading in materials of high interest and appropriate difficulty can help students grow by as much as six months per year in overall reading fluency. Daily sustained reading builds vocabulary knowledge and sharpens students' reading skills. Group-assisted reading can help build reading fluency with middle schoolers.

Group-Assisted Reading. **Group-assisted reading** (Eldredge, 1990) refers to teachers helping a group of students read text material in unison, emphasizing correct phrasing, intonation, and pitch. In group-assisted reading, teachers read each book many times with students until students can read it fluently with expression. In a variation of group-assisted reading called **dyad reading,** the teacher's role is assumed by a peer "lead reader." Both group-assisted and dyad reading groups have been shown to be more effective with at-risk readers than more traditional methods (Eldredge, 1990; Eldredge & Quinn, 1988).

It is also crucial that a writing workshop be established as part of the comprehensive reading program. Although not empirically tested, we believe a writing-dyad system would be helpful to students having learning problems. Because of the reciprocal nature of reading and writing, the natural development of word–spelling knowledge and phonic awareness fostered in students through the writing process, as well as the accompanying interest in books and authors that springs from writing experiences, make writing a mainstay in any literacy program for students having reading problems.

How Can We Help English Learners (ELs) Do Well with Content Texts

English language learners can be particularly challenged by nonfiction text. This section describes research-proven methods of helping ELs interact with informational text.

Modifying Linguistic Variables

"Adjusting the Complexity of Text Language" allows a teacher to accommodate students in a classroom with varying reading abilities. Access *Strategies and Lessons—Reading Methods/Organizing for Reading Instruction* on the Teacher Prep Website *(www.prenhall.com/teacherprep)*.

Limited knowledge of a second language can prevent learners from making full use of semantic, syntactic, and other clues in content reading materials. Kang (1994) suggests the following tactics to help ELs with content demands.

- Reduce the vocabulary load.
- Preteach key vocabulary concepts before students read an assigned passage.
- Use prereading questions, highlight text, notes, or questions in the margins, and create graphic organizers to help students attend to important information.
- Use postreading discussion groups to expose ELs to more complex language input.

Modifying Knowledge Variables

Cooperative learning and differentiated instruction are featured in "A Cooperative Leaning Lesson Journey to Jo'burg" on the Teacher Prep Website *(www.prenhall.com/teacherprep)*. Select *Strategies and Lessons—Reading Methods/Vocabulary* to learn more.

A second variable affecting an EL's ability to learn from reading content area texts is background knowledge. In some cases, a text may presuppose culture-specific background knowledge that is not part of these students' experiences. Likewise, some ELs may focus their reading too heavily on the print (decoding), thus failing to activate their prior knowledge to assist in understanding content area text. In either of these scenarios, Kang (1994) suggests strategies for before, during, and after reading that may help ELs succeed in reading content area texts.

Before Reading
- Use semantic mapping.
- Conduct structured overviews.
- Discuss contradictions, opposing examples, exceptions, categories, and comparisons related to concepts in the native language.

During Reading
- Supply pattern guides
- Use marginal glosses

After Reading
- Conduct semantic feature analysis
- Structure small-group discussion

How Can We Involve Parents in Supporting Children in Learning to Read Content Texts?

Deborah Diffily (2004), in her book titled *Teachers and Families Working Together*, provides one of the most extensive summaries of ideas on how to connect families and communities to student learning. In this section we summarize and expand on some of her proven strategies we feel are particularly applicable to students in grades 4 through 8.

Interactive Homework

Interactive homework (Epstein, 2001) is a tool whereby parents work with their child to complete an assigned homework task. Much like the "joint productive activity (JPA)" idea we discussed elsewhere as a small group instruction method for classroom use, interactive homework inspires a conversation about ideas between the parent and child and connects the primary caregiver to the classroom. Following is one example of an interactive homework assignment related to science on the theme of global warming (see Figure 12.28)

Homework Hot Line and Homework Voicemail

Diffily (2004) explains that telephone calls are often used by teachers to connect with families, but often this tool is used only when there is a problem. Many school districts offer **homework hot lines** for parents and students to provide help for completion of homework assignments. These hotlines are typically staffed by volunteer teachers on a rotation basis and should be promoted where they are available.

Another kind of telephone connection tool used by some teachers to connect with families is the **homework voicemail.** In this instance, teachers use the telephone voicemail system provided to teachers by many school systems (as an answering machine) to record daily homework assignments. In this way parents are able to check each day to find out what their child's homework assignments are so as to insure follow through at home. This is an easy way for teachers to provide whole class assignments to parents with just one short recording.

Websites

Many families have access to the Internet either at home, at their jobs, or through the public library (Diffily, 2004). It is becoming more commonplace for teachers to have their own website as part of their school's website, of through their own resources. One tool provided FREE to teachers as a community service is **school notes.com.** Here teachers can create notes for homework assignments and post them online in just seconds. They also provide many other free resources for elementary and middle school teachers and their students.

Parent Lending Library

Many parents do not have access to appropriate books on school subjects for their children, or book that help "coach" parents on effective learn-at-home strategies they can use. A **parent lending library** (Diffily, 2004) can be housed in a special parent resource room or in the school's library for easy access anytime during the school day.

Students are studying the Civil Rights Movement as a semantic map is created. Read more about activating prior knowledge leading to a preview of text material on the Teacher Prep Website (*www.prenhall.com/ teacherprep*). Select *Strategies and Lessons—Reading Methods/ Comprehension* to locate "Semantic Maps."

Figure 12.28 Interactive Homework Assignment: Global Warming

Dear Parents,

Please read with your child the attached article on *global warming* titled "Signs from Earth" by Tim Appenzeller and Dennis R. Dimick from *National Geographical Magazine.* After you have read the article, talk about possible answers and then write your responses to the following questions in the space provided (or on another sheet of paper):

1. Why do these authors feel global warming is real? How much of the warming do these authors feel is our fault? Write down at least two facts the authors give as their "proof" of global warming.

2. Why do you think some people feel that global warming is not really happening? Write down at least two reasons you have heard people say is "proof" that global warming is either NOT true, or why human beings have nothing to do with global warming.

Parents, please be sure your child brings with him/her the written answers to these homework questions tomorrow for our classroom discussion. Both you and your child are asked to sign and date the homework answers.

If you would like to learn more about global warming, you may find a copy of this article online at http://magma. nationalgeographic.com/ngm/0409/feature1/. You may also want to watch the Academy Award winning film "An Inconvenient Truth" which is now available on DVD.

Thank you for your assistance!

Ms. Brown

Parent's Signature/Date _____

Student's Signature/Date _____

Summary

We have just concluded a very rich chapter detailing how students in grade 4 through 8 can be helped to apply reading skills to learn more about the world around them. Research informs us that there are indeed special reading challenges associated with *expository* or informational texts. In the field of *content area reading* instruction, teachers must help students learn how to apply reading and writing skills in mathematics, science, social studies, and the English/Language Arts texts. This is reading terrain complicated by the distinctive expository text writing patterns used by nonfiction authors. There are marked increases in concept load (i.e., more ideas in smaller chunks of text), unique readability considerations, and significant higher-level comprehension demands.

In preparing to teach, we learned that it is wise to begin with a *content analysis*. Here teachers assess the important knowledge and vocabulary to be learned: the facts, concepts, and generalizations. This provides the kind of pre-teaching knowledge needed to organize ideas and plan scaffolded instruction. At this stage of preparation teachers also seek out supplemental texts and materials to insure understanding by learners who read on variety of reading levels.

We learned about successful strategies for delivering instruction. One powerful way to organize instruction is the *reading workshop,* a way of scaffolding reading and writing instruction that includes the use of mini-lessons for skill development. A proven interdisciplinary strategy presented in this chapter was *themed studies*. Themed studies integrate the content areas (e.g., science, mathematics, literature, and social studies) with reading and writing instruction. The advantages of this kind of curriculum integration are numerous. Reading and writing abilities are acquired and refined within a rich context of real world significance, which in turn inspires students to want to know more. In themed studies skills are not taught in isolation as rote drill, but are learned as tools for communicating ideas. Integration of the curriculum results in a blend of instruction that plants the seeds for future learning throughout life. A third organizational scheme, *themed literature units,* was also presented which builds reading abilities using mainly fiction and nonfiction texts not necessarily connected to the content areas.

A number of other research-proven strategies were presented that help students conquer content texts. For instance, we explored how writing process instruction, which we learned about in Chapter 8, can be explained to help students generate their own expository texts to improve content learning. Study strategies that help students improve their reading comprehension were also explained. These included the use of graphic organizers, study guides, efficient/speed reading strategies, skimming, matching rate to text type and purpose, and learning how to understand and use expository text structures.

In this chapter we saw how struggling readers can be helped to succeed in content area reading. There are commercial programs available that help struggling readers improve basic reading abilities such as Scholastic's *Read 180.* We can also help struggling readers by teaching them to use comprehension skills in unison or "strategy families," by helping them improve reading fluency, and by providing group-assisted reading (dyads and buddy reading). We likewise saw how English Learners (ELs) can be helped to succeed in reading content texts by modifying linguistic and knowledge variables. In this way we put research to work in our classrooms and insure reading success for all learners.

Finally, we found meaningful ways to involve parents in the education process. Teachers can stay connected to parents through interactive homework assignments, and by using volunteer homework hotlines and teacher-created homework voicemails. Many teachers are creating their own Internet websites that are connected to their school's website, others are using free online tools like *schoolnotes.com.* We also discussed the creation of parent lending libraries to help parents have access to books for reading at home, as well as adult-oriented books that help provide "coaching" on effective strategies they can use to help their chid read to learn.

Classroom Applications

1. Select a chapter from a middle school social studies book on a level of your choice. Using the descriptors for expository text patterns discussed in this chapter, identify the patterns of development (e.g., description, comparison) used in the chapter. How often does each pattern occur in the chapter? Are any patterns missing? If so, what might you do to compensate for these omissions? Is it possible that omission of some patterns could lead to learning difficulties for some children? If so, why?

2. A thorough content analysis is the foundation for the successful teaching in the content areas. To practice and refine this ability, try the following: Form a group with two or three of your colleagues. Select several lengthy magazine articles having to do with various topics relevant to core subjects (social studies, math, science). You may want to extract your articles from such magazines as *Air & Space* or *National Geographic*. After group members read their article, each should develop a content analysis to present to the rest of the group. By comparing analyses, it will be possible to detect whether important bits of information have been neglected and if superfluous information has been included.

3. Search the Internet to compile a list of useful sites for the teaching of content area vocabulary and concepts for two topics of your choice. Construct an annotated bibliography of these sites to share with your classmates or colleagues. Online sites can be located by accessing the Companion Website for this book.

4. Develop a themed literature unit using one of the following themes: "Courage," "Relationships," "Discovering New Worlds," "Changes," or "Animals." Include a web of the unit, a list of books chosen from popular children's literature, possible reading strategies to be taught in teacher-directed sessions, and ideas for literature-response activities.

5. Develop plans for your own Writing Workshop. Sketch out how you will manage the program within the constraints of a typical classroom environment. What physical facilities (furniture, space) will you need? Draw up a series of lesson plans for demonstrating or modeling to your class how the Writing Workshop will work.

Recommended Readings

Glenn, H. S., & Nelson, J. (2000). *Raising self-reliant children in a self-indulgent world* (2nd ed.). Rocklin, CA: Prima.

Gunning, T. G. (2004). *Creating literacy: Instruction for all students in grades 4 to 8*. Boston: Pearson Allyn and Bacon.

Kroth, R. L., & Edge, D. (2007). *Communicating with parents and families of exceptional children* (4th ed.). Denver: Love Publishing.

Stipek, D., & Seal, K. (2001). *Motivated minds: Raising children to love learning*. New York: Owl Books.

Trelease, J. (2001). *The read-aloud handbook* (5th ed.). New York: Penguin. Note: Also available in Spanish.

Zeman, A., & Kelly, K. (1997). *Everything you need to know about American history homework*. New York: Scholastic. Note: Other titles are available on the different subjects areas (see online at *http://shop.scholastic.com/*).

REFERENCES

Aardema, V. (1975). *Why mosquitoes buzz in people's ears.* New York: Scholastic.

Aaron, R. L., & Gillespie, C. (1990). Gates-MacGinitie Reading Tests, 3rd Ed. [Test review]. In R. B. Cooter, Jr. (Ed.), *The teacher's guide to reading tests.* Scottsdale, AZ: Gorsuch Scarisbrick.

Abedi, J. (2006). Psychometric issues in the ELL assessment and special education eligibility. *Teachers College Record, 108*(11), 2282–2303.

Adams, M. J. (1990a). *Beginning to read: Thinking and learning about print.* Cambridge, MA: MIT Press.

Adams, M. J. (1990b). *Beginning to read: Thinking and learning about print—a summary.* Urbana, IL: Center for the Study of Reading.

Adams, M. J. (1994). *Beginning to read: Thinking and learning about print.* Cambridge, MA: MIT Press.

Adams, M. J. (2001). Alphabetic anxiety and explicit, systematic phonics instruction: A cognitive science perspective. In S. B. Neuman & D. K. Dickinson (Eds.), *Handbook of early literacy research* (pp. 66–80). New York: Guildford Press.

Adams, M. J. (2002, November). *The promise of speech recognition.* Presentation at A Focus on Fluency Forum, San Francisco, CA. Available at *www.prel. org/programs/rel/fluency/Adams.ppt*

Adams, M. J., Allington, R. L., Chaney, J. H., Goodman, Y. M., Kapinus, B. A., McGee, L. M., et al. (1991). Beginning to read: A critique by literacy professionals and a response by Marilyn Jager Adams. *The Reading Teacher, 44*(6), 370–395.

Adams, M. J., Foorman, B. R., Lundberg, I., & Beeler, T. (1998). *Phonemic awareness in young children: A classroom curriculum.* Baltimore, MD: Paul H. Brookes.

Ahlberg, J., & Ahlberg, A. (1986). *The jolly postman or other people's letters.* Boston: Little, Brown.

Aldridge, J. T., & Rust, D. (1987). A beginning reading strategy. *Academic Therapy, 22*(3), 323–326.

Alexander, J. E. (Ed.). (1983). *Teaching reading,* 2nd Ed. Boston: Little, Brown.

Alexander, J. E., & Filler, R. C. (1976). *Attitudes and reading.* Newark, DE: International Reading Association.

Alexander, J. E., & Heathington, B. S. (1988). *Assessing and correcting classroom reading problems.* Glenview, IL: Scott, Foresman.

Alexander, P. A., & Jetton, T. L. (2000). Learning from text: A multidimensional perspective. In M. L. Kamil, P. B. Mosenthal, P. D. Pearson, and R. Barr (Eds.), *Handbook of reading research* (Vol. 3, pp. 285–310). Mahwah, NJ: Erlbaum.

Aliki. (1985). *Mummies made in Egypt.* New York: Harper Trophy.

Allan, K. K. (1982). The development of young children's metalinguistic understanding of the word. *Journal of Educational Research,* 76, 89–93.

Allington, R. (1997, August/September). Commentary: Overselling phonics. *Reading Today,* 15–16.

Allington, R. L. (1977). If they don't read much, how they ever gonna get good? *Journal of Reading, 21,* 57–61.

Allington, R. L. (1980). Teacher interruption behaviors during primary grade oral reading. *Journal of Educational Psychology, 72,* 371–377.

Allington, R. L. (1983). Fluency: The neglected goal of reading. *Reading Teacher, 36,* 556–561.

Allington, R. L. (1983a). Fluency: The neglected reading goal. *The Reading Teacher, 36*(6), 556–561.

Allington, R. L. (1983b). The reading instruction provided readers of differing reading ability. *Elementary School Journal, 83,* 255–265.

Allington, R. L. (1984). Oral reading. In R. Barr, M. L. Kamil, & P. Mosenthal (Eds.), *Handbook of reading research,* Vol. 1, (pp. 829–864). New York: Longman.

Allington, R. L. (1992). How to get information on several proven programs for accelerating the progress of low-achieving children. *The Reading Teacher, 46*(3), 246–248.

Allington, R. L. (1997, August–September). Overselling phonics. *Reading Today, 14,* 15.

Allington, R. L. (2001). *What really matters for struggling readers: Designing research-based programs*. New York: Addison-Wesley Longman.

Allington, R. L. (2002). *Big brother and the national reading curriculum: How ideology trumped evidence*. Portsmouth, NH: Heinemann Educational Books.

Allington, R. L. (2006). Fluency: Still waiting after all these years. In S. J. Samuels & A. E. Farstrup (Eds.). *What research has to say about fluency instruction* (pp. 94–105). Newark, DE: International Reading Association.

Allington, R. L., & Cunningham, P. (1996). *Schools that work*. New York: HarperCollins College Publishers.

Allington, R. L., & Cunningham, P. M. (1996). *Schools that work: Where all children read and write*. New York: HarperCollins.

Allington, R. L., & Johnston, P. H. (2002). *Reading to learn: Lessons from exemplary fourth-grade classrooms*. New York: Guilford Press.

Allington, R. L., & Woodside-Jiron, H. (1998). Thirty years of research in reading: When is a research summary not a research summary? In K. S. Goodman (Ed.), *In defense of good teaching: What teachers need to know about the "reading wars"* (pp. 143–158). York: ME: Stenhouse.

Altwerger, B., Edelsky, C., & Flores, B. M. (1987). Whole language: What's new? *The Reading Teacher, 41*(2), 144–154.

Altwerger, B., & Flores, B. (1989). Abandoning the basal: Some aspects of the change process. *Theory Into Practice, 28*(4), 288–294.

Alvermann, D. E. (1991). The discussion web: A graphic aid for learning across the curriculum. *The Reading Teacher, 45*(2), 92–99.

Alvermann, D. E., & Boothby, P. R. (1982). Text differences: Children's perceptions at the transition stage in reading. *The Reading Teacher, 36*(3), 298–302.

Alvermann, D. E., Dillon, D. R., & O'Brien, D. G. (1987). *Using discussion to promote reading comprehension*. Newark; DE: International Reading Association.

Alvermann, D. E., & Phelps, S. F. (1994). *Content reading and literacy*. Boston: Allyn & Bacon.

Alvermann, D. E., & Phelps, P. (2001). *Content reading and literacy: Succeeding in today's diverse classrooms*, 3rd Ed. New York: Allyn & Bacon.

Alvermann, D. E., Smith, L. C., & Readence, J. E. (1985). Prior knowledge activation and the comprehension of compatible and incompatible text. *Reading Research Quarterly, 20*(4), 420–436.

Amarel, M., Bussis, A., & Chittenden, E. A. (1977). *An approach to the study of beginning reading: Longitudinal case studies*. Paper presented at the National Reading Conference, New Orleans, LA.

American Federation of Teachers. (1999). *Teaching reading is rocket science. What expert teachers of reading should know and be able to do*. Washington, DC: Author.

American people, The (Grade 6). (1982). New York: American.

Ancona, G. (1994). *The piñata maker: Piñatero*. San Diego, CA: Harcourt Brace.

Andersen, H. C. (1965). *The ugly duckling* (R. P. Keigwin, Trans., & A. Adams, Illustrator). New York: Scribner.

Anderson, L., Evertson, C., & Brophy, J. (1979). An experimental study of effective teaching in first-grade reading groups. *The Elementary School Journal, 79,* 193–222.

Anderson, R. C. (1970). Control of student mediating processes during verbal learning and instruction. *Review of Educational Research, 40,* 349–369.

Anderson, R. C., & Freebody, P. (1981). Vocabulary knowledge. In J. T. Guthrie (Ed.), *Comprehension and teaching: Research reviews* (pp. 80–82). Newark, DE: International Reading Association.

Anderson, R. C., Hiebert, E. F., Scott, J. A., & Wilkinson, I. A. G. (1985). *Becoming a nation of readers: The report of the commission on reading*. Washington, DC: The National Institute of Education.

Anderson, R. C., Mason, J., & Shirey, L. (1984). The reading group: An experimental investigation of a labyrinth. *Reading Research Quarterly, 20*(1), 6–38.

Anderson, R. C., Osborn, J., & Tierney, R. J. (1984). *Learning to read in American schools*. Hillsdale, NJ: Erlbaum.

Anderson, R. C., Reynolds, R. E., Schallert, D. L., & Goetz, E. T. (1977). Frameworks for comprehending discourse. *American Educational Research Journal, 14,* 367–382.

Anderson, R. C., Wilkinson, I. A. G., & Mason, J. M. (1991). A microanalysis of the small-group, guided reading lesson: Effects of an emphasis on global story meaning. *Reading Research Quarterly, 26,* 417–441.

Anderson, R. C., Wilson, P. T., & Fielding, L. G. (1988). Growth in reading and how children spend their time outside of school. *Reading Research Quarterly, 23*(3), 285–303.

Anderson, T. H., & Armbruster, B. B. (1980). Studying. In P. D. Pearson (Ed.), *Handbook of reading research* (pp. 657–680). New York: Longman.

Anderson, V. (1991). *A teacher development project in transactional strategy instruction for teacher of severely reading disabled adolescents.* Paper presented at the National Reading Conference annual meeting. Palm Springs, CA.

Anton, W. (1999). *Corn: From farm to table.* New York: Newbridge.

Apple Computer. (1984). *Macwrite* [Computer program]. Cupertino, CA: Author.

Applebee, A. N. (1979). *The child's concept of story: Ages two to seventeen.* Chicago, IL: The University of Chicago Press.

Applebee, A. N., Langer, J. A., & Mullis, I. V. S. (1988). *Who reads best.* Princeton, NJ: Educational Testing Service.

Appleby, E. (2001). *The three billy goats gruff: A Norwegian folktale.* New York: Scholastic, Inc.

Armbruster, B., & Anderson, T. (1981). *Content area textbooks* (Reading Education Report No. 23). Urbana-Champaign: University of Illinois at Urbana-Champaign, Center for the Study of Reading.

Armbruster, B. B. (1984). The problem of "inconsiderate text." In G. G. Duffy, L. R. Roehler, & J. Mason (Eds.), *Comprehension instruction: Perspective and suggestions.* New York: Longman.

Armbruster, B. B., Lehr, F., & Osborn, J. (2001). *Put reading first: The research building blocks for teaching children to read.* Washington, DC: U.S. Department of Education.

Asbjornsen, P. C. (1973). *The three billy goats gruff* (Paul Galdone, Illustrator). New York: Seaburry Press.

Asch, F. (1993). *Moondance.* New York: Scholastic.

Asheim, L., Baker, D. P., & Mathews, V. H. (1983). *Reading and successful living: The family school partnership.* Hamden, CT: Library Professional.

Asher, S. R. (1977). *Sex differences in reading achievement.* (Reading Education Report No. 2). Urbana-Champaign: University of Illinois at Urbana-Champaign, Center for the Study of Reading.

Asher, S. R. (1980). Topic interest and children's reading comprehension. In R. J. Spiro, B. C. Bruce, & W. F. Brewer (Eds.), *Theoretical issues in reading comprehension* (pp. 525–534). Hillsdale, NJ: Erlbaum.

Ashton-Warner, S. (1963). *Teacher.* New York: Touchstone Press.

Atwell, N. (1987). *In the middle: Writing, reading, and learning with adolescents.* Portsmouth, NH: Heinemann.

Au, K. H. (1993). *Literacy instruction in multicultural settings.* Fort Worth, TX: Harcourt Brace.

Au, K. H. (1997). *Literacy instruction in multicultural settings.* Belmont, CA: Wadsworth.

Au, T. K., Depretto, M., & Song, Y. K. (1994). Input vs. constraints: Early word acquisition in Korean and English. *Journal of Memory and Language, 33,* 567–582.

August, D., & Shanahan, T. (2006). *Developing literacy in second-language learners: A report of the national literacy panel on language-minority children and youth.* Mahwah, NJ: Lawrence Erlbaum Associates, Inc.

Aukerman, R. (1981). *The basal reader approach to reading.* New York: Wiley.

Ausubel, D. P. (1959). Viewpoints from related disciplines: Human growth and development. *Teachers College Record, 60,* 245–254.

Avi, W. (1984). *The fighting ground.* Philadelphia: Lippincott.

Bacharach, N., & Alexander, P. (1986). Basal reader manuals: What do teachers think of them? *Reading Psychology, 3,* 163–172.

Bader, L. A. (1984). Instructional adjustments to vision problems. *The Reading Teacher, 37* (7), 566–569.

Baker, L., & Brown, A. L. (1984). Cognitive monitoring in reading. In J. Flood (Ed.), *Understanding reading comprehension* (pp. 21–44). Newark, DE: International Reading Association.

Baker, L., Dreher, M. J., & Guthrie, J. T. (2000). *Engaging young readers: Promoting achievement and motivation.* New York: Guilford Press.

Baldwin, R. S., & Kaufman, R. K. (1979). A concurrent validity study of the Raygor readability estimate. *Journal of Reading, 23,* 148–153.

Bank Street Writer [Computer program]. (1990). Jefferson City, MO: Scholastic Software.

Bantam. (1985). *Choose your own adventure.* New York: Bantam.

Barker, R. (1978). Stream of individual behavior. In R. Barker & Associates (Eds.), *Habitats, environments, and human behavior* (pp. 3–16). San Francisco: Jossey-Bass.

Barracca, D., & Barracca, S. (1990). *Taxi dog.* New York: Dial Books.

Barrentine, S. B. (1996). Engaging with reading through interactive read-alouds. *The Reading Teacher, 50* (1), 36–43.

Barrentine, S. J. (1999). *Reading assessment: Principles and practices for elementary teachers.* Newark, DE: International Reading Association.

Barrett, F. L. (1982). *A teacher's guide to shared reading.* Richmond Hill, Ontario, Canada: Scholastic-TAB.

Barrett, J. (1978). *Cloudy with a chance of meatballs* (R. Barrett, Illustrator). Hartford, CT: Atheneum.

Barrett, N. S. (1984). *Trucks* (Tony Bryan, Illustrator). London, NY: F. Watts.

Barrett, N. S. (1989). *Spiders.* London, NY: F. Watts.

Barrett, T. (1972). Taxonomy of reading comprehension. *Reading 360 Monograph.* Boston: Ginn.

Barron, R. F. (1969). The use of vocabulary as an advance organizer. In H. L. Herber & P. L. Sanders (Eds.), *Research in reading in the content areas: First year report.* Syracuse, NY: Reading and Language Arts Center, Syracuse University.

Bartlett, B. J. (1978). *Top-level structure as an organizational strategy for recall of classroom text.* Unpublished doctoral dissertation, Arizona State University.

Barton, D., Miller, R., & Macken, M. A. (1980). Do children treat clusters as one unit or two? *Papers and Reports on Child Language Development, 18,* 137.

Basal reading texts. What's in them to comprehend? (1984). *The Reading Teacher,* 194–195.

Base, G. (1986). *Animalia.* New York: Harry N. Abrams.

Baum, L. F. (1972). *The Wizard of Oz.* World.

Bauman, J. F., & Bergon, B. S. (1993). Story map instruction using children's literature: Effects on first graders' comprehension of central narrative elements. *Journal of Reading Behavior, 25*(4), 407–437.

Baumann, J. F. (1992). Basal reading programs and the deskilling of teachers: A critical examination of the argument. *Reading Research Quarterly, 27*(4), 390–398.

Baumann, J. F. (1993). Letters to the editor: Is it "You just don't understand," or am I simply confused? A response to Shannon. *Reading Research Quarterly, 28*(2), 86–87.

Baumann, J. F. (1996). Do basal readers deskill teachers: A national survey of educators' use and opinions of basals. *Elementary School Journal, 96*(5), 511–526.

Baumann, J. F., & Bergeron, B. S. (1993). Story map instruction using children's literature: Effects on first graders' comprehension of central narrative elements. *Journal of Reading Behavior, 25,* 407–437.

Baumann, J. F., Edwards, E. C., Boland, E. M., Olejnik, S., & Kame'enui, E. (2003). Vocabulary tracks: Effects of instruction in morphology and context on fifth-grade students' ability to derive and infer word meanings. *American Educational Research Journal, 40*(2), 447–494.

Baumann, J. F., Jones, L. A., & Siefert-Kessell, N. (1993). Using think alouds to enhance children's comprehension monitoring abilities. *The Reading Teacher, 47*(3), 184–193.

Baumann, J. F., & Stevenson, J. A. (1986). Teaching students to comprehend anaphoric relations. In J. W. Irwin (Ed.), *Understanding and teaching cohesion comprehension* (pp. 3–8). Newark, DE: International Reading Association.

Baylor, B. (1976). *Hawk, I'm your brother.* New York: Macmillan.

Bear, D. R., Inverizzi, M., Templeton, S., & Johnston, F. (2000). *Words their way: Word study for phonics, vocabulary, and spelling instruction.* Upper Saddle River, NJ: Merrill/Prentice-Hall.

Bear, D. R., Templeton, S., Invernizzi, M., & Johnston, F. (1996). *Words their way: Word study for phonics, vocabulary, and spelling instruction.* Upper Saddle River, NJ: Merrill/Prentice-Hall.

Bear, D. R., Templeton, S., Invernizzi, M., & Johnston, F. (2004). *Words their way: Word study for phonics, vocabulary, and spelling instruction* (3rd ed.). Upper Saddle River, NJ: Merrill/Prentice-Hall.

Beaver, J. (2001). *Developmental reading assessment.* Parsippany, NJ: Celebration Press.

Beaver, J. (2006). *Developmental reading assessment —2.* Upper Saddle River, NJ: Pearson Learning Group.

Beck, I. L. (1986). Using research on reading. *Educational Leadership, 43*(7), 13–15.

Beck, I. L. (1997). Response to "Overselling phonics" [Letter to the editor]. *Reading Today,* p. 17.

Beck, I. L., Armbruster, B., Raphael, T., McKeown, M. G., Ringler, L., & Ogle, D. (1989). *Reading today and tomorrow: Treasures. Level 3.* New York: Holt, Rinehart and Winston.

Beck, I. L., & McKeown, M. G. (1981). Developing questions that promote comprehension: The story map. *Language Arts, 58,* 913–918.

Beck, I. L., & McKeown, M. G. (2001). Text talk: Capturing the benefits of read-aloud experiences for young children. *Reading Teacher, 55*(1), 10–20.

Beck, I. L., McKeown, M. G., Omanson, R. C., & Pople, M. T. (1984). Improving the comprehensibility of stories: The effects of revisions that improve coherence. *Reading Research Quarterly, 19,* 263–277.

Beck, I. L., Omanson, R. C., & McKeown, M. G. (1982). An instructional redesign of reading lessons: Effects on comprehension. *Reading Research Quarterly, 17,* 462–481.

Beck, I. L., Perfetti, C. A., & McKeown, M. G. (1982). Effects of long-term vocabulary instruction on lexical access and reading comprehension. *Journal of Educational Psychology, 74,* 506–521.

Bennett, W. J. (2001, April 24). A cure for the illiteracy epidemic. *Wall Street Journal,* p. A24.

Benson & Cummins (2000). *The Power of retelling.* Wright Group/McGraw-Hill, NY.

Berger, M. (1996). *Amazing water.* New York: Newbridge.

Berlak, H. (1992). The need for a new science of assessment. In H. Berlak et al., *Toward a new science of educational testing and assessment.* New York: State University of New York Press.

Betts, E. A. (1946). *Foundation of reading instruction.* New York: American Book.

Biddulph, F., & Biddulph, J. (1992). *How do spiders live?* Bothell, WA: The Wright Group.

Biemiller, A. (2006). Vocabulary development and instruction: A prerequisite for school learning. In D. K. Dickinson & S. B. Neuman (Eds.), *Handbook of early literacy* (Vol. 2) pp. 41–51. New York: Guilford Press.

Bilingual writing center, The. (1992). Fremont, CA: The Learning Company. (Aidenwood Tech Park, 493 Kaiser Drive, Fremont, CA 94555, [800] 852-2255.)

Bintz, W. P. (1991). Staying connected—Exploring new functions for assessment. *Contemporary Education, 62*(4), 307–312.

Birdshaw, D., Burns, S., Carlisle, J. F., Duke, N. K., Garcia, G. E., Hoffman, J. V. et al. (2001). *Teaching every child to read: Frequently asked questions.* Ann Arbor, MI: Center for the Improvement of Early Reading Achievement.

Bissex, G. L. (1980). *Gnys at wrk: A child learns to write and read.* Cambridge, MA: Harvard University Press.

Blachman, B. A. (1984). Relationship of rapid naming ability and language analysis skills to kindergarten and first-grade reading achievement. *Journal of Educational Psychology, 76,* 610–622.

Blachowicz, C. L. Z. (1977). Cloze activities for primary readers. *The Reading Teacher, 31*(3), 300–302.

Blachowicz, C. L. Z. (1986). Making connections: Alternatives to the vocabulary notebook. *Journal of Reading, 29*(7), 643–649.

Blackburn, L. (1997). *Whole music: A whole language approach to teaching music.* Westport, CT: Heinemann.

Blair, S. M., and Williams, K. A. (1999). *Balanced reading instruction: Achieving success with every child.* Newark, DE: International Reading Association.

Blanchard, J., & Rottenberg, C. J. (1990). Hypertext and hypermedia: Discovering and creating meaningful learning environments. *The Reading Teacher, 43*(9), 656–661.

Blanchard, J. S., Mason, G. E., & Daniel, D. (1987). *Computer applications in reading.* Newark, DE: International Reading Association.

Blanton, W. E., & Moorman, G. B. (1985). *Presentation of reading lessons. Technical Report No. 1.* Boone, NC: Center for Excellence on Teacher Education, Appalachian State University.

Blanton, W. E., Moorman, G. B., & Wood, K. D. (1986). A model of direct instruction applied to the basal skills lesson. *The Reading Teacher, 40,* 299–305.

Blecher, S., & Jaffee, K. (1998). *Weaving in the arts: Widening the learning circle.* Westport, CT: Heinemann.

Bleich, D. (1978). *Subjective criticism.* Baltimore, MD: Johns Hopkins University Press.

Blevins, W. (1997). *Phonemic awareness activities for early reading success.* New York: Scholastic.

Blevins, W. (1998). *Phonics from A to Z: A practical guide.* New York: Scholastic Professional Books.

Block, C. C. (1993). Strategy instruction in a literature-based program. *Elementary School Journal, 94,* 103–120.

Block, C. C. (2001, December). *Distinctions between the expertise of literacy teachers preschool through grade 5.* Paper presented at the annual meeting of the National Reading Conference, San Antonio, TX.

Block, C. C., Gambrell, L. B., Hamilton, V., Hartman, D. K., Hasselbring, T. S., Klein, A., et al. (2000). *Scholastic literacy place.* New York: Scholastic.

Block, C. C., & Mangieri, J. (1996). *Reasons to read: Thinking strategies for life through literature* (Vols. 1–3), Menlo Park, CA: Addison.

Block, C. C., Oakar, M., & Hurt, N. (2002). The expertise of literacy teachers: A continuum from preschool to grade 5. *Reading Research Quarterly, 37*(2), 178–206.

Block, J. H. (1989). *Building effective mastery learning schools.* New York: Longman.

Blok, H., Oostdam, R., Otter, M. E., & Overmaat, M. (2002). Computer-assisted instruction in support of beginning reading instruction: A review. *Review of Educational Research, 72*(1), 101–130.

Bloom, A. (1987). *The closing of the American mind: How higher education has failed democracy and impoverished the souls of today's students.* New York: Simon & Schuster.

Bloom, B. (1956). *Taxonomy of educational objectives.* New York: David McKay.

Blum, I. (1995). Using audiotaped books to extend classroom literacy instruction into the homes of second-language learners. *Journal of Reading Behavior, 27*(4), 535–563.

Blume, J. (1972). *Tales of a fourth grade nothing.* New York: Dell.

Bohning, G. (1986). The McGuffey eclectic readers: 1836–1986. *The Reading Teacher, 40,* 263–269.

Bond, G. L., & Dykstra, R. (1967). The cooperative research program in first-grade reading instruction. *Reading Research Quarterly, 2,* 5–142.

Bonne, R. (1985). *I know an old lady.* New York: Scholastic.

Bonners, S. (1989). *Just in passing.* New York: Lothrop, Lee & Shepard.

Booth, J. (1985). *Impressions.* Toronto: Holt, Rinehart and Winston.

Bourgeois, P., & Clark, B. (1986). *Franklin in the dark.* New York: Scholastic.

Boyer, E. L. (1995). *The basic school: A community for learning.* Princeton, NJ: Carnegie Foundation for the Advancement of Teaching.

Boyle, O. F., & Peregoy, S. F. (1990). Literacy scaffolds: Strategies for first- and second-language readers and writers. *The Reading Teacher, 44*(3), 194–200.

Brackett, G. (1989). *Super story tree.* Jefferson City, MO: Scholastic.

Branley, F. (1983). *Saturn: The spectacular planet.* New York: HarperCollins.

Bransford, J. C., & Johnson, M. K. (1972). Contextual prerequisites for understanding: Some investigations of comprehension and recall. *Journal of Verbal Learning and Verbal Behavior, 11,* 717–726.

Bransford, J. D., & Franks, J. J. (1971). The abstraction of linguistic ideas. *Cognitive Psychology, 2,* 331–350.

Braun, C. (1969). Interest-loading and modality effects on textual response acquisition. *Reading Research Quarterly, 4,* 428–444.

Braunger, J., & Lewis, J. P. (2006). *Building a knowledge base in reading* (2nd ed.). Newark, DE: International Reading Asssociation.

Brennan, J. (1994, September 3). Been there done that: Three John Grisham stories, one John Grisham plot. *Fort Worth Star Telegram,* p. 1E.

Brent, D. (1994). Writing classes, writing genres, and writing textbooks. *Textual Studies in Canada, 4*(1), 5–15.

Bridge, C. (1978). Predictable materials for beginning readers. *Language Arts, 55,* 593–597.

Bridge, C. A., Winograd, P. N., & Haley, D. (1983). Using predictable materials vs. preprimers to teach beginning sight words. *The Reading Teacher, 36,* 84–91.

Brigance, A. H. (1999). *Brigance® comprehensive inventory of basic skills–revised.* North Billerica, MA: Curriculum Associates.

Brimner, L. D. (1992). *A migrant family.* Minneapolis, MN: Lerner.

Bromley, K. D. (1991). *Webbing with literature: Creating story maps with children's books.* Boston: Allyn & Bacon.

Bronfenbrenner, U. (1977). Toward an experimental ecology of human development. *American Psychologist, 32,* 513–531.

Bronfenbrenner, U., McClelland, P., Wethington, E., Moen, P., & Ceci, S. J. (1996). *The state of Americans.* New York: Free Press.

Brooks, G., Cole, P., Davies, P., Davis, B., Frater, G., Harman, J., et al. (2002). *Keeping up with the children.* London: Basic Skills Agency Publishers.

Brown, A., & Smiley, S. S. (1978). The development of strategies for studying texts. *Child Development, 49,* 1076–1088.

Brown, A. (1982). Learning how to learn from reading. In J. A. Langer & M. T. Smith-Burke (Eds.), *Reader meets author: Bridging the gap* (pp. 26–54). Newark, DE: International Reading Association.

Brown, A. L., Day, J. D., & Jones, R. S. (1983). The development of plans for summarzing texts. *Child Development, 54,* 968–979.

Brown, D. J., Engin, A. W., & Wallbrown, F. J. (1979). Developmental changes in reading attitudes during the intermediate grades. *Journal of Experimental Education, 47,* 262–279.

Brown, H., & Cambourne, B. (1987). *Read and retell.* Portsmouth, NH: Heinemann Educational Books.

Brown, K. J. (1999). What kind of text—for whom and when? Textual scaffolding for beginning readers. *The Reading Teacher, 53*(4).

Brown, K. J. (2000). What kind of text—For whom and when? Textual scaffolding for beginning readers. *The Reading Teacher, 53*(4), 292–307.

Brown, M. (1947). *Stone soup.* New York: Scribner.

Brown, R., Pressley, M., Van Meter, P., & Schuder, T. (1996). A quasi-experimental validation of transactional strategies instruction with low-achieving second grade readers. *Journal of Educational Psychology, 88,* 18–37.

Brown, T. (1986). *Hello, amigos.* New York: Holt, Rinehart and Winston.

Brozo, W. G., & Simpson, M. L. (1995). *Readers, teachers, learners: Expanding literacy in secondary schools.* Upper Saddle River, NJ: Merrill/Prentice-Hall.

Bruner, J. (1978). The role of dialog in language acquisition. In A. Sinclair, R. J. Jarvella, & W. M. Levelt (Eds.), *The child's conception of language* (pp. 241–256). New York: Springer-Verlag.

Bruner, J. (1986). *Actual minds, Possible worlds.* Cambridge, MA: Harvard University Press.

Bryan, G., Fawson, P. C., & Reutzel, D. R. (2003). Sustained silent reading: Exploring the value of literature discussion with three non-engaged readers. *Reading Research and Instruction, 43*(1), 47–73.

Burke, C. (1987). Burke reading interview. In Goodman, Y., Watson, D., & Burke, C. (Eds.), *Reading miscue inventory: Alternative procedures.* New York: Owen.

Burkhart, A. L. (2000). Breaking the parental barrier. In T. V. Rasinski, N. D. Padak et al. (Eds.), *Motivating recreational reading and promoting home–school connections* (pp. 110–113). Newark, DE: International Reading Association.

Burnford, S. (1960). *The incredible journey.* Boston: Little, Brown.

Burns, M. (1987). *The I hate mathematics book* (Martha Hairston, Illustrator). Cambridge, MA: Cambridge University Press.

Burns, M. S., Griffin, P., & Snow, C. E. (Eds.). (1999). *Starting out right: A guide to promoting children's reading success.* Committee on the Prevention of Reading Difficulties in Young Children, Commission on Behavioral and Social Sciences and Education, National Research Council. Washington, DC: National Academy Press.

Burns, P. C., Roe, B. D., & Ross, E. P. (1992). *Teaching reading in today's elementary schools,* 5th Ed. Dallas: Houghton Mifflin.

Byars, B. (1970). *The summer of the swans.* New York: Viking.

Byars, B. (1981). *The Cybil war.* New York: Viking.

Byrne, B., & Fielding-Barnsley, R. (1989). Phonemic awareness and letter knowledge in the child's acquisition of the alphabetic principle. *Journal of Educational Psychology, 81,* 313–321.

Byrne, B., & Fielding-Barnsley, R. (1990). Acquiring the alphabetic principle: A case for teaching recognition of phoneme identity. *Journal of Educational Psychology, 82*(4), 805–812.

Byrne, B., Freebody, P., & Gates, A. (1992). Longitudinal data on the relations of word-reading strategies to comprehension, reading time, and phonemic awareness. *Reading Research Quarterly, 27*(2), 140–151.

Cafolla, R., Kauffman, D., & Knee, R. (1997). *World Wide Web for teachers: An interactive guide.* Boston: Allyn & Bacon.

California Department of Education. (1980). *Report on the special studies of selected ECE schools with increasing and decreasing reading scores.* (Available from Publication Sales, California State Department of Education, P.O. Box 271, Sacramento, CA 95802.)

California Reading Task Force. (1995). *Every child a reader: The report of the California Reading Task Force.* Sacramento, CA: California Department of Education.

Calkins, L. (1986). *The art of teaching writing.* Portsmouth, NH: Heinemann.

Calkins, L. (1994). *The art of teaching writing.* Westport, CT: Heinemann.

Calkins, L. (2001). *The art of teaching reading.* New York: Addison Wesley.

Calkins, L. M. (1980). When children want to punctuate: Basic skills belong in context. *Language Arts, 57,* 567–573.

Calkins, L. M., & Harwayne, S. (1987). *The writing workshop: A world of difference* [Video]. Portsmouth, NH: Heinemann.

Cambourne, B. (1988). *The whole story: Natural learning and the acquisition of literacy in the classroom.* New York: Ashton-Scholastic.

Cambourne, B., & Turbill, J. (1990). Assessment in whole-language classrooms: Theory into practice. *Elementary School Journal, 90*(3), 337–349.

Campbell, R. (1992). *Reading real books.* Philadelphia: Open University Press.

Campbell, R. (2001). *Read-alouds with young children.* Newark, DE: International Reading Association.

Canney, G., & Winograd, P. (1979). *Schemata for reading and reading comprehension performance* (Technical Report No. 120). Urbana-Champaign: University of Illinois at Urbana-Champaign, Center for the Study of Reading. (ERIC Document Reproduction Service).

Cantrell, S. C. (1999). Effective teaching and literacy learning: A look inside primary classrooms. *The Reading Teacher, 52* (4), 370–378.

Cantrell, S. C. (1999a). The effects of literacy instruction on primary students' reading and writing achievement. *Reading and Research Instruction, 39*(1), 3–26.

Cantrell, S. C. (1999b). Effective teaching and literacy learning: A look inside primary classrooms. *The Reading Teacher, 52*(4), 370–379.

Carbo, M. (1988). The evidence supporting reading styles: A response to Stahl. *Phi Delta Kappan, 70,* 323–327.

Carle, E. (1986). *The very hungry caterpillar.* New York: Scholastic, Inc.

Carle, E. (1986). *The grouchy ladybug.* New York: HarperCollins.

Carlisle, J. F. (2004). Morphological processes that influence learning to read. In C. A. Stone, E. R. Silliman, B. J. Ehren, & K. Apel (Eds.), *Handbook of language and literacy: Development and disorders* (pp. 318–339). New York: Guilford Press.

Carr, E. (1985). The vocabulary overview guide: A metacognitive strategy to improve vocabulary comprehension and retention. *Journal of Reading, 28*(8), 684–689.

Carr, E., Dewitz, P., & Patberg, J. (1989). Using cloze for inference training with expository text. *The Reading Teacher, 43*(6), 380–385.

Carr, E., & Wixson, K. K. (1986). Guidelines for evaluating vocabulary instruction. *Journal of Reading, 29*(7), 588–589.

Carr, H. K. (1986). *Developing metacognitive skills: The key to success in reading and learning.* For the MERIT, Chapter 2 project, The School District of Philadelphia, H. K. Carr, MERIT supervisor. Philadelphia: School District of Philadelphia.

Carroll, J. B., Davies, P., & Richman, B. (1971). *Word frequency book.* Boston: Houghton Mifflin.

Carroll, L. (1872). *Through the looking glass.* New York: Macmillan.

Cassidy, J. (1981). Grey power in the reading program—a direction for the eighties. *The Reading Teacher, 35,* 287–291.

Cattell, J. M. (1885). Ueber die Zeit der Erkennung und Bennenung von Schriftzeichen, Bildern und Farben. *Philosophische Studien, 2,* 635–650.

Caverly, D. C., & Buswell, J. (1988). Computer assisted instruction that supports whole language instruction. *Colorado Communicator, 11*(3), 6–7.

Center for Research on Education, Diversity and Excellence (CREDE). (2006). *The five standards for effective pedagogy.* Available at the Center for Research on Education, Diversity and Excellence (CREDE) Web site: *http://crede.berkeley.edu/standards/standards.html.*

Chall, J. S. (1967). *Learning to read: The great debate.* New York: McGraw-Hill.

Chall, J. S. (1979). The great debate: Ten years later, with a modest proposal for reading stages. In Resnick, L. B., & Weaver, P. A. (Eds.), *Theory and practice of early reading* (pp. 29–55). Hillsdale, NJ: Erlbaum.

Chall, J. S. (1983). *Stages of reading development.* New York: McGraw-Hill.

Chall, J. S. (1998). My life in reading. In E. Sturtevant, J. Dugan, P. Linder, & W. Linek (Eds.), *Literacy and community, the twentieth yearbook of the College Reading Association, USA,* 12–24.

Chapman, L. J., & Hoffman, M. (1977). *Developing fluent reading.* Milton Keynes, England: Open University Press.

Chard, S. C. (1998). *The project approach: Making curriculum come alive,* Book 1. New York: Scholastic Professional Books.

Chase, R. (1948). *Grandfather tales.* Boston: Houghton Mifflin.

Cheney, L. V. (1990). *Tyrannical machines.* Washington, DC: National Endowment for the Humanities.

Chisom, F. P. (1989). *Jump start: The federal role in adult literacy.* Southport, CT: Southport Institute for Policy Analysis.

Choi, S. N. (1991). *Year of impossible goodbyes.* Boston: Houghton Mifflin.

Chomsky, C. (1971). Write first, read later. *Childhood Education, 47,* 230–237.

Chomsky, N. (1974). *Aspects of the theory of syntax.* (2nd ed.). Cambridge, MA: MIT Press.

Chomsky, N. (1975). *The logical structure of linguistic theory.* Chicago: The University of Chicago Press.

Chomsky, N. (1979). Human language and other semiotic systems. *Semiotica, 25,* 31–44.

Chomsky, N. (1997). *Perspectives on power.* Montreal, Canada: Black Rose Books.

Chomsky, N. A. (1957). *Syntactic structures.* The Hague, The Netherlands: Mouton.

Christopher, J. (1967). *The white mountains.* New York: Macmillan.

Churchland, P. M. (1995). *The engine of reason: The seat of the soul.* Cambridge, MA: MIT Press.

Clark, A. (1997). *Being there: Putting brain, body, and world together again.* Cambridge, MA: MIT Press.

Clark, E. (1993). *The lexicon in acquisition.* Cambridge, UK: Cambridge University Press.

Clark, H. H., & Clark, E. V. (1977). *Psychology and language: An introduction to psycholinguistics.* New York: Harcourt Brace Jovanovich.

Clarke, M. A. (1989). Negotiating agendas: Preliminary considerations. *Language Arts, 66*(4), 370–380.

Clay, M. (1966). *Emergent reading behavior.* Unpublished doctoral dissertation, University of Auckland.

Clay, M. M. (1967). The reading behaviour of five year old children: A research report. *New Zealand Journal of Educational Studies, 2*(1), 11–31.

Clay, M. M. (1972). *Reading: The patterning of complex behaviour.* Exeter, NH: Heinemann.

Clay, M. M. (1972). *Sand* and *Stones.* Exeter, NH: Heinemann Educational Books, Inc.

Clay, M. M. (1975). *What did I write? Beginning writing behaviour.* Portsmouth, NH: Heinemann.

Clay, M. M. (1979). *Reading: The patterning of complex behaviour.* Exeter, NH: Heinemann Educational Books, Inc.

Clay, M. M. (1985). *The early detection of reading difficulties* (3rd ed.). Portsmouth, NH: Heinemann.

Clay, M. M. (1987). *Writing begins at home: Preparing children for writing before they go to school.* Portsmouth, NH: Heinemann.

Clay, M. M. (1990a). The Reading Recovery Programme, 1984–88: Coverage, outcomes and Education Board district figures. *New Zealand Journal of Educational Studies, 25,* 61–70.

Clay, M. M. (1990b). What is and what might be in evaluation (Research currents). *Language Arts, 67*(3), 288–298.

Clay, M. M. (1991). *Becoming literate: The construction of inner control.* Portsmouth, NH: Heinemann Educational Books.

Clay, M. M. (1993). *An observation survey of early literacy achievement.* Portsmouth, NH: Heinemann.

Clay, M. M. (1993b). *Reading recovery: A guidebook for teachers in training.* Portsmouth, NH: Heinemann.

Clay, M. M. (1997). *Running records for classroom teachers.* Portsmouth, NH: Heinemann.

Clay, M. M. (1998). *By different paths to common outcomes.* York, ME: Stenhouse.

Clay, M. M. (2000a). *New shoes* and *Follow me, moon.* Portsmouth, NH: Heinemann.

Clay, M. M. (2000b). *Concepts about print: What have children learned about the way we print language?* Portsmouth, NH: Heinemann.

Cleary, B. (1952). *Henry and Beezus.* New York: William Morrow.

Clifford, J. (1991). *The experience of reading: Louise Rosenblatt and reader-response theory.* Portsmouth, NH: Heinemann.

Clyne, M., & Griffiths, R. (2005). *Sand.* Parsippany, NJ: Pearson Education.

Cochrane, O., Cochrane, D., Scalena, D., & Buchanan, E. (1984). *Reading, writing and caring.* New York: Owen.

Cohen, M. (1980). *First grade takes a test.* New York: Dell Books.

Cole, B. (1983). *The trouble with mom.* New York: Coward-McCann.

Cole, J. (1986). *This is the place for me.* New York: Scholastic.

Cole, J. (1990). *The magic school bus lost in the solar system.* New York: Scholastic.

Cole, J. E. (2003). What motivates students to read? Four literacy personalities. *The Reading Teacher, 56*(4), 326–336.

Cole, J., & Calmenson, S. (1990). *Miss Mary Mack.* New York: Morrow Junior Books.

Cole, R. (1997). *The world of matter.* New York: Newbridge Educational.

Coleman, E. (1996). *White socks only.* Morton Grove, IL: Albert Whitman & Co.

Coles, G. (2000). *Misreading reading: The bad science that hurts children.* Portsmouth, NH: Heinemann Educational Books.

Collier, J., & Collier, C. (1981). *Jump ship to freedom.* New York: Delacorte.

Collins, A., & Smith, E. (1980). *Teaching the process of reading comprehension* (Tech. Rep. No. 182). Urbana-Champaign: University of Illinois at Urbana-Champaign, Center for the Study of Reading.

Collins, A. M., & Quillian, M. R. (1969). Retrieval time from semantic memory. *Journal of Verbal Learning and Verbal Behavior, 8,* 240–247.

Collins, C. (1988). Research windows. *The Computing Teacher, 15,* 15–16, 61.

Collins C. (1991). Reading instruction that increases thinking abilities. *Journal of Reading, 34,* 510–515.

Collins-Block, C., Gambrell, L. B., & Pressley, M. (2003). *Improving comprehension instruction: Advances in research, theory, and classroom practice.* San Francisco, CA: Jossey-Bass.

Collins-Block, C., & Mangeri, J. (1996). *Reason to read: Thinking strategies for life through literature,* Palo Alto, CA: Addison-Wesley.

Collins-Block, C., Oaker, M., & Hurt, N. (2002). The expertise of literacy teachers: A continuum from preschool to grade 3. *Reading Research Quarterly, 37*(2), 178–206.

Collins-Block, C., & Pressley, M. (2002). *Comprehension instruction: Research-based best practices.* New York: Guilford Press.

Collins-Block, C., Gambrell, L. B., & Pressley, M. (2002). *Improving comprehension instruction: Rethinking research, theory, and classroom practice.* San Francisco, CA: Jossey-Bass.

Commeyras, M., & DeGroff, L. (1998). Literacy professionals' perspectives on professional development and pedagogy: A United States survey. *Reading Research Quarterly, 33*(4), 434–472.

Cone, M. (1964). *A promise is a promise.* Boston: Houghton Mifflin.

Cook, L. K., & Mayer, R. E. (1988). Teaching readers about the nature of science text. *Journal of Educational Psychology, 80*(4), 448–456.

Cooter, K. S. (2003). *Preparing middle school students for the TAKS in writing: A professional development seminar.* Dallas, TX: Seminar series presented for selected middle schools in the Dallas Independent School District. Unpublished manuscript.

Cooter, K. S. (2006). *Pedagogy to andragogy: CREDE standards in the university classroom.* CREDE Summit, April 7, 2006. University of California at Berkeley, CA.

Cooter, K. S. (2006). *Tinkertoy writing: A systematic approach for grades K–5.* Memphis, TN: Unpublished manuscript.

Cooter, K. S. (2006). When mama can't read: Counteracting intergenerational illiteracy. *The Reading Teacher, 59*(7), 698–702.

Cooter, R. B. (Ed.). (2003). *Perspectives on rescuing urban literacy education: Spies, saboteurs & saints.* Mahwah, NJ: Erlbaum.

Cooter, R. B. (2004) The pillars of urban literacy instruction: Prerequisites for change. In R. C. Cooter (Ed.), *Perspectives on rescuing urban literacy education: Spies, saboteurs, and saints.* Mahwah, NJ: Lawrence Erlbaum Associates.

Cooter, R. B., & Cooter, K. S. (2002). *The fluency formula: A comprehensive model of instruction. Creating Comprehensive Reading Programs: Symposium Series for Title I Teachers and Administrators.* Wichita, KS.

Cooter, R. B., Flynt, E. S., & Cooter, K. S. (2007). *The comprehensive reading inventory.* Upper Saddle River, NJ: Pearson Merrill Prentice-Hall.

Cooter, R. B., & Griffith, R. (1989). Thematic units for middle school: An honorable seduction. *Journal of Reading, 32*(8), 676–681.

Cooter, R. B., Jr. (1988). Effects of Ritalin on reading. *Academic Therapy, 23,* 461–468.

Cooter, R. B., Jr. (1993). *Improving oral reading fluency through repeated readings using simultaneous recordings.* Unpublished manuscript, PDS Urban Schools Project, Texas Christian University.

Cooter, R. B., Jr. (1994). Assessing affective and conative factors in reading. *Reading Psychology, 15*(2), 77–90.

Cooter, R. B., Jr. (1998). *Balanced literacy instructional strands.* Reading Research Report #91, Dallas, TX.

Cooter, R. B., Jr. (1999). *Realizing the dream: Meeting the literacy needs of Dallas children.* Dallas, TX: Unpublished manuscript.

Cooter, R. B., Jr. (Ed.). (1990). *The teacher's guide to reading tests.* Scottsdale, AZ: Gorsuch Scarisbrick.

Cooter, R. B., Jr., & Cooter, K. S. (1999). *BLAST!: Balanced Literacy Assessment System and Training.* Ft. Worth, TX: Unpublished manuscript, Ft. Worth TX.

Cooter, R. B., Jr., & Flynt, E. S. (1989). Blending basal reader and whole language instruction. *Reading Horizons, 29*(4), 275–282.

Cooter, R. B., Jr., & Flynt, E. S. (1996). *Teaching reading in the content areas: Developing content literacy for all students.* Upper Saddle River, NJ: Merrill/Prentice-Hall.

Cooter, R. B., Jr., & Griffith, R. (1989). Thematic units for middle school: An honorable seduction. *Journal of Reading, 32*(8), 676–681.

Cooter, R. B., Jr., & Reutzel, D. R. (1987). Teaching reading skills for mastery. *Academic Therapy, 23*(2), 127–134.

Cooter, R. B., Jr., & Reutzel, D. R. (1990). *Yakity-yak: A reciprocal response procedure for improving reading comprehension.* Unpublished manuscript, Brigham Young University, Department of Elementary Education, Provo, UT.

Cooter, R. B., Jr., Diffily, D., Gist-Evans, D., & Sacken, M. A. (1994). *Literacy development milestones research project* (Report No. 94–100). Unpublished manuscript, Texas Christian University, Fort Worth, TX.

Cooter, R. B., Jr., Jacobson, J. J., & Cooter, K. S. (1998). *Technically simple and socially complex: Three school-based attempts to improve literacy achievement.* Paper presented at The National Reading Conference Annual Convention, Austin, TX, December 5, 1998.

Cooter, R. B., Jr., Joseph, D. G., & Flynt, E. S. (1987). Eliminating the literal pursuit in reading comprehension. *Journal of Clinical Reading, 2*(1), 9–11.

Cooter, R. B., Mathews, B., Thompson, S., & Cooter, K. S. (2004). Searching for lessons of mass instruction? Try reading strategy continuums. *The Reading Teacher, 58*(4), 388–393.

Cooter, R. B., Jr., Mills-House, E., Marrin, P., Mathews, B., & Campbell, S. (1999). Family and community involvement: The bedrock of reading success. *The Reading Teacher, 52*(8), 891–896.

Cooter, R. B., Jr., Reutzel, D. R., & Cooter, K. S. (1998). *Sequence of development and instruction for phonemic awareness.* Unpublished paper.

Cooter, R. B., Mills-House, E., Marrin, P., Mathews, B. A., Campbell, S., and Baker, T. (1999). Family and community involvement: The bedrock of reading. *The Reading Teacher, 52*(8), 891–896.

Cornejo, R. (1972). *Spanish high frequency word list.* Austin, TX: Southwestern Educational Laboratory.

Corno, L., & Randi, J. (1997). Motivation, volition, and collaborative innovation in classroom literacy. In J. T. Guthrie & A. Wigfield (Eds.), *Reading engagement: Motivating readers through integrated instruction.* Newark, DE: International Reading Association.

Cousin, P. T., Weekly, T., & Gerard, J. (1993). The functional uses of language and literacy by students with severe language and learning problems. *Language Arts, 70*(7), 548–556.

Cowley, J. (1980). *Hairy bear.* San Diego, CA: The Wright Group.

Cowley, J. (1982). *What a mess!* San Diego, CA: The Wright Group.

Cox, C. (2002). *Teaching language arts* (4th ed.). Boston: Allyn & Bacon.

Cox, C., & Zarillo, J. (1993). *Teaching reading with children's literature.* Upper Saddle River, NJ: Merrill/Prentice-Hall.

Craft, H., & Krout, J. (1970). *The adventure of the American people.* Chicago, IL: Rand McNally.

CREDE. (2002). *The five standards for effective pedagogy.* Berkeley, CA: Center for Research on Education, Diversity & Excellence, University of California

at Berkeley. Retrieved December 21, 2006, from *http://crede.berkeley.edu/standards/standards.html*

Crist, B. I. (1975). One capsule a week—A painless remedy for vocabulary ills. *Journal of Reading, 19*(2), 147–149.

Cronin, V., Farrell, D., & Delaney, M. (1999). Environmental print and word reading. *Journal of Research in Reading, 22*(3), 271–282.

CTB Adams, M. J., & Treadway, J. (2000). *Fox in a box.* Monterey, CA: CTB McGraw-Hill.

CTB McGraw-Hill. (2000). *Fox in a box.* Monterey, CA: CTB McGraw-Hill.

Cudd, E. T., & Roberts, L. L. (1987). Using story frames to develop reading comprehension in a 1st grade classroom. *The Reading Teacher, 41*(1), 74–81.

Cudd, E. T., & Roberts, L. L. (1993). A scaffolding technique to develop sentence sense and vocabulary. *The Reading Teacher, 47*(4), 346–349.

Cunningham, A. E., Perry, K. E., Stanovich, K. E., & Stanovich, P. J. (2004). Disciplinary knowledge of K–3 teachers and their knowledge calibration in the domain of early literacy. *Annals of Dyslexia, 54*(1), 139–167.

Cunningham, A. E., & Stanovich, K. E. (1998). What reading does for the mind. *American Educator, 22,* 8–15.

Cunningham, P. (1980). Teaching were, with, what, and other "four-letter" words. *The Reading Teacher 34,* 160–163.

Cunningham, P. A., Hall, D. P., & Defee, M. (1998). Non-ability-grouped, multi-level instruction: Eight years later. *The Reading Teacher, 51*(8), 652–664.

Cunningham, P. M. (1980). Teaching *were, with, what,* and other "four-letter" words. *The Reading Teaching, 34,* 160–163.

Cunningham, P. M. (1995). *Phonics they use: Words for reading and writing* (2nd ed.). New York: HarperCollins.

Cunningham, P. M. (2000). *Phonics they use: Words for reading and writing* (3rd ed.). Boston, MA: Allyn and Bacon.

Cunningham, P. M. (2005). *Phonics they use: Words for reading and writing.* Boston, MA: Allyn and Bacon.

Cunningham, P. M., Hall, D. P., & Sigmon, C. M. (2001). *The teacher's guide to the four-blocks: A multimethod, multilevel framework for grades 1–3.* Greensboro, NC: Carson Dellosa.

Cutting, B., & Cutting, J. (2002). *Is it a fish?* – Sunshine Science Series. Bothell, WA: Wright Group/ McGraw-Hill Publishing.

D. E. S. (1975). *A language for life (The Bulloch Report)*. London: H.M.S.O.

daCruz-Payne, C. (2005). *Shared reading for today's classroom*. NY: Scholastic, Inc.

Dahl, R. (1961). *James and the giant peach: A children's story* (Nancy Ekholm Burkert, Illustrator). New York: Alfred A. Knopf.

Dahl, R. (1964). *Charlie and the chocolate factory*. New York: Alfred A. Knopf.

Dale, E. (1969), *Audiovisual methods in teaching* (3rd ed.). New York: Holt, Rinehart and Winston.

Dallin, L., & Dallin, L. (1980). *Heritage songster*. Dubuque, IA: William C. Brown.

Dana, C. (1989). Strategy families for disabled readers. *Journal of Reading, 33*(1), 30–35.

Daniels, H. (2002). *Literature circles: Voice and choice in book clubs and reading groups,* 2nd Ed. York, ME: Stenhouse.

Darling-Hammond, L., Wise, A. E., & Klein, S. P. (1999*). A license to teach*. San Francisco, CA: Jossey-Bass.

Davis, D. (1990). *Listening for the crack of dawn*. Little Rock, AR: August House.

Day, K. C., & Day, H. D. (1979). Development of kindergarten children's understanding of concepts about print and oral language. In M. L. Damil & A. H. Moe (Eds.), *Twenty-eighth yearbook of the National Reading Conference* (pp. 19–22). Clemson, SC: National Reading Conference.

DeBruin-Parecki, A., & Krol-Sinclair, B. (2003). *Family literacy: From theory to practice*. Newark, DE: International Reading Association.

Dechant, E. V. (1970). *Improving the teaching of reading* (2nd ed.). Upper Saddle River, NJ: Prentice-Hall.

DeFord, D., & Harste, J. C. (1982). Child language research and curriculum. *Language Arts, 59*(6), 590–601.

DeFord, D. E. (1985). Validating the construct of theoretical orientation in reading instruction. *Reading Research Quarterly, 20*(3), 351–367.

DeFord, D. E., Lyons, C. A., & Pinnell, G. S. (1991). *Bridges to literacy: Learning from Reading Recovery*. Portsmouth, NH: Heinemann.

DeGroff, L. (1990). Is there a place for computers in whole language classrooms? *The Reading Teacher, 43*(8), 568–572.

DeJong, M. (1953). *Hurry home, Candy*. New York: Harper.

Delacre, L. (1996). *Golden tales: Myths, legends and folktales from Latin America*. New York: Scholastic.

Delpit, L. D. (1988). The silenced dialogue: Power and pedagogy in educating other people's children. *Harvard Educational Review, 58*(3), 280–298.

Denny, T. P., & Weintraub, S. (1966). First graders' responses to three questions about reading. *Elementary School Journal, 66*, 441–448.

Denton, C. A., Ciancio, D. J., & Fletcher, J. M. (2006). Validity, reliability, and utility of the *Observation Survey of Early Literacy Achievement*. *Reading Research Quarterly, 41*(1), 8–34.

dePaola, T. (1978). *The popcorn book*. New York: Holiday House.

Department of Education. (1985). *Reading in junior classes. Wellington, New Zealand*. New York: Owen.

DeRidder, I. (2002). Visible or invisible links: Does the highlighting of hyperlinks affect incidental vocabulary learning, text comprehension, and the reading process? *Language Learning & Technology, 6*(1), 123–146.

D. E. S. (1975). *A language for life (The Bulloch Report)*. London: H.M.S.O.

Developmental Learning Materials. (1985). *The writing adventure*. Allen, TX: Developmental Learning Materials.

Devillar, R. A., Faltis, C. J., & Cummins, J. P. (1994). *Cultural diversity in schools: From rhetoric to practice*. Albany, NY: SUNY Press.

Dewey, J. (1913). *Interest and effort in education*. New York: Houghton Mifflin.

Dewey, J., & Bentley, A. F. (1949). *Knowing and the known*. Boston: Beacon Press.

Dewitz, P., & Carr, E. M. (1987). Teaching comprehension as a student directed process. In P. Dewitz (Chair), *Teaching reading comprehension, summarizing and writing in content area*. Symposium conducted at the National Reading Conference, Orlando, Florida.

Dewitz, P., Stammer, J., & Jensen, J. (1980). *The development of linguistic awareness in young children from label reading to word recognition*. Paper presented at the annual meeting of the National Reading Conference, San Diego, CA.

Dickinson, D. K., McCabe, A., & Sprague, K. (2003). Teacher Rating of Oral Language and Literacy (TROLL): Individualizing early literacy instruction with a standards-based rating tool. *The Reading Teacher, 56*(6), 554–564.

Dickinson, D. K., & Smith, M. W. (1994). Long-term effects of preschool teachers' book readings on low-income children's vocabulary and story comprehension. *Reading Research Quarterly, 29,* 104–122.

Dickinson, D. K., & Tabors, P. O. (Eds.). (2001). *Young children learning at home and school: Beginning literacy with language.* Baltimore, MD: Paul H. Brookes.

Dickson, S. V., Simmons, D. C., & Kame'enui, E. J. (1998a). Text organization: Instructional and curricular basics and implications. In D. C. Simmons & E. J. Kame'enui (Eds.), *What reading research tells us about children with diverse learning needs.* (pp. 279–302). Mahwah, NJ: Erlbaum;

Dickson, S. V., Simmons, D. C., & Kame'enui, E. J. (1998b). Text organization: Research bases. In D. C. Simmons and E. J. Kame'enui (Eds.), *What reading research tells us about children with diverse learning needs* (pp. 239–278). Mahwah, NJ: Erlbaum.

Dickson, S. V., Simmons, D. C., & Kame'enui, E. J. (1998b). Text organization: Instructional and curricular basics and implications (279–294). In D. C. Simmons & E. J. Kame'enui (Eds.), *What reading research tells us about children with diverse learning needs: Bases and basics.* Mahwah, NJ: Lawrence Erlbaum Associates.

Diederich, P. B. (1974). *Measuring growth in English.* Urbana, IL: National Council of Teachers of English.

Diffily, D. (1994, April). *Portfolio assessment in early literacy settings.* Paper presented at a professional development schools workshop at Texas Christian University, Fort Worth, TX.

Diffily, D. (2004). *Teachers and families working together.* Boston: Pearson Education/Allyn and Bacon.

Dillner, M. (1993–1994). Using hypermedia to enhance content area instruction. *Journal of Reading, 37*(4), 260–270.

Dixon-Krauss, L. (1996). *Vygotsky in the classroom: Mediated literacy instruction and assessment.* New York: Longman.

Doctorow, M., Wittrock, M. C., & Marks, C. (1978). Generative processes in reading comprehension. *Journal of Educational Psychology, 70*(2), 109–118.

D'Odorico, L. (1984). Nonsegmental features in prelinguistic communications: An analysis of some types of infant cry and noncry vocalizations. *Journal of Child Language, 11,* 17–27.

Dole, J. A., Brown, K. J., & Trathen, W. (1996). The effects of strategy instruction on the comprehension performance of at-risk students. *Reading Research Quarterly, 31,* 62–88.

Dole, J. A., Osborn, J., & Lehr, F. (1990). *A guide to selecting basal reader programs.* Champaign, IL: Center for the Study of Reading.

Dole, J. A., Rogers, T., & Osborn, J. (1987). Improving the selection of basal reading programs: A report of the textbook adoption guidelines project. *Elementary School Journal, 87,* 282–298.

Donelson, K. L., & Nilsen, A. P. (1985). *Literature for today's young adults.* Boston: Scott, Foresman.

Donovan, C. A., & Smolkin, L. B. (2002). Considering genre, context, and visual features in the selection of trade books for science instruction. *The Reading Teacher, 55*(6), 502–520.

Dowd, C. A., & Sinatra, R. (1990). Computer programs and the learning of text structure. *Journal of Reading, 34*(2), 104–112.

Dowhower, S. (1987). Effects of repeated readings on second-grade transitional readers' fluency and comprehension. *Reading Research Quarterly, 22,* 389–406.

Dowhower, S. (1991). Speaking of prosody: Fluency's unattended bedfellow. *Theory Into Practice, 30*(3), 158–164.

Dowhower, S. L. (1989). Repeated reading: Research into practice. *The Reading Teacher, 42*(7), 502–507.

Downing, J. (1970). The development of linguistic concepts in children's thinking. *Research in the Teaching of English, 4,* 5–19.

Downing, J. (1971–72). Children developing concepts of spoken and written language. *Journal of Reading Behavior, 4,* 1–19.

Downing, J. (1977). How society creates reading disability. *The Elementary School Journal, 77,* 274–279.

Downing, J., & Oliver, P. (1973). The child's concept of a word. *Reading Research Quarterly, 9,* 568–582.

Downing, J., & Thomson, D. (1977). Sex role stereotypes in learning to read. *Research in the Teaching of English, 11,* 149–155.

Downing, J. G. (1990). *A study of the relationship between literacy levels and institutional behaviors of incarcerated male felons*. Unpublished doctoral dissertation, Ball State University, Muncie, IN.

Doyle, C. (1988). Creative applications of computer assisted reading and writing instruction. *Journal of Reading, 32*(3), 236–239.

Dreher, M. J., & Gambrell, L. B. (1985). Teaching children to use a self-questioning strategy for studying expository prose. *Reading Improvement, 22,* 2–7.

Drew, D. (1989). *The life of the butterfly*. Crystal Lake, IL: Rigby.

Driscoll, M. P. (1994). *Psychology of learning for instruction*. Boston: Allyn & Bacon.

Drucker, P. F. (1998, August 24). The next information revolution. *Forbes ASAP*. 47–58.

Duffy, G. G. (2003). *Explaining reading: A resource for teaching concepts, skills, and strategies*. New York: Guilford Press.

Duffy, G. G. (2004). *Explaining reading: A resource for teaching concepts, skills, and strategies*. New York: Guilford Press.

Duffy, G. G., Roehler, L. R., & Putnam, J. (1987). Putting the teacher in control: Basal reading textbooks and instructional decision making. *The Elementary School Journal, 87*(3), 357–366.

Duke, N. K. (2000). 3.6 minutes per day: The scarcity of informational texts in first grade. *Reading Research Quarterly, 35*(2), 202–224.

Duke, N. K. (2000a). For the rich it's richer: print experiences and environments offered to children in very low- and very high-socioeconomic status first-grade classrooms. *American Educational Research Journal, 37,* 441–478.

Duke, N. K. (2000b). 3.6 minutes per day: The scarcity of informational texts in first grade. *Reading Research Quarterly, 35*(2), 202–224.

Duke, N. K., & Bennett-Armistead, V. S. (2003). *Reading and writing informational text in the primary grades: Research-based practices*. New York: Scholastic, Inc.

Duke, N. K., Bennett-Armistead, S., Roberts, E. M. (2002). Incorporating informational text in the primary grades 40–54. In C. M. Roller (Ed.), *Comprehensive reading instruction across the grade levels: A collection of papers from the 2001 reading research conference*. Newark, DE: International Reading Association.

Duke, N. K., & Purcell-Gates, V. (In press). Genres at home and at school: Bridging the new to the known. *The Reading Teacher*.

Dunn, L., & Dunn, L. M. (1997). *Peabody picture vocabulary test—third edition* (PPVT-III). Circle Pines, MN: American Guidance Service.

Dunn, L., Lugo, D. E., Padilla, E. R., & Dunn, L. M. (1986). *Test de Vocabulario en Imágenes Peabody* (TVIP). Circle Pines, MN: American Guidance Service.

Dunn, L. M., & Markwardt, F. C. (1970). *Peabody individual achievement test*. Circle Pines, MN: American Guidance Service.

Dunn, R. (1988). Teaching students through their perceptual strengths or preferences. *Journal of Reading, 31,* 304–309.

Dunn, S. (1987). *Butterscotch dreams*. Markham, Ontario: Pembroke.

Durkin, D. (1966). *Children who read early: Two longitudinal studies*. New York: Teachers College Press.

Durkin, D. (1974). A six year study of children who learned to read in school at the age of four. *Reading Research Quarterly, 10,* 9–61.

Durkin, D. (1978). What classroom observations reveal about reading comprehension instruction. *Reading Research Quarterly, 14*(4), 482–533.

Durkin, D. (1981a). Reading comprehension in five basal reader series. *Reading Research Quarterly, 16*(4), 515–543.

Durkin, D. (1981b). What is the value of the new interest in reading comprehension? *Language Arts, 58,* 23–43.

Durkin, D. (1983). *Reading comprehension instruction: What the research says*. Presentation at the first Tarleton State University Reading Conference, Stephenville, TX.

Durkin, D. (1984). Is there a match between what elementary teachers do and what basal reader manuals recommend? *The Reading Teacher, 37,* 734–745.

Durkin, D. (1987). *Teaching young children to read,* (4th ed.) New York: Allyn & Bacon.

Durkin, D. (1989). *Teaching them to read,* 5th Ed. New York: Allyn & Bacon.

Durrell, D. D. (1940). *Improvement of basic reading abilities*. New York: World Book.

Duthie, J. (1986). The web: A powerful tool for the teaching and evaluation of the expository essay. *The History and Social Science Teacher, 21,* 232–236.

Dutro, S., & Moran, C. (2003). Rethinking English language instruction: An architectural approach.

In G. G. Garcia (Ed.), *English learning: Reaching the highest level of English literacy* (pp. 227–258). Newark, DE: International Reading Association.

Dyer, P. C. (1992). Reading Recovery: A cost-effectiveness and educational-outcomes analysis. *ERS Spectrum, 10*, 10–19.

Early Childhood-Head Start Taskforce. (2002). *Teaching our youngest: A guide for preschool teachers and child care and family providers.* Washington, DC: U.S. Departments of Education and Health and Human Services.

Eastlund, J. (1980). Working with the language deficient child. *Music Educators Journal, 67*(3), 60–65.

Eckhoff, B. (1983). How reading affects children's writing. *Language Arts, 60*(5), 607–616.

Edelsky, C. (1988). Living in the author's world: Analyzing the author's craft. *The California Reader, 21,* 14–17.

Edelsky, C., Altwerger, B., & Flores, B. (1991). *Whole language: What's the difference?* Portsmouth, NH: Heinemann.

Eder, D. (1983). Ability grouping and student's academic self-concepts: A case study. *The Elementary School Journal, 84,* 149–161.

Educational Testing Service. (1988). *Who reads best?* Princeton, NJ: Educational Testing Service.

Edwards, P. (1999). *A path to follow: Learning to listen to parents.* Portsmouth, NH: Heinemann.

Efta, M. (1984). Reading in silence: A chance to read. In A. J. Harris & E. R. Sipay (Eds.), *Readings on reading instruction* (3rd ed.), (pp. 387–391). New York: Longman.

Ehri, L. C. (1984). How orthography alters spoken language competencies in children. In J. Downing & R. Valtin (Eds.), *Language awareness and learning to read* (pp. 118–147). New York: Springer-Verlag.

Ehri, L. C. & Sweet, J. (1991). Fingerpoint-reading of memorized text: What enables beginners to process the print? *Reading Research Quarterly, 26,* 442–462.

Ehri, L. C., & Wilce, L. C. (1980). The influence of orthography on readers' conceptualization of the phonemic structure of words. *Applied Psycholinguistics, 1,* 371–385.

Ehri, L. C., & Wilce, L. C. (1985). Movement into reading: Is the first stage of printed word learning visual or phonetic? *Reading Research Quarterly, 20,* 163–179.

Ekwall, E. E., & Shanker, J. L. (1989). *Teaching reading in the elementary school* (2nd ed.). Upper Saddle River, NJ: Merrill/Prentice-Hall.

Elbow, P. (1994). Will the virtues of portfolios blind us to their potential dangers? In L. Black, D. Daiker, J. Sommers, & G. Stygall (Eds.), *New directions in portfolio assessment* (pp. 40–55). Portsmouth, NH: Boynton/Cook.

El-Dinary, P. B. (2002). Challenges implementing transactional strategies instruction for reading comprehension. In C. Collins-Block & M. Pressley (Eds.), *Comprehension instruction: Research-based best practices* (pp. 201–218). New York: Guilford Press.

Eldredge, J. L. (1990). Increasing the performance of poor readers in the third grade with a group assisted strategy. *Journal of Educational Research, 84*(2), 69–77.

Eldredge, J. L., & Quinn, D. W. (1988). Increasing reading performance of low-achieving second graders with dyad reading groups. *Journal of Educational Research, 82,* 40–46.

Eldredge, J. L., Reutzel, D. R., & Hollingsworth, P. M. (1996, Summer). Comparing the effectiveness of two oral reading practices: Round-robin reading and the shared book experience. *Journal of Literacy Research, 28*(2), 201–225.

Ellis, A. K., & Fouts, J. T. (1993). *Research on educational innovations.* Princeton Junction, NJ: Eye on Education.

Ellison, C. (1989, January). PCs in the schools: An American tragedy. *PC/Computing,* 96–104.

Engelmann, S., & Bruner, E. C. (1995). *Reading mastery I: Presentation book C,* Rainbow Edition. Columbus, OH: Science Research Associates/Macmillan/McGraw-Hill.

Engelmann, S., & Bruner, E. C. (2002). *SRA reading mastery plus.* Columbus, OH: SRA-McGraw-Hill.

Englert, C. S., & Tarrant, K. L. (1995). Creating collaborative cultures for educational change. *Remedial and Special Education, 16*(6), 325–336.

Enz, B. J. (2003). The ABCs of family literacy. In A. DeBruin-Parecki & B. Krol-Sinclair (Eds.), *Family literacy: From theory to practice* (pp. 50–67). Newark, DE: International Reading Association.

Epstein, J. L. (2001). *School, family, and community partnerships: Preparing educators and improving schools.* Boulder, CO: Westview Press.

Ericson, L., & Juliebo, M. F. (1998). *The phonological awareness handbook for kindergarten and primary teachers*. Newark, DE: International Reading Association.

Ervin, J. (1982). *How to have a successful parents and reading program: A practical guide*. New York: Allyn & Bacon.

Esch, M. (1991, February 17). Whole language teaches reading. *The Daily Herald* (Provo, UT), p. D1.

Estes, T. H., & Vaughn, J. L. (1978). *Reading and learning in the content classroom*. Boston: Allyn & Bacon.

Fader, D. N. (1976). *The new hooked on books*. New York: Berkley.

Farnan, N., & Dahl, K. (2003). Children's writing: Research and practice. In J. Flood, D. Lapp, J. R. Squire, & J. M. Jensen (Eds.), *Handbook of research on teaching the English language arts* (pp. 993–1007). Mahwah, NJ: Lawrence Erlbaum Associates.

Farr, R. (1991). *Portfolios: Assessment in the language arts*. ED334603.

Farr, R., & Tone, B. (1994). *Portfolio and performance assessment*. Fort Worth, TX: Harcourt Brace.

Farr, R., & Tulley, M. (1989). State level adoption of basal readers: Goals, processes, and recommendations. *Theory Into Practice, 28*(4), 248–253.

Farr, R., Tulley, M. A., & Powell, D. (1987). The evaluation and selection of basal readers. *The Elementary School Journal, 87*, 267–281.

Farrar, E. B. (1985). *Accelerating the oral language of children of low socio-economic status*. Belle Glade, FL: Unpublished Dissertation. (ERIC Document Reproduction Service No. ED 262 913).

Farrar, M. T. (1984). Asking better questions. *The Reading Teacher, 38*, 10–17.

Fawson, P. C., Ludlow, B., Reutzel, D. R., Sudweeks, R., & Smith, J. A. (in press). Examining the reliability of running records: Attaining generalizable results. *Journal of Educational Research*.

Fawson, P. C., & Reutzel, D. R. (2000). But I only have a basal: Implementing guided reading in the early grades. *The Reading Teacher, 54*(1), 84–97.

Fay, L. (1965). Reading study skills: Math and science. In J. A. Figurel (Ed.), *Reading and inquiry*. Newark, DE: International Reading Association.

Felmlee, D., & Eder, D. (1983). Contextual effects in the classroom: The impact of ability groups on student attention. *Sociology of Education, 56*, 77–87.

Ferguson, R. F. (1991). Paying for public education: New evidence on how and why money matters. *Harvard Journal of Legislation, 282*, 465–498.

Ferreiro, E., & Teberosky, A. (1982). *Literacy before schooling*. Portsmouth, NH: Heinemann.

Fielding, L., Kerr, N., & Rosier, P. (1998). *The 90% reading goal*. Kennewick, WA: National Reading Foundation.

Fields, M. V., & Spangler, K. L. (2000). *Let's begin reading right: A developmental approach to emergent literacy*. Upper Saddle River, NJ: Merrill.

Fillmore, D. (1968). The case for case. *Universals of linguistic theory*. New York: Holt, Rinehart and Winston.

Fillmore, L. W., & Snow, C. E. (2000). *What teachers need to know about language*. Special report from ERIC Clearing House on Languages and Linguistics [Online]. Available at *http://www.cal.org/ericcll/teachers/teachers.pdf*

Finchler, J. (2001). *Testing Miss Malarkey*. New York: Walker & Company.

Fisher-Nagel, H. (1987). *The life of a butterfly*. Minneapolis: Carolrhoda Books.

Fitzgerald, J. (1993). Literacy and students who are learning English as a second language. *The Reading Teacher, 46*(8), 638–647.

Fitzgerald, J. (1994). Crossing boundaries: What do second-language-learning theories say to reading and writing teachers of English-as-a-second-language learners? *Reading Horizons, 34*(4), 339–355.

Fitzgerald, J. (1995). English-as-a-second-language reading instruction in the United States: A research review. *Journal of Reading Behavior, 27*(2), 115–152.

Fitzgerald, J. (1999). What is this thing called "balance"? *The Reading Teacher, 53*(2), 100–115.

Fleischman, S. (1986). *The whipping boy*. Mahwah, NJ: Troll Associates.

Flesch, R. (1955). *Why Johnny can't read*. New York: HarperCollins.

Flesch, R. (1979, November 1). Why Johnny still can't read. *Family Circle, 26*, 43–46.

Flesch, R. (1981). *Why Johnny still can't read*. New York: HarperCollins.

Flippo, R. F. (2001). *Reading researchers in search of common ground*. Newark, DE: International Reading Association.

Flippo, R. F. (2003). *Assessing readers: Qualitative diagnosis and instruction*. Portsmouth, NH: Heinemann.

Flood, J., & Lapp, D. (1986). Types of texts: The match between what students read in basals and what they encounter in tests. *Reading Research Quarterly, 21*, 284–297.

Flynt, E. S., & Cooter, R. B. (1987). Literal comprehension: The cognitive caboose? *The Kansas Journal of Reading, 3*(1), 8–12.

Flynt, E. S., & Cooter, R. B. (2001). *The Flynt/Cooter Reading Inventory for the Classroom* (4th ed.). Upper Saddle River, NJ: Merrill/Prentice-Hall.

Flynt, E. S., & Cooter, R. B, Jr. (1999). *The Flynt/Cooter English * Español reading inventory.* Upper Saddle River, NJ: Merrill/Prentice-Hall.

Flynt, E. S., & Cooter, R. B., Jr. (2004). *The Flynt/Cooter Reading Inventory for the Classroom* (5th ed.). Upper Saddle River, NJ: Merrill/Prentice-Hall.

Follett, R. (1985). The school textbook adoption process. *Book Research Quarterly, 1,* 19–23.

Foorman, B. R., et al. (1997). Early intervention for children with reading problems: Study designs and preliminary findings. *Learning Disabilities: A Multidisciplinary Journal, 8*(1), 63–71.

Foorman, B. R., Francis, D. J., Fletcher, J. M., Schatschneider, C., & Mehta, P. (1998). The role of instruction in learning to read: Preventing reading failure in at-risk children. *Journal of Educational Psychology, 90,* 37–55.

Forbes, E. (1943). *Johnny Tremain.* Boston: Houghton Mifflin.

Fosnot, C. T. (1996). *Constructivism: Theory, perspectives, and practice.* New York: Teachers College Press.

Fountas, I. C., & Pinnell, G. S. (1996). *Guided reading instruction: Good first teaching for all children.* Portsmouth, NH: Heinemann Educational Books.

Fountas, I. C., & Pinnell, G. S. (1999). *Matching books to readers: Using leveled books in reading, K–3.* Portsmouth, NH: Heinemann Educational Books.

Fountas, I. C., & Pinnell, G. S. (2001). *Guiding readers and writers: Grades 3–6. Teaching comprehension genre, and content literacy.* Portsmouth, NH: Heinemann.

Fowler, G. L. (1982). Developing comprehension skills in primary students through the use of story frames. *The Reading Teacher, 36*(2), 176–179.

Fox, B. J. (1996). *Strategies for word identification: Phonics from a new perspective.* Upper Saddle River, NJ: Merrill/Prentice-Hall.

Fox, B. J. (2004). *Strategies for word identification: Phonics from a new perspective* (3rd ed.). Upper Saddle River, NJ: Merrill/Prentice-Hall.

Fox, B. J., & Hull, M. A. (2002). *Phonics for the teacher of reading* (8th ed.). Upper Saddle River, NJ: Prentice-Hall.

Fox, P. (1973). *The slave dancer.* New York: Bradbury.

Fox, P. (1986). *The moonlight man.* New York: Bradbury.

Fractor, J. S., Woodruff, M. C., Martinez, M. G., & Teale, W. H. (1993). Let's not miss opportunities to promote voluntary reading: Classroom libraries in the elementary school. *The Reading Teacher, 46,* 476–484.

Fredericks, A. D., & Rasinski, T. V. (1990). Working with parents: Involving the uninvolved: How to. *The Reading Teacher, 43*(6), 424–425.

Freeman, D. E., & Freeman, Y. S. (1994). *Between worlds: Access to second language acquisition.* Portsmouth, NH: Heinemann.

Freeman, D. E., & Freeman, Y S. (2000). *Teaching reading in multilingual classrooms.* Portsmouth, NH: Heinemann.

Freeman, Y. S., & Freeman, D. E. (1992). *Whole language for second language learners.* Portsmouth, NH: Heinemann.

Freppon, P. A., & Dahl, K. L. (1998). Balanced instruction: Insights and considerations. *Reading Research Quarterly, 33*(2), 240–251.

Friedman, T. (2005). *The world is flat: A brief history of the twenty-first century.* New York: Farrar, Straus, and Giroux.

Fry, E. (1977). Fry's readability graph: Clarifications, validity, and extension to level 17. *Journal of Reading, 21,* 242–252.

Fry, E. (1980). The new instant word list. *The Reading Teacher, 34,* 284–289.

Fry, E. (2004). Phonics: A large phoneme-grapheme frequency count revisited. *Journal of Literacy Research, 36*(1), 85–98.

Fry, E. B., Kress, J. E., & Fountoukidis, D. L. (2000). *The reading teacher's book of lists* (4th ed.). New York: Jossey-Bass.

Fry, E. B., Polk, J. K., & Fountoukidis, D. (1984). *The reading teacher's book of lists.* Upper Saddle River, NJ: Prentice-Hall.

Gahn, S. M. (1989). A practical guide for teaching writing in the content areas. *Journal of Reading, 33,* 525–531.

Galdone, Paul. *The little red hen.* L. McQueen, Illustrator. New York: Scholastic.

Galindo, R., & Escamilla, K. (1995). A biographical perspective on Chicano educational success. *Urban Review, 27*(1), 1–25.

Gall, M. D., Ward, B. A., Berliner, D. C., Cahen, L. S., Crown, K. A., Elashoff, J. D., et al. (1975). *The effects of teacher use of questioning techniques on student achievement and attitude.* San Francisco: Far West Laboratory for Educational Research and Development.

Gallant, M. G. (1986). *More fun with Dick and Jane.* New York: Penguin Books.

Gallup, G. (1969). *The Gallup poll.* New York: American Institute of Public Opinion.

Gamberg, R., Kwak, W., Hutchings, M., & Altheim, J. (1988). *Learning and loving it: Theme studies in the classroom.* Portsmouth, NH: Heinemann.

Gambrell, L. B. (1978). Getting started with sustained silent reading and keeping it going. *The Reading Teacher, 32,* 328–331.

Gambrell, L. B. (1985). Dialogue journals: Reading-writing instruction. *The Reading Teacher, 38*(6), 512–515.

Gambrell, L. B., & Almasi, J. F. (1996). *Lively discussions: Fostering engaged reading.* Newark, DE: International Reading Association.

Gambrell, L. B., & Bales, R. J. (1986). Mental imagery and the comprehension-monitoring performance of fourth- and fifth-grade poor readers. *Reading Research Quarterly, 21*(4), 454–464.

Gambrell, L. B., & Marnak, B. A. (1997). Incentives and intrinsic motivation to read. In J. T. Guthrie & A. Wigfield (Eds.), *Reading engagement: Motivating readers through integrated instruction* (pp. 205–217). Newark, DE: International Reading Association.

Gambrell, L. B., Morrow, L. M., Neuman, S. B., & Pressley, M. (1999). *Best practices in literacy instruction.* New York: Guilford Press.

Gambrell, L. B., Pfeiffer, W., & Wilson, R. (1985). The effects of retelling upon reading comprehension and recall of text information. *Journal of Educational Research, 78,* 216–220.

Gambrell, L. B., Wilson, R. M., & Gnatt, W. N. (1981). Classroom observations of task-attending behaviors of good and poor readers. *Journal of Educational Research, 74,* 400–404.

Garan, E. M. (2002). *Resisting reading mandates: How to triumph with the truth.* Portsmouth, NH: Heinemann Educational Books.

García, G. E., McKoon, G., & August, D. (2006a). Synthesis: Language and literacy assessment. In D. August & T. Shanahan (Eds.), *Developing literacy in second-language learners: Report of the National Literacy Panel on language-minority children and youth* (pp. 583–596). Mahwah, NJ: Lawrence Erlbaum.

García, G. E., McKoon, G., & August, D. (2006b). Language and literacy assessment of language-minority students. In D. August & T. Shanahan (Eds.), *Developing literacy in second-language learners: Report of the National Literacy Panel on language-minority children and youth* (pp. 597–624). Mahwah, NJ: Lawrence Erlbaum.

Garcia, S. B., & Malkin, D. H. (1993). Toward defining programs and services for culturally and linguistically diverse learners in special education. *Teaching Exceptional Children,* Fall, 52–58.

Gardener, H. (1993). *Frames of mind: The theory of multiple intelligences.* New York: Basic Books.

Garza, C. L. (1990). *Cuadros de familia: Family pictures.* San Francisco: Children's Book Press.

Gates, A. I. (1921). An experimental and statistical study of reading and reading tests (in three parts). *Journal of Educational Psychology, 12,* 303–314, 378–391, 445–465.

Gates, A. I. (1937). The necessary mental age for beginning reading. *Elementary School Journal, 37,* 497–508.

Gates, A. I. (1961). Sex differences in reading ability. *Elementary School Journal, 61,* 431–434.

Gelman, R. G. (1976). *Why can't I fly?* New York: Scholastic.

Gelman, R. G. (1977). *More spaghetti, I say!* New York: Scholastic.

Gelman, R. G. (1985). *Cats and mice.* New York: Scholastic.

Gentile, L. M. (2003). *The oracy instructional guide: Linking research and theory to assessment and instruction.* Carlsbad, CA: Dominie Press, Inc.

Gentry, R. (1987). *Spel... is a four-letter word.* Portsmouth, NH: Heinemann.

George, J. (1972). *Julie of the wolves.* New York: HarperCollins.

Gersten, R., & Baker, S. (2000). *Effective instruction for English-language learners: What we know about effective instructional practices for English-language learners.* Eugene, OR: University of Oregon, Eugene Research Institute.

Gertson, R., Fuchs, L. S., Williams, J. P., & Baker, S. (2001). Teaching reading comprehension strategies to students with learning disabilities: A review of research. *Review of Educational Research, 71*(2), 279–320.

Gibson, E. J., & Levin, H. (1975). *The psychology of reading.* Cambridge, MA: MIT Press.

Gillet, J. W., & Temple, C. (1986). *Understanding reading problems: Assessment and instruction.* Boston: Little, Brown.

Gingerbread man, The. (1985). (K. Schmidt, Illustrator). New York: Scholastic.

Giordano, G. (2001). *Twentieth-century reading education: Understanding practices of today in terms of patterns of the past.* New York: JAI Press.

Gipe, J. P. (1980). Use of a relevant context helps kids learn new word meanings. *The Reading Teacher, 33,* 398–402.

Gipe, J. P. (1987). *Corrective reading techniques for the classroom teacher.* Scottsdale, AZ: Gorsuch Scarisbrick.

Glatthorn, A. A. (1993). Outcome-based education: Reform and the curriculum process. *Journal of Curriculum and Supervision, 8*(4), 354–363.

Glazer, S. M. (1989). Oral language and literacy development. In D. S. Strickland & L. M. Morrow (Eds.), *Emerging literacy: Young children learn to read and write* (pp. 16–26). Newark, DE: International Reading Association.

Glazer, S. M., & Brown, C. S. (1993). *Portfolios and beyond: Collaborative assessment in reading and writing.* Norwood, MA: Christopher-Gordon.

Gleason, J. B. (1989). *The development of language* (2nd ed.). Upper Saddle River, NJ: Merrill/Prentice-Hall.

Glowacki, D., Lanucha, C., & Pietrus, D. (2001). *Improving vocabulary acquisition through direct and indirect teaching.* Syracuse, NY: Educational Resources Information Center (ERIC) Document Reproduction Service.

Goetz, E. T., Reynolds, R. E., Schallert, D. L., & Radin, D. I. (1983). Reading in perspective: What real cops and pretend burglars look for in a story. *Journal of Educational Psychology, 75*(4), 500–510.

Golden, J. M. (1992). The growth of story meaning. *Language Arts, 69*(1), 22–27.

Good, R. H., & Jefferson, G. (1988). Contemporary perspectives on curriculum-based measurement validity. In M. R. Shinn (Ed.), *Advanced applications of curriculum-based measurement* (pp. 61–88). NY: Guilford Press.

Good, R. H., & Kamiski, R. A. (Eds.). (2002). *Dynamic indicators of basic early literacy skills* (6th ed.). Eugene, OR: Institute for the Development of Educational Achievement. Available: *http://dibelsuoregon.edu/*

Good, R. H., Simmons, D. C., & Kame'enui, E. J. (2001). The importance and decision-making utility of a continuum of fluency-based indicators of foundational reading skills for third-grade high-stakes outcomes. *Scientific Studies of Reading, 5*(3), 257–288.

Good, T. (1979). Teacher effectiveness in the elementary school. *The Journal of Teacher Education, 30,* 52–64.

Goodman, K., Shannon, P., Freeman, Y., & Murphy, S. (1988). *Report card on basal readers.* Katona, NY: Owen.

Goodman, K., Smith, E. B., Meredith, R., & Goodman, Y. M. (1987). *Language and thinking in school: A whole-language curriculum.* Katona, NY: Owen.

Goodman, K. S. (1967). Reading: A psycholinguistic guessing game. *Journal of the Reading Specialist, 6,* 126–135.

Goodman, K. S. (1968). *Study of children's behavior while reading orally* (Final Report, Project No. S 425). Washington, DC: U.S. Department of Health, Education, and Welfare.

Goodman, K. S. (1976). Behind the eye: What happens in reading. In H. Singer & R. B. Ruddell (Eds.), *Theoretical models and processes of reading,* 2nd Ed. (pp. 470–496). Newark, DE: International Reading Association.

Goodman, K. S. (1985). Unity in reading. In H. Singer & R. B. Ruddell (Eds.), *Theoretical models and processes of reading* (3rd ed.). Newark, DE: International Reading Association.

Goodman, K. S. (1986). *What's whole in whole language?* Ontario, Canada: Scholastic.

Goodman, K. S. (1987). Look what they've done to Judy Blume!: The "basalization" of children's literature. *The New Advocate, 1*(1), 29–41.

Goodman, K. S., & Goodman, Y. M. (1983). Reading and writing relationships: Pragmatic functions. *Language Arts, 60*(5), 590–599.

Goodman, Y. M. (1986). Children coming to know literacy. In W. H. Teale & E. Sulzby (Eds.), *Emergent literacy: Writing and reading* (pp. 1–14). Norwood, NJ: Ablex.

Goodman, Y. M., & Altwerger, B. (1981). *Print awareness in preschool children: A study of the development of literacy in preschool children.* Occasional paper, Program in Language and Literacy. Tucson, AZ: University of Arizona.

Gopnik, A., Meltzoff, A. N., & Kuhl, P. K. (1999). *The scientist in the crib: Minds, brains, and how children learn.* New York: William Morrow and Co.

Gordon, C. J., & Braun, C. (1983). Using story schema as an aid to reading and writing. *The Reading Teacher, 37*(2), 116–121.

Gordon, D. (2001). Practical suggestions for supporting speaking and listening in classrooms. In P. G. Smith (Ed.), *Talking classrooms: Shaping children's learning through oral language instruction* (pp. 57–73). Newark, DE: International Reading Association.

Gordon, N. (Ed.). (1984). *Classroom experiences: The writing process in action.* Exeter, NH: Heinemann.

Goswami, U. (2000). Phonological and lexical processes. In M. L. Kamil, P. B. Mosenthal, P. D. Pearson, & R. Barr (Eds.), *Handbook of reading research* (Vol. 3) (pp. 251–268). Mahwah, NJ: Lawrence Erlbaum Associates.

Goswami, U. (2001). Early phonological development and the acquisition of literacy. In S. B. Neuman & D. K. Dickinson (Eds.), *Handbook of early literacy research* (pp. 111–125). New York: Guildford Press.

Goswami, U., & Bryant, P. (1990). *Phonological skills and learning to read.* East Sussex, UK: Erlbaum.

Goswami, U., & Mead, F. (1992). Onset and rime awareness and analogies in reading. *Reading Research Quarterly, 27*(2), 152–163.

Gough, P. B. (1972). One second of reading. In J. F. Kavanagh & I. G. Mattingly (Eds.), *Language by ear and by eye.* Cambridge, MA: MIT Press.

Gove, M. K. (1983). Clarifying teacher's beliefs about reading. *The Reading Teacher, 37*(3), 261–268.

Graesser, A., Golding, J. M., & Long, D. L. (1991). Narrative representation and comprehension. In R. Barr, M. L. Kamil, P. Mosenthal, & P. D. Pearson (Eds.), *Handbook of reading research:* Vol. 2. (pp. 171–205). New York: Longman.

Graves, D. H. (1983). *Writing: Teachers and children at work.* Portsmouth, NH: Heinemann.

Graves, M. F., & Slater, W. H. (1987). Development of reading vocabularies in rural disadvantaged students, intercity disadvantaged students and middle class suburban students. Paper presented at AERA conference, Washington, DC.

Greaney, V. (1994). World illiteracy. In F. Lehr & J. Osborn (Eds.), *Reading, language, and literacy: Instruction for the twenty-first century.* Hillsdale, NJ: Erlbaum.

Greene, F. P. (1970). *Paired reading.* Unpublished manuscript, Syracuse University, New York.

Greene, F. P. (1973). *OPIN.* Unpublished paper, McGill University, Montreal, Quebec, Canada.

Greenhalgh, K. S., & Strong, C. J. (2001). Literate language features in spoken narratives of children with typical language and children with language impairments. *Language, Speech, & Hearing Services in Schools, 32*(2), 114–126.

Greenwald, R., Hedges, L., & Laine, R. (1996). The effect of school resources on student achievement. *Review of Educational Research, 66,* 361–396.

Gregg, M., & Sekeres, D. C. (2006). Supporting children's reading of expository text in the geography classroom. *The Reading Teacher, 60*(2), 102–110.

Gregory, G. H., & Chapman, C. (2002). *Differentiated instructional strategies: One size doesn't fit all.* Thousand Oaks, CA: Corwin Press.

Griffith, L. W., & Rasinski, T. V. (2004). A focus on fluency: How one teacher incorporated fluency with her reading curriculum. *The Reading Teacher 58*(2), 126–137.

Griffith, P. L., & Olson, M. W. (1992). Phonemic awareness helps beginning readers break the code. *The Reading Teacher, 45,* 516–523.

Grigg, W. S., Daaine, M. C., Jin, Y., & Campbell, J. R. (2003). *The nation's report card: Reading 2002* (NCES Report No. 2003-521). Washinton, DC: U.S. Department of Education, National Center for Educational Statistics.

Groff, P. J. (1984). Resolving the letter name controversy. *The Reading Teacher, 37*(4), 384–389.

Groom, W. (1986). *Forrest Gump.* New York: Pocket Books.

Gross, A. D. (1978). The relationship between sex differences and reading ability in an Israeli kibbutz system. In D. Feitelson (Ed.), *Cross-cultural perspectives on reading and reading research* (pp. 72–88). Newark, DE: International Reading Association.

Grossen, B. (1997). *30 years of research: What we know about how children learn to read.* Santa Cruz, CA: The Center for the Future of Teaching and Learning.

Guilfoile, E. (1957). *Nobody listens to Andrew.* Cleveland, OH: Modern Curriculum Press.

Gunderson, L. (1991). *ESL literacy instruction: A guidebook to theory and practice.* Upper Saddle River, NJ: Prentice-Hall.

Gunn, B., Biglan, A., Smolkowski, K., & Ary, D. (2000). The efficacy of supplemental instruction in decoding skills for Hispanic and non-Hispanic students in early elementary school. *The Journal of Special Education, 34,* 90–103.

Gunn, B. Smolkowski, K., Biglan, A., & Black, C. (2002). Supplemental instruction in decoding skills for

Hispanic and non-Hispanic students in early elementary school: A follow-up. *The Journal of Special Education, 36,* 69–79.

Guskey, T. R., Smith, J. K., Smith, L. F., Crooks, T., & Flockton, L. (2006). Literacy assessment, New Zealand style. *Educational Leadership, 64*(2), 74–79.

Guszak, F. J. (1967). Teacher questioning and reading. *The Reading Teacher, 21*(1), 227–234.

Guthrie, J. T. (1982). Effective teaching practices. *The Reading Teacher, 35*(7), 766–768.

Guthrie, J. T., & McCann, A. D. (1997). Characteristics of classrooms that promote motivations and strategies for learning. In J. T. Guthrie & A. Wigfield (Eds.), *Reading engagement: Motivating readers through integrated instruction.* Newark, DE: International Reading Association.

Guthrie, J. T., Seifert, M., Burnham, N. A., & Caplan, R. J. (1974). The maze technique to assess and monitor reading comprehension. *The Reading Teacher, 28*(2), 161–168.

Guthrie, J. Y., Hoa, L. W., Wigfield, A., Tonks, S. M., & Perencevich, K. C. (2006). From spark to fire: Can situational reading interest lead to long-term reading motivation? *Reading Research and Instruction, 45*(2), 91–117.

Gwynne, F. (1970). *A chocolate moose for dinner.* New York: Windmill Books.

Gwynne, F. (1976). *The king who rained.* New York: Windmill Books.

Gwynne, F. (1999). *A chocolate moose for dinner.* New York: Bt Bound.

Hagerty, P. (1992). *Reader's workshop: Real reading.* New York: Scholastic.

Haggard, M. R. (1986). The vocabulary self-collection strategy: Using student interest and world knowledge to enhance vocabulary growth. *Journal of Reading, 29*(7), 634–642.

Hagood, B. F. (1997). Reading and writing with help from story grammar. *Teaching Exceptional Children, 29*(4), 10–14.

Hall, L. (2004). Comprehending expository text: Promising strategies for struggling readers and students with reading disabilities? *Reading Research and Instruction, 44*(2), 75–95.

Hall, M. A. (1978). *The language experience approach for teaching reading: A research perspective.* Newark, DE: International Reading Association.

Hall, M. A. (1981). *Teaching reading as a language experience,* 3rd Ed. Upper Saddle River, NJ: Merrill/Prentice-Hall.

Hall, N. (1987). *The emergence of literacy.* Portsmouth, NH: Heinemann.

Hall, R. (1984). *Sniglets.* New York: Collier Books.

Haller, E. J., & Waterman, M. (1985). The criteria of reading group assignments. *The Reading Teacher, 38,* 772–781.

Halliday, M. A. K. (1975). *Learning how to mean: Explorations in the development of language.* London: Edward Arnold.

Hallinan, M. T., & Sorensen, A. B. (1985). Ability grouping and student friendships. *American Educational Research Journal, 22,* 485–499.

Halpern, H. (1981). An attitude survey of uninterrupted sustained silent reading. *Reading Horizons, 21,* 272–279.

Hammill, D., & Larsen, S. C. (1974). The relationship of selected auditory perceptual skills and reading ability. *Journal of Learning Disabilities, 7,* 429–435.

Handel, R. D. (1999). The multiple meanings of family literacy. *Education of Urban Society, 32*(1), 127–144.

Hansen, J. (1981). The effects of inference training and practice on young children's reading comprehension. *Reading Research Quarterly, 16*(3), 391–417.

Hansen, J. (1987). *When writers read.* Portsmouth, NH: Heinemann.

Hare, V. C, & Borchordt, K. M. (1984). Direct instruction of summarization skills. *Reading Research Quarterly, 20*(1), pp. 62–78.

Harkrader, M. A., & Moore, R. (1997). Literature preferences of fourth graders. *Reading Research and Instruction, 36*(4), 325–339.

Harp, B. (1988). When the principal asks: "Why are your kids singing during reading time?" *The Reading Teacher, 41*(4), 454–457.

Harp, B. (1989). What do we do in the place of ability grouping? *The Reading Teacher, 42,* 534–535.

Harp, B. (1989a). What do we do in the place of ability grouping? *The Reading Teacher, 42,* 534–535.

Harp, B. (1989b). When the principal asks: "Why don't you ask comprehension questions?" *The Reading Teacher, 42*(8), 638–639.

Harris, A. J., & Hodges, R. E. (Eds.). (1981). *A dictionary of reading and related terms.* Newark, DE: International Reading Association.

Harris, A. J., & Sipay, E. R. (1990). *How to increase reading ability: A guide to developmental and remedial methods* (9th ed.). New York: Longman.

Harris, T., Matteoni, L., Anderson, L., & Creekmore, M. (1975). *Keys to reading.* Oklahoma City: Economy.

Harris, T. L., & Hodges, R. E. (Eds.). (1981). *A dictionary of reading and related terms.* Newark, DE: International Reading Association.

Harris, T. L., & Hodges, R. E. (Eds.). (1995). *The literacy dictionary: The vocabulary of reading and writing.* Newark, DE: International Reading Association.

Harste, J. C., & Burke, C. L. (1977). A new hypothesis for reading teacher research: Both the teaching and learning of reading are theoretically based. In Pearson, D. P. (Ed.). *Reading: Theory, research, and practice* (pp. 32–40). Clemson, SC: National Reading Conference.

Harste, J. C., Short, K. G., & Burke, C. (1988). *Creating classrooms for authors: The reading writing connection.* Portsmouth, NH: Heinemann.

Harste, J. C., Woodward, V. A., & Burke, C. L. (1984). *Language stories and literacy lessons.* Portsmouth, NH: Heinemann.

Hart, B., & Risley, T. R. (1995). *Meaningful differences in the everyday experience of young American children.* Baltimore, MD: Paul H. Brookes.

Hart, B., & Risley, T. R. (2002). *The social world of children: Learning to talk.* Baltimore, MD: Paul H. Brookes.

Harwayne, S. (1992). *Lasting impressions.* Portsmouth, NH: Heinemann.

Hasbrouck, J., & Tindal, G. (2006). Oral reading fluency norms: A valuable assessment tool for reading teachers. *The Reading Teacher, 59*(7), 636–645.

Hasbrouck, J. E., & Tindal, G. (1992). Curriculum-based oral reading fluency for students in grades 2 through 5. *Teaching Exceptional Children, 24*(3), 41–44.

Haselkorn, D., & Harris, L. (2001). *The essential profession: American education at the crossroads.* Belmont, MA: Recruiting New Teachers.

Hawking, S. W. (1988). *A brief history of time: From the big bang to black holes.* Toronto: Bantam.

Heald-Taylor, G. (1989). *The administrator's guide to whole language.* Katona, NY: Owen.

Heald-Taylor, G. (1991). *Whole language strategies for ESL students.* San Diego, CA: Dominie Press.

Heald-Taylor, G. (2001). *The beginning reading handbook: Strategies for success.* Portsmouth, NH: Heinemann.

Healy, J. M. (1990). *Endangered minds: Why children don't think and what can be done about it.* New York: Touchstone.

Heath. (no date). *Quill* [computer program]. Lexington, MA: Heath.

Heathington, B. S. (1990). Test review: Concepts about print test. In R. B. Cooter, Jr. (Ed.). *The teacher's guide to reading tests* (pp. 110–114). Scottsdale, AZ: Gorsuch Scarisbrick.

Heckleman, R. G. (1966). Using the neurological impress remedial reading technique. *Academic Therapy, 1,* 235–239, 250.

Heckleman, R. G. (1969). A neurological impress method of remedial reading instruction. *Academic Therapy, 4,* 277–282.

Heide, F. P., & Gilliland, J. H. (1990). *Day of Ahmed's secret.* New York: Lothrop, Lee & Shepard Books.

Heilman, A. W., Blair, T. R., & Rupley, W. H. (2001). *Principles and practices of teaching reading,* 10th Ed. Upper Saddle River, NJ: Merrill/Prentice-Hall.

Henderson, J. (2001). *Incidental vocabulary acquisition: Learning new vocabulary from reading silently and listening to stories read aloud.* Syracuse, NY: Educational Resources Information Center (ERIC) Document Reproduction Service.

Henk, W. A. (1983). Adapting the NIM to improve comprehension. *Academic Therapy, 19,* 97–101.

Henk, W. A., & Holmes, B. C. (1988). Effects of content-related attitude on the comprehension and retention of expository text. *Reading Psychology, 9*(3), 203–225.

Hennings, K. (1974). Drama reading: An on-going classroom activity at the elementary school level. *Elementary English, 51,* 48–51.

Henwood, C. (1988). *Frogs* (Barrie Watts, Photographer). London, NY: Franklin Watts.

Herber, H. L. (1978). *Teaching reading in the content areas,* 2nd Ed. Upper Saddle River, NJ: Prentice-Hall.

Heymsfeld, C. R. (1989, March). Filling the hole in whole language. *Educational Leadership,* pp. 65–68.

Hiebert, E. (1978). Preschool children's understanding of written language. *Child Development, 49,* 1231–1241.

Hiebert, E. (1981). Developmental patterns and interrelationships of preschool children's print awareness. *Reading Research Quarterly, 16,* 236–260.

Hiebert E., & Ham, D. (1981). *Young children and environmental print.* Paper presented at the annual meeting of the National Reading Conference, Dallas, TX.

Hiebert, E. H. (1983). An examination of ability grouping for reading instruction. *Reading Research Quarterly,* 18, 231–255.

Hiebert, E. H. (1999). Text matters in learning to read. *The Reading Teacher, 52*(6), 552–566.

Hiebert, E. H. (2006). Becoming fluent: Repeated reading with scaffolded texts. In S. J. Samuels & A. E. Farstrup (Eds.), *What research has to say about fluency instruction* (pp. 204–226). Newark, DE: International Reading Association.

Hiebert, E. H., & Colt, J. (1989). Patterns of literature-based reading. *The Reading Teacher, 43*(1), 14–20.

Hiebert, E. H., & Fisher, P. (2006). Fluency from the first: What works with first graders. In T. V. Rasinski, C. Blachowicz, & K. Lems (Eds.). *Fluency instruction: Research-based best practices* (pp. 279–294). New York: Guilford Press.

Hiebert, E. H., & Martin, L. A. (2001). The texts of beginning reading instruction. In S. B. Neuman & D. K. Dickinson (Eds.), *Handbook of Early Literacy.* New York: Guildford Press.

Hiebert, E. H., Pearson, P. D., Taylor, B. M. Richardson, V., & Paris, S. G. (1998). *Every child a reader: Applying reading research in the classroom.* Ann Arbor, MI: Center for the Improvement of Early Reading Achievement.

Hill, B., & Ruptic, C. (1994). *Practical aspects of authentic assessment: Putting the pieces together.* Norwood, MA: Christopher-Gordon.

Hill, S. (1990a). *Raps and rhymes.* Armadale, Victoria, Australia: Eleanor Curtain.

Hill, S. (1990b). *Readers theatre: Performing the text.* Armadale, Victoria, Australia: Eleanor Curtain.

Hintze, J. M., & Christ, T. J. (2004). An examination of variability as a function of passage variance in CBM progress monitoring. *School Psychology Review, 33*(2), 204–217.

Hirsch, E. D. (1987). *Cultural literacy: What every American needs to know.* Boston: Houghton Mifflin.

Hirschfelder, A. B., & Singer, B. R. (1992). *Rising voices: Writing of young Native Americans.* New York: Scribner's.

Hobbs, R. (2005). Literacy for the information age. In J. Flood, S. B. Heath, & D. Lapp (Eds.), *Handbook of research on teaching literacy through the communicative and visual arts* (pp. 7–14). Mahwah, NJ: Lawrence Erlbaum Associates.

Hoffman, J. V. (1987). Rethinking the role of oral reading in basal instruction. *The Elementary School Journal, 87*(3), 367–374.

Hoffman, J. V. (2001). *WORDS (on words in leveled texts for beginning readers).* Ann Arbor, MI: Center for the Improvement of Early Reading Achievement. Available at *http://www.ciera.org/library/presos/2001/*

Hoffman, J. V. (2001). *WORDS (on Words in Leveled Texts for Beginning Readers).* Paper presented at 2001 National Reading Conference, San Antonio, Texas.

Hoffman, J. V. (2003). Foreword. In T. V. Rasinski's *The Fluent Reader: Oral reading strategies for building word recognition, fluency, and comprehension* (pp. 5–6). New York: Scholastic.

Hoffman, J. V., McCarthey, S. J., Abbott, J., Christian, C., Corman, L., Curry, et al. (1994). So what's new in the new basals? A focus on first grade. *Journal of Reading Behavior, 26*(1), 47–73.

Hoffman, J. V., Roser, N., & Battle, J. (1993). Reading aloud in classrooms: From the modal to a "model." *The Reading Teacher, 46*(6), 496–503.

Hoffman, J. V., Sailors, M., Duffy, G., & Beretvas, S. N. (2004). The effective classroom literacy environment: Examining the validity of the TEX-IN3 Observation System. *Journal of Literacy Research, 36*(3), 303–334.

Hoffman, J. V., & Segel, K. W. (1982). *Oral reading instruction: A century of controversy.* (ERIC Document Reproduction Service).

Hoffman, M. (1991). *Amazing grace.* New York: Dial Books.

Holdaway, D. (1979). *The foundations of literacy.* Exeter, NH: Heinemann.

Holdaway, D. (1981). Shared book experience: Teaching reading using favorite books. *Theory Into Practice, 21,* 293–300.

Holdaway, D. (1984). *Stability and change in literacy learning.* Portsmouth, NH: Heinemann.

Hollingsworth, P. M. (1970). An experiment with the impress method of teaching reading. *The Reading Teacher, 24,* 112–114.

Hollingsworth, P. M. (1978). An experimental approach to the impress method of teaching reading. *The reading Teacher, 31,* 624–626

Hollingsworth, P. M., & Reutzel, D. R. (1988). Get a grip on comprehension. *Reading Horizons, 29*(1), 71–78.

Hollingsworth, P. M., & Reutzel, D. R. (1990). Prior knowledge, content-related attitude, reading comprehension: Testing Mathewson's affective model of reading. *The Journal of Educational Research, 83*(4), 194–200.

Holmes, J. A. (1953). *The substrata-factor theory of reading.* Berkeley, CA: California Books.

Homan, S. P., Klesius, J. P., & Hite, C. (1993). Effects of repeated readings and non-repetitive strategies on students' fluency and comprehension. *Journal of Educational Research, 87*(2), 94–99.

Honig, B., Diamond, L., & Gutlohn, L. (2000). *Teaching reading: Sourcebook for kindergarten through eighth grade.* Novato, CA: Arena Press.

Hook, P. E., & Jones, S. (2002). The importance of automaticity and fluency for efficient reading comprehension. *Perspectives, 28*(1), 9–14.

Hopkins, C. (1979). Using every-pupil response techniques in reading instruction. *The Reading Teacher, 33,* 173–175.

Hoskisson, K., & Tompkins, G. E. (1987). *Language arts: Content and teaching strategies.* Upper Saddle River, NJ: Merrill/Prentice-Hall.

Houston, J. (1977). *Frozen fire.* New York: Atheneum.

Hoyt, L. (1999). *Revisit, reflect; retell: Strategies for improving reading comprehension.* Portsmouth, NH: Heinemann.

Huber, J. A. (2004). A closer look at SQ3R. *Reading Improvement, 41*(2), 108–112.

Huck, C. S., Helper, S., & Hickman, J. (1987). *Children's literature in the elementary school.* New York: Holt, Rinehart and Winston.

Huck, C. S., & Kuhn, D. Y. (1968). *Children's literature in the elementary school.* New York: Holt, Rinehart and Winston.

Hudson, R. F., Lane, H. B., & Pullen, P. C. (2005). Reading fluency assessment and instruction: What, why, and how? *The Reading Teacher, 58*(8), 702–714.

Huebner, C. E. (2000). Promoting toddlers language development: A randomized trial of a community-based intervention. *Journal of Applied Developmental Psychology, 21,* 513–535.

Huebner, C. E. (2001). *Hear-and-say reading with toddlers.* Bainbridge Island, WA: Bainbridge Island Rotary (instructional video). To order, contact: Hear and Say Reading Program, Rotary Club of Bainbridge Island, PO Box 11286, Bainbridge Island, WA 98110.

Huebner, C. E., & Meltzoff, A. N. (2005). Intervention to change parent-child reading syle: A comparison of instructional methods. *Applied Developmental Psychology, 26,* 296–313.

Huey, E. B. (1908). *The psychology and pedagogy of reading.* New York: Macmillan.

Hughes, T. O. (1975). *Sentence-combining: A means of increasing reading comprehension.* Kalamazoo: Western Michigan University, Department of English.

Hull, M. A. (1989). *Phonics for the teacher of reading.* Upper Saddle River, NJ: Merrill/Prentice-Hall.

Hunt, J. (2004). *Volcano!* Northborough, MA: Sundance.

Hunt, L. C. (1970). Effect of self-selection, interest, and motivation upon independent, instructional, and frustrational levels. *Reading Teacher, 24,* 146–151.

Hunter, M. (1984). Knowing, teaching and supervising. In P. L. Hosford (Ed.), *Using what we know about teaching.* Alexandria, VA: Association for Supervision and Curriculum Development.

Hunter, P. (2003). "A tale of two schools" takes an intimate look at the national reading crisis. Available at *http://www.readingrockets.org/pressrelease/632*

Huot, B., & Neal, M. (2006). Writing assessment. In C. A. MacArthur, S. Graham, & J. Fitzgerald (Eds.), *Handbook of writing research.* New York: Guilford.

Hymes, D. (Ed.). (1964). *Language in culture and society.* New York: HarperCollins.

Invernizzi, M., Juel, C., & Rosemary, C. (1997). A community volunteer tutorial that works. *Reading Teacher, 50*(4), 304–311.

Irvin, J. L. (2001). Assisting struggling readers in building vocabulary and background knowledge. *Voices from the Middle, 8*(4), 37–43.

Irwin, J. W. (1996). *Teaching reading comprehension processes,* 2nd Ed. Englewood Cliffs, NJ: Prentice-Hall.

Jachym, N. K., Allington, R. L., & Broikou, K. A. (1989). Estimating the cost of seatwork. *The Reading Teacher, 43,* 30–37.

Jacobs, H. H., & Borland, J. H. (1986). The interdisciplinary concept model: Theory and practice. *Gifted Child Quarterly, 30*(4), 159–163.

Jaffe, N. (1993). *The uninvited guest and other Jewish holiday tales.* New York: Scholastic.

Jancoloa, L. (n.d.). *Six-trait writing.* Retrieved November 3, 2006, from *http://www.kent.k12.wa.us/staff/LindaJancola/6Trait/6-trait.html*

Jenkins, J. R., Fuchs, L. S., Van den Broek, P., Espin, C., & Deno, S. L. (2003). Accuracy and fluency in list and context reading of skilled and RD groups: Absolute and relative performance levels. *Learning Disabilities Research and Practice, 18*(4), 237–245.

Jenkins, R. (1990). *Whole language in Australia.* Scholastic Co. workshop at Brigham Young University, Provo, UT.

Jennings, J. H., Caldwell, J., & Lerner, J. W. (2006). *Reading problems: Assessment and teaching strategies* (5th ed.). Boston: Pearson Allyn and Bacon.

Jobe, F. W. (1976). *Screening vision in schools.* Newark, DE: International Reading Association.

Johns, J. L. (1980). First graders' concepts about print. *Reading Research Quarterly, 15,* 529–549.

Johns, J. L. (1986). Students: Perceptions of reading: Thirty years of inquiry. In D. B. Yaden, Jr. & S. Templeton (Eds.), *Awareness and beginning literacy: Conceptualizing what it means to read and write* (pp. 31–40). Portsmouth, NH: Heinemann.

Johns, J. L., & Ellis, D. W. (1976). Reading: Children tell it like it is. *Reading World, 16,* 115–128.

Johns, J. L., & Johns, A. L. (1971). How do children in the elementary school view the reading process? *The Michigan Reading Journal, 5,* 44–53.

Johns, J. L., & Lunn, M. K. (1983). The informal reading inventory: 1910–1980. *Reading World, 23*(1), 8–18.

Johnson, D. (1989). *Pressing problems in world literacy: The plight of the homeless.* Paper presented at the 23rd annual meeting of the Utah Council of the International Reading Association, Salt Lake City, UT.

Johnson, D., & Pearson, P. D. (1984). *Teaching reading vocabulary.* New York: Holt, Rinehart and Winston.

Johnson, D. D. (1973). Sex differences in reading across cultures. *Reading Research Quarterly, 9*(1), 67–86.

Johnson, D. D. (2001). *Vocabulary in the elementary and middle school.* Needham Heights, MA: Allyn & Bacon.

Johnson, D. D., & Baumann, J. F. (1984). Word identification. In P. D. Pearson (Ed.), *Handbook of reading research* (pp. 583–608). New York: Longman.

Johnson, D. D., & Pearson. P. D. (1975). Skills management systems: A critique. *The Reading Teacher, 28,* 757–764.

Johnson, D. D., & Pearson, P. D. (1984). *Teaching reading vocabulary.* New York: Holt, Rinehart and Winston.

Johnson, D. W. (1976). *Jack and the beanstalk* (D. William Johnson, Illustrator). Boston: Little, Brown.

Johnson, D. W., & Johnson, R. T. (1999). *Learning together and alone: Cooperative, competitive, and individualistic learning* (5th ed.). Boston: Allyn & Bacon.

Johnson, D. W., Maruyama, G., Johnson, R. T., Nelson, D., & Skon, L. (1981). Effects of cooperative, competitive, and individualistic goal structures on achievement: A meta-analysis. *Psychological Bulletin, 89,* 47–62.

Johnson, T. D., & Louis, D. R. (1987). *Literacy through literature.* Portsmouth, NH: Heinemann.

Johnston, F. R. (1998). The reader, the text, and the task: Learning words in first grade. *The Reading Teacher, 51,* 666–676.

Johnston, P. H. (1992). *Constructive evaluation of literate activity.* New York, NY: Longman Publishers.

Jones, M. B., & Nessel, D. D. (1985). Enhancing the curriculum with experience stories. *The Reading Teacher, 39,* 18–23.

Jongsma, K. S. (1989). Questions & answers: Portfolio assessment. *The Reading Teacher, 43*(3), 264–265.

Jongsma, K. S. (1990). Questions & Answers: Collaborative Learning, *The Reading Teacher, 43*(4), 346–347.

Jordan, G. E., Snow, C. E., & Porche, M. V. (2000). Project EASE: The effect of a family literacy project on kindergarten students' early literacy skills. *Reading Research Quarterly, 35,* 524–546.

Joseph, D. G., Flynt, E. S., & Cooter, R. B., Jr. (1987, March). *Diagnosis and correction of reading difficulties: A new model.* Paper presented at the National Association of School Psychologists annual convention, New Orleans, LA.

Juel, C. (1988). Learning to read and write: A longitudinal study of the fifty-four children from first through fourth grade. *Journal of Educational Psychology, 80*(4), 437–447.

Juel, C. (1991). Cross-age tutoring between student athletes and at-risk children. *Reading Teacher, 45*(3), 178–186.

Juel, C., & Minden-Cupp, C. (2004). Learning to read words: Linguistic units and instructional strategies. In R. B. Ruddell, & N. J. Unrau (Eds.), *Theoretical models and processes of reading* (5th ed.) (pp. 313–364). Newark DE: International Reading Association.

Juster, N. (1961). *The phantom tollbooth.* New York: Random House.

Justice, L. M., Pence, K., Bowles, R. B., & Wiggins, A. (2006). An investigation of four hypotheses concerning the order by which 4-year-old children learn the alphabet letters. *Early Childhood Research Quarterly, 21*(3), 374–389.

Kaderavek, J. N., & Justice, L. M. (2005). The effect of book genre in repeated readings of mothers and their children with language impairment: A pilot investigation. *Child Language Teaching and Therapy, 21*(1), 75–92.

Kagan, J. (1966). Reflection-impulsivity: The generality and dynamics of conceptual tempo. *Journal of Abnormal Psychology, 71,* 17–24.

Kame'enui, E. J., & Simmons, D. C. (2001). The DNA of reading fluency. *Scientific Studies of Reading, 5*(3), 203–210.

Kang, H. W. (1994). Helping second language readers learn from content area text through collaboration and support. *The Journal of Reading, 37*(8), 646–652.

Karlsen, B., & Gardner, E. F. (1984). *Stanford diagnostic reading test* (3rd ed.). New York: Harcourt Brace.

Kaufman, A. S., & Kaufman, N. L. (1997). *Kaufman Test of Educational Achievement-Normative Update (K-TEA/NU).* Circle Pines, MN: AGS.

Kearsley, R. (1973). The newborn's response to auditory stimulation: A demonstration of orienting and defensive behavior. *Child Development, 44,* 582–590.

Keegan, M. (1991). *Pueblo boy: Growing up in two worlds.* New York: Cobblehill Books.

Keene, E. O., & Zimmerman, S. (1997). *Mosaic of thought: Teaching comprehension in a reader's workshop.* Portsmouth, NH: Heinemann.

Keillor, G., Pankake, J., & Pankake, M. (1988). *A prairie home companion folk song book.* New York: Viking.

Keith, S. (1981). *Politics of textbook selection* (Research report No. 81-AT). Stanford, CA: Stanford University School of Education, Institute for Research on School Finance and Governance.

Kemp, M. (1987). *Watching children read and write.* Portsmouth, NH: Heinemann.

Kessen, W., Levine, J., & Wendrich, K. (1979). The imitation of pitch in infants. *Infant Behavior and Development, 2,* 93–100.

Kiefer, Z., Levstik, L. S., & Pappas, C. C. (1998). *An integrated language perspective in the elementary school: An action approach* (3rd ed.). Boston: Addison-Wesley.

Killilea, M. (1954). *Karen.* New York: Dodd, Mead.

Kintsch, W. (1974). *The representation of meaning in memory.* Hillsdale, NJ: Erlbaum.

Kintsch, W. (1998). *Comprehension: A paradigm for cognition.* Cambridge: Cambridge University Press.

Kintsch, W. (2004). The construction-integration model of text comprehension and its implications for instruction. In R. B. Ruddell & N. J. Unrau (Eds.), *Theoretical models and processes of reading* (5th ed.) (pp. 94–120). Newark, DE: International Reading Association.

Kintsch, W., & Kintsch, E. (2005). Comprehension. In S. G. Paris & S. A. Stahl (Eds.), *Children's reading comprehension and assessment* (pp. 71–92). Mahwah, NJ: Lawrence Erlbaum Associates.

Kirsch, I. S., Jungeblut, A., Jenkins, L., & Kolstad, A. (1993). *Adult literacy in America: A first look at the results of the national adult literacy survey.* Washington, DC: National Center for Educational Statistics.

Kirshner, D., & Whitson, J. A. (1997). *Situated cognition: Social, semiotic, and psychological perspectives.* Mahwah, NJ: Lawrence Erlbaum Associates.

Klare, G. R. (1963). Assessing readability. *Reading Research Quarterly, 10,* 62–102.

Klenk, L., & Kibby, M. W. (2000). Remediating reading difficulties: Appraising the past, reconciling the present, constructing the future. In M. L. Kamil, P. B. Mosenthal, P. D. Pearson, and R. Barr (Eds.), *Handbook of reading research,* Vol. 3. (pp. 667–690). Mahwah, NJ: Lawrence Erlbaum Associates.

Klobukowski, P. (2000). Parents, buddy journals, and teacher response. In T. V. Rasinski, N. D. Padak, et al. (Eds.), *Motivating recreational reading and promoting home-school connections* (pp. 51–52). Newark, DE: International Reading Association.

Knapp, M. S. (1991). *What is taught, and how, to the children of poverty: Interim report from a two-year investigation.* Menlo Park, CA: SRI.

Kornblith, G. J., & Lasser, C. (2005). "The truth, the whole truth, and nothing but the truth": Writing, producing, and using college-level American history textbooks. *Journal of American History, 91*(4), 1380–1382.

Koskinen, P., Wilson, R., & Jensema, C. (1985). Closed-captioned television: A new tool for reading instruction. *Reading World, 24,* 1–7.

Koskinen, P. S., Blum, I. H., Bisson, S. A., Phillips, S. M., Creamer, T. S., & Baker, T. K. (1999). Shared reading, books, and audiotapes: Supporting diverse students in school and at home. *The Reading Teacher, 52*(5), 430–444.

Kownslar, A. O. (1977). *People and our world: A study of world history.* New York: Holt, Rinehart and Winston.

Kozol, J. (1985). *Illiterate America*. New York: New American Library.

Kozol, J. (1991). *Savage inequalities*. New York: Harper Perennial.

Krashen, S. (1982). *Principles and practices in second language acquisition*. New York: Pergamon Press.

Krashen, S. (1992). *The power of reading*. Englewood, CO: Libraries Unlimited.

Krashen, S. (1993). *The power of reading: Insights from the research*. Englewood. CO: Libraries Unlimited.

Krashen, S., & Biber, D. (1988). *On course*. Sacramento, CA: CABE.

Krashen, S. D. (1985). *The input hypothesis: Issues and implication*. New York: Longman.

Krauss, R. (1945). *The carrot seed*. New York: Scholastic, Inc.

Krech, B. (2000). *Fresh & fun: Teaching with kids' names* (Grades K–2). New York: Scholastic, Inc.

Krulik, N. E. (1991). *My picture book of the planets*. New York: Scholastic.

Kuby, P., & Aldridge, J. (1994). Direct vs. indirect environmental print instruction and early reading ability in kindergarten children. *Reading Psychology 18*(2), 91–104.

Kuby, P., & Aldridge, J. (1997). Direct vs. indirect environmental print instruction and early reading ability in kindergarten children. *Reading Psychology 15*(1), 1–9.

Kuby, P., Aldridge, J., & Snyder, S. (1994). Developmental progression of environmental print recognition in kindergarten children. *Reading Psychology 18*(2), 91–104.

Kuby, P., Kirkland, L., & Aldridge, J. (1996). Learning about environmental print through picture books. *Early Childhood Education Journal, 24*(1), 33–36.

Kuchinskas, G., & Radencich, M. C. (1986). *The semantic mapper*. Gainesville, FL: Teacher Support Software.

Kuhn, M. (2005a). Helping students become accurate, expressive readers: Fluency instruction for small groups. *The Reading Teacher, 58*(4), 338–345.

Kuhn, M. (2005b). A comparative study of small group fluency instruction. *Reading Psychology, 26,* 127–146.

Kuhn, M. R., & Schwanenflugel, P. J. (2006). Fluency-oriented reading instruction: A merging of theory and practice. In K. A. Stahl & M. C. McKenna (Eds.), *Reading research at work: Foundations of effective practice* (pp. 205–216). New York: Guilford Press.

Kuhn, M. R., & Stahl, S. A. (2000). *Fluency: A review of developmental and remedial practices*. Center for the Improvement of Early Reading Achievement—Report #2-008, University of Michigan, Ann Arbor, Michigan.

Kulik, C. C., & Kulik, J. A. (1982). Effects of ability grouping on secondary students: A meta-analysis of evaluation findings. *American Educational Research Journal, 19,* 415–428.

L'Engle, M. (1962). *A wrinkle in time*. New York: Dell.

Labbo, L. D. (2001). Supporting children's comprehension of informational text through interactive read alouds. *Literacy and Nonfiction Series, 1*(2), 1–4.

Labbo, L. D., & Teale, W. H. (1990). Cross age reading: A strategy for helping poor readers. *The Reading Teacher, 43,* 363–369.

LaBerge, D., & Samuels, S. J. (1974). Toward a theory of automatic information processing in reading. *Cognitive Psychology, 6,* 293–323.

LaBerge, D., & Samuels, S. J. (1985). Toward a theory of automatic information processing in reading. In H. Singer & R. B. Ruddell (Eds.), *Theoretical models and processes of reading* (pp. 689–718). Newark, DE: International Reading Association.

Lamme, L. L., & Hysmith, C. (1991). One school's adventure into portfolio assessment. *Language Arts, 68,* 629–640.

Lamoreaux, L., & Lee, D. M. (1943). *Learning to read through experience*. New York: Appleton-Century-Crofts.

Langer, J. (1981). From theory to practice: A prereading plan. *Journal of Reading, 25,* 152–156.

Langer, J. A. (1984). Examining background knowledge and text comprehension. *Reading Research Quarterly, 19,* 468–481.

Langer, J. A. (1985). Levels of questioning: An alternative view. *Reading Research Quarterly, 20*(5), 586–602.

Langer, P., Kalk, J. M., & Searls, D. T. (1984). Age of admission and trends in achievement: A comparison of blacks and Caucasians. *American Educational Research Journal, 21,* 61–78.

Larsen, N. (1994). *The publisher's chopping block: What happens to children's trade books when they are published in a basal reading series?* Unpublished master's projects, Brigham Young University.

Lass, B., & Davis, B. (1985). *The remedial reading handbook*. Upper Saddle River, NJ: Prentice-Hall.

Lathlaen, P. (1993). A meeting of minds: Teaching using biographies. *The Reading Teacher, 46*(6), 529–531.

Law, B., & Eckes, M. (1990). *The more than just surviving handbook: ESL for every classroom teacher.* Winnipeg, Canada: Peguis.

Lee-Daniels, S. L., & Murray, B. A. (2000). DEAR me: What does it take to get my children reading? *The Reading Teacher, 54*, 154–155.

Leinhardt, G., Zigmond, N., & Cooley, W. (1981). Reading instruction and its effects. *American Educational Research Journal, 18*, 343–361.

Lemann, N. (1997, November). The reading wars. *The Atlantic Monthly, 280*(5), 128–134.

Lenneberg, E. H. (1964). *New directions in the study of language.* Cambridge, MA: MIT Press.

Leslie, L., & Caldwell, J. (2001). *Qualitative reading inventory–3.* New York: Longman.

Leu, D. J. (2006). *Preparing all students for the new literacies of online reading comprehension: Ten easy steps.* Presentation at the Texas State Reading Association Annual Conference, November 10, 2006.

Levin, J.-R., Johnson, D. D., Pittelman, S. D., Levin, K., Shriberg, L. K., Toms-Bronowski, S., & Hayes, B. (1984). A comparison of semantic- and mnemonic-based vocabulary-learning strategies. *Reading Psychology, 5*, 1–15.

Levin, J. R., Levin, M. E., Glasman, L. D., & Nordwall, M. B. (1992). Mnemonic vocabulary instruction: Additional effectiveness evidence. *Contemporary Educational Psychology, 17*, 156–174.

Levine, S. S. (1976). *The effect of transformational sentence-combining exercises on the reading comprehension and written composition of third-grade children.* Unpublished doctoral dissertation, Hofstra University, NY.

Lewis, C. S. (1961). *The lion, the witch, and the wardrobe.* New York: Macmillan.

Liberman, I. Y., Shankweiler, D., Liberman, A., Fowler, C., & Fischer, F. (1977). Phonetic segmentation and decoding in the beginning reader. In A. S. Reber & D. L. Scarborough (Eds.), *Toward a psychology of reading* (pp. 207–225). Hillsdale, NJ: Erlbaum.

Lightbrown, P. M., & Spada, N. (1999). *How languages are learned* (Rev. ed.). New York: Oxford University Press.

Lima, C., & Lima, J. (1993). *A to zoo: A subject access to children's picture books.* New York: Bowker.

Lindsay, P. H., & Norman, D. A. (1977). *Human information processing: An introduction to psychology.* New York: Academic Press.

Lipson, M. Y. (1983). The influence of religious affiliation on children's memory for text information. *Reading Research Quarterly, 18*(4), 448–457.

Lipson, M. Y. (1984). Some unexpected issues in prior knowledge and comprehension. *The Reading Teacher, 37*(8), 760–764.

Lisle, J. T. (1989). *Afternoon of the elves.* New York: Franklin Watts.

Littlejohn, C. (1988). *The lion and the mouse.* New York: Dial Books for Young Readers.

Livingston, N., & Birrell, J. R. (1994). Learning about cultural diversity through literature. *BYU Children's Book Review, 54*(5), 1–6.

Loban, W. (1976). *Teaching language and literature: Grades seven–twelve* (NCTE Research Report No. 18). Urbana, IL: National Council of Teachers of English.

Loban, W. D. (1963). *The language of elementary school children* (Research Report No. 1). Urbana, IL: National Council of Teachers of English.

Loban, W. D. (1964). *Language ability: Grades seven, eight, and nine.* Berkeley, CA: University of California. ERIC Ed 001275.

Lobel, A. (1981). *On market street.* New York: Scholastic.

Lobel, A. (1983). *Fables.* New York: Harper & Row.

Lock, S. (1980). *Hubert hunts his hum* (J. Newnham, Illustrator). Sydney, Australia: Ashton Scholastic.

Lomax, R. G., & McGee, L. M. (1987). Young children's concepts about print and reading: Toward a model of word reading acquisition. *Reading Research Quarterly, 22*(2), 237–256.

Long, M. H. (1991). Focus on form: Design features in language teaching methodology. In K. de Bot, D. Coste, R. Ginsberg, & C. Kramsch (Eds.), *Foreign language research in cross-cultural perspective* (pp. 39–52). Amsterdam: John Benjamins.

Loranger, A. L. (1997). Comprehension strategies instruction: Does it make a difference? *Reading Psychology, 18*(1), 31–68.

Loughlin, C. E., & Martin, M. D. (1987). *Supporting literacy: Developing effective learning environments.* New York: Columbia Teachers College Press.

Lowery, L. F., & Grafft, W. (1967). Paperback books and reading attitudes. *The Reading Teacher, 21*(7), 618–623.

Luria, A. R., & Yudovich, F. I. (1971). *Speech and the development of mental processes in the child.* London: Staples press.

Lyman, F. (1988). Think-Pair-Share, Wait time two, and on . . . *Mid-Atlantic Association for Cooperation in Education Cooperative News, 2,* 1.

Lyon, G. R. (1997). Statement of G. Reid Lyon to The Committee on Education and the Workforce, U.S. House of Representatives (July 19, 1997). Washington, DC.

Lyon, G. R. (1998). Why reading is not a natural process. *Educational Leadership, 55*(6), 14–18.

Lyon, G. R. (1999). Reading development, reading disorders, and reading instruction: Research-based findings. ASHA Special Interest Division I Newsletter. *Language Learning and Education, 6*(1), 8–16.

Lyon, R. (1977). Auditory-perceptual training: The state of the art. *Journal of Learning Disabilities, 10,* 564–572.

Lyons, C. A., & Beaver, J. (1995). Reducing retention and learning disability placement through reading recovery: An educationally sound, cost-effective choice. In R. L. Allington & S. A. Walmsley (Eds.), *No quick fix: Rethinking literacy programs in America's elementary schools.* New York: Teachers College Press.

MacGinitie, W. H. (1969). Evaluating readiness for learning to read: A critical review and evaluation of research. *Reading Research Quarterly, 4,* 396–410.

MacGinitie, W. H., & MacGinitie, R. K. (1989). *Gates-MacGinitie reading tests* (3rd ed.). Chicago: Riverside.

Macmillan/McGraw-Hill. (1993). *Macmillan/McGraw-Hill reading/language: A new view.* New York: Author.

Manarino-Leggett, P., & Salomon, P. A. (1989, April–May). *Cooperation vs. competition: Techniques for keeping your classroom alive but not endangered.* Paper presented at the Thirty-Fourth Annual Convention of the International Reading Association, New Orleans, LA.

Mandler, J. M., & Johnson, N. S. (1977). Remembrance of things parsed: Story structure and recall. *Cognitive Psychology, 9,* 111–151.

Manning, G. L., & Manning, M. (1984). What models of recreational reading make a difference? *Reading World, 23,* 375–380.

Manzo, A. V. (1969). The request procedure. *The Journal of Reading, 13,* 123–126.

Manzo, A. V., & Manzo, U. C. (1990). *Content area reading: A heuristic approach.* Upper Saddle River, NJ: Merrill/Prentice-Hall.

Manzo, A. V., Manzo, U. C., & Estes, T. (2000). *Content area literacy: Interactive teaching for active learning,* 3rd Ed. San Francisco, CA: John Wiley & Sons.

Marchionini, G. (1988). Hypermedia and learning: Freedom and chaos. *Educational Technology, 28,* 8–12.

Martin, B. (1990). *Brown bear, brown bear, what do you see?* New York: Henry Holt.

Martin, B. (1991). *Polar bear, polar bear, what do you hear?* New York: Henry Holt.

Martin, B., & Archambault, J. (1987). *Knots on a counting rope.* New York: Holt, Rinehart and Winston.

Martin, J. H. (1987). *Writing to read* [Computer program]. Boca Raton, FL: IBM.

Martinez, M. (1993). Motivating dramatic story reenactments. *The Reading Teacher, 46*(8), 682–688.

Martinez, M., & Nash, M. F. (1990). Bookalogues: Talking about children's literature. *Language Arts, 67,* 576–580.

Martorella, P. H. (1985). *Elementary social studies.* Boston: Little, Brown.

Martorella, P. H. (2000). *Teaching social studies in middle and secondary schools.* Upper Saddle River, NJ: Prentice-Hall.

Maryland Evaluation Committee. (2006). *Final report of the Maryland Evaluation Committee for selecting supplemental and intervention programs and materials.* Baltimore, MD: Maryland State Department of Education.

Marzano, R. J. (1993–1994). When two world views collide. *Educational Leadership, 51*(4), 6–11.

Marzano, R. J. (1998). *A theory-based meta-analysis of research on instruction* (Contract No. RJ96006101). Aurora, CO: Office of Educational Research and Improvement, Department of Education, Mid-continent Regional Educational Laboratory.

Marzano, R. J. (2004). *Building background knowledge for academic achievement: Research on what works in schools.* Alexandria, Virginia: Association for Supervision and Curriculum Development.

Marzollo, J., & Marzollo, C. (1982). *Jed's junior space patrol: A science fiction easy to read.* New York: Dial.

Mason, J. (1983). An examination of reading instruction in third and fourth grades. *The Reading Teacher, 36*(9), 906–913.

Mason, J., Herman, P. A., & Au, K. H. (1991). Reading: Children's developing knowledge of words. In J. Flood, J. M. Jensen, D. Lapp, & J. R. Squire (Eds.), *Handbook of research on teaching the language arts.* New York: Macmillan.

Mason, J. M. (1980). When do children begin to read: An exploration of four-year-old children's letter and word reading competencies. *Reading Research Quarterly, 15,* 203–227.

Masonheimer, P. E., Drum, P. A., & Ehri, L. C. (1984). Does environmental print identification lead children into word reading? *Journal of Reading Behavior, 16,* 257–271.

Math, I. (1981). *Wires and watts: Understanding and using electricity.* New York: Scribner's.

Mathes, P. G. (1997). Cooperative story mapping. *Remedial and Special Education, 18*(1), 20–27.

Mathes, P. G., Denton, C. A., Fletcher, J. M., Anthony, J. L., Francis, D. J., & Schatschneider, C. (2005). The effects of theoretically different instruction and student charactertistics on the skills of struggling readers. *Reading Research Quarterly, 40*(2), 148–183.

Mathes, P. G., Simmons, D. C., & Davis, B. I. (1992). Assisted reading techniques for developing reading fluency. *Reading Research and Instruction, 31*(4), 70–77.

Mathewson, G. C. (1985). Toward a comprehensive model of affect in the reading process. In H. Singer & R. B. Ruddell (Eds.), *Theoretical models and processes of reading* (3rd ed.). (pp. 841–856). Newark, DE: International Reading Association.

Mathewson, G. C. (1994). Model of attitude influence upon reading and learning to read. In H. Singer & R. B. Ruddell (Eds.), *Theoretical models and processes of reading* (4th Ed.) (pp. 1131–1161). Newark, DE: International Reading Association.

Maxim, G. (1989). *The very young: Guiding children from infancy through the early years* (3rd ed.). Upper Saddle River, NJ: Merrill/Prentice-Hall.

May, F. B., & Elliot, S. B. (1978). *To help children read: Mastery performance modules for teachers in training* (2nd ed.). Upper Saddle River, NJ: Merrill/Prentice-Hall.

May, F. B., & Rizzardi, L. (2002). *Reading as communication* (6th ed.). Upper Saddle River, NJ: Merrill/Prentice-Hall.

Mayer, M. (1976a). *Ah-choo.* New York: Dial Books.

Mayer, M. (1976b). *Hiccup.* New York: Dial Books.

McCallum, R. D. (1988). Don't throw the basals out with the bath water. *The Reading Teacher, 42,* 204–209.

McCardle, P., & Chhabra, V. (2004). *The voice of evidence in reading research.* Baltimore, MD: Paul H. Brookes.

McCarrier, A., Pinnell, G. S., & Fountas, I. C. (1999). *Interactive writing: How language and literacy come together, K–2.* Portsmouth, NH: Heinemann.

McCarthey, S. J., Hoffman, J. V., Christian, C., Corman, L., Elliott, B., Matherne, D., & Stahle, D. (1994). Engaging the new basal readers. *Reading Research and Instruction, 33*(3), 233–256.

McCormick, C. E., & Mason, J. (1986). Intervention procedures for increasing preschool children's interest in and knowledge about reading. In W. H. Teale & E. Sulzby (Eds.), *Emergent literacy: Writing and reading* (pp. 90–115). Norwood, NJ: Ablex Publishing.

McCormick, S. (1995). *Instructing students who have literacy problems.* Upper Saddle River, NJ: Merrill/Prentice-Hall.

McCracken, R. A., & McCracken, M. J. (1978). Modeling is the key to sustained reading. *The Reading Teacher, 31,* 406–408.

McDermott, G. (1993). *Raven: Trickster tale from the Pacific Northwest.* San Diego, CA: Harcourt Brace.

McGee, L. M. (1982). Awareness of text structure: Effects on children's recall of expository text. *Reading Research Quarterly, 17*(4), 581–590.

McGee, L. M., Lomax, R. G., & Head, M. H. (1988). Young children's written language knowledge: What environmental and functional print reading reveals. *Journal of Reading Behavior, 20*(2), 99–118.

McGee, L. M., Ratliff, J. L., Sinex, A., Head, M., & LaCroix, K. (1984). Influence of story schema and concept of story on children's story compositions. In J. A. Niles & L. A. Harris (Eds.), *Thirty-third yearbook of the National Reading Conference* (pp. 270–277). Rochester, NY: National Reading Conference.

McGee, L. M., & Richgels, D. J. (2000). *Literacy's beginnings: Supporting young readers and writers* (3rd ed.). Needham, MA: Allyn & Bacon.

McGee, L. M., & Richgels, D. J. (2003). *Designing early literacy programs: Strategies for at-risk preschool and kindergarten children.* New York: Guilford.

McGuire, F. N. (1984). How arts instruction affects reading and language: Theory and research. *The Reading Teacher, 37*(9), 835–839.

McInnes, J. (1983). *Networks.* Toronto: Nelson of Canada.

McKee, D. (1990). *Elmer.* London: Red Fox.

McKenna, M. C., & Stahl, S. A. (2003). *Assessment for reading instruction*. New York: Guilford Press.

McKeown, M. G., & Beck, I. L. (1988). Learning vocabulary: Different ways for different goals. *Remedial and Special Education, 9*(1), 42–52.

McKeown, M. G., Beck, I. L., Omanson, R. C., & Pople, M. T. (1985). Some effects of the nature and frequency of vocabulary instruction on the knoweldge and use of words. *Reading Research Quarterly, 20,* 522–535.

McKeown, M. G., Beck, I. L., & Worthy, M. J. (1993). Grappling with text ideas: Questioning the author. *The Reading Teacher, 46*(7), 560–565.

McKissack, P. C. (1986). *Flossie & the fox*. New York: Dial Books for Young Readers.

McKuen, R. (1990). Ten books on CD ROM. *MacWorld, 7*(12), 217–218.

McMahon, S. I., & Raphael, T. E. (1997). *The book club connection: Literacy learning and classroom talk*. New York: Teachers College Press.

McNabb, M. (2006). *Evaluation study of Language, Literacy, & Vocabulary!* St. Charles, IL: Learning Gauge.

McNeil, J. D. (1987). *Reading comprehension* (2nd ed.). Glenview, IL: Scott, Foresman.

McQueen, L. (1985). *The little red hen*. New York, NY: Scholastic Books, Inc.

McQuillan, J. (1998). *The literacy crisis: False claims, real solutions*. Portsmouth, NH: Heinemann Educational Books.

McTighe, J., & Lyman, F. T. (1988). Cueing thinking in the classroom: The promise of theory-embedded tools. *Educational Leadership, 45*(7), 18–24.

Meade, E. L. (1973). The first R-A point of view. *Reading World, 12,* 169–180.

MECC. (1984). *Writing a narrative* (computer program). St. Paul, MN: Minnesota Educational Computing Consortium.

Medina, M., & Escamilla, K. (1994). Language acquisition and gender for limited-language-proficient Mexican Americans in a maintenance bilingual program. *Hispanic Journal of Behavioral Sciences, 16*(4), 422–437.

Meisinger H., Schwanenflugel, P. J., Bradley, E., Kuhn, M. R., & Stahl, S. A. (2002). *Interaction quality during partner reading*. Paper presented at the Annual Meeting of the National Reading Conference, Miami, FL.

Meltzer, N. S., & Himse, R. (1969). The boundaries of written words as seen by first graders. *Journal of Reading Behavior, 1,* 3–13.

Menke, D. J., & Pressley, M. (1994). Elaborative interrogation: Using "why" questions to enhance learning from text. *Journal of Reading, 37*(8), 642–645.

Menon, S., & Hiebert, E. H. (2005). A comparison of first graders' reading with little books or literature-based basal anthologies. *Reading Research Quarterly, 40*(1), 12–36.

Menyuk, P. (1988). *Language development knowledge and use*. Glenview, IL: Scott, Foresman/Little, Brown College Division.

Merrill Mathematics (Grade 5). (1985). Upper Saddle River, NJ: Merrill/Prentice-Hall.

Merrill Science (Grade 3). (1989). Upper Saddle River, NJ: Merrill/Prentice-Hall.

Messaris, P. (2005). Introduction. In J. Flood, S. B. Heath, & D. Lapp (Eds.), *Handbook of research on teaching literacy through the communicative and visual arts* (pp. 3–6). Mahwah, NJ: Lawrence Erlbaum Associates.

Meyer, B., Brandt, D., & Bluth, G. (1980). Use of top-level structure in text for reading comprehension of ninth-grade students. *Reading Research Quarterly, 16,* 72–103.

Meyer, B. J. (1979). Organizational patterns in prose and their use in reading. In M. L. Kamil & A. J. Moe (Eds.), *Reading research: Studies and applications* (pp. 109–117). Twenty-eighth Yearbook of the National Reading Conference.

Meyer, B. J. F., & Freedle, R. O. (1984). Effects of discourse type on recall. *American Educational Research Journal, 21*(1), 121–143.

Meyers, P. A. (2006). The princess storyteller, Clara clarifier, Quincy questioner, and the wizard: Reciprocal teaching adapted for kindergarten students. *The Reading Teacher, 59*(4), 314–325.

Mezynski, K. (1983). Issues concerning the acquisition of knowledge: Effects of vocabulary training on reading comprehension. *Review of Educational Research, 53*(2), 253–279.

Michaels, J. R. (2001). *Dancing with words: Helping students love language through authentic vocabulary instruction*. Urbana, IL: National Council of Teachers of English.

Miesels, S. J., & Piker, R. A. (2001). *An analysis of early literacy assessments used for instruction, CIERA Report #2-013*. Ann Arbor, MI: Center for the Improvement of Early Reading Achievement.

Miller, B. F., Rosenberg, E. B., & Stackowski, B. L. (1971). *Investigating your health*. Boston: Houghton Mifflin.

Mindplay. (1990). *Author! Author!* Danvers, MA: Methods and Solutions.

Missal, K. N., & McConnell, S. R. (2004). *Technical report: Psychometric characteristics of individual growth and development indicators: Picture naming, rhyming, and alliteration.* Minneapolis, MN: University of Minnesota.

Moats, L. (1999) *Teaching Reading IS Rocket Science.* Washington, DC: American Federation of Teachers.

Moats, L. C. (1994). The missing foundation in teacher education: Knowledge of the structure of spoken and written language. *Annuals of Dyslexia, 44,* 81–102.

Moats, L. C. (1999). *Teaching reading is rocket science: What expert teachers of reading should know and be able to do.* Washington, DC: American Federation of Teachers.

Moats, L. C. (2000). *Speech to print: Language essentials for teachers.* Baltimore, MD: Paul H. Brookes.

Moe, A. J., & Irwin, J. W. (1986). Cohesion, coherence, and comprehension. In J. W. Irwin (Ed.), *Understanding and teaching cohesion comprehension* (pp. 3–8). Newark, DE: International Reading Association.

Moffett, J. (1983). *Teaching the universe of discourse.* Boston: Houghton Mifflin.

Moffett, J., & Wagner, B. J. (1976). *Student-centered language arts and reading K–13. A handbook for teachers,* 2nd Ed. Boston: Houghton Mifflin.

Mohr, K. A. J. (2003). Children's choices: A comparison of book preferences between Hispanic and non-Hispanic first-graders. *Reading Psychology: An International Quarterly, 24*(2), 163–176.

Mohr, K. A. J. (2006). Children's choices for recreational reading: A three-part investigation of selection preferences, rationales, and processes. *Journal of Literacy Research, 38*(1), 81–104.

Monjo, F. N. (1970). *The drinking gourd.* New York: HarperCollins.

Montelongo, J., Jiménez, L. B., Hernández, A. C., & Hosking, D. (2006). Teaching expository text structures. *The Science Teacher, 73*(2), 28–31.

Mooney, M. E. (1990). *Reading to, with, and by children.* Katonah, NY: Owen.

Moore, G. (1986). Effects of the spatial definition of behavior settings on children's behavior: A quasi-experimental field study. *Journal of Personality and Social Psychology, 6,* 205–231.

Moore, J. C., Jones, C. J., & Miller, D. C. (1980). What we know after a decade of sustained silent reading. *The Reading Teacher, 33,* 445–450.

Moore, M. A. (1991). Electronic dialoguing: An avenue to literacy. *The Reading Teacher, 45*(4), 280–286.

Moran, C. (1996). *Content area instruction for students acquiring English: Power of two languages.* New York: MacMillan/McGraw-Hill.

Morphett, M. V., & Washburne, C. (1931). When should children begin to read? *Elementary School Journal, 31,* 496–503.

Morris, D., Bloodgood, J. M., Lomax, R. G., & Perney, J. (2003). Developmental steps in learning to read: A longitudinal study in kindergarten and first grade. *Reading Research Quarterly, 38*(3), 302–328.

Morris, D., Shaw, B., & Perney, J. (1990). Helping low readers in grades 2 & 3: An after-school volunteer tutoring program. *Elementary School Journal, 91,* 133–150.

Morrow, L. M. (1984). Reading stories to young children: Effects of story structure, and traditional questioning strategies on comprehension. *Journal of Reading Behavior, 16,* 273–288.

Morrow, L. M. (1985). Retelling stories: A strategy for improving children's comprehension, concept of story structure, and oral language complexity. *Elementary School Journal, 85,* 647–661.

Morrow, L. M. (1988a). Retelling as a diagnostic tool. In S. M. Glazer, L. W. Searfoss, & L. Gentile (Eds.), *Re-examining reading diagnosis: New trends and procedures in classrooms and clinics* (pp. 128–149). Newark, DE: International Reading Association.

Morrow, L. M. (1988b). Young children's responses to one-to-one story reading in school settings. *The Reading Teacher, 23*(1), 89–107.

Morrow, L. M. (1990). Preparing the classroom environment to promote literacy during play. *Early Childhood Education Research Quarterly, 5,* 537–554.

Morrow, L. M. (1993). *Literacy development in the early years: Helping children read and write* (2nd ed.). Boston: Allyn & Bacon.

Morrow, L. M. (1995). *Family literacy: Connections in schools and communities.* Newark, DE: International Reading Association.

Morrow, L. M. (2001). *Literacy development in the early years: Helping children read and write* (4th ed.). Needham Heights, MA: Allyn & Bacon.

Morrow, L. M. (2002). *The literacy center: Contexts for reading and writing* (2nd ed.). Portland, ME: Stenhouse.

Morrow, L. M. (2005). *Literacy development in the early years: Helping children read and write* (5th ed.). Boston, MA: Allyn & Bacon.

Morrow, L. M., & Casey, H. K. (2003). A comparison of exemplary characteristics in 1st and 4th grade teachers. *The California Reader, 36*(3), 5–17.

Morrow, L. M., & Gambrell, L. B. (2001). Literature-based instruction in the early years. In S. B. Neuman & D. K. Dickinson (Eds.), *Handbook of early literacy research* (pp. 348–360). New York: Guilford Press.

Morrow, L. M., & Rand, M. K. (1991). Promoting literacy during play by designing early childhood classroom environments. *The Reading Teacher, 44*(6), 396–402.

Morrow, L. M., Gambrell, L. B., Kapinus, B., Koskinen, P. S., Marshall, N., & Mitchell, J. N. (1986). Retelling: A strategy for reading instruction and assessment. In J. A. Niles and R. V. Lalik (Eds.), *Solving problems in literacy: Learners, teachers and researchers: Thirty-fifth yearbook of the National Reading Conference* (pp. 73–80). Rochester, NY: National Reading Conference.

Morrow, L. M., Reutzel, D. R., & Casey, H. (2006). Organization and management of language arts teaching: Classroom environments, grouping practices, and exemplary instruction. In C. Evertson (Ed.), *Handbook of classroom management* (pp. 559–582). Mahwah, NJ: Lawrence Erlbaum Associates.

Morrow, L. M., Tracey, D. H., Woo, D. G., & Pressley, M. (1999). Characteristics of exemplary first-grade literacy instruction. *The Reading Teacher, 52*(5), 462–476.

Mosenthal, J., Lipson, M., Torncello, S., Russ, B., & Mekkelsen, J. (2004). Contexts and practices of six schools successful in obtaining reading achievement. *Elementary School Journal, 104*(5),343–367.

Mosenthal, P. B. (1989a). From random events to predictive reading models. *The Reading Teacher, 42*(7), 524–525.

Mosenthal, P. B. (1989b). The whole language approach: Teachers between a rock and a hard place. *The Reading Teacher, 42*(8), 628–629.

Moskal, B. M. (2003). Developing classroom performance assessments and scoring rubrics: Part II. College Park, MD: ERIC Clearinghouse on Assessment and Evaluation. ED 481715.

Moss, B. (1997). A qualitative assessment of first graders' retelling of expository text. *Reading Research and Instruction, 37*(1), 1–13.

Moss, B. (2004). Teaching expository text structures through information trade book retellings. *The Reading Teacher, 57*(8), 710–718.

Moss, B., & Newton, E. (2001). An examination of the information text genre in basal readers. *Reading Psychology, 23*(1), 1–13.

Moustafa, M. (1997). *Beyond traditional phonics: Research discoveries and reading instruction.* Portsmouth, NH: Heinemann.

Moustafa, M., & Maldonado-Colon, E. (1999). Whole-to-parts phonics instruction: Building on what children know to help them know more. *The Reading Teacher, 52*(5), 448–458.

Mullis, I. V. S., Campbell, J. R., & Farstrup, A. E. (Eds.). (1993). *NAEP 1992 reading report card for the nation and the states* (Report No. 23-ST06). Washington, DC: National Center for Education Statistics, USDOE.

Munsch, R. (1980). *The paper bag princess.* Toronto: Annick Press.

Murray, A. D. (1990). Fine-tuning of utterance length to preverbal infants: Effects on later language development. *Journal of Child Language, 17*(3), 511–525.

Mustafa, M. (1997). *Beyond traditional phonics: Research discoveries and reading instruction.* Portsmouth, NH: Heinemann.

Muth, K. D. (1989). *Children's comprehension of text: Research into practice.* Newark, DE: International Reading Association.

Myers, W. D. (1975). *Fast Sam, Cool Clyde, and Stuff.* New York: Puffin Books.

Nagy, W. (1988). *Teaching vocabulary to improve reading comprehension.* Unpublished manuscript, Champaign, IL: Center for the Study of Reading.

Nagy, W. E., Anderson, R., & Herman, P. (1987). Learning word meanings from context during normal reading. *American Educational Research Journal, 24,* 237–270.

Nagy, W. E., & Anderson, R. C. (1984). How many words are there in printed school English? *Reading Research Quarterly, 19*(3), 304–330.

Nagy, W. E., Herman, P. A., & Anderson, R. C. (1985). Learning words from context. *Reading Research Quarterly, 20,* 233–253.

Naiden, N. (1976). Ratio of boys to girls among disabled readers. *The Reading Teacher, 29*(6), 439–442.

Namioka, L. (1992). *Yang the youngest and his terrible ear.* Boston: Little, Brown.

Nash, B., & Nash, G. (1980). *Pundles.* New York: Stone Song Press.

Nash, B., & Nash, G. (1983). *Pundles.* New York: GD/ Perigee Book.

Naslund, J. C., & Samuel, J. S. (1992). Automatic access to word sounds and meaning in decoding written text. *Reading and Writing Quarterly, 8*(2), 135–156.

National assessment of educational progress report, 1994: Reading. Washington, DC: National Center for Educational Statistics and the U.S. Department of Education.

National Assessment of Educational Progress, Reading Report Card. (2002). Washington, DC: U.S. Department of Education.

National Assessment of Educational Progress. (1990). *Learning to read in our nation's schools: Instruction and achievement in 1988 at grades 4, 8, and 12.* Princeton, NJ: Author.

National Assessment of Educational Progress. (2000). Washington, DC: Department of Education.

National Assessment of Educational Progress NAEP. (1996). *Results from the NAEP 1994 reading assessment—at a glance.* Washington, DC: National Center for Educational Statistics.

National Association for the Education of Young Children. (1986). Position statement on developmentally appropriate practice in programs for 4- and 5-year-olds. *Young Children, 41*(6), 20–29.

National Center for Education Statistics. (1999). *NAEP 1998 Reading Report Card: National & state highlights.* Washington, DC: National Center for Education Statistics.

National Commission on Teaching and America's Future. (1996). *What matters most: Teachers for America's future.* Woodbridge, VA: Author.

National Commission on Teaching and America's Future (NCTAF). (2006). *NCTAF emphasizes need for 21st century teaching and learning: Meeting summary.* St. Paul, MN: NCTAF.

National Education Association (NEA). (2000). *Report of the National Education Association's Task Force on Reading 2000.* Washington, DC: Author.

National Education Association. *Report of the NEA Task Force on Reading 2000.* Washington, DC. Retrieved from *https://www.nea.org/reading/images/readingtaskforce2000.pdf*

National Institute of Child Health and Human Development. (2000). *Report of the National Reading Panel: Teaching children to read.* Washington, DC.

National Institute of Child Health and Human Development. (2000). *Why children succeed or fail at reading. Research from NICHD's program in learning disabilities.* Retrieved from *http://wwwnichd.nih.gov/publications/pubs/readbro.htm*

National Institutes of Health. (Ed.). (2006). Retrieved from *http://www.nih.gov/.*

National Reading Panel (NRP). (2000). *Report of the National Reading Panel: Teaching children to read.* Washington, DC: National Institute of Child Health and Human Development.

National Research Council. (1998). Preventing Reading Difficulties in Young Children. Washington, DC: National Academy Press.

National Research Council. (2001). *Scientific research in education.* (Report of the Committee on Scientific Principles for Education Research). Washington, DC: National Academy Press.

Nelson, T. (1988, January). Managing immense storage. *Byte,* 225–238.

Neuman, S. B. (1981). Effect of teaching auditory perceptual skill on reading achievement in first grade. *The Reading Teacher, 34,* 422–426.

Neuman, S. B. (1999). Books make a difference: A study of access to literacy. *Reading Research Quarterly, 34,* 286–311.

Neuman, S. B. (1999). *The importance of classroom libraries: Research monograph.* New York: Scholastic, Inc.

Neuman, S. B. (2001). The role of knowledge in early literacy. *Reading Research Quarterly, 36*(4), 468–475.

Neuman, S. B., & Celano, D. (2001). Access to print in low-income and middle-income communities: An ecological study of four neighborhoods. *Reading Research Quarterly, 36*(1), 8–26.

Neuman, S. B., & Celano, D. (2006). The knowledge gap: Implications of leveling the playing field for low-income and middle-income children. *Reading Research Quarterly, 42*(2), 176–201.

Neuman, S. B., & Koskinen, P. (1992). Captioned television as comprehensible input: Effects of incidental word learning from context for language minority students. *Reading Research Quarterly, 27*(1), 94–106.

Neuman, S., & Koskinen, P. (1992). Captioned television as comprehensible input: Effects of incidental word learning from context for language minority students. *Reading Research Quarterly, 27*(3), 94–106.

Neuman, S. B., & Roskos, K. (1990). Play, print, and purpose: Enriching play environments for literacy development. *The Reading Teacher, 44*(3), 214–221.

Neuman, S. B., & Roskos, K. (1990). The influence of literacy-enriched play settings on preschooler's engagement with written language. In J. Zutell & S. McCormick (Eds.), *Literacy theory and research: Analysis from multiple paradigms* (pp. 179–187). Chicago, IL: National Reading Conference.

Neuman, S. B., & Roskos, K. (1992). Literacy objects as cultural tools: Effects on children's literacy behaviors in play. *Reading Research Quarterly, 27*, 202–225.

Neuman, S. B., & Roskos, K. (1993). Access to print for children of poverty: Differential effects of adult mediation and literacy-enriched play settings on environmental and functional print tasks. *American Educational Research Journal, 30*(1), 95–122.

Neuman, S. B., & Roskos, K. (1993). *Language and literacy learning in the early years: An integrated approach*. New York: Harcourt Brace.

Neuman, S. B., & Roskos, K. (1997). Literacy knowledge in practice: Contexts of participation for young writers and readers. *Reading Research Quarterly, 32*(1), 10–33.

Neuman, S., & Roskos, K. (1992). Literacy objects as cultural tools: Effects on children's literacy behaviors in play. *Reading Research Quarterly, 27*(3), 203–225.

Neuman, S., & Roskos, K. (1997). Literacy knowledge in practice: Contexts of participation for young writers and readers. *Reading Research Quarterly, 32*(1), 10–33.

Newman, J. M. (1985a). Yes, that's an interesting idea, but. . . . In J. M. Newman (Ed.), *Whole language: Theory in use* (pp. 181–186). Portsmouth, NH: Heinemann.

Newman, J. M. (Ed.). (1985b). *Whole language: Theory in use*. Portsmouth, NH: Heinemann.

Newman, M. L. (1996). *The association of academic achievement, types of offenses, family, and other characteristics of males who have been adjudicated as juvenile delinquents*. Unpublished masters thesis, California State University, Long Beach, CA.

Nilsen, A. P., & Nilsen, D. L. F. (2002). Lessons in the teaching of vocabulary from September 11 and Harry Potter. *Journal of Adolescent & Adult Literacy, 46*(3), 254–260.

Nist, S. L., & Simpson, M. L. (1993). *Developing vocabulary concepts for college thinking*. Lexington, MA: Heath.

Nolan, E. A., & Berry, M. (1993). Learning to listen. *The Reading Teacher, 46*(7), 606–608.

Nordquist, V. M., & Twardosz, S. (1990). Preventing behavior problems in early childhood special education classrooms through environmental organization. *Education and Treatment of Children, 13*(4), 274–287.

Norton, D. (2007). *Through the eyes of a child: An introduction to children's literature* (7th ed.). Upper Saddle River, NJ: Pearson/Merrill/Prentice-Hall.

Norton, D. E. (1998). *Through the eyes of a child: An introduction to children's literature* (5th ed.). Upper Saddle River, NJ: Merrill/Prentice-Hall.

Norton, D. E., & Norton, S. (2003). *Through the eyes of a child: An introduction to children's literature* (6th ed.). Upper Saddle River, NJ: Merrill/Prentice-Hall.

Norton, D. E., & Norton, S. E. (2003). *Language arts activities for children* (4th ed.). Upper Saddle River, NJ: Merrill Prentice-Hall.

Novick, R. (2002). Learning to read the heart: Nurturing emotional literacy. *Young Children, 57*(3), 84–89.

Noyce, R. M., & Christie, J. F. (1989). *Integrating reading and writing instruction*. Boston: Allyn & Bacon.

Numeroff, L. J. (1985). *If you give a mouse a cookie*. New York: Scholastic.

Nurss, J. R., Hough, R. A., & Goodson, M. S. (1981). Prereading/language development in two day care centers. *Journal of Reading Behavior, 13*, 23–31.

O'Bruba, W. S. (1987). Reading through the creative arts. *Reading Horizons, 27*(3), 170–177.

O'Huigin, S. (1988). *Scary poems for rotten kids*. New York: Firefly Books.

Oakes, J. (1992). Can tracking research inform practice? *Educational Researcher, 21*(4), 12–21.

Oczkus, L. (2003). *Reciprocal teaching at work: Strategies for improving reading comprehension*. Newark, DE: International Reading Association.

Ogle, D. M. (1986). K-W-L: A teaching model that develops active reading of expository text. *The Reading Teacher, 39*(6), 564–570.

Ohanian, S. (1984). Hot new item or same old stew? *Classroom Computer Learning, 5,* 30–31.

O'Haigin, S. (1988). Scary poems for rotten kids. New York: Firefly Books.

Olson, M. W., & Gee, T. C. (1988). Understanding narratives: A review of story grammar research. *Childhood Education, 64*(4), 302–306.

Olson, M. W., & Longnion, B. (1982). Pattern guides: A workable alternative for content teachers. *Journal of Reading, 25,* 736–741.

Opitz, M. F. (1992). The cooperative reading activity: An alternative to ability grouping. *The Reading Teacher, 45*(9), 736–738.

Opitz, M. F. (1998). *Flexible grouping in reading: Practical ways to help all students become better readers.* New York: Scholastic.

Opitz, M. F., & Ford, M. P. (2001). *Reaching readers: Flexible and innovative strategies for guided reading.* Portsmouth, NH: Heinemann.

Opitz, M. F., & Rasinski, T. V. (1998). *Good-bye round robin: 25 effective oral reading strategies.* Portsmouth, NH: Heinemann.

Orellana, M. F., & Hernandez, A. (1999). Talking the walk: Children reading urban environmental print. *The Reading Teacher, 52*(6), 612–619.

ORFC Curriculum Review Panel. (2004). *Oregon Reading First Center (ORFC): Review of comprehensive programs.* Eugene, OR: University of Oregon.

Osborn, J. (1984). The purposes, uses, and contents of workbooks and some guidelines for publishers. In R. C. Anderson, J. Osborn, & R. J. Tierney (Eds.), *Learning to read in American schools* (pp. 45–112). Hillsdale, NJ: Erlbaum.

Osborn, J. (1985). Workbooks: Counting, matching, and judging. In J. Osborn, P. T. Wilson, & R. C. Anderson (Eds.), *Reading education: Foundations for a literate America* (pp. 11–28). Lexington, MA: Lexington Books.

Osborn, J., Lehr, M. A., & Hiebert, E. H. (2003). *Focus on fluency: Research-based practices in early reading series.* Honolulu, HI: Pacific Resources for Education and Learning (PREL).

Otto, J. (1982). The new debate in reading. *The Reading Teacher, 36*(1), 14–18.

Palincsar, A. M. (2003). Collaborative approaches to comprehension instruction. In C. E. Snow & A. P. Sweet (Eds.), *Rethinking reading comprehension* (pp. 99–114). New York: Guilford Press.

Palincsar, A. M., & Brown, A. L. (1984). Reciprocal teaching of comprehension-fostering and monitoring activities. *Cognition and Instruction, 1,* 117–175.

Palincsar, A. S., & Brown, A. L. (1985). Reciprocal teaching: A means to a meaningful end. In J. Osborn, P. T. Wilson, & R. C. Anderson (Eds.), *Reading education: Foundations for a Literate America* (pp. 299–310). Lexington, MA: Heath.

Pankake, M., & Pankake, J. (1988). *A Prairie Home Companion folk song book.* New York: Viking.

Pappas, C. C., Kiefer, B. Z., & Levstik, L. S. (1990). *An integrated language perspective in the elementary school.* New York: Longman.

Paradis, E., & Peterson, J. (1975). Readiness training implications from research. *The Reading Teacher, 28*(5), 445–448.

Paradis, E. E. (1974). The appropriateness of visual discrimination exercises in reading readiness materials. *Journal of Educational Research, 67,* 276–278.

Paradis, E. E. (1984). *Comprehension: Thematic units* (videotape). Laramie: University of Wyoming.

Paratore, J. R. (2003). Building on family literacies: Examining the past and planning the future. In A. DeBruin-Parecki & B. Krol-Sinclair (Eds.), *Family literacy: From theory to practice* (pp. 8–27). Newark, DE: International Reading Association.

Paris, S. G., Carpenter, R. D., Paris, A. H., & Hamilton, E. E. (2005). Spurious and genuine correlates of children's reading comprehension. In S. G. Paris & S. A. Stahl (Eds.), *Children's reading comprehension and assessment* (pp. 131–160). Mahwah, NJ: Lawrence Erlbaum Associates.

Paris, S. G., Lipson, M. Y., & Wixson, K. K. (1983). Issues concerning the acquisition of knowledge: Effects of vocabulary training on reading comprehension. *Review of Educational Research, 53,* 293–316.

Paris, S. G., & Stahl, S. A. (2005). *Children's reading comprehension and assessment.* Mahwah, NJ: Lawrence Erlbaum Associates.

Parish, P. (1963). *Amelia Bedelia.* New York: Harper-Collins.

Park, L. S. (2001). *A single shard.* New York: Clarion.

Parker, A., & Paradis, E. (1986). Attitude development toward reading in grades one through six. *Journal of Educational Research, 79*(5), 313–315.

Parkes, B. (1986a). *The enormous watermelon.* Crystal Lake, IL: Rigby.

Parkes, B. (1986b). *Who's in the shed?* Crystal Lake, IL: Rigby.

Parsons, L. (1990). *Response journals.* Portsmouth, NH: Heinemann.

Partnership for Reading (2001). Put reading first: The research building blocks for teaching children to read. Washington. DC: The Partnership for

Reading. Report available online at *www.nifl.gov/partnershipforreading*

Pashler, H. (2006). *Optimizing resistance to forgetting.* Paper presented at the 2006 Institute of Education Sciences 2006 Research Conference, Washington, DC.

Paterson, K. (1977). *Bridge to Terabithia.* New York: Thomas Y. Crowell.

Paterson, W. A., Henry, J. J., O'Quin, K., Ceprano, M. A., & Blue, E. V. (2003). Investigating the effectiveness of an integrated learning system on early emergent readers. *Reading Research Quarterly, 38*(2), 172–207.

Paul, R. (2001). *Language disorders from infancy through adolescence* (2nd ed.). St. Louis, MO: Mosby.

Paulsen, G. (1987). *Hatchet.* New York: Simon & Schuster.

Payne, C. (2005). *Shared reading for today's classroom.* NY: Scholastic, Inc.

Payne, C. D., & Schulman, M. B. (1998). *Getting the most out of morning message and other shared writing lessons.* New York: Scholastic. Inc.

Payne, R. (1998). *A framework for understanding poverty.* Highlands, TX: RFT.

Payne, R. K. (1998). *A framework for understanding poverty.* Highlands, TX: RFT Publishing Co.

Pearson, P. D. (1974). The effects of grammatical complexity on children's comprehension, recall, and conception of certain semantic relations. *Reading Research Quarterly, 10*(2), 155–192.

Pearson, P. D. (1985). Changing the face of reading comprehension instruction. *The Reading Teacher, 38*(8), 724–738.

Pearson, P. D. (1989a). *Improving national reading assessment: The key to improved reading instruction.* Paper presented at the 1989 annual reading conference of the Utah Council of the International Reading Association, Salt Lake City, UT.

Pearson, P. D. (1989b). Reading the whole language movement. *Elementary School Journal, 90*(2), 231–242.

Pearson, P. D. (2000). *What sorts of programs and practices are supported by research? A reading from the radical middle.* Ann Arbor, MI: Center for the Improvement of Early Reading Instruction.

Pearson, P. D. (2006). Forward. In K. S. Goodman (Ed.), *The truth about DIBELS: What it is–What it does.* (pp. v–xx) Portsmouth, NH: Heinemann.

Pearson, P. D., & Duke, N. (2002). Comprehension instruction in the primary grades. In C. Collins-Block & M. Pressley (Eds.), *Comprehension instruction: Research-based best practices* (pp. 247–258). New York: Guildford Press.

Pearson, P. D., & Fielding, L. (1982). Listening comprehension. *Language Arts, 59*(6), 617–629.

Pearson, P. D., & Gallagher, M. C. (1983). The instruction of reading comprehension. *Contemporary Educational Psychology, 8*(3), 317–344.

Pearson, P. D., & Johnson, D. D. (1978). *Teaching reading comprehension.* New York: Holt, Rinehart and Winston.

Pearson, P. D., Hansen, J., & Gordon, C. (1979). The effect of background knowledge on children's comprehension of implicit and explicit information. *Journal of Reading Behavior, 11*(3), 201–209.

Peregoy, S. F., & Boyle, O. F. (1993). *Reading, writing, and learning in ESL.* New York: Longman.

Perez, S. A. (1983). Teaching writing from the inside: Teachers as writers. *Language Arts, 60*(7), 847–850.

Perfetti, C. A., & Lesgold, A. M. (1977). Discourse comprehension and sources of individual differences. In M. A. Just & P. A. Carpenter (Eds.), *Cognitive processes in comprehension* (pp. 141–184). Hillsdale, NJ: Erlbaum.

Perkins, J. H. (2001). Listen to their teachers' voices: Effective reading instruction for fourth grade African American students. *Reading Horizons, 41*(4), 239–255.

Perspectives on basal readers (Special issue). (1989). *Theory Into Practice, 28*(4).

Peterson, B. (1991). Selecting books for beginning readers. In D. E. DeFord, C. A. Lyons, & G. S. Pinnell (Eds.), *Bridges to literacy: Learning from reading recovery* (pp. 119–147). Portsmouth, NH: Heinemann.

Peterson, P., Carta, J., & Greenwood, C. (2005). Teaching milieu language skills to parents in multiple-risk families. *Journal of Early Intervention, 27,* 94–109.

Peterson, R., & Eeds, M. (1990). *Grand conversations: Literature groups in action.* New York: Scholastic.

Pfeffer, S. B. (1989). *Future forward.* New York: Holt.

Piaget, J. (1955). *The language and thought of the child.* New York: World.

Piaget, J. (1959). *The language and thought of the child* (3rd ed.). London: Routledge & Kegan.

Pikulski, J. J. (1985). Questions and answers. *The Reading Teacher, 39*(1), 127–128.

Pikulski, J. J. (2006). Fluency: A developmental and language perspective. In S. J. Samuels & A. E. Farstrup (Eds.), *What research has to say about fluency instruction* (pp. 70–93). Newark, DE: International Reading Association.

Pikulski, J. J., & Chard, D. J. (2005). Fluency: Bridge between decoding and reading comprehension. *The Reading Teacher, 58*(6), 510–519.

Pikulski, J. J., & Templeton, S. (1997). The role of phonemic awareness in learning to read. *Invitations to Literacy*. Boston: Houghton Mifflin.

Pinkney, A. D. (1993). *Alvin Ailey*. New York: Hyperion Books for Children.

Pinnell, G. S. (1998). *The language foundation of reading recovery*. Keynote address to the Third International Reading Recovery Institute: Cairns, Australia.

Pinnell, G. S., Deford, D. E., & Lyons, C. A. (1994). Comparing instructional models for the literacy education of high-risk first graders. *Reading Research Quarterly, 29*(1), 8–39.

Pinnell, G. S., & Fountas, I. C. (1997a). *A handbook for volunteers: Help America read*. Portsmouth, NH: Heinemann.

Pinnell, G. S., & Fountas, I. C. (1997b). *Help America read: Coordinator's guide*. Portsmouth, NH: Heinemann.

Pinnell, G. S., & Fountas, I. C. (1998). *Word matters*. Portsmouth, NH: Heinemann.

Pinnell, G. S., & Fountas, I. C. (2002). *Leveled books for readers grades 3–6: A companion volume to guiding readers and writers*. Portsmouth, NH: Heineman.

Pinnell, G. S., Fried, M. D., & Estice, R. M. (1990). Reading recovery: Learning how to make a difference. *The Reading Teacher, 43*, 282–295.

Pinnell, G. S., & Jaggar, A. M. (2003). Oral language: Speaking and listening in elementary classrooms. In J. Flood, D. Lapp, J. R. Squire, & J. M. Jensen (Eds.), *Handbook of research on teaching the English language arts* (2nd ed.) (pp. 881–913). New York: MacMillan.

Pinnell, G. S., Lyons, C. A., DeFord, D. E., Bryk, A. S., & Seltzer, M. (1994). Comparing instructional models for the literacy education of high-risk first graders. *Reading Research Quarterly, 29*(1), 8–39.

Pino, E. (1978). *Schools are out of proportion to man*. Seminar on discipline, Utah State University, Logan, UT.

Pintrich, P. R., & DeGroot, E. V. (1990). Motivational and self-regulated learning components of classroom academic performance. *Journal of Educational Psychology, 82*, 33–40.

Piper, T. (1993). *Language for all our children*. New York: Merrill/Macmillan.

Piper, T. (1998). *Language and learning: The home and school years* (2nd ed.). Upper Saddle River, NJ: Merrill/Prentice-Hall.

Point/counterpoint. The value of basal readers. (1989, August–September). *Reading Today, 7*, 18.

Polacco, P. (2002). *When lightning comes in a jar*. New York: Philomel.

Pollack, P. (1982). *Keeping it secret*. New York: Putnam.

Potter, B. (1903). *The tale of Peter Rabbit*. New York: F. Warne.

Potter, B. (1986). *The tale of Peter Rabbit*. New York: Scholastic, Inc.

Powell, D. A. (1986). *Retrospective case studies of individual and group decision making in district-level elementary reading textbook selection*. Unpublished doctoral dissertation, Indiana University, Bloomington, IN.

Pray, R. T. (1983). *A comparison of good and poor readers in an adult, incarcerated population*. Unpublished doctoral dissertation, Harvard University, Cambridge, MA.

Prelutsky, J. (1976). *Nightmares: Poems to trouble your sleep*. New York: Greenwillow Books.

Prelutsky, J. (1984). *A new kid on the block*. New York: Greenwillow Books.

Prelutsky, J. (1990). *Something big has been here*. New York: Greenwillow Books.

Prelutsky, J. (1991). *Poems for laughing out loud*. New York: Alfred A. Knopf.

Prelutsky, J. (1996). *A pizza the size of the sun*. New York: Greenwillow Books.

Pressley, M. (2000). What should comprehension instruction be the instruction of? In M. L. Kamil, P. B. Mosenthal, P. D. Pearson, & R. Barr (Eds.), *Handbook of reading research,* Vol. 3 (pp. 545–561). Mahwah, NJ: Erlbaum.

Pressley, M. (2002). *Beginning reading instruction: The rest of the story from research*. Washington, DC: National Education Association. *http://www nea.org/reading/images/beginningreading.pdf*

Pressley, M. (2002). Comprehension strategies instruction: A turn-of-the-century status report. In C. Collins-Block & M. Pressley (Eds.), *Comprehension instruction: Research-based best practices,* (pp. 11–27). New York: Guilford Press.

Pressley, M. (2002). *Reading instruction that works: The case for balanced teaching* (2nd ed.). New York: Guilford Press.

Pressley, M. (2002a). Comprehension strategies instruction: A turn-of-the-century status report. In C. Collins-Block, & M. Pressley (Eds.) *Improving comprehension instruction: Advances in research, theory, and classroom practice* (pp. 11–27). New York: Guilford Press.

Pressley, M. (2006). *Reading instruction that works: The case for balanced teaching* (3rd ed.). New York: Guilford Press.

Pressley, M., Allington, R. L., Wharton-McDonald, R., Collins-Block, C., and Morrow, L. M. (2001). *Learning to read: Lessons from exemplary first-grade classrooms.* New York: Guildford Press.

Pressley, M., Gaskin, I. W., Wile, D., Cunicelli, E. A., & Sheridan, J. (1991). Teaching literacy strategies across the curriculum: A case study at Benchmark School. In J. Zutell & S. McCormick (Eds.), *Learner factors/teacher factors: Issues in literacy research and instruction: Fortieth yearbook of the National Reading Conference* (pp. 219–228). Chicago: National Reading Conference.

Pressley, M., Rankin, J., & Yokoi, L. (1996). A survey of instructional practices of primary teachers nominated as effective in promoting literacy. *Elementary School Journal, 96*(4), 363–383.

Prince, A. T., & Mancus, D. S. (1987). Enriching comprehension: A schema altered basal reading lesson. *Reading Research and Instruction, 27,* 45–53.

Proudfoot, G. (1992). Pssst! There is literacy at the laundromat. *English Quarterly, 24*(1), 10–11.

Provensen, A., & Provensen, M. (1983). *The glorious flight: Across the channel with Louis Bleriot.* New York: Viking Penguin.

Puckett, M. B., & Black, J. K. (1994). *Authentic assessment of the young child.* Upper Saddle River, NJ: Merrill/Prentice-Hall.

Pulver, C. J. (1986). Teaching students to understand explicit and implicit connectives. In J. W. Irwin (Ed.), *Understanding and teaching cohesion comprehension* (pp. 3–8). Newark, DE: International Reading Association.

Put reading first: The research building blocks for teaching children to read. Washington, DC: The Partnership for Reading. Report available online at *www.nifl.gov/partnershipforreading*

Radencich, M., Beers, P., & Schumm, J. S. (1995). *Handbook for the K–12 reading specialist.* Boston, MA: Allyn and Bacon.

Radencich, M. C. (1995). *Administration and supervision of the reading/writing program.* Boston: Allyn & Bacon.

Ramey, S. L., & Ramey, C. T. (2006). Early educational interventions: Principles of effective and sustained benefits from targeted early educational programs. In D. K. Dickenson & S. B. Neuman (Eds.), *Handbook of early literacy research* (Vol. 2) (pp. 445–459). New York: Guilford Press.

Ramirez, G., & Ramirez, J. L. (1994). *Multiethnic literature.* Albany, NY: Delmar.

RAND Reading Study Group. (2001). *Reading for understanding: Towards an R & D program in reading comprehension.* Washington, DC: Author/OERI/Department of Education.

RAND Reading Study Group. (2002). *Reading for understanding: Toward an R & D program in reading comprehension.* Santa Monica, CA: Science and Technology Policy Institute, RAND Education.

Raphael, T. E. (1982). Question-answering strategies for children. *The Reading Teacher, 36,* 186–191.

Raphael, T. E. (1986). Teaching question answer relationships, revisited. *The Reading Teacher, 39*(6), 516–523.

Raphael, T. E., & Au, K. H. (2005). QAR: Enhancing comprehension and test-taking across grade and content areas. *The Reading Teacher, 59*(3), 206–221.

Raphael, T. E., Florio-Ruane, S., Kehus, M. J., George, M., Hasty, N. L., & Highfield, K. (2003). Constructing curriculum for differentiated instruction: Inquiry in the teachers' learning collaborative. In R. L. McCormick & J. R. Paratore (Eds.), *After early intervention, then what? Teaching struggling readers in grades 3 and beyond* (pp. 94–116). Newark, DE: International Reading Association.

Raphael, T. E., Pardo, L., Highfield, K., & McMahon, S. I. (1997). *Book club: A literature-based curriculum.* Littleton, MA: Small Planet Communications.

Raphael, T. E., & Pearson, P. D. (1982). *The effect of metacognitive awareness training on children's question answering behavior* (Tech. Rep. No. 238).

Urbana-Champaign: University of Illinois at Urbana-Champaign, Center for the Study of Reading.

Rasinski, T. (1989). Fluency for everyone: Incorporating fluency instruction in the classroom. *The Reading Teacher, 42*(9), 690–693.

Rasinski, T. (1990b). Investigating measure of reading fluency. *Educational Research Quarterly, 14*(3), 37–44.

Rasinski, T. (1998, September). *Reading to learn: Vocabulary development strategies.* Paper presented at the Fall Session of the Dallas Reading Plan Grades 4–6 Professional Development Series, Dallas, TX.

Rasinski, T. (2000). Speed does matter. *The Reading Teacher, 54*(2), 146–151.

Rasinski, T. V. (1984). *Developing Models of Reading Fluency.* ERIC Document Reproduction Service No. ED269721.

Rasinski, T. V. (1990). Effects of repeated reading and listening-while-reading on reading fluency. *Journal of Educational Research, 83*(2), 147–150.

Rasinski, T. V. (1995). *Parents and teachers: Helping children learn to read and write.* New York: Harcourt Brace.

Rasinski, T. V. (2000). Speed does matter. *The Reading Teacher, 54*(2), 146–151.

Rasinski, T. V. (2006). A brief history of reading fluency. In S. J. Samuels & A. E. Farstrup (Eds.), *What research has to say about fluency instruction* (pp. 4–23). Newark, DE: International Reading Association.

Rasinski, T. V. (2006). Reading fluency instruction: Moving beyond accuracy, automaticity, and prosody. *The Reading Teacher, 59*(7), 704–707.

Rasinski, T. V. & Fredericks, A. D. (1988). Sharing literacy: Guiding principles and practices for parent involvement. *The Reading Teacher, 41,* 508–512.

Rasinski, T. V., & Fredericks, A. D. (1989). Working with parents: What do parents think about reading in the schools? *The Reading Teacher, 43*(3), 262–263.

Rasinski, T. V., & Hoffman, J. V. (2006). Seeking understanding about reading fluency: The contributions of Steven A. Stahl. In K. A. Stahl & M. C. McKenna (Eds.), *Reading research at work: Foundations of effective practice,* (pp.169–176). New York: Guilford Press.

Rasinski, T. V., & Padak, N. (1996). Five lessons to increase reading fluency. In L. R. Putnam (Ed.), *How to become a better reading teacher: Strategies for assessment and intervention,* (pp. 255–266) Columbus, OH: Merrill/Prentice-Hall.

Raskinski, T. V. (2003). *The fluent reader: Oral reading strategies for building word recognition, fluency, and comprehension.* NY: Scholastic, Inc.

Rasinski, T. V., Blachowicz, C., & Lems, K. (2006). *Fluency instruction: Research-based best practices.* New York: Guilford Press.

Rasinski, T., & Opitz, M. F. (1998). *Good-bye round robin: 25 effective oral reading strategies.* Portsmouth, NH: Heinemann.

Rasinski, T., & Padak, N. D. (1990). Multicultural learning through children's literature. *Language Arts, 69,* 14–20.

Rathvon, N. (2004). *Early reading assessment: A practitioner's handbook.* New York: Guilford Press.

Raven, J. (1992). A model of competence, motivation, and behavior, and a paradigm for assessment. In H. Berlak, *Toward a new science of educational testing and assessment.* New York: State University of New York Press.

Ravitch, D., & Finn, C. E., Jr. (1987). *What do our 17-year-olds know?* New York: HarperCollins.

Rawls, W. (1961). *Where the red fern grows.* New York: Doubleday.

Raygor, A. L. (1977). The Raygor readability estimate: A quick and easy way to determine difficulty. In P. D. Pearson (Ed.), *Reading: Theory, research and practice* (pp. 259–263). Clemson, SC: National Reading Conference.

Rayner, K., Foorman, B. R., Perfetti, C. A., Pesetsky, D., and Seidenberg, M. S. (2001). How psychological science informs the teaching of reading. *Psychological Science in the Public Interest 2*(2), 31–74.

Rayner, K., Foorman, B. R., Perfetti, C. A., Pesetsky, D., and Seidenberg, M. S. (2002, March). How should reading be taught? *Scientific American,* 85–91.

Read, C. (1971). Preschool children's knowledge of English phonology. *Harvard Educational Review, 41,* 1–34.

Read, S. J., & Rosson, M. B. (1982). Rewriting history: The biasing effects of attitudes on memory. *Social Cognition, 1,* 240–255.

Reid, J. F. (1966). Learning to think about reading. *Educational Research, 9,* 56–62.

Reimer, B. L. (1983). Recipes for language experience stories. *The Reading Teacher, 36*(4), 396–401.

Reinking, D. (Ed.) (1987). *Computers and reading: Issues for theory and practice.* New York: Teachers College Press.

Reinking, D., & Rickman, S. S. (1990). The effects of computer-mediated texts on the vocabulary learning and comprehension of intermediate-grade readers. *Journal of Reading Behavior, 22*(4), 395–409.

Remaly, B. K. (1990). *Strategies for increasing the expressive vocabulary of kindergarten children.* Fort Lauderdale, FL: Nova University. (ERIC Document Reproduction Service No. ED 332 234).

Reutzel, D. R. (1985a). Reconciling schema theory and the basal reading lesson. *The Reading Teacher, 39,* 194–197.

Reutzel, D. R. (1985b). Story maps improve comprehension. *The Reading Teacher, 38*(4), 400–405.

Reutzel, D. R. (1991). Understanding and using basal readers effectively. In Bernard L. Hayes (Ed.), *Reading instruction and the effective teacher* (pp. 254–280). New York: Allyn & Bacon.

Reutzel, D. R. (1992). Breaking the letter a week tradition: Conveying the alphabetic principle to young children. *Childhood Education, 69*(1), 20–23.

Reutzel, D. R. (1995). Fingerpoint-reading and beyond: Learning about print strategies (LAPS). *Reading Horizons, 35*(4), 310–328.

Reutzel, D. R. (1996a). A balanced reading approach. In J. Baltas & S. Shafer (Eds.), *Scholastic guide to balanced reading: Grade 3–6,* 7–11. New York: Scholastic.

Reutzel, D. R. (1996b). A balanced reading approach. In J. Baltas & S. Shafer (Eds.), *Scholastic guide to balanced reading: K–2.* New York: Scholastic.

Reutzel, D. R. (1999a). On balanced reading. *The Reading Teacher, 52*(4), 2–4.

Reutzel, D. R. (1999b). Organizing literacy instruction: Effective grouping strategies and organizational plans. In L. M Morrow, L. B. Gambrell, S. Neuman, & M. Pressley (Eds.), *Best practices for literacy instruction.* New York: Guilford Press.

Reutzel, D. R. (2006). Hey teacher, when you say fluency, what do you mean?: Developing fluency and meta-fluency in elementary classrooms. In T.V. Rasinski, C. Blachowicz, & K. Lems (Eds.), *Fluency instruction: Research-based best practices* (pp. 62–85). New York: Guilford Press.

Reutzel, D. R., Camperell, K., & Smith, J. A. (2002). Helping struggling readers make sense of reading. In C. Collins-Block, L. B. Gambrell, & M. Pressley (Eds.), *Improving comprehension instruction: Advances in research, theory, and classroom practice.* San Francisco, CA: Jossey-Bass.

Reutzel, D. R., & Cooter, R. B. (2000). *Teaching children to read: Putting the pieces together* (3rd ed.). Upper Saddle River, NJ: Merrill/Prentice-Hall.

Reutzel, D. R., & Cooter, R. B. (2003). *Strategies for reading assessment and instruction: Helping every child succeed* (2nd ed.). Upper Saddle River, NJ: Merrill/Prentice-Hall.

Reutzel, D. R., & Cooter, R. B. (2003). *Strategies for assessment & intervention.* Upper Saddle River, NJ: Merrill/Prentice-Hall.

Reutzel, D. R., & Cooter, R. B. (2004). *Teaching children to read: Putting the pieces together* (4th ed.). Upper Saddle River, NJ: Merrill/Prentice-Hall.

Reutzel, D. R., & Cooter, R. B. (2005). *Essentials of teaching children to read.* Upper Saddle River, NJ: Merrill/Prentice-Hall.

Reutzel, D. R., & Cooter, R. B. (2007). *Strategies for reading assessment and instruction: Helping every child succeed* (3rd ed.). Upper Saddle River, NJ: Merrill/Prentice-Hall.

Reutzel, D. R., & Cooter, R. B., Jr. (1990). Whole language: Comparative effects on first-grade reading achievement. *Journal of Educational Research, 83,* 252–257.

Reutzel, D. R., & Cooter, R. B., Jr. (1991). Organizing for effective instruction: The reading workshop. *The Reading Teacher, 44*(8), 548–555.

Reutzel, D. R., & Cooter, R. B., Jr. (1999). *Balanced reading strategies and practices: Assessing and assisting readers with special needs.* Upper Saddle River, NJ: Merrill/Prentice-Hall.

Reutzel, D. R., & Daines, D. (1987a). The instructional cohesion of reading lessons in seven basal reading series. *Reading Psychology, 8,* 33–44.

Reutzel, D. R., & Daines, D. (1987b). The text-relatedness of seven basal reading series. *Reading Research and Instruction, 27,* 26–35.

Reutzel, D. R., & Fawson, P. C. (1989). Using a literature webbing strategy lesson with predictable books. *The Reading Teacher, 43*(3), 208–215.

Reutzel, D. R., & Fawson, P. C. (1990). Traveling tales: Connecting parents and children in writing. *The Reading Teacher, 44,* 222–227.

Reutzel, D. R., & Fawson, P. C. (1991). Literature webbing predictable books: A prediction strategy that helps below-average, first-grade readers. *Reading Research and Instruction, 30*(4), 20–30.

Reutzel, D. R., & Fawson, P. C. (1998). Global literacy connections: Stepping into the future. *Think, 8*(2), 32–34.

Reutzel, D. R., & Fawson, P. C. (2002). *Your classroom library—giving it more teaching power: Research-based strategies for developing better readers and writers.* New York: Scholastic Professional Books.

Reutzel, D. R., Fawson, P. C., & Smith, J. A. (2006). *Words to Go!:* Evaluating a firstgrade parent involvement program for "making" words at home. *Reading Research and Instruction 2,* 119–159.

Reutzel, D. R., Fawson, P., Young, J., & Morrison, T. (2003). Reading environmental print: What is the role of concepts about print in discriminating young readers' responses? *Reading Psychology, 24*(2), 123–162.

Reutzel, D. R., & Gali, K. (1998). The art of children's book selection: A labyrinth unexplored. *Reading Psychology, 19*(1), 3–50.

Reutzel, D. R., & Hollingsworth, P. M. (1988a). Highlighting key vocabulary: A generative-reciprocal procedure for teaching selected inference types. *Reading Research Quarterly, 23*(3), 358–378.

Reutzel, D. R., & Hollingsworth, P. M. (1988b). Whole language and the practitioner. *Academic Therapy, 23*(4), 405–416.

Reutzel, D. R., & Hollingsworth, P. M. (1991a). Investigating the development of topic-related attitude: Effect on children's reading and remembering text. *Journal of Educational Research, 84*(5), 334–344.

Reutzel, D. R., & Hollingsworth, P. M. (1991b). Reading comprehension skills: Testing the skills distinctiveness hypothesis. *Reading Research and Instruction, 30*(2), 32–46.

Reutzel, D. R., & Hollingsworth, P. M. (1991c). Reading time in school: Effect on fourth graders' performance on a criterion-referenced comprehension test. *Journal of Educational Research, 84*(3), 170–176.

Reutzel, D. R., & Hollingsworth, P. M. (1991d). Using literature webbing for books with predictable narrative: Improving young readers' predictions, comprehension, & story structure knowledge. *Reading Psychology, 12*(4), 319–333.

Reutzel, D. R., & Hollingsworth, P. M. (1993). Effects of fluency training on second graders' reading comprehension. *Journal of Educational Research, 86*(6), 325–331.

Reutzel, D. R., Hollingsworth, P. M., & Eldredge, J. L. (1994). Oral reading instruction: The impact on student reading development. *Reading Research Quarterly, 23*(1), 40–62.

Reutzel, D. R., & Larsen, N. S. (1995). Look what they've done to real children's books in the new basal readers. *Language Arts, 72*(7), 495–507.

Reutzel, D. R., & Mitchell, J. P. (2005). High-stakes accountability themed issue: How did we get here from there? *The Reading Teacher, 58*(4), 2–4.

Reutzel, D. R., & Morgan, B. C. (1990). Effects of prior knowledge, explicitness, and clause order on children's comprehension of causal relationships. *Reading Psychology: An International Quarterly, 11,* 93–114.

Reutzel, D. R., & Morrow, L. M. (in press). Promoting and assessing effective literacy learning classroom environments. In J. Paratore & C. McCormick (Eds.), *Classroom literacy assessment: Making sense of what students know and do.* New York: Guilford Press.

Reutzel, D. R., & Morrow, L. M. (in press). Promoting and assessing effective literacy learning classroom environments. In R. McCormick & J. M. Paratore (Eds.), *In-classroom literacy assessment.* New York: Guilford Press.

Reutzel, D. R., Oda, L. K., & Moore, B. H. (1989). Developing print awareness: The effect of three instructional approaches on kindergartners: Print awareness, reading readiness, and word reading. *Journal of Reading Behavior, 21*(3), 197–217.

Reutzel, D. R., & Sabey, B. (1995). Teacher beliefs about reading and children's conceptions: Are there connections? *Reading Research and Instruction, 35*(4), 323–342.

Reutzel, D. R., Smith, J. A., & Fawson, P. C. (2005). An evaluation of two approaches for teaching reading comprehension strategies in the primary years using science information texts. *Early Childhood Research Quarterly, 20,* 276–305.

Reutzel, D. R., & Wolfersberger, M. (1996). An environmental impact statement: Designing supportive literacy classrooms for young children. *Reading Horizons, 36*(3), 266–282.

Reutzel, D. R., Smith, J. A., & Fawson, P. C. (in preparation). *Reconsidering silent sustained reading (SSR): A comparative study of modified SSR with oral repeated reading practice.* Logan, UT: Utah State University.

Reznitskaya, A., & Anderson, R. C. (2002). The argument schema and learning to reason. In C. Collins-Block, L. B. Gambrell, & M. Pressley (Eds.) *Improving comprehension instruction: Advances in research, theory, and classroom practice* (pp. 319–334). San Francisco, CA: Jossey-Bass.

Rhodes, L. K., & Dudley-Marling, C. (1988). *Readers and writers with a difference.* Portsmouth, NH: Heinemann.

Rhodes, L. K., & Shanklin, N. (1993). *Windows into literacy: Assessing learners K–8.* Portsmouth, NH: Heinemann.

Ribowsky, H. (1985). *The effects of a code emphasis approach and a whole language approach upon emergent literacy of kindergarten children* (Report No. CS-008-397). (ERIC Document Reproduction Service)

Rice, P. E. (1991). Novels in the news. *The Reading Teacher, 45*(2), 159–160.

Rich, E. S. (1964). *Hannah Elizabeth.* New York: HarperCollins.

Richards, M. (2000). Be a good detective: Solve the case of oral reading fluency. *The Reading Teacher, 53*(7), 534–539.

Richek, M. A. (1978). Readiness skills that predict initial word learning using 2 different methods of instruction. *Reading Research Quarterly, 13,* 200–222.

Richgels, D. J. (2001). Invented spelling, phonemic awareness, and reading and writing instruction. In Neuman, S. B., & Dickinson, D. K. (Eds.), *Handbook of early literacy research* (pp. 142–155). New York: Guilford Press.

Richgels, D. J., & Wold, L. S. (1998). Literacy on the road: Backpacking partnerships between school and home. *The Reading Teacher, 52*(1), 18–29.

Rijlaarsdam, G., & van den Bergh, H. (2006). Writing process theory. In C. A. MacArthur, S. Graham, & J. Fitzgerald (Eds.), *Handbook of writing research.* New York: Guilford.

Riley, R. E. (1993). *Adult literacy in America.* Washington, DC: United States Department of Education.

Rinehart, S. D., Stahl, S. A., & Erickson, L. G. (1986). Some effects of summarization training on reading and studying. *Reading Research Quarterly, 21*(4), 422–438.

Ring, S. (2003). *Bridges.* Boston, MA: Newbridge.

Roberts, B. (1992). The evolution of the young child's concept of word as a unit of spoken and written language. *Reading Research Quarterly, 27*(2), 124–139.

Roberts, T. (1975). Skills of analysis and synthesis in the early stages of reading. *British Journal of Educational Psychology, 45,* 3–9.

Robertson, C., Keating, I., Shenton, L., & Roberts, I. (1996). Uninterrupted, sustained, silent reading: The rhetoric and the practice. *Journal of Research in Reading, 19,* 25–35.

Robinson, A. (In press). *American Reading Instruction.* Newark, DE: International Reading Association.

Robinson, B. (1972). *The best Christmas pageant ever.* New York: HarperCollins.

Robinson, F. (1946). *Effective study.* New York: Harper Brothers.

Robinson, H. M. (1972). Perceptual training—does it result in reading improvement? In R. C. Aukerman (Ed.), *Some persistent questions on beginning reading* (pp. 135–150). Newark, DE: International Reading Association.

Rogg, L. J. (2001). *Early literacy instruction in kindergarten.* Newark, DE: International Reading Association.

Roller, C. M. (2002). *Comprehensive reading instruction across the grade levels: A collection of papers from the Reading Research 2001 Conference.* Newark, DE: International Reading Association.

Romero, G. G. (1983). *Print awareness of the preschool bilingual Spanish English speaking child.* Unpublished doctoral dissertation, University of Arizona Tucson.

Rosenbaum, J. (1980). *Making inequality: The hidden curriculum of high school tracking.* New York: Wiley.

Rosenblatt, L. M. (1978). *The reader, the text, and the poem.* Carbondale, IL: Southern Illinois University Press.

Rosenblatt, L. M. (1989). Writing and reading: The transactional theory. In J. M. Mason (Ed.), *Reading and writing connections* (pp. 153–175). Boston: Allyn & Bacon.

Rosenblatt, L. M. (2004). The transactional theory of reading and writing. In R. B. Ruddell & N. J. Unrau (Eds.), *Theoretical models and processes of reading* (5th ed.) (pp. 1363–1398). NWP Publications.

Rosenhouse, J., Feitelson, D., & Kita, B. (1997). Interactive reading aloud to Israeli first graders: its contribution to literacy development. *Reading Research Quarterly, 32,* 168–183.

Rosenshine, B., & Meister, C. (1994). Reciprocal teaching: A review of nineteen experimental studies. *Review of Educational Research, 64,* 479–530.

Rosenshine, B. V. (1980). Skill hierarchies in reading comprehension. In R. J. Spiro, B. C. Bruce, & W. F. Brewer (Eds.), *Theoretical issues in reading comprehension* (pp. 535–554). Hillsdale, NJ: Erlbaum.

Roser, N. L., Hoffman, J. V., & Farest, C. (1990). Language, literature, and at-risk children. *The Reading Teacher, 43*(8), 554–561.

Roskos, K., & Neuman, S. B. (2001). Environment and its influences for early literacy teaching and learning. In S. B. Neuman & D. K. Dickinson (Eds.), *Handbook of Early Literacy Research* (pp. 281–294). New York: Guildford Press.

Roswell, F. G., & Chall, J. S. (1963). *Auditory Blending Test.* New York: Essay Press.

Rouse, H. L., & Fantuzzo, J. W. (2006). Validity of the *Dynamic Indicators for Basic Early Literacy Skills* as an indicator of early literacy for urban kindergarten children. *The School Psychology Review, 35*(3) 341–355.

Routman, R. (1988). *Transitions: From literature to literacy.* Portsmouth, NH: Heinemann.

Routman, R. (1996). *Literacy at the crossroads: Crucial talk about reading, writing, and other teaching dilemmas.* Portsmouth, NH: Heinemann.

Routman, R. (2003). *Reading Essentials: The specifics you need to know to teach reading well.* Portsmouth, NH: Heinemann.

Rowe, M. B. (1974). Wait-time and rewards as instructional variables, their influence on language, logic, and fate control: Part one—wait time. *Journal of Research in Science Teaching, 11,* 81–94.

Rowling, J. K. (1998). *Harry Potter and the Sorcerer's Stone.* New York: Scholastic.

Ruddell, R. (1974). *Reading-language instruction: Innovative practices.* Upper Saddle River, NJ: Prentice-Hall.

Ruddell, R. B., & Ruddell, M. R. (1995). *Teaching children to read and write: Becoming an influential teacher.* Boston: Allyn & Bacon.

Ruddell, R. B., & Unrau, N. J. (1997). The role of responsive teaching in focusing reader intention and developing reader motivation. In J. T. Guthrie & A. Wigfield (Eds.), *Reading engagement: Motivating readers through integrated instruction.* Newark, DE: International Reading Association.

Ruddell, R. B., & Unrau, N. J. (2004). *Theoretical models and processes of reading* (5th ed.). Newark, DE: International Reading Association.

Rule, A. C. (2001). Alphabetizing with environmental print. *The Reading Teacher, 54*(6), 558–562.

Rumelhart, D. E. (1975). Notes on a schema for stories. In D. G. Bobrow & A. Collins (Eds.), *Representation and understanding: Studies in cognitive science* (pp. 211–236). New York: Academic Press.

Rumelhart, D. E. (1980). Schemata: The building blocks of cognition. In R. J. Spiro (Ed.), *Theoretical issues in reading comprehension* (pp. 33–58). Hillsdale, NJ: Erlbaum.

Rumelhart, D. E. (1981). Schemata: The building blocks of cognition. In Guthrie, J. T. (Ed.), *Comprehension and teaching: Research reviews* (pp. 3–26). Newark, DE: International Reading Association.

Rumelhart, D. E. (1984). Understanding understanding. In J. Flood (Ed.), *Understanding reading comprehension* (pp. 1–20). Newark, DE: International Reading Association.

Rupley, W., & Blair, T. (1987). Assignment and supervision of reading seatwork: Looking in on 12 primary teachers. *The Reading Teacher, 40*(4), 391–393.

Rupley, W. H., & Blair, T. R. (1978). Teacher effectiveness in reading instruction. *The Reading Teacher, 31,* 970–973.

Ryder, R. J., & Graves, M. F. (1994). Vocabulary instruction presented prior to reading in two basal readers. *Elementary School Journal, 95,* 139–153.

Rye, J. (1982). *Cloze procedure and the teaching of reading.* Portsmouth, NH: Heinemann.

Sadoski, M., & Pavio, A. (2004). A dual coding theoretical model of reading. In R. B. Ruddell & N. J. Unrau (Eds.), *Theoretical models and processes of reading* (5th ed.) (pp. 1329–1362). Newark, DE: International Reading Association.

Sadoski, M., & Quast, Z. (1990). Reader response and long-term recall for journalistic text: The roles of imagery, affect, and importance. *Reading Research Quarterly, 24*(4), 256–272.

Sadow, M. W. (1982). The use of story grammar in the design of questions. *The Reading Teacher, 35,* 518–523.

Salvia, J., & Ysseldyke, J. E. (2004). *Assessment in special and inclusive education* (9th ed.). Boston: Houghton Mifflin.

Samuels, S. J. (1967). Attentional process in reading: The effect of pictures on the acquisition of reading responses. *Journal of Educational Psychology, 58,* 337–342.

Samuels, S. J. (1970). Effects of pictures on learning to read, comprehension, and attitudes. *Review of Educational Research, 40,* 397–408.

Samuels, S. J. (1979). The method of repeated reading. *The Reading Teacher, 32,* 403–408.

Samuels, S. J. (2006). Toward a model of reading fluency. In S. J. Samuels & A. E. Farstrup (Eds.), *What research has to say about fluency instruction* (pp. 24–46). Newark, DE: International Reading Association.

Samuels, S. J., & Farstrup, A. E. (2006). *What research has to say about fluency instruction.* Newark, DE: International Reading Association.

Sanders, W. A., & Rivers, J. C. (1996). *Cumulative and residual effects of teachers on future student academic achievement.* Knoxville: University of Tennessee Value-Added Research and Assessment Center.

Sandora, C., Beck, I. L, & McKeown, M. G. (1999). A comparison of two discussion strategies on students' comprehension and interpretation of complex literature. *Reading Psychology, 20*(3), 177–212.

Sanford, A. J., & Garrod, S. C. (1981). *Understanding written language.* New York: Wiley.

Santa, C. (1990). *Reporting on the Montana Teacher Change Project: Kallispell reading/language initiative.* Utah Council of the International Reading Association, Salt Lake City, UT.

Santa, C. M. (1997). School change and literacy engagement: Preparing teaching and learning environments. In J. T. Guthrie & A. Wigfield (Eds.), *Reading engagement: Motivating readers through integrated instruction.* Newark, DE: International Reading Association.

Santa, C. M., & Heien, T. (1998). An assessment of Early Steps: A program for early interventions of reading problems. *Reading Research Quarterly, 34*(1), 54–79.

Savage, J. F. (1994). *Teaching reading using literature.* Madison, WI: Brown & Benchmark.

Scarborough, H. S. (2001). Connecting early language and literacy to later reading (dis) abilities: Evidence, theory, and practice. In S. B. Neuman & D. K. Dickinson (Eds.), *Handbook of early literacy research* (Vol. 1) (pp. 97–110). New York: Guilford.

Scarborough, H. S., & Dobrich, W. (1994). On the efficacy of reading to preschoolers. *Developmental Review, 14,* 245–302.

Schmidt, K. (1985). *The gingerbread man.* New York, NY: Scholastic Books.

Schneider, W., & Shiffrin, R. M. (1977). Controlled and automatic human information processing: 1. Detection, search, and attention, *Psychological Review, 84*(1), 1–66.

Scholastic. (1986). *Talking text* (computer program). Jefferson City, MO: Scholastic.

Scholastic. (1990). *Bank Street writer III* (computer program). Jefferson City, MO: Scholastic Software.

Scholastic. (1995). *Literary place program.* New York: Author.

Schreiber, A., & Tuchman, G. (1997). *Scholastic Phonics Readers The Big Hit: Book 14.* New York: Scholastic.

Schunk, D. H., & Zimmerman, B. J. (1997). Developing self-efficacious readers and writers: The role of social and self-regulatory processes. In J. T. Guthrie and A. Wigfield (Eds.), *Reading engagement: Motivating readers through integrated instruction* (pp. 34–50). Newark, DE: International Reading Association.

Schwartz, D. M. (1985). *How much is a million?* Richard Hill, Ontario: Scholastic-TAB.

Schwartz, R. M., & Raphael, T. E. (1985). Concept of definition: A key to improving students' vocabulary. *The Reading Teacher, 39*(2), 198–205.

Scieszka, J. (1989). *The true story of the 3 little pigs: By A. Wolf.* New York: Viking Kestrel.

Searfoss, L. W. (1975). Radio reading. *The Reading Teacher, 29,* 295–296.

Searfoss, L. W., & Readence, J. E. (1989). *Helping children learn to read* (2nd ed.). Upper Saddle River, NJ: Prentice-Hall.

Seefeldt, C., & Barbour, N. (1986). *Early childhood education: An introduction.* Upper Saddle River, NJ: Merrill/Prentice-Hall.

Seidenberg, P. L. (1989). Relating text-processing research to reading and writing instruction for learning disabled students. *Learning Disabilities Focus, 5*(1), 4–12.

Sendak, M. (1962). *Chicken soup with rice.* New York: Scholastic.

Sendak, M. (1963). *Where the wild things are*. New York: HarperCollins.

Senechal, M., & Cornell, E. H. (1993). Vocabulary acquisition through shared reading experiences. *Reading Research Quarterly, 28*(4), 361–373.

Seuss, D. (1954). *Horton hears a Who!* New York: Random House.

Shake, M. (1986). Teacher interruptions during oral reading instruction: Self-monitoring as an impetus for change in corrective feedback. *Remedial and Special Education, 7*(5), 18–24.

Shake, M. C., & Allington, R. L. (1985). Where do teacher's questions come from? *The Reading Teacher, 38*, 432–439.

Shanahan, T. (1984). Nature of the reading-writing relation: An exploratory multi-variate analysis. *Journal of Educational Psychology, 76*, 466–477.

Shanahan, T. (2003a). Research-based reading instruction: Myths about the National Reading Panel report. *The Reading Teacher, 56*(7), 646–655.

Shanahan, T. (2003b). *A framework for improving reading achievement*. Paper presented at the National Conference on Family Literacy and the California Family Literacy Conference. Long Beach, California, March 16, 2003.

Shanahan, T. (2004). Critiques of the National Reading Panel report: Their implications for research, policy, and practice. In P. McCardle & V. Chhabra (Eds.), *The voice of evidence in reading research* (pp. 235–266). Baltimore: MD: Paul H. Brookes.

Shanahan, T. (2004, November). *How do you raise reading achievement?* Paper presented at the Utah Council of the International Reading Association Meeting, Salt Lake City, UT.

Shanahan, T. (2006). Relations among oral language, reading, and writing. In C. A. MacArthur, S. Graham, & J. Fitzgerald (Eds.), *Handbook of writing research* (pp. 171–186). New York: Guilford Press.

Shanahan, T. (2006). Relations among oral language, reading, and writing development. In C. A. MacArthur, S. Graham, & J. Fitzgerald (Eds.), *Handbook of writing research* (pp. 171–186). New York: Guilford Press.

Shanahan, T., & Barr, R. (1995). Reading Recovery: An independent evaluation of the effects of an early intervention for at-risk learners. *Reading Research Quarterly, 30*(40), 958–996.

Shanahan, T., & Lomax, R. G. (1986). An analysis and comparison of theoretical models of the reading-writing relationship. *Journal of Educational Psychology, 78*, 116–123.

Shanahan, T., Mulhern, M., & Rodriquez-Brown, F. (1995). Project FLAME: Lessons learned from a family literacy program for minority families. *The Reading Teacher, 48*, 40–47.

Shanklin, N. L., & Rhodes, L. K. (1989). Comprehension instruction as sharing and extending. *The Reading Teacher, 43*(7), 496–500.

Shannon, P. (1983). The use of commercial reading materials in American elementary schools. *Reading Research Quarterly, 19*, 68–85.

Shannon, P. (1989a). Basal readers: Three perspectives. *Theory Into Practice, 28*(4), 235–239.

Shannon, P. (1989b). *Broken promises*. Granby, MA: Bergin & Garvey.

Shannon, P. (1992). *Becoming political: Readings and writings in the politics of literacy education*. Portsmouth, NH: Heinemann.

Shannon, P. (1993). Letters to the editor: Comments on Baumann. *Reading Research Quarterly, 28*(2), 86.

Shannon, P., & Goodman, K. (1994). *Basal readers: A second look*. New York: Owen.

Sharmat, M. W. (1980). *Gila monsters meet you at the airport*. New York: Aladdin.

Shaywitz, S. E., & Shaywitz, B. A. (2004). Neurobiologic basis for reading and reading disability. In P. McCardle & V. Chhabra (Eds.), *The voice of evidence in reading research* (pp. 417–444). Baltimore: MD: Paul H. Brookes.

Shermis, M. D., Burstein, J., & Leacock, C. (2006). Applications of computers in assessment and analysis of writing. In C. A. MacArthur, S. Graham, & J. Fitzgerald (Eds.), *Handbook of writing research*. New York: Guilford.

Shinn, M. R. (Ed.). (1989). *Curriculum-based measurement: Assessing special children*. NY: Guilford.

Shockley, B., Michalove, B., & Allen, J. (1995). *Engaging Families*. Portsmouth, NH: Heinemann.

Short, K. G., Harste, J. C., & Burke, C. (1996). *Creating classrooms for authors and inquirers*. Portsmouth, NH:Heinemann.

Shulman, L. (2001). *Ways of measuring: Then and now*. Northborough, MA: Sundance Publishers.

Siegel, M. (1983). *Reading as signification*. Unpublished doctoral dissertation, Indiana University.

Silvaroli, N. J. (1986). *Classroom reading inventory* (5th ed.). Dubuque, IA: William C. Brown.

Silverstein, S. (1974). *Where the sidewalk ends.* New York: HarperCollins.

Silverstein, S. (1996). *Falling Up.* New York: Harper-Collins.

Simmons, D. C., & Kame'enui, E. J. (1998). *What reading research tells us about children with diverse learning needs: Bases and basics.* Mahwah, NJ: Erlbaum.

Simmons, D. C., & Kame'enui, E. J. (2003). *A consumer's guide to evaluating a core reading program, Grades K–3: A critical elements analysis.* Eugene, OR: University of Oregon.

Sinatra, R. C., Stahl-Gemake, J., & Berg, W. (1984). Improving reading comprehension of disabled readers through semantic mapping. *Reading Teacher, 38*(1), 22–29.

Singer, H. (1960). *Conceptual ability in the substrata-factor theory of reading.* Unpublished doctoral dissertation, University of California at Berkeley.

Singer, H. (1978a). Active comprehension: From answering to asking questions. *The Reading Teacher, 31,* 901–908.

Singer, H. (1978b). Research in reading that should make a difference in classroom instruction. In *What research has to say about reading instruction* (pp. 57–71). Newark, DE: International Reading Association.

Singer, H., & Donlan, D. (1989). *Reading and learning from text* (2nd ed.). Hillsdale, NJ: Erlbaum.

Sippola, A. E. (1994). Holistic analysis of basal readers: An assessment tool. *Reading Horizons, 34*(3), 234–246.

Skaar, G. (1972). *What do the animals say?* New York: Scholastic.

Slaughter, H. B. (1988). Indirect and direct teaching in a whole language program. *The Reading Teacher, 42*(1), 30–35.

Slaughter, J. J. (1993). *Beyond storybooks: Young children and the shared book experience.* Newark, DE: International Reading Association.

Slavin, R. E. (1987). Ability grouping and student achievement in elementary schools: A best-evidence synthesis. *Review of Educational Research, 57*(3), 293–336.

Slavin, R. E. (1988). Cooperative learning and student achievement. *Educational Leadership, 45,* 31–33.

Slavin, R. E. (1991). Are cooperative learning and "untracking" harmful to the gifted? *Education Leadership, 48*(6), 68–71.

Slavin, R. E. (1995). *Cooperative learning: Theory, research, and practice.* Needham Heights, MA: Allyn & Bacon.

Slavin, R. E., & Madden, N. (1995). Effects of success for all on the achievement of English language learners. Paper presented at the annual meeting of the American Educational Research Association, San Francisco, CA, April, 1995.

Slavin, R. E., Madden, N. A., Karweit, N. L., Livermon, B. J., & Dolan, L. (1990). Success for all: First-year outcomes of a comprehensive plan for reforming urban education. *American EducationalResearch Journal, 27,* 255–278.

Slavin, R. E., Madden, N. L., Dolan, L., & Wasik, B. A. (1996). *Every child, every school: Success for all.* Thousand Oaks, CA: Corwin.

Slavin, R. E., Madden, N. L., Karweit, N. L., Dolan, L., & Wasik, B. A. (1992). *Success for all: A relentless approach to prevention and early intervention in elementary schools.* Arlington, VA: Educational Research Services.

Slosson, R. L. (1971). *Slosson intelligence test.* East Aurora, NY: Slosson Educational Publications.

Sloyer, S. (1982). *Reader's theater: Story dramatization in the classroom.* Urbana, IL: National Council of Teachers of English.

Smith, D. E. P. (1967). *Learning to learn.* New York: Harcourt Brace.

Smith, E. B., Goodman, K. S., & Meredith, R. (1976). *Language and thinking in school* (2nd ed.). New York: Holt, Rinehart and Winston.

Smith, F. (1977). The uses of language. *Language Arts, 54*(6), 638–644.

Smith, F. (1983). *Essays into literacy.* Exeter, NH: Heinemann.

Smith, F. (1985). *Reading without nonsense* (2nd ed.). New York: Teachers College Press.

Smith, F. (1987). *Insult to intelligence.* New York: Arbor House.

Smith, F. (1988). *Understanding reading* (4th ed.). Hillsdale, NJ: Erlbaum.

Smith, K. A. (1989). *A checkup with the doctor.* New York: McDougal, Littell.

Smith, M. W. & Dickinson, D. K. (2002). *Early language and literacy classroom observation (ELLCO).* Baltimore, MD: Paul H. Brookes.

Smith, M. W., Dickinson, D. K., Sangeorge, A., & Anastasopoulos, L. (2002). *Early language and literacy classroom observation (ELLCO) toolkit.* Baltimore, MD: Paul H. Brookes.

Smith, N. B. (1965). *American reading instruction.* Newark, DE: International Reading Association.

Smith, N. B. (1986). *American reading instruction.* Newark, DE: International Reading Association.

Smith, N. B. (2002). *American reading instruction—special edition.* Newark, DE: International Reading Association.

Smith, P. G. (2001). *Talking classrooms: Shaping children's learning through oral language instruction.* Newark, DE: International Reading Association.

Smith, R. K. (1981). *Jelly belly.* New York: Dell.

Smolkin, L. B., & Donovan, C. A. (2000). *The contexts of comprehension: Information book read alouds and comprehension acquisition.* (CIERA Report #2-009). Ann Arbor, MI: Center for the Improvement of Early Reading Achievement.

Smoot, R. C., & Price, J. (1975). *Chemistry, a modern course.* Upper Saddle River, NJ: Merrill/Prentice-Hall.

Snow, C. (1999). *Preventing reading difficulties.* Keynote address at the Second Annual Commissioner's Reading Day, Austin, TX.

Snow, C. E., Burns, M. N., & Griffin, P. (1998). *Preventing reading difficulties in young children.* Washington: National Academy Press.

Snow, C. E., Griffin, P., & Burns, M. S. (2005). *Knowledge to support the teaching of reading: Preparing teachers for a changing world.* San Francisco, CA: Jossey-Bass.

Snow, C. E., Scarborough, H. S., & Burns, M. S. (1999). What speech-language pathologists need to know about early reading. *Topics in Language Disorders, 20*(1), 48–58.

Snowball, D., & Bolton, F. (1999). *Spelling K–8: Planning and teaching.* York, ME: Stenhouse.

Soto, G. (1993). *Local news.* San Diego, CA: Harcourt Brace.

Spache, G., & Spache, E. (1977). *Reading in the elementary school* (4th ed.). Boston: Allyn & Bacon.

Spady, W., & Marshall, K. J. (1991). Beyond traditional outcome-based education. *Educational Leadership, 48,* 67–72.

Spangler, K. L. (1983). Reading interests vs. reading preferences: Using the research. *The Reading Teacher, 36*(9), 876–878.

Speare, E. G. (1958). *The witch of Blackbird Pond.* New York: Dell.

Sperry, A. (1940). *Call it courage.* New York: Macmillan.

Spiegel, D. L. (1981). Six alternatives to the directed reading activity. *The Reading Teacher, 34,* 914–922.

Spiegel, D. L. (1999). The perspective of the balanced approach. In S. M. Blair-Larsen & K. A. Williams (Eds.), *The balanced reading program: Helping all students achieve success* (pp. 8–23). Newark, DE: International Reading Association.

Spier, P. (1977). *Noah's ark.* Garden City, NY: Doubleday.

Spinelli, J. (1991). Catching Maniac Magee. *The Reading Teacher, 45*(3), 174–176.

Spivak, M. (1973). Archetypal place. *Architectural Forum, 140,* 44–49.

Squire, J. R. (1983). Composing and comprehending: Two sides of the same basic process. *Language Arts, 60*(5), 581–589.

Squire, J. R. (1989). A reading program for all seasons. *Theory into Practice, 28*(4), 254–257.

St. John, E. P., & Loescher, S. A. (2001). *Improving early reading: A resource guide for elementary schools.* Bloomington, IN: Indiana Education Policy Center.

St. Pierre, R. G., Gamse, B., Alamprese, J., Rimdzius, T., & Tao, F. (1998). *National evaluation of the Even Start family literacy program: Evidence from the past and a look to the future.* Washington, DC: U.S. Department of Education Planning and Evaluation Service.

Stage, S., Sheppard, J., Davidson, M. M., & Browning, M. M. (2001). Prediction of first-graders' growth in oral reading fluency using kindergarten letter fluency. *Journal of School Psychology, 39*(3), 225–237.

Stahl, K. (2004). Proof, practice, and promise: Comprehension strategy instruction in the primary grades. *The Reading Teacher, 57*(7), 598–609.

Stahl, K. A., & McKenna, M. C. (2006). *Reading research at work: Foundations of effective practice.* New York: Guilford Press.

Stahl, S. (2004). What do we do about fluency? In P. McCardle & V. Chhabra (Eds.), *The voice of evidence in reading research* (pp. 187–211). Baltimore: MD: Paul H. Brookes.

Stahl, S. A. (1986). Three principles of effective vocabulary instruction. *Journal of Reading, 29*(7), 662–668.

Stahl, S. A., Bradley, B., Smith, C. H., Kuhn, M. R., Schwanenglugel, P., Meisinger, E., et al. (2003). *Teaching children to become fluent and automatic readers*. Paper presented at the annual meeting of the American Educational Research Association, Chicago.

Stahl, S. A., & Fairbanks, M. M. (1986). The effects of vocabulary instruction: A model-based meta-analysis. *Review of Educational Research, 56*(1), 72–110.

Stahl, S. A., Hare, V. C., Sinatra, R., & Gregory, J. F. (1991). Defining the role of prior knowledge and vocabulary in reading comprehension: The retiring of number 41. *Journal of Reading Behavior, 23*(4), 487–507.

Stahl, S. A., Heuback, K., & Cramond, B. (1997). *Fluency-oriented reading instruction*. Athens, GA and Washington, D.C.: National Reading Research Center and U.S. Department of Education, Office of Educational Research and Improvement, Educational Resources Information Center.

Stahl, S. A., & Jacobson, M. G. (1986). Vocabulary difficulty, prior knowledge, and text comprehension. *Journal of Reading Behavior, 18*(4), 309–319.

Stahl, S. A., & Kapinus, B. (2001). *Word power: What every educator needs to know about teaching vocabulary.*Washington, DC: National Education Association.

Stahl, S. A., & Miller, P. D. (1989). Whole language and language experience approaches for beginning reading: A quantitative research synthesis. *Review of Educational Research, 59*, 87–116.

Stahl, S. A., & Murray, B. A. (1993). Environmental print, phonemic awareness, letter recognition, and word recognition. In D. J. Leu & C. I. Kinzer (Eds.), *Examining central issues in literacy research, theory, and practice* (pp. 227–233). Chicago: National Reading Conference.

Standard for the English Language Arts. (1996). A project of The International Reading Association and National Council of Teachers of English. Newark, DE: International Reading Association.

Stanovich, E., & West, R. F. (1989). Exposure to print and orthographic processing. *Reading Research Quarterly, 24*, 402–433.

Stanovich, K. (1980). Toward an interactive-compensatory model of individual differences in the development of reading fluency. *Reading Research Quarterly, 16*(1), 37–71.

Stanovich, P. J., & Stanovich, K. E. (2003). *Using research and reason in education: How teachers can use scientifically-based research to make curricular and instructional decisions*. Washington, DC: National Institute for Literacy.

Stauffer, R. G. (1969). *Directing reading maturity as a cognitive process*. New York: HarperCollins.

Stauffer, R. G. (1975). *Directing the reading-thinking process*. New York: HarperCollins.

Stayter, F., & Allington, R. (1991). Fluency and the understanding of texts. *Theory Into Practice, 30*(3), 143–148.

Stayter, F. Z., & Allington, R. L. (1991). Fluency and the understanding of texts. *Theory Into Practice, 30*(3), 143–148.

Stead, T. (2001). *Is that a fact? Teaching nonfiction writing K–3*. Portland, ME: Stenhouse.

Stead, T. (2006). *The use of non-fiction informational text in developing comprehension*. Presentation at the Texas State Reading Association Annual Conference, November 11, 2006.

Stedman, L. C., & Kaestle, C. E. (1987). Literacy and reading performance in the United States from 1880 to the present. *Reading Research Quarterly, 22*, 8–46.

Steele, W. O. (1958). *The perilous road*. Orlando, FL: Harcourt Brace.

Stein, M. (1993). *The beginning reading instruction study*. Syracuse, NY: Educational Resources Information Center (ERIC) Document Reproduction Service.

Stein, N. L., & Glenn, C. G. (1979). An analysis of story comprehension in elementary school children. In R. O. Freedle (Ed.), *New directions in discourse processing* (pp. 53–120). Hillsdale, NJ: Erlbaum.

Steinbeck, J. (1937). *The red pony*. New York: Bantam Books.

Stenner, A. J. (1996). *Measuring reading comprehension with the Lexile framework*. Washington, DC: Paper presented at the 4th North American Conference on Adolescent/Adult Literacy.

Stenner, A. J., & Burdick, D. S. (1997). *The objective measurement of reading comprehension*. Durham, NC: MetaMetrics.

Steptoe, J. (1987). *Mufaro's beautiful daughters: An African tale*. New York: Lothrop, Lee, & Shepard Books.

Stern, D. N., & Wasserman, G. A. (1979). *Maternal language to infants*. Paper presented at a meeting of the Society for Research in Child Development. Ann Arbor, MI.

Stevens, R., & Rosenshine, B. (1981). Advances in research on teaching. *Exceptional Education Quarterly, 2*, 1–9.

Stevens, R. J., Madden, N. A., Slavin, R. E., & Farnish, A. (1987a). *Cooperative integrated reading and* composition: *A brief overview of the CIRC program.* Baltimore, MD: Johns Hopkins University, Center for Research on Elementary and Middle Schools.

Stevens, R. J., Madden, N. A., Slavin, R. E., & Farnish, A. M. (1987b). Cooperative integrated reading and composition: Two field experiments. *Reading Research Quarterly, 22*(4), 433–454.

Stevens, R. J., & Slavin, R. E. (1995). Effects of a cooperative learning approach in reading and writing on academically handicapped and nonhandicapped students. *Elementary School Journal, 95*(3), 241–262.

Stolz, M. (1963). *Bully on Barkham Street.* New York: HarperCollins.

Stoodt, B. D. (1989). *Reading instruction.* New York: HarperCollins.

Straub, S. B. (2003). Read to me: A family literacy program for young mothers and their babies. In A. DeBruin-Parecki & B. Krol-Sinclair (Eds.), *Family literacy: From theory to practice* (pp. 184–201). Newark, DE: International Reading Association.

Straub, S. B., & DeBruin-Parecki, A. (2002, May). *Read to me: A unique high school program linking teenage mothers, their babies, and books.* Paper presented at the 47th Annual Convention of the International Reading Association, San Francisco, CA.

Strickland, D. S. (1998). *Teaching phonics today: A primer for educators.* Newark, DE: International Reading Association.

Strickland, D. S., Feeley, J. T., & Wepner, S. B. (1987). *Using computers in the teaching of reading.* New York: Teachers College Press.

Strickland, D. S., Snow, C., Griffin, P., Burns, M. S., & McNamara, P. (2002). *Preparing our teachers: Opportunities for better reading instruction.* Washington, DC: John Henry Press.

Sucher, F., & Allred, R. A. (1986). *Sucher-Allred group reading placement test.* Oklahoma City: Economy.

Sukhomlinsky, V. (1981). *To children I give my heart.* Moscow, USSR: Progress.

Sulzby, E. (1985). Children's emergent reading of favorite storybooks: A developmental study. *Reading Research Quarterly, 20*(4), 458–481.

Sulzby, E. (1991). Assessment of emergent literacy: Storybook reading. *The Reading Teacher, 44*(7), 498–500.

Sulzby, E., Hoffman, J., Niles, J., Shanahan, T., & Teale, W. (1989). *McGraw-Hill reading.* New York: McGraw-Hill.

Sunburst. (1987). *The puzzler.* Pleasantville, NY: Sunburst Communications.

Swafford, J. (1995). I wish all my groups were like this one: Facilitating peer interaction during group work. *Journal of Reading, 38*(8), 626–631.

Sweet, A. (1997). Teacher perceptions of student motivation and their relation to literacy learning. In J. T. Guthrie & A. Wigfield (Eds.), *Reading engagement: Motivating readers through integrated instruction.* Newark, DE: International Reading Association.

Sweet, A. P., & Snow, C. E. (2003). *Rethinking reading comprehension.* New York: Guilford Press.

Szymusiak, K., & Sibberson, F. (2001). *Beyond leveled books: Supporting transitional readers in grades 2–5.* Portland, ME: Stenhouse.

Taba, H. (1975). *Teacher's handbook for elementary social studies.* Reading, MA: Addison-Wesley.

Tarver, S. G., & Dawson, M. M. (1978). Modality preference and the teaching of reading: A review. *Journal of Learning Disabilities, 11*(1), 5–17.

Taxel, J. (1993). The politics of children's literature: Reflections on multiculturalism and Christopher Columbus. In V. J. Harris (Ed.), *Teaching multicultural literature in grades K–8* (pp. 1–36). Norwood, MA: Christopher Gordon.

Taylor, B., Harris, L. A., & Pearson, P. D. (1988). *Reading difficulties: Instruction and assessment.* New York: Random House.

Taylor, B. M., & Pearson, P. D. (2002). *Teaching reading: Effective schools, accomplished teachers.* Mahwah, NJ: Lawrence Erlbaum Associates.

Taylor, B. M., Frye, B. J., & Gaetz, T. M. (1990). Reducing the number of reading skill activities in the elementary classroom. *Journal of Reading Behavior, 22*(2), 167–180.

Taylor, B. M., Graves, M. F., & Van den Broek, P. (2000). *Reading for meaning: Fostering comprehension in the middle grades.* New York: Teachers College Press.

Taylor, B. M., Pearson, P. D., & Clark, K. (2000). Effective schools and accomplished teachers: Lessons about primary-grade reading instruction in low-income schools. *Elementary School Journal, 101*(2), 121–165.

Taylor, B. M., Pearson, P. D., Clark, K. E., & Walpole, S. (1999). *Beating the odds in teaching all children to read* (Ciera Report No.2–006). Ann Arbor, MI: Center for the Improvement of Early Reading Achievement.

Taylor, B. M, Pearson, P. D., Clark, K. F., & Walpole, S. (2000). Effective schools and accomplished teachers: Lessons about primary grade reading instruction in low-income schools. *Elementary School Journal, 101,* 121–165.

Taylor, B. M. Pearson, P. D., Peterson, D. S., & Rodriguez, M. C. (2005). The CIERA School Change Framework: An evidence-based approach to professional development and school reading improvement. *Reading Research Quarterly, 40*(1), 40–69.

Taylor, D. (1983). *Family literacy: Young children learning to read and write.* Portsmouth, NH: Heinemann.

Taylor, D., & Strickland, D. S. (1986). *Family storybook reading.* Portsmouth, NH: Heinemann.

Taylor, G. C. (1981). ERIC/RCS report: Music in language arts instruction. *Language Arts, 58,* 363–368.

Taylor, M. D. (1990). *Road to Memphis.* New York: Dial Books.

Taylor, N. E. (1986). Developing beginning literacy concepts: Content and context. In D. B. Yaden, Jr., & S. Templeton (Eds.), *Metalinguistic awareness and beginning literacy* (pp. 173–184). Portsmouth, NH: Heinemann.

Taylor, N. E., Blum, I. H., & Logsdon, M. (1986). The development of written language awareness: Environmental aspects and program characteristics. *Reading Research Quarterly, 21*(2), 132–149.

Taylor, W. L. (1953). Cloze procedure: A new tool for measuring readability. *Journalism Quarterly, 30,* 415–433.

Teale, W. H. (1987). Emergent literacy: Reading and writing development in early childhood. In J. E. Readence, R. S. Baldwin, J. P. Konopak, & H. Newton (Eds.), *Research in literacy: Merging perspectives* (pp. 45–74). Rochester, NY: National Reading Conference.

Teale, W. H., & Martinez, M. (1986a). Reading in a kindergarten classroom library. *The Reading Teacher, 41*(6), 568–573.

Teale, W. H., & Martinez, M. (1986b). *Teachers reading to their students: Differing styles, different effects?* ERIC Document Reproduction Service.

Teale, W. H., & Sulzby, E. (1986). *Emergent literacy: Writing and reading.* Norwood, NJ: Ablex.

Temple, C., & Gillet, J. (1996). *Language and literacy: A lively approach.* New York: HarperCollins.

Temple, C., Nathan, R., Burris, N., & Temple, F. (1993). *The beginnings of writing* (3rd ed.). Newton, MA: Allyn & Bacon.

Templeton, S. (1995). *Children's literacy: Contexts for meaningful learning.* Princeton, NJ: Houghton Mifflin.

Texas Education Agency. (2003–2004). *Texas primary reading inventory* (TPRI). Austin, TX: Author. Available online, in both English and Spanish, at Reading Initiative at *http://www.tea.state.tx.us/ reading/*

Thaler, M. (1989). *The teacher from the Black Lagoon.* New York: Scholastic.

Tharp, R. (1982). The effective instruction of comprehension: Results and description of the Kamehameha Early Education Program. *Reading Research Quarterly, 17*(4), 503–527.

Tharpe, R. G., & Gallimore, R. (1988). *Rousing minds to life.* Cambridge, MA: Cambridge University Press.

Thelen, J. N. (1984). *Improving reading in science.* Newark, DE: International Reading Association.

Thomas, D. G., & Readence, J. E. (1988). Effects of differential vocabulary instruction and lesson frameworks on the reading comprehension of primary children. *Reading Research and Instruction, 28,* 1–13.

Thompson, R. (1997). The philosophy of balanced reading instruction. *The Journal of Balanced Reading Instruction, 4*(D1), 28–29.

Thorndike, E. L., & Lorge, I. (1944). *Thorndike-Lorge magazine count: Entries from* The teacher's word book of 30,000. New York: Columbia University.

Thorndike, R. L. (1973). *Reading comprehension education in fifteen countries: An empirical study.* New York: Wiley.

Thorndyke, P. N. (1977). Cognitive structure in comprehension and memory of narrative discourse. *Cognitive Psychology, 9*(1), 77–110.

Tierney, R. J. (1992). Setting a new agenda for assessment. *Learning, 21*(2), 61–64.

Tierney, R. J., Carter, M. A., & Desai, L. E. (1991). *Portfolio assessment in the reading-writing classroom.* Norwood, MA: Christopher-Gordon.

Tierney, R. J., & Cunningham, J. W. (1984). Research on teaching reading comprehension. In P. D. Pearson (Ed.), *Reading research handbook* (pp. 609–656). New York: Longman.

Tierney, R. J., & Pearson, P. D. (1983). Toward a composing model of reading. *Language Arts, 60*(5), 568–580.

Tierney, R. J., Readence, J. E., & Dishner, E. K. (1985). *Reading strategies and practices: A compendium* (2nd ed.). Boston: Allyn & Bacon.

Tierney, R. J., & Shanahan, T. (1991). Research on the reading-writing relationship: Interactions, transactions, and outcomes. In R. Barr, M. L. Kamil, P. Mosenthal, & P. D. Pearson (Eds.), *Handbook of reading research* (Vol. II). New York: Longman, Inc.

Tierney, R. J., & Shanahan, T. (1996). Research on the reading-writing relationship: Interactions, transactions, and outcomes. In R. Barr, M. L. Kamil, P. Mosenthal, & P. D. Pearson (Eds.), *Handbook of reading research* (Vol. 2, pp. 246–280). Mahwah, NJ: Erlbaum.

Tindal, G., Martson, D., & Deno, S. L. (1983). *The reliability of direct and repeated measurement.* (Research Rep. No. 109). Minneapolis: University of Minnesota Institute for Research on Learning Disabilities.

Tomasello, M. (1996). Piagetian and Vygotskian approaches to language acquisition. *Human Development, 39,* 269–276.

Tomlinson, C. A. (1999). *The differentiated classroom: Responding to the needs of all learners.* Alexandria, VA: Association for Supervision and Curriculum Development.

Tomlinson, C. A. (2001). *How to differentiate instruction in mixed-ability classrooms* (2nd ed.). Alexandria, VA: Association for Supervision and Curriculum Development.

Tompkins, G. (2006). *Literacy for the 21st century: A balanced approach.* Upper Saddle River, NJ: Merrill Prentice-Hall.

Tompkins, G. E. (1998). *Language arts: Content and teaching strategies* (4th ed.). Upper Saddle River, NJ: Merrill Prentice-Hall.

Tompkins, G. E. (2000). *Teaching writing: Balancing process and product* (3rd ed.). Upper Saddle River, NJ: Merrill/Prentice-Hall.

Tompkins, G. E. (2003). *Literacy for the 21st Century*, 3rd Ed. Upper Saddle River, NJ: Merrill/Prentice-Hall.

Tompkins, G. E. (2004). *Teaching writing: Balancing process and product* (4th ed.). Upper Saddle River, NJ: Merrill Prentice-Hall Pearson.

Tompkins, G. E. (2005). *Language arts essentials.* Upper Saddle River, NJ: Merrill Prentice-Hall.

Tompkins, G. E. (2006). *Literacy for the 21st century: A balanced approach.* Upper Saddle River, NJ: Merrill Prentice-Hall.

Tompkins, G. E., & Hoskisson, K. (1995). *Language arts: Content and teaching strategies* (3rd ed.). Upper Saddle River, NJ: Merrill/Prentice-Hall.

Topping, K. (1989). Peer tutoring and paired reading: Combining two powerful techniques. *The Reading Teacher, 42,* 488–494.

Torgesen, Wagner, Rashotte, Alexander, & Conroy, 1997. Prevention and remediation of severe reading disabilities: Keeping the end in mind. *Scientific Studies of Reading, 1*(3), 217–234.

Torrey, J. W. (1979). Reading that comes naturally. In G. Waller & G. E. MacKinnon (Eds.), *Reading research: Advance in theory and practice,* Vol. 1, (pp. 115–144). New York: Academic Press.

Tovey, D. R., & Kerber, J. E. (Eds.) (1986). *Roles in literacy learning.* Newark, DE: International Reading Association.

Towers, J. M. (1992). Outcome-based education: Another educational bandwagon. *Educational Forum, 56*(3), 291–305.

Towle, (1993). *The real McCoy: The life of an African American inventor.* New York: Scholastic.

Town, S., & Holbrook, N. M. (1857). *Progressive Primer.* Boston: Carter, Bazin & Company.

Trabasso, T. (1980). *On the making of inferences during reading and their assessment.* (Tech. Rep. No. 157). Urbana-Champaign: University of Illinois, Center for the Study of Reading.

Tracey, D. H., & Morrow, L. M. (2006). *Lenses on reading: An introduction to theories and models.* New York: Guilford Press.

Treiman, R. (1985). Onsets and rimes as units of spoken syllables: Evidence from children. *Journal of Experimental Child Psychology, 39,* 161–181.

Trelease, J. (1995). *The new read-aloud handbook* (4th ed.). New York: Penguin.

Tunnell, M. O., & Jacobs, J. S. (1989). Using "real" books: Research findings on literature based reading instruction. *The Reading Teacher, 42,* 470–477.

Turner, J., & Paris, S. (1995). How literacy tasks influence children's motivation for literacy. *The Reading Teacher, 48*(8), 662–673.

Tutolo, D. (1977). The study guide: Types, purpose and value. *Journal of Reading, 20,* 503–507.

Tyner, B. (2004). *Small-group reading instruction: A differentiated teaching model for beginning and struggling readers.* Newark, DE: International Reading Association.

U.S. Bureau of Labor. (1995). *Final report: Governor's Council on School-to-Work Transition.* Washington, DC: U.S. Department of Education.

U.S. Department of Education. (1997). *President Clinton's America's Reading Challenge.* Washington, DC: U.S. Department of Education.

U.S. Department of Education. *National Assessment of Educational Progress: The Nation's Report Card Reading 2000.* Washington, DC: U.S. Department of Education, Office of Educational Research and Improvement.

United States and the other Americas, The (Grade 5). (1980). Upper Saddle River, NJ: Merrill/Prentice-Hall.

United States: Its history and neighbors, The (Grade 5). (1985). San Diego. CA: Harcourt Brace.

Unsworth, L. (1984). Meeting individual needs through flexible within-class grouping of pupils. *The Reading Teacher, 38*(3), 298–304.

Vacca, J. L., Vacca, R. T., & Gove, M. K. (1995). *Reading and learning to read* (3rd ed.). Boston: Little, Brown.

Vacca, R. T., & Vacca, J. L. (2001). *Content area reading: Literacy and learning across the curriculum* (7th ed.). New York: Allyn & Bacon.

Vacca, R. T., Vacca, J. L., Gove, M. K., Burkey, L. C., Lenhart, L. A., & McKeon, C. A. (2003). *Reading and learning to read* (5th ed.). Needham Heights, MA: Allyn & Bacon.

Valencia, S. (1990). A portfolio approach to classroom reading assessment: The whys, whats, and hows. *The Reading Teacher, 43*(4), 338–340.

Valencia, S. (1998). *Portfolios in action.* New York: HarperCollins.

Valencia, S., McGinley, W., & Pearson, P. D. (1990). *Assessing reading and writing: Building a more complete picture for middle school assessment* (Tech. Rep. No. 500). Urbana, IL: Center for the Study of Reading. (ERIC Document Reproduction Service).

Valencia, S., & Pearson, P. D. (1987). Reading assessment: Time for a change. *The Reading Teacher, 40*(8), 726–733.

Vallecorsa, A. L., & deBettencourt, L. U. (1997). Using a mapping procedure to teach reading and writing skills to middle grade students with learning disabilities. *Education and the Treatment of Children, 20*(2), 173–188.

Van Allsburg, C. (1985). *The polar express.* Boston: Houghton Mifflin.

Van Allsburg, C. (1987). *The Z was zapped.* Boston: Houghton Mifflin.

Van Dijk, T. A. (1999). *Context models in discourse processing.* Mahwah, NJ: Lawrence Erlbaum Associates.

Van Manen, M. (1986). *The tone of teaching.* Ontario: Scholastic.

Van Meter, P., Aleksic, M., & Schwartz, A. (2006). Learner-generated drawing as a strategy for learning from content area text. *Contemporary Educational Psychology, 31*(2), 142–166.

Varble, M. E. (1990). Analysis of writing samples of students taught by teachers using whole language and traditional approaches. *Journal of Educational Research, 83*(5), 245–251.

Veatch, J. (1968). *How to teach reading with children's books.* New York: Owen.

Veatch, J. (1978). *Reading in the elementary school,* 2nd Ed. New York: Owen.

Veatch, J., & Cooter, R. B., Jr. (1986). The effect of teacher selection on reading achievement. *Language Arts, 63*(4), 364–368.

Viorst, J. (1972). *Alexander and the terrible, horrible, no good, very bad day* (R. Cruz, Illustrator). New York: Atheneum.

Viorst, J. (1972). *Alexander and the terrible, horrible, no good, very bad day.* New York: Atheneum.

Viorst, J. (1987). *Alexander and the terrible, horrible, no good, very bad day.* New York: Aladdin.

Voltz, D. L., & Demiano-Lantz, M. (1993, Summer). Developing ownership in learning. *Teaching Exceptional Children,* pp. 18–22.

Vopat, J. (1994). *The parent project: A workshop approach to parent involvement.* York, ME: Stenhouse.

Vopat, J. (1998). *More than bake sales: The resource guide for family involvement in education.* York: ME: Stenhouse.

Vukelich, C. (1994). Effects of play interventions on young children's reading of environmental print. *Early Childhood Research Quarterly, 9*(2), 153–170.

Vygotsky, L. S. (1939). Thought and speech. *Psychiatry, 2,* 29–54.

Vygotsky, L. S. (1962). *Thought and language.* Cambridge, MA: MIT Press.

Vygotsky, L. S. (1978). *Mind in society.* Cambridge, MA: Harvard University Press.

Vygotsky, L. S. (1986). *Thought and language.* Boston: MIT Press.

Vygotsky, L. S. (1990). *Mind in society.* Boston: Harvard University Press.

Wade, S. E., & Moje, E. B. (2000). The role of text in classroom learning. In M. L. Kamil, P. B. Mosenthal, P. D. Pearson, & R. Barr (Eds.), *Handbook of Reading Research*, Vol. 3. Mahwah, NJ: Erlbaum.

Wagner, R., Torgesen, J., & Rashotte, C. (1999). *Comprehensive Test of Phonological Processing (CTOPP)*. Circle Pines, MN: AGS.

Walker, B. J. (2004). *Diagnostic teaching of reading: Techniques for instruction and assessment.* Upper Saddle River, NJ: Merrill/Prentice-Hall.

Walker, J. E. (1991, May). *Affect in naturalistic assessment: Implementation and implications.* Paper presented at the 36th annual convention of the International Reading Association, Las Vegas, NV.

Wallach, L., Wallach, M. A., Dozier, M. G., & Kaplan, N. E. (1977). Poor children learning to read do not have trouble with auditory discrimination but do have trouble with phoneme recognition. *Journal of Educational Psychology, 69,* 36–39.

Walley, C. (1993). An invitation to reading fluency. *The Reading Teacher, 46*(6), 526–527.

Walpole, S., & McKenna, M. C. (2004). *The literacy coach's handbook: A guide to research-based practice.* New York: Guilford Press.

Walters, K., & Gunderson, L. (1985). Effects of parent volunteers reading first language (L1) books to ESL students. *The Reading Teacher, 39*(1), 66–69.

Wang, C. X., & Dwyer, F. M. (2006). Instructional effects of three concept mapping strategies in facilitating student achievement. *International Journal of Instructional Media, 33*(2), 135–151.

Wang, M., Haertel, G., & Walberg, H. (1994, December). What helps students learn? *Educational Leadership,* 74–79.

Warren, S. F. (2001). The future of early communication and language intervention. *Topics in Early Childhood Special Education, 20*(1), 33–38.

Warren, S. F., & Yoder, P. J. (1997). Emerging model of communication and language intervention. *Mental Retardation and Developmental Disabilities Research Reviews, 3,* 358–362.

Washington, DC: National Institute of Child Health and Human Development.

Wasik, B. A. (1998). Using volunteers as reading tutors: Guidelines for successful practices. *The Reading Teacher, 51*(7), 562–573.

Watson, D., & Crowley, P. (1988). How can we implement a whole-language approach? In C. Weaver (Ed.), *Reading process and practice* (pp. 232–279). Portsmouth, NH: Heinemann.

Watson, R. (2001). Literacy and oral language: Implications for early literacy acquisition. In S. B. Neuman & D. K. Dickinson (Eds), *Handbook of Early Literacy Research* (pp. 43–53). New York: Guilford Press.

Watson, S. (1976). *No man's land.* New York: Greenwillow.

Watt, M. G. (2005). *Standards-based reforms in the United States of America: An overview.* Online Submission. (ERIC Document Reproduction Service No. ED490562)

Weaver, C. (1994). *Reading process and practice: From socio-psycholinguistics to whole language* (2nd ed.). Portsmouth, NH: Heinemann.

Weaver, C. (1998). *Reconsidering a balanced approach to reading.* Urbana, IL: National Council of Teachers of English.

Weaver, C. A., & Kintsch, W. (1996). Expository text. In R. Barr, M. L. Kamil, P. Mosenthal, & P. D. Pearson (Eds.), *Handbook of reading research, volume II* (pp. 230–245). Mahwah, NJ: Lawrence Erlbaum.

Weaver, C., Chaston, J., & Peterson, S. (1993). *Theme exploration: A voyage of discovery.* Portsmouth, NH: Heinemann.

Webb, K., & Willoughby, N. (1993). An analytic rubric for scoring graphs. *The Texas School Teacher, 22*(3), 14–15.

Webb, M., & Schwartz, W. (1988, October). Children teaching children: A good way to learn. *PTA Today,* 16–17.

Weimans, E. (1981). *Which way courage?* New York: Atheneum.

Weinstein, R. S. (1976). Reading group membership in first grade: Teacher behaviors and pupil experience over time. *Journal of Educational Psychology, 68,* 103–116.

Weintraub, S., & Denny, T. P. (1965). What do beginning first graders say about reading? *Childhood Education, 41,* 326–327.

Wells, R. (1973). *Noisy Nora.* New York: Scholastic.

Wepner, S. B. (1985). Linking logos with print for beginning reading success. *The Reading Teacher, 38*(7), 633–39.

Wepner, S. B. (1990). Holistic computer applications in literature-based classrooms. *The Reading Teacher, 44*(1), 12–19.

Wepner, S. B. (1992). Technology and text sets. *The Reading Teacher, 46*(1), 68–71.

Wepner, S. B. (1993). Technology and thematic units: An elementary example on Japan. *The Reading Teacher, 46*(5), 442–445.

Wepner, S. B., & Feeley, J. T. (1993). *Moving forward with literature: Basals, books, and beyond.* Upper Saddle River, NJ: Merrill/Prentice-Hall.

Wepner, S. B., Feeley, J. T., & Strickland, D. S. (1995). *The administration and supervision of reading programs* (2nd ed.). New York: Teacher's College Columbia Press.

Wepner, S. B., Valmont, W. J., & Thurlow, R. (2000). *Linking literacy and technology: A guide for K–8 classrooms.* Newark, DE: International Reading Association.

Wessells, M. G. (1990). *Computer, self, and society.* Upper Saddle River, NJ: Prentice-Hall.

West, L. S., & Egley, E. H. (1998). Children get more than a hamburger: Using labels and logos to enhance literacy. *Dimensions of Early Childhood, 26*(3–4), 43–46.

Whaley, J. F. (1981). Readers' expectations for story structures. *Reading Research Quarterly, 17,* 90–114.

Wharton-McDonald, R., Pressley, M., Rankin, J., & Mistretta, J. (1997). Effective primary-grades literacy instruction equals balanced literacy instruction. *The Reading Teacher, 6*(50), 518–521.

Wharton-McDonald, R., Pressley, M., Rankin, J., Mistretta, J., Yokoi, L., & Ettenberger, S. (1997). Effective primary-grades literacy instruction = balanced literacy instruction. *The Reading Teacher, 50*(6), 518–521.

Wheatley, E. A., Muller, D. H., & Miller, R. B. (1993). Computer-assisted vocabulary instruction. *Journal of Reading, 37*(2), 92–102.

Whitaker, B. T., Schwartz, E., & Vockell, E. (1989). *The computer in the reading curriculum.* New York: McGraw-Hill.

White, C. S. (1983). Learning style and reading instruction. *The Reading Teacher, 36,* 842–845.

White, E. B. (1952). *Charlotte's web.* New York: HarperCollins.

White, E. B. (1970). *The trumpet of the swan.* New York: HarperCollins.

Whitehurst, G. J., Arnold, D. S., & Epstein, J. N. (1994). A picture book reading intervention in day care and home for children from low income families. *Developmental Psychology, 30,* 679–689.

Whitehurst, G. J., Falco, F. L., & Lonigan, C. J. (1988). Accelerating language development through picture book reading. *Developmental Psychology, 24,* 552–559.

Wiener, R. B., & Cohen, J. H. (1997). *Literacy portfolios: Using assessment to guide instruction.* Upper Saddle River, NJ: Merrill/Prentice-Hall.

Wiesendanger, W. D. (1986). Durkin revisited. *Reading Horizons, 26,* 89–97.

Wigfield, A. (1997). Motivations, beliefs, and self-efficacy in literacy development. In J. T. Guthrie & A. Wigfield (Eds.), *Reading engagement: Motivating readers through integrated instruction.* Newark, DE: International Reading Association.

Wigfield, A. (1997b). Children's motivations for reading and reading engagement. In J. T. Guthrie and A. Wigfield (Eds.), *Reading engagement: Motivating reading through integrated instruction* (pp. 14–33). Newark, DE: International Reading Association.

Wigfield, A. (2000). Facilitating children's reading motivation. In L. Baker, M. J. Dreher, and J. T. Guthrie (Eds.), *Engaging young readers: Promoting achievement and motivation* (pp. 140–158). New York: Guilford Press.

Wigfield, A., & Guthrie, J. T. (1997). Relations of children's motivation for reading to the amount and breadth of their reading. *Journal of Educational Psychology, 89,* 420–432.

Wiggins, R. A. (1994). Large group lesson/small group follow-up: Flexible grouping in a basal reading program. *The Reading Teacher, 47*(6), 450–460.

Wiig, E. H., Becker-Redding, U., & Semel, E. M. (1983). A cross-cultural comparison of langauge abilities of 7-to 8- and 12-to-13-year-old children with learning disabilities. *Journal of Learning Disabilities, 16*(10) 576–585.

Wilde, S. (1997). *What's a schwa sound anyway?* Portsmouth, NH: Heinemann Educational Books.

Williams, J. P. (2005). Instruction in reading comprehension for primary-grade students: A focus on text structure. *Journal of Special Education, 39*(1), 6–18.

Williams, J. P., Brown, L. G., Silverstein, A. K., & deCari, J. S. (1994). An instructional program in comprehension of narrative themes for adolescents with learning disabilities. *Learning Disability Quarterly, 17,* 205–221.

Willman, A. T. (2000). "Hello, Mrs. Willman, it's me!: Keep kids reading over the summer by using voice mail." In T. V. Rasinski, N. D. Padak, et al. (Eds.), *Motivating recreational reading and promoting home-school connections* (pp. 51–52). Newark, DE: International Reading Association.

Wilson, R. M., & Gambrell, L. B. (1988). *Reading comprehension in the elementary school.* Boston: Allyn & Bacon.

Wilson, R. M., Hall, M. A., Leu, D. J., & Kinzer, C. K. (2001). *Phonics, phonemic awareness, and word analysis for teachers: An interactive tutorial* (7th ed.). Upper Saddle River, NJ: Prentice-Hall.

Winograd, P. (1989). Improving basal reading instruction: Beyond the carrot and the stick. *Theory Into Practice, 28*(4), 240–247.

Winograd, P. N. (1989). Introduction: Understanding reading instruction. In P. N. Winograd, K. K. Wixson, & M. Y. Lipson (Eds.). *Improving basal reader instruction* (pp. 1–20). New York: Teachers College Press.

Winograd, P. N., Paris, S., & Bridge, C. (1991). Improving the assessment of literacy. *The Reading Teacher, 45*(2), 108–116.

Winograd, P. N., Wixson, K. K., & Lipson, M. Y. (Eds.). (1989). *Improving basal reader instruction.* New York: Teachers College Press.

Wiseman, D. L. (1992). *Learning to read with literature.* Boston: Allyn & Bacon.

Wittrock, M. C. (1974). Learning as a generative process. *Educational Psychologist, 11,* 87–95.

Wixson, K. K., Peters, C. W., Weber, E. M., & Roeber, E. D. (1987). New directions in statewide reading assessment. *The Reading Teacher, 40*(8), 749–755.

Wolf, M., & Katzir-Cohen, T. (2001). Reading fluency and its intervention. *Scientific Studies of Reading, 5*(3), 211–229.

Wolfersberger, M., Reutzel, D. R., Sudweeks, R., & Fawson, P. F. (2004). Developing and validating the Classroom Literacy Environmental Profile (CLEP): A tool for examining the "print richness" of elementary classrooms. *Journal of Literacy Research, 36*(2), 211–272.

Wong, H., & Wong, R. (1998). *The first days of school: How to be an effective teacher.* Mountain View, CA: Harry K. Wong.

Wong, H. K., & Wong, R. (1998). *The first days of school: How to be an effective teacher.* Mountain View, CA: Harry K. Wong.

Wong, J. W., & Au, K. H. (1985). The concept-text-application approach: Helping elementary students comprehend expository text. *The Reading Teacher, 38*(7), 612–618.

Wood, A. (1984). *The napping house* (Don Wood, Illustrator). San Diego, CA: Harcourt Brace.

Wood, A. (1990). *Weird parents.* New York: Dial Books for Young Readers.

Wood, A., & Wood, D. (1988). *Elbert's bad word.* New York: Harcourt, Brace, & Jovanovich.

Wood, E., Pressley, M., & Winne, P. H. (1990). Elaborative interrogation effects on children's learning of factual content. *Journal of Educational Psychology, 82,* 741–48.

Wood, K. D. (1983). A variation on an old theme: 4-way oral reading. *The Reading Teacher, 37*(1), 38–41.

Wood, K. D. (1987). Fostering cooperative learning in middle and secondary level classrooms. *Journal of Reading, 31,* 10–18.

Woodcock, R., Mather, N., & Barnes, E. K. (1987). *Woodcock reading mastery tests–revised.* Circle Pines, MN: American Guidance Service.

Woodcock, R. W. (1997). *Woodcock Reading Mastery Tests–Revised (WRMT–R).* Circle Pines, MN: AGS.

Woodcock, R. W., & Muñoz-Sandoval, A. F. (1993). *Woodcock-Muñoz language survey* (WMLS), English and Spanish forms. Chicago: Riverside.

Worby, D. Z. (1980). *An honorable seduction: Thematic studies in literature.* Arlington, VA: ERIC Document Reproduction Service. (ERIC Document Reproduction Service).

Worthy, J., & Broaddus, K. (2002). Fluency beyond the primary grades: From group performance to silent, independent reading. *The Reading Teacher, 55*(4), 334–343.

Worthy, J., Moorman, M., & Turner, M. (1999). What Johnny likes to read is hard to find in school. *Reading Research Quarterly, 34*(1), 12–27.

Yaden, D. B., Jr. (1982). A multivariate analysis of first graders' print awareness as related to reading achievement, intelligence, and gender. *Dissertation Abstracts International, 43,* 1912A. (University Microfilms No. 82–25, 520)

Yaden, D. B., Jr., & S. Templeton (Eds.). (1986). *Reading research in metalinguistic awareness: A classification of findings according to focus and methodology.* Portsmouth, NH: Heinemann Educational Books.

Yashima, T. (1983). *Crow boy.* New York: Viking.

Yeh, S. (2003). An evaluation of two approaches for teaching phonemic awareness to children in Head Start. *Early Childhood Research Quarterly, 18*(1), 511–529.

Yellin, D., & Blake, M. E. (1994). *Integrating language arts: A holistic approach.* New York: Harper-Collins.

Yep, L. (1989). *The rainbow people.* New York: Harper-Collins.

Ylisto, I. P. (1967). An empirical investigation of early reading responses of young children (doctoral dissertation, The University of Michigan, 1967). *Dissertation Abstracts International, 28,* 2153A. (University Microfilms No. 67–15, 728).

Yolen, J. (1976). *An invitation to a butterfly ball: A counting rhyme.* New York: Philomel.

Yolen, J. (1988). *The devil's arithmetic.* New York: Viking Kestrel.

Yopp, H. K. (1988). The validity and reliability of phonemic awareness tests. *Reading Research Quarterly, 23,* 159–177.

Yopp, H. K. (1992). Developing phonemic awareness in young children. *The Reading Teacher, 45*(9), 696–703.

Yopp, H. K., & Troyer, S. (1992). *Training phonemic awareness in young children.* Unpublished manuscript.

Yopp, R. H., & Yopp, H. K. (2000). *Literature-based reading activities* (3rd Ed.). New York: Allyn & Bacon.

Young, E. (1989). *Lon Po Po.* New York: Philomel Books.

Young, T. A., & Vardell, S. (1993). Weaving readers theatre and nonfiction into the curriculum. *The Reading Teacher, 46,* 396–406.

Zahar, R., Cobb, T., & Sapda, N. (2001). Acquiring vocabulary through reading: Effects of frequency and contextual richness. *Canadian Modern Language Review, 57*(4), 541–572.

Zarillo, J. (1989). Teachers' interpretations of literature-based reading. *The Reading Teacher, 43*(1), 22–29.

Zemelman, S., Daniels, H., & Hyde, A. (1993). *Best practice: New standards for teaching and learning in America's schools.* Portsmouth, NH: Heinemann.

Zeno, S. M., Ivens, S. H., Millard, R. T., & Duvvuri, R. (1995). *The educator's word guide.* New York: Touchstone Applied Science Associates, Inc.

Zentall, S. S. (1993). Research on the educational implications of attention deficit hyperactivity disorder. *Exceptional Children, 60*(2), 143–153.

Zintz, M. V., & Maggart, Z. R. (1989). *The reading process: The teacher and the learner.* Dubuque, IA: William C. Brown.

Zlatos, B. (1993). Outcomes-based outrage. *Executive Educator, 15*(9), 12–16.

Zutell, J., & Rasinski, T. (1991). Training teachers to attend to their students' oral reading fluency. *Theory Into Practice, 30*(3), 211–217.

Zuzovsky, R., & Libman, Z. (2006). Standards of teaching and teaching tests: Is this the right way to go? *Studies in Educational Evaluation, 32*(1), 37–52.

Zwann, R. A. (1999). Embodied cognition, perceptual symbols, and situated cognition. *Discourse Processes, 28*(1), 81–88.

NAME INDEX

Abbott, J., 375
Adams, M. J., 74, 75, 78, 88,
　　91, 110, 176, 194,
　　198–199, 376
Alamprese, J., 16
Albom, 16
Aldridge, J., 84
Aleksic, 471
Allington, R. L., 8, 19, 24, 73, 81, 144,
　　150, 158, 181, 193, 194, 276,
　　377, 378, 392, 408
Almasi, J. F., 271
Alvermann, D. E., 31, 471, 502
American Federation of
　　Teachers, 73
American Library Association, 471
Anastasopoulos, L., 411
Anderson, 511
Anderson, R. C., 7, 9, 28,
　　151, 193, 194, 235, 378,
　　399, 410
Anderson, V., 259
Anthongy, J. L., 448
Anton, W., 418
Appleby, E., 443
Archambault, J., 182
Armbruster, B. B., 13–14, 26, 74, 88,
　　89, 377, 439
Arnold, D. S., 65
Ary, D., 395
Ashton-Warner, S., 199, 319
Atwell, N., 317, 318, 487
Au, K. H., 257, 259, 282, 328
Au, T. K., 39, 225, 226
August, D., 98, 138, 357

Baines, 370
Baker, S., 63
Baldwin, 352, 461
Barbour, N., 41

Barnes, E. K., 126, 357
Barracca, D., 111
Barracca, Sal, 111
Barrett, F. L., 85, 442
Barrett, T., 257
Barron, 471, 472
Barton, D., 110
Battle, J., 439, 441
Baum, F., 493, 500
Baumann, J. F., 27, 238
Bean, 352
Bear, D. R., 78, 284, 415
Beaver, J., 131, 244, 354, 392
Beck, I. L., 194, 197, 246, 250, 259,
　　260, 269, 270, 375
Becker-Redding, U., 41
Beeler, T., 78
Bennett-Armistead, S., 97, 243, 469
Beretvas, S. N., 11
Berg, W., 223
Bergon, B. S., 238
Berliner, D. C., 257
Betts, E. A., 130, 353
Biber, D., 401
Biddulph, F., 256
Biddulph, J., 256
Biemiller, A., 41, 64
Biglan, A., 395
Bintz, W. P., 334
Blachman, B. A., 110
Blachowicz, C., 149, 157, 158, 202,
　　203, 395
Blair, 459
Blair, T. R., 292
Blake, M. E., 327, 330
Bleich, D., 271
Blevins, W., 78, 89, 92, 110, 122
Block, C. C., 19, 81, 408
Bloodgood, J. M., 74, 76, 84
Bloom, B., 257, 258

Boland, E. M., 27
Borchordt, K. M., 264
Borland, 495
Bowles, R. B., 94
Boyer, E., 5
Boyle, O. F., 222, 401
Bradley, E., 416
Bransford, J. C., 29
Braunger, J., 6, 10, 18
Brent, D., 458
Bridge, C. A., 377
Broaddus, K., 157
Broikou, K. A., 378
Brooks, G., 99
Brown, A. L., 239, 245, 264
Brown, H., 241
Brown, K. J., 158, 238
Brown, R., 238
Browning, M. M., 75, 94
Brozo, 470
Bruner, J., 37
Bryan, G., 158, 178
Burke, C. L., 39, 342
Burnham, N. A., 205
Burns, C. E., 149–150
Burns, M. S., 5, 6, 7, 9, 10, 13, 14, 18,
　　25, 26, 41, 50, 64, 73, 74, 76,
　　80, 88, 98, 136, 145, 165, 194,
　　195, 238, 294, 439, 441
Byars, B., 483, 501
Byrne, B., 106

Cahen, L. S., 257
Caldwell, J., 131, 244, 338
Calkins, L., 282, 305, 308, 311,
　　316, 446
Cambourne, B., 241
Camperell, K., 262
Cantrell, S. C., 19
Caplan, R. J., 205

SUBJECT INDEX

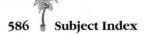

Grade 4. *See* Fourth grade
Grade 5. *See* Fifth grade
Grammar
  defined, 9, 27–28
  regional differences in, 32
Grand conversations, 271
Graphemes, 9, 26
Graphic organizers
  complex story structure, 254
  constructing, 471–472
  examples of, 473–474
  expository text structure, 255–257
  limiting number of, 473
  oral retellings and, 456
  semantic maps, 223, 224, 225
  simple story structure, 253
  web sites on, 473
Graphophonemic knowledge, 105
Graphophonic cues, 123
Grids, miscue, 126, 128
Grouchy Ladybug, The (Carle), 215–216
Group conversations, 54
Group Literature Response, 489
Group-assisted reading, 511–512
Grouping students
  companion CD on, 13
  for effective K–3 reading instruction, 424–425
  for guided oral reading, 170
  for neurological impress method, 175
  reading workshop, 483
Guide to Selecting Basal Reading Programs, A, 385
Guided oral reading, 168, 170–176, 489
  with audio cassettes and CDs, 176
  choral reading, 173
  lesson overview for, 174
  lesson planning for, 172–174
  neurological impress method (NIM), 175
  partner/paired reading, 173, 175
  purpose of, 168, 170
  reading levels and, 171–172
  with teacher feedback, 170–172
  teacher feedback for, 172–173
  technology-assisted, 176
Guided practice, 37
Guided practice phase of mini-lesson, 485
Guided Reading Leveling Comparisons, 172

Handbook of Writing Research (Shanahan), 282
Hands-on learning experiences, 459–461
Harcourt, 382, 391
Hard c sound, 107–108
Hard g sound, 108
Harry Potter and the Sorcerer's Stone (Rowling), 197, 484–486
Hatchet (Paulsen), 483
Henry and Beezus (Cleary), 491
Heuristic oral language instruction, 55–58
Hiearchies for classroom activities, 460–460
Higher order thinking, 510
High-frequency words, 137. *See also* Sight words
  list of 25, 152–153
  list of 107, 153, 165
Holidays, 443
Holistic scoring rubrics, 301, 302, 303
Holophrases, 35, 39
Homework
  interactive, 513
  posted online, 513–514
Homework hot lines, 513
Homework voicemail, 513
Honey Baby Sugar Child (Duncan), 223, 224
Houghton Mifflin, 382, 391
How Do Spiders Live?, 256
Humorous oral language activities, 60, 61

"I Can Read" books, 84
"I Know an Old Lady Who Swallowed a Fly," 135
I Openers information series, 255
"I Spy" game, 96
Iconic memory, 236
Idiomatic expressions, 201
IF-THEN Thinking, 339, 340, 360, 364–365
IIS (individual interest sheet), 221
Imaginative oral language instruction, 58
Independent fluency practice, 176–180
Independent level, 122
Independent practice, 37
Indiana, 391
Indirect vocabulary instruction, 196–197

Individual diagnostic reading tests, 357
Individual Growth and Development Indicators, 47
Individual interest sheet (IIS), 221
Individual Reading Conferences (IRCs), 491
Individually administered achievement tests, 357–358
Infants, baby talk used with, 38–39
Inflated euphemisms, 217
Inflected morphemes, 27
Informal interviews, 52
Informal reading inventory (IRI), 130, 353–355
Information books, text structure instruction with, 251, 255. *See also* Expository texts
Information text, basal reading program, 375–376
Information-gathering, for writing, 306
Innatist theory of oral language development, 34–35
Insights: Reading Fluency (computer-based program), 176
Instructional conversations, 51
Instructional level, 122
Instructional management systems, 381–382
Instructional reading level, 136
Instructional strategies. *See also* Fluent reading instruction; Reading comprehension teaching strategies
  early reading, 82–96
  efficient study, 505–507
  interactive read-aloud, 439, 441
  language experience approach, 443–444
  oral language, 51–62
  phonics, 132–134
  reading comprehension, 237–239, 238
  shared reading, 442–443
  vocabulary instruction, 207–218
  writing, 313–322
Instructions, oral language instruction and, 58–60
Integrated curriculum, 476, 482
Integrated learning centers, 418
Integration phase of mental processing, 237

Transitional stage of writing/spelling, 289–291

Traveling tales backpack, 327, 328, 329

TROLL (Teacher Rating of Oral Language and Literacy), 43–47

Trumpet of the Swan, The (White), 500

Ugly Duckling, The, 248

Unaided recall, 243, 244

Unison reading, 173

The Unknown Character, 489

Unknown level of word knowledge, 195, 196

Unknown vocabulary, 168, 197

Upper elementary grades. *See* Intermediate grades, effective literacy instruction in

U.S. Department of Education, 13, 161, 209

Utah, 391

Validity, measures of, 338

Vanderbilt University, 510

VCE (final silent E) generalization, 109

Vegetative sounds, 39

Verbal prompts, oral story retellings using, 242

Very Hungry Caterpillar, The (Carle), 315–316

Village English activity, 226

Visual cues, 123

Vocabulary
  of three- to four-year-old, 40
  constructivist view of oral language development and, 35
  in early reading instruction, 73
  in expository texts, 459
  of four- to six-year-old, 40–41
  four types of, 195
  reading comprehension and, 246
  relationship with reading comprehension, 239
  three levels of knowledge in, 168

Vocabulary acquisition
  assessing, 202–207
  family involvement in, 226–229
  indirect, 196–197
  levels of, 195–196
  shared reading experiences and, 218
  sources of rare words in, 193

  sources of student's, 193–194
  for students with special needs, 222–226
  student's word-learning strategies, 219–220
  through language interactions, 194–195
  through vocabulary overviews, 222
  through wide reading, 220–221
  through word consciousness, 197
  through word-learning strategies, 196–197

Vocabulary center, 416–417

Vocabulary cluster strategy, 223

Vocabulary flash cards, 206

Vocabulary in the Elementary and Middle School (Johnson), 229

Vocabulary instruction
  computer-assisted, 195, 221–222
  evaluation of core reading programs for, 388–389
  extended instruction, 211
  levels of processing for, 208–209
  Making Words, 212–213, 214
  preteaching vocabulary, 210–211
  principles of effective, 207–208
  repeated exposures to vocabulary, 212
  research findings on, 195, 196–197
  shared reading experiences and, 218
  specific word instruction, 209–210
  of unknown words, 197
  with word banks, 209, 210
  word functions and changes, 215–218
  word maps for, 202–203
  word to teach in, 197–201

Vocabulary notebooks, 136–137

Vocabulary overview, 222

Vocabulary tests, 203, 205, 206–207

Vocabulary words
  antonyms, 216–217
  creative words, 218
  discovery words, 199
  euphemisms, 217–218
  function words, 213–215
  idiomatic expressions, 201
  key vocabulary, 199
  most difficult to learn, 199, 201
  sight words, 198–199, 200
  synonyms, 215–216

Vocal pitch, 25

Vocal play, 39

Vowel digraphs (CVVC), 109

Vowels
  coming together in a word, 109
  ranked by frequency, 95
  R-controlled, 109

Vygotsky's theory, 38

Waterford Early Reading Program, 396–397

Ways of Measuring: Then and Now, 260

Web sites
  book award, 471
  on computer-based guided reading programs, 176
  DIBELS, 154
  on graphic organizers, 473
  on homework assignments, 513–514
  joke and riddle, 61
  on software for reading fluency, 177

Webs
  brainstorming, 477
  discussion, 502–503
  semantic, 475
  semantic maps, 223, 224, 225
  themed literature unit, 493, 494
  themed studies, 478, 480, 481, 482

Weird Parents (Wood), 216

What Did I Write (Clay), 15

Where the Sidewalk Ends (Silverstein), 197

White Socks Only (Coleman), 269–270, 270

Whole language movement, 73

Whole-class instructional area, 412–414

Wide oral reading, 177

Wide readings
  reading comprehension and, 246
  reading fluency and, 159
  vocabulary acquisition and, 220–221

Wide silent readings, 151

Wikki stiks, 86

Wizard of Oz, The (Baum), 493, 500

Woodcock Reading Mastery Tests-Revised (WRMT-R/NU), 126, 129–130, 357

Woodcock-Muñoz Language Survey (WMLS), 207, 357

Word attack skills, 105
  IF-THEN chart for, 364–365

D. Ray Reutzel

D. Ray Reutzel is the Emma Eccles Jones Distinguished Professor and Endowed Chair of Early Childhood Education at Utah State University. Ray is a former Provost and Vice President for Academic Affairs at Southern Utah University; Associate Dean of Teacher Education in the David O. McKay School of Education; and former Chair of the Department of Elementary Education at Brigham Young University. While at BYU, he was the recipient of the 1992 Karl G. Maeser Distinguished Research and Creative Arts Professor Award and was an integral part of developing BYU's nationally celebrated Public School Partnership, the field-based Elementary Education program, the Center for Improvement of Teacher Education and Schooling (CITES) and the Utah/CITES Balanced Literacy initiative as a part of the U.S. and Utah's Goals 2000 funding. He has served as technical assistant to the Reading Excellence Act and the Reading First federal reading reform projects in the state of Utah. Several years ago, he took a leave from his university faculty position to return to full-time, first-grade classroom teaching in Sage Creek Elementary School. Ray has taught in Kindergarten, 1st grade, 3rd grade, and 6th grade.

Dr. Reutzel is the author of more than 165 refereed research reports, articles, books, book chapters, and monographs published in *Early Childhood Research Quarterly, Reading Research Quarterly, Journal of Literacy Research, Journal of Educational Research, Reading Psychology, Reading Research and Instruction, Language Arts, Journal of Adolescent and Adult Literacy,* and *The Reading Teacher,* among others. He has received more than $5.5 million in research/professional development funding from private, state, and federal funding agencies. He was recently awarded a $1 million research grant as principal investigator under the Teacher Quality Research Program of the Institute of Education Sciences, U.S. Department of Education.

He is the past editor of *Reading Research and Instruction,* the journal of the College Reading Association. He is co-author, with Robert B. Cooter, Jr., of *The Essentials for Teaching Children to Read,* First Edition*, Teaching Children to Read: The Teacher Makes* *the Difference,* Fifth Edition and *Strategies for Reading Assessment and Instruction: Helping Every Child Succeed,* Third Edition published by Merrill/Prentice-Hall. He has written a professional book titled, *Your Classroom Library: How to Give It More Teaching Power,* with Parker C. Fawson, published by Scholastic, Inc. He is or has been a reviewer for *The Reading Teacher, Reading Research Quarterly, Reading Psychology, Journal of Educational Research, Early Childhood Research Quarterly, Reading Research and Instruction, Journal of Reading Behavior, Journal of Literacy Research* and *the Elementary School Journal.* He was an author of Scholastic Incorporated's Literacy Place, 1996, 2000® school reading program.

Dr. Reutzel received the A.B. Herr Award from the College Reading Association in 1999 for Outstanding Research and Published Contributions to Reading Education. He was the editor of the International Reading Association's professional elementary section journal *The Reading Teacher* from 2002–2007. He was awarded the Researcher/Scholar of the Year Award by the College of Education and Human Services at Utah State University in May, 2004. And he was elected Vice-President of the College Reading Association in April of 2005 and will serve as that organization's President in 2007. Dr. Reutzel was recognized as a recipient of the College of Education's 2006 Distinguished Alumni Award at the University of Wyoming in Laramie, Wyoming and is the D. Wynne Thorne Outstanding University Researcher Award recipient from Utah State University in April 2007. Dr. Reutzel was given the John C. Manning Public School Service Award from the International Reading Association in May 2007. Ray will also serve as a member of the Board of Directors of the International Reading Association from 2007–2010.

Dr. Robert B. Cooter, Jr.

Dr. Robert B. Cooter, Jr., holds the position of Distinguished Professor of Urban Literacy Research at The University of Memphis. In March of 2006, Robert Cooter and J. Helen Perkins, also of The University of Memphis, were selected by the International Reading Association to serve as editors through 2011 of *The Reading Teacher,* the largest literacy education journal in the world. His primary research focus pertains to research-based reading instruction for children living at the poverty level.

Professor Cooter founded The Memphis Literacy Academy, an outreach program in Memphis City Schools dedicated to raising the expertise of hundreds of inner-city teachers of reading, and is also co-principal investigator for the Memphis Striving Readers Program (grades 6–9 content areas), a $16 million middle school literacy research project in Memphis City Schools funded under a major grant by the U.S. Department of Education for 2006–2011. Dr. Cooter formerly served as the first "Reading Czar" (associate superintendent) for the Dallas Independent School

District (TX) and engineered the district's highly acclaimed Dallas Reading Plan involving the training of approximately 3,000 teachers in comprehensive literacy instruction.

Cooter has authored or co-authored nearly 100 journal articles and some 19 books in reading education. His books include *Strategies for Reading Assessment and Instruction: Helping Every Child Succeed* (Merrill/Prentice Hall), which is at present the top text in reading assessment in the U.S.; *Perspectives on Rescuing Urban Literacy Education: Spies, Saboteurs, & Saints* (Lawrence Erlbaum Associates); *The Flynt/Cooter Reading Inventory for the Classroom* (Merrill/Prentice-Hall); and the new *Comprehensive Reading Inventory* (Merrill/Prentice Hall), a norm-referenced reading assessment for classroom use.

Bob lives in Memphis with his wife, Dr. Kathleen Spencer Cooter, a popular Early Childhood/Special Education professor and researcher at The University of Memphis. They enjoy vacationing on their houseboat, (our last child), along with Mitchell and Spencer (golden retrievers of dubious function), and their twelve grandchildren.